LEARNING FROM DATA
AN INTRODUCTION TO STATISTICAL REASONING

THIRD EDITION

LEARNING FROM DATA
AN INTRODUCTION TO STATISTICAL REASONING
THIRD EDITION

ARTHUR M. GLENBERG

MATTHEW E. ANDRZEJEWSKI

LEA Lawrence Erlbaum Associates
Taylor & Francis Group

New York   London

Lawrence Erlbaum Associates
Taylor & Francis Group
270 Madison Avenue
New York, NY 10016

Lawrence Erlbaum Associates
Taylor & Francis Group
2 Park Square
Milton Park, Abingdon
Oxon OX14 4RN

© 2008 by Taylor & Francis Group, LLC
Lawrence Erlbaum Associates is an imprint of Taylor & Francis Group, an Informa business

Printed in the United States of America on acid-free paper
10 9 8 7 6 5 4 3 2 1

International Standard Book Number-13: 978-0-8058-4921-9 (Hardcover)

Library of Congress Cataloging-in-Publication Data

Glenberg, Arthur M.
    Learning from data : an introduction to statistical reasoning / Arthur M. Glenberg and Matthew E. Andrzejewski. -- 3rd ed.
        p. cm.
    Includes bibliographical references and index.
    ISBN-13: 978-0-8058-4921-9 (alk. paper)
    1. Statistics. I. Andrzejewski, Matthew E. II. Title.

HA29.G57 2008
001.4'22--dc22   2007022035

**Visit the Taylor & Francis Web site at
http://www.taylorandfrancis.com**

Contents

CHAPTER *7*

Sampling Distributions   119

CHAPTER *8*

Logic of Hypothesis Testing   141

CHAPTER *9*

Power   177

CHAPTER *10*

Logic of Parameter Estimation   199

PART *III*

Applications of Inferential Statistics   213

CHAPTER *11*

Inferences About Population Proportions Using the z Statistic   215

CHAPTER *12*

Inferences About μ When σ Is Unknown: The Single-sample t Test   241

CHAPTER *13*

Comparing Two Populations: Independent Samples   263

CHAPTER *14*

Random Sampling, Random Assignment,
and Causality   299

CHAPTER *15*

Comparing Two Populations: Dependent Samples   311

CHAPTER *16*

Comparing Two Population Variances: The *F* Statistic   345

CHAPTER *17*

Comparing Multiple Population Means: One-factor ANOVA   359

CHAPTER *18*

Introduction to Factorial Designs   399

CHAPTER *19*

Computational Methods for the Factorial ANOVA   425

CHAPTER *20*

Describing Linear Relationships: Regression   441

CHAPTER *21*

Measuring the Strength of Linear Relationships: Correlation   477

CHAPTER **22**

Inferences From Nominal Data: The χ^2 Statistic   505

Preface

Statistics is a difficult subject. There is a lot to learn, and much of it involves new thinking. As the title implies, *Learning From Data: An Introduction to Statistical Reasoning* teaches you a new way of thinking about and learning about the world. Our goal is to put readers in a good position to understand psychological data and their limitations. Another more important goal is to evaluate data that affect all aspects of life—psychological, social, educational, political, and economic—to better prepare readers to question and to challenge. Yet another goal is to help readers retain the material. Psychologists have developed (from data) techniques that facilitate learning and comprehension, and we have incorporated three of these techniques into the book.

First, we have devoted extra attention to explaining difficult-to-understand concepts in detail. For example, some textbooks attempt to combine important concepts such as sampling distributions, hypothesis testing, power, and parameter estimation in one chapter. In this book, each concept has its own chapter. Yes, this means more reading, but it also means greater understanding.

Second, the book uses repetition extensively to help students learn and retain concepts. There are multiple fully explained examples of each major procedure. Many concepts (for example, power, Type I errors) are repeated from chapter to chapter. The problem sets at the ends of most chapters require students to apply principles introduced in earlier chapters.

The third major learning aid is the use of a consistent schema (the six-step procedure) for describing all statistical tests from the simplest to the most complex. The schema provides a valuable heuristic for learning from data. Students learn (1) to consider the assumptions of a statistical test, (2) to generate null and alternative hypotheses, (3) to choose an appropriate sampling distribution, (4) to set a significance criterion and generate a decision rule, (5) to compute the statistic of interest, and (6) to draw conclusions. Learning the schema at an early stage (in Chapter 8) will ease the way through Chapters 11 through 22, in which the schema is applied to many different situations. This schema also provides a convenient summary for each hypothesis-testing procedure. A table with a summary schema is included in the last section of each chapter containing the hypothesis-testing procedure. Inside the front cover of the book is a "Statistical Selection Guide" to further assist students in determining which statistical test is most appropriate for the situation.

ABOUT THE BOOK

There are many aspects to *Learning From Data* that differentiate it from other statistics textbooks. In addition to the three teaching/learning methods mentioned earlier, the content and organization of the book may be quite different from what students are used to. First, nonparametric statistical tests are integrated into the chapters in which analogous parametric tests are described. With this organization, students can better appreciate the situations in which particular tests apply. In fact, throughout the book there is an emphasis on practicing how to choose the best statistical procedure. The choice of the procedure is discussed in examples, and students are required to make the correct choice as they solve the problems at the end of the chapter. The endpapers of the book provide guidelines for choosing procedures.

Second, the initial parts of the chapters on regression (Chapter 20) and correlation (Chapter 21) are self-contained sections that include discussions of regression and correlation as descriptive procedures. Instructors may present these topics along with other descriptive statistics or delay their introduction until later in the course.

Third, the book contains two independent treatments of power. The major treatment begins in Chapter 9 with graphical illustrations of how power changes under the influence of such factors as the significance level and sample size. The chapter also introduces formulas for computing power and estimating sample size needed to obtain a particular level of power. These formulas are repeated and generalized for many of the statistical procedures discussed in later chapters. Often, however, there may not be enough time for an extensive treatment of power. In that case, instructors can choose to treat power less extensively and omit Chapter 9 (and the relevant formulas in the other chapters). This less extensive treatment of power is part of each new inferential procedure. It consists of a non-mathematical discussion of how power can be enhanced for that particular procedure.

Fourth, factorial designs, interactions, and the ANOVA are explained in greater detail than in most introductory textbooks. Our goal is to give students enough information so that they will be able to understand the statistics used in many professional journal articles. Of course, it would be foolish for the authors of any introductory textbook to try to cover the statistical analyses of complex situations. Instead, Chapter 18 discusses how two-factor and three-factor factorial experiments are designed, and how to interpret main effects and two-factor and three-factor interactions. Chapter 19 presents a description of computational procedures for the relatively simple two-factor, independent sample ANOVA.

Last, but most important to us, is Chapter 14, "Random Sampling, Random Assignment, and Causality." A major reason for writing the first two editions of this book was to address the issues discussed in this chapter. All of us who teach statistics courses and conduct research have been struck by the incongruity between what we practice and what we preach. When we teach a statistics course, we emphasize random sampling from populations. But in most experiments we do no such thing. Instead, we use some form of random assignment to conditions. How can we perform statistical analyses of our experiments when we have ignored the most important assumption of the statistical tests? In Chapter 14, we develop a rationale for this behavior, but the rationale extracts severe payment by placing restrictions on the interpretation of the results when random assignment is used instead of random sampling.

NEW TO THE THIRD EDITION

In addition to the features already described, there are a number of new features. First, the third edition of *Learning From Data* is designed to be used seamlessly with Excel™. Unlike other texts that concentrate on statistical software, we choose to focus on Excel, a spreadsheet program. Recent versions of statistical programs produce output that are far more complicated than needed for the undergraduate level. The output from Excel is straightforward; however, the statistical tools available are not complete. Thus, we have written an Add-in ("LFD3 Data Analysis Add-in") for Excel so all the analyses presented in the book can be conducted in Excel. Excel is widely available and can also be used as a database, data manager, and graphics program; experience with these functions may provide a valuable set of skills for undergraduates in a number of professions, including psychology. Thus, files containing all the data used in the book are provided on a companion CD in Excel format. However, because other programs are still widely used, text-based files are also available for use in other statistical programs, like SPSS™, SAS™, and Systat™.

Second, the book attempts to capture the student's interest by focusing on what can be learned from a statistical analysis, not just on how it is done. This is most apparent in the treatment of hypothesis testing. Using the six-step schema, the last step in hypothesis-testing is described as deciding whether to reject the null hypothesis *and then* concluding what that decision implies about the world and what the implications for future action might be. Another way that the book attempts to capture the student's interest is by continually referring back to two real data sets. These data sets are intrinsically interesting and save time because new experimental scenarios do not need to be continually introduced. The first data set on the effectiveness of Zyban® and nicotine-replacement gum on smoking comes from Dr. Timothy Baker. Data from 608 participants are included on the companion CD. The second data set on the effects of having a child on marriage comes from Dr. Janet Hyde and Dr. Marilyn Essex. The data from 244 families are also included on the companion CD. Data from these studies are used throughout the book in illustrating important concepts. The fact that these are real data sets strikes a chord with students that statistics plays an important role in *Learning From Data.*

Finally, we have provided instructors with substantial resources. To begin with, we have added approximately 20 new problems to the end-of-chapter exercises and provided many more on the companion CD. Included on the instructor CD are sample test questions, exercises, and sample data sets. We have also generated Powerpoint® lectures for each chapter for instructors to use or edit, as they choose. There are a number of very useful graphics and illustrations that mirror the ones in the book. There are also fun, interactive exercises/demonstrations and tools that we have found useful (for example, data generation algorithms, Gaussian random number generators, etc.). As additional items become available, our Web site (www.LFD3.net) will provide users of the textbook access to them.

MANY THANKS

Many people have contributed to this book. We thank our students and colleagues at the University of Wisconsin–Madison and those instructors who used the first two editions and provided valuable comments. We also thank Laura D. Goodwin (University of Colorado, Denver), Richard E. Zinbarg (Northwestern University), Daniel S. Levine (University of Texas, Arlington), and Randall De Pry (University of Colorado, Colorado Springs) for their valuable reviews of many of the chapters and of the proposal for a third edition of the book. AMG thanks his instructors at the University of Michigan and Miami University. MEA thanks his instructors at Temple University, especially Ralph Rosnow, Alan Sockloff, and Phil Bersh. Thanks are due to the editorial and production staffs at Lawrence Erlbaum Associates, who tolerated delay after delay. Finally, thanks to Mina and Anna for their love and support.

Arthur M. Glenberg

Matthew E. Andrzejewski

Why Statistics?

*T*here are many ways to learn about the world and the people who populate it. Learning can result from critical thinking, asking an authority, or even from a religious experience. However, collecting data (that is, measuring observations) is the surest way to learn about how the world really is.

Unfortunately, data in the behavioral sciences are messy. Initial examination of data reveals no clear facts about the world. Instead, the data appear to be nothing but an incoherent jumble of numbers. To learn about the world from data, you must first learn how to make sense out of data, and that is what this textbook will teach you. *Statistical procedures are tools for learning about the world by learning from data.*

To help you to understand the power and usefulness of statistical procedures, we will explore two real (and important!) data sets throughout the course of the book. One of the data sets is courtesy of Professor Timothy Baker at the University of Wisconsin Center for Tobacco Research and Intervention (which we will call the Smoking Study). The data were collected to investigate several questions about smoking, addiction, withdrawal, and how best to quit smoking. The data set consists of a sample of 608 people who wanted to quit smoking. These people were randomly assigned (see Chapter 14 for the benefits of random assignment) to three groups. The participants in one group were given the drug bupropion

SR (Zyban) along with nicotine replacement gum. In a second group, the participants were given the bupropion along with a placebo gum that did not contain any active ingredients. The final group received both a placebo drug and a placebo gum. The major question of interest is whether people are more successful in quitting smoking when the the the active gum is added to the bupropion. These data are exciting for a couple of reasons. First, given the tremendous social cost of cigarette smoking, we as a society need to figure out how to help people overcome this addiction, and these data do just that. Second, the study included measurements of about 30 other variables to help answer ancillary questions. For example, there are data on how long people have smoked and how much they smoked; data on health factors and drug use; and demographic data such as gender, ethnicity, age, education, and height. These variables are described more fully within the Excel and SPSS data files on the CD that comes with this book and in Appendix A. The statistical tools you will learn about will give you the opportunity to explore these data to the fullest extent possible. You can ask important questions—some that may never have been asked before—such as whether drug use affects people's ability to quite smoking, and you can get the answers. In addition, these data will be used to illustrate various statistical procedures, and they will be used in the end-of-chapter exercises.

The second data set is courtesy of Professors Janet Hyde and Marilyn Essex of the University of Wisconsin–Madison. The data set is a subset of the data from the Wisconsin Maternity Leave and Health Project and the Wisconsin Study of Families and Work (we will refer to it as the Maternity Study). This project was designed to answer questions about how having a baby affects family dynamics such as marital satisfaction, and how various factors affect child development. The data set consists of measurements of 26 variables for 244 families. Some of these variables are demographic, such as age, education, and family income. Marital satisfaction was measured separately for mothers and fathers both before the child was born (during the 5th month of pregnancy) and at three times after the birth (1, 4, and 12 months postpartum). There are also data on how much the mother worked outside the house and how equally household tasks were divided among the mothers and fathers. Finally, there are eight measures of the quality of mother–child interactions at 12 months after birth, and three measures of child temperament (for example, hyperactivity) measured when the child was 4.5 years old. These variables are described more fully on the CD that comes with this book and in Appendix B. As with the smoking data, you are free to use these data to answer important questions, such as whether the amount of time that a mother works affects child development.

This chapter introduces a number of topics that are basic to statistical analyses. We begin with a discussion of variability, the cause of messy data, and move on to the distinctions between population and sample, descriptive and inferential statistics, and types of measurement found in the behavioral sciences.

VARIABILITY

The first step in learning how to learn from data is to understand why data are messy. A concrete example is useful. Consider the CESD (Center for Epidemiologic Studies Depression) scores from the Smoking Study (see Appendix A). Each participant rated 20 questions such as "I felt lonely" using a rating of 0 (rarely or none of the time during the past week) to 3 (most of the time during the past week). The score is the sum of the ratings for the participant. For the 601 participants for whom we have CESD scores, the scores range from 0 to 23. About a quarter of the scores are below 2, but another quarter are above 9. These data are messy in the sense that the scores are very different from one another.

> **Variability** is the statistical term for the degree to which scores (such as the depression scores) differ from one another.

Chapter 3 presents statistical procedures for precisely measuring the variability in a set of scores. For now, only an intuitive understanding of variability is needed. When the scores differ from one another by quite a lot (such as the depression scores), variability is high. When the scores have similar values, variability is low. When all the scores are the same, there is no variability.

Sources of Variability

It is easy enough to see that the CESD data are variable, but why are they variable? In general, variability arises from several sources. One source of variability is individual differences: Some smokers are more depressed than others; some have difficulty reading and understanding the items on the test; some smokers' answers on the inventory are more honest than the answers of other smokers. There are as many potential sources of variability due to individual differences as there are reasons for why one person differs from another in intelligence, personality, performance, and physical characteristics.

Another source of variability is the procedure used in collecting the data. Perhaps some of the smokers were more rushed than others; perhaps some were tested at the end of the day and were more tired than others. Any change in the procedures used for collecting the data can introduce variability. Finally, some variability may be due to conditions imposed on the participants, such as whether they are taking the placebo gum.

Variables and Constants

Variability does not occur only in textbook examples; it is characteristic of all data in the behavioral sciences. Whenever a behavioral scientist collects data, whether on the incidence of depression, the effectiveness of a psychotherapeutic technique, or the reaction time to respond to a stimulus, the data will be variable; that is, not all the scores collected will be the same. In fact, because data are variable, collecting data is sometimes referred to as measuring a variable (or a random variable).

> **A variable** is a measurement that changes from one observation to the next.

CESD is a variable because it changes from one smoker (observation) to the next. "Effectiveness of a psychotherapeutic technique" is another example of a variable, because a given technique will be more effective for some people than for others.

Variables should be distinguished from constants.

Constants are measurements that stay the same from one observation to the next.

The boiling point of pure water at sea level is an example of a constant. It is always 100 degrees Centigrade. Whether you use a little water or a lot of water, whether the water is encouraged to boil faster or not, no matter who is making the observation (as long as the observer is careful!), the water always boils at the same temperature. Another constant is Newton's gravitational constant, the rate of acceleration of an object in a gravitational field (whether the object is large or small, solid or liquid, and so on).

Many of the observations made in the physical sciences are observations of constants. Because of this, it is easy for the beginning student in the physical sciences to learn from data. A single careful observation of a constant tells the whole story.

You may be surprised to learn that there is not one constant in all of the behavioral sciences. There is no such thing as *the* effectiveness of a psychotherapeutic technique, or *the* depression score, because measurements of these variables change from person to person. In fact, because what is known in the behavioral sciences is always based on measuring variables, even the beginning student must have some familiarity with statistical procedures to appreciate the body of knowledge that comprises the behavioral sciences and the limitations inherent in that body of knowledge. In case you were wondering, this is why you are taking an introductory statistics course, and your friends majoring in the physical sciences are not.

The concept of variability is absolutely basic to statistical reasoning, and it will motivate all discussions of learning from data. In fact, the remainder of this chapter introduces concepts that have been developed to help cope with variability.

POPULATIONS AND SAMPLES

The psychologists studying addiction *might* be interested in the CESD scores of the specific smokers from whom they collected data. However, it is likely that they are interested in more than just those individuals. For example, they may be interested in the incidence of depression among all smokers in Wisconsin, or all smokers in the United States, or even all smokers in the world. Because depression is a variable that changes from person to person, the specific observations cannot reveal everything the researchers might want to know about all of these depression scores.

Statistical Populations

A statistical **population** is a collection or set of measurements of a variable that share some common characteristic.

One example of a population is the set of CESD scores of all smokers in Wisconsin. These scores are measurements of a variable (CESD), and they have the common characteristic of being from a particular group of people: smokers in Wisconsin. A different statistical population consists of the CESD scores for smokers in the United States. And, a very different population consists of the marital satisfaction scores for new mothers who work full-time outside of the home. The point is that you should not think of statistical populations as groups of people, such as the people in the United States. There is only one population of people for the United States, but there are an infinite number of statistical populations depending on what variables are measured (for example, CESD or marital satisfaction), and how those scores might be grouped (for example, smokers or working mothers).

Thinking of statistical populations as sets of measurements may appear cold and unfeeling. Nonetheless, thinking this way has a tremendous advantage in that it facilitates the application of the same statistical procedure to a variety of populations. Instead of having to learn one technique for analyzing and learning from depression scores, and another technique for analyzing IQ scores, and yet another for analyzing errors rats make in learning mazes, many of the same procedures can be applied in all of these cases. In every case we are dealing (statistically) with the same stuff, a set of measurements.

Unfortunately, thinking of statistical populations as sets of numbers can cause some people to become bored and lose interest in the enterprise. The way to counter this boredom is to remember that the statistical procedures are operating on numbers that have meaning: The numbers are scores that represent something interesting about the world (for example, the incidence of depression in smokers). As you read through this book, think about applying your new knowledge to problems that are of interest to you, and not just as manipulation of numbers.

The Problem of Large Populations

Some statistical populations consist of a manageable number of scores. Usually, however, statistical populations are very large. For example, there are potentially millions of CESD scores of smokers. When dealing with large populations, it is difficult and time consuming to actually collect all of the scores in the population. Sometimes, for ethical reasons, all the scores in the population cannot be obtained. For example, suppose that a medical researcher believes that she has discovered a drug that safely and effectively reduces high blood pressure. One way to determine the drug's effectiveness is to administer it to all people suffering from high blood pressure and then to measure their blood pressures. (The population of interest consists of the blood pressure scores of people suffering from high blood pressure who have taken the new drug.) Clearly, this would be time consuming and expensive. It would also be very unethical. After all, what if the medical researcher were wrong, and the drug did more harm than good? Also, even with a great national effort, not all the scores could be collected, because some of the people would die before they took the drug, others would have their blood pressures lowered by other drugs, and others would develop high blood pressure over the course of data collection.

We appear to have run across a problem. Usually, we are not interested in just a few scores, but in all the scores in a population. Yet, because behavioral scientists are interested in learning about variables (not constants), it is impossible to know for sure about all the scores in a population from measuring just a few of them. On the other hand, it is time consuming and expensive to collect all the scores in a population, and it may be unethical or impossible. What to do?

Samples

The solution to this problem is provided by statistical procedures based on sampling from populations.

> **A sample** is a subset of measurements from a population.

That is, a sample contains some, but usually not all, of the scores in the population. The 608 CESD scores are a sample from the population of CESD scores of all smokers.

An important type of sample is a random sample.

> **A random sample** is selected so that every score in the population has an equal chance of being included.

Whether a sample is random or not does not depend on the actual scores included in the sample, but on how the scores in the sample are selected. Only if the scores are selected in such a way that each score in the population has an equal chance of being included in the sample is the sample a random sample. The CESD scores are not a random sample of CESD scores of all smokers. These scores are only from people living in Madison and Milwaukee, Wisconsin, and there was no attempt to ensure that CESD scores of people living elsewhere were included. Procedures for producing random samples are discussed in Chapter 5.

As you will see in Chapters 5–22, random samples are used to help solve the problem of large populations. That is, with the data in a random sample, we can learn about the population from which the sample was obtained by using inferential statistical procedures.

DESCRIPTIVE AND INFERENTIAL STATISTICAL PROCEDURES

Descriptive Statistical Procedures

Because of variability, in order to learn anything from data, the data must be organized.

> **Descriptive statistical procedures** are used to organize and summarize the measurements in samples and populations.

In other words, descriptive statistical procedures do what the name implies—they describe the data. These procedures can be applied to samples and to populations. Most often, they are applied to samples, because it is rare to have *all* the scores in a population.

Descriptive statistical procedures include ways of ordering and grouping data into distributions (discussed in Chapter 2) and ways of calculating single numbers that summarize the whole set of scores in the sample or population (discussed in Chapters 2 and 3). Some descriptive statistical procedures are used to represent data graphically, because as everyone knows, a picture is worth a thousand words.

Inferential Statistical Procedures

The most powerful tools available to the statistician are inferential statistical procedures.

> **Inferential statistical procedures** are used to make educated guesses (inferences) about populations based on random samples from the populations.

These educated guesses are the best way to learn about a population short of collecting all of the scores in the population.

All of this may sound a bit like magic. How can you possibly learn about a whole population that may contain millions and millions (or, theoretically, an infinity) of scores by examining a small number of scores contained in a random sample from that population? It is not magic, however, and it is even understandable. Part II of this book presents a detailed description of how inferential statistical procedures work.

Inferential statistical procedures are so pervasive in our society that you have undoubtedly read about them and made decisions based on them. For example, think about the last time you heard the results of an opinion poll, such as the percentages of the registered voters who favor Candidates A, B, or C. Supposedly, your opinion is included in those percentages (assuming that you are a registered voter so that your opinion is included in the population). But on what grounds does the pollster presume to know your opinion? It is a safe bet that only rarely, if ever, has a pollster actually contacted you and asked you your opinion. Instead, the percentages reported in the poll are educated guesses based on inferential statistical procedures applied to a random sample.

In recent years, it has become fashionable for the broadcast and print media to acknowledge that conclusions from opinion polls are educated guesses (rather than certainties). This acknowledgment is in the form of a "margin of error." The "margin of error" is how much the reported percentages may differ from the actual percentages in the population (see Chapter 11 for details).

Another example of the impact of inferential statistical procedures on our daily lives is in our choices of foods and medicines. Many new food additives and medicines are tested for safety and approved by government agencies such as the Food and Drug Administration (FDA). But how does the FDA know that the new product is safe for you? In fact, the FDA does not know for sure. The decision that a new drug is safe is based on inferential statistical procedures. The FDA example raises several sobering issues about the data used by government agencies to set standards on which our lives literally depend. It is only recently that government agencies have insisted that data be collected from women, and without such data, it is uncertain if a particular drug is actually safe or effective for women. The terrible birth defects attributed to the drug Thalidomide occurred because no one had bothered to collect the data that would verify the safety of the drug with pregnant woman. Similarly, very little data on safe levels of environmental pollutants such as PCBs and pesticides have been collected from children. Consequently, our society may be setting the scene for a disaster by allowing into the environment chemicals that are relatively safe for adults but disastrous for children whose immune systems are immature and whose rapidly developing brains are sensitive to disruption by chemicals.[1]

---

[1] For an excellent discussion of these issues, see C. F. Moore (2003), *Silent scourge*. New York: Oxford University Press.

The final example of the use of inferential procedures is the behavioral sciences themselves. Most knowledge in the behavioral sciences is derived from data. The data are analyzed using inferential statistical procedures, because interest is not confined to just the sample of scores, but extends to the whole population of scores from which the sample was selected. If you are to understand the data of the behavioral sciences, then you need to understand how statistical procedures work.

MEASUREMENT

Data are collected by measuring a variable. But what does it mean to measure a variable?

> **Measurement** is the use of a rule to assign a number to a specific observation of a variable.

As an example, think about measuring the length of your desk. The rule for measuring length is, "Assign a number equal to the number of lengths of a standard ruler that fit exactly from one end of the desk to the other." In this example, the variable being measured is "length." The observation is the length of a specific desk, your desk. The rule is to assign a value (for example, 4 feet) equal to the number of lengths of a standard ruler that fit from one end of the desk to the other.

As another example, consider measuring the weight of a newborn baby. The variable being measured is weight. The specific observation is the weight of the specific baby. The measurement rule is something like, "Put the baby on one side of a balance scale, and assign to that baby a weight equal to the number of pound weights placed on the other side of the scale to get the scale to balance."

Measuring variables in the behavioral sciences also requires that we use a rule to assign numbers to observations of a variable. For example, one way to measure depression is to assign a score equal to the sum of the ratings of the CESD questions. The variable is depression, the specific observation is the depression of the person being assessed, and the rule is to assign a value equal to the sum of the ratings. Similarly, measuring intelligence means assigning a number based on the number of questions answered correctly on an intelligence test.

Considering Measurement in a Social and Political Context

The choice of what variables to measure in a study is no accident; usually those choices entail a lot of discussion and planning, and are often influenced by social or political motives of the researcher. The measurement rules, as well, usually involve much discussion, but the details are rarely stated in a study's results. At the very least, there's usually some ambiguity. Take, for example, the LONG variable in the Smoking Study, which measures the longest time without smoking. Let's say that a study participant answers "8 months," which would result in a score of 7 (6–12 months). But, if we probe further, we may find that the participant actually answered: "Well, I didn't smoke for 4 months, but then one night I had one cigarette, and then didn't have another for 4 months. I say 8 months because it was just a minor slip-up." Is the longest time without smoking for this individual 8 months or 4 months? Is "smoking" defined as "one cigarette" or "one drag" or "buying a pack"? If the researcher is interested in the effectiveness of a particular antismoking program, she may give this participant "a break" and count it as 8 months, because clearly, to her, this participant didn't relapse (it was only one cigarette, after all). A different researcher, interested in showing that all addicts wind up using again (relapsing) might say that one cigarette constitutes a relapse, and score this as 4 months. Political motives may enter a study in this way because for some people the only solution for drug addiction may be abstinence (for example, Alcoholics Anonymous), but for others, recreational drug use may be seen as OK in certain situations (for example, "harm reduction" approaches). In addition, a researcher's grant funding may be dependent on *having* and *solving* a social problem, and maybe even a "growing problem," even though the "problem" is not as big as one might think. Therefore, we should remain critical of how psychologists measure and contemplate what might have been included and what might have been left out.

Differences Among Measurement Rules

All rules for measuring variables are not equally good. They differ in three important ways. First, they differ in validity.

> **Validity** refers to how well the measurement rule actually measures the variable under consideration as opposed to some other variable.

Some intelligence tests are better than others because they measure intelligence rather than (accidentally) being influenced by creativity or memory for trivia. Similarly, some measures of depression are better than others because they measure depression rather than introversion or aggressiveness.

Measurement rules also differ in reliability.

> **Reliability** is an index of how consistently the rule assigns the same number to the same observation.

For example, an intelligence test is reliable if it tends to assign the same number to individuals each time they take the test. Books on psychological testing discuss validity and reliability in detail.[2]

Finally, a third difference among measurement rules is that the properties of the numbers assigned as measurements depend on the rule. At first blush, this statement may sound like nonsense. After all, numbers are numbers; how can their properties differ?

---

[2] A classic text is A. Anastasi (1988), *Psychological testing* (6th ed.). New York: Macmillan.

Properties of Numbers Used as Measurements

When numbers are measurements, they can have four properties. The first of these is the category property.

> The **category property** is that observations assigned the same number are in the same category, and observations assigned different numbers are in different categories.

For example, suppose that you are collecting data on the types of cars that American citizens drive, and you are most interested in the country in which the cars were manufactured. You could "measure" the country of manufacture (the variable) by using the following rule to assign numbers to observations: If the car was manufactured in the United States, assign it a 1; if manufactured in Japan, assign it a 2; if in Germany, a 3; if in France, a 4; if in Italy, a 5; and if manufactured anywhere else, a 0. These numbers have the category property because each observation assigned the same number (for example, 2) is in the same category (made in Japan).

These country-of-manufacture numbers are different from the numbers that we usually encounter. Typically, assigning a number to an observation (say, Observation A) means more than just assigning observation A to a specific category. For example, if Observation A is assigned a value of 1 and Observation B is assigned a value of 2, it usually means that Observation A is shorter, lighter, or less valuable than Observation B. This is not the case for the measurements of country of manufacture. A car manufactured in the United States (and assigned a number 1) is not necessarily shorter, lighter, or less valuable than a car manufactured in Japan (assigned the number 2). The point is, how we interpret the measurements depends on the properties of the numbers, which in turn depend on the rule used in assigning the numbers.

> Measurements have the **ordinal property** when the numbers can be used to order the observations from those that have the least of the variable being measured to those that have the most.

Consider another example. Suppose that a social psychologist investigating cooperation has a preschool teacher rank the four pupils in the class from least cooperative (first) to most cooperative (fourth). These cooperation scores (ranks) have two properties. First, the scores have the category property, because children assigned different scores are in different categories of cooperation. Second, the scores have the ordinal property because the scores can be used to order the observations from those that have the least to those that have the most cooperation. It is only when measurements have the ordinal property that we know that observations with larger measurements have *more* of whatever is being measured.

A third property that measurements may have is the equal intervals property.

> The **equal intervals property** means that whenever two observations are assigned measurements that differ by exactly one unit, there is always an equal interval (difference) between the observations in the actual variable being measured.

To understand what is meant by equal intervals, consider again measuring the cooperativeness of the four preschool children. The four children (call them Alana, Bob, Carol, and Dan) have cooperation scores of 1, 2, 3, and 4. The difference between Alana's cooperation *score* (1) and Bob's cooperation *score* (2) is 1. Likewise, the difference between Carol's cooperation *score* (3) and Dan's cooperation *score* (4) is 1. The important question is whether the actual difference in *cooperation* (not just the score) between Alana and Bob equals the actual difference in cooperation between Carol and Dan.

It is very unlikely that the difference in cooperation between Alana and Bob equals the difference in cooperation between Carol and Dan. The teacher simply ranked the children from least to most cooperative. The teacher did not take any precautions to ensure equal intervals. Alana and Bob may both be very uncooperative, with Bob being just a bit more cooperative than Alana (the actual difference in cooperation between Alana and Bob is a "bit"). Carol may also be on the uncooperative side, but just a bit more cooperative than Bob (the actual difference between Carol and Bob is a "bit"). Suppose, however, that Dan is the teacher's helper and is very cooperative. In this case, the difference in cooperation between Carol and Dan may be very large, much larger than the difference in cooperation between Alana and Bob. Because the differences in scores are equal (the difference in cooperation *scores* between Alana and Bob equals the difference in cooperation *scores* between Carol and Dan), but the differences in amount of cooperation (the variable) are not equal, these cooperation *scores do not* have the equal interval property.

Now consider using a ruler to measure the lengths of the four lines in Figure 1.1. The lines A, B, C, and D have lengths of 1, 2, 3, and 6 centimeters, respectively. Using a ruler to measure length generates measurements with the equal intervals property: For each pair of observations for which the measurements differ by exactly one unit, the differences in length are exactly equal. That is, the measurements assigned lines A (1) and B (2) differ by one, as do the measurements assigned lines B (2) and C (3); and, important to note, the actual difference in lengths between lines A and B exactly equals the actual difference in length between lines B and C.

FIGURE 1.1
Length measured using two different measurement rules.

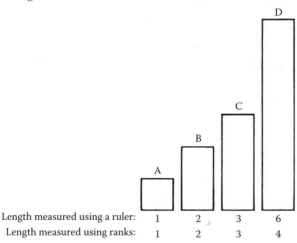

| Length measured using a ruler: | 1 | 2 | 3 | 6 |
| Length measured using ranks: | 1 | 2 | 3 | 4 |

A difficulty in understanding the equal intervals property is in maintaining the distinction between the variable being measured (length or cooperation) and the number assigned as a measurement of the variable. The numbers *represent* or stand for certain properties of the variable. The numbers are not the variable itself. The number 1 is no more the cooperation of Alana (it is a measure of her cooperation) than is the number 1 the actual length of line A (it is a measure of its length). Whether or not the measurements have properties such as equal intervals depends on how the numbers are assigned to represent the variable being measured. Using a ruler to measure length of a desk assigns numbers that have the equal intervals property; using rankings to measure cooperation of preschool children assigns numbers that do not have the equal intervals property.

The difference between the length and cooperation examples is not in what is being measured, but in the rule used to do the measuring. A ranking rule can be used to measure the lengths of lines (this is what we do when we need a rough measure of length—compare two lengths to see which is longer). In this case, the measured lengths of lines A, B, C, and D would be 1, 2, 3, and 4, respectively (see Figure 1.1). These measurements of length do *not* have the equal intervals property, because for each pair of observations for which the measurements differ by exactly one unit, the real differences in length are *not* exactly equal.

The fourth property that measurements may have is the absolute zero property.

> The **absolute zero property** means that a value of zero is assigned as a measurement only when there is nothing at all of the variable that is being measured.

When length is measured using a ruler (rather than ranks), the score of zero is an absolute zero. That is, the value of zero is assigned only when there is no length. When measuring country of car manufacture, zero is not an absolute zero. In that example, zero does not mean that there is no country of manufacture, only that the country is not the United States, Japan, Germany, France, or Italy.

Another example of a measurement scale that does not have an absolute zero is the Fahrenheit (or Centigrade) scale for measuring temperature. A temperature of 0°F does not mean that there is no heat. In fact, there is still some heat at temperatures of −10°F, −20°F, and so on. Because there is still some heat (the variable being measured) when zero is assigned as the measurement, the zero is not an absolute zero.[3]

Types of Measurement Scales

In addition to the four properties of measurements (category, ordinal, equal intervals, and absolute zero), there are four types of measurement rules (or scales), determined by the properties of the numbers assigned by the measurement rules.

> **A nominal scale** is formed when the numbers assigned by the measurement rule have only the category property.

---

[3] The Kelvin scale of temperature does have an absolute zero. On this scale, 0 means absolutely no heat. Zero degrees Kelvin equals −459.69°F.

"Nominal" comes from the word *name*. The numbers assigned using a nominal scale name the category to which the observation belongs but indicate nothing else. Thus, the measurements of country of manufacture of cars form a nominal scale, because the numbers name the category (country), but have no other properties.

Several of the variables in the Smoking Study are measured using nominal scales. For example, TYPCIG (type of cigarette smoked) is measured using a nominal scale defined as 1 = regular filter; 2 = regular no filter; 3 = light; 4 = ultra light; 5 = other. Another nominally measured variable is SPOUSE, that is, whether the smoker's spouse smokes (1) or does not smoke (0). The GENDER variable in the Maternity Study (is the child male or female) is also measured using a nominal scale.

> **An ordinal scale** is formed when the measurement rule assigns numbers that have the category and the ordinal properties, but no other properties.

Many of the variables in the Smoking and Maternity studies are measured using ordinal scales. The longest time without smoking (LONG) variable is measured as 1 = less than a day; 2 = 1–7 days; 3 = 8–14 days; 4 = 15 days to a month; 5 = 1–3 months; 6 = 3–6 months; 7 = 6–12 months; 8 = more than a year. As the assigned score increases from 1 to 8, the length of time without smoking increases, so the numbers have the ordinal property. However, the difference between a measurement of 1 and 2 (LONG 1 – LONG 2 = about 3 days) is not comparable to a difference between a measurement of, say, 5 and 6 (LONG 5 – LONG 6 = about 3 months), thus the measurements do not have the equal intervals property. The researchers might have attempted to measure LONG using a ratio scale by asking participants to estimate the longest number of days without smoking, from 0 to thousands of days. Unfortunately, people's estimates are often clouded by faulty memory processes and faulty estimates. One person who knows that he quit once for more than a year might estimate LONG as 500 days. Another person who had been abstinent for the same amount of time, but who can't remember whether he quit in the year 2001 or 1999, and who can't quite remember how to translate years into days, might estimate LONG as 10,000 days. Thus, these measurements are not as valid or reliable as the simpler ordinal measurements of the LONG scale.

Many behavioral scientists (and businesses that conduct marketing research) collect data by having people rate observations for specific qualities. For example, a clinical psychologist may be asked to rate the severity of his patients' psychopathologies on a scale from 1 (extremely mild) to 10 (extremely severe). As another example, a consumer may be asked to rate the taste of a new ice cream from 1 (awful) to 100 (sublime). In both cases, the measurements represent ordinal properties. For the clinical psychologist, the larger numbers represent more severe psychopathology than the smaller numbers; for the ice-cream raters, the larger numbers represent better-tasting ice cream than the smaller numbers. In neither example, however, do the measurements have the equal intervals property. *As a general rule, ratings and rankings form ordinal scales.*

The third type of scale is the interval scale.

> **Interval scales** are formed when the numbers assigned as measurements have the category, ordinal, and equal intervals properties, but not an absolute zero.

Two examples of interval scales are the Fahrenheit and Centigrade scales of temperature. Neither has an absolute zero because 0° (F or C) does not mean absolutely no heat. The measurements do have the category property (all observations assigned the same number of degrees have the same amount of heat), the ordinal property (larger numbers indicate more heat), and the equal intervals property (on a particular scale, a difference of 1° always corresponds to a specific amount of heat).

Many psychological variables are measured using scales that are between ordinal and interval scales. This statement holds for many of the variables included in the Maternity Study, such as marital satisfaction (for example, M1MARSAT), mother's positive affect during free play (MPOS), infant dysregulation during free play (IDYS), and child's internalizing behavior during free play (M7INT). Consider M7INT in a little more detail. To measure the variable, a mother was asked to rate her child's behavior in regard to nine questions such as, "Tends to be fearful or afraid of new things or new situations." The rating scale was 0 = does not apply; 1 = sometimes applies; 2 = frequently applies. Thus, the rating of each question forms an ordinal scale without the equal intervals property. But what happens when we sum the ratings from nine questions to get the M7INT score? It is unlikely that the difference in internalizing behavior between M7INT 10 and M7INT 11 is exactly the same as the difference between, say, M7INT 20 and M7INT 21. Nonetheless, it may well be that these two differences in internalizing behavior are fairly comparable, that is, that the scale is close to having the equal intervals property.

The conservative (and always correct) approach to these "in between" scales is to treat them as ordinal scales. As we will see in Part II, however, ordinal scales are at a disadvantage compared to interval scales when it comes to the range and power of statistical techniques that can be applied to the data. Recognizing this disadvantage, many psychologists treat the data from these in-between scales as interval data; that is, they treat the data as if the measurements were collected using an interval scale. One rule of thumb is that scores from the middle of an in-between scale are more likely to have the equal intervals property than scores from either end. If the data include scores from the ends of an in-between scale, it is best to treat the data conservatively as ordinal.

Many scales for measuring physical qualities (length, weight, time) are ratio scales.

> **A ratio scale** is formed when the numbers assigned by the measurement rule have all four properties: category, ordinal, equal interval, and absolute zero.

The reason for the name "ratio" is that statements about ratios of measurements are meaningful only on a ratio scale. It makes sense to say that a line that is 2.5 centimeters long is *half* (a ratio) the length of a 5-centimeter line. Similarly, it makes sense to say that 20 seconds is *twice* (a ratio) the duration of 10 seconds.

On the other hand, it does not make sense to say that 68°F is twice as hot as 34°F. This is easily demonstrated by converting to Centigrade measurements. Suppose that the temperature of Object A is 34°F (corresponding to 1°C) and that the temperature of Object B is 68°F (corresponding to 20°C). Comparing the amount of heat in the objects using the Fahrenheit measurements seems to indicate that Object B is twice as hot as Object A, because 68 is twice 34. Comparing the measurements on the Centigrade scale (which of course does not change the real amount of heat in the objects), it seems that Object B is 20 times as hot as Object A. Object B cannot be 20 times as hot as object A and at the same time be twice as hot. The problem is that statements about ratios are not meaningful unless the measurements are made using a ratio scale. Neither ratio (2:1 or 20:1) is right, because neither set of measurements was made using a ratio scale.

This problem does not occur when using a ratio scale. A 5-centimeter (2-inch) line *is* twice as long as a 2.5-centimeter (1-inch) line, and that is true whether the measurements are made in centimeters, inches, or any other ratio measurement of length.

Several variables in the Smoking Study are measured using ratio scales. One example is the carbon monoxide level at the end of treatment measured in parts per million (CO_EOT), and another is the number of times the participant has tried to quit smoking (QUIT).

Importance of Scale Types

The question that may be uppermost in your mind is, "So what?" There are three reasons why knowing about scale types is important. First, now that you know about scale types you will be less likely to make unsupportable statements about data. One such statement is the use of ratio comparisons when the data are not measured using a ratio scale. For example, consider a teacher who gives a spelling test and observes that Alice spelled 10 words correctly, whereas Bill spelled only 5 words correctly. Certainly, Alice spelled twice as many words correctly as did Bill. Nevertheless, the number of words correct on a spelling test is not a ratio measurement of spelling ability (zero words correct does not necessarily mean zero spelling ability). So, although it is perfectly correct to say that Alice spelled twice as many words correctly as did Bill, it is silly to say that Alice is twice as good a speller as is Bill. Similarly, it is not legitimate to claim that a child with an internalizing score (M7INT) of 20 internalizes twice as much as a child with a score of 10.

Second, the types of descriptive statistical procedures that can be applied to data depend in part on the scale type. Although some types of descriptions can be applied to data regardless of the scale type, others are appropriate only for interval or ratio scales, and still others are appropriate for ordinal, interval, and ratio scales, but not nominal scales.

Third, the types of inferential statistical procedures that can be applied to data depend in part on the measurement scale.

Given these three reasons, it is clear that if you want to learn from data you must be able to determine what sort of scale was used in collecting the data. The only way to know the scale type is to determine the properties of the numbers assigned using that rule. If the only property of the measurements is the category property, then the data are nominal; if the measurements have both the category and ordinal properties, then the data are ordinal; if, in addition, the data have the equal interval property, then the data are interval. Only if the data have all four properties are they ratio.

Now that you understand the importance of scale types, it may be helpful to read this section again. Your ability to distinguish among scale types will be used throughout this textbook and in all of your dealings with behavioral data.

USING COMPUTERS TO LEARN FROM DATA

Data analysis often involves some pretty tedious computations, such as adding columns of numbers. Much of this drudgery can be eliminated by using a computer program such as Excel, and *Learning From Data* is written to be used with that program. The CD that comes with this book provides the files that your Excel program requires to mesh with the book. First, open up the Read Me file and follow the instructions for loading the Excel Add-ins. These Add-ins provide computer routines that exactly match those used in the book. Second, if you are not familiar with basic Excel operations (e.g, for entering data in a spreadsheet or for selecting rows and columns), you should run the Excel tutorial. Third, the CD includes numerous data files. Two large data files provide the data from the Maternity and Smoking studies. Other data files provide the data used in all of the major worked-out examples and the end-of-chapter exercises.

What Statistical Analysis Programs Can Do for You

The programs have two main benefits. First, they eliminate the drudgery of doing lots of calculations. Second, they ensure accuracy of calculation. A benefit that flows from these two is that the programs make it easy to explore data by conducting multiple analyses.

What the Programs Cannot Do for You

Almost everything that is important is *not* done by the programs. The essence of statistical analysis is choice (choosing the right statistical method and interpretation of the outcome of the chosen method). The programs cannot choose the appropriate methods for you. Similarly, the programs do not know whether a data set is a sample, a random sample, or a population. Consequently, the program cannot adequately interpret the output. *Learning From Data* teaches you how to make good choices and how to interpret the outcome of the statistical methods; the computer eliminates the drudgery.

Because the computer program does the calculations, you might think that you can ignore the formulas in the text. That would be a big mistake for several reasons. First, for small sets of data it is easier to do calculations by hand (or using a calculator) rather than using a computer. But to do the calculations by hand, you need to know the formulas. Second, following the formulas is often the best way to figure out exactly what the statistical technique is doing and how it works. Working through the formulas can be hard intellectual labor, but that is the only way to understand what they do.

SUMMARY

The behavioral sciences are built on a foundation of data. Unfortunately, because behavioral data consist of measurements of variables, individual measurements will differ from one another so that no clear picture is immediately evident. Fortunately, we can learn from variable data by applying statistical procedures.

Descriptive statistical procedures organize, describe, and summarize data. Descriptive statistical procedures can be applied to samples or to populations, but because we rarely have all the scores in a population, descriptive procedures are generally applied to data from samples. We use inferential statistical procedures to make educated guesses (inferences) about a population of scores based on a random sample of scores from the population. Although these inferences are not error-free, appropriate use of inferential statistical procedures can reduce the chance of error to acceptable levels (for example, the margin of error in a poll).

Appropriateness of a statistical procedure depends in part on the type of measurement scale used in collecting the data. The measurement scale is determined by the properties of the numbers (assigned by the measurement). If the measurements have the category, ordinal, equal interval, and absolute zero properties, then a ratio scale is formed; if the measurements have all but the absolute zero property, an interval scale is formed. If the measurements have only the category and ordinal properties, they form an ordinal scale. Finally, if the measurements have only the category property, they form a nominal scale.

EXERCISES

Terms   *Define these new terms.*

variable	measurement
constant	category property
sample	ordinal property
random sample	equal intervals property
population	absolute zero property
descriptive statistical procedure	nominal scale
inferential statistical procedure	ordinal scale
validity	interval scale
reliability	ratio scale

Questions   *Answer the following questions.*
(Answers are given in the back of the book for questions marked with "†".)

1. Why would there be no need for descriptive or inferential statistical procedures if behavioral scientists could measure constants instead of variables?
2. List 10 different variables and 1 constant in the behavioral sciences.
3. Classify each of the following as a population, a sample, or both. When the answer is both, describe the circumstances under which the data should be considered a population and under which they should be considered a sample.
   a. Family incomes of all families in the United States.
   †b. Family incomes of all families in Wisconsin.
   c. The number of words recalled from a list of 50 words by 25 first-year college students who volunteer to take part in an experiment.
   d. The number of days spent in intensive care for all people who have undergone heart transplant surgery.
   e. The number of errors made by rats learning a maze.

4. Describe two examples of each of the four types of measurement scales. Indicate why each is an example of its type.

5. If you had a choice between using nominal, ordinal, interval, or ratio scales to measure a variable, what would be the best choice? Why?

6. A set of scores can be one type of scale or another, depending on what the set of scores represents. Consider the number of errors made by rats in learning a maze. If the data represent simply the number of errors, then the scores form a ratio scale. The numbers have all four properties, and it makes perfectly good sense to say that if Rat A made 30 errors and Rat B made 15 errors, then Rat A made twice as many errors as Rat B. Suppose, however, that the scores are used as a measure of rat intelligence. Are these scores a ratio measure of intelligence? Explain your answer. What are some of the implications of your answer?

7. Determine the type of measurement scale used in each of the following situations:

   a. A supervisor ranks his employees from least to most productive.

  †**b.** Students rate their statistics teacher's teaching ability using a scale of 1 (awful) to 10 (magnificent).

   c. A sociologist classifies sexual preference as 0 (heterosexual), 1 (homosexual), 2 (bisexual), 3 (asexual), 4 (other).

   d. A psychologist measures the time to complete a problem-solving task.

Descriptive Statistics

*T*he three chapters in Part I provide an introduction to descriptive statistical techniques. All of these techniques are designed to help you organize and summarize your data without introducing distortions. As you will see, once the data have been organized, it is far easier to make sense of them; that is, it is far easier to understand what the data are telling you about the world.

Three general types of descriptive techniques are covered. We begin in Chapter 2 with frequency distributions—a technique for arranging the scores in a sample or a population to reveal general trends. We will also learn how to use graphs to illustrate frequency distributions.

A second descriptive technique is computing statistics that summarize frequency distributions with just a few numbers. In Chapter 3, we will learn how to compute several indices of central tendency, the most typical scores in a distribution. We will also learn how to summarize the variability of the scores in a distribution.

Finally, we will consider two methods for describing relative location of individual scores within a distribution—that is, where a particular score stands relative to the others. Percentiles are introduced in Chapter 2. They are often used when reporting the results of standardized tests such as the Scholastic Aptitude Test (SAT) and American College Test (ACT). The other measure of relative standing is the standard score (or z score) discussed in Chapter 4. Standard scores are generally more useful than percentiles, but they require the same background to understand.

All of these descriptive techniques form the underpinning for the remainder of this book, which deals with inferential statistical techniques. Statistical inference begins with a description of the data in a sample, and it is this description that is used to make inferences about a broader population.

Frequency Distributions and Percentiles

*C*ollecting data means measuring observations of a variable. And, of course, these measurements will differ from one another. Given this variability, it is often difficult to make any sense of the data until they are analyzed and described. This chapter examines a basic technique for dealing with variability and describing data: forming a frequency distribution. When formed correctly, frequency distributions achieve the goals of all descriptive statistical techniques: They organize and summarize the data without distorting the information the data provide about the world.

This chapter also introduces two related topics, graphical representation of distributions and percentiles. Graphical representations highlight the major features of distributions to facilitate learning from the data. Percentiles are a technique for determining the relative standing of individual measurements within a distribution.

While reading this chapter, keep in mind that the procedures for constructing frequency distributions can be applied to populations and to samples. Because it is so rare to actually have all the scores in a population, however, frequency distributions are usually constructed from samples. Reflecting this fact, most of the examples in the chapter will involve samples.

FREQUENCY DISTRIBUTIONS

Suppose that you are working on a study of social development. Of particular interest is the age at which aggressive tendencies first appear in children. You begin data collection (measuring the aggressiveness variable) by asking the teacher of a preschool class to rate the aggressiveness of the 20 children in the class using the scale:

Meaning	Score Value
potential for violence	5
very aggressive	4
somewhat aggressive	3
average	2
timid	1
very timid	0

The data are in Table 2.1. As is obvious, the data are variable; that is, the measurements differ from one another. It is also obvious that it is difficult to learn anything from these data as they are presented in Table 2.1. So as a first step in learning from the data, they can be organized and summarized by arranging them in the form of a frequency distribution.

> A **frequency distribution** is a tabulation of the number of occurrences of each score value.

The frequency distribution for the aggressiveness data is given in Table 2.2. The second column lists the score values. The third column in Table 2.2 lists the frequency with which each score value appears in the data. Constructing the frequency distribution involves nothing more than counting the number of occurrences of each score value. There is a simple way to check whether the distribution has been properly constructed: The sum of the frequencies in the distribution should equal the number of observations in the sample (or population). As indicated in Table 2.2, the frequencies sum to 20, the number of observations.

TABLE 2.1
Aggressiveness Ratings for 20 Preschoolers

Child	Rating	Child	Rating	Child	Rating	Child	Rating
a	4	f	0	k	3	p	2
b	3	g	3	l	0	q	3
c	1	h	3	m	4	r	3
d	1	i	4	n	2	s	1
e	2	j	2	o	3	t	3

TABLE 2.2
Frequency Distributions for the Aggressiveness Data in Table 2.1

Meaning	Score Values	Frequency	Relative Frequency	Cumulative Frequency	Cumulative Relative Frequency
Very Timid	0	2	.10	2	.10
Timid	1	3	.15	5	.25
Average	2	4	.20	9	.45
Aggressive	3	8	.40	17	.85
Very Aggressive	4	3	.15	20	1.00
Potential for Violence	5	0	.00	20	1.00
		20	1.00		

It is clear that the frequency distribution has a number of advantages over the listing of the data in Table 2.1. The frequency distribution organizes and summarizes the data, thereby highlighting the major characteristics. For example, it is now easy to see that the measurements in the sample range from a low of 0 to a high of 4. Also, most of the measurements are in the middle range of score values, and there are fewer measurements in the ends of the distribution.

Another benefit provided by the frequency distribution is that the data are now easily communicated. To describe the data, you need to report only five pairs of numbers (score values and their frequencies).

Try not to confuse the numbers representing the score values and the numbers representing the frequencies of the particular score values. For example, in Table 2.2 the number "4" appears in the column labeled "score value" and the column labeled "frequency." The meaning of this number is quite different in the two columns, however. The score value of 4 means a particular level of aggressiveness (*very aggressive*). The frequency of 4 means the number of times a particular score value was observed in the data. In this case, a score value of 2 (*average*) was observed four times.

To help overcome any confusion, be sure that you understand the distinctions among the following terms. "Score value" refers to a possible value on the measurement scale. Not all score values will necessarily appear in the data, however. If a particular score value is never assigned as a measurement (for example, the score value 5, *potential for violence*), then that score value would have a frequency of zero. "Frequency" refers to the number of times a particular score value occurs in the data. Finally, the terms "measurement," "observation," and "score" are used interchangeably to refer to a particular datum—the number assigned to a particular individual. Thus, in Table 2.2, the score value of 1 (*timid*) occurs with a frequency of 3. Similarly, there are three scores (measurements, observations) with the score value of 1 (*timid*).

Relative Frequency

An important type of frequency distribution is the relative frequency distribution.

Relative frequency of a score value is the proportion of observations in the distribution at that score value. **A relative frequency distribution** is a listing of the relative frequencies of each score value.

The relative frequency of a score value is obtained by dividing the score value's frequency by the total number of observations (measurements) in the distribution. For example, the relative frequency of aggressive children (score value of 3) is 8/20 = .40.

Relative frequency is closely related to percentage. Multiplying the relative frequency by 100 gives the percentage of observations at that score value. For these data, the percentage of children rated aggressive is .40 × 100 = 40%.

The fourth column in Table 2.2 is the relative frequency distribution for the aggressiveness data. Note that all of the relative frequencies are between 0.0 and 1.0, as they must be. Also, the sum of the relative frequencies in the distribution will always equal 1.0. Thus, computing the sum is a quick way to ensure that the relative frequency distribution has been properly constructed.

Relative frequency distributions are often preferred over raw frequency distributions because the relative frequencies combine information about frequency with information about the number of measurements. This combination makes it easier to interpret the data. For example, suppose that an advertisement for Nationwide Beer informs you that in a "scientifically selected" sample, 90 people preferred Nationwide, compared to only 10 who preferred Brand X. You may conclude from these data that most people prefer Nationwide. Suppose, however, that the sample actually included 10,000 people, 90 of whom preferred Nationwide, 10 of whom preferred Brand X, and 9,900 of whom could not tell the difference. In this case, the relative frequencies are much more informative (for the consumer). The relative frequency of preference for Nationwide is only .009.

The same argument in favor of relative frequency can also be made (in a more modest way) for the data on aggressiveness. It is more informative to know that the relative frequency of aggressive children is .15 than to simply know that three children were rated as aggressive.

When describing data from *random* samples, relative frequency has another advantage. The relative frequency of a score value in a random sample is a good guess for the relative frequency of that score value in the population from which the random sample was selected. There is no corresponding relation between frequencies in a sample and frequencies in a population.

Cumulative Frequency

Another type of distribution is the cumulative frequency distribution.

A cumulative frequency distribution is a tabulation of the frequency of all measurements at or smaller than a given score value.

The fifth column in Table 2.2 is the cumulative frequency distribution for the aggressiveness scores. The cumulative frequency of a score value is the frequency of that score value plus the frequency of all smaller score values. The cumulative frequency of a score value of zero (*very timid*) is 2. The cumulative frequency of a score value of 1 (*timid*) is obtained by adding 3 (the frequency of *timid*) plus 2 (the frequency of *very timid*) to get 5. Note that the cumulative frequency of the largest score value (5) equals 20, the total number of observations. This must be the case, because cumulative frequency is the frequency of all observations at smaller than a given score value, and all of the observations must be at or smaller than the largest score value. Also, note that the cumulative frequencies can never decrease when going from the lowest to the highest score value. The reason is that the cumulative frequency of the next higher score value is always obtained by *adding* to the lower cumulative frequency.

The notion of "at or smaller" implies that the score values can be ordered so that we can determine what is "smaller." Thus, cumulative frequency distributions are usually not appropriate for nominal data.

> **A cumulative relative frequency** distribution is a tabulation of the relative frequencies of all measurements at or below a given score value.

The last column in Table 2.2 lists the cumulative relative frequencies for the aggressiveness data. These numbers are obtained by adding up the relative frequencies of all score values at or smaller than a given score value.

Cumulative frequency distributions are most often used when computing percentiles. We shall postpone further discussion of these distributions until that section of the chapter.

GROUPED FREQUENCY DISTRIBUTIONS

The aggressiveness data were particularly amenable to description by frequency distributions in part because there were only a few score values. Sometimes, however, the data are not so accommodating, and a more sophisticated approach is called for.

Consider, for example, the first 60 measurements on the YRSMK variable in the Smoking Study (Table 2.3). Because the measurements are variable, it is difficult to learn anything from the data as presented in this table.

The frequency distribution is presented in Table 2.4. As you can see, the frequency distribution for these data does not provide a very useful summary of the data. The problem is that there are too many different score values.

TABLE 2.3
YRSMK—Number of Years Smoking Daily From the First 60 Participants in the Smoking Study

5	13	17	20	19	35	21	28	3	22
26	13	30	30	30	32	40	27	14	4
27	33	28	45	29	25	38	35	33	39
5	4	20	24	25	27	16	25	38	9
36	20	18	11	12	23	22	27	32	49
22	30	0	32	4	23	9	29	22	23

TABLE 2.4
Frequency Distribution of First 60 YRSMK Scores

Score Value	Frequency	Score Value	Frequency	Score Value	Frequency
0	1	17	1	34	0
1	0	18	1	35	2
2	0	19	1	36	1
3	1	20	3	37	0
4	3	21	1	38	2
5	2	22	4	39	1
6	0	23	3	40	1
7	0	24	1	41	0
8	0	25	3	42	0
9	2	26	1	43	0
10	1	27	4	44	0
11	1	28	2	45	1
12	0	29	2	46	0
13	2	30	4	47	0
14	1	31	0	48	0
15	0	32	3	49	1
16	1	33	2		

The solution is to group the data into clusters called class intervals.

A class interval is a range of score values. **A grouped frequency distribution** is a tabulation of the number of measurements in each class interval.

The grouped frequency distribution is presented in Table 2.5. The class intervals are listed on the left. The lowest interval, 0–4, contains all of the measurements between (and including) 0 and 4. The next interval, 5–9, contains the measurements between 5 and 9, and so on.

Clearly, the data in the grouped distribution are much more easily interpreted than when the data are ungrouped. We can now see that most of the people in this sample have been smoking for 20–30 years, although there are a few who have been smoking for more than 45 years and a few who have been smoking only a couple of years.

Relative and cumulative frequency distributions can also be formed from grouped data. Relative frequencies are formed by dividing the frequency in each class interval by the total number of measurements. Cumulative distributions are formed by adding up the frequencies (or relative frequencies) of all class intervals at or below a given class interval. These distributions are also given in Table 2.5.

Constructing Grouped Distributions

A grouped frequency distribution should summarize the data without distorting them. Summarization is accomplished by forming class intervals; if the intervals are inappropriate (for

TABLE 2.5
Grouped Frequency Distributions for YRSMK Scores in Table 2.3

Class Interval	Frequency	Relative Frequency	Cumulative Frequency	Cumulative Relative Frequency
0–4	5	.083	5	.083
5–9	4	.067	9	.150
10–14	5	.083	14	.233
15–19	4	.067	18	.300
20–24	12	.200	30	.500
25–29	12	.200	42	.700
30–34	9	.150	51	.850
35–39	6	.100	57	.950
40–44	1	.017	58	.967
45–49	2	.033	60	1.00
Total	60	1.000		

TABLE 2.6
Grouped Frequency Distributions for YRSMK Scores in Table 2.3

Interval	f(YRSMK)
0–19	18
20–39	39
40–59	3
Total	60

example, too big), however, the data are distorted. As an example of distortion, Table 2.6 summarizes the YRSMK data from Table 2.3 using three large intervals. Indeed, the data are summarized, but important information regarding how the measurements are distributed is lost. The following steps should be used to construct grouped distributions that summarize but do not distort.

Guidelines for grouped frequency intervals:

1. There should be between 8 and 15 intervals.
2. Use convenient class interval sizes, like 2, 3, 5, or multiples of 5.
3. Start the first interval at or below your lowest score.

To construct a good grouped frequency distribution:

1. Compute the range of your scores by subtracting the lowest score from the highest score (Range = High Score – Low Score).
2. Divide the range by 8 and 15. Find a convenient number in between those two values. That will be your class interval. This is also known as your "bin width."

3. Select a starting value. The starting value could be your lowest score, but if your class interval is a multiple of 5, then you may want to select a more convenient, and hence lower starting point. For example, the intervals 0–9, 10–19, 20–29, etc., work very well if you have determined that a class interval of 10 is appropriate. If your lowest score is 3, the intervals 3–12, 13–22, 23–32, etc., do not seem as intuitive as 0–9, 10–19, 20–29, etc. (or 1–10, 11–20, 21–30, etc.).

4. Beginning with your starting value, construct intervals of increasing value.

5. Count the number (frequency) of scores in each interval.

One other step is needed when the measurements contain decimals instead of whole numbers. In these cases, all of the measurements should be rounded so that they have the same number of decimal places.

These steps were used to construct the grouped frequency distribution in Table 2.5. For Step 1, the range was computed as 49 (49 – 0). For Step 2, the range was divided by 8 (49/8 = 6.125) and 15 (49/15 = 3.267), and a convenient number in between those two (5) was selected as the class interval. For Step 3, because the lowest score was 0, the starting value was set at 0. For Step 4, starting with 0, consecutive intervals, of width 5, were constructed: 0–4, 5–9, 10–14, etc.

Note that the interval 5–9 includes the five score values 5, 6, 7, 8, and 9. Thus, the interval size really is 5, even though the difference between 9 and 5 is 4.

Once the lowest interval is specified, the remaining class intervals are easily constructed. Each successive interval is formed by adding the interval size (5) to the bounds of the preceding interval. For example, the interval 10–14 was obtained by adding 5 to both the lower and upper bounds of the interval 5–9. Finally, tabulate the number of measurements within each interval to construct the frequency distribution.

For a second example of grouping, consider the data in Table 2.7. The 60 measurements in this table are from the Smoking Study. Each measurement is a participant's score on the Wisconsin Inventory of Smoking Dependence Motives (WISDM), which are ratings on 65 questions such as "Does smoking make a good mood better?"

TABLE 2.7
First 60 Scores on the Wisconsin Inventory of Smoking Dependence Motives (WISDM)

52.9952	60.7071	53.2262	82.0333	65.9119	59.7071
44.4405	38.3167	62.2333	39.6786	46.2762	52.1119
68.4571	66.4476	28.2667	60.6667	50.0857	44.5690
33.6786	55.1119	21.8190	27.6929	53.1310	36.5500
57.4857	63.9262	60.0548	50.8071	61.2405	66.5810
55.3071	28.4643	43.9143	67.8524	54.7310	52.9429
60.8405	60.7238	51.0786	35.5071	54.2524	65.5429
60.1310	78.9357	65.1976	32.4833	51.2381	48.5786
62.5905	80.6071	54.0476	68.8190	52.1738	55.4214
61.4619	53.3571	35.8976	59.3190	68.1143	62.9429

Because these measurements contain decimals, we begin by making sure that all have the same number of decimal places, as they do. For Step 1, we compute the range of scores by subtracting the lowest score (21.8190) from the highest score (82.0333) to arrive at 60.2143.

In Step 2, we divide the range by 8 and 15: 60.2143/8 = 7.526788 and 60.2143/15 = 4.041287. We choose a number between these two results, preferably a multiple of 2, 3, or 5. We might choose 5.6901, which is a number between 7.526788 and 4.041287, and is divisible by 3, but 5.6901 will not serve as a convenient class interval. Rather, 5 is between 7.526788 and 4.041287, divisible by 5 (obviously), and convenient.

The third step, selecting a starting value, could be set at the lowest score, 21.8190, but 20.0000 seems more intuitive. The first interval, therefore, will be 20.0000–24.9999, the next 25.0000–29.9999, and so on. The final step is to tabulate the number of measurements in each interval to obtain the frequency distribution, and then divide each frequency by the total number of observations to obtain the relative frequency distribution.

As you can tell from Table 2.8, these data are very interesting. The distribution appears "top heavy." In other words, more than half of the scores are greater than 50. This may not be unexpected, though, for it is a measure of "smoking motives" and smokers (which all the participants in the study are) may have many motives to smoke. Nevertheless, these data may be important to the study's designers because they can show that their participants were highly motivated to smoke, as opposed to participants who weren't motivated to smoke. In the end, the study's authors, if the experiment is successful, can claim that their intervention works for people highly motivated to smoke.

TABLE 2.8
Relative Frequency Distribution for
WISDM Scores (First 60 Subjects)

Class Interval	Relative Frequency
20.0000–24.9999	0.017
25.0000–29.9999	0.050
30.0000–34.9999	0.033
35.0000–39.9999	0.083
40.0000–44.9999	0.050
45.0000–49.9999	0.033
50.0000–54.9999	0.233
55.0000–59.9999	0.100
60.0000–64.9999	0.200
65.0000–69.9999	0.150
70.0000–74.9999	0.000
75.0000–79.9999	0.017
80.0000–84.9999	0.033
Total	1.000

FIGURE 2.1
Relative frequency histogram for the aggressiveness scores in Table 2.2.

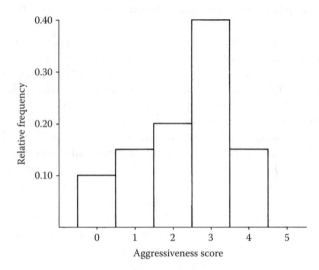

GRAPHING FREQUENCY DISTRIBUTIONS

Displaying a frequency distribution as a graph can highlight important features of the data. Graphs of frequency distributions are always drawn using two axes.

> The **abscissa** or **x-axis** is the horizontal axis. For frequency and relative frequency distributions, the abscissa is marked in units of the variable being measured, and it is labeled with the variable's name. The **ordinate** or **y-axis** is marked in units of frequency or relative frequency, and so labeled.

In Figure 2.1, the abscissa is labeled with values of the aggressiveness variable for the distribution in Table 2.2. The ordinate is marked to represent relative frequency of the measurements. Techniques for graphing frequency and relative frequency distributions are almost exactly the same. The only difference is in how the ordinate is marked. Because relative frequency is generally more useful than raw frequency, the examples that follow are for relative frequency distributions.

Histograms

Figure 2.1 is a relative frequency histogram for the aggressiveness data.

> **A relative frequency histogram** uses the heights of bars to represent relative frequencies of score values (or class intervals).

FIGURE 2.2
Relative frequency histogram for the number of years smoking scores in Table 2.5.

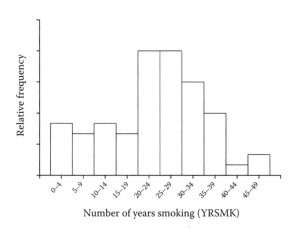

Number of years smoking (YRSMK)

To construct the histogram, place a bar over each score value. The bar extends up to the appropriate frequency mark on the ordinate. Thus, a bar's height is a visual analogue of the score value's relative frequency: the higher the bar, the greater the relative frequency.

Relative frequency histograms can also be drawn for grouped distributions. For these distributions, a bar is placed over each class interval.

Figure 2.2 is a relative frequency histogram of the YRSMK scores in Table 2.5. Sometimes, only the midpoints of each interval are shown on the abscissa. The midpoint of a class interval is the average of the interval's lower bound and the upper bound. Again, the height of each bar corresponds to its relative frequency.

The relative frequency histogram illustrated in Figure 2.2 makes particularly clear some of the salient characteristics of the distribution. For example, it is easy to see that most of the scores are in the middle of the distribution and that there is a decrease in frequency from the moderate scores to the higher scores.

Frequency Polygons

Figure 2.3 is an example of a relative frequency polygon using the WISDM scores in Table 2.8. The axes of a relative frequency polygon are the same as for a histogram. However, instead of placing a bar over each midpoint (or score value), a dot is placed over the midpoint so that the height of the dot corresponds to the relative frequency of the class interval. Next, adjacent dots are connected by straight lines.

As a convention, an additional midpoint (or score value) is added to each end of the distribution (the intervals "15–19" and "85–89" in Figure 2.3). These extra intervals are always drawn with a frequency of zero because no measurements are actually in the intervals. Using the zero-frequency midpoints "closes" the figure made by connecting the dots,

FIGURE 2.3
Relative frequency polygon for the scores on the WISDM in Table 2.8.

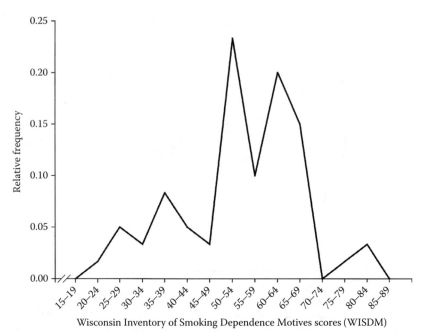

Wisconsin Inventory of Smoking Dependence Motives scores (WISDM)

producing a more visually pleasing figure. (A many-sided closed figure is a polygon, which is why this sort of graph is called a relative frequency polygon.)

Traditionally, the abscissa and the ordinate are drawn so that they intersect at a value of 0 on the ordinate and a value of 0 on the abscissa. In Figure 2.3, the double slash marks on the abscissa indicate that there is a "break" in the axis so that the first mark, 15, is not actually 15 units from the intersection.

In general, graphs highlight the salient characteristics of distributions more effectively than do tables. Comparison of Figure 2.3 and the distribution in Table 2.8 demonstrates this point nicely. Starting with the table, it takes some effort to appreciate that the distribution has high frequencies of high scores (intervals 50–54, 60–64, etc.). Figure 2.3 portrays this unusual quality dramatically and without requiring any effort to appreciate it.

When to Use Histograms and Frequency Polygons

We must answer two questions: When should we use graphing techniques? Given that a graph is appropriate, when should a histogram be used and when should a polygon be used? In answer to the first question, graphs of distributions are used whenever it is important to highlight features of the distribution such as the shape, the range (the number of score values), and the location of the distribution on the measurement scale (the typical or middle score values). Each of these features is easily grasped from a picture, but harder to obtain from just the tabular form of the distribution.

Often, graphs are used when two or more distributions must be compared. Because information such as shape of the distribution is easily obtained from a graph, you can actually see that graphs of two distributions are similar or dissimilar in shape. Comparison of two distributions in tabular form is usually more difficult.

The choice between the use of histograms and polygons is often a matter of personal taste. There is one generally accepted rule, however, that depends on the distinction between discrete and continuous variables.

> A **discrete variable** can take on a limited number of score values (such as whole numbers) and can be measured exactly. **A continuous variable** can take on any score value and requires an infinite number of decimal places to specify.

The distinction between continuous and discrete does not depend on the measurement scale, but on the nature of the variable. For example, the variable "family size" is a discrete variable because it can take on only a limited number of score values (whole numbers). This is true whether we measure family size using an ordinal scale (small, medium, or large) or a ratio scale (the actual count of family members).

On the other hand, a variable such as "time to make a grammaticality judgment" is a continuous variable—time can take on an unlimited number of score values. The variable is continuous even if our measuring device (clock) gives measurements only to the nearest whole second.

The rule for deciding between histograms and polygons is that histograms should be used when the variable is discrete or when the variable is measured on a nominal scale; otherwise, it may be preferable to use a polygon. The reason for this is simple. Connecting the points together in the polygon suggests that there are possible score values between the points. Furthermore, the lines connecting the points in a polygon suggest that the relative frequencies of these in-between score values can be estimated by the heights of the lines. Indeed, these suggestions are often appropriate for continuous variables. However, these suggestions are misleading for discrete variables, because there are no score values in between those indicated in the graph. Thus, histograms should be used for discrete variables.

CHARACTERISTICS OF DISTRIBUTIONS

Distributions differ in three major characteristics: shape, central tendency, and variability. Over the next few pages, we will practice comparing distributions by using these characteristics and you will see that they play a major role in the study of statistics.

All of the illustrations that follow will use relative frequency polygons. However, dots will not be placed over specific score values, and continuous lines will be used to illustrate the general shapes of the distributions. The purpose of this departure from standard procedure is to illustrate general principles that do not depend on specific distributions.

Shape

The shape of a distribution can be broadly classified as symmetric, positively skewed, or negatively skewed.

FIGURE 2.4
Relative frequency distributions of various shapes.

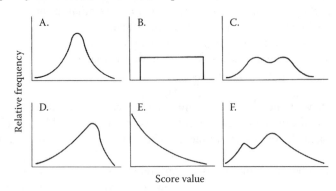

A symmetric distribution can be divided into two halves that are mirror images of each other.

The distributions illustrated in the top row of Figure 2.4 are symmetric distributions. The distribution of years smoking in Figure 2.2 can be characterized as "somewhat symmetric."

In contrast, a skewed distribution cannot be divided into halves that are mirror images. The distributions illustrated in the bottom row of Figure 2.4 are skewed, as is the distribution of WISDM scores in Figure 2.3.

> **A positively skewed distribution** has score values with low frequencies that trail off toward the positive numbers (to the right). **A negatively skewed distribution** has score values with low frequencies that trail off toward the negative numbers (to the left).

Distributions E and F in Figure 2.4 are positively skewed; Distribution D has a negative skew. Note that a skewed distribution has one "tail" that is longer than the other. If the longer tail is pointing toward the positive numbers, then the distribution has a positive skew; if the longer tail is pointing toward the negative numbers, then the distribution has a negative skew.

Salary distributions are often positively skewed. Salaries cannot be less than $0.00, so the tail on the left cannot trail off very far. Most people have salaries in the midrange, but some people have very large salaries, and some (although relatively few) have enormous salaries. The people with enormous salaries produce a positive skew in the distribution.

Modality is another aspect of the shape of a distribution. Modality is the number of clearly distinguishable peaks in the distribution.

> A **unimodal distribution** has one peak. A **bimodal distribution** has two peaks. A **multimodal distribution** has more than two peaks.

In Figure 2.4, Distributions A, D, and E are unimodal, and Distributions C and F are bimodal.

Some shapes of distributions have special names. A distribution that is unimodal and symmetric (such as Distribution A in Figure 2.4) is called a bell-shaped distribution. (A normal distribution is a special type of bell-shaped distribution that we will discuss in Chapter 4.) Many psychological variables (such as intelligence) have bell-shaped distributions.

Distribution B in Figure 2.4 is called a rectangular distribution. Note that this distribution is symmetric, but it does not have a well-defined mode. Rectangular distributions indicate that all of the score values have the same relative frequency. Rectangular distributions often arise in gambling situations, such as tossing a fair coin (relative frequency of heads = relative frequency of tails = .5) and rolling a fair die (each number has a relative frequency of one sixth).

Distribution E in Figure 2.4 is called a J-curve (although backward J-curve would be more appropriate). This distribution is positively skewed, and is frequently seen in the relative frequencies of rare events, such as number of lotteries won. Most of us have never won a lottery, so the score value of zero has the greatest relative frequency. Some people have won one or two lotteries, and a few have won even more, producing the long tail on the right.

Central Tendency

In addition to shape, distributions differ in central tendency.

> The **central tendency of a distribution** is the score value near the center of the distribution. It is a typical or representative score value.

You may think of the central tendency as the score value that is most representative of the distribution—that is, the score value that you would choose to give the general flavor of the distribution. On the other hand, you may think of the central tendency as the location of the center of the distribution on the measurement scale (represented by the abscissa in a graph). In Chapter 3, we will discuss the mean, the median, and the mode, which are numerical indices of central tendency.

The distributions in the top row of Figure 2.5 have the same shape, but differ in central tendency (the central tendencies are indicated by arrows). In the bottom of the figure, the distributions differ in both shape and central tendency. In both the top and the bottom, the central tendency increases from left to right.

Variability

As you will recall, variability is the driving force behind statistics. Indeed, distributions arise because we measure variables so that not all the measurements are the same.

> **Variability** is the degree to which the measurements in a distribution differ from one another.

When all the measurements in a distribution are similar, the distribution has little variability. In fact, in the rare instance when all of the measurements in the distribution are the

FIGURE 2.5
Top: **Distributions that differ only in central tendency.** *Bottom:* **Distributions that differ in shape and central tendency.**

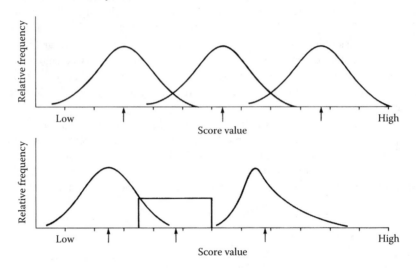

same, the distribution has no variability. When the measurements in a distribution deviate greatly from one another, the distribution has much variability. In Chapter 3, we will learn how to compute the variance and the standard deviation, two particularly useful numerical indices of variability.

The top half of Figure 2.6 illustrates how distributions can have the same general shape and the same central tendency, but differ in variability. Variability increases from Distribution A to B to C.

The bottom of Figure 2.6 illustrates how distributions can have different central tendencies and different variabilities. From left to right, the distributions increase in central tendency. However, Distribution D has the greatest variability and Distribution E has the least variability.

Comparing Distributions

Now that you have learned how distributions can differ, you have the skills needed to quickly compare and summarize distributions. Simply determine how the distributions compare in terms of shape, central tendency, and variability.

Recall that in the beginning of this chapter we started with an example of a psychologist investigating the development of aggressive behavior. Suppose that the psychologist had segregated the data by sex of the children and had constructed separate relative frequency distributions for the girls and the boys. Figure 2.7 illustrates two possible distributions.

The distribution for the girls is more symmetric than that for the boys; the distribution for the boys is positively skewed. Both distributions are unimodal. The two distributions have similar central tendencies, but they differ in variability; the distribution for the boys is more variable than that for the girls.

FIGURE 2.6
Top: **Distributions that differ only in variability.** *Bottom:* **Distributions that differ in both variability and central tendency.**

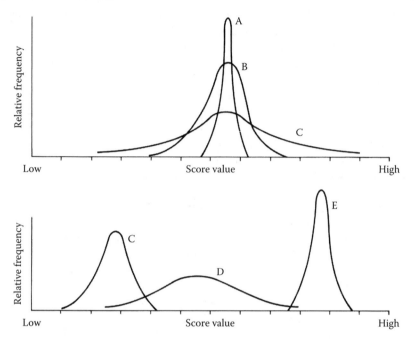

FIGURE 2.7
Distributions of aggressiveness scores for boys and girls.

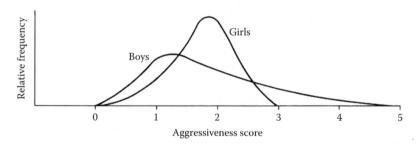

Now that the data have been described, it is up to you to determine their importance. Why is the distribution for the boys more variable than that for the girls? Does this represent a basic difference between the sexes, or is it due to socialization? Should these data be used to argue for social change? Of course, these particular questions are not statistical questions, and statistical analyses will not provide answers to them. The point is that statistical analysis can transform the data into a form that helps *you* to ask good questions. But it is up to you to ask the questions.

PERCENTILES

We have been working with whole distributions and paying little attention to individual measurements within a distribution. At times, however, the individual measurements are of great importance. Consider this example. One of your professors has just handed back your exam. On the top, in bold red ink, is the number 32. At first you are worried. But when you see the 25 on your neighbor's paper, you begin to feel a little better. Still, is 32 a good score?

How good an exam score is depends in part on how you define "good." As a first approximation, you might think that a good score on a test corresponds to achieving close to the maximum possible. Thus, if the exam had a total of 50 points possible, your score of 32 corresponds to 64% correct, which is not very good.

Suppose, however, that the exam was extremely difficult and your score of 32 is one of the best in the class. In this case, you are justified in thinking that your score of 32 (or 64%) is really very good.

The point is this: An informative index of the goodness of a score is the standing of that score relative to the other scores in a distribution. Scores that are near the top of the distribution are "good," regardless of the actual score value or the percent correct. Scores near the bottom of the distribution are "poor," regardless of the actual score value. (If you obtained 90% correct on a test, that would be a "poor" score if everyone else in the class obtained 100% correct.)

Percentile ranks provide just such an index of goodness by giving the *relative standing* of a score—the score's location in the distribution relative to the other measurements in the distribution. More formally:

> The **percentile rank** of a score value is the percent of measurements in the distribution below that score value.

Note that percentile rank and percent correct are not the same. A score value of 80% correct might have any percentile rank between 0 and 100, depending on the number of measurements in the distribution less than 80% correct.

When exam grades are given as percentiles, you have an easily interpreted index of relative standing—how well you did relative to the others in the distribution. If your score has a percentile rank of 95%, then you did better than 95% of the others in the distribution. If your score has a percentile rank of 30%, you did better than 30% of the others.

Percentile ranks are often used to report the results of standardized tests such as the SAT (Scholastic Aptitude Test) and the GRE (Graduate Record Examination). Your percentile rank indicates the percentage of students who received scores lower than yours. So, in terms of your relative performance, you should be happier with higher percentile ranks than lower percentile ranks.

Of course, percentile ranks are not always associated with just exam scores. As we will see, percentile ranks can be determined for scores in any distribution (as long as the measurement scale is not nominal). Thus, you can determine the percentile rank of an aggressiveness score of 4, or the percentile rank of a WISDM score of 62.4963.

Percentile Ranks and Percentiles

As you now know, the percentile rank of a score value indicates the percent of measurements smaller than that score value. In the context of percentile ranks, the score values themselves are often called percentiles.

> The Pth **percentile** is the score value with $P\%$ of the measurements in the distribution below it.

Three Precautions

There are three things to be aware of when you use percentiles and percentile ranks. First, percentile ranks and percentiles are only approximate; for grouped distributions, particularly, answers will be approximate.

Second, percentile ranks are an ordinal index of relative standing. That is, the percentile rank of a score value indicates that $P\%$ of the measurements are smaller than the score value; the percentile rank does not indicate *how* far below.

Third, percentile ranks can be interpreted only within the context of a specific distribution. An example will help to make this precaution clear. Suppose that your score on an English-language achievement test has a percentile rank of 15% (that is, your score is in the 15th percentile). Such a low score might at first be alarming.

However, if all the other measurements in the distribution come from graduate students in English, your score is perfectly reasonable. That same score value may be in the 75th percentile if the test were given to high school students. Remember, percentile ranks are a measure of relative standing—the location of a particular score value relative to the other measurements in the *distribution*. Thus, interpretation of a percentile rank depends on careful consideration of the sample (or population) described by the distribution.

COMPUTATIONS USING EXCEL

Constructing Frequency Distributions

Constructing a frequency distribution can be a tedious enterprise, especially if a data set contains a large number of scores. Take, for example, the Smoking Study data on the CD provided with the book. In a previous example, we looked at the first 60 scores on the YRSMK variable (Number of Years Smoking Daily) from the Smoking Study, but there are 608 total scores in the data set. It would probably take hours to construct a frequency distribution, and then there will likely be errors.

Constructing a frequency distribution in Excel can be accomplished using the LFD3 Analysis Add-in. Open the Smoking data set in Excel, then click on "Tools" and select "LFD Analyses," which will bring up a window with a number of additional analysis tools. "Frequency Distribution" is the first option. When you select this option, a new window

FIGURE 2.8

Completed frequency distribution analysis using YRSMK data and the LFD3 Add-in.

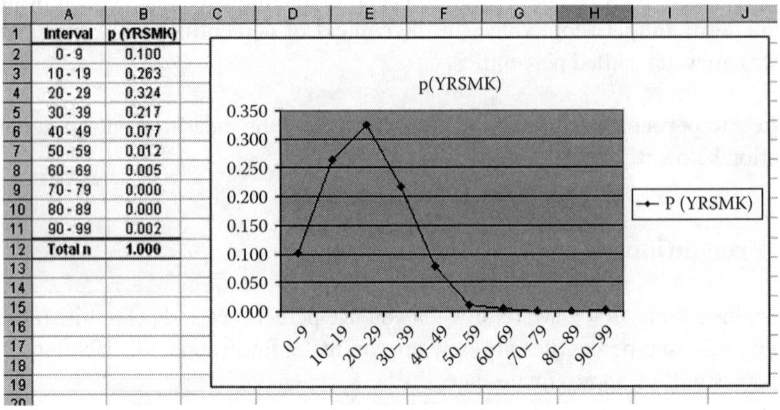

will open that is divided into five sections (all of the analyses in the LFD3 Add-in will look similar). The program that completes the frequency distribution is a complicated program—to take you through every option would take many pages and figures. Some of the options may be self-explanatory; others may be confusing. Don't worry—we've provided very detailed help with the add-in. In other words, if you don't know what "Grouped By" means, click on the Help button and find out!

By entering the appropriate range of data, starting value, and interval width, you should be able to produce something like Figure 2.8.

As you can see, running the frequency distribution add-in quickly summarizes a large data set in both tabular and graphical form. The graph of the YRSMK data is especially revealing: The distribution has a positive skew with a central tendency in the interval 20–29.

However, like any convenient procedure, the results produced by an add-in can be inappropriate and deceiving. Interpreting the results of an analysis that has not been well thought out (What should the class interval size be? What should the starting value be?) may be difficult or ineffective. For example, if you look closely at the frequency distribution in Figure 2.8, the interval 90–99 contains a proportion of .002 of the scores. The proportion .002 represents a single score out of the 608 total scores (rounded up). Therefore, there is a single person in the Smoking Study who has smoked for 90 or more years (92 years, actually). Is it possible that a person in the study has been smoking for 92 years? If so, they must be at least 100 years old! Upon closer inspection of the data set, though, you can see that this participant is 45 years old. In this case, it appears that there was a data entry error (it should read 29, not 92).

Although this is a relatively minor mistake, which was subsequently caught by the experimenters, its impact on our frequency distribution shouldn't be overlooked. Note that the two preceding intervals, 70–79 and 80–89, are empty (contain a 0.000 proportion of the scores). Thus, our "summary" of this data set may have too few intervals, thereby obscuring some potentially interesting features (if we removed the last three intervals, there would be seven remaining, which, according to the guidelines is too few).

Estimating Percentile Ranks With Excel

In Table 2.2, each of 20 children was given an "aggressiveness score" from 0 to 5. Let's say that you are interested in the percentile rank of a score of 3. Using Excel to estimate the percentile rank of the aggressive score "3," use the worksheet function "PERCEN-TRANK," which *requires* two arguments, "ARRAY" and "X." If you enter appropriate values for these arguments, Excel will estimate the percentile rank of the value X in the distribution of values specified by ARRAY. For this function to work, ARRAY has to be a "Range" in Excel, or a group of cells that contain numbers. X also has to be a number, although it doesn't have to be a number in the ARRAY.

By entering all the aggressiveness scores in a single column in an Excel spreadsheet and using the PERCENTRANK function, the value "0.473" appears. Multiplying by 100% = 47.30%. In other words, the percentile rank of the score of 3 in the aggressiveness scores is 47.3%.

Estimating Percentiles

Lastly, what is the score value with *P%* of the measurements below it, or the *P*th percentile? Using Excel's "PERCENTILE" function, the 35th percentile of YRSMK, for example, requires entering the range of data and percentile as arguments in the function. Doing this, Excel returns a value 19. In other words, 35% of the scores are at or smaller than 19. Put another way, a score of 19 is the 35th percentile.

SUMMARY

The purpose of descriptive statistics is to organize and summarize data without distortion. One way of achieving this goal is to construct a frequency distribution or a relative frequency distribution. A frequency distribution is a tally of the number of times a particular score value appears in a sample or population. Relative frequency is obtained by dividing these tallies by the total number of measurements. Because relative frequency combines information about frequency and the total number of scores, it is generally more useful than raw frequency. Cumulative frequency (and cumulative relative frequency) distributions tally the number of occurrences of measurements at or below a given score value. They are most useful in calculating percentiles and percentile ranks.

When the measurements in a distribution are scattered across a large number of different score values, frequencies are tabulated for class intervals rather than for individual score values. Choice of interval size is not automatic; the intervals must be chosen so that they do not distort the data. Although there are heuristic suggestions for choosing interval size, the ultimate decision rests on your analysis of the specific distribution with which you are working.

Graphs of frequency distributions highlight major characteristics of distributions and facilitate comparison among distributions. Histograms use the heights of bars to indicate frequency or relative frequency and are often used for nominal scales and when the measured variable is discrete. Polygons use connected points to indicate frequency and relative frequency. Polygons are often used for measurements of continuous variables. Most commonly, distributions are described and compared in terms of shape (whether the distribution is symmetric or skewed and modality), central tendency (typical score value), and variability (degree to which the scores differ from each other).

Percentile ranks are a measure of relative standing. The percentile rank of a score value indicates the percent of measurements in the distribution below that score value. A score value with a percentile rank of *P*% is called the *P*th percentile. Reporting the percentile rank of a score provides much more information than the score value alone, because the percentile rank indicates the position of that score within the distribution.

Nonetheless, three precautions should be used when interpreting percentile ranks. First, percentile ranks are only approximate. Second, percentile ranks are an ordinal index of relative standing, even when the original measurements are interval or ratio. Third, interpretation of percentile ranks depends on the particular sample (or population) that is described by the distribution.

EXERCISES

Terms   *Define these new terms.*

frequency distribution	upper real limit
relative frequency	abscissa
cumulative frequency	ordinate
cumulative relative frequency	histogram
class interval	frequency polygon
midpoint	discrete variable
lower real limit	continuous variable
symmetric distribution	central tendency
positive skew	variability
negative skew	percentile rank
unimodal	percentile
bimodal	

Questions   *Answer the following questions.*

1. Table 2.9 contains three sets of scores. For each set construct
   a. frequency and relative frequency distributions.
   b. a cumulative relative frequency distribution.
2. Assume that the first set of scores in Table 2.9 represents the IQ scores of children who have been participating in a school lunch program, and the second set of scores represent the IQs of a similar group of children who have not participated in the program.

TABLE 2.9

Set 1			Set 2			Set 3		
75	95	103	82	101	89	0	2	0
100	93	91	114	128	118	1	0	0
90	92	89	105	91	100	0	0	1
105	86	85	99	113	106	0	0	0
81	96	103	106	102	95	0	0	0
99	94	95	120	97	106	2	0	0
91	97	92	103	105	112	0	0	2
107	75	106	98	85	93	0	1	0
92	97	88	107	119	104	0	0	4
87	89	104	110	97	109	1	0	0
97	113	93	100	109	95	1	0	0
108	101	84	115	83	103	0	1	0
96	83	98	90	108	83			
115	109	98						
88	110	99						
94	103	79						
95	114	118						
102	104							

    a. Prepare appropriate graphical representations of the frequency and relative frequency distributions.

    †**b.** Is the relative frequency or the frequency distribution more appropriate when making comparisons between the two sets?

    c. Compare the two distributions.

    †**d.** What conclusions do you draw from these data?

3. Assume that the third set in Table 2.9 is data from a survey of riders of a city bus system. Each rider was asked to indicate the number of times he or she had taken a bus on a Sunday during the previous month.

    a. Prepare a graphical representation of the relative frequency data.

    b. What conclusions do you draw from these data?

4. Data in Table 2.10 were collected by an agency responsible for ensuring nondiscrimination in housing in a particular city. For each measurement, a young couple inquired about an apartment that had been advertised as available for rent. The data labeled "minority" are the measurements made when the young couple was a member of a minority group. The measurement scale was: 1, shown the apartment and asked to sign a lease; 2, shown the apartment; 3, told that the manager was unavailable for showing the apartment; 4, told that the apartment was no longer for rent; 5, received no response.

    a. Construct a graphic representation of the data.

    †**b.** What do you conclude from a comparison of the distributions?

TABLE 2.10

Minority			Majority		
1	4	2	1	2	1
2	2	3	2	1	1
2	2	1	1	5	5
1	1	2	1	1	2
3	2	1	1	1	1
2	1	2	2	1	1
4	2	2	1	2	3
2	2	2	3	1	2
5	3	4	2	1	1
2	1	1	1	4	2

†5. For each of the sets of data in Table 2.9, use Excel to find the following percentiles: 5th, 25th, 70th, and 90th.

†6. For the first two sets of data in Table 2.9, find the percentile ranks of the score values 80, 100, and 115.

7. Use Excel to find the median (50th percentile) number of bus rides for the third distribution in Table 2.9.

8. A student obtained a score of 77 on a 100-point test. He was also told that his percentile rank was 56. The student complained that because he got 77 out of 100, it was clear that his percentile rank should be 77. Explain how his score could have a percentile rank of 56.

9. Using the data from the Smoking Study and Excel:
   a. Construct a frequency distribution and graphical representation of the "TYPCIG" scores.
   b. Can you find the 45th percentile of the "TYPCIG" scores? What does this mean?
   c. Construct a relative frequency distribution of the "CIGDAY" scores.
   d. Determine the 25th, 50th, and 75th percentiles of the "CIGDAY" scores.
   e. What are the percentile ranks of 12, 17, 27, and 35 in the distribution of "CIGDAY" scores?
   f. Construct a relative frequency distribution and graphical representation of the ages of the participants in the Smoking Study.
   g. What are the percentile ranks of 24, 36, 48, and 55 years old in the distribution of ages?
   h. What are the 5th, 10th, 90th, and 95th percentiles in the distribution of ages?

10. Your friend, who is taking a remedial math course, is proud that he was at the 85th percentile on the last exam. He points out that because you were at the 75th percentile on your last statistics exam, he is actually better in math than you. What is your response to his reasoning?

11. Sketch two relative frequency distributions in which Distribution A has a greater central tendency than Distribution B, Distribution A has less variability than Distribution B, and both are negatively skewed.
12. Sketch two relative frequency distributions in which Distribution A is symmetric, has a small central tendency, and large variability, and Distribution B is skewed, has a large central tendency, and large variability.

Central Tendency and Variability

*T*hree important characteristics of a distribution are its shape, central tendency, and variability. In Chapter 2, we discussed how to determine the shape of a distribution; this chapter will explain how to compute measures of central tendency and variability. It is a key chapter because these concepts play an important role in the study of statistics. For example, a variety of inferential statistical techniques attempt to infer the value of the population central tendency from data in a random sample.

The chapter begins with a slight digression to introduce a mathematical shorthand called sigma notation. As you will see, it is useful in simplifying the presentation of equations for computing central tendency and variability.

SIGMA NOTATION

A Σ is the Greek capital letter *sigma*. When used in equations it is shorthand for the phrase, "sum up the indicated sequence of quantities." The important question is, of course, what sequence?

To make this discussion concrete, suppose that you are a sports psychologist who is studying why some people seem to be more prone to injuries than others. You measure the variable "number of injuries sustained during sports activities in the last year" for members of the university baseball team. The data are:

Player	1	2	3	4	5	6	7	8	9
Number of injuries (X)	0	3	1	0	2	2	2	5	1

In sigma notation, the direction to "add up the number of injuries for all of the players" is:

$$\sum_{i=1}^{n} X_i$$

The "X" stands for the variable that is being measured, whether it is number of injuries, aggressiveness scores, or whatever. The subscript "i" is a position index; it specifies the positions of the scores that go into the sum. The starting value of the index (the position of the first score that goes into the sum) is indicated by the "$i = 1$" at the bottom of the Σ. The final value of the index (the position of the last score that goes into the sum) is given by the number at the top of the Σ. If the letter n is at the top of the Σ, it indicates that the final value of the position index is the last (nth) score. Each change in the index from the starting value to the final value indicates that a new measurement is to be added into the sum.

The shorthand expression can be expanded by writing out the Xs for all of the values of the index between the starting value (of the index) and the final value. Expanding the expression gives:

$$\sum_{i=1}^{n} X_i = X_1 + X_2 + X_3 + X_4 + X_5 + X_6 + X_7 + X_8 + X_9$$

The final step is to substitute for each of the subscripted Xs the actual measurements of the variable and then add them up.

$$\sum_{i=1}^{n} X_i = 0 + 3 + 1 + 0 + 2 + 2 + 2 + 5 + 1 = 16$$

To summarize, sigma notation is a direction to add up the sequence of measurements indicated by the subscripted Xs, where the subscript begins at the starting value and continues (by ones) to the final value.

For most of the equations used in this book, the index will start at $i = 1$ and continue to n, meaning to add up all of the scores in the sample (or population). Whenever it is clear which scores are to be added, the subscript will be dropped. Thus, ΣX means "sum up all of the measurements of X." For the sports injuries data, $\Sigma X = 16$.

A few other forms of sigma notation are particularly useful. The expression ΣX^2 means to square each of the measurements, and then add them up. Because the index is missing, you know to include all of the measurements. Thus, for the sports injury data:

$$\Sigma X^2 = 0^2 + 3^2 + 1^2 + 0^2 + 2^2 + 2^2 + 2^2 + 5^2 + 1^2 = 48$$

The expression $(\Sigma X)^2$ looks similar to ΣX^2, but is quite different in meaning. Note that for $(\Sigma X)^2$ the summation is within the parentheses and the power of 2 is outside the parentheses. The meaning is to first add all of the measurements and then to square the sum. For the sports injury data:

$$(\Sigma X)^2 = (0 + 3 + 1 + 0 + 2 + 2 + 2 + 5 + 1)^2 = 16^2 = 256$$

The expression $(\Sigma X)^2$ is sometimes called the square of the sum.

The quantity ΣX^2 (48) does not equal $(\Sigma X)^2$ (256) for the sports injury data. This is not an accident. For almost all sets of data, the two quantities will not be equal, so it is important to keep them distinct. The fact that the two quantities are not equal is often expressed by the phrase, "the sum of the squares does not equal the square of the sum."

The last form of sigma notation to be introduced in this chapter is $\Sigma(X - C)^2$. In this expression, the C stands for a constant. The value of C must be determined before carrying out the instructions given in the expression, but once it is determined, the value stays the same (constant) while following the instructions. The sigma notation indicates three things: First, the value of C should be subtracted from each of the measurements of the variable (each X); second, after the subtraction, each of the remainders (that is, differences) should be squared; and, third, all of the squared differences should be added up. Clearly, this is a rather complicated expression. On the other hand, you can see why sigma notation is such a handy shorthand. The expression $\Sigma(X - C)^2$ can be used instead of writing out Steps 1 through 3.

Suppose that $C = 2$. Then, for the sports injury data:

$$\Sigma(X - C)^2 = (0-2)^2 + (3-2)^2 + (1-2)^2 + (0-2)^2 + (2-2)^2$$

$$+ (2-2)^2 + (2-2)^2 + (5-2)^2 + (1-2)^2$$

$$= (-2)^2 + 1^2 + (-1)^2 + (-2)^2 + 0^2 + 0^2 + 0^2 + 3^2 + (-1)^2$$

$$= 20$$

Now suppose that $C = 5$.

$$\Sigma(X - C)^2 = (0-5)^2 + (3-5)^2 + (1-5)^2 + (0-5)^2 + (2-5)^2$$

$$+ (2-5)^2 + (2-5)^2 + (5-5)^2 + (1-5)^2$$

$$= (-5)^2 + (-2)^2 + (-4)^2 + (-5)^2 + (-3)^2$$

$$+ (-3)^2 + (-3)^2 + 0^2 + (-4)^2$$

$$= 113$$

Because sigma notation may be new to you, it is worthwhile to take a few moments to practice it and make sure that the concepts are well learned. Use the data in Table 2.1 (the aggressiveness data) to calculate ΣX, ΣX^2, and $(\Sigma X)^2$.[1] Does the sum of the squares equal the square of the sum? Suppose that C is 1. Calculate $\Sigma(X - C)^2$ (be careful when you get to the two scores of zero).

MEASURES OF CENTRAL TENDENCY

As you know from Chapter 2, the central tendency of a distribution is the score value (or location on the abscissa) that corresponds to the center of the distribution. It is a typical or representative score value. Knowledge of a distribution's central tendency is useful in three ways.

First, the central tendency is a handy way to summarize a distribution. Of course, a single number (score value) cannot provide a complete description of a whole distribution, but it can give a general impression. Second, distributions can be easily compared by comparing central tendencies. Finally, central tendency is used in many inferential statistical procedures.

There are three commonly used measures of central tendency: the mean, the median, and the mode. We will apply all three to the following sample of data: Suppose that you are in charge of social activities for the student government. You decide that you need to know the ages of the students on campus to plan appropriately. You go to the student union and ask the ages of the first 15 people you meet. The data are in Table 3.1 and Figure 3.1.

TABLE 3.1
Sample of Ages of Students

17, 18, 18, 18, 19, 19, 19, 19, 19, 20, 20, 21, 22, 23, 28

FIGURE 3.1
Frequency of ages of students sampled.

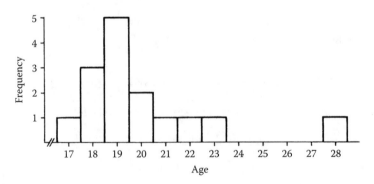

---

[1] For the data in Table 2.1, $\Sigma X = 47$, $\Sigma X^2 = 139$, $(\Sigma X)^2 = 2209$, and for $C = 1$, $\Sigma(X - C)^2 = 57$.

The Mean

The first measure of central tendency is the mean.

> The **mean** of a distribution is the numerical average. It is obtained by summing all of the measurements in the distribution and dividing by the number of measurements in the distribution.

Using a formula:

$$\text{mean} = \Sigma X/n.$$

According to the formula, the mean is calculated by adding all the scores in the distribution, and then dividing the sum by n, the number of scores in the distribution. For the data in Table 3.1,

$$\text{mean} = 300/15 = 20.$$

Computing a mean in Excel can be accomplished very easily. Simply enter the scores in consecutive cells in a spreadsheet and use the function "AVERAGE."

The mean is so important that it has two symbols. The first, M, is used to represent the mean of a sample.[2] So, for the sample data in Table 3.1, $M = 20$.

The second symbol, μ (the Greek lowercase letter *mu*), represents the mean of a population. The formula for the mean of a population is almost identical to the formula for M; the only difference is that the denominator is a capital N, which indicates division by the number of measurements in the population rather than the number of measurements in the sample. Thus,

████████████

FORMULA 3.1   The Population Mean and the Sample Mean

$$\mu = \Sigma X/N \qquad M = \Sigma X/n$$

The distinction between M and μ leads to two important definitions.

> **A statistic** is a quantity computed from the scores in a sample. **A parameter** is a quantity computed from the scores in a population.

Thus, M is a statistic and μ is the corresponding population parameter. The notation can be used to help remember which is which: Statistics are represented by letters of the Roman (English) alphabet and parameters are usually represented by letters of the Greek alphabet.

---

[2] For many years, the symbol $\overline{X}$ ("X-bar") was commonly used to represent the sample mean. The fifth edition of the *Publication Manual of the American Psychological Association* now recommends using the symbol M.

The subtitle of this book is "An Introduction to Statistical Reasoning," not "An Introduction to Parametrical Reasoning." There is a good reason for this. It is very rare that we have available all of the scores from a population, so it is rare to be able to compute parameters. On the other hand, we can easily collect samples of measurements from populations and compute statistics from the samples. In this chapter, you are learning how to use statistics (such as M) to describe samples. Later, we will discuss how to use statistics (such as M) to make inferences (educated guesses) about population parameters (such as μ).

The mean has three advantages over the other measures of central tendency (the median and mode, to be discussed shortly). First, the mean is computed using all of the data in the sample (or population). Other measures disregard some of the data.

Second, the mean has certain mathematical properties that make it very useful in computing other statistics.

Third, and most important, when M is calculated from a *random* sample, then M is an unbiased estimator of the mean of the population (μ) from which the sample was taken. You may think of an unbiased estimator as the best guess for a population parameter based on the evidence available (measurements in the random sample). More technically,

> when all possible random samples of the same size are collected from a population and an **unbiased estimator** is computed from each of the samples, then the mean of the unbiased estimators is guaranteed to equal the population parameter being estimated.

Because M is an unbiased estimator for μ, the average M from all random samples of the same size is guaranteed to equal μ, the mean of the population from which the random samples were selected. In terms of our example, suppose that you took a random sample of the ages of 15 students and found M for the sample. Then, you took another random sample of 15 ages and computed M again (so that you now have two Ms), and another random sample, and another, and so on. Once you have determined M for all possible random samples, the average (mean) of the Ms is guaranteed to equal the mean age of students in the population, μ.

The mean does have certain disadvantages, however. Primarily, it is sensitive to outlying scores when the distribution is skewed. This problem can be illustrated with the data in Figure 3.1. Note that the mean of the distribution, 20, is greater than the more intuitive center of the distribution, around 19. The problem is that the mean is influenced by the single outlier, the measurement of 28. Similarly, if the distribution is made even more skewed by changing the 28 to a 58, the mean, 22 (330/15), is pulled even farther away from the center of the distribution. Thus, when a distribution is highly skewed, the mean is generally a poor measure of central tendency. Second, there is some conceptual difficulty in interpreting the mean when the data are nominal or interval. The difficulty is that calculation of the mean assumes the equal interval property.[3]

---

[3] In Chapter 1, we discussed in-between scales in which the equal intervals property is only approximated. The mean is often used as a measure of central tendency when a variable is measured on such a scale.

The Median

A second measure of central tendency is the median.

> The **median** of a distribution is the 50th percentile, the score value that has below it half of the measurements in the distribution, and above it half the measurements.

The formula for computing the median is tedious, and like percentiles, is only approximate. Several other methods exist. Perhaps you remember from your high school math courses that you should line up the scores, and starting from the outside, count inward toward the median. For example, if you had the scores:

$$1, 6, 7, 9, 11$$

7 would be the median, because it's the middle score. However, what if you have an even number of scores, like:

$$3, 4, 4, 7, 8, 9 \,?$$

Moving from the outside in, you'll wind up at 4 and 7. At this point, the median would be in between 4 and 7, or 5.5 ((4 + 7)/2 = 5.5).

The methods described above are exactly what the Excel worksheet function MEDIAN does. Unfortunately, these methods don't work very well when you have many scores near the median. For example, let's look back at the data from Table 3.1:

$$17, 18, 18, 18, 19, 19, 19, 19, 19, 20, 20, 21, 22, 23, 28$$

Because there are an odd number of scores, we may say that the median age is 19. Although this is close to the middle value, there seem to be more scores that are higher than 19 (six scores) than there are lower than 19 (four scores). If you look at the distribution in Figure 3.1, this intuition is played out further—the score that divided the distribution in half is higher than 19. Indeed, the median is probably closer to 20 than to 18. But is the value 19.5 or 19.2 or 19.8? Technically, the best approximation for the median is computed using the complex formula:

$$median = LRL + \frac{\dfrac{50 \times n}{100} - n_b}{n_w} \times I$$

where LRL is the lower real limit of the interval of interest, n_b is the number of observations below the interval of interest, n_w is the number of observations within the interval of interest, and I is the interval width. Fortunately, we have included on the companion CD a custom worksheet function "MDN" that you can add to Excel. The MDN function will compute the median using the above formula. (Did you get a median of 19.2?)

The median has three advantages relative to the mean. First, when the distribution is skewed (as in Table 3.1), the median is less sensitive to outliers than is the mean. For this reason, the median, 19.2, is closer to the center of the distribution than is the mean, 20. Note also, the median would be the same no matter what the value of the last score. The reason for this lack of sensitivity to outliers is that the median is the score value that has half of the measurements above it (and half below it). How far above (or below) is inconsequential.

Second (but for the same reason), the median can be used when measurements at the ends of the distribution are inexact. For example, suppose that one of the students refused to give his age, saying instead, "Just write down that it is over 25." Not knowing the exact age precludes computation of *M*, but not the median (at least when the inexact scores are near the ends of the distribution).

Finally, the median can be used even when the data are measured on an ordinal scale (but not a nominal scale).

These advantages result from the fact that computation of the median disregards some information in the data (information about the scores at the ends of the distribution and the equal intervals property of interval and ratio data). Thus, from the perspective of trying to use as much information as possible, these advantages can be seen as a disadvantage: The median is based on less information than is the mean.

The median has one other clear disadvantage compared to the mean. The sample median is not an unbiased estimator of any population parameter. Thus, the role of the median in statistical inference is limited.

The Mode

The third measure of central tendency is the mode.

> The **mode** of a distribution is the score value (or class interval) with the greatest frequency. A distribution with two frequently occurring score values is a **bimodal distribution.**

The mode of the distribution in Table 3.1 is 19.

The great advantage of the mode compared to the median and the mean is that it can be computed for any type of data—nominal, ordinal, interval, or ratio. The greatest disadvantage is that the mode ignores much information (magnitude, equal intervals, and scores near the ends of the distribution). Also, the sample mode is not an unbiased estimator of the population mode.

Comparison of the Mean, Median, and Mode

These three measures of central tendency are typically not the same score value. In fact, only when the distribution is unimodal and symmetric will the three be the same. Figure 3.2 illustrates the location of the mean, median, and mode for various shapes of distributions.

Estimating the mode from a frequency (or relative frequency) polygon is easy. Simply find the score value that has the greatest frequency (or relative frequency). The median

FIGURE 3.2
Mean, median, and mode in distributions of various shapes.

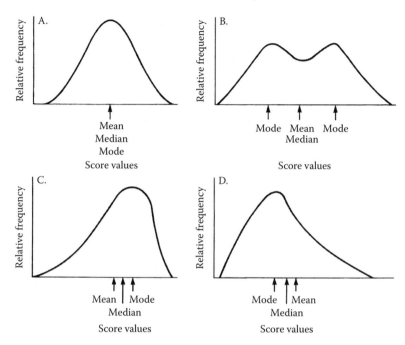

can be estimated visually by finding the point on the abscissa that has half of the area of the distribution to its right and half to its left. Estimating the mean is a little trickier. For a symmetric distribution, the mean, like the median, will be the score value that divides the distribution in half. For a skewed distribution, the mean (because it is sensitive to outliers) will be closer to the longer tail than is the median. A rule to help you remember all of this is that when the distribution is unimodal and skewed, the three measures of central tendency occur in alphabetical (or reverse alphabetical) order. You can see this for yourself in Figure 3.2.

Which one is best? The answer depends on the situation. When the data are measured using a nominal scale, then the mode is the best measure because it is the only one that is appropriate. When the data are ordinal, the median is preferred over the mode because it is based on more information. When the data are interval or ratio, the mean is generally preferred because it is an unbiased estimator of μ. However, when the distribution is highly skewed, the median provides a more reasonable index of central tendency than does the mean.

Of course, there is nothing wrong with using more than one measure of central tendency to describe your data. For instance, if a distribution is bimodal but symmetric, the central tendency is best conveyed by mentioning the modes and computing the mean. On the other hand, if a distribution is unimodal but highly skewed, central tendency is conveyed well by reporting both the median and the mean. Remember, the goal of descriptive statistics is to summarize the data without introducing distortions. Use the measure (or measures) that best achieve this goal.

MEASURES OF VARIABILITY

As a general rule, whenever a variable is measured (whenever data are collected in the social sciences), the measurements will not all be the same.

> **Variability** is the extent to which the measurements in a distribution differ from one another.

In some distributions, the measurements are similar so that variability is low. In fact, if all the scores in a distribution happen to be the same, the distribution has no variability. In other distributions, when the scores are very different from one another, variability is great. The techniques developed in this section can be used to characterize precisely (that is, numerically) the variability of a distribution.

We begin with an example that illustrates that when describing data, variability can be just as important as central tendency. Suppose that you are investigating the effects of smoking marijuana on driving skill. Although it seems that many traffic accidents are associated with drug abuse, you have also heard the conflicting claim that moderate amounts of marijuana may improve driving ability. To investigate these conflicting claims you measure driving ability under four conditions. In Condition A (placebo), six subjects smoke a cigarette with no active marijuana and then drive a standard course. You measure the number of barriers knocked down by each driver. Each of the six participants in Conditions B–D smokes cigarettes having progressively more active ingredients before driving the course.

The data for the four conditions are illustrated in Figure 3.3.[4] Note that all of the conditions have the same central tendency (the means all equal 4). Clearly, however, the distributions differ in an important respect: As the amount of drug increases (from Conditions A to D), variability also increases. Apparently, some people become more cautious drivers under marijuana intoxication, and some become more reckless. That is, the central tendency remains stable, but variability increases.

The Range

A particularly simple measure of variability is the range.

> The **range** is the largest score minus the smallest score.

From A to D, the ranges for the distributions are 0, 2, 4, and 4.

Although the range is easy to compute, it is not a particularly useful measure of variability because it ignores so much of the data. It is determined solely by the two most extreme scores. You can see this for yourself by comparing the two distributions at the bottom of Figure 3.3. The distributions have the same range, but Distribution C seems less variable than Distribution D. Many of the scores are similar to one another in Distribution C, but the scores are mostly different from one another in Distribution D. Also, the range

---

[4] This example is completely fictitious.

FIGURE 3.3
Four distributions that differ in variability but have the same mean.

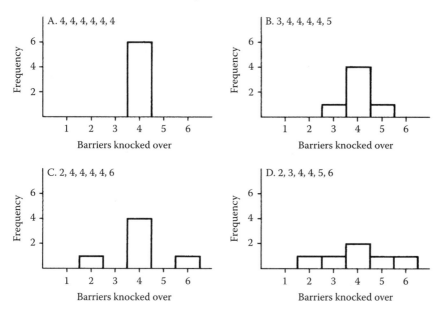

is not very useful because the range of a sample is not an unbiased estimator of the population range.

Population Variance and Standard Deviation

A more useful measure of variability is the variance. Computation of the variance is slightly different for populations and samples. We begin with the population variance because it is a little easier to understand.

The population variance is the degree to which the scores differ from the mean of the population. More formally:

> The **population variance** is the average of the squared deviations of each score from the population mean (μ). The symbol for the population variance is the Greek lowercase letter *sigma* raised to the power of two, σ^2, pronounced "sigma squared" (a Greek letter is used because the population variance is a parameter).

Note that variance is not the same as variability. In general, variability indicates how much the scores in a distribution *differ from one another*. The population variance is one way to measure variability based on how much the scores *differ from μ*.

The variance of a population can be computed as follows: (a) Find the difference between each score and μ; (b) square all of the differences and add them up; (c) divide the sum by the number of measurements in the population, N, to obtain the average of the squared differences. This procedure is summarized in Formula 3.2.

━━━━━━━━

FORMULA 3.2   Definitional Formula for the Population Variance

$$\sigma^2 = \frac{\Sigma(X - \mu)^2}{N} = \frac{SS(X)}{N}$$

The numerator in the definitional formula for population variance, or the quantity $\Sigma(X - \mu)^2$, is often called the "sum of squares" and abbreviated $SS(X)$.

> The **sum of squares ($SS(X)$)** is the sum of the squared deviations of each score from the mean.

Although $SS(X)$ is difficult to interpret, it is very useful in many subsequent computations. It may be the second most frequently computed statistic after the sample mean. Thus, population variance is the average sum of squares.

The computation of σ^2 for Distribution D (Figure 3.3) is illustrated in Table 3.2. Note that applying Formula 3.2 to these data makes the highly questionable assumption that these data form a whole population (in other words, the investigator is interested in the scores from these particular subjects and no others). More reasonably, the investigator would treat these data as a sample from a broader population of driving scores under marijuana intoxication (that is, the population of scores of all drivers driving under marijuana intoxication). Nonetheless, Table 3.2 illustrates how to use the formula for computing the population variance.

At first glance, the notion of population variance may seem needlessly complex. Why should the difference of each score from μ be squared? Why not simply compute the average difference between each score and μ? As it turns out, there is a very good reason. The average difference between each score and μ is always 0.0 (see Table 3.2). Clearly then, the average difference would not be a very useful index of variability.

TABLE 3.2
Computation of σ^2 for Distribution D (Figure 3.3) Using Definitional Formula

Score (X)	μ	$X - \mu$	$(X - \mu)^2$
2	4	−2	4
3	4	−1	1
4	4	0	0
4	4	0	0
5	4	1	1
6	4	2	4
		$\Sigma(X - \mu) = 0$	$\Sigma(X - \mu)^2 = SS(X) = 10$

$$\sigma^2 = \frac{\sum(X - \mu)^2}{N} = \frac{SS(X)}{N} = \frac{10}{6} = 1.67$$

The variances of Distributions A–D (Figure 3.3) are 0, .33, 1.33, and 1.67, respectively. Note that when all the scores are the same, as in Distribution A, the population variance is 0. As the scores become more spread out from one another (and μ), the population variance increases. Also, note the difference in variance for Distributions C and D, even though the ranges are identical. In Distribution C, many scores are near μ, so that the variance is smaller than in Distribution D, where many scores are far from μ. Finally, note that each σ^2 is positive. Because σ^2 is an average of *squared* deviations (which are always positive), it will always be a positive number.

As a measure of variability, the population variance has three great advantages over the range. First, it uses much more of the data than does the range. Second, the variance plays a role in further statistical computations. Finally, as we shall see shortly, the sample variance is an unbiased estimator of the population variance.

Nonetheless, σ^2 is not quite perfect. The population variance should be computed only for interval and ratio data. Note that σ^2 is computed by taking differences between each score and the mean. Implicit in this procedure is the assumption that a difference of one unit has the same meaning at all locations on the scale (the equal intervals property).[5]

When μ is not a whole number, σ^2 and $SS(X)$ can be difficult to compute. This is because μ must be subtracted from each measurement in the distribution, and subtracting a number with a long decimal part can be laborious and error-prone. The solution is to use the computing formula for $SS(X)$ and then compute σ^2.

■■■■■■■■■

FORMULA 3.3   Computing Formula for Population Variance

$$\sigma^2 = \frac{SS(X)}{N} = \frac{\sum X^2 - N\mu^2}{N}$$

The computing formula is mathematically equivalent to the definitional formula (Formula 3.2). That is, the two will always produce the same answer. The computing formula is easier to work with, however, because only one subtraction is involved. Table 3.3 illustrates how to use the computing formula for computing σ^2 for Distribution D. Note that σ^2, 1.67, is exactly the same as computed in Table 3.2.

When you are thinking about what the population variance is, think in terms of the definitional formula. That formula directly represents the idea of an average (squared) deviation from the mean, because the formula directs you to subtract the mean from each score. On the other hand, use the computing formula or Excel whenever you actually have to compute a population variance to save yourself time (and errors).

Sometimes, σ^2 is difficult to interpret because it is in *squared* units. For example, consider the data in Figure 3.3, Distribution D. The mean of the distribution is 4 *barriers* knocked down. The population variance is 1.67 *barriers squared*! Clearly, the concept of a "squared barrier" is unusual. To ease interpretation, another measure of variability is commonly used. It is the standard deviation.

---

[5] The variance is often used as a measure of variability when the data are only approximately interval, conforming to an in-between scale.

TABLE 3.3
Computation of σ^2 for Distribution D (Figure 3.3)
Using Computing Formula

Score (X)	X^2	
2	4	$SS(X) = \Sigma X^2 - NM^2$
3	9	
4	16	$SS(X) = 106 - 6(4)^2$
4	16	$SS(X) = 106 - 96 = 10$
5	25	
6	36	$\sigma^2 = \dfrac{SS(X)}{N} = \dfrac{10}{6} = 1.67$
$N = 6$	$\Sigma X^2 = 106$	
$\Sigma X = 24$		

$$\mu = \frac{\sum X}{N} = \frac{24}{6} = 4$$

The **population standard deviation** is the positive square root of the population variance. The symbol for the population standard deviation is σ, the lowercase Greek *sigma*.

The population standard deviation can be found in a number of equivalent ways.

∎∎∎∎∎

FORMULA 3.4   Formulas for the Population Standard Deviation

$$\sigma = \sqrt{\sigma^2} = \sqrt{\frac{\sum (X - \mu)^2}{N}} = \sqrt{\frac{\sum X^2 - N\mu^2}{N}} = \sqrt{\frac{SS(X)}{N}}$$

Because it does not involve squared units, σ is easier to conceptualize than is the population variance. For the measurements of driving ability, the population standard deviation is 1.29 *barriers,* the square root of 1.67 *barriers squared.*

The value of σ is typically about one fourth of the range when the distribution is bell-shaped. For example, the range of Distribution D is 4, and $\sigma = 1.29$, a little more than one fourth of the range. You can use this approximation as a rough check on your calculation of σ. Also, when you graph a distribution, you can visualize σ as about one fourth of the distance along the abscissa.

As with σ^2, computation of σ is more appropriate for interval and ratio data than for ordinal data. It is inappropriate for nominal data.

Formulas 3.2 and 3.3 (for σ^2) and 3.4 (for σ) should be used only when you have all of the scores in a population. Do not use the formulas on samples. The problem is that using these formulas on sample data does *not* result in unbiased estimates of σ^2 or σ.

Sample Variance and Standard Deviation

Given a random sample from a population, an unbiased estimator of the population variance (σ^2) can be computed, but *not* by using Formula 3.2 or 3.3.

> The **sample variance** is the sum of squared deviations of each score from M divided by $n - 1$. The symbol for the sample variance is s^2 (a Roman letter is used because the sample variance is a statistic).

FORMULA 3.5   Definitional Formula for the Sample Variance

$$s^2 = \frac{\sum (X - M)^2}{n - 1} = \frac{SS(X)}{n - 1}$$

Except for two changes, the formula for s^2, the sample variance, is identical to Formula 3.2 for σ^2, the population variance. The first change is that M is subtracted from each score instead of μ. The quantity $\Sigma (X - M)^2$ is also called the sum of squares or $SS(X)$, the only difference being that the sample mean, M, is subtracted from every score rather than the population mean, μ. The second change is more important. To obtain s^2, the sum of squares is divided by $n - 1$, the number of scores in the sample minus one, rather than by the total number of scores in the sample. Dividing by $n - 1$ rather than by n makes the sample variance an unbiased estimator of the population variance. Without this change, the sample variance would be systematically too small, rather than an unbiased estimator of σ^2.

Because it is so rare to actually have all of the scores in a population, the sample variance is computed much more often than the population variance. In fact, throughout this textbook (and in practice) the term variance (without a modifier) means the sample variance (s^2).

The sample variance can be computed using the definitional formula (Formula 3.5). However, as with σ^2, it is easier to use the computing formula.

FORMULA 3.6   Computing Formulas for Sample Variance

$$s^2 = \frac{\sum X^2 - nM^2}{n - 1} = \frac{SS(X)}{n - 1}$$

Table 3.4 illustrates the use of both the definitional and the computing formulas for the variance using Distribution C from Figure 3.3. Note that the values of s^2 are identical, even though the formulas look quite different.

Like the population variance, the sample variance is in strange units (such as barriers squared). The solution is to use the positive square root of the variance, the standard deviation.

TABLE 3.4
Two Computations of s^2 Using Distribution C (from Figure 3.3)

Definitional Formula

Score (X)	M	$X - M$	$(X - M)^2$	
2	4	−2	4	
4	4	0	0	$s^2 = \dfrac{\sum (X - M)^2}{n - 1} = \dfrac{8}{5} = 1.6$
4	4	0	0	
4	4	0	0	
4	4	0	0	
6	4	2	4	
		$\Sigma(X - M) = 0$	$\Sigma(X - M)^2 = 8$	

Computing Formula

Score (X)	X^2	
2	4	$SS(X) = \displaystyle\sum X^2 - nM^2$
4	16	$= 104 - 6(4)^2$
4	16	$= 104 - 96$
4	16	$= 8$
4	16	
6	36	
$\Sigma X = 24$	$\Sigma X^2 = 104$	$s^2 = \dfrac{SS(X)}{n - 1}$
		$= \dfrac{8}{5}$
		$= 1.6$

The **standard deviation** (that is, the sample standard deviation) is the positive square root of the variance. The symbol for the standard deviation is s.

The standard deviation, s, can be computed in a variety of ways, some of which are listed below. The computing formula (at the far right) is the easiest way to compute s when starting from scratch.

FORMULA 3.7   Computing Formulas for Standard Deviation

$$s = \sqrt{s^2} = \sqrt{\frac{\sum (X - M)^2}{n - 1}} = \sqrt{\frac{\sum X^2 - nM^2}{n - 1}} = \sqrt{\frac{SS(X)}{n - 1}}$$

Like σ, s is the original units, rather than squared units. Also, s is about one fourth of the range (when the distribution is bell-shaped), so it is easy to estimate.

In summary, the variance is close to a perfect measure of variability. When the computing formulas are used, both s^2 and σ^2 are easy to compute; the units can be made interpretable by calculating the square roots to obtain s and σ; and s^2 can be used as an unbiased estimator of σ^2. In addition, remember that all four quantities (s, σ, s^2, σ^2) are based on all of the measurements in the distribution and that the variance is used in many other statistical formulas. The only restriction is that s, s^2, σ, and σ^2 are inappropriate for ordinal and nominal data.

When to Use the Various Measures of Variability

As discussed in Chapter 2, some measure of variability is usually required to provide a clear description of the data. If the data are measured on an ordinal scale, the range is more easily interpreted than the variance. When the data are interval or ratio, the variance is generally preferred because it uses all of the data and because s^2 is an unbiased estimator of σ^2.

Once you have decided on the variance as the appropriate measure of variability, should you compute s^2 (using $n - 1$) or σ^2 (using N)? The answer depends on whether you have all of the data in a population or a sample from a population.

If the scores you have on hand are the only scores of interest to you, then they are a population and σ^2 should be computed. On the other hand, if there is a larger group of scores that is of interest, but you have only a subset (sample) from the larger group, then s^2 is more appropriate. Some examples should help to make the distinction clearer.

When an instructor hands back an exam, she often presents descriptive statistics such as a grouped frequency distribution, the mean, and the standard deviation. Should the instructor compute s or σ? Typically, the instructor (and the students) are interested only in these specific scores (the scores of the class). Therefore, the scores form a population and the σ formula should be used.

Suppose, however, that the instructor is conducting a research project on ways of teaching the course. The students in the class were selected to be a random sample of all students who normally enroll in the course. In this case, the instructor may wish to treat the exam scores as a sample, and calculate s^2. This s^2 could then be used as an unbiased estimator of σ^2, the variance of the scores of all of the students in the population.

As another example, consider the scores in Figure 3.3, which illustrate the effects of marijuana intoxication on driving skill. These scores might have been collected as part of a research program, so that the specific scores represent a random sample from the population of scores for people who are driving while intoxicated. In this case, s^2 should be calculated and used as an unbiased estimator of the population parameter.

A small (albeit unlikely and probably illegal) change in the scenario makes σ^2 the appropriate index of variability. Suppose that a group of friends wanted to discover the effects of marijuana intoxication on their own driving skills. The group of friends is not a random sample from any population, nor are they interested in any scores other than their own. In this case, the scores should be treated as comprising the whole population, and σ^2 calculated.

A final question is when to use the variance and when to use the standard deviation as a descriptive statistic. It makes little difference which is used, because it is so easy to convert from one to the other.

In the Media: Skew Skewers the President

When a distribution is skewed, the mean is not a very good index of central tendency because it is pulled away from the middle of the distribution in the direction of skew. Because distributions of income tend to be very skewed (most people have modest incomes, but a few are fabulously wealthy), distributions of taxes paid and refunds also tend to be very skewed.

In the article "Dividends" (*The New Yorker*, January 20, 2003), Hendrik Hertzberg is commenting on President George W. Bush's defense of his plan to eliminate taxes on stock dividends. The defense was delivered the week before at the Economic Club of Chicago. Many people believe that this type of tax cut will tremendously benefit the very rich at the expense of the middle class and poor. For example, "According to Citizens for Tax Justice, whose computations are generally regarded as reliable, half the cash will flow to the richest one per cent of taxpayers. Another quarter of the benefits will go to the rest of the top five percent." So, how can the president defend these cuts? Bush is quoted as saying, "These tax reductions will bring real and immediate benefits to middle-income Americans ... Ninety-two million Americans will keep an average of $1083 more of their own money." Hertzberg notes that this claim is true because the mean amount saved by a taxpayer will be $1083, but remember that the mean is greatly affected by skew. If one computes the median amount saved, it is "a couple of hundred dollars. And a worker in the bottom twenty per cent will get next to nothing—at most, a dime or a quarter a week." Hertzberg then goes on to note that Bush himself will get a "windfall of as much as $44,500 ... more in fact than the total income, before taxes, of a substantial majority of American families. (Vice President) Dick Cheney does even better. His tax break comes to $327,000—more than the before-tax income of ninety-eight per cent of his fellow-citizens."

Thus, using just basic statistical knowledge, Hertzberg makes several tremendously important points, not the least of which is that politicians can use statistics inappropriately to attempt to mislead the public. Could there be a better illustration of H. G. Wells's claim that "statistical thinking will one day be as necessary for efficient citizenship as the ability to read and write"? It would have been nice if Hertzberg had included the full distribution relating taxes saved to current income, perhaps in the form of a histogram. But, that is not the style of *The New Yorker*.

SUMMARY

A statistic is the result of computations using the scores in a sample; a parameter is the result of computations using the scores in a population. A statistic is an unbiased estimator of the corresponding population parameter if the average of the statistic from all possible random samples of the same size equals the population parameter. The property of unbiased estimation is important because it indicates which statistics are good guesses for population parameters.

Of the three measures of central tendency—mean, median, and mode—only the sample mean (M) is an unbiased estimator of the population mean (μ). In addition, the mean is generally preferred as an index of central tendency because it is based on all of the measurements in the distribution. Nonetheless, the median is a more appropriate descriptive statistic when the distribution is highly skewed, when scores near the ends of the distribution are inexact, or when the data are measured on an ordinal scale. The mode is often reported when the distribution is multimodal and when the data are nominal.

Two measures of variability are the range and the variance. The range is easy to understand, easy to compute, and appropriate for all but nominal data. Unfortunately, it ignores much data and is not an unbiased estimator. The (sample) variance is an unbiased estimator of the population variance and it is based on all of the data. The population variance is the average squared deviation of scores from μ; the (sample) variance is a little larger than the average squared deviation of scores from M. The positive square root of the variance is the standard deviation. For a bell-shaped distribution, the standard deviation is about one fourth of the range.

EXERCISES

Terms *Define these new terms and symbols.*

statistic	population standard deviation
parameter	sample standard deviation
unbiased estimator	Σ
mean	M
median	μ
mode	s
range	σ
population variance	s^2
sample variance	σ^2
$SS(X)$	

Questions *Answer the following questions.*

†1. Complete Steps a through d for each of the sets of scores in Table 3.5. Assume that Sets A and B are populations and that Sets C and D are samples.
   a. Compute the mean, median, and mode.
   b. Compute the range.
   c. Estimate the standard deviation using the range.
   d. Compute the standard deviation and variance using the definitional formulas. Why are some estimates (from Step c) better than others?
   e. Compute the standard deviation and the variance by using the computing formulas. Was it easier to use the definitional formulas or the computing formulas?

TABLE 3.5

A		B		C		D	
0	1	23	79	.00	.37	−5	−4
5	3	30	21	.01	.33	−6	−4
1	5	21	27	.43	.45	−5	−3
3	2	20	31	.23	.44	−5	−5
4	4	23	19	.24	.51	−7	−6
2	3	29	28	.46	.53		
2	4	17	25				
3	2	35	26				

TABLE 3.6

Score Value	Frequency
15	3
14	5
13	8
12	3
11	1

†2. Compute the sample mean and standard deviation for the distribution in Table 3.6. (Hint: Remember that the frequency of each score value indicates the number of measurements of that score value. Because $n = 20$, 20 measurements will be used in computing M and s, even though there are only 5 score values.)

3. Which measure of central tendency is preferred for the following situations? Why?

   a. A political scientist assigns a score of 0 to Independents, 1 to Democrats, 2 to Republicans, and 3 to all others.

   b. A social psychologist measures group productivity by rating the quality of group decisions on a scale of 1 to 10.

   c. A social psychologist measures group productivity by counting the number of decisions reached in a 1-hour period.

   d. A cognitive psychologist measures the amount of time needed to decide if two metaphors have the same meaning. Because several subjects have difficulty with the task, a few of the times are very long.

4. Summarize the relative advantages and disadvantages of the mean, median, and mode as measures of central tendency. Describe different situations in which each would be the best measure of central tendency.

5. A psychologist engaging in cross-cultural research is investigating the ability of people to recognize culture-specific patterns. He shows his subjects a large number of pictures of Persian-style rugs, and then determines for each subject the number of pictures that can be recognized a day later. He has data from subjects living in the United States and subjects living in the Middle East. What measures of central tendency and variability should he compute to compare the distributions? Why are those measures particularly appropriate?

6. Describe a situation in which computation of s^2 is more appropriate than computation of σ^2. Describe a situation in which σ^2 is more appropriate than s^2.

7.†a. If Distribution A has a mean of 50 and Distribution B has a mean of 100, can the variance of Distribution A be larger than the variance of Distribution B? Explain your answer by reference to the definitional formula for variance.

    b. If Distribution C has 100 observations and Distribution D has 200 observations, which do you think has the greater variance? Explain your answer.

8. Suppose that you are a statistician working for a TV advertising firm. You have three sets of data in front of you. Set A consists of the number of hours of television watched (weekly) by each of 100 randomly selected people living on the West Coast. Set B consists of the number of hours of television watched by each of 150 randomly sampled Midwesterners. Set C consists of the number of hours watched by each of 200 randomly sampled people living on the East Coast. Your job is to apply statistical techniques to make sense out of these data. What would you do? For each step, describe why you would choose that statistical procedure over alternatives, and what you hope to learn from application of that procedure.

9. For each of the following situations, discuss whether it is more appropriate to compute σ or s, or whether neither is appropriate.

    a. A teacher gives a reading rate test to his 30 students. In reporting the results to the class, he wishes to give a measure of variability.

    b. A researcher gives a reading rate test to a random sample of 30 students from a school. She wishes to determine the variability of the reading scores for the school.

    c. A researcher gives a reading rate test to 30 students in one class. He wishes to determine the variability of the reading scores for the school.

10. Is the mean of the data in Table 3.1 ($M = 20$) an unbiased estimator of μ? Justify your answer.

11. Considering the Smoking Study data set as a sample:

    a. Compute the mean, median, and mode of the WISDM scores.

    b. Compute the range, $SS(X)$, variance, and standard deviation of the WISDM scores.

    c. What is the average age and standard deviation of the participants of the smoking study? What is the average length of time (and standard deviation) that participants in the study have smoked? What is the median number of cigarettes smoked per day by the participants in the study? What is the mean of the number of cigarettes smoked per day?

z Scores and Normal Distributions

*T*his chapter introduces the concept of a ~~standard score~~, or *z* score. Standard scores, like percentiles, are a measure of relative standing. That is, a *z* score indexes the location of one observation in a distribution relative to the other observations in the distribution. Unlike percentiles, *z* scores are easy to compute. Also, *z* scores are extremely useful in the context of a special type of distribution, the normal distribution. In fact, all of the next section of the book (Chapters 5 through 10) uses *z* scores in conjunction with the normal distribution to develop techniques of statistical inference.

STANDARD SCORES (*z* SCORES)

Suppose that you have taken three tests in your course on statistics, and your scores are 85, 70, and 56 (see Table 4.1). At first glance, the trend appears dismal; your grades seem to be getting worse and worse. Fortunately, you remember that raw scores do not always give an accurate picture of performance—a measure of relative standing is called for.

TABLE 4.1
Descriptive Statistics for Three Statistics Tests

	Test 1	Test 2	Test 3
Your Score	85	70	56
μ (mean)	90	60	50
Difference Score	−5	10	6
Points per Question	2	5	1
Questions Above μ	−2.5	2	6 / 3
σ	5	20	2
σ Above μ (z scores)	−1	.5	3

Interpretation of Zero

Your scores on the statistics tests seem to be worse and worse because they are becoming smaller numerically. However, this comparison implicitly assumes that a score of zero has the same interpretation on the three tests. That is, your score on the first test (85) is 85 points *above zero,* whereas your score on the second test is only 70 points *above zero.* Suppose, however, that the first test was so easy that the lowest score any student obtained was 50, whereas on the second test, the lowest obtained score was zero. In this case, score values of zero do not have the same interpretation on the two tests. On the first test, a score value of zero means "50 points below the lowest score," whereas on the second test, a score value of zero means "the lowest score." Because the interpretation of zero is different for the two tests, the raw scores are not directly comparable.

Now, consider how to standardize the meaning of a score value of zero so that it has the same meaning in all distributions. For each score in a distribution, subtract μ, the mean. We will call these new scores difference scores. Note that a difference score of zero always has the same interpretation; it is a score exactly equal to the mean of the distribution. (Remember, each raw score has μ subtracted from it. Therefore, raw scores that were exactly equal to μ become difference scores of zero.) Similarly, a difference score greater than zero indicates performance above the mean, and a difference score less than zero indicates performance below the mean.

Because the meaning of a difference score of zero is standardized for all distributions, comparing difference scores is safer than comparing raw scores. For example, look at the difference scores in Table 4.1. Based on the difference scores, your performance actually increased from the first test to the second test. In other words, *relative to the means of the distributions* (difference scores of zero), your performance has increased from the first test to the second.

The point of this section is easily summarized: Raw scores are difficult to compare directly because the meaning of zero changes from distribution to distribution. Forming difference scores by subtracting μ from each raw score standardizes the meaning of zero. For all distributions, a difference score of zero is equal to μ.

Interpretation of One: The Unit of a Scale

Examination of the difference scores in Table 4.1 seems to indicate that performance improved from the first to the second test, but then decreased on the third test. Once again, however, our interpretation of the scores is based on a hidden assumption. This time we are assuming that the meaning of "one point" (the unit of measurement) is the same on each test.

Suppose that each question on the second test was worth 5 points, whereas each question on the third test was worth 1 point. Therefore, although your score on the second test is 10 "points" above the mean, it is only two "questions" (10 points divided by 5 points per question) above the mean. On the other hand, your score on the third test is not only 6 "points" above the mean, it is also 6 "questions" above the mean.

Whenever the scores in a distribution are divided (or multiplied) by a constant (such as points per question), the unit of measurement is changed. Given that the unit of measurement can be changed, we can choose a unit that has the same meaning for all distributions. One such unit is the population standard deviation, σ. Dividing each difference score by σ indicates how many standard deviations above (or below) the mean the score is.

Referring to Table 4.1, σ on the third test is 2.0, so that the difference score of 6 is 3.0 (6/2) standard deviations above the mean. On the second test, the difference score of 10 is .5 (10/20) standard deviations above the mean. On the first test, the difference score of –5 is actually below the mean. Dividing the difference score by $\sigma = 5$ yields $-5/5 = -1$. The negative sign indicates that the score is below the mean (in this case, one standard deviation unit below the mean).

Comparing your performance on the tests by using the number of standard deviations above or below the mean presents a very cheerful picture. Your performance has improved from below the mean (–1) on Test 1, to somewhat above the mean (.5) on Test 2, to well above the mean (3.0) on Test 3.

Is this all statistical legerdemain and nonsense? Why, at first, did it seem that performance on the tests got worse, but now, looking at the transformed scores, performance gets better? Remember, the raw scores in Table 4.1 are difficult to compare because they differ in both the meaning of zero and the meaning of one point (the unit of measurement). The transformed scores at the bottom of the table have comparable interpretations of zero (a score equal to μ) and comparable units of measurement (one standard deviation). Thus, we started out trying to compare apples and oranges, and ended up with a more reasonable basis for comparison.

Figure 4.1 graphically illustrates the situation. Each relative frequency distribution displays the scores from one test. The "X" in each graph indicates the location of your test score. Relative to the other scores in the distribution, your score on Test 1 is poor. That is, your score is below the mean of the distribution, as is indicated by the negative transformed score. On Test 3, relative to the other scores in the distribution, your score is very good. It is near the top of the distribution, three standard deviations above the mean.

In summary, difference scores standardize the meaning of zero (an observation equal to μ), but not the unit of measurement. Dividing the difference score by σ standardizes the meaning of the unit of measurement. The result is a transformed score that indicates how many standard deviations the score is above (or below) the mean.

FIGURE 4.1

Distributions of scores on three statistics tests.

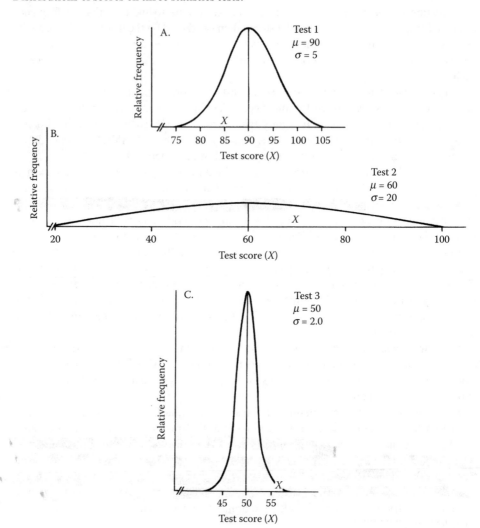

Standard Scores (z Scores)

A **standard score** or z score is a score that has been standardized by subtracting μ and dividing the difference by σ. A z score indicates the number of standard deviations the observation is above (or, when negative, below) the mean of the distribution.

As you may have guessed by now, the scores in the bottom row of Table 4.1 are *z* scores. They indicate exactly where a score is, relative to the other scores in the distribution. Positive *z* scores indicate scores that are located above μ; negative *z* scores indicate scores that are located below μ. The actual value of the *z* score indicates how many standard deviations above or below μ a score is located.

Although the discussion of *z* scores has been rather drawn out, the computation is really quite easy. A *z* score is just the difference between the raw score (X) and the mean μ, divided by the population standard deviation σ. Thus, any score can be converted to a *z* score by using Formula 4.1.

━━━━━━━━

FORMULA 4.1   Computing *z* Scores

$$z = \frac{X - \mu}{\sigma}$$

Note that the numerator (top) of the formula computes the difference score ($X - \mu$) to standardize the meaning of zero, and the denominator divides the difference score by σ to standardize the unit of measurement.

Working With *z* Scores

Consider a researcher who is investigating heart rate. For the population he is considering, $\mu = 70$ beats per minute (bpm) and $\sigma = 3$ bpm. If you are part of that population and you have a heart rate of 65 bpm, what is your relative standing? The *z* score corresponding to 65 bpm is

$$z = \frac{65 - 70}{3} = \frac{-5}{3} = -1.67$$

In other words, your heart rate is 1.67 standard deviations below the mean heart rate.

Suppose that your friend is told that her heart rate has a *z* score of .6. What is her heart rate in bpm? This problem involves a little algebra. Starting with Formula 4.1 for *z* scores, we can derive a formula for computing raw scores (X). First, multiply both sides of Formula 4.1 by σ.

$$\frac{X - \mu}{\sigma} = z$$

$$X - \mu = z\sigma$$

Then, add μ to each side.

$$X = \mu + z\sigma$$

Now we have a new formula for obtaining raw scores from *z* scores.

████████████

FORMULA 4.2   Computing Raw Scores From z Scores

$$X = \mu + z\sigma$$

For your friend with the z score of .6, the corresponding raw score is

$$X = \mu + z\sigma$$
$$= 70 + (.6)(3)$$
$$= 71.8$$

As another example, suppose you can run 100 yards in 12.5 seconds, and the parameters of the running time distribution are $\mu = 13$ seconds and $\sigma = .5$ seconds. Using Formula 4.1, your z score is

$$z = \frac{12.5 - 13}{.5} = \frac{-.5}{.5} = -1$$

This means that your running time is one standard deviation below (faster than) the mean.

Your friend is told once again that her z score is .6. Using Formula 4.2, her time to run the hundred-yard dash is

$$X = 13 + (.6)(.5) = 13.3 \text{ seconds}$$

CHARACTERISTICS OF z SCORES

So far, we have noted the following characteristics of z scores. First, they are a measure of relative standing in a distribution. Second, they facilitate comparison across distributions because they standardize the meaning of zero (μ) and the meaning of one unit (σ). Third (and this follows directly from the preceding), a z score of zero corresponds to the mean of the distribution, positive z scores indicate the number of standard deviations above the mean, and negative z scores indicate the number of standard deviations below the mean. Now we will consider distributions of z scores, in addition to individual z scores.

Characteristics of Distributions of z Scores

We can apply the z-score transformation to every score in a distribution. The result is a distribution of z scores with some remarkable characteristics. First, a distribution of z scores always has a mean of zero and a standard deviation of one. Second, the shape of a distribution of z scores is always exactly the same as the shape of the corresponding distribution of raw scores (Xs).

is this for normal distributions?

TABLE 4.2
Distributions of Raw Scores (*X*) and *z* Scores

X	z Score
6	−2
8	−1
8	−1
10	0
10	0
10	0
10	0
10	0
10	0
12	1
12	1
14	2
N = 12	N = 12

$$\sum X = 120 \qquad\qquad \sum z = 0$$

$$\sum X^2 = 1248 \qquad\qquad \sum z^2 = 12$$

$$\mu_X = \frac{\sum X}{N} = \frac{120}{12} = 10.0 \qquad\qquad \mu_z = \frac{\sum z}{N} = \frac{0}{12} = 0$$

$$SS(X) = \sum X^2 - N\mu_X^2 \qquad\qquad SS(z) = \sum z^2 - N\mu_z^2$$

$$SS(X) = 1248 - 12(10)^2 = 48 \qquad\qquad SS(z) = 12 - 12(0)^2 = 12$$

$$\sigma_X = \sqrt{\frac{SS(X)}{N}} = \sqrt{\frac{48}{12}} = 2.0 \qquad\qquad \sigma_z = \sqrt{\frac{SS(z)}{N}} = \sqrt{\frac{12}{12}} = 1$$

The left-hand column of Table 4.2 presents a (small) population of scores. The values of $\mu = 10.0$ and $\sigma = 2.0$ (computed at the bottom of the column) are used to convert each and every *X* into a *z* score. For example, the *z* score corresponding to a raw score of 14 is $z = (14 - 10)/2 = 2$. Once all of the *z* scores are computed, the mean and the standard deviation of the *z* scores can be calculated (see the bottom of the right-hand column of Table 4.2).

Note that the mean of the *z* scores (μ_z) equals 0.0, and the standard deviation of the *z* scores (σ_z) equals 1.0. This result is mathematically guaranteed. The mean of a distribution of *z* scores always equals 0.0, and the standard deviation always equals 1.0.

Figure 4.2 is an illustration of the distributions formed from the scores in Table 4.2. The frequency polygon on the left shows the distribution of raw scores and the polygon on the right illustrates the corresponding distribution of *z* scores. Each *X* and *z* in the figure corresponds to one score in Table 4.2. The arrow in the figure indicates the transformation of a single *X* into a single *z* through the use of Formula 4.1. The result of transforming every *X* is the distribution of *z* scores.

FIGURE 4.2

Frequency polygons of raw scores and z scores illustrating data from Table 4.2.

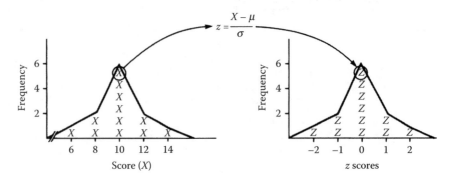

Note that all of the Xs at the mean of the distribution (10) have a z score of zero, in the center of the z-score distribution. Similarly, all of the Xs that are located one standard deviation below 10 (that is, at 8) have z scores of -1, and all of the Xs one standard deviation above 10 (at 12) have z scores of $+1$. Thus, the z-score transformation preserves the relative distances between the scores, thereby preserving the shape of the distribution.

Lest you think that these relationships hold only for distributions with simple shapes, Table 4.3 and Figure 4.3 provide another example. Each X in Table 4.3 is converted to a z score, and the mean and standard deviation of the z scores are computed. Again, $\mu_z = 0.0$ and $\sigma_z = 1$. Figure 4.3 graphically illustrates the transformations and the fact that the shape of the distribution is not changed by the converting to z scores.

NORMAL DISTRIBUTIONS

Standard scores take on added significance in the context of a specific kind of distribution that is called a normal distribution. We will digress briefly to study normal distributions, and then combine z scores and normal distributions in a useful (and even exciting) way.

Characteristics of Normal Distributions

There is no such thing as "the normal distribution." Instead, there is a family of distributions that share certain characteristics. In fact, all of the distributions illustrated in Figure 4.4 are normal distributions.

The most important characteristic of all normal distributions is that they can be described by the following formula:

$$\text{Height of the curve} = \left[\frac{1}{\sqrt{2\pi\sigma^2}} \right] e^{-(X-\mu)^2/2\sigma^2}$$

TABLE 4.3
Distributions of Raw Scores (X) and z Scores

X	z Score
60	−1.33
60	−1.33
80	−0.67
100	0
100	0
120	.67
140	1.33
140	1.33
$N = 8$	$N = 8$

$$\sum X = 800 \qquad\qquad \sum z = 0$$

$$\sum X^2 = 87,200 \qquad\qquad \sum z^2 = 8$$

$$\mu_X = \frac{\sum X}{N} = \frac{800}{8} = 100 \qquad\qquad \mu_z = \frac{\sum z}{N} = \frac{0}{8} = 0$$

$$SS(X) = \sum X^2 - N\mu_X^2 \qquad\qquad SS(z) = \sum z^2 - N\mu_z^2$$

$$SS(X) = 87,200 - 8(100)^2 = 7200 \qquad SS(z) = 8 - 8(0)^2 = 8$$

$$\sigma_X = \sqrt{\frac{SS(X)}{N}} = \sqrt{\frac{7200}{8}} = 30 \qquad\qquad \sigma_z = \sqrt{\frac{SS(z)}{N}} = \sqrt{\frac{8}{8}} = 1.0$$

FIGURE 4.3
Frequency polygons of raw scores and z scores illustrating data from Table 4.3.

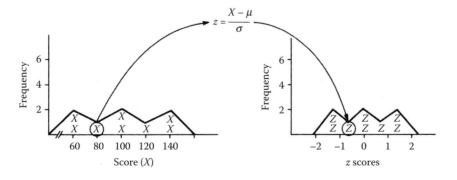

FIGURE 4.4
A variety of normal distributions.

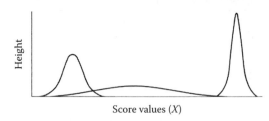

Score values (*X*)

On the left, "height of the curve" refers to the value on the ordinate. You may think of this as relative frequency, although, as we will see shortly, this is not strictly correct. On the right of the equation, the terms π and e are constants, approximately 3.1416 and 2.7183, respectively. Each curve in Figure 4.4 is generated by applying the formula to every possible value of X (from negative infinity to positive infinity) to obtain the corresponding height.

Important to note is the fact that μ and σ^2 appear in the equation without having specific values. This means that any value can be substituted for μ (for example, 0, −5.344, 3,897,656.0008, and so on) and any non-negative value can be substituted for σ^2 (for example, 1, .001, 578.99, and so on) and a normal curve would be generated. Amazingly, a normal distribution generated by the formula always has a mean exactly equal to the value of μ used in the equation and a variance exactly equal to the value of σ^2. Thus, there is an infinite number of normal distributions, one for each combination of μ and σ^2 that can be inserted into the formula.

All normal distributions share three additional characteristics:

1. Normal distributions are symmetric.
2. Normal distributions are bell-shaped. However, when σ^2 is very large (such as in the second distribution in Figure 4.4), the distribution can be flatter than a prototypical bell, and when σ^2 is very small, the distribution is thinner than a prototypical bell.
3. The tails of a normal distribution extend to positive infinity (to the right) and negative infinity (to the left). That is, although the tails appear to come very close, they never touch the abscissa.[1]

Why Normal Distributions Are Important

There are two reasons why normal distributions are important. First, many statistics are normally distributed. Imagine selecting a random sample from a population of scores and computing a statistic such as M. Then select another random sample from the same population and compute another M. After doing this many, many times you would have many,

---

[1] An exception is the "degenerate" case in which $\sigma^2 = 0.0$. Because the variance is 0.0, all of the observations are exactly the same, namely, μ. In this case, there are no tails.

many Ms. Interestingly, the relative frequency distribution of these Ms is normally distributed. This fact plays an important role in statistical inference.

Second, the distributions of many naturally occurring variables approximate normal distributions. As diverse examples, the distribution of the heights of all kindergarten children approximates a normal distribution, the distribution of all grade point averages (GPAs) at your university approximates a normal distribution, and the distribution of all responses in a psychological experiment on memory approximates a normal distribution.

Why do the distributions of these variables only "approximate" a normal distribution? For one reason, the distributions of these naturally occurring variables do not have tails that extend to infinity (as does a true normal distribution). For example, you have never seen a child in kindergarten with a height less than 24 inches, nor greater than 60 inches. Nonetheless, because the distribution is relatively bell-shaped and symmetric, it approximates a normal distribution.

You might well ask what good it does to know that a distribution approximates a normal distribution? The answer is that by using z scores in conjunction with a normal distribution, you can easily find out anything that you might wish to know about the distribution. We will discuss how to do that after we introduce the standard normal distribution.

Standard Normal Distribution

Suppose that you transform every X in a normal distribution into a z score (using Formula 4.1). As always, the distribution of z scores will have a mean of 0.0 and a standard deviation of 1.0. Also, because the distribution of Xs is normally distributed, the distribution of z scores will be normally distributed (remember, the z-score transformation preserves the shape of the distribution). Therefore, whenever you start out with a normal distribution and apply the z-score formula, the result is a normal distribution with $\mu = 0.0$ and $\sigma = 1.0$, and this distribution is called the standard normal distribution.

The **standard normal distribution** is a normal distribution with $\mu = 0.0$ and $\sigma = 1.0$.

Figure 4.5 illustrates the transformation of a normal distribution into the standard normal distribution. On the left, the distribution (of Xs) has a mean of 5 and a standard deviation of 3. The standard normal distribution results from applying the z-score formula to

FIGURE 4.5
Transforming a normal distribution of scores (Xs) into the standard normal distribution.

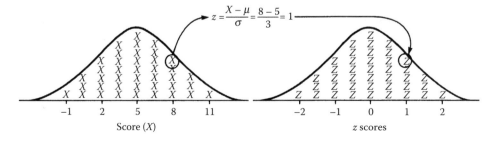

every X in the distribution of Xs. Of course, you do not really have to apply the z-score formula to each and every X because we know what the result will be. Nonetheless, in thinking about the standard normal distribution it may be useful to envision transforming each X into a z score.

A caution is in order. The z-score formula is not magic. If the distribution of Xs is not normally distributed, then the distribution of z scores will not be normally distributed, and thus the distribution of z scores will not be the standard normal distribution. Of course, if the original distribution of scores approximates a normal distribution (as do the heights of kindergartners), then the result of applying the z-score formula will be an approximation of the standard normal distribution.

USING THE STANDARD NORMAL DISTRIBUTION

Once a normal distribution is transformed into the standard normal distribution, you can calculate anything you might wish to know about the scores in the distribution. In particular, the relative frequency (or percentile rank) of any set of scores can be determined. That may not sound like much now, but you will see shortly how useful these calculations can be.

When using the standard normal distribution, the most important idea to keep in mind is that relative frequency corresponds to *area* under the curve rather than height on the ordinate. That is, the relative frequency of observations between any two z scores is exactly equal to the area under the curve between those two z scores. Remember (from Chapter 2) that the sum of relative frequencies in a distribution always equals 1.0. Therefore, as illustrated in Figure 4.6, the total area under the standard normal curve is 1.0.

Also, remember that normal distributions are symmetric; therefore, the total area to the right of the mean is exactly equal to the total area to the left of the mean, and both of these areas equal .50. Thus, the relative frequency of z scores between negative infinity and 0.0 (μ) is .50, and the relative frequency of z scores between positive infinity and 0.0 is .50.

The correspondences between z scores and all other relative frequencies are given in Table A, on page 531. Turn to that page now and place a bookmark there. It is almost impossible to understand the rest of this chapter without constantly referring to the table.

The numbers in the body of Table A are areas under the standard normal distribution between negative infinity and a particular z score. In other words, the numbers tell you

FIGURE 4.6
Areas in the standard normal distribution.

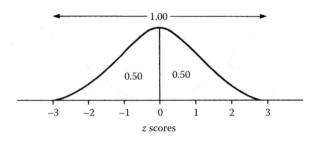

z scores

the area under the curve to the left of, or less than, a *z* score. The first column of Table A gives the first decimal place of a particular *z* score, and the top row of the table gives the second decimal place. For example, suppose you want to find the area under the standard normal distribution less than a *z* score of 0.44. First, put your finger on the row beginning with 0.4 (the first decimal place of the particular *z* score). Next, move your finger to the column headed by the 0.04 (the second decimal place). The number .6700 is the area under the standard normal distribution to the left of a *z* score of 0.44. In other words, the relative frequency of *z* scores at or below 0.44 is .6700. Equivalently, the percentage of *z* scores less than or equal to 0.44 is 67.00%.

Now, find the relative frequency of *z* scores less than 1.96. First, find the row that begins with 1.9, and move to the column headed by 0.06 (1.9 + 0.06 = 1.96). The .9750 is the relative frequency of *z* scores less than or equal to 1.96. In other words, in the standard normal distribution, the percentage of observations (*z* scores) between -∞ and 1.96 is 97.50%.

What if you wanted to know the proportion of scores between two *z* scores in the standard normal distribution? For example, what proportion of scores are between *z* scores of −1.50 and +1.50? Just find the area to the left of +1.50 and subtract the area to the left of −1.50. Figure 4.7 graphically shows the logic of this example.

Looking in Table A, we find a proportion .9332 of the scores are less than a *z* of +1.50 and that a proportion .0668 of the scores are below a *z* score of −1.50. The area between +1.50 and −1.50 is .9332 − .0668 = .8664, or 86.84% of the scores are between *z* scores of +1.50 and −1.50.

Finding the area under of the curve of a normal distribution or standard normal distribution can also be accomplished with Excel. In fact, Table A was generated using the worksheet function NORMSDIST. The function NORMSDIST takes just one argument, a *z* score, and returns the proportion of scores, or area under the curve, to the left of the *z* score. Don't confuse NORMSDIST with the function NORMDIST (the "S" stands for standard). The NORMDIST function returns the height of the curve of a particular score *X*, provided the mean (μ) and standard deviation (σ) of a normally distributed variable. The NORMDIST function is useful because you don't need to do the intermediate step of converting raw scores to *z* scores.

FIGURE 4.7
Graphical representation of the procedure for finding the area under the standard normal distribution between two *z* scores.

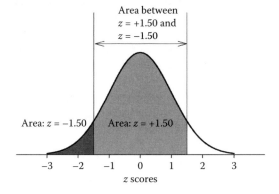

In the Media: A *z* Score, Please!

Simply comparing one raw score to another gives very little information. Often, a comparison of *z* scores would be much more informative. As an example, consider an article by Natasha Kassulke published in the *Wisconsin State Journal* on September 14, 1993, "City Seniors Outscore State." Kassulke writes, "Madison students taking the ACT in spring 1993 earned an average composite score of 23 of a possible 36 points. The average composite score of all Wisconsin students is 21.8 and that of the nation is 20.7 ... 'Wisconsin students scored 0.2 points higher this year than last year,' said Jane Grinde, director of the Bureau of School and Community Relations for the state Department of Public Instruction."

Is the difference between 23 (the average score for city seniors) and 21.8 (the average for the state) large or small? It certainly looks small! As illustrated in Table 4.1, however, it can be misleading to compare raw scores without any consideration of the standard deviations. The standard deviation of ACT scores is approximately 4.7. Thus, the difference between 23 and 21.8 corresponds to a *z*-score difference of .45, almost half a standard deviation. If the distribution of ACT scores is approximately normal, then we can use Table A to determine that a *z* score of .45 has about 67% of the other scores below it. That is, the average city senior (at the 67th percentile) is doing much better than an average senior in the state (at the 50th percentile).

And what about the 0.2-point gain cited by Jane Grinde? It looks tiny. A difference of 0.2 corresponds to a *z*-score difference of .04. Here the impression given by the raw scores is correct: There has been very little change from one year to the next.

Determining Relative Frequencies Given Scores

To see how to use these facts in an interesting way, we will work with a specific distribution. Suppose that for your school the distribution of GPAs (in which each student contributes one GPA) has $\mu = 2.5$ and $\sigma = .5$. Further, suppose that the distribution approximates a normal distribution. Of course, the distribution is not a true normal distribution because GPAs have finite limits; usually the lowest GPA is 0.0 (rather than negative infinity) and the highest GPA is 4.0 (rather than positive infinity). Nonetheless, as illustrated on the left of Figure 4.8, the distribution is bell-shaped and approximates a normal distribution.

Suppose that your GPA is 3.0. What is the relative frequency of scores in the distribution below your score? (In other words, what is the percentile rank of your score?) To answer this question, we need to transform the original distribution because we do not have a table of relative frequencies for the GPA distribution, but we do have one for the *z*-score distribution, Table A.

Conceptually, transforming the distribution involves calculating a *z* score for each GPA in the original distribution (as in Tables 4.2 and 4.3). Fortunately, the actual work is unnecessary. We know that the result of transforming each and every GPA is the standard normal distribution with $\mu = 0.0$ and $\sigma = 1.0$.

Now, picture the problem in terms of areas under the curve (remember, areas correspond to relative frequencies). The question, "What is the relative frequency of scores

FIGURE 4.8

Using the standard normal distribution to determine the percentile rank of a GPA of 3.0.

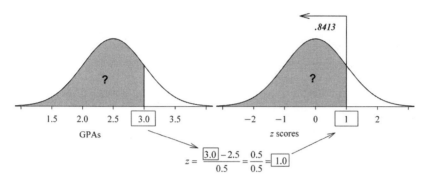

below a GPA of 3.0?" is the same as "What is the area under the curve below a score of 3.0?" This area is shaded in Figure 4.8.

Next, use the standard normal distribution to determine the area. To do this, we need the z score corresponding to a GPA of 3.0.

$$z = \frac{3.0 - 2.5}{.5} = 1.0$$

This transformation is illustrated at the bottom of the figure. Now you can see (from Figure 4.8) that the answer to the question "What is the area under the GPA distribution below a GPA of 3.0?" is the same as the answer to the question "What is the area under the z-score distribution below a z score of 1.0?"

The answer is provided by using Table A. From Table A, we know that the relative frequency of z scores less than $z = 1.00$ is .8413. Therefore, the relative frequency of z scores below $z = 1.0$ is .8413, and the relative frequency of GPAs less than 3.0 (corresponding to a z score of 1.0) is .8413. In other words, the percentile rank of your GPA is 84.13%.

Although 84.13% seems very exact, remember that the GPA distribution only approximates a normal distribution, so this answer is only an approximation. As long as the raw-score distribution is mound-shaped and symmetric, your answer will be accurate to within a few percentage points of the real value.

Now, suppose that you have a friend whose GPA is 1.75. What is the percentile rank of his GPA (what is the relative frequency of GPAs below his)? The situation is portrayed in Figure 4.9, with the distribution of GPAs on the left and the transformed distribution of z scores on the right. Again, you must picture the question in terms of areas: What is the area under the GPA curve below a score of 1.75?

$$z = \frac{1.75 - 2.5}{.5} = -1.5$$

Note that the z score is negative, indicating that it is below the mean.

FIGURE 4.9
Using the standard normal distribution to determine the percentile rank of a GPA of 1.75.

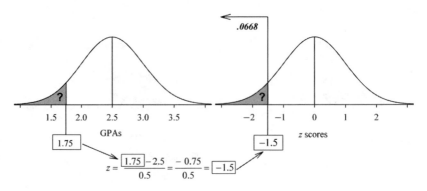

FIGURE 4.10
Using the standard normal distribution to determine the percentage of GPAs between 2.25 and 3.5.

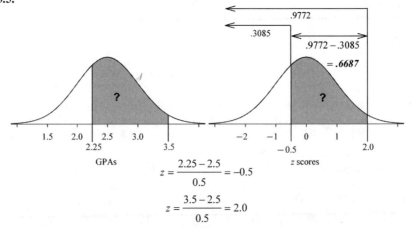

Table A indicates that the relative frequency of z scores below −1.5 is .0668. Thus, the relative frequency of z scores less than z = −1.50 is .0668; the relative frequency of GPAs less than 1.75 is .0668; and the percentile rank of the GPA is 6.68%.

As a final problem using the GPA distribution, suppose that you and a friend are debating whether or not most students have GPAs between 2.25 and 3.5. To settle the debate, you decide to compute the relative frequency of GPAs between 2.25 and 3.5. The situation is illustrated in Figure 4.10. The relative frequency corresponds to the area between these two GPAs.

Finding the shaded area requires computation of the two z scores that correspond to GPA = 2.25 and GPA = 3.5.

$$z = \frac{2.25 - 2.5}{.5} = -.5 \qquad z = \frac{3.5 - 2.5}{.5} = 2.0$$

Using Table A, the area below $z = -.5$ is .3085, and the area below $z = 2.0$ is .9772. The area between the two z scores is $.9772 - .3085 = .6687$, corresponding to the relative frequency between the two GPAs. Thus the majority of the students (66.87%) have GPAs between 2.25 and 3.5.

Reflecting back over the last three problems, you will begin to appreciate the power of z scores in conjunction with the normal distribution. Indeed, when a distribution is normally distributed (or approximates a normal distribution), just knowing μ and σ allows you to determine everything else about the distribution.

Before continuing to read about other types of z-score problems, it may help to take a few moments to see if you really do understand the techniques discussed so far. Try to solve the following problems. The answers are given below.[2]

Suppose that you are a legislative analyst working with the state government. You must calculate the relative frequency of people within certain income categories to help estimate the effects of proposed tax changes. You know that the distributions of incomes in your state approximates a normal distribution, $\mu = \$23,000$ and $\sigma = \$6,000$. $\dfrac{23000-11000}{6000} =$

1. What is the relative frequency of incomes less than $11,000?
2. What is the relative frequency of incomes greater than $41,000?
3. What is the relative frequency of incomes between $14,000 and $32,000?
4. Why might your calculations not be completely accurate?

Determining Scores Given Relative Frequencies

The z-score problems discussed so far have all required computation of relative frequencies. Another form of problem begins with relative frequency and requires computation of specific scores. As an example, again suppose that you are the legislative analyst. You are told that the state treasury has a surplus so that people with incomes in the lowest 10% of the distribution do not need to pay taxes. Your problem is to determine which incomes correspond to the lowest 10% of all incomes.

Figure 4.11 illustrates the situation. On the left is the distribution of incomes, and on the right is the corresponding distribution of z scores. The lowest 10% (relative frequency of .10) is shaded in each figure. The problem is to determine the income corresponding to the lowest .10, indicated by the box with a question mark in it. In outline, the process is to find the z score corresponding to the lowest 10% of the z-score distribution, and then to transform that z score into an income.

Look in the body of Table A for an *area* close to .1000. The area closest to .1000 is .1003, corresponding to $z = -1.28$.

The next step is to transform this z score into an income (X) using Formula 4.2.

$$\begin{aligned} X &= \mu + z\sigma \\ &= \$23,000 + (-1.28)(\$6,000) \\ &= \$15,320 \end{aligned}$$

Therefore, the lowest 10% of the incomes are those below $15,320.

---

[2] 1. .0228; 2. .0013; 3. .8664; 4. The distribution of incomes only approximates a normal distribution.

FIGURE 4.11
Using the standard normal distribution to determine the income with a percentile rank of 10%.

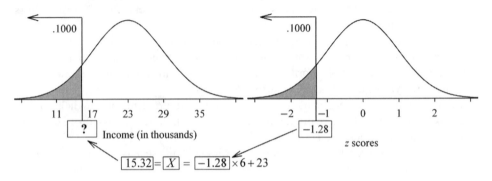

FIGURE 4.12
Using the standard normal distribution to determine the reading scores in the top 5% and the bottom 5% of the distribution of reading scores.

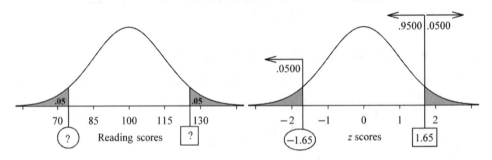

As a final example, suppose that you are designing reading programs for an elementary school. You propose that students who score in the middle 90% on a test of reading ability are receiving adequate training. Those students in the lowest 5% should be given remedial instruction, and those students in the top 5% should receive advanced instruction. Given that the distribution of reading scores has $\mu = 100$ and $\sigma = 15$, and that it approximates a normal distribution, find the reading scores that define the top 5% and the bottom 5%.

The problem is illustrated in Figure 4.12. The shaded areas indicate the top 5% and the bottom 5% (relative frequencies of .0500). The shapes with question marks correspond to the reading scores we are trying to determine. The z score that has 5% of the scores higher than it also has 95% of the scores below it (1.0000 − .0500 = .9500). Looking in the body of Table A, we find that the z score of 1.65 is the closest to .9500 (actually .9505). The z score with 5% of the scores below it is closest to −1.65 (a proportion of .0495). Thus, $z = 1.65$ has the top 5% of the distribution above it, and $z = -1.65$ has the bottom 5% of the distribution below it. These z scores are converted into reading test scores (Xs) using Formula 4.2:

$$X = 100 + (-1.65)(15) = 75.25 \quad X = 100 + (1.65)(15) = 124.75$$

Students who score below 75.25 (bottom 5%) should receive remedial instruction, and those who score above 124.75 (top 5%) should receive advanced instruction.

Summary of Steps for z-Score Problems

Although it may seem that a confusing array of techniques was used to solve the z-score problems, the steps are easily summarized. Remember, to use Table A, the distribution of raw scores must approximate a normal distribution.

1. Sketch a diagram of the raw score (X) distribution and the z-score distribution. The z-score distribution always has a mean of zero.
2. If you are given scores and must calculate areas (percentile ranks or relative frequencies), then include the scores on your diagram of the X distribution, and sketch the required areas on both distributions. Convert the scores into z scores, and use Table A to determine the area needed.
3. If you have the areas (percentile ranks or relative frequencies) and must calculate the scores, then sketch and label the areas in both distributions. Use boxes to indicate the z score(s) and raw score(s) needed. Refer to Table A to find the z score for this area. Finally, convert the z score to the required raw score using Formula 4.2. (See Figures 4.10 and 4.11 for examples.)

OTHER STANDARDIZED SCORES

Although z scores solve many of the problems associated with comparing scores, they pose one difficulty: z scores, particularly negative z scores, are difficult for an unsophisticated person to understand. This difficulty is eliminated by transforming z scores in a way that preserves the desirable features, but eliminates the necessity for negative numbers. In fact, scores on the Scholastic Aptitude Test (SAT) and the Graduate Record Examination (GRE) are based on this sort of transformation.

SAT and GRE scores are related to z scores by the following transformation:

$$\text{SAT or GRE} = 500 + (z)(100)$$

This transformation has two effects. First, the mean of the transformed scores is now 500 rather than 0. Second, the standard deviation of the transformed scores is now 100 rather than 1. Therefore, a score of 500 on the SAT test indicates performance equal to the mean. A score of 600 is one standard deviation above the mean, and a score of 400 is one standard deviation below the mean.

Because the distribution of SAT scores approximates a normal distribution, Table A can be used to calculate percentile ranks for SAT scores. For example, an SAT score of 450 corresponds to a z score of $-.5$ [$(450 - 500)/100 = -.5$]. Using Table A, the area less than $z = -.5$ is .3085. The percentile rank of an SAT score of 450 is approximately 30.85%.

SUMMARY

Standard scores (z scores) standardize the meaning of zero as the mean of the distribution and standardize the meaning of one unit as the standard deviation. The mean of a distribution of z scores is always 0.0, the standard deviation of a distribution of z scores is always 1.0, and the shape of a z-score distribution is always the same as the shape of the original distribution of Xs.

z scores are useful for three reasons. They indicate at a glance the relative standing of a score in a distribution. They can be used to compare scores across distributions. Finally, z scores can be used to compute frequencies and percentiles in conjunction with the standard normal distribution.

EXERCISES

Terms   *Define these new terms.*

standard score   normal distribution
z score   standard normal distribution

Questions   *Answer the following questions.*

1. Consider a normal distribution with $\mu = 75$ and $\sigma = 5$.
   †a. What percentage of the scores is below a score of 85?
   b.   What percentage of the scores is above 65?
   c.   What percentage of the scores is between 70 and 90?
   †d. What score is at the 9th percentile?
   e.   What scores enclose the middle 99% of the distribution?
2. Consider a normal distribution with $\mu = 20$ and $\sigma^2 = 9$ (be careful).
   †a. What proportion of the scores is below 17?
   b.   What proportion of the scores is above 15.5?
   c.   What is the relative frequency of scores between 18 and 26?
   †d. What is the 40th percentile?
   e.   What proportion of scores has z scores greater than 0?
3. Suppose that your score on a test is 95. From which of the following distributions would you prefer your score to be? Why?
   a. $\mu = 95$ $\sigma = 10$
   b. $\mu = 95$ $\sigma = 15$
   c. $\mu = 85$ $\sigma = 10$
   d. $\mu = 85$ $\sigma = 15$
   e. $\mu = 105$ $\sigma = 10$
   f. $\mu = 105$ $\sigma = 15$

†**4.** Suppose that a friend of yours is in a very competitive chemistry course. On the first test, there are far more grades above the mean than below. Knowing that you are taking statistics, your friend asks you to help her compute the percentile rank of her score, 58. She tells you that $\mu = 50$ and $\sigma = 8$. How would you proceed?

5. Jane scored at the 90th percentile on her psychology test. Bill scored at the 40th percentile on his botany test. Is it possible for Bill's raw score to be greater than Jane's raw score? Explain your answer.

†**6.** Jane's z score on her history exam is 0.0. Bill's z score on his math exam is $-.1$. Is it possible for Bill's percentile rank to be greater than Jane's percentile rank? Is it likely? Explain your answers.

7. In Distribution A, a score of 73 is at the 50th percentile and has a z score of .80. In Distribution B, a score of 73 is at the 50th percentile and has a z score of 0.0. Which distribution is definitely not normally distributed? How do you know?

8. z scores are a measure of relative standing. z scores measure the standing of what, relative to what, in units of what?

†**9.** You are working for the quality control division of a lightbulb manufacturer. One of your jobs is to ensure that no more than 1% of the lightbulbs are defective. A defective lightbulb is defined as one with a lifetime of less than 1,000 hours. The lifetimes of lightbulbs approximate a normal distribution with a standard deviation of 50 hours. What should you suggest to the engineers as a mean lifetime to ensure that no more than 1% of the lightbulbs are defective?

†**10.** You are working for a school system that is beginning to institute special education classes. State law mandates that all children with IQ scores of less than 80 be given the opportunity to enroll in special after-school enrichment programs. The school district has a total of 10,000 students. Assuming that the distribution of IQ scores approximates a normal distribution with $\mu = 100$ and $\sigma = 15$, what would you estimate to be the maximum enrollment in the enrichment program?

PART *II*

Introduction to Inferential Statistics

*T*he five chapters in Part II present the foundations of statistical inference making. In short, you will learn how to learn about (that is, make inferences about) broad populations from the data in relatively small samples. If you think about it, this knowledge confers on you a fantastic ability. Because samples are easier and cheaper to collect than *all* of the scores in a broad population, inferential techniques give you the ability to learn about aspects of the world that would otherwise be beyond the reach of even the richest of kings. All of this for the cost of a little study.

Most of the specific procedures discussed in Part II are used infrequently when people actually make statistical inferences. Why, then, are they presented here? And why are they presented first and in detail? Because these procedures are among the most straight-forward and easiest to understand, learning about them will help you to develop a solid understanding of the foundations of statistical inference. Then, Part III of this book, which deals with many practical inferential procedures, will be much easier to follow.

Before continuing, you should be certain that you understand concepts that are used repeatedly in Part II. In particular, review the following concepts if you have any uncertainty about them: sample, population, variability, distribution, mean, variance, *z* score, and normal distribution.

CHAPTER **5**

Overview of Inferential Statistics

*I*n this chapter we have two goals. The first is to give you a basic orientation to statistical inference, the topic of the remainder of this textbook. We will include discussions of why inferential techniques are needed, and explain the variety of inferential procedures available.

The second goal of the chapter is to introduce the topic of random sampling. All statistical procedures described here require random sampling, and yet random sampling is frequently difficult to achieve. The disclaimer "nonscientific results" or "nonscientific sampling" attached to reports in the popular media usually means that results have been obtained without random sampling. We will find out why such results should be treated with extreme skepticism.

WHY INFERENTIAL PROCEDURES ARE NEEDED

The first step in learning from data is describing the measurements in the sample. Often, the second step is using the data in the sample to make inferences about the population from which the sample was obtained.

> An **inferential statistical procedure** uses a random sample from a population to make inferences (educated guesses) about the population.

Inferential procedures are needed because of two related problems. First, we are usually interested in populations of scores, not just the few scores in a sample. Nonetheless, because populations are typically very large, collecting all the scores in a population (that is, making all of the necessary measurements) is time consuming, expensive, sometimes unethical, and often impossible.

Consider the two examples introduced in Chapter 1. Recall that Professor Tim Baker at the University of Wisconsin Center for Tobacco Research and Intervention is conducting research on how to help people best quit smoking. The data set from this study (the Smoking Study), though large (608 people), does not include all the people in Wisconsin, much less the United States or the world, who want to quit smoking. Ultimately, Dr. Baker and his colleagues are really interested in how well their methods work for a larger group of people. Similarly, Drs. Janet Hyde and Marilyn Essex, of the Wisconsin Maternity Leave and Health Project and the Wisconsin Study of Families and Work (the Maternity Study), are interested in how having a baby affects family dynamics, such as marital satisfaction, and how various factors affect child development. Although they have data from 244 families (an enormous data set!), they do not have measurements for all the families in Wisconsin, or the United States or the world. Inferential procedures help these researchers make inferences about the population based on data from their samples. And this point cannot be understated: With inferential statistics, Dr. Baker and Drs. Hyde and Essex can draw conclusions about many important questions that trouble our society. The results of the Smoking Study will help a lot of people quit smoking, not just the 608 people in the study, but potentially the millions who try to quit each year. Likewise, the Maternity Study will help us understand the impact of having a child on just about any family, not just the 244 families that Drs. Hyde and Essex studied.

The second problem solved by inferential statistical procedures has to do with variability. Remember, data collection consists of measuring variables, and the nature of variables is to be variable (that is, to change from observation to observation). Thus, the scores in a sample need not be exactly the same as the scores in the population. Inferential procedures are designed to assess the variability of the scores in the sample and to use that variability as an aid to inference making.

What You Learn From Inferential Procedures

The inferences produced by inferential procedures are educated guesses about characteristics of populations—namely, the shape of the population relative frequency distribution, its central tendency, and its variability. As was demonstrated in Chapter 4, knowing the shape, central tendency, and variability of a population gives you just about all the information that you need to know about that population.

Going back to the Smoking Study example, the important question that Dr. Baker would like to answer is whether people given Zyban and/or nicotine replacement gum are more likely to remain smoke-free than those who received neither. Asking the question statistically, is the *central tendency* of the population of smoke-free days of people given Zyban/nicotine gum higher than the *central tendency* of the population of smoke-free days of people not given Zyban/nicotine gum? Thus, answering the statistical question about central tendency provides the answer to an important psychological question, and that is exactly how one learns from data.

VARIETIES OF INFERENTIAL PROCEDURES

Parameter Estimation

Inferential procedures can be divided into two broad categories. One of the categories is parameter estimation.

> **Parameter estimation** uses data in a random sample to estimate a parameter of the population from which the sample was drawn.

A parameter, you will recall, is a numerical description of a population such as μ, the population mean. The category of parameter estimation procedures is subdivided into different procedures for estimating different parameters (for example, μ and σ).

Hypothesis Testing

The second type of inferential procedure is hypothesis testing.

> **Hypothesis-testing** procedures require the formulation of two opposing hypotheses about the population of interest. Data from random samples are used to determine which of the opposing hypotheses is more likely to be correct.

Hypothesis testing may seem needlessly complicated. Why bother formulating opposing hypotheses when population parameters can be estimated? The answer is that hypothesis testing provides an elegant way of answering many research questions. Refer back to the Maternity Study example. Drs. Hyde and Essex are interested in discovering, broadly, which of the following hypotheses is correct:

1. Having a child changes your marital satisfaction.
2. Having a child does not change your marital satisfaction.

The important question is whether or not there is a change in a person's feelings of marital satisfaction (the central tendency of the population of marital satisfaction scores); the actual values of the population parameters may be of little interest to Drs. Hyde and Essex.

The category of hypothesis-testing procedures is subdivided into parametric hypothesis testing and nonparametric hypothesis testing.

> **Parametric hypothesis testing** means that the hypotheses refer to population parameters, usually the mean or the variance of the population.

Parametric hypothesis testing requires computation of means and variances. As you know from Chapter 3, these computations are most easily interpreted when the data are interval or ratio. Consequently, the results of parametric procedures are most easily interpreted when the data are measured on interval or ratio scales. Also, parametric procedures typically require that the population of scores meets several assumptions (for example, that the population is normally distributed). When these assumptions are not met, the parametric procedures should not be used.

> **Nonparametric hypothesis testing** means that the specific hypotheses refer to the shape or location (central tendency) of the populations, rather than specific parameters.

Nonparametric procedures have two advantages: They can be used even when the data are ordinal (and sometimes nominal), and they do not make any assumptions regarding the population. They have the disadvantage of being generally less powerful than parametric procedures. That is, for a given sample size, nonparametric procedures are slightly less likely than parametric procedures to result in a correct decision regarding which hypothesis is correct. There are several reasons for this difference in power. One is that interval and ratio data used in parametric hypothesis testing contain more information (the information provided by the equal intervals property of the measurements) than the ordinal or nominal data used in nonparametric hypothesis testing. As is reasonable, the more information on which a decision is based, the more likely the decision will be correct. Because of this difference in accuracy of decision making, parametric procedures are preferred over nonparametric procedures.

RANDOM SAMPLING

Inferential statistical procedures will produce accurate inferences only when they are based on random samples. The reason is that all inferential procedures depend on probability theory, which, in turn, requires random samples in order to work.

> **A random sample** is one that has been obtained in such a way that each observation in the population has an equal chance of being included in the sample, and the selection of one observation does not influence the selection of any other observation.

Of course, not every observation in the population has to be included in a random sample, but the sample must be chosen so that every observation could have been included. Thus, whether or not a sample is random does not depend on what is actually included in the sample; it depends only on the procedure used in obtaining the sample. If the procedure guarantees that each observation in the population is equally likely to be included in the sample, then the sample is a random sample.

A random sample is likely to be representative of (similar to) the population from which it is drawn. That is, the sample and population are likely to have similar central tendencies, variabilities, and shapes. In contrast, **a biased sample** is selected from a population in such a way that some scores are more likely to be chosen than others. A biased sample is unlikely to be representative of its population.

How to Sample Randomly

The hardest part of applying inferential statistical procedures to real situations (as opposed to textbook examples) is the procurement of truly random samples. It is so difficult that those who can do it well are famous, highly paid, and in great demand (for example, Gallup polls or Nielson television ratings).

The following procedure can be used to produce a random sample:

1. Take each and every observation in the population and write it down on a standard-size slip of paper. At this stage, you may not have the actual scores that comprise the statistical population. You may, however, write down the names of the people (or animals) from whom those scores can be obtained. Once the random sample is selected, the desired scores are obtained from the people or animals.
2. Put all the slips of paper into a large hat and thoroughly mix them.
3. Close your eyes, stick in your hand, and pull out one slip of paper. Record the observation (or name) from this slip of paper, then put the slip back into the hat and thoroughly remix the slips of paper.
4. Continue to repeat Step 3 until you have recorded n observations, where n is the number of scores you intend to have in your random sample. Because each slip of paper has an equal chance of being included in the sample (each is a standard size and all are well mixed), each score in the population has an equal chance of being included in the sample.

The procedure just described is called **random sampling with replacement** or **independent (within-sample) random sampling**.[1] The name sampling with replacement is used because after a slip of paper is selected, it is replaced in the hat before the next draw. The other name, independent (within-sample) random sampling, highlights the fact that what is selected in one draw from the hat has absolutely no effect on what is selected in the next draw: The draws within each sample are independent of each other. Imagine the case in which there are only two slips of paper in the hat. Before the first draw, each slip of paper is equally likely to be drawn. After the first draw, if the first slip is replaced, then each slip is again equally likely to be drawn on the second draw. Thus, what happened on the first draw has absolutely no effect on the second draw; the two draws are independent.

Now consider what would happen if the first slip had *not* been replaced. In this case, the slip remaining in the hat after the first draw must be drawn on the second draw. In other words, whatever slip is drawn first completely determines which slip is drawn second; the draws are not independent, but dependent. The important point is that all of the inferential procedures that we will discuss require independent (within-sample) random sampling. The accuracy of your inferences will depend on the degree to which this ideal is met.

The requirement for independent (within-sample) random sampling along with the notion of replacement leads to an apparent problem, which is best illustrated with an example. Suppose that you are conducting research on the efficacy of a psychotherapeutic technique. You randomly sample (names) with replacement from a population in need of psychotherapy. To your surprise, the same name turns up twice. Should that person be included in the research twice? Should the patient receive two doses of the psychotherapeutic technique? The answer is no. The important criterion is to sample *scores* independently. If the same person is given the psychotherapy twice, the scores are certainly not

---

[1] The phrase "within-sample" is needed because another form of independent random sampling, independent-groups sampling, will be introduced in Chapter 13.

independent—the experience the person gains by virtue of the first dose of therapy will surely influence the second score.

So what does it mean to sample with replacement if whenever a name is resampled we cannot use it? The problem is that we are confusing the statistical population of scores with the human population of people. When randomly sampling with replacement from a set of scores, it is perfectly legitimate to use the same *score* more than once. Sampling the score the first time does not influence the probability that the score is resampled, nor will the score be influenced if it is resampled (the score will be the same). Thus, when randomly sampling from a population of scores, independence is achieved by sampling with replacement. When names of people (or animals) are randomly sampled and then the scores are collected from the people, independence is best approximated by including a person in the sample one time at most.

The procedure for random sampling outlined above is not very practical. With a large population, it would be extremely time consuming to actually write each observation on a separate sheet of paper. Also, it would be doubtful that the individual slips of paper could be thoroughly mixed to the extent that each had an equal chance of being included in the sample (those put in last would tend to be closest to the top). The procedures discussed next are more practical, but each is conceptually related to the slips of paper in the hat.

In the Media: Huge Worthless (and Frightening) Samples

Inferential statistics give you the tools to generalize to broad populations, but only if you randomly sample from that population. Don't be fooled by large samples: Even a small random sample is a better guide than a huge biased one. Apparently, however, either many media moguls do not know this simple rule, or they hope that their consumers do not know it. How else can we explain the vast number of polls and surveys conducted by the media in which, for example, people are urged to call one telephone number to express one opinion and a different number to express another opinion? Because these data do not conform to a random sample, they are worthless for making inferences.

As an example of the worthlessness of even huge nonrandom samples, consider the results of a survey conducted by the magazine *Better Homes and Gardens,* published in June 1978. The lengthy survey of demographic and "family values" issues had been published in the magazine several months prior to this date, and readers were asked to fill it out and mail it in. To the credit of the magazine, the editors did publish, along with the results, a sidebar disclaimer. "Also keep in mind that our respondents are obviously all readers of *Better Homes and Gardens.* Certain segments of the American population—the economically disadvantaged, for example—are not adequately represented in our magazine's readership … And even among our readers, there is a limiting factor. Not everyone had the time or inclination to complete our lengthy questionnaire—only those with a particularly strong interest in the subject. Technically, this isn't a cross section of national opinion. The views expressed here are strictly those of 302,602 readers of *Better Homes and Gardens* who give evidence of caring deeply about the American family."

In other words, 302,602 people wasted their time! A much more informative (and less expensive) procedure would have been to randomly sample 100 readers. At least then the results could be generalized to the readership of the magazine.

Another, more frightening, example is contained in an article by Paul Raeburn that was published in the *Denver Post,* November 2, 1995. The headline was "AIDS Invented to Kill Blacks? Many African-Americans Say Yes." It begins, "A survey of about 1000 black church members in five cities found that more than one-third of them believed the AIDS virus was produced in a germ-warfare laboratory as a form of genocide against blacks." It is only in the fifth paragraph that we learn, "The surveyed group was not necessarily a representative sample of America's black population, and the findings cannot be applied to blacks as a whole." The frightening aspect of this article is not that people hold false beliefs; after all, who knows what lies they might have been told (or read) recently? Instead, the frightening aspect is that the editors of a respected newspaper would choose to publish an article with such an inflammatory headline based on such poor data.

Random Sampling Using a Random Number Table

Sampling using a random number table such as Table H on page 543 is more sophisticated (and less burdensome) than random sampling from a hat. This table was produced so that each digit occurs randomly in each column. Random numbers of any size can be constructed by putting together adjacent columns. For example, if you need numbers in the range of 1–5000, group together four columns. The digits in the four columns combine to make numbers between 0000 and 9999. You may ignore the numbers that are greater than you need (for example, greater than 5000) and less than you need (less than 0001).

The first step in using a random number table is to assign each and every observation in the population a unique number, usually starting with 1 and continuing sequentially up to N, the number of observations in the population. (Again, people can be assigned the numbers and the scores measured later.) As an example, suppose that $N = 5382$.

Next, turn to the table of random numbers (Table H). Choose a starting location in the table by selecting a page, and then close your eyes and plop your finger down on the table. Let us suppose that your finger lands on page 543 on the very last column, on the 11th row down. Immediately to the left of your finger is the number 73,998. Because N equals 5382, we need consider only the first four columns of digits. Putting the first four together generates the random number 3998. Therefore, the first observation included in the sample is the measurement from the person assigned the number 3998.

To obtain the next observation, move your finger down the column to the next row. The first four digits in this row form the number 7851. Because there are no observations in the population assigned this number (it is too large), it is ignored.

Do not ignore the first digit, 7, and use observation 851. Dropping the first digit makes observations assigned three-digit numbers too likely to be included in the sample. For example, observation 851 would be included if the random number 0851 occurred, or if the random number 6851 occurred, or if the random number 7851 occurred, and so on.

The next number, 7817, is also too large, and so it is ignored. The next is 1062. The person assigned this number is measured to produce the next observation for the random sample. This process is continued until you have n (the size of the sample) random numbers.

Using the random numbers table to select observations is equivalent to independent (within-sample) random sampling of slips of paper from a hat. Assigning each observation in the population a single number is equivalent to writing each on a standard-size slip of paper. The process used to generate the table is equivalent to thoroughly mixing the slips in the hat. Finally, because selecting a random number does not, in any sense, remove it from the table (the very next random number is just as likely to be the one that was just chosen as any other particular number), sampling is independent. (Once again, however, if you are sampling names of people rather than scores, the same person should not be used twice.)

Random Sampling and Computers

Probably the most common procedure for producing random samples is to use a computer. Many implementations of computer languages such as BASIC or Pascal have built-in routines for producing random numbers.[2] The computer can be used to assign a unique number to each observation in the population, and it can also be used to generate the n random numbers corresponding to the n observations to include in the random sample.

BIASED SAMPLING

We can contrast the procedures for producing random samples with procedures that produce biased samples. For example, suppose that a university administrator is interested in the opinions of students regarding a change in graduation requirements. The administrator may attempt to produce a random sample by stopping every fifth student who enters the student union, and asking for that student's opinion. The administrator reasons (incorrectly) that "every fifth student" sounds random and without bias. Unfortunately, this sample will be biased because it includes only scores from students who happen to frequent the student union. Those who spend their time in the library will be systematically (although perhaps unintentionally) excluded.

As another example, suppose that the mayor of a city is interested in the opinions of the residents regarding a new bond issue. The mayor's aide attempts to draw a random sample by using a random number table to select pages in the city telephone directory and randomly select names from the chosen pages. This sample will be biased because it will exclude those too poor to own a telephone and overrepresent those families that are rich enough to have more than one telephone number. Also, it is likely that married women will be systematically excluded from the sample if only their husbands are listed in the directory.

As a final example, consider the "polls" conducted by television shows (call one number to vote yes and another to vote no) and surveys conducted by mass-circulation magazines (often variants of "How's Your Sex Life?"). The data collected by these procedures are extraordinarily biased because the sampling procedures exclude people who do not watch that specific television show or read that specific magazine. Also excluded are those too

---

[2] Some built-in routines for generating random numbers do not do a very good job; that is, the numbers generated are not really random. The statistical procedures described in Chapter 22 can be used to check on the randomness of a random number routine.

poor to respond, and those who do not care to respond. Even though one of these surveys may produce hundreds of thousands of responses, the data are useless because they do not form any population of interest, nor are they a random sample from any population. There is very little to be learned from data of this sort. Thus, an immediately useful and practical bit of advice is to be extremely cautious when you interpret the results of nonrandom ("nonscientific") sampling reported in newspapers, magazines, and broadcasts.

At times, we may have available a sample that is not random (because the sampling procedure did not conform to the definition of a random sample), but does not appear to have any special bias. For example, you may randomly select a list of names from a population and send a survey to each person on the list. Only 25% of the people respond. Examination of the responses does not reveal any systematic bias. Why not proceed as if you actually had a random sample?

The problem is that the examination of the responses for bias is, itself, biased. You are likely only to look for the types of bias that you believe are important (for example, age, sex, income). However, a great variety of biases, some of which you may never have considered, may be influencing who returned the survey. There is virtually no way to guarantee that the sample obtained has no biases; hence, proceeding as if it were a random sample is a risky undertaking without any formal ("scientific") justification.

OVERGENERALIZING

Not only do inferential statistical procedures require random samples, it is also the case that inferences must be restricted to the population that was randomly sampled. An example will help make this point clear. Suppose that a doctor is attempting to determine characteristics (such as weight) of people with high blood pressure. Rather than attempting to measure the weights of all people with high blood pressure, the doctor selects a random sample of weights of people attending the high blood pressure clinic at University Hospital. Based on this random sample, the doctor can make inferences about a population. But what is the population? The only population that the doctor can legitimately make inferences about is the population of weights of people *attending the high blood pressure clinic at University Hospital*. Inferences cannot be made about the population of weights of *all* people with high blood pressure, nor can inferences be made about the population of weights of people with high blood pressure, even in the same city as University Hospital.

There is a good reason for limiting inferences to the specific population from which the random sample is drawn. Namely, the sample is random with respect to the specific population, but biased with respect to other (even closely related) populations. For example, when the sample is constrained to measurements of people attending the high blood pressure clinic, certain groups are systematically excluded. People with milder cases of high blood pressure are excluded; people with such severe problems that they are hospitalized are excluded. People with high blood pressures who do not live close to University Hospital are excluded. Some of these people may lead a more rural lifestyle (and, therefore, they may have different patterns of weight) than people who live close to the hospital. To reiterate the main point, inferences should be made only about the population from which the sample was randomly drawn.

An **overgeneralization** is an inference made about a population other than the one that was randomly sampled.

Overgeneralization is a matter of serious concern because we often would like to make inferences (or generalizations) to broad populations, even if the random sample is from a narrower population. As an example, consider a special education instructor who develops techniques for teaching socialization skills to mildly retarded 10-year-olds in a specific school district. Will the techniques work for mildly retarded 11-year-olds? Will it work for more severely retarded children? Will it work in another school system? Whenever discoveries are made for one population, you should be at least slightly skeptical as to whether the discoveries will generalize to a different population. Statistical procedures provide license to make inferences only about the specific population that is randomly sampled.

There are two approaches to the problem of overgeneralization. The first is to avoid it by carefully determining the population about which you wish to make inferences and randomly sampling from that population. The second is to be aware of the possible dangers of overgeneralization, both when you are reporting inferences you have made and when you are analyzing the inferences others have made.

Sampling in Psychology

Although the problems of biased sampling and overgeneralization are well known, they occur frequently. Perhaps the most flagrant violations occur in research in psychology using volunteer human subjects. Often, experimenters will obtain volunteer subjects from among the students enrolled in an introductory psychology class. Thus, the statistical population is very constrained—the population of scores of students who are taking introductory psychology at a specific university who volunteer for service in experiments. Nonetheless, any inference to other populations is an overgeneralization.

Even with this constrained population, the samples frequently used in psychological research are not random. Instead, students sign up for experiments depending on factors such as convenience, or rumors as to which experiments are fun. Clearly, extreme caution should be exercised in drawing conclusions from data of this sort. There are two partial solutions to this problem. The first is to use inferential procedures specifically designed for this sort of sampling, such as randomization tests.[3] A second (partial) solution is the random assignment of subjects to conditions within an experiment. Random assignment and its limitations are discussed in Chapter 14.

SUMMARY

Inferential statistical procedures are used to learn about a population when a random sample from the population is available. The inferences are educated guesses about characteristics of the population, such as shape of the frequency distribution, central tendency,

---

[3] See S. E. Eddington (1980), *Randomization tests*. New York: Marcel Dekker.

and variability. The two broad classes of inferential procedures are parameter estimation and hypothesis testing. Hypothesis-testing procedures are used to distinguish between two contrasting hypotheses about the population. When the hypotheses specify parameters of the population, parametric hypothesis testing is used. Parametric hypothesis testing usually requires interval or ratio data and that the sampled population is normally distributed. Parametric procedures are more powerful (that is, more likely to result in a correct decision regarding the hypotheses) than nonparametric procedures. However, nonparametric procedures can be used with ordinal data and require fewer assumptions about the population. Nonparametric hypothesis testing generally tests hypotheses about the shape of the population frequency distribution rather than hypotheses about specific parameters.

All inferential procedures described in this book require independent (within-sample) random sampling from the population of interest. Procedures for obtaining a random sample ensure that all observations in the population have the same chance of being included in the sample; otherwise, the sample is biased. Overgeneralization can be avoided by confining claims to the specific population from which the random sample was drawn.

EXERCISES

Terms *Define these new terms and symbols.*

parameter estimation	sampling with replacement
hypothesis testing	independent (within-sample) random sampling
nonparametric hypothesis testing	overgeneralization
parametric hypothesis testing	n
random sampling	N

Questions *Answer the following questions.*

1. What is a statistical inference?
2. What good does it do to make inferences about statistical populations when those populations are just a bunch of numbers?
3. How can you tell if a sample is random or biased?
4. Use Table H to find random numbers for selecting a random sample when
   a. $n = 3$ and $N = 50$
   b. $n = 5$ and $N = 500$
   c. $n = 4$ and $N = 50,000$
   d. $n = 6$ and $N = 500,000$
5. For each of the following situations, indicate if the sample is biased or random. If it is a biased sample, indicate why it is biased. If it is a random sample, describe the population from which it was drawn.
   †a. An animal behavior psychologist went to the rat colony in her laboratory and selected the first rat she could catch from each of the first 10 cages (assume that each cage holds five rats). She then measured how long it took each rat to run through a maze.

      b. A sociologist who is examining regional use of hospitals consulted a recent census to determine all cities with populations over 100,000 in a five-state region. He obtained a telephone directory for each of these cities and listed all the hospitals. He then used a table of random numbers to select a sample of 15 hospitals to study. For each hospital, he determined the average daily occupancy during the preceding year.

      c. An engineering psychologist measured reaction times of five volunteers from a class in human factors psychology. Each volunteer was randomly selected from among those who volunteered.

      d. A university administrator sent surveys to all faculty members at the university. Only 15% of the faculty bothered to respond. The administrator examined the responses and noted that there was no obvious bias; that is, the responses came from a variety of academic departments, they came from faculty at all levels, and they came from both male and female faculty members. The administrator decided to treat the returned surveys as a random sample.

6. In June of 1978, the magazine *Better Homes and Gardens* published the results of a survey originally printed in an earlier issue of the magazine. Readers of the earlier issue were requested to fill out the survey and send in their responses by mail. In all, 302,602 (n) responded. This is an enormous sample that cost, in aggregate, much time and money. What can be learned from these data? Why?

Probability

*I*nferential statistical procedures are used to make educated guesses (inferences) about a population based on a random sample drawn from that population. As we talked about in the last chapter, the various *statistics* that describe a sample's central tendency, variability, etc., would be much more helpful if we could say something about the *parameters* of the population from which the sample was drawn. For example, if the mean (M) of a sample was 10, what is the mean (μ) of the population from which the sample was drawn? Unfortunately, we don't know from the information provided by the sample what μ really is, but M is one good guess. You may next ask, how good a guess is M? And the answer is, "It depends, on a bunch of things." And using something known as "probability theory," we can take some things and combine them to answer the more interesting question of "what is μ?" (and questions about other parameters as well). So, we need to review, briefly, probability theory, or one form of the theory (sometimes called the "frequentist" theory of probability) to help us put together the inferential methods we're going to learn. Because probability, in this account, is closely related to relative frequency (hence the name "frequentist"), it won't be a difficult topic (probably).

Interestingly, there is no universally accepted definition of what a probability really is. We will take advantage of this situation by discussing probabilities in a way that makes them most relevant for use in inferential statistics. That is, we will conceptualize probability as dealing with the possible outcomes of random sampling from populations. In all of the examples in this chapter (and in the rest of the book), you may think of the population as a set of numbers (measurements of a variable), each written on a standard-size slip of paper, and all of the slips well mixed in a huge hat. Probabilities refer to what might happen when independent (within-sample) random samples are drawn from that hat.

PROBABILITIES OF EVENTS

Imagine that you are a health psychologist working with Dr. Baker on the Smoking Study. You are working on finding ways to help people quit smoking. Some of the basic data that Dr. Baker's team collected include the number of years that each participant smoked ("YRSMK") and the expired-air carbon monoxide content ("CO_EOT") of each participant at the end of the study ("end of treatment" or "EOT"). Carbon monoxide (CO) content is often used as a dependent measure in smoking studies because it indicates how much a person has been smoking, and it is more reliable than a person's report of how much he or she has been smoking. If you were to collect these measures on all smokers, the measurements would form a population of scores.

The concept of an event is useful in thinking about probabilities.

> An **event** is a value, or range of values, on the variables being measured.

For example, one event relevant to the population of CO_EOT scores is "carbon monoxide content of less than 5 parts per million (ppm)." All observations of CO content less than 5 ppm are instances of this event. Another event is "CO content between 17 and 25 ppm." Although many different people have expired-air CO content of between 17 and 25 ppm, each is an observation of the same event.

> **Simple probabilities** are numbers that indicate the likelihood that an event occurs in a single random observation from a population (a random sample with $n = 1$).

The probability of having a "CO content less than 5 ppm" is the likelihood of obtaining a measurement of less than 5 ppm in a random sample of one measurement of CO content from the population of people who smoke (a huge population).

The symbol for the probability of an event is p(event). So, the probability that "a single random observation (X) of CO_EOT is less than 5 ppm is written as $p(X < 5)$. Using this type of abbreviation, the X stands for any single random observation from the population of CO measurements.

The next point is so important it is called the *first axiom of probability theory:* Probabilities are always between 0 and 1. (An axiom is an accepted, but undemonstrated principle. In this case, it is a principle that we have to assume to be true for probability theory to work.) A probability of 0 means that there is no likelihood (it is impossible) for the event to occur. For example, if there are no observations in a population corresponding to a specified value of a variable (for example, no smoker will have a CO content less than 0 ppm), then the event of randomly choosing an observation with that value has a probability of 0. Using symbols, $p(X < 0 \text{ ppm}) = 0$. At the other extreme, a probability of 1.0 means that the event will always occur. For example, if all smokers in the population had expired-air CO content of greater than 0 ppm, $p(X > 0) = 1.0$. That is, any single observation (X) chosen from the population is guaranteed to be greater than 0 ppm (even nonsmokers expire some CO).

Probabilities between 0 and 1 indicate relative amounts of certainty that the event will occur. An event with a probability of .25 will occur on a quarter of the random samples (of single observations) from the population; for an event with a probability of .5, one half of the random samples will be instances of the event.

Calculating Simple Probabilities

Simple probabilities are calculated using the following formula:

FORMULA 6.1   Simple Probabilities

$$p(\text{event}) = \frac{\text{Number of equally likely observations of event in the population}}{\text{Number of equally likely observations in the population}}$$

If we use a procedure for randomly sampling from the population of expired-air CO content in the smokers, then each of the observations is equally likely to be chosen (remember, that is what random sampling means). Therefore, $p(X > 5 \text{ ppm})$ = number of smokers with CO content greater than 5 ppm divided by the total number of smokers in the population. As of now, we cannot calculate $p(X > 5 \text{ ppm})$ because we do not know the number of smokers in the population who have CO content greater than 5 ppm, nor do we know the total number of smokers in the population (but we will return to this problem later in the chapter). In a sense, we are back to the problem we started with: It is very hard to get all the measurements of a population.

Let's start with a more manageable population to illustrate how one might calculate a simple probability. Imagine six same-size pieces of paper in a top hat each with a number from 1 to 6 printed on it. The slips of paper are well-mixed. This setup might be used for drawing random samples from a small population in which there are only six observations.

Now, suppose that you are about to stick your hand into the hat and draw out a single slip of paper. The probability that you will draw any given number can be calculated before you actually draw a slip. This is possible because of the *second axiom of probability:* The probability that you will select an event in the population is 1. In other words, you are guaranteed to select a slip of paper with a 1, 2, 3, 4, 5, or 6, but not a 0, 7, or 4582 (more on this in a moment). So, what is the probability that you will draw a 3? There is only one way to draw a 3—picking the piece of paper with a "3" on it. There are six equally likely observations. Using Formula 6.1, the probability of drawing a 3 is 1/6, or in symbols, $p(X = 3) =$ 1/6. In words, the probability (likelihood) that a piece of paper has a 3 on it is 1/6, or .167.

PROBABILITY AND RELATIVE FREQUENCY

Similarities

Probabilities and relative frequencies are very similar. Indeed, as we shall see, probabilities of events and relative frequencies of events are almost identical, except for their interpretations. Probabilities refer to the chance of some event occurring in the future; relative frequency refers to what has been observed in the past.

The first similarity is that the probability of an event is equal to the event's relative frequency *in the population*. That is, the actual numbers you end up with are the same when you calculate the probability of an event and when you calculate the event's relative frequency in the population. In the example with $N = 6$, not only does $p(X = 3) = 1/6$, but the relative frequency of 3 is also 1/6.

It is not difficult to see why the probability of an event will always equal its relative frequency in the population. Remember, relative frequency of a value of a variable (an event) in a population is the number of observations of that value in the population (the numerator of Formula 6.1) divided by the total number of observations in the population (the denominator of Formula 6.1).

A second similarity between relative frequency and probability is that neither is ever smaller than 0 nor larger than 1.

Recall that the relative frequencies of events form a distribution and that the sum of the relative frequencies in the distribution always equals 1. This is also true of probabilities: The probabilities of (nonoverlapping or mutually exclusive) events form a distribution, and the sum of the probabilities of the events in the distribution always equals 1. This is a third similarity between relative frequency and probability.

Fourth, a relative frequency distribution can be summarized by its μ and σ^2. In fact, the mean and variance of a probability distribution are exactly the same as the mean and variance of the population relative frequency distribution for the same events.

Finally, a probability distribution and its corresponding relative frequency distribution have exactly the same shape. Indeed, as far as the *numbers* are concerned, relative frequencies in a population and probabilities are exactly the same, and the distributions are exactly the same.

Differences Between Relative Frequency and Probability

There are two major differences. One difference is that relative frequencies are obtained by collecting data, whereas probabilities are calculated by using Formula 6.1. There is no way to know the relative frequencies of events in random samples without actually making observations and calculating the relative frequencies from those observations. Probabilities are theoretical, and can be calculated without ever making an observation. If a population has six equally likely observations, then the probability of choosing any one of the observations is 1/6, and this can be calculated without ever taking any samples.

The greatest difference between relative frequencies and probabilities is in interpretation. Relative frequency refers to the result of having made many observations *in the past*. Probability (or at least simple probability) refers to the chance that an event will occur *in the future* in a random sample from the population. A probability of 0 means that there is no chance that the event will occur. A probability of 1 means that the event will occur with absolute certainty. Numbers between 0 and 1 indicate increasing degrees of certainty that the event will occur in the future.

Probability may also be interpreted as giving an *estimated* relative frequency of an event in future random sampling from the population. Why just an estimate and not the real relative frequency? Probability is only an estimate of relative frequency in a to-be-taken random sample because the to-be-taken random sample (like any random sample) may not be exactly like the population from which it was drawn. Relative frequency of an event in a to-be-taken random sample is likely to be close to the relative frequency of the event in the population (its probability), but the two may not be exactly equal.

TABLE 6.1
Probability Distribution

event	0	1	2	3	4	5	6	7
$p(X = \text{event})$	0	1/6	1/6	1/6	1/6	1/6	1/6	0

DISCRETE PROBABILITY DISTRIBUTIONS

A few examples will help to make the notion of probability clearer. These examples will use probability distributions based on discrete variables. You will recall (from Chapter 2) that discrete variables take on a limited number of values. An example of a discrete variable is the number of children in a family. A family can have 1 or 2 or 3 (or more) children, but not 1.58 children. Another example of a discrete variable is the value of an observation from the population of 6 numbers in the top hat; an observation can be a 1 or a 2, but not a 1.5.

In the top-hat example, what is the probability of drawing a 1? There is one way of obtaining the event 1; there are six equally likely observations, so $p(X = 1) = 1/6$. What is the probability of drawing a 7? Because there are no observations that could lead to the event 7, $p(X = 7) = 0$.

Probabilities for drawing all the numbers 1–6 (and any other number) can be calculated in a similar fashion. Putting these probabilities together forms a probability distribution for this variable (drawing a number from the top hat.) See Table 6.1 for the probability distribution.

Figure 6.1 is a histogram representing the same distribution. The rules for constructing a probability histogram are exactly the same as the rules for constructing a relative frequency histogram.

There are a few characteristics of this distribution that you should note. First, all of the probabilities are between 0 and 1, which must be if the calculations are correct. Second, the sum of the probabilities equals 1. Third, the mean of the distribution can be calculated using Formula 6.2.

FIGURE 6.1

Probability distribution for data in Table 6.1.

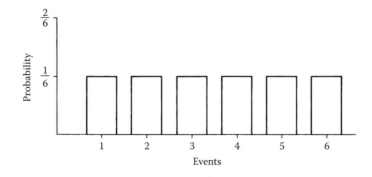

■■■■■■■

FORMULA 6.2   Mean of a Probability Distribution

$$\mu = \Sigma(X)p(X)$$

According to this formula, the mean of a probability distribution is equal to the sum of each value of the variable (*X*) times its corresponding probability. For the example,

$$\mu = 1 \times 1/6 +$$
$$2 \times 1/6 +$$
$$3 \times 1/6 +$$
$$4 \times 1/6 +$$
$$5 \times 1/6 +$$
$$6 \times 1/6$$
$$= 3.5$$

All other values of the variable (for example, 0, 7, −5) can be ignored. These other values have probabilities of zero and will not contribute to the sum.

You can think about this mean in different ways. First, it is a measure of central tendency of the probability distribution. As such, it tells you a value of the variable that is close to the center of distribution on the horizontal axis. Indeed, referring to Figure 6.1, the mean of 3.5 is a good index of central tendency because it is right at the center of the distribution's location on the horizontal axis.

It is a little awkward to think about the mean of a probability distribution as an average. Remember, probabilities refer to the chance of obtaining a specific event on a single observation randomly drawn from a population, and what is the average of a single observation other than the value of the observation? Instead, you can think about the mean of a probability distribution as what you can expect *in the long run*. That is, the mean of a probability distribution is a prediction of the average of many individual random samples from the population. In fact, the mean of a probability distribution is sometimes called the **expected value** of the distribution. For example, in repeated random sampling from the population of six numbers, we can expect that the average of the random samples will be 3.5.

Similarly, the variance of a probability distribution is an estimate of the variance of the events in future random samplings from the population. Formula 6.3 is used for calculating the variance of a probability distribution.

■■■■■■■

FORMULA 6.3   Variance of a Probability Distribution

$$\sigma^2 = \Sigma(X - \mu)^2 p(X)$$

For the example,

$$\sigma^2 = (1 - 3.5)^2 \times 1/6 +$$
$$(2 - 3.5)^2 \times 1/6 +$$
$$(3 - 3.5)^2 \times 1/6 +$$
$$(4 - 3.5)^2 \times 1/6 +$$
$$(5 - 3.5)^2 \times 1/6 +$$
$$(6 - 3.5)^2 \times 1/6$$
$$= 2.92$$

Again, values of the variable other than 1–6 can be ignored because they have probabilities of zero and will contribute nothing to the sum.

This 2.92 is the variance of the probability distribution. You may think of it as a **prediction** of the variance of many random samples (each with $n = 1$) to be taken in the future. As you might expect, the predicted standard deviation, σ, is simply the square root of σ^2.

Now imagine the same hat, but add to it four more slips of paper, two with the number 3 on them and two with the number 4. The hat now contains a different population, one that has 10 measurements. What is the probability of randomly drawing a 1? Because there is only one way of observing the event of drawing a 1, but 10 equally likely observations, $p(X = 1) = 1/10 = .1$. Similarly, the probability of drawing a 5 is .1. What is $p(X = 4)$? Because there are 3 equally likely observations that contribute to the event "drawing a 4" and 10 equally likely observations in all, $p(X = 4) = 3/10 = .3$. The complete probability distribution can be seen in Table 6.2.

Figure 6.2 is a histogram of this probability distribution. As with all probability distributions, the probabilities are all between 0 and 1, and the sum of the probabilities of the events equals 1.

The mean of the distribution can be calculated using Formula 6.2.

TABLE 6.2
Probability Distribution

event	1	2	3	4	5	6
$p(X = \text{event})$	.1	.1	.3	.3	.1	.1

FIGURE 6.2
Probability distribution for the data in Table 6.2.

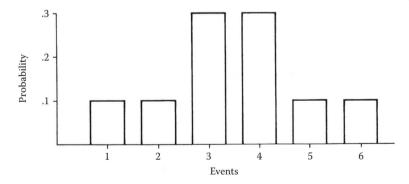

$$\mu = 1 \times .1 +$$
$$2 \times .1 +$$
$$3 \times .3 +$$
$$4 \times .3 +$$
$$5 \times .1 +$$
$$6 \times .1$$
$$= 3.5$$

Visual comparison of Figures 6.1 and 6.2 suggests that the distribution in Figure 6.2 is less variable than the distribution in Figure 6.1 (which has a variance of 2.92). In Figure 6.2, the most probable values of the variable are clumped around the central tendency, whereas in Figure 6.1 the values of the variable are spread out. Using Formula 6.3 to calculate the variance bears out this comparison. For the distribution in Figure 6.2:

$$\sigma^2 = (1 - 3.5)^2 \times .1 +$$
$$(2 - 3.5)^2 \times .1 +$$
$$(3 - 3.5)^2 \times .3 +$$
$$(4 - 3.5)^2 \times .3 +$$
$$(5 - 3.5)^2 \times .1 +$$
$$(6 - 3.5)^2 \times .1$$
$$= 1.85$$

THE OR-RULE FOR MUTUALLY EXCLUSIVE EVENTS

Sometimes (for example, when inferential procedures are used) it is necessary to calculate probabilities of events that are more complex than those we have considered so far. More complex events are also characteristic of games of chance (such as card games and dice games).[1] One type of complex event consists of combining simple events with the conjunction *or*. For example, what is the probability of drawing a "5 or 6," on a single draw, from the hat containing six slips of paper? Referring to Figure 6.1, we can see that $p(X = 6) = 1/6$ and that $p(X = 5) = 1/6$. But, what is the probability of a 5 or 6 [$p(X = 5$ or $X = 6)$]?

The or-rule is used for calculating probabilities of complex events that use the conjunction *or*. Before describing the rule itself, however, there is an important constraint on its application. The constraint is that the or-rule applies only when calculating the probability of a complex event composed of simpler events that are mutually exclusive.

> **Mutually exclusive events** cannot occur on the same observation (a random sample with $n = 1$ from the population).

---

[1] Probabilities for events such as throwing a die, flipping a coin, or drawing a card from a well-shuffled deck of cards can be determined using the following hat analogy. Imagine that each of the possible events (for example, heads or tails when flipping a coin) is written on a slip of paper and the slips are well mixed in the hat. Flipping a coin once, throwing a die once, or drawing one card from a deck corresponds to randomly drawing one slip of paper from the hat.

The complex event of drawing a "5 or 6" on the next draw from the hat is composed of two mutually exclusive simple events, "observing a 5 on the next draw from the hat" and "observing a 6 on the next draw from the hat." These events are mutually exclusive because they cannot occur together on the same observation; it is impossible to observe both a 5 and a 6 on the next draw from the hat, although it is possible to observe a 5 *or* a 6.

Two events that are *not* mutually exclusive are "observing a 5 on the next draw from the hat" and "observing a number less than 6 on the next draw from the hat."

The *third axiom of probability* applies to mutually exclusive events and states that the probability of one event or another is the sum of the probabilities of the simpler events (the "or-rule" of mutually exclusive events).

So, using the distribution in Figure 6.1, $p(X = 5 \text{ or } X = 6)$ is equal to $p(X = 5) + p(X = 6)$, which equals 2/6. It is easy to see why the or-rule works; it is really only an extension of the basic formula for calculating probabilities (Formula 6.1). There are two equally likely ways to observe a 5 or a 6 on the next draw (if either a 5 or a 6 shows up on the slip of paper), whereas there are six equally likely observations in all. Using Formula 6.1 to calculate $p(X = 5 \text{ or } X = 6)$ gives the same answer, 2/6.

What is $p(X = 1 \text{ or } X = 5 \text{ or } X = 6)$? The or-rule can be extended as long as all of the events are mutually exclusive. Because $p(X = 1) = 1/6$ and $p(X = 5 \text{ or } X = 6) = 2/6$, $p(X = 1 \text{ or } X = 5 \text{ or } X = 6) = 3/6$.

The or-rule can also be applied to mutually exclusive events from less regular distributions, such as that in Figure 6.2. Based on the distribution in that figure, what is $p(X = 1 \text{ or } X = 4)$? Because $p(X = 1) = .1$ and $p(X = 4) = .3$, $p(X = 1 \text{ or } X = 4) = .4$.

Probability theory provides more complex rules to apply to more complex events. For example, there is a rule for determining the probability of or-type events that are not mutually exclusive. There is also a rule for determining probabilities for and-type events such as observing, in two successive observations, a 5 *and* a 6.

CONDITIONAL PROBABILITIES

The discussion of simple probabilities was needed to bring us to one of the most important concepts in inferential statistics, conditional probabilities.

A **conditional probability** is the probability of an event conditional upon the occurrence of some other event or the existence of a particular state of affairs.

For example, we might want to compute the probability that a participant in Dr. Baker's Smoking Study will quit smoking if the participant has smoked for less than 1 year. It is probably easier to quit after smoking 1 year than after smoking many years. Consequently, we would expect that the probability of quitting conditional upon having smoked for 1 year is greater than the simple probability of quitting.

Conditional probabilities are symbolized as $p(A|B)$ and read as "the probability of A given B." Note that the $p(A|B)$ is not necessarily equal to the $p(B|A)$ (the probability of B given A). To illustrate, what is the probability of rain given clouds in the sky [p(rain |clouds)]? It is certainly far less than 1.0 because often there are clouds but no rain. In contrast, the p(clouds | rain) = 1.0. That is, when it is raining, it is almost certain that there are clouds in the sky. Thus, $p(A|B) \neq p(B|A)$.

Returning to the smoking example, the conditional probability of quitting given that a person has been smoking for less than 1 year is symbolized p(quitting | smoked for <1 year). Our reasoning leads us to suspect that p(quitting | smoked for <1 year) > p(quitting).

One way to calculate conditional probabilities is given in Formula 6.4.

FORMULA 6.4   Conditional Probability

$$p(A|B) = \frac{\text{number of equally likely observations of events that are both A and B}}{\text{number of equally likely observations of event B}}$$

For example, consider the population consisting of the 10 events that led to the distribution in Figure 6.2 (1, 2, 3, 3, 3, 4, 4, 4, 5, 6). What is $p(X = 3|X < 4)$? There are five observations of the event $X < 4$ (1, 2, 3, 3, 3). There are three observations that are both $X = 3$ and $X < 4$ (3, 3, 3). Thus, $p(X = 3|X < 4) = 3/5 = .6$. What is $p(X = 3|X > 4)$? Because there are no observations that are both $X = 3$, and $X > 4$, $p(X = 3|X > 4) = 0/2 = 0$.

PROBABILITY AND CONTINUOUS VARIABLES

A continuous variable can take on any value within a specified range, such as 1.5839, in addition to values such as 1 or 2. Height, weight, and intelligence are examples of continuous variables. In Chapter 4, we learned how relative frequencies of continuous variables can be determined by calculating areas. The exact same techniques can be applied to calculate probabilities of continuous variables.

z Scores and Probability

To continue with the Smoking Study introduced at the beginning of this chapter, suppose that the distribution of CO in smokers approximates a normal distribution with $\mu = 25$ ppm and $\sigma = 10$ ppm.[2] To find the probability of randomly drawing a single observation of CO content less than 15 ppm, we can calculate the relative frequency of CO content less than 15 ppm in the population. This is done using z scores exactly as in Chapter 4.

The calculations are illustrated in Figure 6.3. On the left is the original relative frequency distribution; the distribution on the right is the result of transforming each score in the original distribution using the z transformation. The score of 15 ppm corresponds to a

---

[2] The distribution of expired air CO content in smokers is certainly not normally distributed, because the tails do not extend to infinity. No smoker has less than 0 ppm CO in his expired air, for example, and no smoker has 300 ppm CO, either (that would be fatal). Nonetheless, as discussed in Chapter 4, if a distribution is symmetric and mound-shaped, the normal distribution is a close approximation.

FIGURE 6.3
Determining the probability of randomly selecting a single smoker with expired air CO content less than 15 ppm. *Left panel*: **the population of expired air CO content.** *Right panel*: **the population transformed into** *z* **scores.**

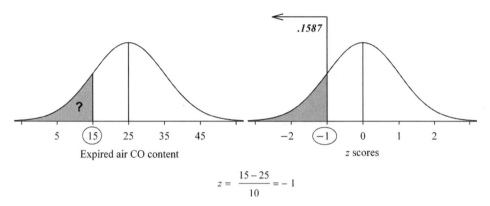

$$z = \frac{15-25}{10} = -1$$

z score of −1.0 ([15 − 25] / 10 = −1.0). Therefore, the relative frequency of expired air CO content of less than 15 ppm corresponds to the relative *z* scores of than less −1.0. Using Table A, a *z* score of −1.0 has a proportion of .1587 of the scores below it.

In other words, the relative frequency of *z* scores less than −1.0 (and consequently, the relative frequency of smokers with expired air CO content less than 15 ppm) is .1587. This number is also the probability that a single randomly selected observation from the population of smokers is less than 15 ppm; that is, $p(X < 15 \text{ ppm}) = .1587$.

What is the probability of selecting a CO content of between 30 and 40 (what is the $p(30 < X < 40)$)? This probability corresponds to the relative frequency of observations between 30 and 40. Calculation of this relative frequency is illustrated in Figure 6.4. The scores 30 and 40 correspond to *z* scores of .5 and 1.5, respectively. The relative frequency of scores less than the *z* score of 1.5 is .9332, and the relative frequency of a *z* score less than .5 is .6915. The relative frequency of *z* scores between .5 and 1.5 is .9332 − .6915 = .2417 (the shaded area). Thus, the probability of randomly selecting a smoker with expired air CO content between 30 ppm and 40 ppm is .2417.

The Or-rule and Continuous Distributions

The or-rule can also be applied to continuous frequency distributions as long as the events are mutually exclusive: The probability of a complex event composed of mutually exclusive simple events conjoined by "or" is the sum of the probabilities of the simple events. In applying the or-rule to continuous frequency distributions you first use Table A to calculate the probabilities of the simple events, and then add those probabilities. For example, the probability of selecting an observation that is less than 15 ppm or between 30 and 40 ppm is .1587 + .2417 = .4004.

As another example, consider randomly drawing from the population of grade point averages (GPAs) of students attending Great Midwestern University. Suppose that the

FIGURE 6.4
Determining the probability of randomly selecting a single smoker with a CO content between 30 and 40 ppm. *Left panel*: the populations of CO content. *Right panel*: the population transformed into *z* scores.

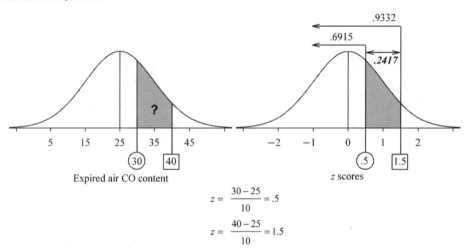

$$z = \frac{30 - 25}{10} = .5$$

$$z = \frac{40 - 25}{10} = 1.5$$

relative frequency distribution is (close to) normally distributed with $\mu = 2.5$ and $\sigma = .5$. What is the probability that a single observation randomly drawn from the population is greater than 2.5? That is, what is $p(X > 2.5)$? Because 2.5 is the mean of the distribution (and for a normal distribution the mean is also the median), half of the observations are above it. Therefore, the relative frequency (and probability) of randomly drawing a single observation greater than 2.5 is .5.

What is the probability that a student randomly selected from the population is either on the dean's list (GPA > 3.25) or on probation (GPA < 1.5)? In symbols, what is $p (X > 3.25$ or $X < 1.5)$? Because these events are mutually exclusive, the or-rule can be applied. A GPA of 3.25 corresponds to a *z* score of $(3.25 - 2.5)/.5 = 1.5$. From Table A, the relative frequency of observations less than a *z* score of 1.5 is .9332, so the relative frequency of observations greater than 1.5 is $1 - .9932 = .0668$ (see Figure 6.5). A GPA of 1.5 corresponds to a *z* score of $(1.5 - 2.5)/.5 = -2$. The relative frequency of observations less than a *z* score of −2, from Table A, is .0228. Putting these probabilities together using the or-rule, $p(X > 3.25$ or $X < 1.5) = .0668 + .0228 = .0896$.

SUMMARY

The probability of a simple event is equal to the number of equally likely observations of the event (in the population) divided by the total number of equally likely observations in the population. This definition emphasizes the relationship between relative frequency and probability. Indeed, when dealing with a population, relative frequencies and probabilities are exactly the same numbers, differing only in interpretation. Relative frequencies refer

FIGURE 6.5
**Determining the probability of randomly selecting a single student with a GPA less than 1.5
or greater than 3.25.** *Left panel*: **the population of GPAs.** *Right panel*: **the population transformed into** *z* **scores.**

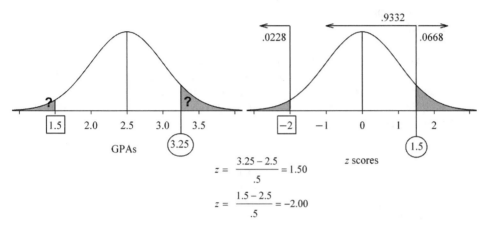

$$z = \frac{3.25 - 2.5}{.5} = 1.50$$

$$z = \frac{1.5 - 2.5}{.5} = -2.00$$

to actual observations made in the past; probabilities are predictions about what will occur
in future random sampling from the population. That is, the probability of a simple event is
the likelihood that the event will occur in a to-be-taken random sample of one observation.
The or-rule can be used to calculate the probabilities of complex events specifying that
one event *or* another occurs in a random sample of one observation from the population.
When the individual events are mutually exclusive, the probability of the complex event is
the sum of the probabilities of the individual simple events. As we will see in the following
chapters, probabilities are used whenever statistical inferences are made.

EXERCISES

Terms   *Define these new terms and symbols.*

expected value   mutually exclusive
simple event   or-rule
complex event $p(X = \text{event})$
probability

Questions   *Answer the following questions.*

†1. Imagine a population consisting of 30 observations that are distributed as follows
    (the event is given first, followed by the number of observations of that event in
    the population): 1–5, 2–6, 3–7, 4–0, 5–0, 6–0, 7–2, 8–5, 9–2, 10–3. Determine the
    probability distribution and represent it as a histogram. What are the mean and
    variance of the distribution?

2. Use the distribution formed in Question 1 to calculate
  a. $p(X = 1 \text{ or } X = 2)$
†**b.** $p(X = 3 \text{ or } X = 6)$
  c. $p(X = \text{odd number})$
  d. $p(X = 8 \text{ or } X = 11)$
†**e.** $p(X > 6)$
  f. $p(X = \text{any number except 7})$

3. A standard deck of playing cards has 52 cards divided equally into four suits. Two suits are red (hearts and diamonds), and two are black (clubs and spades). Within each suit are cards labeled 1 (ace) to 10, jack, queen, and king. Given random sampling (with replacement) of a single card from a deck, calculate (see Footnote 1 on p. 112)
†**a.** $p(X = 5)$
  b. $p(X = 5 \text{ of clubs})$
†**c.** $p(X = 5 \text{ of clubs or } X = 5 \text{ of diamonds})$
  d. $p(X = \text{jack or } X = \text{queen or } X = \text{king})$
†**e.** $p(X = \text{black card})$
  f. $p(X = \text{black card or } X = \text{red card})$

4. Imagine drawing random samples of one observation from a population that is normally distributed with a mean of 75 and a standard deviation of 20. For each question, determine if an answer can be found using the methods described in this chapter. If an answer can be found, calculate it. Otherwise, explain why an answer cannot be calculated using the methods described in this chapter.
†**a.** $p(X > 65)$
  b. $p(X < 65)$
†**c.** $p(65 < X < 95)$
†**d.** $p(z \text{ score} > 1.25)$
†**e.** $p(z \text{ score} < -1 \text{ or } X < 35)$
  f. $p(z \text{ score} > 2 \text{ or } X < 75)$
  g. $p(z \text{ score} < -1.96 \text{ or } z \text{ score} > 1.96)$
  h. $p(z \text{ score} < 1 \text{ or } z \text{ score} < -1)$

5. Scores on the Graduate Record Examination (GRE) are normally distributed with a mean of 500 and a standard deviation of 100. Determine if the probability of each of the following events can be calculated using the methods introduced in this chapter. Calculate those probabilities.
†**a.** $p(X > 700)$
†**b.** $p(X = 653)$
†**c.** $p(400 < X < 450)$
  d. $p(X < 450)$
†**e.** $p(X < 450 \text{ or } 400 < x < 450)$
  f. $p(X > 650)$
  g. $p(550 < X < 600)$
  h. $p(X > 650 \text{ or } 550 < X < 600)$
  i. $p(400 < X < 450 \text{ or } X < 500)$

7

Sampling Distributions

$\mathcal{S}$ampling distributions are special types of probability distributions that are important in inferential statistics. In fact, the concept of a sampling distribution may well be the key concept in understanding how inferential procedures work. In this chapter, we will discuss what sampling distributions are and how they are used. Also, a particularly important type of sampling distribution, the sampling distribution of the sample mean, is discussed in detail.

CONSTRUCTING A SAMPLING DISTRIBUTION

Definition of a Sampling Distribution

What is a sampling distribution?

> Formally, **a sampling distribution of a statistic** is the probability distribution of the statistic computed from all possible random samples of the same size from the same population.

Before giving up on trying to understand this definition, let's break it down into its parts. First, we're talking about a distribution of a *statistic*.

A *statistic* is a quantitative characteristic of a sample, computed from a sample of measurements; *M* (sample mean) or *s* (standard deviation) are examples of statistics that describe features of a sample quantitatively.

The next part of the definition says that a sampling distribution is a *probability distribution*. A probability distribution is like a relative frequency distribution that plots the probability (likelihood) of some measure. Sampling distributions show the probability of a statistic.

Which brings us to the last part of the definition that says that the statistics that are used to construct the sampling distribution are computed from *all possible random samples of the same size from the same population*. As we'll learn shortly, a sampling distribution changes in important ways depending on the size of sample; therefore we construct a sampling distribution for all samples of the *same size (n)*. And, because probability distributions show the likelihood of every possible outcome (remember the second axiom of probability: The probability that you will select an event in the population is 1), a sampling distribution represents *all* the possibilities. This last part of the definition also means that there is not just one sampling distribution, but many; there is a different sampling distribution for each combination of statistic, sample size, and population.

The Five-step Procedure for Constructing Sampling Distributions

We can clarify the concept of a sampling distribution by considering a procedure that can be used to construct them. The procedure consists of five steps.

1. Choose a specific population of measurements (for example, the expired-air CO content of smokers), a specific sample size (for example, 3), and a specific statistic (for example, *M*). Each choice defines a new sampling distribution. The choices you make depend on a number of factors, such as the population you are interested in and your resources for sampling. Later, we will discuss in detail how to make these choices.

2. Draw a random sample of size *n* (the size you chose in Step 1) from the population you chose in Step 1. Think of each of the observations in the population as being written on a standard-size slip of paper, and that all the slips are well mixed in a huge hat. Use independent (within-sample) random sampling to select the sample: Draw one slip of paper, record the measurement, put the slip back in the hat, and mix up the slips; randomly select another slip, record the measurement, put the slip back in the hat, and so on, until you have *n* observations.

3. Compute the statistic you chose in Step 1. You now have one statistic based on one random sample of size *n* from a specific population.

4. Do Steps 2 and 3 over and over again. In fact, if you were to really construct the sampling distribution of the statistic based on *all* random samples of the same size from the same population, you would have to do Steps 2 and 3 an infinite

number of times to ensure that you did indeed have all possible random samples.[1] For now, think about doing Steps 2 and 3 several hundred times. After doing this, you would have several hundred statistics, all computed from random samples of size n drawn from the same population.

5. Take all of the statistics that you have computed and construct the relative frequency distribution for the statistic. This step is completed by following the procedures discussed in Chapter 2 for constructing relative frequency distributions. Although each of the several hundred numbers that you have are statistics, they are treated just like any other numbers: Group the statistics into intervals, count the frequency of statistics in each interval, and divide the frequency in each interval by the total number of statistics (several hundred).

The relative frequency distribution constructed in Step 5 is a sampling distribution (that is, a probability distribution) if it is based on all possible random samples; if it is based on several hundred random samples, then the relative frequency distribution is a close approximation to a sampling distribution. In either case, we can treat the relative frequencies as probabilities; that is, we can treat the relative frequencies as predictions about what will happen in future random sampling.

In Chapter 6, we defined a simple probability as the chance of obtaining an event in a random sample of size $n = 1$ from a population. Because the sample size used in constructing the sampling distribution can be greater than $n = 1$, it may appear that a sampling distribution cannot be a probability distribution. This difficulty disappears, however, by conceptualizing the sampling distribution as the probability distribution for a *population of statistics*. Thus, probabilities obtained from a sampling distribution refer to the chance of obtaining a specific statistic from a *single* random sample from the population of statistics. To reiterate, even though the single random sample may be based on a large sample size (n), the sampling distribution can be used to calculate the probability of obtaining a specific value of the statistic in the single random sample.

For example, suppose we choose the expired-air carbon monoxide (CO) content of smokers as our population, $n = 3$ as the sample size, M as the statistic, and apply the five-step procedure to construct the sampling distribution. We can then compute from the sampling distribution various probabilities such as the probability that a single future random sample of size 3 will have M less than 20 ppm. Note that the probabilities obtained from this sampling distribution are not probabilities for drawing specific scores, as in Chapter 6. For example, we cannot obtain from the sampling distribution the probability of drawing a single smoker with CO content less than 20 ppm, because the sampling distribution is a distribution of sample means, not individual scores.

Now, imagine going through the five steps to construct a slightly different sampling distribution. This time, $n = 4$, but we sample again from the population of smokers and compute the mean as the statistic. Draw a random sample of 4 measurements, compute M, draw a second random sample and compute a second M, and so on. Once you have drawn many, many random samples and have computed many, many sample means, construct the

---

[1] There are mathematical techniques (using combinations and permutations) that can be used to determine all possible random samples of the same size without necessarily taking an infinite number of random samples. These techniques may be found in more advanced statistics or probability texts.

relative frequency (probability) distribution of the Ms. This distribution is the sampling distribution of the sample mean (the statistic you computed), based on random samples of n = 4 drawn from the population of expired-air CO content of smokers. This new distribution is different from the relative frequency distribution of scores in the population; it is also different from the sampling distribution based on n = 3. This new distribution can be used to calculate probabilities such as the probability of drawing from the population a single random sample with n = 4 that has a mean less than 20 ppm [($p(M < 20)$)], or the probability of drawing from the population a single random sample with n = 4 that has a mean between 30 and 40 ppm [$p(30 < M < 40)$], and so on.

Of course, it is not obvious why in the world you would ever go through the five steps to construct a sampling distribution simply to calculate the probability of choosing a random sample with a mean between 30 and 40! The why will be provided later in this chapter and in Chapter 8.

Sampling distributions do not always have to be distributions of sample means; all statistics have sampling distributions. For example, suppose that when we took the samples of CO content with n = 4 we computed the sample variance, s^2, in addition to M. The relative frequency distribution of all of those sample variances is the sampling distribution of sample variance based on random samples with n = 4 from the population of expired-air CO content from smokers. We have many, many samples from the population of smokers. Each of the many samples has four measurements in it. For each sample, we compute s^2 using Formula 3.6. Now we have many sample variances (each computed from a sample with four measurements). These sample variances are grouped into intervals, and the relative frequency distribution of the sample variances is constructed. If we actually had all the possible random samples for the population of CO content, then this relative frequency distribution would actually be the sampling distribution of the sample variances. If we just have several hundred random samples, the relative frequency distribution is a close approximation to the sampling distribution.

What exactly is this sampling distribution? It is the probability distribution of the sample variance (the statistic computed from each sample) based on random samples with n = 4 drawn from the population of expired-air CO content of smokers.

For what can this distribution be used? It can be used to calculate probabilities of future events, such as the probability of drawing a single random sample (n = 4) from the population of CO content that has a sample variance of less than 5.4, in symbols, $p(s^2 < 5.4)$. Or, the distribution could be used to determine the probability of drawing a single random sample (n = 4) from the population of expired-air CO content that has a sample variance between 7 and 8, $p(7 < s^2 < 8)$.

To review, a sampling distribution is a probability distribution of a statistic for a specific sample size and a specific population. The probability distribution can be used to calculate the probability that a future random sample of that specific size from that specific population will have a statistic (for example, M) that meets certain characteristics. There are multiple sampling distributions, because each time you change the statistic (for example, from M to s^2), you specify a different sampling distribution; and each time you change the sample size, you get a different sampling distribution; and each time you change the population from which the random samples are drawn (for example, the population of CO content to the population of weights to the population of IQ scores), you get a different sampling distribution.

There are many things that a sampling distribution is not. It is not a single number—it is a distribution. It is not the distribution of scores in a sample. Simply drawing a random sample (of any size) and constructing the relative frequency distribution of the scores in that sample does not give you a sampling distribution. Finally, a sampling distribution is not the distribution of scores in the population. What is it? It is the probability (relative frequency) distribution of a statistic computed from all possible random samples, all of the same size, all drawn from the same population.

TWO SAMPLING DISTRIBUTIONS

Constructing a Sampling Distribution of the Sample Mean

Imagine a population with a total of 25 observations. The population consists of one 1, one 2, one 3, two 4s, three 5s, four 6s, six 7s, four 8s, and three 9s. Each of the 25 observations is written on a standard-size slip of paper, and the slips are well mixed in a hat. The relative frequency distribution of this population is illustrated as a histogram at the top of Figure 7.1. Note that the distribution is negatively skewed (skewed to the left). The mean of this population (computed in the usual way) is 6.16. The standard deviation of the population can be computed using the computing formula

$$\sigma = \sqrt{\frac{SS(X)}{N}}$$

Note that N, not $n - 1$, is used in the formula because we have all the scores in the population. The standard deviation of the population is 2.09.

We will construct a sampling distribution based on this population. Although the population is specified (the one in Figure 7.1), we still must choose a statistic and a sample size. Suppose that we choose M, the sample mean, as a statistic, and use a sample size of 4.

The next step is to pick a random sample from the population and then compute the statistic (M). The random sample can be chosen by randomly selecting a slip of paper from the hat, recording the observation, putting the slip back into the hat, mixing up the slips, selecting another slip, recording the observation, and so on, until four observations (the first sample) have been selected. The first sample (see the middle part of Figure 7.1) consists of the scores 8, 7, 2, and 8. The next step is to compute $M = 6.25$.

Now we choose another random sample of the same size from the same population. The scores in the second random sample are 5, 6, 6, and 7. The mean of this random sample is 6.00.

In all, 100 random samples (each with $n = 4$) were selected from the same population. For each random sample, M was computed, and, of course, the Ms were not all the same; the Ms ranged from 3.25 to 8.75. These 100 samples and their Ms are all listed in the middle part of Figure 7.1.

The final step is to construct the relative frequency distribution for these sample means. Using the suggestions for grouping given in Chapter 2, the Ms were grouped using an

FIGURE 7.1

Steps in constructing a sampling distribution of the sample mean. *Top*: the original population; *middle*: 100 random samples and their *M*s; *bottom*: approximate sampling distribution
based on the 100 *M*s.

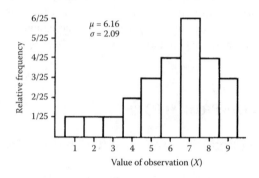

Sample	M		Sample	M		Sample	M		Sample	M
1. 8, 7, 2, 8	6.25		26. 9, 7, 7, 5	7.00		51. 7, 5, 6, 7	6.25		76. 8, 7, 6, 7	7.00
2. 5, 6, 6, 7	6.00		27. 8, 9, 9, 9	8.75		52. 9, 6, 2, 7	6.00		77. 9, 6, 6, 7	7.00
3. 9, 8, 3, 5	6.25		28. 6, 6, 4, 5	5.25		53. 7, 3, 8, 3	5.25		78. 8, 2, 6, 8	6.00
4. 7, 3, 8, 7	6.25		29. 5, 7, 7, 4	5.75		54. 4, 7, 9, 7	6.75		79. 7, 4, 1, 5	4.25
5. 7, 7, 7, 5	6.50		30. 5, 8, 6, 8	6.75		55. 7, 6, 4, 9	6.50		80. 8, 7, 9, 9	8.25
6. 8, 7, 7, 1	5.75		31. 6, 4, 1, 2	3.25		56. 7, 3, 7, 8	6.25		81. 5, 7, 8, 9	7.25
7. 3, 6, 7, 7	5.75		32. 9, 3, 6, 9	6.75		57. 7, 6, 7, 7	6.75		82. 6, 4, 7, 3	5.00
8. 6, 6, 8, 7	6.75		33. 1, 8, 6, 2	4.25		58. 9, 6, 7, 6	7.00		83. 8, 7, 7, 8	7.50
9. 7, 5, 7, 9	7.00		34. 6, 9, 6, 2	5.75		59. 8, 7, 6, 8	7.25		84. 8, 8, 5, 7	7.00
10. 2, 8, 6, 8	6.00		35. 4, 8, 5, 8	6.25		60. 4, 7, 6, 6	5.75		85. 1, 6, 7, 7	5.25
11. 1, 1, 6, 7	3.75		36. 1, 6, 7, 5	4.75		61. 1, 7, 9, 2	4.75		86. 4, 6, 7, 9	6.50
12. 3, 7, 5, 7	5.50		37. 7, 6, 6, 6	6.25		62. 7, 7, 8, 5	6.75		87. 7, 8, 8, 9	8.00
13. 8, 1, 7, 7	5.75		38. 9, 6, 7, 6	7.00		63. 7, 4, 5, 9	6.25		88. 7, 6, 9, 4	6.50
14. 7, 3, 7, 8	6.25		39. 7, 5, 4, 9	6.25		64. 2, 6, 7, 9	6.00		89. 7, 9, 5, 9	7.50
15. 5, 6, 8, 2	5.25		40. 5, 9, 7, 7	7.00		65. 9, 5, 4, 8	6.50		90. 6, 6, 2, 4	4.50
16. 7, 7, 5, 5	6.00		41. 2, 7, 7, 7	5.75		66. 9, 7, 6, 3	6.25		91. 4, 7, 8, 4	5.75
17. 5, 1, 8, 8	5.50		42. 4, 7, 4, 3	4.50		67. 7, 6, 9, 7	7.25		92. 7, 1, 9, 8	6.25
18. 9, 8, 4, 7	7.00		43. 6, 9, 4, 9	7.00		68. 7, 8, 7, 3	6.25		93. 2, 7, 7, 8	6.00
19. 5, 5, 4, 9	5.75		44. 1, 5, 7, 5	4.50		69. 7, 6, 6, 5	6.00		94. 6, 9, 8, 4	6.75
20. 7, 8, 8, 7	7.50		45. 7, 7, 8, 2	6.00		70. 7, 4, 3, 6	5.00		95. 7, 5, 7, 4	5.75
21. 5, 8, 8, 7	7.00		46. 6, 9, 5, 6	6.50		71. 7, 6, 8, 6	6.75		96. 3, 5, 7, 9	6.00
22. 6, 7, 8, 9	7.50		47. 7, 6, 7, 5	6.25		72. 7, 6, 3, 7	5.75		97. 8, 3, 8, 7	6.50
23. 7, 6, 6, 6	6.25		48. 9, 8, 6, 3	6.50		73. 9, 7, 1, 9	6.50		98. 8, 6, 9, 1	6.00
24. 7, 5, 4, 5	5.25		49. 6, 7, 8, 6	6.75		74. 9, 5, 6, 7	6.75		99. 8, 8, 6, 7	7.25
25. 8, 8, 9, 7	8.00		50. 7, 4, 6, 7	6.00		75. 6, 4, 5, 8	5.75		100. 7, 2, 4, 8	5.25

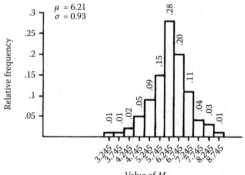

interval size of .5. The relative frequency distribution for these sample means is illustrated by the histogram at the bottom of Figure 7.1. This relative frequency histogram is an approximation of the sampling distribution of M based on $n = 4$. It is not exactly the sampling distribution because we have not taken all possible random samples, only 100.[2]

There are both similarities and differences between the sampling distribution (bottom part of Figure 7.1) and the population relative frequency distribution (top part of the figure). A major difference is that the sampling distribution is a distribution of Ms, not individual scores. Second, the sampling distribution of M is relatively symmetric, whereas the distribution of the population is negatively skewed. Third, the standard deviation of the sampling distribution (that is, the standard deviation of the 100 Ms), which equals 0.93, is smaller than the standard deviation of the population, 2.09. There is one important similarity between the two distributions: The mean of the sampling distribution, 6.21, is similar to the mean of the population, 6.16. In general, however, the sampling distribution is not much like the distribution of scores in the population.

Using the Sampling Distribution of the Sample Means

If we pretend that the approximate sampling distribution is the real thing, then we can use it to calculate probabilities. For example, what is the probability that a future random sample of four scores from this population will have a mean between 4.495 (the lower real limit of the interval labeled 4.745) and 4.995 (the upper real limit of the interval)? The answer, obtained directly from the sampling distribution, is .05. In symbols, $p(4.495 < M < 4.995) = .05$.

What is the probability that a future random sample of four scores will have a mean less than 3.995 (the upper real limit of the interval labeled 3.745) or greater than 7.995 (the lower real limit of the interval labeled 8.245)? Because these two events are mutually exclusive, the or-rule can be applied. $p(M < 3.995) = .02(.01 + .01)$, and $p(M > 7.995) = .04$ $(.03 + .01)$, so the probability of one or the other is .06.

What is the probability that a future random sample of five scores will have a mean between 4.875 and 5.375? We cannot use the sampling distribution in Figure 7.1 to answer this question because it applies for sampling from the population only when $n = 4$. If you really need to know the answer to this question, you can use the five-step procedure to compute the sampling distribution for random samples with $n = 5$ and then compute the probability, or you can wait until later in this chapter where we will learn a much easier way of constructing sampling distributions of sample means.

Constructing a Sampling Distribution of the Sample Variance

A second example of constructing a sampling distribution is illustrated in Figure 7.2. At the top of the figure is the relative frequency histogram of the population from which

---

[2] Although 100 samples is a lot, it is easy to see that all possible random samples from the population in Figure 7.1 are *not* listed. The sample 1, 1, 1, 1 does not appear in Figure 7.1, nor does the sample 9, 9, 9, 9. Because all possible random samples are not included in these 100 samples, the sampling distribution in the figure is only approximate.

FIGURE 7.2
Steps in constructing a sampling distribution of the sample variance. *Top*: **the original popula-**
tion; *middle*: **100 random samples and their** s^2**s;** *bottom*: **approximate sampling distribution**
based on the 100 s^2**s.**

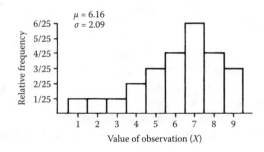

Sample	s^2	Sample	s^2	Sample	s^2	Sample	s^2
1. 3, 6, 4	2.33	26. 9, 9, 9	0.00	51. 9, 5, 9	5.33	76. 8, 7, 4	4.33
2. 8, 7, 7	0.33	27. 7, 9, 7	1.33	52. 7, 7, 6	0.33	77. 6, 9, 7	2.33
3. 4, 6, 4	1.33	28. 8, 5, 8	3.00	53. 8, 8, 9	0.33	78. 5, 7, 9	4.00
4. 6, 6, 5	0.33	29. 6, 7, 5	1.00	54. 9, 5, 7	4.00	79. 3, 9, 6	9.00
5. 3, 7, 7	5.33	30. 2, 7, 8	10.33	55. 7, 9, 4	6.33	80. 7, 7, 5	1.33
6. 4, 1, 7	9.00	31. 7, 6, 7	0.33	56. 9, 8, 6	2.33	81. 6, 6, 7	0.33
7. 9, 8, 8	0.33	32. 9, 7, 7	1.33	57. 4, 7, 4	3.00	82. 9, 5, 8	4.33
8. 7, 5, 8	2.33	33. 6, 1, 9	16.33	58. 6, 3, 5	2.33	83. 7, 9, 6	2.33
9. 8, 4, 8	5.33	34. 8, 7, 7	0.33	59. 7, 6, 8	1.00	84. 1, 7, 6	10.33
10. 9, 8, 6	2.33	35. 9, 3, 1	17.33	60. 6, 5, 9	4.33	85. 8, 5, 5	3.00
11. 7, 6, 5	1.00	36. 6, 9, 5	4.33	61. 7, 4, 5	2.33	86. 7, 4, 7	3.00
12. 7, 8, 2	10.33	37. 8, 7, 6	1.00	62. 7, 5, 7	1.33	87. 7, 2, 7	8.33
13. 7, 6, 7	0.33	38. 8, 6, 5	2.33	63. 5, 7, 7	1.33	88. 1, 7, 9	17.33
14. 5, 6, 1	7.00	39. 1, 7, 9	17.33	64. 8, 4, 9	7.00	89. 6, 3, 9	9.00
15. 6, 7, 6	0.33	40. 9, 1, 2	19.00	65. 5, 9, 5	5.33	90. 9, 7, 7	1.33
16. 4, 7, 7	3.00	41. 8, 9, 4	7.00	66. 8, 2, 5	9.00	91. 2, 7, 6	7.00
17. 5, 5, 4	0.33	42. 2, 7, 6	7.00	67. 7, 6, 2	7.00	92. 8, 7, 8	0.33
18. 7, 5, 5	1.33	43. 8, 6, 1	13.00	68. 7, 5, 5	1.33	93. 9, 5, 2	12.33
19. 5, 3, 7	4.00	44. 2, 4, 7	6.33	69. 7, 8, 7	0.33	94. 7, 8, 8	0.33
20. 6, 8, 1	13.00	45. 6, 8, 7	1.00	70. 4, 9, 4	8.33	95. 1, 7, 2	10.33
21. 8, 5, 4	4.33	46. 7, 6, 7	0.33	71. 2, 2, 6	5.33	96. 6, 6, 8	1.33
22. 7, 2, 6	7.00	47. 5, 7, 7	1.33	72. 9, 2, 8	14.33	97. 6, 4, 7	2.33
23. 1, 8, 6	13.00	48. 7, 1, 4	9.00	73. 5, 8, 2	9.00	98. 3, 8, 7	7.00
24. 6, 7, 7	0.33	49. 1, 6, 6	8.33	74. 7, 9, 5	4.00	99. 8, 5, 1	12.33
25. 7, 8, 2	10.33	50. 9, 7, 6	2.33	75. 5, 1, 1	5.33	100. 1, 4, 8	12.33

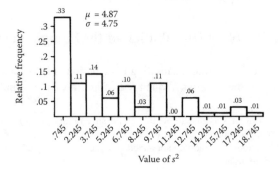

the random samples will be drawn. It is the same population as was used in Figure 7.1. Although the population is the same, this example uses a different sample size, $n = 3$, and a different statistic, the sample variance, s^2.

For this example, 100 random samples of $n = 3$ were selected. For each sample, the variance was computed using the computing formula given in Chapter 3

$$s^2 = \frac{SS(X)}{n-1}$$

Note that the formula uses $n - 1$ in the denominator, because we are computing from a sample, not a population.

The 100 s^2s were grouped and a relative frequency histogram constructed. It is illustrated at the bottom of Figure 7.2. This relative frequency distribution is an approximate sampling distribution of the sample variance (the statistic) based on random samples of $n = 3$ drawn from the population. Note again that the sampling distribution is very different from the distribution of the population. The sampling distribution is positively skewed (to the right), whereas the population is negatively skewed. The standard deviation of the sampling distribution (that is, the standard deviation of the 100 scores in Figure 7.2 that just happen to be variances) is 4.75, larger than the standard deviation of the population. Not even the mean of this sampling distribution (the mean of the 100 variances is 4.87) is close to the mean of the population. The point is that sampling distributions and populations of raw scores are very different.

Using the Sampling Distribution of the Sample Variances

Ignoring for the moment that the distribution in the bottom of Figure 7.2 is only an approximate sampling distribution, we can treat it as a probability distribution. What is the probability that in the future a random sample of $n = 3$ is drawn from the population, and that the random sample's s^2 is less than 1.495 (the upper real limit of the interval labeled .745)? $p(s^2 < 1.495) = .33$. What is the probability that s^2 is greater than 14.995 (the lower real limit of the interval labeled 15.745)? $p(s^2 > 14.995) = .01 + .03 + .01 = .05$.

SAMPLING DISTRIBUTIONS USED IN STATISTICAL INFERENCE

Sampling distributions are used in all inferential statistical procedures. But, as you have seen, they are difficult to construct using the five-step procedure, especially if you intend to construct real sampling distributions using all possible random samples. If you think about it, there is a dilemma lurking here. Supposedly, inferential techniques are useful because they help you to make inferences about the population without having to go through the onerous task of collecting all of the measurements in the population. But inferential techniques use sampling distributions that require an infinite number of random samples, and that seems even worse!

As you might suspect, there is a solution to this dilemma. Statisticians have determined the characteristics of some special sampling distributions so that the five-step procedure is not needed. In fact, most of the tables in the back of this book (such as the tables for the *z, t, F,* and χ² statistics) are sampling distributions in tabular form. Part III of this text consists of information on how to use these sampling distributions in statistical inference.

So why did we spend so much time on the five-step procedure and approximate sampling distributions? To understand how inferential procedures work, it is necessary to understand what sampling distributions are. Although we will be learning about easier ways to construct sampling distributions, there is no better way to understand the concept than to work with the five-step procedure. The sampling distributions in the back of the book were determined mathematically, but they represent the same thing as if they were based on statistics computed from all possible random samples of the same size from the same population. As such, each of those sampling distributions can be used to predict what will be found in future random sampling, and that is the important point. A sampling distribution tells you about what you are likely to find in a future random sample of a specific size from a specific population.

SAMPLING DISTRIBUTION OF THE SAMPLE MEAN

One of the special sampling distributions that can be determined mathematically is the sampling distribution of the sample mean. The sampling distribution in Figure 7.1 is an approximate sampling distribution of the sample mean. As we shall see in the following chapters, the sampling distribution of the sample mean is a particularly useful sampling distribution.

There are three amazing facts to learn about the sampling distribution of the sample mean.[3] These facts can be used instead of the five-step procedure to construct a sampling distribution of a sample mean whenever it is needed (which is often in statistical inference). The three amazing facts are first summarized, and then each is discussed in depth.

1. The mean of the sampling distribution of the sample mean, μ_M, is exactly equal to the mean of the population from which the samples were drawn.
2. The standard deviation of the sampling distribution of the sample mean, σ_M, is exactly equal to the standard deviation of the population divided by the square root of the sample size.
3. As the sample size increases, the sampling distribution of the sample mean becomes a better and better approximation of a normal distribution.

Amazing Fact Number 1, $\mu_M = \mu$

Amazing Fact Number 1 is that the mean of the sampling distribution of sample means is equal to the mean of the population from which the random samples were drawn. This

---

[3] You may think it hokey to call these facts "amazing," but after reading this chapter you will probably agree that they are truly amazing. Also, because there are so many facts to memorize, it is helpful to make some of them particularly memorable by making them distinctive.

does not mean that all of the *M*s that make up the sampling distribution all equal μ, the population mean. In fact, we can see in Figure 7.1 that many of the individual *M*s do not equal the population mean. The amazing fact is that it is the mean (the average) of all of the *M*s in the sampling distribution that equals μ.

The concept of the mean of the sampling distribution of means is so important that it has its own symbol, μ_M. As you recall from Chapter 2, when a Greek letter is used as a symbol, it signifies a population parameter. In this case, the *mu* tells us that it is a population mean. The subscript *M* tells us exactly what it is the mean of: It is the mean of sample means.

The mean of the approximate sampling distribution in Figure 7.1 is 6.21. It is not exactly equal to the mean of the population, 6.16 because the distribution is only an approximate sampling distribution based on 100 samples of $n = 4$, rather than the real sampling distribution based on all possible random samples of $n = 4$. Because of Amazing Fact Number 1, we do not have to keep sampling to know *for sure* the real value of μ_M. For this sampling distribution, $\mu_M = 6.16$. In fact, any sampling distribution of sample means from the population illustrated in the top of Figure 7.1 will have a μ_M equal to 6.16, because the original population has a mean of 6.16.

Of course, not all sampling distributions based on this population will have means equal to 6.16. As an example, the mean of the sampling distribution of sample *variances* (see Figure 7.2) will not necessarily equal 6.16. Only the mean of a sampling distribution of the *sample mean* is guaranteed to equal the population mean.

Amazing Fact Number 2, $\sigma_M = \sigma/\sqrt{n}$

Amazing Fact Number 2 concerns the standard deviation of the sampling distribution of sample means. The standard deviation of the sampling distribution of the sample mean is so important that it is also given its own symbol and name. The symbol is σ_M. Again, the use of the Greek letter signifies that the quantity is a population parameter, and the specific Greek letter, σ, means that it is a standard deviation. Of what is it a standard deviation? It is the standard deviation of all of the *M*s that go into making up the sampling distribution. This is signified by the subscript *M*. The special name given σ_M is the **standard error of the mean,** or when the context makes it unambiguous, simply the standard error.

What exactly is σ_M? It is a measure of variability among the *M*s in the sampling distribution. Referring back to Figure 7.1, you can see that not all of the *M*s are the same; they are variable. The σ_M is a measure of that variability. If we had all of the *M*s in the sampling distribution, we could calculate σ_M using a formula for a standard deviation very similar to that used for calculating σ (see Chapter 3). So that you can see the similarity, the formula for σ is reproduced below (Formula 7.1) along with a formula for σ_M (Formula 7.2).

FORMULA 7.1   Standard Deviation of a Population

$$\sigma = \sqrt{\frac{\sum (X - \mu)^2}{N}}$$

FORMULA 7.2   Standard Deviation of a Sampling Distribution of *M*s (the Standard Error of the Sample Means)

$$\sigma_M = \sqrt{\frac{\sum (M - \mu_M)^2}{N_M}}$$

where N_M = number of sample means in the sampling distribution.

The formulas for σ_M and σ are similar because they are both standard deviations. σ is the standard deviation of the population of raw scores. σ_M is the standard deviation of the population *M*s (the sampling distribution of the sample mean).

Calculating σ_M using Formula 7.2 would be a lot of work because the sampling distribution contains so many scores (many *M*s). Fortunately, this is just where Amazing Fact Number 2 comes to the rescue. Amazing Fact Number 2 is that σ_M is guaranteed to equal the standard deviation of the original population (from which the samples were drawn) divided by the square root of the sample size (Formula 7.3).

FORMULA 7.3   Standard Error of the Sample Means

$$\sigma_M = \frac{\sigma}{\sqrt{n}}$$

The standard error can be computed using either Formula 7.2 or 7.3. Of course, Formula 7.3 is much simpler; this is what makes it so amazing.

According to Amazing Fact Number 2, the standard error of the sampling distribution in Figure 7.1 should equal 1.045 (that is, 2.09, the population standard deviation, divided by 2, the square root of the sample size). However, the standard deviation of the scores in Figure 7.1 equals .93 instead. Why the discrepancy? The discrepancy arises because the distribution in Figure 7.1 is only an approximation of the real sampling distribution based on all possible random samples of the same size. If we had the real sampling distribution, its standard deviation (standard error) is guaranteed to equal $\sigma/\sqrt{n}$.

As the sample size increases, the denominator in Formula 7.3 also increases. Thus, as the sample size increases, the standard error will get smaller. Because this relationship between the sample size and the magnitude of the standard error is very important for inferential statistics (see discussion of power in Chapters 8 and 9), we will spend some time understanding why it comes about.

Consider what happens to the sampling distribution when the sample size is 1. Each random sample from the population will be a single score and so each *M* will simply be the score itself. So, when $n = 1$, the sampling distribution of the sample means is exactly the same as the original population, and the standard error of the sampling distribution will be exactly the same as the standard deviation of the population. Of course, this is just what Amazing Fact Number 2 implies, when $n = 1$, $\sigma_M = \sigma/\sqrt{1} = \sigma$.

Now, consider what happens to the standard error when the sample size is a little larger, say, 4. With larger sample sizes, it is unlikely for the random sample to consist of just the infrequent scores (from the tails). For example, in Figure 7.1 there are no random samples comprised of only 1s, or only 1s and 2s. The point is that with larger sample sizes the Ms from the samples will tend to cluster near μ_M. As you know, when scores cluster near the mean of the distribution, the standard deviation (standard error in this case) is small. So, with a larger sample size the standard error will be smaller than when the sample size equals 1.

Now, consider the size of the standard error when the sample size is infinitely large. An infinitely large sample will include all of the scores in the population. Thus, the first random sample consists of all the scores in the population, and so the M of this sample will equal μ (and μ_M). The second random sample will also consist of all the scores in the population, and so it will also have an M equal to μ_M. Similarly, the third random sample, and all others, will have Ms equal to μ_M. Because all of the Ms are the same, there is no variability in the distribution, and the standard error equals zero. Again, this is consistent with Amazing Fact Number 2. When σ is divided by the square root of an infinitely large sample size (and the square root of infinity is also infinity), the resulting σ_M is zero.

In summary, when the sample size is 1, each M is equal to one of the scores in the population. Because the Ms are not closely grouped around μ_M, the standard error is large. When the sample size is a little larger, the Ms tend to cluster closer to μ_M, and so the variability (standard error) decreases. When the sample size is infinitely large, all the Ms equal μ_M, and so the standard error equals zero. In short, as the sample size grows larger, the standard deviation of the sample means (σ_M) grows smaller.

As we proceed, keep in mind that it is only the standard deviation of the sampling distribution of the sample *means* that equals $\sigma/\sqrt{n}$. The standard deviation of other sampling distributions (for example, Figure 7.2) need not have any special relationship to σ.

Amazing Fact Number 3, the Central Limit Theorem

This is really the most amazing fact of them all. It has two parts. First, if the population from which the random samples are drawn is a normal distribution, then the sampling distribution of the sample means is guaranteed to be a normal distribution. The second part is so amazing that it has a special name: the Central Limit Theorem. According to the Central Limit Theorem, no matter what shape the population is, as the sample size grows larger, the sampling distribution of the sample mean gets closer and closer to a normal distribution. You can begin with a population that is skewed, or multimodal, or any weird shape, but if the sample size is large enough, the sampling distribution of the sample mean will, in the limit, be a normal distribution. How large does the sample size have to be to have a sampling distribution that is normally distributed? With most distributions, a sample size of 10 or 20 will do. Even with very strangely shaped population distributions, a sample size of about 20 will virtually guarantee a normally distributed sampling distribution.

Figure 7.1 provides a partial illustration of this amazing fact. Although the original population was skewed (top of the figure), the sampling distribution of the sample means is decidedly more symmetrical (bottom of the figure). Even with a sample size as small as 4, the sampling distribution of the sample means approaches a normal distribution.

FIGURE 7.3
The three amazing facts about the sampling distribution of the sample mean. (Adapted from original prepared by Theodore J. Sielaff. Reprinted with permission of Lansford Publishing.)

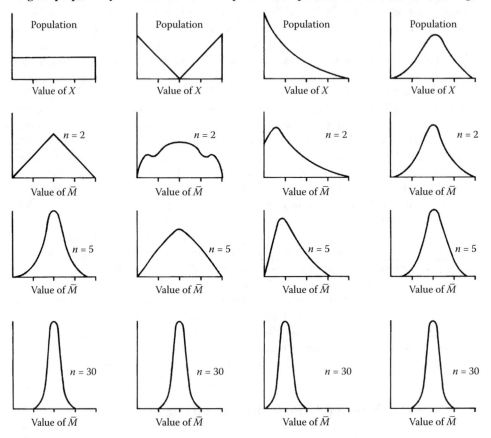

All three amazing facts are illustrated in Figure 7.3. Along the top of the figure are relative frequency polygons for four different populations. The other distributions in each column are sampling distributions of the sample mean based on various sample sizes.

Amazing Fact Number 1 is that μ_M always equals μ. You can see this in Figure 7.3 by noting that each sampling distribution has the same mean as its parent population distribution.

Amazing Fact Number 2 is that

$$\sigma_M = \frac{\sigma}{\sqrt{n}}$$

Going down each column, the sampling distributions become thinner (less variable) as the sample sizes get larger.

Finally, consistent with Amazing Fact Number 3, as the sample size gets larger, the sampling distribution becomes more and more like a normal distribution (with a small variance).

Because you now know these three amazing facts, as long as you have an adequate sample size, you never have to use the five-step procedure to construct a sampling distribution of sample means. You know that it will be virtually normally distributed, you know that μ_M equals μ and that σ_M equals $\sigma/\sqrt{n}$, and that is all you ever need to know. Recall from Chapter 4 that if a distribution is normally distributed and you know its mean and variance, you can then figure out anything else you might want to know using *z* scores and Table A.

REVIEW OF SYMBOLS AND CONCEPTS

You may have noticed that the symbols are starting to accumulate, and that it is becoming difficult to keep them all straight. Unfortunately, it is *not* the case that they all mean pretty much the same thing and so you can ignore subtle technical differences. The truth is that there are major differences that you have to understand.

We have made the distinction between three types of collections of scores. First, we can have a sample, which, as you know, is usually a relatively small set of measurements from a much larger population of measurements. Second, we can have a population that consists of all the measurements of interest (for a specific question or problem). The third type of collection is a sampling distribution. The scores in a sampling distribution are not individual measurements as in samples and populations. The scores in a sampling distribution are statistics (such as *M*), each calculated from a random sample.

Associated with a sample are two symbols of interest. The mean of a sample is represented by *M*. The standard deviation of a sample is represented by *s*. Similarly, a population has two important symbols associated with it, the population mean, μ, and the population standard deviation, σ. As you may recall, *M* for a random sample is an unbiased estimator for (in other words, a good guess for) μ, the mean of the population from which the sample was drawn. This does not mean that *M* will necessarily equal μ, just that it is a good guess. In fact, as you can see in Figure 7.1, different random samples from the *same* population will have different *M*s. Similarly, s^2 calculated from a random sample is an unbiased estimator of σ^2.

A sampling distribution of sample means also has a mean, μ_M, and a standard deviation, σ_M. The average of the *M*s in the sampling distribution of sample means is μ_M. Although μ_M will always have the same value as μ (Amazing Fact Number 1), the concepts are distinct.

Because not all of the *M*s in the sampling distribution are the same (when *n* is not infinitely large), the sampling distribution has a nonzero standard deviation, σ_M. This standard deviation is called the standard error. Although σ and σ_M are both standard deviations, they are standard deviations of very different distributions. It is simply an amazing fact that the two quantities can be related by a formula as simple as $\sigma_M = \sigma/\sqrt{n}$.

The various relationships among the symbols are summarized in Table 7.1.

z SCORES AND THE SAMPLING DISTRIBUTION OF THE SAMPLE MEAN

As long as the sample size is adequate (say 20 or larger), then the sampling distribution of the sample mean will be virtually normally distributed. Therefore, *z* scores and Table A can be used to calculate the probability of various events.

TABLE 7.1

Relations Between the Different Types of Means, Standard Deviations, and Variances

Collection of Scores	Name	Symbol	Formulas	What Is Estimated
Sample	Sample mean (statistic)	M	$\dfrac{\sum X}{n}$	μ
	Standard Deviation (statistic)	s	$\sqrt{\dfrac{\sum (X-M)^2}{n-1}}, \sqrt{\dfrac{SS(X)}{n-1}}$	σ
	Variance (statistic)	s^2	$\dfrac{\sum (X-M)^2}{n-1}, \dfrac{SS(X)}{n-1}$	σ^2
Population	Population Mean (parameter)	μ	$\dfrac{\sum X}{N}$	
	Population Standard Deviation (parameter)	σ	$\sqrt{\dfrac{\sum (X-\mu)^2}{N}}, \sqrt{\dfrac{SS(X)}{N}}$	
	Population Variance (parameter)	σ^2	$\dfrac{\sum (X-\mu)^2}{N}, \dfrac{SS(X)}{N}$	
Sampling Distribution	Mean of the Sampling Distribution of M (parameter)	μ_M	$\mu, \dfrac{\sum M}{N_M}$	
	Standard Deviation of the Sampling Distribution of M "Standard Error" (parameter)	σ_M	$\dfrac{\sigma}{\sqrt{n}}, \sqrt{\dfrac{\sum (M-\mu_M)^2}{N_M}}$	
	Variance of the Sampling Distribution of M (parameter)	σ_M^2	$\dfrac{\sigma^2}{n}, \dfrac{\sum (M-\mu_M)^2}{N_M}$	

Suppose, for example, that we are interested in sampling from a population of reading times for freshmen at Great Midwestern University. To be more specific, suppose that the population consists of how long it takes (in seconds) to read a standard page of prose, and we have the scores for all the freshmen at the university. Furthermore, suppose that the mean of the population (μ) equals 90 seconds, and the standard deviation (σ) is 30 seconds.

One question about sampling from this population is, "What is the probability that a single score drawn randomly is greater than 92?" In symbols, what is $p(X > 92)$? *If* we knew that the population was normally distributed, then answering this question would be easy, because obtaining the answer would require only the standard z-score techniques practiced in Chapters 4 and 6. Unfortunately, from the information given, we do not know anything about the shape of the distribution.

Here is another sort of question. Suppose that we took a random sample of 100 scores from the population. What is $p(M > 92)$? To answer this question we need the probability distribution of sample means from samples with $n = 100$. This probability distribution is, of course, the sampling distribution of the sample mean based on $n = 100$. If we had lots of time, we could use the five-step procedure to construct the sampling distribution, but a more efficient way is to use the three amazing facts. First, we know that the mean of the sampling distribution, μ_M, equals the mean of the population, μ, which is 90 seconds. Second, we know that the standard error (standard deviation) of the sampling distribution is

$$\sigma_M = \sigma/\sqrt{n} = 30/\sqrt{100} = 3$$

FIGURE 7.4

Determining $p(M \geq 92)$ when $\mu = 90$, $\sigma = 30$, and $n = 100$. *Left panel*: **the sampling distribution of the sample mean.** *Right panel*: **the sampling distribution transformed into *z* scores.**

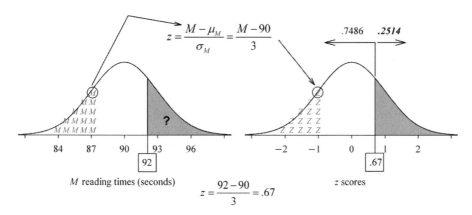

Third, we know that with a sample size this large, the sampling distribution of the sample mean is virtually a normal distribution.

This sampling distribution is illustrated on the left of Figure 7.4. Because this distribution is a normal distribution, it can be converted to the standard normal distribution by transforming each score (each *M* in the distribution) to a *z* score (indicated by the arrow in the figure). As usual, a *z* score is a score minus the mean of the distribution divided by the standard deviation of the distribution. In this case, each score is an *M,* the mean of the distribution is μ_M, and the standard deviation is σ_M.

FORMULA 7.4　*z* Scores for the Sampling Distribution of *M*

$$z = \frac{M - \mu_M}{\sigma_M}$$

The result of transforming each of the original *M*s into a *z* score is the standard normal distribution illustrated on the right of Figure 7.4. Now that the sampling distribution has been transformed into the standard normal distribution, the problem can be solved much like any *z*-score problem discussed in Chapters 4 and 6.

First, let us transform the raw score of 92 into a *z* score using Formula 7.4.

$$z = \frac{M - \mu_M}{\sigma_M} = \frac{92 - 90}{3} = .67$$

Looking at Figure 7.4, we can see that $p(M > 92)$ equals the shaded area in the distribution on the left, and this area corresponds to the shaded area in the *z*-score distribution on the right. Using Table A, the area below a *z* score of .67 is .7486, so the shaded area is 1 − .7486 = .2514. Thus, given a random sample with $n = 100$, $p(M > 92) = .2514$.

FIGURE 7.5

Determining $p(84 \leq M \leq 87)$ when $\mu = 90$, $\sigma = 30$, and $n = 100$. *Left panel*: the sampling distribution of the sample mean. *Right panel*: the sampling distribution transformed into z scores.

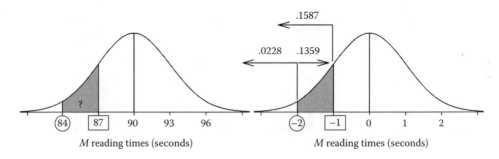

M reading times (seconds)   M reading times (seconds)

$$z = \frac{84 - 90}{3} = \frac{-6}{3} = -2$$

$$z = \frac{87 - 90}{3} = \frac{-3}{3} = -1$$

What is the probability that a random sample of $n = 100$ scores from the population of reading times has a mean between 84 and 87? This probability corresponds to the shaded area in Figure 7.5. Use Formula 7.4 to convert 84 and 87 into the z scores −2 and −1, respectively. Referring to Table A, the proportion of scores less than a z score of −1 is .1587, whereas the proportion of scores less than a z score of −2 is .0228. Therefore, the shaded area is the area to the left of a z score of −1, minus the area to the left of a z score of −2 or .1587 − .0228 = .1359. In words, the probability that the sample of 100 scores has a mean between 84 and 87 is .1359; in symbols, $p(84 \leq M \leq 87) = .1359$.

One more example with a slight change: Suppose that the mean of the population of reading times is 83 seconds and the standard deviation is, again, 30 seconds. What is the probability that a random sample of 100 scores will have a mean greater than or equal to 92? The relevant sampling distribution of sample means will have $\mu_M = 83$ seconds (Amazing Fact Number 1), $\sigma_M = 30/10 = 3$ (Amazing Fact Number 2), and it will be normally distributed (Amazing Fact Number 3). This sampling distribution is illustrated on the left of Figure 7.6.

An M of 92 is equivalent to a z score of 3 ([92−83]/3). Therefore, $p(M > 92)$ is equivalent to the relative frequency of z scores greater than 3. Using Table A, this relative frequency equals .0013 (1 − .9987). In other words, when sampling from a population with $\mu = 83$ and $\sigma = 30$, it is extremely rare to find a random sample of 100 scores with an M greater than or equal to 92.

A PREVIEW OF INFERENTIAL STATISTICS

We have spent time on sampling distributions with only the promise that they will be useful for making statistical inferences. This final section of the chapter describes an example that uses sampling distributions to make an inference about a population. Although the

FIGURE 7.6
Determining $p(M \geq 92)$ **when** $\mu = 83$, $\sigma = 30$, **and** $n = 100$. *Left panel*: **the sampling distribution of the sample mean.** *Right panel*: **the sampling distribution transformed into** z **scores.**

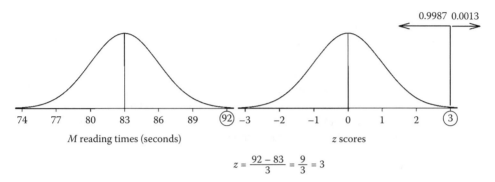

$$z = \frac{92 - 83}{3} = \frac{9}{3} = 3$$

example is clearly contrived, it does share some important features with hypothesis testing described more fully in Chapter 8.

Imagine that it is a warm and windy spring day, and you are walking past the university administration building. Because it is such a lovely day, you are surprised to hear a soft whimper coming from one of the open windows. Curious, you peer in to see the dean of the College of Letters and Science teary-eyed and sobbing. Because you are a kindly sort, you say, "Excuse me, dean. Is there anything I can do to help?" The dean responds by inviting you into his office.

He explains to you that he has spent an enormous amount of college money collecting data on reading for all freshmen in the college. In particular, each freshman was timed while reading a standard page of prose. The dean had the whole population of scores on his desk (each on an individual slip of paper, no less) when a gust of wind blew them out the window. All that he was able to salvage was a random sample of 100 slips of paper retrieved from around campus. Also, he remembers that the standard deviation of the population is 30 seconds. "But," he says, "for the life of me, I can't remember exactly the population mean. And I have to give a presentation before the board of regents in less than an hour. Please, please, is there anything you can do to help me?"

You say to him, "What do you mean you can't remember the population mean exactly? What do you remember?"

The dean replies, "For some reason, I can remember that the population mean is either 83 seconds or 90 seconds."

Confidently you respond, "Given this information, I think that I can help. Essentially we have two hypotheses about the mean of the population. Hypothesis A is that $\mu = 83$ seconds. Hypothesis B is that $\mu = 90$ seconds. What we have to do is to determine which hypothesis is more likely to be correct, given the data on hand."

"Data?" he says.

"Certainly. We have a random sample of 100 observations. Let's see what we can learn from the data. What is the mean of the sample?"

"92 seconds," he replies, somewhat intrigued.

"OK," you say. "Using a couple of amazing facts that I know, I can figure out the probability that a random sample of 100 scores with $M = 92$ seconds came from a population with

$\mu = 83$ seconds and $\sigma = 30$ seconds. Curiously, I recently computed that probability, and it turns out that when $\sigma = 30$ seconds, $\mu = 83$ seconds and $n = 100$, $p(M \geq 92) = .0013$. In other words, the random sample that we have is extremely *unlikely if* Hypothesis A is correct.

"I can also figure out, assuming that $\mu = 90$ seconds and $n = 100$, the probability of getting an M greater than or equal to 92 seconds. It turns out that that probability is .2514. In other words, the random sample that we have is fairly *likely if* Hypothesis B is correct."

"So now what?"

"It's easy," you say. "It is very unlikely that we would have obtained a random sample with a mean as great as 92 seconds if Hypothesis A were correct (.0013). On the other hand, it is reasonable to have obtained a random sample with a mean as great as 92 seconds if Hypothesis B were correct (.2514). Since Hypothesis A is so unlikely in the face of our data, I think that we can safely reject it and conclude that Hypothesis B is correct."

"How can I ever thank you?" exclaims the dean.

"I'll think of something," you say.

As illustrated in this example, the essence of statistical hypothesis testing consists of formulating two hypotheses about the population of interest. Then, the data in a random sample from the population are used to evaluate which of the hypotheses is more likely to be correct. This evaluation procedure involves comparing a statistic computed from the sample (for example, M) to the sampling distributions derived from the two hypotheses. Each sampling distribution is a prediction about what is likely to be found in the random sample *if* the hypothesis is correct. When the data in the random sample demonstrate that the prediction made by one of the hypotheses is a poor one, we are then justified in concluding that that hypothesis is incorrect. In the example, Hypothesis A predicted that a sample with a mean as large as 92 seconds was extremely improbable (.0013). Nonetheless, 92 seconds was the mean of the random sample. Because Hypothesis A made a poor prediction, we are justified in concluding that it is incorrect. In statistical terminology, concluding that a hypothesis is incorrect is called rejecting the hypothesis. Because Hypothesis B made a fairly reasonable prediction, we do not reject it.

By rejecting one hypothesis in favor of the other, you are making a statistical inference about the population. The inference is that the rejected hypothesis is an unreasonable guess about the population, whereas the remaining hypothesis is a reasonable guess about the population.

SUMMARY

A sampling distribution is a probability distribution of a statistic based on all possible random samples of the same size drawn from the same population. Each change in the statistic, the sample size, or the population produces a different sampling distribution. One way to conceptualize sampling distributions is in terms of the five-step procedure, which involves repeatedly drawing random samples of the same size from the same population and then calculating the statistic for each of the random samples. The relative frequency distribution of these statistics is the sampling distribution of the statistic.

Although the five-step procedure is a good way to think about what a sampling distribution is, the procedure is inconvenient for actually constructing one. Fortunately, many important sampling distributions can be obtained analytically. For example, using the three amazing facts about sampling distributions of the sample means we can produce the sampling distribution without ever actually taking a random sample.

Whether the sampling distribution is obtained by actually taking random samples or analytically, it can be used to calculate the probability of drawing in the future a *single* random sample that has a statistic within a particular range of value [for example, $p(M > 92)$]. The sampling distribution of the sample mean is particularly easy to work with because the sampling distribution is normally distributed (when the sample size is large). Therefore, probabilities can be calculated using z scores.

Hypothesis testing requires formulating hypotheses that are used to derive predictions (sampling distributions) of what will be found in a future random sample. Then, a statistic from an actual random sample is compared to the sampling distributions (predictions). If the statistic conflicts with a prediction, then the hypothesis that generated the prediction can be rejected.

EXERCISES

Terms   *Define these new terms and symbols.*

sampling distribution   Central Limit Theorem
sampling distribution of the sample mean μ_M
standard error of the mean σ_M

Questions   *Answer the following questions.*

1. Starting with a population that is normally distributed with a mean of 100 and a standard deviation of 12, answer the following questions (if possible).
   †a. What is the probability of randomly drawing a single score between 100 and 106, $p(100 < X < 106)$?
   †b. What is the probability of drawing a random sample of 9 observations with a mean between 100 and 106, $p(100 < M < 106)$?
   c. What is the probability of drawing a random sample of 36 observations with a mean between 100 and 106, $p(100 < M < 106)$?
   d. What is the probability of drawing a random sample of 36 observations with a standard deviation between 10 and 14, $p(10 < s < 14)$?
2. Suppose that the population in Question 1 was not normally distributed.
   †a. Which part(s)—a, b, c, d—could you answer without actually taking any random samples? What are the answers?
   b. Describe how you could answer the other parts of Question 1 if given the time and resources to engage in random sampling.
3. Suppose that a population has $\mu = 50$, $\sigma = 25$, and that you draw random samples of 25 scores from the population. Some of the Ms will be quite close to μ. Others will be quite discrepant.
   a. Which Ms are so large that they would occur only in the 5% of the samples with the largest means?
   b. Which Ms are so small that they would occur only in the 5% of the samples with the smallest means?

†**4.** Suppose that you draw a random sample of 100 scores from a population with a standard deviation of 30, and that $M = 25$. What is the probability that you would obtain a sample with a mean this large or larger if $\mu = 20$? 25? 19?

5. The meanium is a mythical statistic calculated by taking the square root of the sample median and dividing it by half of the sample size. Describe how you could construct a sampling distribution for the meanium.

6. Describe the relationships among the terms M, μ, and μ_M.

7. Describe the relationships among the terms s, σ, σ_M, and standard error.

8. Write each of the following numbers on a separate slip of paper: 3, 4, 4, 5, 5, 5, 5, 6, 6, 7. Mix the slips thoroughly and draw five random samples (sampling with replacement), each with a sample size of three slips. Compute the mean of each of the random samples.

    a. What is the value of μ_M?

    b. How can you estimate μ_M from the sample means? (Hint: See definition of μ_M.)

    c. Why is your estimate unlikely to exactly equal μ_M?

    d. What is your estimate of μ_M?

    e. What is the value of σ_M?

    f. How can you estimate σ_M using the sample means? (Hint: See Formula 7.2.)

    g. What is your estimate of σ_M?

9. Using the slips of paper made for Question 8, draw five random samples (sampling with replacement), each with a sample size of six scores, and compute the mean of each of the random samples. Answer Questions a–g from Question 8 using these new Ms. To what do you attribute the different answers?

Logic of Hypothesis Testing

A Third Example
  Step 1: Check the Assumptions
  Step 2: Formulate the Hypotheses
  Step 3: The Sampling Distributions
  Step 4: Set the Significance Level and
    the Decision Rule
Step 5: Randomly Sample and Compute
    the Statistic
Step 6: Decide and Draw Conclusions
Summary
Exercises
  Terms
  Questions

*T*esting hypotheses about populations is not a magical procedure, but one that depends on a type of logic. This logic is comprehensible (now that you know about sampling distributions), and it is always the same. Although you will be learning how to apply this logic to different situations (such as testing hypotheses about means or variances, for example), the basic logic remains the same.

The logic of hypothesis testing has six steps. As you read through this chapter, you should ask yourself periodically, "Do I understand why this step is important? Do I understand how this step relates to the previous step?" Only if you can answer these questions in the affirmative should you be satisfied with your level of understanding. Remember, it is important to understand the logic of hypothesis testing now, because it will be used repeatedly later.

The six-step logic is easier to understand when it is presented in the context of a specific procedure. In this chapter, we will focus on testing hypotheses about a single population mean when we happen to know the variance of the population. Admittedly, this is an unusual situation. If we do not know anything about the population mean (and that is why we are testing hypotheses about it), we usually don't know anything about the population variance. Nonetheless, application of the six-step logic to this type of hypothesis testing is particularly easy. Table 8.1 at the end of the chapter summarizes this procedure. You may find it helpful to refer to this table periodically while reading. Also, in later chapters other hypothesis-testing procedures will be summarized in a similar fashion to facilitate comparison among procedures. We turn now to a concrete example of testing hypotheses about μ when σ is known.

At the close of Chapter 7, we left the dean of the College of Letters and Science at Great Midwestern University (GMU) after helping him to determine that for freshmen the mean time to read a standard page of text was 90 seconds with $\sigma = 30$ seconds. The dean had collected that data for the following purpose. At Another Midwestern University (AMU), all freshmen enroll in a reading improvement program. The dean at GMU must determine if such a program is effective. If it is, he will incorporate the program into his own school's curriculum. If the program is ineffective (or even detrimental), he will advise the dean of AMU to drop the program.

The dean's plan is to compare the mean reading time of freshmen at GMU to the mean reading time for freshmen at AMU (who have all had the reading program). The dean has already obtained the mean for freshmen at GMU. But how is he to determine the mean reading time for freshmen at the other university? One solution is to test all of the freshmen attending AMU. This solution—collecting all of the scores in the population—is expensive and time consuming.

A second solution is to take a random sample of n scores from the population of reading times of freshmen at AMU (randomly choose n freshmen attending AMU and measure their reading times) and to use hypothesis-testing techniques to make an inference regarding the population mean. There are three hypotheses of interest about μ for freshmen at AMU. The first is that $\mu = 90$ seconds. If this hypothesis is correct, then the mean at AMU is not different from the mean at GMU, implying that the reading program is probably ineffective. The second hypothesis is that $\mu < 90$ seconds. If this hypothesis is correct, then the mean reading time for freshmen at AMU is less than the mean at GMU, implying that that the program is probably effective (that is, on the average, freshmen at AMU read faster than freshmen at GMU). The third hypothesis is that $\mu > 90$ seconds, implying that the program at AMU may actually be detrimental.[1]

Suppose that a random sample of $n = 36$ freshmen is selected and the reading time of each of these students is measured. In order to keep this example going, we will postulate that σ for the AMU freshmen reading times equals 30 seconds. Certainly, in real situations no one ever hands you a standard deviation out of thin air; either you know it based on measuring the whole population, or, more often, you estimate it (using s). Unfortunately, estimating σ complicates the picture (a complication dealt with in Chapter 12), and so for now we will opt for simplicity at the expense of realism.

Given this sample of 36 scores (and the fact that $\sigma = 30$), how can we learn about the mean of the population of reading times for freshmen at AMU? The six-step logic of hypothesis testing is used.

STEP 1: CHECK THE ASSUMPTIONS OF THE STATISTICAL PROCEDURE

Assumptions Are Requirements

All inferential procedures demand that the data being analyzed meet certain requirements. These requirements are called **assumptions,** although that is a poor choice of wording. In general, you should not *assume* that the requirements are met; rather, you should *know* that the requirements are met, because meeting the requirements guarantees that the inferential procedure works accurately. Nonetheless, for the sake of tradition, we will use the word *assumption* instead of *requirement.*

There are three kinds of assumptions: assumptions about the population from which the sample is drawn, assumptions about the sample itself, and assumptions about the

---

[1] The statistical hypothesis-testing procedure provides information as to the value of μ such as whether it is greater than 90 seconds. The hypothesis-testing procedure provides *absolutely no* information as to why μ happens to be that value. Perhaps the students at AMU just happen to be slower (or faster) readers than the students at GMU, and the difference has nothing to do with the reading program. In other words, on the basis of statistical reasoning, the dean will be able to determine if μ is different from 90, but he will not be able to determine if the difference is due to the reading program. The logical considerations needed to attribute a difference to a specific factor (such as the reading program) are discussed in texts on experimental methodology. A brief discussion of these considerations is included in Chapter 14.

measurement scale of the data. The population and sample assumptions are needed to guarantee that the procedure works. Assumptions about the scale type of the data are of lesser importance, but help as in deciding what specific type of test to conduct. The results of procedures dealing with means and variances are often more easily interpreted when the scale assumptions are met, but the results can be meaningful even when these assumptions are not met.

Assumptions for Testing Hypotheses About μ When σ Is Known

Population Assumptions

1. The population from which the sample is drawn is normally distributed, or the sample size is large. In Step 3, we will construct a sampling distribution for M. When this assumption is met, Amazing Fact Number 3 ensures that the sampling distribution will be normally distributed.
2. σ, the standard deviation of the population from which the sample is obtained, is known, not estimated. This σ will be used to calculate σ_M, using Amazing Fact Number 2.

Sampling Assumption   The sample is obtained using independent (within-sample) random sampling. This assumption is required for probability theory to work.

Data Assumption   The data should be measured using an interval or a ratio scale. The procedure requires computation of means and, as you will recall from Chapter 3, interpretation of means and variances is most clear-cut when the data are interval or ratio.

Does the reading time example meet these assumptions? Regarding the first population assumption, with a sample size of 36, even if the population is not normally distributed, the sample is large enough to guarantee that the sampling distribution of M will be (essentially) normally distributed. The second population assumption is also met because we know that $\sigma = 30$. The sampling assumption is met because we have a random sample from the population of reading times of freshmen at AMU. Finally, because reading time measured in seconds results in a ratio scale, the example satisfies the data assumption.

When the Assumptions Cannot Be Met

What should you do if you cannot meet the assumptions? In general, you should not bother to proceed. Certainly, you can crank out the numbers, but whatever conclusion you reach at the end will have no justification. The inferential procedures are guaranteed to be accurate only when all the assumptions are met.

However, there may be alternatives, depending on which assumptions cannot be met. For example, if you do not know σ, there are procedures using the t statistic for testing hypotheses about a single population mean when σ is estimated. These procedures will be discussed in Chapter 12.

STEP 2: GENERATE THE NULL AND ALTERNATIVE HYPOTHESES

Function of the Hypotheses

All hypothesis-testing procedures require that you generate two hypotheses about the population. The purpose of hypothesis testing is to decide which of these two hypotheses is more likely to be correct. Clearly, choosing the appropriate hypotheses is important. Fortunately, there are a number of heuristic rules to help you formulate them.

Most important, you have to decide what aspect of the population your hypotheses will concern: central tendency, variability, or shape of the population. When the hypotheses are about specific population parameters, you are conducting a **parametric test.** When the hypotheses specify shape of the population, you are conducting a **nonparametric test.** In our example, the dean is particularly interested in the mean of the population of reading times. Therefore, we will formulate hypotheses about the population mean and conduct a parametric statistical test.

The Null Hypothesis

One of the hypotheses is always called the *null hypothesis*. It has the following characteristics:

- The null hypothesis specifies that there is no change or no difference from a standard or theoretical value. That is why it is called the *null* (meaning none) hypothesis.
- The null hypothesis always proposes something specific about the population. For instance, when the null hypothesis is about a population parameter, the null hypothesis proposes a specific value for the parameter.
- The null hypothesis has an essential role in helping to construct the sampling distribution used in hypothesis testing (as you will see in Step 3).

In the reading example, the null hypothesis is that *the mean of the population of reading times at AMU equals 90 seconds*. This hypothesis is about the population parameter (the mean) that we decided was of interest; it proposes that there is no change from a standard (the standard is the 90-second mean reading time at GMU); it is specific in that it proposes that the mean of the population is a particular value, 90 seconds.

Because the null hypothesis is referred to frequently, it is convenient to have a symbol for it. That symbol is H_0, read as *null hypothesis* or pronounced *aitch sub oh*. The H stands for hypothesis, the subscript 0 is not really an "oh" but a zero or nought (for null). Often, the null hypothesis will be written as

$$H_0: \mu = 90 \text{ seconds}$$

Note the use of the colon; it should be read as *is that*. Thus, the null hypothesis *is that* $\mu = 90$ seconds. It is inappropriate to say the "null hypothesis is 90 seconds," or "the null hypothesis equals 90 seconds"; it is μ that equals 90 seconds.

The Alternative Hypothesis

The second hypothesis is called the *alternative hypothesis*. Its symbol is H_1 (aitch sub one). The alternative hypothesis also has a number of characteristics, which are as follows:

- The alternative is about the same aspect of the population as H_0. If H_0 is about the mean, then so is H_1; if H_0 is about the variance, then so is H_1.
- Although H_0 is specific, H_1 is always general.
- H_1 is always in opposition to H_0. That is, H_1 and H_0 must be formulated so that they cannot both be true at the same time. It is the hypothesis-testing procedure that helps us to decide which of these contrasting hypotheses is more likely to be correct.
- H_1 plays an important role in Step 4 of the hypothesis-testing procedure. In that step, a decision rule is formulated that specifies how the data in the sample are used to decide between H_0 and H_1.

An alternative hypothesis for the reading time example is that the mean of the population of reading times at AMU is not equal to 90 seconds. In symbols,

$$H_1: \mu \neq 90 \text{ seconds}$$

This alternative hypothesis is about the same aspect of the population as is the null hypothesis; it is a general hypothesis in that it does not suggest a specific value for the mean. It opposes the null hypothesis, because they both cannot be correct.

This form of the alternative is called a nondirectional alternative hypothesis.

> **A nondirectional alternative hypothesis** does not specify the direction in which the null hypothesis is incorrect, although, like all alternative hypotheses, it does propose that the null hypothesis is incorrect.

In the example, the alternative hypothesis indicates that μ is greater than 90 seconds or less than 90 seconds, implying that H_0 is incorrect. The alternative does not specify, however, the specific direction (greater than or less than) in which the null hypothesis is wrong. For reasons that will become clear later, the nondirectional alternative hypothesis is sometimes called a two-tailed alternative hypothesis.

Another option is to use a directional alternative.

> **A directional alternative hypothesis** specifies the direction (greater than or less than) in which the null hypothesis is incorrect.

For our example, a directional alternative could be $H_1: \mu > 90$ seconds. According to this alternative, not only is H_0 incorrect (because this alternative is saying that μ is greater than 90 seconds, not equal to 90 seconds), but it is incorrect in a specific direction (greater than). Another directional alternative could be $H_1: \mu < 90$ seconds.

It may at first seem perverse to use a nondirectional H_1. Why not simply state the direction? Important to note, the nondirectional H_1 encompasses both of the directional alternatives: $H_1: \mu \neq 90$ seconds is equivalent to both $H_1: \mu > 90$ seconds and $H_1: \mu < 90$ seconds at the same time. Therefore, the nondirectional alternative hypothesis should be used whenever you are interested in *either* way in which the null hypothesis can be incorrect. The directional alternative hypothesis should be used only when you are interested in one direction in which the H_0 may be wrong, but not the other. Because the nondirectional H_1 is more general, it is used most frequently. An expanded discussion of the considerations involved in choosing an alternative hypothesis is presented later in the chapter.

In our example, the dean of GMU would like to know if $\mu = 90$ seconds (the null hypothesis), if $\mu < 90$ seconds (indicating that the reading program is effective), or if $\mu > 90$ seconds (indicating that the reading program is detrimental). That is, the dean is interested in deviations from H_0 in *either direction,* so the appropriate H_1 is the nondirectional H_1: $\mu \neq 90$ seconds.

Now that we have formulated the two hypotheses, we have a good idea of where we are going. The remaining steps are set up to help us decide which of the two hypotheses is more likely to be correct. That is, is the mean of the population of reading times at AMU (the population from which we will randomly sample) equal to 90 seconds (as specified by the null hypothesis), or different from 90 seconds (as specified by the alternative hypothesis)? Making this decision is tantamount to making a statistical inference.

STEP 3: SAMPLING DISTRIBUTION OF THE TEST STATISTIC

The Test Statistic

In deciding between H_0 and H_1, we will be calculating a test statistic from a random sample.

> **A test statistic** is a specific value computed from a sample (thus making it a statistic) that is used in deciding between H_0 and H_1.

When testing hypotheses about a single population mean when σ is known (the situation under discussion), the test statistic is the z score formed by transforming the sample mean using Formula 8.1.

FORMULA 8.1 z Score for Testing Hypotheses About μ

$$z = \frac{M - \mu_0}{\sigma_M}$$

The one new term in the equation is μ_0. This symbol stands for the value of the mean of the population specified by H_0. Otherwise, the equation is the same as we used in Chapter 7 for transforming Ms into z scores. Rather than forming the sampling distributions of the test statistic (z) directly, we will begin with a discussion of the sampling distributions of M.

Sampling Distributions of M

Suppose for the moment that H_0 is correct. In this case, the three amazing facts can be used to construct the sampling distribution of M based on samples from the population of reading times. Amazing Fact Number 1 is that the mean of the sampling distribution equals the mean of the population. Therefore, when H_0 is correct, the mean of the sampling distribution will equal 90 seconds. Amazing Fact Number 2 is that the standard error of the sampling distribution is equal to the standard deviation of the population divided by the square root of the sample size. Because we know that $\sigma = 30$ seconds and $n = 36$,

$$\sigma_M = 30/\sqrt{36} = 5$$

Finally, because the sample size is relatively large, Amazing Fact Number 3 guarantees that the sampling distribution is essentially normally distributed.

Now it should be clear why the population assumptions were needed in Step 1: When the assumptions are met, the shape and standard error of the sampling distribution can be determined. It should also be clear why the null hypothesis must propose a specific value for μ (Step 2): That value is used as the mean of the sampling distribution.

The dark curve in Figure 8.1 represents the sampling distribution of the sample mean *if the null hypothesis is correct.* Because this sampling distribution is a probability distribution, it predicts which values of M are likely to be found in the random sample *(if the null hypothesis is correct).* Working roughly from the figure, if the null hypothesis is correct, likely values for M are around 90 seconds, and unlikely values are those many standard deviations above or below 90 seconds. To express this differently, if the null hypothesis is true, we expect an M around 90 seconds in a to-be-taken random sample. We would be surprised if the mean of the sample actually drawn is much above or much below 90 seconds, because these values have low probabilities when H_0 is correct.

Now, suppose for a moment that H_1 is correct, rather than H_0. The alternative hypothesis states that the mean of the population of reading times is either greater than 90 seconds or less than 90 seconds. We cannot use this alternative to formulate a specific sampling distribution because it does not provide a specific value for the mean. Instead, we can think of the alternative as suggesting a number of different sampling distributions. Some of these sampling distributions are illustrated by the light curves in Figure 8.1. Each curve

FIGURE 8.1
Sampling distributions of M specified by H_0: $\mu = 90$ and H_1: $\mu \neq 90$.

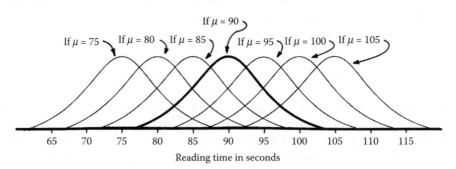

represents one of the many possible sampling distributions consistent with the supposition that H_1 is correct.

The distributions representing H_1 also make predictions about likely values for M in the random sample drawn from the population. Namely, *if H_1 is correct,* we expect M to be either greater than 90 seconds or less than 90 seconds. Even very large values for M are highly probable when $\mu > 90$ seconds (part of H_1), and very small values for M are highly probable when $\mu < 90$ seconds (the other part of H_1).

Sampling Distributions of the Test Statistic, z

Imagine that each M in the distribution representing H_0 is run through Formula 8.1 and turned into a z score. The relative frequency distribution of those z scores is illustrated in the middle of Figure 8.2. As usual, the mean of the z-score distribution is 0.0 and the shape is the same as the shape of the original distribution (normal). Of course, this is still a sampling distribution, but in this case it is a sampling distribution of z scores. Because it is a sampling distribution, it makes predictions about what is likely to be found in the random sample that will actually be drawn. Namely, if H_0 is correct, then the test statistic computed from the random sample should be around 0.0 (corresponding to an M of 90 seconds). Also, if H_0 is correct, it is very unlikely that the test statistic would be much greater than 2 or much less than −2 (because these are z scores with very low probabilities of occurring when H_0 is correct).

Next, we will transform the sampling distributions representing H_1 into z scores. Again, we run each of the Ms in the sampling distributions through Formula 8.1. At first, this may seem wrongheaded, because Formula 8.1 indicates that we are to subtract from each M the mean (μ_0) of the population specified by H_0, even though the sampling distribution is based on H_1! The reason for doing this is that Formula 8.1 will actually be applied to the random sample we draw from the population (in Step 5). Therefore, we must determine what H_1 *predicts* we will find when Formula 8.1 is applied to the sample.

Applying Formula 8.1 to the light-line distributions in Figure 8.1 results in the light-line distributions in Figure 8.2. All of the distributions in Figure 8.1 maintain their *relative*

FIGURE 8.2
Sampling distributions of z scores specified by H_0: $\mu = 90$ and H_1: $\mu \neq 90$. The $\alpha = .05$ rejection region is also illustrated.

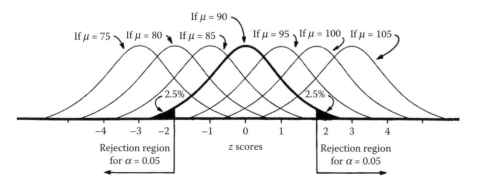

locations. It is not difficult to understand why this occurs. Take, for example, the distribution in Figure 8.1 centered on 95 seconds. All of the Ms equal to 95 seconds (at the mean of the distribution) will, when run through Formula 8.1, result in z scores of 1.0 (95 seconds − 90 seconds/5). Thus, the distribution that was originally centered on 95 seconds, one standard error above the M distribution specified by H_0, will now be centered on a z score of 1 (one standard error above the z-score distribution specified by H_0). Similarly, the distribution originally centered on 85 (one standard error below the M distribution specified by H_0) will now be centered on a z score of −1 (one standard error below the z-score distribution specified by H_0).

These z-score distributions are also making predictions. Namely, when H_1 is correct, values of the test statistic computed from the random sample should be either large positive z scores (corresponding to those distributions on the right) or large negative z scores (corresponding to those z scores on the left). To summarize, the sampling distribution for H_0 predicts that the z score from the random sample will be around zero; the sampling distributions for H_1 predict that the z score will be different from zero.

STEP 4: SET THE SIGNIFICANCE LEVEL AND FORMULATE THE DECISION RULE

The Decision Rule

The decision rule is used to decide which hypothesis provides a better description of the population. In Step 5, you will draw a random sample from the population and calculate a test statistic (z). The decision rule is then applied to the test statistic to determine whether this statistic is more likely to have come from a population described by H_0 or a population described by H_1. A simple formula for the decision rule is presented later in this section. Before introducing it, we will go through the reasoning that leads to the formula.

The decision rule specifies values of the test statistic that simultaneously meet two conditions: (a) The values have a low probability of occurring when H_0 is correct, and (b) the values have a high probability of occurring when H_1 is correct. Then, suppose that you draw a random sample, compute the test statistic, and find that the test statistic is one of the values specified by the decision rule. Because the value of the statistic you have is (a) unlikely when H_0 is correct, but (b) very likely when H_1 is correct, the most reasonable decision is to reject H_0 (decide that it is incorrect) in favor of H_1.

> The values specified by the decision rule are called the **rejection region** for the null hypothesis. If the test statistic (calculated in Step 5) is in the rejection region, then H_0 is rejected in favor of H_1.

Choose a Significance Level

Examining Figure 8.2, we can see which values of z are (a) unlikely when H_0 is correct, but (b) very likely when H_1 is correct. These are the z scores that are far from zero (both large positive z scores and large negative z scores).

But how far from zero is far enough? Surely, z scores greater than 4 or 5, for example, are (a) unlikely when H_0 is correct and yet (b) very likely when H_1 is correct. The same is true for z scores around −4 or −5. But what about z scores such as 1.8, or −2.1? These z scores do have low probabilities of occurring when H_0 is correct, but are they low enough? Stated differently, if the z scores you actually get from your random sample were 1.8, would you be willing to reject H_0?

Choice of the values of the test statistic forming the rejection region is, in part, a personal decision. You must decide, for yourself, what it takes to convince you that H_0 should be rejected. Would you reject H_0 if the z score from the random sample were 1.8 or −2.1? Do these z scores have a low enough probability (based on the sampling distribution for H_0) that if you actually got one of them it would convince you that H_0 is unlikely to be correct?

Fortunately, there are guidelines to help you formulate the rejection region and the decision rule. In psychology, a probability of .05 is often used in constructing the decision rule. That is, the rejection region consists of those values of the test statistic that occur with a relative frequency of only .05 when H_0 is correct, but are very likely when H_1 is correct.

> The probability value associated with the decision rule (for example, .05) is called the **significance level** of the test. The significance level of a statistical test is represented by the Greek letter *alpha, α*.

To reiterate, the choice of a significance level (α) is up to you. It is your own personal statement of what it takes to convince you that H_0 is incorrect. If the test statistic from your random sample is unlikely (has a probability less than α) when H_0 is correct, but very likely when H_1 is correct, then you will decide to reject H_0 in favor of H_1.

Formulating the Decision Rule: Use the Significance Level to Determine the Rejection Region

After setting the significance level, the rejection region is found by solving a z-score problem. For a significance level of .05, which z scores are so far from zero that (a) they have only a .05 chance of occurring, supposing H_0 is correct, and (b) are very likely, supposing that H_1 is correct? These are the z scores in the tails of the sampling distribution specified by H_0. Namely, the .025 of the z scores in the upper tail of the sampling distribution and the .025 of the z scores in the lower tail of the sampling distribution have (a) a total probability of only .05, supposing that H_0 is correct, and (b) they are very probable, supposing that H_1 is correct (see Figure 8.2).

The z score having .025 of the distribution above it will have .9750 below it ($1 - .025 = .9750$). If we look in the body of Table A, we find that a z score of 1.96 has a proportion of .9750 of the scores below it. Similarly, a z score of −1.96 has .025 of the distribution below it. Therefore, the rejection region consists of z scores greater than or equal to 1.96, as well as z scores less than or equal to −1.96. The decision rule that corresponds to this rejection region is:

$$\text{Reject } H_0 \text{ if } z \geq 1.96 \text{ or } z \leq -1.96$$

More generally, when testing hypotheses about μ when σ is known, the decision rule for the nondirectional alternative hypothesis is

$$\text{Reject } H_0 \text{ if } z \geq z_{\alpha/2} \text{ or if } z \leq -z_{\alpha/2}$$

The symbol $z_{\alpha/2}$ indicates the z score with $\alpha/2$ proportion of the normal distribution above it. This z score is also called a **critical value**—the value of the test statistic that begins the rejection region.

For $\alpha = .05$, $z_{\alpha/2} = z_{.025} = 1.96$. A z score of 1.96 is the critical value.

Formulating the Decision Rule: Summary

The decision rule can be formed in two steps. First, choose a significance level (α). Second, for a nondirectional alternative hypothesis (the directional alternative is discussed later in this chapter), use Table A to find the critical value, $z_{\alpha/2}$.

It is important to understand what these two steps represent. The significance level is your own personal statement of what it takes to convince you to reject H_0. If the test statistic you calculate has (a) a low probability (α) of occurring when H_0 is correct, but (b) a high probability when H_1 is correct, then it is much more reasonable to believe that H_1 is correct than that H_0 is correct.

Applying the Decision Rule

Suppose that you draw a random sample and find that the z score is 3.0. Because this test statistic falls into the rejection region (it is larger than 1.96), H_0 would be rejected, and you would conclude that H_1 is a better guess about the population than is H_0. Indeed, looking at Figure 8.2, you can see that a z score of 3.0 is very unlikely when H_0 is correct, but that it is very probable when H_1 is correct.

As another example, suppose that the z score obtained from the random sample were 1.0. This z score is not part of the rejection region, so H_0 would not be rejected. In other words, this z score is one of those that is quite likely to be found when H_0 is correct, and so there is no reason to reject H_0.

STEP 5: RANDOMLY SAMPLE FROM THE POPULATION AND COMPUTE THE TEST STATISTIC

This step consists of both the hardest and the easiest parts of hypothesis testing. The first part, drawing a random sample of size n from the population, is the hardest part. As we discussed in Chapter 5, it can be very difficult to ensure that each score in the population has an equal chance of being included in the sample. One possibility is for the dean at GMU to obtain a list of all freshmen at AMU, and then randomly select 36 names (perhaps using a random number table) from this list. These individuals would then be contacted, and their reading times obtained. The 36 scores would then comprise the actual sample from the population.

The second part of Step 5, computing the test statistic, is the easiest part of hypothesis testing. Each inferential procedure comes with a formula that specifies how to calculate the appropriate test statistic. Some students believe that the formula is the most important part of an inferential procedure. This is a mistake. The formula can be applied in a rote fashion, just by plugging in the numbers. By contrast, the other steps in the logic of statistical inference are the ones that call for thinking.

Formula 8.1 specifies how to calculate the test statistic for testing hypotheses about a population mean when σ is known. The formula specifies three quantities needed to compute the test statistic: the standard error of the sampling distribution, which we know from Step 3 is 5, the mean of the population as specified by H_0, which we know is 90, and the mean of the sample, M. As you know, $M = \Sigma X / n$.

Suppose that we actually had a random sample of $n = 36$ scores and $M = 102$. Then,

$$z = \frac{M - \mu_0}{\sigma_M} = \frac{102 - 90}{5} = 2.4$$

STEP 6: APPLY THE DECISION RULE AND DRAW CONCLUSIONS

The last step is to apply the decision rule from step 4 to the test statistic computed in Step 5. The decision rule is to reject H_0 if $z \geq 1.96$ or if $z \leq -1.96$. Because 2.4 is greater than 1.96, H_0 is rejected. In other words, because the test statistic falls into the rejection region, it is simply too discrepant with what H_0 predicts to believe that H_0 is correct. In this case, we reject the claim that $\mu = 90$ seconds.

Conclusions: Learning From Data

Now that we have decided to reject H_0, what sort of conclusions can we draw? First, not only is H_0 rejected, but the decision also implies that H_1 is correct. We can be even a little more specific. The test statistic, 2.4, is to the right of the distribution specified by H_0 (see Figure 8.2); that is, it is in the upper part of the rejection region. This upper part of the rejection region not only is inconsistent with H_0, it is consistent with the alternative hypotheses specifying $\mu > 90$ seconds. We can conclude, therefore, that μ is in fact greater than 90 seconds.

Note that we cannot claim that $\mu = 102$ seconds, the value of M. Remember, the value "102 seconds" is based on just one sample from the population. Because there is sampling error—that is, samples differ from one another—we cannot, on the basis of a single finite sample, know an exact value for μ. Examining Figure 8.2, you can see that $M = 102$ seconds is consistent with a number of possible values for μ, such as 100 seconds and 105 seconds.

The best we can do for now is to say that H_0 is rejected, and that $\mu > 90$ seconds. In Chapter 10, we discuss parameter estimation techniques in which data from random samples are used to generate a reasonable range of values for μ.

Another way of stating these conclusions is that *on the average,* the reading times of freshmen at AMU are slower than the reading times at GMU. Apparently, the reading program is not very effective for these students (but see Footnote 1 on p. 143).

An implication of these data is that the reading program should not be adopted at GMU. Note that we cannot claim that the reading program is totally ineffective; it may work at some universities. It simply was not very effective in the population that we examined. If we had claimed that the reading program was ineffective for all students, we would be overgeneralizing (that is, inappropriately extending our claims to populations from which we did not randomly sample).

Although the conclusions are limited, the data have taught us a lot. From the dean's point of view, a possibly costly mistake (adopting an ineffective program) was prevented by learning from data that cost relatively little.

Statistical Significance

Sometimes you read the statement that results are statistically significant.

The phrase **statistically significant** means that the null hypothesis was rejected.

Do not confuse statistical significance with practical significance. Although the null hypothesis may be rejected, the finding may be trivial if it has no practical, intellectual, or theoretical value.

WHEN H_0 IS NOT REJECTED

Now consider what decision we would have made, and what we would have concluded, if the mean of the random sample had been equal to 92 seconds. First, recompute z.

$$z = \frac{M - \mu_0}{\sigma_M} = \frac{92 - 90}{5} = .4$$

In this case, we cannot reject H_0, because .4 is not part of the rejection region. Can we conclude that H_0 is correct? The answer is an emphatic *no*.

Hypothesis testing is an asymmetrical procedure. We can reject H_0 if the test statistic is part of the rejection region, but if it is not, we cannot decide that H_0 is correct. The problem is that a z score of .4 is consistent with hypotheses other than H_0. For example, a z score of .4 is very consistent with the hypothesis that $\mu = 95$ seconds (see Figure 8.2), as well as the hypothesis that $\mu = 90$ seconds (the null hypothesis). Even a z score of 0.0, which is consistent with H_0, is *not* inconsistent with the hypothesis that $\mu = 95$ seconds, or $\mu = 91$ seconds, or $\mu = 89$ seconds, or $\mu = 88$ seconds. The rejection region is special because it consists of values of the test statistic that are (a) inconsistent with H_0 and (b) consistent with H_1. So, when a test statistic is part of the rejection region, it is good evidence that H_0 is incorrect and H_1 is correct. On the other hand, values of the test statistic not in the rejection region (values of z around 0 in Figure 8.2) are consistent with *both* H_0 and H_1. We cannot decide which is correct and which is incorrect.

The asymmetric nature of hypothesis testing is true of all hypothesis-testing procedures. Although a test statistic may allow us to reject H_0 when it falls into the rejection region, a test statistic that does not fall into the rejection region never by itself allows the claim that H_0 is correct. This fact is summarized in the aphorism, "You can't prove the null hypothesis."

What can you conclude when the test statistic does not fall into the rejection region? The best that can be said is that there is not enough evidence in the random sample to reject H_0. It does not mean that H_0 is correct, nor does it mean that H_0 is incorrect. The conclusion is that you simply do not know. Clearly, this is an unsatisfying conclusion. Strategies for decreasing the frequency with which you have to make this conclusion are discussed briefly in the section on errors in hypothesis testing, and in more detail in Chapter 9.

BRIEF REVIEW

The general features of the six-step hypothesis-testing procedure apply to all hypothesis-testing situations. The first step is to determine if the situation satisfies the assumptions (requirements) of the hypothesis-testing procedure. Satisfying the assumptions is important because they are used later to help derive sampling distributions of the test statistic. If the assumptions of a particular hypothesis-testing procedure cannot be satisfied, then that hypothesis-testing procedure should not be used, and alternative (often nonparametric) procedures must be investigated.

The second step is to formulate the null and alternative hypotheses. H_0 is always a specific statement about the population. It often specifies "no change" or "no difference" from other populations. H_1 is always a general statement about the population that is in opposition to H_0. H_0 and H_1 cannot both be true. The purpose of hypothesis testing is to determine which hypothesis is a better description of the population.

The third step involves formulating sampling distributions of the test statistic. We temporarily suppose that H_0 is correct, and we determine the sampling distribution of the test statistic. This distribution predicts the likely values of the test statistic if H_0 is indeed correct. Next, we temporarily suppose that H_1 is correct, and we determine the various sampling distributions associated with it. These distributions predict likely values for the test statistic if H_1 is correct.

The fourth step is to set up a decision rule: Determine those values of the test statistic that would convince you that H_0 is incorrect. In general, the values of the test statistic that form the rejection region are those values that have a very low probability of occurring, according to the sampling distribution for H_0, and have a very high probability of occurring, according to the sampling distributions for H_1. Then, if the test statistic from the random sample falls into the rejection region, H_0 is rejected, and you conclude that H_1 provides a better description of the population.

The specific values of the test statistic included in the rejection region depend on α, the significance level. Although it is usually .05, the choice of the significance level is up to you. You must decide how small the probability of the test statistic must be to convince you that H_0 is incorrect and H_1 is correct. Once you have made this decision, the specific values of the test statistic that form the rejection region can be determined.

The fifth step requires taking a random sample from the population and computing the test statistic.

The sixth step is to apply the decision rule to the test statistic computed from the random sample, and to decide whether or not to reject H_0. If the test statistic falls into the rejection region, H_0 is rejected, and the conclusion is that H_1 is correct. Another way of saying this is that the results are statistically significant. On the other hand, if the test statistic does not fall into the rejection region, H_0 cannot be rejected, nor is it proven true. The only conclusion in this case is that there is not enough evidence to decide between the two hypotheses. In either case, remember that the conclusions you draw are only about the specific population from which the random sample was drawn.

At this point the statistical reasoning is over, but now you must consider the implications of your decision to reject (or not reject) H_0. Your decision may suggest that a reading program is ineffective (for a particular population), or that one psychotherapy is better than another (for a particular population), or that watching a particular type of violent film leads to aggression (for a particular population). The challenge is to take what you have learned from the data and apply it to solving real problems.

In the Media: You Can Prove the Null Hypothesis!

Hypothesis testing is designed to determine if there is enough evidence to reject the null hypothesis, but it cannot be used to determine if the null hypothesis is correct. Why? It may be that the real population mean differs from the hypothesized value (μ_0) by only a small amount; that is, the effect size is small. When effects are small, rejecting the null hypothesis requires very strong data in the form of either a very small variance or a very large sample (details are provided in Chapter 9). How do you know whether the null is correct or the effect is just small and the data not strong enough to detect this small effect? Generally, you don't, hence the aphorism: You can't prove the null hypothesis.

In light of this discussion, consider headlines such as, "Study: Low Levels of Mercury Did Not Harm Pregnancies," in an article by Paul Driscoll (*Wisconsin State Journal,* August 26, 1998). This headline implicitly claims that the null hypothesis is correct. A similar claim is made in the first sentence of the article, "Children whose mothers ate lots of ocean fish containing low levels of mercury while they were pregnant suffered no ill effects in a study conducted in the Indian Ocean Country of Seychelles." To his credit, Driscoll does provide some relevant information and some important caveats. For example, he reports that the sample size is 711 observations. Although this seems like a large number, it may not be large enough to detect very small effects (see Chapter 9). He also notes that "fish are contaminated with mercury to different degrees throughout the world." That is, it is not safe to generalize these findings to people who live outside the Seychelles.

ERRORS IN HYPOTHESIS TESTING: TYPE I ERRORS

Unfortunately, the hypothesis-testing procedure is not error-free; even when all the assumptions are met and all the calculations are performed correctly, erroneous decisions can be made. The two types of errors that can be made are called, reasonably enough, Type I and Type II errors.

A Type I error occurs when H_0 is rejected when it really is correct.

Interestingly, the probability of Type I error always equals α, the significance level. In fact, another definition for *alpha* is that it is the probability of a Type I error. It is not difficult to see why this is so. Take a look at Figure 8.2. An α of .05 corresponds to the shaded portion of the figure. Now, in order to make a Type I error, H_0 must be correct, and yet the test statistic must fall into the rejection region so that H_0 is (erroneously) rejected. What is the probability that the test statistic falls into the rejection region when H_0 is correct? It is exactly α.

How can this happen? Remember, we picked the rejection region to consist of those values of the test statistic that are very probable when H_1 is correct, but very improbable when H_0 is correct. Well, indeed, having the test statistic fall into the rejection region is improbable when H_0 is correct, but it can happen! And the probability that the test statistic falls into the rejection region when H_0 is correct is exactly α.

Although errors are unpleasant, there are two comforting features in regard to Type I errors. First, α is small. Most of the time when H_0 is correct, the test statistic will not fall into the rejection region so that you will not make Type I errors. Indeed, when H_0 is correct, the proportion of times that you will make Type I errors is only α (typically, .05), whereas the proportion of times that you will make the correct decision is $1 - \alpha$ (typically, .95).

The second comforting feature is that you get to set the value for α for yourself. If you are comfortable with .05, fine. If you want to lower the probability of a Type I error, then you can use a smaller value of α. The choice is yours, although as we will see in a moment, the choice does have important consequences.

Being able to set the probability of making a Type I error is one of the great advantages of statistical decision making over intuition. It does not take a statistical genius to know that if M is very discrepant with a hypothesized value of μ, then the hypothesis is likely to be wrong. What the impressive machinery of statistical decision making adds to intuition is a mechanism for exactly setting the probability of a Type I error. Because *you* set α, you can make it as small as you want. That is something that intuition just cannot do for you.

p Values

As we have seen, setting α is a personal decision and will vary from person to person. In recognition of this, many investigators include in the report of statistical tests a *p* value.

A *p* value is the smallest α that would allow rejection of the null hypothesis.

The *p* value is also the conditional probability of obtaining your results when the null hypothesis is true [p(Results | H_0 is true)].

You can think of p as standing for "the probability of a Type I error." Thus, $p < .025$, for example, means that the probability of a Type I error is less than .025.

Imagine you are reading the report of an experiment and find the statement, "$p < .025$." Should you reject H_0 or not? If your *alpha* is .025 or greater, then this H_0 should be rejected. For example, if your $\alpha = .05$, then you are willing to accept a probability of a Type I error of up to .05. Because the probability of a Type I error is less than .025 (and thus less than .05), you should reject H_0.

Suppose, however, that your $\alpha = .01$. In this case, you would not reject H_0. Your $\alpha = .01$ means that you are willing to tolerate a probability of a Type I error of only up to .01. When $p < .025$ there is no guarantee that the probability of a Type I error is also less than .01.

Sometimes, an investigator reports $p > .05$. In this case H_0 is usually not rejected, because α would have to be quite large (that is, larger than .05) for H_0 to be rejected, and most people prefer to set α at .05 or smaller.

What a p Value Is Not

Often p values are misinterpreted and easily misunderstood. A p value is not the probability that the null hypothesis is true [$p(H_0$ is true)], nor is it the probability of your results [p(Results)], nor is it the probability that the null is true given your results [p(H_0 is true | Results)]. The p value is the probability of obtaining your results *if* the null were true [p(Results | H_0 is true)]. In hypothesis testing, we assume that the null is true in order to construct a sampling distribution. Just as the p(rain), the p(clouds), the p(rain | clouds), and the p(clouds | rain) are different quantities, the p(Results | H_0 is true) is different from $p(H_0$ is true | Results).

Setting $\alpha = 0.0$

If α can be set to any probability, why put up with Type I errors at all? Why not just set α at zero? The problem arising from setting α at zero can be demonstrated by noting what happens as α becomes smaller and smaller. As illustrated in Figure 8.3, as α becomes smaller, the rejection region moves out farther into the tails of the distribution specified by H_0.

When α is set at 0.0, the rejection region consists of z scores that have a probability of 0.0 when H_0 is correct. Which z scores are impossible (have a probability of 0.0) when H_0 is correct? There are none: As α approaches 0.0, the rejection region moves so far into the tails of the distribution that it disappears.

When there is no rejection region, that is, when $\alpha = 0.0$, you will never make a Type I error because you will never reject H_0 when it is correct. Unfortunately, when $\alpha = 0.0$ you will not reject H_0 when it is *incorrect* either, because there is no value of the test statistic that requires rejection of H_0. Clearly, not rejecting H_0 when it is incorrect is an error; in particular, it is a Type II error.

TYPE II ERRORS

A Type II error occurs when H_0 is really incorrect, but the test statistic does not fall into the rejection region.

FIGURE 8.3
Sampling distributions and rejections regions for α = .05, .01, and .001.

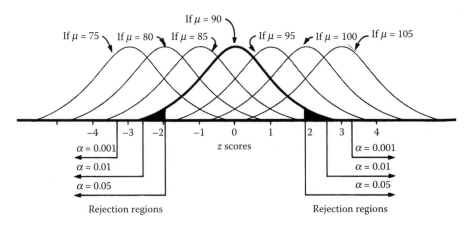

A **Type II error** is made when H_0 is not rejected when it really is incorrect. The symbol for the probability of a Type II error is the Greek letter β (beta).

How can we make a Type II error? We have just seen one way. If α is zero, Type II errors will occur whenever H_0 is incorrect, because the test statistic cannot fall into the (nonexistent) rejection region, and so the incorrect H_0 cannot be rejected. Now you know why α is never 0.0: Although Type I errors would be eliminated, Type II errors would be common.

Even when α is not 0.0 Type II errors can occur. Look at Figure 8.3 and suppose that μ really equals 95 (so that H_0: $\mu = 90$ is incorrect). With $\mu = 95$, we might well obtain an M of 95. Applying Formula 8.1,

$$z = \frac{M - \mu_0}{\sigma_M} = \frac{95 - 90}{5} = 1.0$$

With a test statistic of 1.0, we would be unable to reject H_0 (because z does not fall into the rejection region). In this case, a Type II error would be made; H_0: $\mu = 90$ is incorrect, but we did not reject it.

The probability of a Type II error, β, is not as easy to calculate as α. In fact, much of Chapter 9 is devoted to procedures for calculating β. Nonetheless, there are five general factors that affect β, and some of them can be used to control the size of β.

Reduce β by Increasing α

α and β are inversely related; as α becomes smaller β becomes larger, and as α becomes larger β becomes smaller. It is not true that $\beta = 1 - \alpha$; the relationship is more complicated than that. Nonetheless, one way to make β smaller is to make α larger.

This method for reducing β is not very satisfactory because it just trades one type of error for another. That is, although the probability of Type II errors is reduced by increasing α, this results in an increase in the probability of Type I errors. Chapter 9 includes a discussion of when it might be preferable to have a modest increase in α to gain a decrease in β.

Reduce β by Using Parametric Statistical Tests

The second way to reduce β is to use parametric hypothesis testing (such as testing hypotheses about a population mean when σ is known, as in this chapter) rather than nonparametric hypothesis testing. Generally, the probability of a Type II error is smaller for parametric hypothesis-testing procedures than for nonparametric procedures. Because of this difference, parametric hypothesis-testing procedures should be used whenever you have a choice. Of course, if the situation does not meet the assumptions (requirements) of a parametric procedure, then the appropriate nonparametric procedure should be used.

Reduce β by Decreasing Variability

Third, β can be reduced by decreasing the variability in the sampling distribution. The easiest way to decrease this variability is to increase the sample size. As you know from amazing fact number 2, $\sigma_M = \sigma/\sqrt{n}$. By increasing n, σ_M is reduced, and this reduces β. Although this specific equation holds only for the sampling distribution of the sample mean, it is always true that increasing n reduces β. The practical advice to remember is that the larger the sample size, the smaller the probability of a Type II error.

This relationship between sample size and β explains what may appear to be a curious feature about the logic of hypothesis testing. Namely, only a single sample of size n is drawn. Why not draw two samples, or three samples, or more? The answer is that increasing n decreases β. Therefore, it is better to draw one large sample than many small ones. Thus, hypothesis testing is one of the few instances in which it is better to put all of your eggs into one basket.

Variability in the sampling distribution can also be decreased by reducing the variability in your measurements. Reducing variability in measurement reduces σ, which, in turn, reduces σ_M. This, in turn, reduces β. Variability in measurement can be reduced by collecting all of the measurements under conditions that are as uniform as possible. In the reading time example, this would mean measuring reading times for the same material, presenting exactly the same instructions to all the participants in the sample, obtaining all the measurements in the same location at the same time of day, and so on. Other suggestions as to how to reduce variability introduced by the measurement process can be found in texts on psychological testing and texts on experimental methodology.

Variability in the sampling distribution can also be reduced by using procedures based on dependent-group sampling. These procedures are discussed in Chapter 15.

β and the Alternative Hypothesis

The fourth way to reduce β is the appropriate use of directional alternative hypotheses. We turn to that topic in a later section of this chapter.

β and the Effect Size

β is a concern only when the null hypothesis is *incorrect* (because β is the probability of not rejecting H_0 when it is *incorrect*). The effect size is closely related to the numerical difference between the real population mean and the mean specified by the null hypothesis μ_0). The greater this difference, the smaller β. That is, the more wrong H_0 is, the more likely we are to reject it and not make a Type II error.

Much of the time we have no control over the effect size (but see Chapter 14). Nonetheless, the concept is useful. If you suspect that the effect size is small (so that β is large), then you should attempt to decrease β by other means, such as increasing the sample size and taking care to reduce variability by careful measurement procedures.

OUTCOMES OF A STATISTICAL TEST

Figure 8.4 summarizes the four possible outcomes of statistical hypothesis testing. Focus first on what can happen when H_0 is correct (although in hypothesis testing you do not know this for sure, it is what you are trying to find out). When H_0 is correct, there are only two possible outcomes. If the decision you make in Step 6 is to reject H_0, then you have made a Type I error. The probability of a Type I error (α) can be made very small, however. On the other hand, the decision you make in Step 6 might be to retain (not reject) H_0, and this decision would be correct. The probability of making a correct decision when H_0 is correct is $1 - \alpha$, typically .95.

This result should be very comforting. Although you can make a Type I error when H_0 is correct, it is far more likely that you will make the correct decision. The purpose of all this discussion about errors is to demonstrate that errors in hypothesis testing are possible and to explain how to decrease the probability of making an error. Nonetheless, when H_0 is correct, the probability of making the right decision is much greater than the probability of making an error.

Now, consider what can happen when H_0 is incorrect. Again, there are two possible outcomes to Step 6. If the decision is to retain H_0, then under these circumstances a Type

FIGURE 8.4

Outcomes of statistical hypothesis testing and their probabilities.

		H_0 is correct	H_0 is incorrect
Decision made in Step 6	Reject H_0	Type 1 error probability = α	Correct decision probability = $1 - \beta$ = power
	Do not reject H_0	Correct decision probability = $1 - \alpha$	Type 2 error probability = β

II error is made. On the other hand, the decision might be to reject H_0, which, under these circumstances, would be a correct decision. Although β, the probability of a Type II error, cannot be controlled as directly as α, we do know how to keep it small. Namely, do not make α too small, use parametric tests whenever possible, and decrease variability by using a large sample size, careful measurement procedures, and dependent-group sampling (Chapter 15).

When H_0 is incorrect and you decide to reject it, a correct decision is made. The probability of rejecting H_0 when it is incorrect is $1 - \beta$.

> $1 - \beta$ is called the **power** of a statistical test. Power is the probability of making the correct decision of rejecting an incorrect H_0.

Clearly, it is desirable to have statistical tests with as much power as possible. Because power is simply $1 - \beta$, power is increased by decreasing β, using any of the methods described previously. Chapter 9 presents a more thorough discussion of this important concept.

Figure 8.4 makes one other point of interest: The two types of errors cannot be made at the same time. If you reject H_0, then either you have made a correct decision, or you have made a Type I error. Once you have rejected H_0, you cannot make a Type II error. On the other hand, if you do not reject H_0, then either you have made a correct decision, or you have made a Type II error. Once the decision is made not to reject H_0, a Type I error cannot be made. Again, you should take some comfort in this; although errors can be made, you cannot make more than one of them at a time.

DIRECTIONAL ALTERNATIVE HYPOTHESES

Step 2 of hypothesis testing requires that you formulate a null and an alternative hypothesis. The alternative is always a general hypothesis that contradicts H_0. The difference between the directional and the nondirectional alternative hypotheses is whether or not a direction (< or >) is specified. The nondirectional alternative hypothesis, H_1: $\mu \neq 90$ seconds, contradicts H_0: $\mu = 90$ seconds, but the alternative does not further specify whether μ is greater than 90 seconds or whether μ is less than 90 seconds; it could be either. Because direction is not specified, values of the test statistic forming the rejection region were z scores far from zero on *both* the positive and the negative side.

Directional alternative hypotheses specify a particular direction as an alternative to H_0. For example, a directional alternative for the reading time example is H_1: $\mu < 90$ seconds.

When to Use the Directional Alternative

A directional alternative hypothesis should be used only when you are absolutely uninterested in deviations from H_0 in the direction *opposite* that specified by the alternative. For example, H_1: $\mu < 90$ seconds should be used only when there is absolutely no interest in finding out if $\mu > 90$ seconds. Why? Because if a directional alternative is used, you cannot legitimately ever find deviations from H_0 in the opposite direction.

This claim can be illustrated with the reading time example. Suppose that the dean at GMU reasons that he is interested in the reading program only if it speeds reading; that is, if $\mu < 90$ seconds. If μ is greater than 90 seconds, the dean reasons, he is certainly not going to adopt the program, and so why should he even bother to look for evidence that μ is greater than 90 seconds? How does this sort of reasoning affect the reading time example?

Effect of the Directional Alternative on the Six Steps of Hypothesis Testing

The first step, checking the assumptions, is completely unaffected by the use of a directional alternative. The same assumptions apply, and they are checked in the same way.

The second step, formulating the hypotheses, is of course changed. Based on the dean's contention that he is interested only in the possibility that $\mu < 90$ seconds, and that he is completely uninterested in finding out if $\mu > 90$ seconds, then a directional alternative is called for. Clearly, the appropriate alternative is the one that reflects the dean's interest, namely,

$$H_1: \mu < 90 \text{ seconds}$$

The null hypothesis remains the same, namely,

$$H_0: \mu = 90 \text{ seconds}$$

Step 3 is to construct the sampling distributions. Because H_0 is the same, the sampling distribution specified by H_0 is exactly the same as before. The sampling distributions specified by H_1, are different, however. Only sampling distributions based on means less than 90 seconds are consistent with the directional alternative. These sampling distributions (for M) are illustrated by the light lines in Figure 8.5. Figure 8.6 illustrates the effect of transforming the sampling distributions using z scores (Formula 8.1).

Step 4 consists of setting the significance level (α) and formulating a decision rule consistent with the significance level. Suppose that we set $\alpha = .05$, as before. The rejection region consists of values of the test statistic that are (a) unlikely when H_0 is correct (have a probability as low or lower than α), and (b) are very likely when H_1 is correct. Examination

FIGURE 8.5
Sampling distributions of M for $H_0: \mu = 90$ and the directional alternative, $H_1: \mu < 90$.

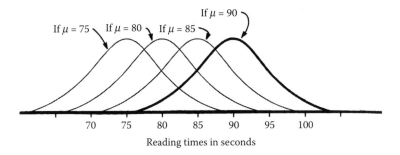

FIGURE 8.6
Sampling distributions of z scores for H_0: $\mu = 90$ and H_1: $\mu < 90$. The $\alpha = .05$ rejection region is also illustrated.

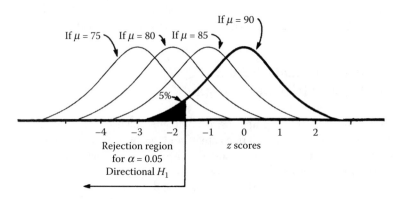

of Figure 8.6 indicates that only values of z less than zero fit the bill. Note that large values of z are unlikely when H_0 is correct, *and* they are unlikely when the directional alternative is correct. Thus, the rejection region consists only of values of z less than zero that have a relative frequency of .05 when H_0 is correct.

The specific values of z in the rejection region are found with the aid of Table A. Enter the body of the table with the area of .05 and find the corresponding z score, -1.65. Remember, the rejection region consists only of z scores less than zero (see Figure 8.6), so the critical z score will be negative; that is, -1.65. The decision rule is

$$\text{Reject } H_0 \text{ if } z \leq -1.65$$

Although we used the same α and H_0 as previously, the decision rule is quite different. First, the rejection region is only on one side of the sampling distribution specified by H_0. Reflecting this, another name for a directional alternative is a **one-tailed alternative.** A nondirectional alternative is sometimes called a **two-tailed alternative.** Be careful with this nomenclature because not all nondirectional tests are two-tailed tests, as we will learn. It is best to use the terms *directional* and *nondirectional*.

A second way in which the decision rule differs from before is in the critical value of z that defines the beginning of the rejection region. With the nondirectional alternative, for $\alpha = .05$, the critical z scores are 1.96 and -1.96 ($z_{\alpha/2}$); with the directional alternative, the critical z score is -1.65. The reason for the difference is that for the directional alternative, the 5% of the z scores that are most consistent with H_1 and least consistent with H_0 are all in one tail.

For the directional alternative, the critical value is z_α, the z score that separates most of the distribution from the α proportion in one tail; which tail, and hence the sign of the z score, depends on the specific directional alternative chosen. Thus, the decision rules for a directional test of hypotheses about μ when σ is known are:

$$\text{for } H_1: \mu > \mu_0 \text{ reject } H_0 \text{ if } z \geq z_\alpha$$

$$\text{for } H_1: \mu < \mu_0 \text{ reject } H_0 \text{ if } z \leq -z_\alpha$$

For the dean's alternative hypothesis, $H_1: \mu < 90$, and $\alpha = .05$, the decision rule is

$$\text{Reject } H_0 \text{ if } z \leq -1.65$$

The fifth step, as before, is to collect a random sample of scores from the population and calculate the test statistic using Formula 8.1. Using the same data as before ($\sigma = 30$, $n = 36$, $M = 5$, $M = 102$),

$$z = \frac{M - \mu_0}{\sigma_M} = \frac{102 - 90}{5} = 2.4$$

the same as previously.

The sixth step is to apply the decision rule. Because 2.4 is not in the rejection region, H_0 cannot be rejected. This is a strange situation. Using a *nondirectional* alternative, a z score of 2.4 would result in rejecting H_0, but with a directional alternative, H_0 cannot be rejected. The problem is that the rejection region must contain values of the test statistic consistent with H_1, and a z score of 2.4 is simply not consistent with the specific, directional alternative $H_1: \mu < 90$.

This is exactly why a directional alternative is dangerous: It commits you to examining deviations from H_0 in only one direction. Thus, the directional alternative should be used only when you are absolutely certain that you are uninterested in deviations in the other direction. Because we are usually interested in finding out if H_0 is incorrect in either direction, the nondirectional alternative is usually used in hypothesis testing.

Do Not Change the Alternative Hypothesis After Examining the Data

It may *seem* that there is an easy solution to the problem of not rejecting H_0 when a directional alternative is used and the test statistic falls into the other tail: Simply switch to the other directional alternative so that H_0 can be rejected. However, switching alternative hypotheses is forbidden. The alternative hypothesis and the rejection region must be set before the test statistic is examined, and then it cannot be changed legitimately.

Switching alternative hypotheses is forbidden because changing the rejection region after examining the data increases α, the probability of a Type I error. The reasoning is as follows: Suppose that H_0 really is correct, so that rejecting H_0 is a Type I error. Furthermore, suppose that if the test statistic falls into the "wrong" rejection region, you switch to the other directional alternative and reject the null hypothesis. What is the real probability of a Type I error? You will reject H_0 if the test statistic is any of the 5% that falls into the original rejection region, *or* if the test statistic is any of the 5% that falls into the other rejection region. Using the or-rule for mutually exclusive events, the total probability of a Type I error is $.05 + .05 = .10$. Thus, even if you say that $\alpha = .05$, the real probability of making a Type I error, if you switch alternatives, is .10. This reasoning holds for just about any sort of switching of alternatives (such as from nondirectional to directional or directional to nondirectional). The point is simple: Do not change the alternative hypothesis after Step 2.

The Directional Alternative and Type II Errors

Because using a directional alternative forces you to stick to a one-tailed rejection region, why should it ever be used? When H_0 is incorrect, using the correct directional alternative reduces β (and increases power) compared to using the nondirectional alternative. However, this method of reducing β should be used only when you are honestly and completely uninterested in rejecting H_0 if the test statistic happens to fall into the other tail. The relationship between the alternative hypothesis and power is developed more formally in Chapter 9.

A SECOND EXAMPLE

For a second example, let's return to the Smoking Study conducted by Dr. Baker. One of the variables that Dr. Baker's team measured was each participant's height (in inches). Smoking has been identified as a risk factor for bone health, especially in women. Osteoporosis is a condition where bones weaken and are more likely to fracture. Again, this condition is especially problematic in women. If bone health is affected by smoking, are women smokers shorter than other women?

Using the M of the heights of the women in Dr. Baker's smoking study, we can test the hypothesis that women smokers are shorter than nonsmokers.

Step 1: Check the Assumptions

One population assumption is that the population (of heights) is normally distributed, or that the sample size is large enough such that the Central Limit Theorem comes into play (amazing fact number 3). Although we have only limited information about the population distribution, the sample size is large enough to guarantee that the sampling distribution of the test statistic (in this case, z score) is virtually normally distributed.

The other population assumption is that σ, the standard deviation of the population, is known. Fortunately, the National Institutes of Health, the Centers for Disease Control and Prevention, and the National Center for Health Statistics conduct studies (like the National Health and Nutrition Examination Surveys or NHANES) that give us a very close approximation of σ for measures like the heights of adult women (18–69 years old). According to the report "Anthropometric Reference Data from Children and Adults: U.S. Population, 1999–2002" from the Division of Health and Nutrition Examination Surveys, $\sigma = 3.28$ inches.

The data assumption is that the data are measured on an interval or ratio scale. This requirement is met because height is measured using a ratio scale.

Lastly, the sampling assumption that the data are obtained using independent (within-sample) random sampling, is, technically, not met. Dr. Baker did not acquire his sample using independent random sampling. Rather, he used volunteers, and only ones from Wisconsin, thereby violating the random sampling assumption. We will proceed with the example for illustrative purposes and talk about limitations of this in later sections of the book.

Step 2: Generate H_0 and H_1

The null hypothesis must specify a particular value for the population mean of heights of women smokers. Also, it should specify a value that is "no change" from a standard or theoretical value. For this example, the NHANES report indicates that the average height of women in the United States is 65.00 inches; thus, a reasonable null hypothesis is

$$H_0: \mu = 65.00 \text{ inches}$$

This null says that women who smoke have an average height of 65.00; in effect, smoking does not affect height.

Formulating H_1 is a little more difficult. As usual, we must decide whether to use a directional or nondirectional alternative. The nondirectional alternative would be $H_1: \mu \neq 65.00$ inches. This alternative is acceptable, but is it best in this specific circumstance? If smoking is a risk factor for decreased bone density and osteoporosis, then smoking would presumably be associated with shorter women. Thus, we are interested in whether smoking makes women shorter, not taller. Given this logic, a preferable alternative is

$$H_1: \mu < 65.00 \text{ inches}$$

or that women who smoke are less than 65.00 inches tall.

Step 3: Generate Sampling Distributions of the Test Statistic

The test statistic is the z score given in Formula 8.1. As in the previous example, we will begin by formulating the sampling distribution for M, and then convert that sampling distribution into a distribution of z scores. When H_0 is correct, the sampling distribution of sample means has

1. $\mu_M = 65.00$
2. $\sigma_M = \sigma / \sqrt{n} = 3.28 / \sqrt{352} = .17$
3. a normal distribution (because the sample size, $n = 352$, is large).

The distribution is illustrated by the dark curve in Figure 8.7.

If the directional alternative is correct, then the Ms would tend to be less than 65.00 inches. The sampling distributions of Ms consistent with H_1 are illustrated by the light lines in Figure 8.7.

Remember, each distribution in Figure 8.7 consists of many separate Ms. Imagine taking all of those Ms and running them through Formula 8.1.

$$z = \frac{M - \mu_0}{\sigma_M} = \frac{M - 65.00}{.17}$$

The results are the sampling distributions illustrated in Figure 8.8.

FIGURE 8.7
Sampling distributions of *M* for H_0: μ = 65.00 inches and the directional alternative, H_1: μ < 65.00 inches.

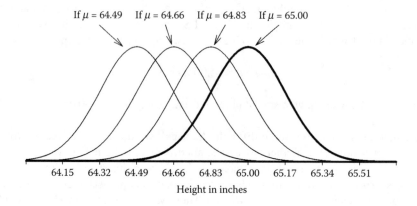

FIGURE 8.8
Sampling distributions of *z* scores for H_0: μ = 65.00 inches H_1: μ < 65.00 inches. Also illustrated is the α = .01 rejection region.

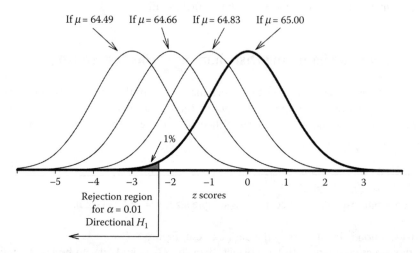

We can now see what the two hypotheses predict about the *z* score (test statistic) that we will obtain from our sample of 352 heights of women smokers. The null hypothesis predicts that the *z* score will be close to 0.0. The alternative hypothesis predicts that the *z* score will be much less than 0.0.

Step 4: Set the Significance Level and the Decision Rule

You may reason that the test has a small probability of a Type II error because the sample size is large and a directional alternative is used. In this case, you may wish to decrease the probability of a Type I error (α) without great risk of inflating the probability of a Type II error (β). Based on this reasoning, set $\alpha = .01$.

The formula for the decision rule for the directional alternative is

$$\text{Reject } H_0 \text{ if } z \leq -z_\alpha$$

Because $\alpha = .01$, the critical value ($z_{.01}$) is the z score that has .01 of the distribution below it. Using Table A, the critical value is -2.33, and decision rule is

$$\text{Reject } H_0 \text{ if } z \leq -2.33$$

Thus, the rejection region consists of those values of the test statistic that are (a) the 1% least likely when H_0 is correct and (b) very likely when H_1 is correct. These are just the z scores less than -2.33.

Step 5: Sample From the Population and Compute the Test Statistic

The sample of women smokers from Dr. Baker's study included 352 heights. Because that is far too many to reproduce here, we have included all of those heights in a file on the data CD accompanying this book. From these data, $M = 64.80$.

The test statistic is calculated by using Formula 8.1. It is

$$z = \frac{M - \mu_0}{\sigma_M} = \frac{64.80 - 65.00}{.17} = -1.18$$

Step 6: Apply the Decision Rule and Draw Conclusions

The null hypothesis cannot be rejected because the test statistic, -1.18, is not in the rejection region. Of course, this does not mean that the null is proven correct, only that there is not enough evidence to demonstrate that it is incorrect.

The sample mean, 64.80, is in the range of probable Ms when H_1 is correct, but it is also within the range specified by H_0 ($\mu = 65.00$).

On the other hand, the decision not to reject H_0 might be a Type II error. For example, suppose that $\mu = 64.66$ inches (see Figure 8.7, the population mean of women smokers is truly 64.66). In this case, a sample mean of 64.80 would not be that unusual. The point is, when H_0 is not rejected, it is difficult to know if a correct decision has been made, or if a Type II error has been made.

Finally, keep in mind that the conclusion holds only for the limited population that was sampled: the population of female participants in the Smoking Study.

A THIRD EXAMPLE

A research psychologist is using monkeys to study the development of aggression. She knows that orphaned monkeys raised in isolation are very aggressive. In fact, when placed in a cage with another monkey for a 30-minute observation period, an isolation-raised orphan will spend an average of 17 minutes (with $\sigma = 8$ minutes) engaged in aggressive behavior. The researcher's question is whether or not exposing the orphaned monkeys to social stimulation will affect their aggressive behavior.

Her plan is to take a random sample of 16 orphaned monkeys and to put each monkey into a social group for 1 hour a day. After 6 months she will record, for each of the 16 monkeys, the number of minutes spent in aggressive behavior during a 30-minute observation period. She will use this measurement as an aggression score. Will the orphaned monkeys exposed to social stimulation be more or less aggressive than orphaned monkeys raised in isolation? In statistical terms, is the mean of the population of aggression scores for orphaned monkeys exposed to social stimulation different from the mean of the population of aggression scores for orphaned monkeys raised in isolation?

Step 1: Check the Assumptions

We do not know if the population of aggression scores for the socially stimulated monkeys is normally distributed. However, as long as the population is not extremely nonnormal, the Central Limit Theorem guarantees that a sample size of 16 will produce a sampling distribution of sample means that is virtually normally distributed (see Figure 7.3 on p. 132).

We will assume that the standard deviation of the population of aggression scores for socially stimulated monkeys is 8 minutes, the same as the standard deviation for the population of isolated monkeys. Note carefully: Outside of a textbook example, this assumption would be foolish. If you do not actually know σ, use the *t* test described in Chapter 12.

The sampling assumption is that the aggression scores are obtained by using independent (within-sample) random sampling. This assumption will be guaranteed by the procedures used in Step 5.

The data assumption is that the scores are measured using an interval or ratio scale. This assumption is met because the aggression scores (time spent aggressing) are measured using a ratio scale.

Step 2: Formulate the Hypotheses

The most reasonable hypotheses are:

$$H_0: \mu = 17 \text{ minutes}$$

$$H_1: \mu \neq 17 \text{ minutes}$$

The psychologist probably suspects (or hopes) that social stimulation will reduce the mean of the aggression scores. Nonetheless, because she is interested in finding out if social stimulation has *any* effect on the mean, the nondirectional alternative is most appropriate.

FIGURE 8.9
Sampling distribution of z scores for H_0: $\mu = 17$ and H_1: $\mu \neq 17$. Also illustrated is the $\alpha = .05$ rejection region.

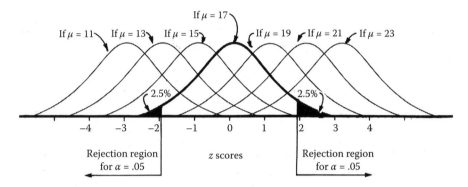

Step 3: The Sampling Distributions

The test statistic is the z score from Formula 8.1.

$$z = \frac{M - \mu_0}{\sigma_M} = \frac{M - 17}{2}$$

If the null hypothesis is correct, then the most likely values for z are around zero. On the other hand, if the alternative hypothesis is correct, then the most likely values for z are large positive numbers and large negative numbers. The distributions are illustrated in Figure 8.9.

Step 4: Set the Significance Level and the Decision Rule

The psychologist decides to use the standard, .05, significance level. For a nondirectional alternative hypothesis, the decision rule is

$$\text{Reject } H_0 \text{ if } z \geq z_{\alpha/2} \text{ or } z \leq -z_{\alpha/2}$$

For $\alpha = .05$, $z_{\alpha/2} = z_{.025} = 1.96$. Thus

$$\text{Reject } H_0 \text{ if } z \geq 1.96 \text{ or } z \leq -1.96$$

Step 5: Randomly Sample and Compute the Statistic

The psychologist selects a random sample of 16 orphaned monkeys and exposes each to social stimulation for an hour a day for 6 months. At the end of the 6-month period, she measures the aggression score for each monkey. Suppose that $M = 11$ minutes.

Because $\sigma = 8$ and $n = 16$,

$$\sigma_M = \sigma/\sqrt{n} = 8/\sqrt{16} = 2$$

Then, computing z,

$$z = \frac{M - \mu_0}{\sigma_M} = \frac{11 - 17}{2} = -3.0$$

Step 6: Decide and Draw Conclusions

Because the z score is in the rejection region, the null hypothesis is rejected. There is enough evidence to conclude that the mean of the population of aggression scores for monkeys exposed to social stimulation is less than 17 minutes. Apparently, social stimulation reduces aggression.

Results such as these have important implications. From a humanitarian point of view, the results imply that orphaned monkeys should not be isolated. To the extent that monkeys and humans are similar, the results also have implications for human development (strictly speaking, however, there is no statistical justification for generalizing the results to humans).

The psychologist might have made a Type I error in rejecting H_0. However, the probability of a Type I error is small (.05). Because H_0 was rejected, she could not have made a Type II error.

SUMMARY

Hypothesis testing is a complex process. Breaking it down into small steps makes it easier to understand how it works. With practice, each of the steps, and then the whole procedure, becomes clear. That practice should begin with trying to understand how each step is related to successive steps, and why each step is necessary in hypothesis testing. Your understanding of hypothesis testing will be complete when you understand how errors are made, and how the probability of making errors can be reduced.

Although the six steps are the same for all hypothesis-testing procedures, in this chapter the six steps were applied only to the specific procedure of testing hypotheses about a population mean when the standard deviation (σ) of that population is known. Later chapters will demonstrate how to apply the six steps in situations that are less constrained. Table 8.1 summarizes the procedure for testing hypotheses about μ when σ is known.

It should be clear by now that hypothesis testing is not a procedure that can be executed in cookbook fashion without any thought. The extent to which the procedure is successful and you learn something from your data depends on critical thinking at almost every

---

TABLE 8.1

Testing Hypotheses About μ When σ Is Known

1. **Assumptions:**

   Population assumptions:
   a. The population is normally distributed, or the sample size is large.
   b. The population standard deviation, σ, is known.

   Sampling assumption:
   A random sample is obtained using independent (within-sample) random sampling.

   Data assumption:
   The data are measured using an interval or a ratio scale.

2. **Hypotheses:**

$$H_0: \mu = \mu_0$$

   where μ_0 is a specific value.

   Alternative hypotheses available:

$$H_1: \mu \neq \mu_0$$
$$H_1: \mu > \mu_0$$
$$H_1: \mu < \mu_0$$

3. **Test statistic and its sampling distribution:**

$$z = \frac{M - \mu_0}{\sigma_M}, \sigma_M = \sigma/\sqrt{n}$$

   When H_0 is correct, likely values of z are near 0.0. When H_1 is correct, likely values for z are discrepant from 0.0.

4. **Decision rule:**
   For $H_1: \mu \neq \mu_0$

$$\text{Reject } H_0 \text{ when } z \geq z_{\alpha/2} \text{ or } z \leq -z_{\alpha/2}$$

   where $z_{\alpha/2}$ is the z score that has $\alpha/2$ of the distribution above it.
   For $H_1: \mu > \mu_0$

$$\text{Reject } H_0 \text{ when } z \geq z_\alpha$$

   For $H_1: \mu < \mu_0$

$$\text{Reject } H_0 \text{ when } z \leq -z_\alpha$$

   where z_α is the z score that has α proportion of distribution above it.

5. **Sample and compute z:**
   Randomly sample from the population and compute the test statistic.

6. **Decide and draw conclusions:**
   If H_0 is rejected, then conclude that the mean of the population is different from μ_0. If H_0 is *not* rejected, do *not* conclude that it is correct.

---

step. For example, if the assumptions are not satisfied, then there is no justification for the conclusions you might draw, and the only guarantee that the assumptions are met is the one you provide by a careful examination of the situation. Formulating the hypotheses is, of course, of utmost importance. The hypotheses are the questions you apply to the data, and the form of the hypotheses determines exactly what you will learn from the data.

Setting the significance level, α, is important because it determines directly the probability of a Type I error, and indirectly it is one of the components that affects the probability of a Type II error. Often, students (and professionals) will automatically set $\alpha = .05$, the standard level. Remember, however, that the choice is yours. You must weigh for yourself the relative costs of Type I and Type II errors in deciding exactly where to set α.

The fifth step—obtaining a random sample from the population—is often the hardest step to complete successfully. As discussed in Chapter 5, true random sampling from a population requires careful planning and execution. Once the sample is obtained, however, it is often a trivial matter to compute the test statistic.

The sixth step is deciding whether or not to reject H_0. If the test statistic falls into the rejection region, then reject H_0. Otherwise, conclude that there is not enough evidence to decide (do not conclude that H_0 is true). Remember, whatever the decision, there is statistical justification only for conclusions about the specific population from which you randomly sampled.

Most people who use inferential statistics have goals other than simply stating a fact about a population. They also want to know the implications of the facts (Should a reading program be started at GMU? What is the best way to reduce aggression?), and they want to use those facts to improve the world in which they live. The statistics provide the facts; it is up to you to apply them to improve your world.

EXERCISES

Terms   *Define these new terms and symbols.*

logic of hypothesis testing	critical value
assumptions	statistically significant
null hypothesis	Type I error
alternative hypothesis	Type II error
directional alternative	power
nondirectional alternative	p value
one-tailed test	H_0
two-tailed test	H_1
parametric hypothesis testing	α
nonparametric hypothesis testing	β
test statistic	μ_0
rejection region	$z_{\alpha/2}$
significance level	z_α
decision rule	

Questions   *Answer the following questions.*

†1. Assume that you are testing hypotheses about a population mean when σ is known, that the alternative hypothesis is nondirectional, and that all of the sampling distributions have been transformed by using Formula 8.1. Formulate the decision rule for each of the following significance levels: .04, .10, .002.

2. Which of the decision rules in Question 1 will produce the largest probability of a Type I error? Which of the decision rules will produce the largest probability of a Type II error? Without changing the significance levels or the alternative hypotheses, how could you attempt to roughly equate the probability of a Type II error in all of the cases?

†3. For each of the decision rules in Question 1, what decisions would you make if the test statistics were −3.0, −2.0, −1.5, 0.1, 1.92, 2.25, 4.0?

4. Answer Questions 1 and 3, assuming that a directional alternative (specifying a mean greater than that given by the null hypothesis) is being used.

5. Explain why it is not legitimate to switch from a directional to a nondirectional alternative even though the rejection region seems to shrink from α to $\alpha/2$ in each tail.

6. Why must the null hypothesis state a specific value for μ?

7. A student testing his first hypothesis made sure that all of the assumptions were satisfied, formulated null and nondirectional hypotheses, set $\alpha = .05$, randomly sampled (with $n = 50$) from the population, and accurately computed the test statistic. Nonetheless, the student was unable to reject the null hypothesis. Given that the student did everything correctly, how can this happen?

8. The student in Question 7 was disappointed with his results, and so he took another random sample of the same size from the same population and still was unable to reject the null hypothesis. Then he took another sample with the same outcome. In all, the student took 100 random samples (each of size 50). Five of the test statistics fell into the rejection region, and so he concluded that H_0 is incorrect.
   a. What is wrong with the student's procedures?
   b. Why is the evidence not only insufficient to reject H_0, but is very strong evidence for the truth of H_0?

9. Because of a mix-up, two laboratory assistants tested the same null and alternative hypotheses using the same α. They used different samples of 100 observations each, although they both obtained their samples by randomly sampling from the same population. One assistant was able to reject the null hypothesis; the other was not.
   a. How can it happen that one assistant can reject the null and the other not?
   b. Without collecting any more data, what can be done to provide the best test of the null hypothesis? (*Hint:* Consider how to conduct a powerful test.)

10. Why can't you prove the null hypothesis by hypothesis testing?

For each of the following questions, determine if the procedure for testing hypotheses about a population mean can be used. If it can, then formulate and test the hypotheses. After testing the hypotheses,

   a. *state whether or not you could be making a Type I or a Type II error.*
   b. *describe the population about which you made an inference.*
   c. *state any conclusions that you draw about the results.*

If the procedure cannot be applied, then state why not.

†11. A social psychologist wishes to determine if exposure to favorable information about a stranger influences the degree of interaction with the stranger. A random sample of 60 college sophomores attending GMU is recruited for the experiment. Each student reads a short favorable description about another student (the

stranger). When the stranger is introduced, the experimenter measures the amount of time the student spends interacting with the stranger. From previous experiments, the psychologist knows that without reading favorable information, sophomores spend an average of 3.5 minutes interacting with the stranger. For these 60 sophomores, $M = 3.8$ minutes, $s = 4$ minutes. Assume that $\sigma = 5$ minutes.

12. A physiological psychologist is investigating mechanisms of weight control in rats. She knows that the average 10-month-old white rat in her laboratory weighs 450 grams with a standard deviation of 60 grams, and that the distribution of weights approaches a normal distribution. She takes a random sample of 16 white rats and surgically removes the brain structures hypothesized to regulate weight. When the rats are 10 months old, she weighs them and finds that $M = 490$ grams, $s = 54$ grams. Assume that $\sigma = 60$ grams. Is the mean of the population of weights of rats that have this particular surgical procedure different from the mean of the population of weights of other 10-month-old rats in the laboratory?

13. A psychologist is attempting to determine if attending a preschool in New York City has any effect on aggressiveness. She knows that the mean aggressiveness score for children in New York City who have not attended preschool is 15.3 on a scale of 1 to 25. She randomly selects 100 children from among those attending preschool and measures their aggressiveness by rating each child using the aggressiveness scale. The mean rating of these 100 children is 13.75, $s = 5.5$. Is the population of aggressiveness scores of children attending preschool different from the population of aggressiveness scores of children who do not attend preschool?

14. An anthropologist is quite certain that the citizens of a particular country do not average more than 12 years of formal education. She wants to know whether there is evidence to claim that the mean is less than 12. She takes a random sample of 100 citizens and determines for each the number of years of formal education. She finds that $M = 8.6$ and $s = 8$. Assume that $\sigma = 8.8$. If her $\alpha = .01$, what should she decide?

Power

*T*he most pleasing outcome when testing a hypothesis is to reject an incorrect null hypothesis—a type of correct decision. Certainly, it is better to make a correct decision than an error (either a Type I or a Type II error). And, rejecting an incorrect null hypothesis is more pleasing than not rejecting a correct null hypothesis (the other type of correct decision). The reason, as we learned in Chapter 8, is that when the null is not rejected, we cannot draw any strong conclusions; the best we can do is the rather insipid "there isn't enough evidence to reject the null."

The moral of this analysis is that we should try to maximize the probability of rejecting incorrect null hypotheses. Of course, that does not mean that we should always reject null hypotheses. Some of the nulls will be correct, and rejecting one of them would be a Type I error. We want to maximize the probability that, when we run up against an incorrect null hypothesis, we will reject it. The probability of rejecting an incorrect H_0 is called power (see Figure 8.4 on p. 161).

This chapter is divided into four major sections. In the first section, we develop a technique for calculating power using z scores. In the second section, this technique is used to mathematically and graphically demonstrate factors that affect power. Although this section uses computational techniques relevant to testing hypotheses about a single population mean when σ is known, the conclusions reached apply to all hypothesis-testing situations. The third section describes practical methods of power analysis that can be used to enhance your own research. These practical methods include computational formulas for calculating power and for estimating the sample size needed to obtain a desired level of power. In the final section, we discuss the situations in which power analyses are useful.

CALCULATING POWER USING z SCORES

The calculation of power is easier to understand within the framework of a specific example. A school psychologist knows that the mean IQ score of all students in the United States is 100 (because of the way the test is constructed and scored), and that $\sigma = 16$. She is most concerned, however, with children in her district, where there are significant environmental pollutants that may be affecting intelligence. She plans to take a random sample of the IQ scores of 64 children in her district and use the data in the sample to test

$$H_0: \mu = 100$$

$$H_1: \mu < 100,$$

where μ stands for the mean IQ of all the children in the psychologist's district.

The situation seems to meet all of the assumptions for testing hypotheses about a population mean when σ is known. Namely, the sample size is large enough to virtually guarantee normality of the sampling distribution, σ is known, the sample will be randomly selected from the population, and the IQ scores, if not exactly measured on an interval scale, are close to being interval (see Chapter 1 for the discussion of "in-between" scales).

The null hypothesis states a specific value for the mean of the population of IQ scores of children in the district. Selection of this value was not arbitrary. First, it is a standard value in that it is the mean of the population of IQ scores in the United States. Second, it is an important value, because if this H_0 is rejected in favor of the alternative, then the psychologist will know that something is wrong, namely, that the children in her district have IQ scores lower than the national average.

Choice of the alternative hypothesis was more difficult. The directional alternative implies that the psychologist is interested in detecting deviations from H_0 in only one direction: lower scores. Certainly, it is important to be able to detect this sort of deviation. But would the psychologist really be uninterested in finding out that the mean IQ score in her district was higher than the national average? Perhaps the environmental pollutants actually enhance intelligence. On reflection, however, she decides that this possibility is so remote that it is not worthy of her consideration, and she opts for the directional alternative.

The test statistic is the z score computed using Formula 8.1 on p. 147. The σ_M required for that formula can be found by applying Amazing Fact Number 2,

$$\sigma_M = \sigma / \sqrt{n} = 16 / \sqrt{64} = 2$$

$$z = \frac{M - \mu_0}{\sigma_M} = \frac{M - 100}{2}$$

The sampling distributions of the test statistic for testing these hypotheses are illustrated in Figure 9.1. This figure is different from those used in Chapter 8 in that the sampling distributions of M and z are represented in the same figure. This can be done because both have the same shape (normal distributions). To use the figure as the sampling distribution of M, read the Ms off the abscissa labeled "M." To use the figure as the sampling distribution of z, use the abscissa labeled "z relative to H_0: $\mu = 100$." In the figure, the dark curve represents the sampling distribution when H_0 is correct. The light curves represent the sampling distributions when H_1 is correct.

The next step for our psychologist is to set the significance level and to formulate the decision rule. Let us suppose that the psychologist chooses $\alpha = .05$. The rejection region will consist of those z scores that (a) are the 5% that are least likely when H_0 is correct and (b) are very likely when H_1 is correct. Examining Figure 9.1 indicates that these z scores are just those in the lower tail of the distribution specified by H_0. Using Table A, the critical value (z_α) associated with the lower 5% is -1.65. Thus the decision rule is

Reject H_0 if $z \le -1.65$

At this point, the psychologist might begin to worry. She is planning to commit much time and energy to this project, but she does not know if there is a reasonable chance that she will learn anything. That is, if H_0 really is wrong, what is the probability that she will reject it? In other words, what is the power of the statistical procedure? If power is small (.20, for example), then she is unlikely to reject H_0 even if it is wrong. In this case, she would be foolish to continue without attempting to increase the power.

FIGURE 9.1
Sampling distributions for H_0: $\mu = 100$ and the directional alternative, H_1: $\mu < 100$. Also illustrated is the $\alpha = .05$ rejection region.

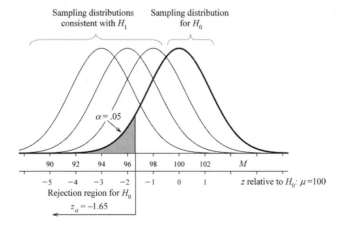

The Specific Alternative

Power is the probability of rejecting H_0 when H_0 is incorrect. In order to reject H_0, the test statistic must fall into the rejection region. Therefore, power is the probability that the test statistic falls into the rejection region when H_1 is correct, not H_0. But which of the H_1 distributions should be used to calculate this probability? $\mu = 94$, $\mu = 92$, $\mu = 98$? *Whenever power (or β) is calculated, you must propose a specific alternative hypothesis.* For example, the school psychologist might propose the specific alternative hypothesis (H_s) that the mean of the population is 96. In symbols,

$$H_s: \mu = 96$$

The specific alternative hypothesis has three characteristics.

1. Like H_0, H_s is always specific.
2. Unlike H_0, H_s is always consistent with H_1.
3. H_s always proposes a reasonable value for the population parameter. That is, the value should be chosen only after consideration of relevant theories, other data, or common sense.

How does $H_s: \mu = 96$ stand up against these criteria? Clearly, this alternative is specific (Criterion 1), and it is consistent with $H_1: \mu < 100$ (Criterion 2). In regard to Criterion 3, H_s proposes a reasonable value for μ: IQ scores generally have a mean of 100, a standard deviation of 16, and are positive. Thus, 96 is certainly more reasonable than, say, −15. It is also reasonable in that it is unlikely that a group of functioning, noninstitutionalized children would have a mean IQ much below 96. Now we can translate the question, "What is the power of the statistical test," into "What is the probability of rejecting H_0 if μ really equals 96?"

Calculating Power

Calculating power using z scores involves three steps, the first of which we have already completed:

1. Specify H_s.
2. Find the values of M that constitute the rejection region.
3. Calculate the probability of obtaining one of these Ms based on the sampling distribution of H_s (for example, the probability of obtaining an M in the rejection region when $\mu = 96$).

The result of the third step is power. It is the probability that H_0 will be rejected (because the M will result in a z score in the rejection region) when H_s is correct, not H_0.

Reference to Figure 9.2 should help you to follow the steps. The figure illustrates the sampling distribution assuming H_0 is correct (the dark curve), the sampling distributions assuming H_1 is correct (the light curves), and the sampling distribution for H_s (the dashed

FIGURE 9.2

Power of the statistical test described on the right of the figure.

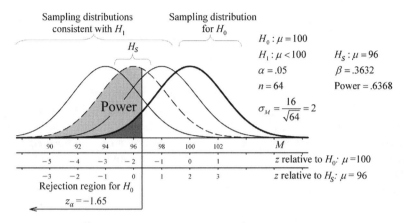

curve). These sampling distributions may be treated as distributions of either *M* or *z*, depending on which abscissa is used. Note that there are two *z*-score abscissas. The upper one labels the *z* scores relative to the mean as specified by H_0 ($\mu_0 = 100$), and the lower one labels the *z* scores relative to the mean specified by H_s. It is convenient to have both when calculating power.

Power corresponds to the shaded area in Figure 9.2. That area is the probability, *when H_s is correct,* that a to-be-taken random sample will produce a test statistic in the rejection region. Note that α is an area under the sampling distribution corresponding to H_0, because it is the probability of falling into the rejection region *when H_0 is correct.*

Step 2 is to find the values of *M* that constitute the rejection region. The rejection region consists of *z* scores ≤ -1.65 (as stated in the decision rule). The *M*s corresponding to these *z* scores can be found by solving a reverse *z*-score problem as in Chapter 4. To review, if

$$z = \frac{M - \mu_0}{\sigma_M}$$

then by algebraic manipulation

$$M = \mu_0 + (z)(\sigma_M)$$

Note the use of μ_0 in this step. We need to convert from a *z* score originally based on μ_0 back to *M*. Thus, the *M* corresponding to a *z* score of -1.65 is

$$M = 100 - 1.65 \times 2 = 96.7$$

For any $M \leq 96.7$, the school psychologist would reject H_0, because the corresponding *z* score would be in the rejection region.

Step 3 is to calculate the probability of obtaining an $M \leq 96.7$ (and thus reject H_0), *assuming that the specific alternative is correct.* What is the probability of obtaining an $M \leq 96.7$ when $\mu = 96$? The z score is

$$z = \frac{M - \mu_s}{\sigma_M} = \frac{96.7 - 96}{2} = .35$$

Note the use of 96 for μ_s: This z score computes the location of 96.7 relative to the mean specified by H_s. Using Table A, the proportion of z scores that are less than .35 is .6368. Thus, the power of this statistical test is .6368. Stated differently, the probability is .6368 that the educational psychologist will be able to reject the incorrect H_0, *if μ really equals 96.*

Is this a reasonable amount of power? Should the educational psychologist continue? Certainly, she has a fighting chance of rejecting H_0 (assuming it is incorrect). However, there is also a substantial probability that the psychologist will make a Type II error and fail to reject H_0. The probability of a Type II error (β) is $1 -$ power, or in this case $1 - .6368 = .3632$. Therefore, even if H_s: $\mu = 96$ is correct, there is about a one in three chance that the psychologist will not be able to reject H_0. We turn next to factors that affect power, some of which can be directly manipulated to increase power.

FACTORS AFFECTING POWER

Demonstrations of how factors (such as the value of α) affect power are presented in this section. Although there are some computations, for the most part the major benefit comes from careful study of Figures 9.3 through 9.6. Each of these figures illustrates how power is affected by various changes in the hypothesis-testing situation. The details are worked out only for testing hypotheses about a single population mean. Nonetheless, the conclusions regarding factors that affect power apply to all hypothesis-testing procedures.

α and β Are Inversely Related; α and Power Are Directly Related

As α increases β decreases. But, because power $= 1 - \beta$, as α increases there is also an increase in power. Some insight into this relationship can be obtained by studying Figure 9.3.

The top panel illustrates the IQ example, but with $\alpha = .01$. In the figure, α corresponds to the area that is darkly shaded, and power corresponds to the lightly shaded area. Because we have H_s (the first step in computing power), all that remains are the z-score problems.

Step 2. The critical value for the $\alpha = .01$ directional test is a z score of -2.33. The M values corresponding to the rejection region are values of $M \leq 95.33$.

Step 3. Given H_s: $\mu = 96$, the z score corresponding to 95.33 is $(95.33 - 96)/2 = -.34$, and the probability of obtaining z scores smaller than $-.34$ (the lightly shaded portion of the figure) is .3669. Thus, power $= .3669$.

FIGURE 9.3
Relationship between α and power. From top to bottom, α (indicated by the dark shading) increases and power (indicated by light shading) increases.

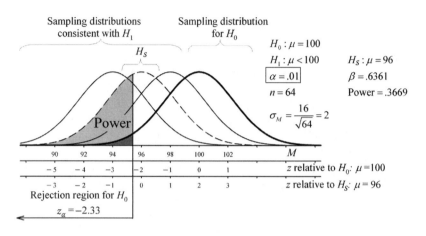

$H_0 : \mu = 100$
$H_1 : \mu < 100$ $H_S : \mu = 96$
$\boxed{\alpha = .01}$ $\beta = .6361$
$n = 64$ Power $= .3669$

$$\sigma_M = \frac{16}{\sqrt{64}} = 2$$

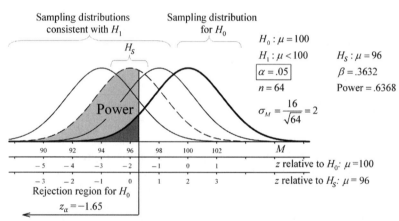

$H_0 : \mu = 100$
$H_1 : \mu < 100$ $H_S : \mu = 96$
$\boxed{\alpha = .05}$ $\beta = .3632$
$n = 64$ Power $= .6368$

$$\sigma_M = \frac{16}{\sqrt{64}} = 2$$

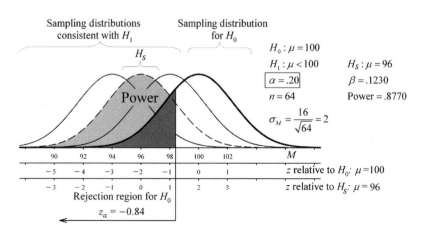

$H_0 : \mu = 100$
$H_1 : \mu < 100$ $H_S : \mu = 96$
$\boxed{\alpha = .20}$ $\beta = .1230$
$n = 64$ Power $= .8770$

$$\sigma_M = \frac{16}{\sqrt{64}} = 2$$

The power of the situation illustrated in the top panel is not very satisfying. If the educational psychologist were to follow through with data collection, then she would have only about a one chance in three of rejecting H_0 if $\mu = 96$.

Now, examine what happens to power as α increases. In the middle panel of Figure 9.3, the situation is exactly the same except that α has been increased to .05 (as in the original presentation of the IQ score example). Note that the darkly shaded area corresponding to α has increased, reflecting the larger rejection region. Because the rejection region is larger, the probability of obtaining an M in the rejection region has also increased. The overall result is that power has increased from .3669 when $\alpha = .01$ to .6368 when $\alpha = .05$.

The final panel in Figure 9.3 illustrates the effect of another increase in α, this time to .20. Again, the rejection region increases in size corresponding to the increase in α. The larger rejection region increases the chances of obtaining an M in the rejection region, and power increases to .8770.

We can learn a number of lessons from Figure 9.3. The first is that even in apparently reasonable situations (for example, the top panel) power can be very small. Because of the low power, the educational psychologist is likely to make a Type II error and miss the very important fact that the mean IQ is below the national average.

The second lesson to be learned from Figure 9.3 is that modest increases in α can produce sizeable increases in power. Note that the increase in power between the top and middle panels (an increase of .27) is purchased with only a modest increase in α (an increase of .04). Although the size of the increase in power gained by increasing α depends on the specific situation, it may be worth considering.

Power and Variability

From a practical standpoint, one of the most important relationships is that between power and variability. As the variability of the sampling distributions decreases, power increases. The relationship is of practical importance because you can decrease variability in three ways. First, variability can be decreased by standardizing data collection procedures to avoid variability produced by the measurement process. For example, the educational psychologist could decrease variability by collecting each IQ using the same IQ test, testing each child in the same room at the same time of day, using the same tester for each child, and so on. Second, variability in the sampling distributions can be decreased by increasing the sample size (remember Amazing Fact Number 2). Third, variability can sometimes be decreased by using dependent sampling, a procedure that will be discussed in Chapter 15.

Figure 9.4 illustrates the effect of decreasing variability by increasing the sample size. In the top panel, a relatively small sample size of 16 is used. Applying Amazing Fact Number 2 generated a value of 4 for σ_M. Note that because the distributions are so variable (fat), they overlap to a large extent, and this reduces power. Indeed, power in the top panel is only .2578.

In the middle panel, the sample size is increased to 64 (our standard example), and power increases to .6368.

In the bottom panel, the sample size has been increased to 256. Note that the standard deviation of the sampling distributions is one fourth that of the top panel. In this case, power is much greater. It may be difficult and/or costly to increase your sample size. We will discuss in a later section of this chapter how to select a sample size.

FIGURE 9.4
Relationship between variability of the sampling distribution and power. From top to bottom, as σ_M decreases (by increasing the sample size, n), power increases.

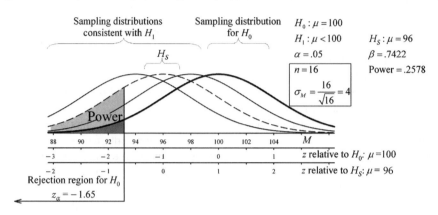

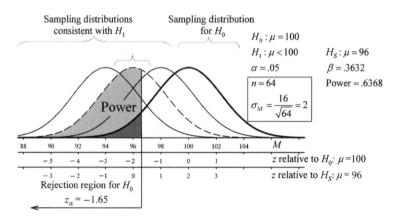

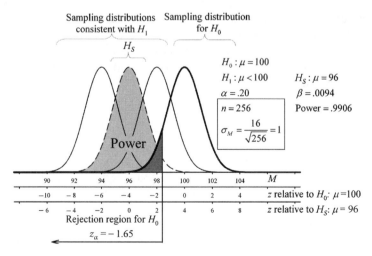

Power and the Alternative Hypothesis

The top panel in Figure 9.5 illustrates an unfortunate situation. A directional test is being used (H_1: $\mu > 100$), but it is on the opposite side of H_0 as the True value of μ (represented by H_s). As usual, α corresponds to the darkly shaded area. Power would correspond to the lightly shaded area, but there is so little power that it does not appear in the figure. Clearly, use of the directional alternative hypothesis can be dangerous!

The middle panel is the standard case with a power of .6368.

The bottom panel illustrates power in the nondirectional, two-tailed situation. Power, corresponding to the shaded area of the figure, is .5160.

Figure 9.5 teaches two lessons. First, the top panel illustrates a danger associated with the directional alternative. If you pick the "wrong" directional alternative, there is almost no chance that you will reject H_0 when it is wrong. Repeating the caution from Chapter 8: Use the directional alternative only when you have absolutely no interest in detecting a deviation from H_0 in the other direction.

The second lesson is that power is greater when using the appropriate directional alternative (middle panel) than when using the nondirectional alternative (bottom panel). This second lesson can be abused. To "gain power," an unscrupulous investigator may switch from a nondirectional alternative to a directional alternative after examining the data (thereby avoiding the possibility of picking the wrong directional alternative). As discussed in Chapter 8, however, switching alternative hypotheses after the data have been examined has the unfortunate effect of increasing α beyond the stated value.

Power and Parametric Tests

When the assumptions of both parametric and nonparametric tests are met, then the parametric test is generally more powerful than the nonparametric test. Typically, parametric tests require that the population (about which you are going to make an inference) meets various assumptions, such as being normally distributed. Also, parametric tests generally require interval or ratio data. Most nonparametric tests do not have either of these requirements. The extra power of parametric tests results, in part, from taking advantage of the extra information (normality, equal intervals) to make more accurate decisions. Why then are nonparametric tests used at all? Because when the parametric assumptions are not met, then nonparametric tests are more likely to result in correct decisions. We will discuss various nonparametric tests in Part III.

Power and the Effect Size

The top panel of Figure 9.6 illustrates the situation in which μ_s (98) is very close to μ_0 (100). A consequence of the small difference between μ_0 and μ_s is that the sampling distributions based on H_0 and H_s overlap to a great extent. As always, the rejection region consists of values of the test statistic that are unlikely when H_0 is correct. Unfortunately, because of the extent of the overlap, the rejection region also consists of values of the test statistic that are *unlikely* when H_s is correct. So, even when H_s is correct, the test statistic is unlikely to

FIGURE 9.5
Relationship between form of the alternate hypothesis and power. Power is the lowest when the directional alternative specifies the wrong direction (top); when the directional alternative specifies the correct direction (middle) power is greater than for the nondirectional alternative (bottom).

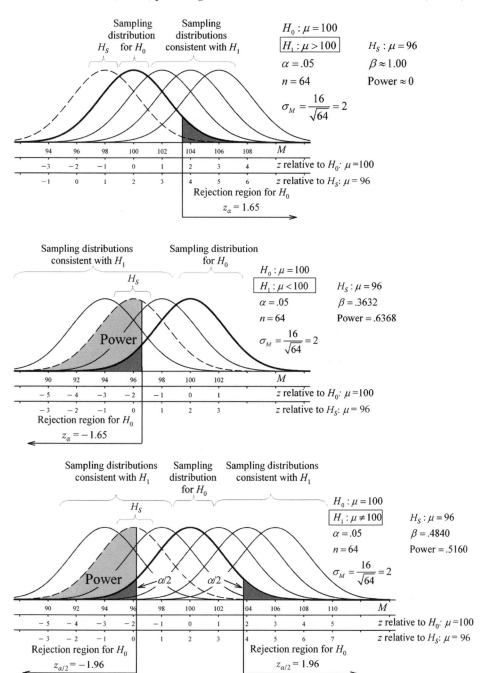

FIGURE 9.6
Relationship between the True value of μ (as guessed by μ_s) and power. As the numerical difference between the μ_s and μ increases (bottom to top), power increases.

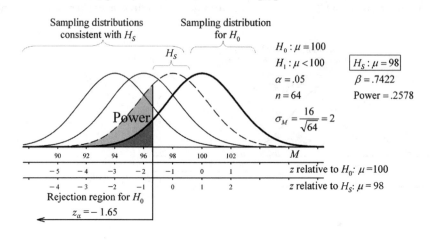

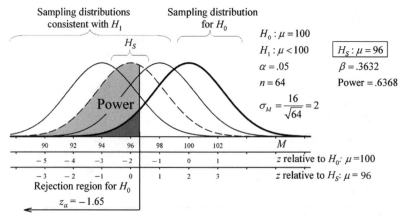

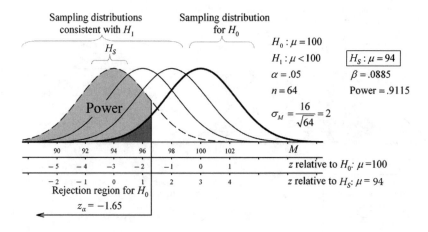

fall into the rejection region and we are unlikely to reject H_0. Power in the top panel is an abysmal .2578.

In the middle panel, our standard situation is illustrated with $\mu_s = 96$. With this larger difference between μ and μ_s, the overlap between the H_s and H_0 distributions decreases. Now, values of the test statistic that are unlikely when H_0 is correct are fairly likely when H_s is correct (which is what we want). Power is .6368.

In the bottom panel, $\mu_s = 94$ so that the difference between μ and μ_s is even greater. Because the overlap between the H_s and H_0 distributions is negligible, values of the test statistic that are unlikely when H_0 is correct are very likely when H_s is correct, and power is .9115.

The major lesson to be learned from Figure 9.4 is that a small difference between μ and μ_s results in low power. In other words, the closer μ_0 is to the True mean, the harder it is to reject H_0. If you are investigating a situation in which you believe that the difference between μ and μ_s is small, then you should attempt to increase power (for example, by using a large sample size).

EFFECT SIZE

As we have learned, there are two possible outcomes of a hypothesis test: rejecting the null or failing to reject the null. When we reject H_0, we base this on the finding that the probability of our test statistic (assuming that H_0 is true) is so low (less than α) that it is unlikely that our sample came from the distribution specified by H_0. It is more likely that our sample came from a distribution specified by H_1.

In Chapter 8, we wondered if there was any evidence that smoking might affect height of women who are more at risk for osteoporosis. Recall that we failed to reject the null. In other words, we did not find evidence for an *effect* of smoking on women's heights. However, the mean height of women in our sample (M) was different from the population mean (μ). It just wasn't different enough to conclude that our M was unlikely given that H_0 was true. Our null hypothesis that the population mean is some specified value (for example, $H_0: \mu = 64.60$ inches) could be restated by saying there is no "effect" of smoking on heights, or that the effect size is zero. In other words, "shortness" does not seem to coincide with smoking. According to Jacob Cohen (1988):

> **Effect size (ES)** is the degree to which the phenomenon is present in the population; it estimates the degree to which the null hypothesis is false.

In our example, the phenomenon in question is "shortness." How much "shortness" is in the smoking population?

To help conceptualize ES, Figure 9.7 shows two distributions of heights of women smokers. The thick curve shows a distribution of the population of scores consistent with H_0: $\mu = 65.00$, whereas the lighter curve represents a distribution of scores consistent with H_1: $\mu < 65.00$. In addition, the lighter curve shows a distribution of scores that we would construct if we obtained the results $M = 64.80$. Remember, we assumed that the distribution of women smokers' heights is normally distributed and that the variance of the distribution is

FIGURE 9.7
Two population distributions of women's heights. The dark curve represents the population of scores when μ = 65.00. The lighter curve represents the distribution of scores when μ = 64.80.

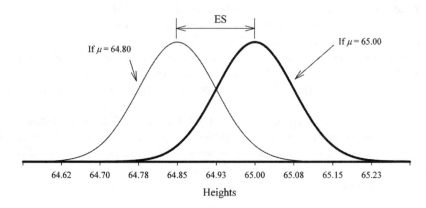

equal to that of the distribution characterized by H_0 (homogeneity of variance assumption). The degree to which the null hypothesis is false, or the effect size, can be estimated as the difference between the two distributions. Note that the distributions in Figure 9.7 are not sampling distributions; they represent the distributions of women's heights. ES estimates the degree to which "shortness" is in the population or how much it differs from the distribution characterized by H_0.

The Importance of Effect Size

Hypothesis testing is a function of four related parameters: significance level (α), power ($1 - \beta$), sample size (n), and effect size (ES). Since we have talked at length about significance level, power, and sample size, let's turn to effect size.

Estimates of ES have become so important that the American Psychological Association now recommends that ES estimates be provided in reports along with the value of the statistic, the p value, and size of sample. There are several reasons for this recommendation. The first is that a hypothesis test can be conceptualized as follows:

Test Statistic = Size of Effect × Size of Study

That is, the value of a statistic (and its p value) is a function of ES and the size of the study. The two dimensions of a statistic work in similar ways: Increasing ES or the size of the study *increases* the absolute value of the statistic (and *decreases* the p value). In the above conception of the hypothesis test, we see the influence of the four parameters mentioned earlier: α, $1 - \beta$, n, and ES. The right side of the formula contains ES and some measure of n, whereas the left side contains the rejection criteria specified by α and $1 - \beta$.

It is important to recognize several consequences of hypothesis testing in the context of the above formulation. It is conceivable that the only reason that you fail to reject the null hypothesis is because the sample size was too small. Some critics of hypothesis testing have pointed to this possibility as reason to reject hypothesis testing altogether. Recall that we had failed to reject the null that women smokers' heights were less than 65.00 inches when we had a sample of 352 women's heights from the Smoking Study. What if we had taken a sample of 4000? The standard deviation of the sampling distribution of the sample mean (the standard error of the mean) under these conditions would be

$$\sigma_M = \frac{\sigma}{\sqrt{n}} = \frac{3.28}{\sqrt{4000}} = .05$$

If our sample of 4000 had a mean height of 64.80 (as our sample of 352 had), then

$$z = \frac{M - \mu_0}{\sigma_M} = \frac{64.80 - 65.00}{.05} = -4.00$$

A value of -4.00 is in the rejection region specified by $\alpha = .01$, thus our decision would be to reject $H_0 : \mu = 65.00$.

However, the size of the effect in a study is independent of whether or not the null is rejected. In terms of women smokers' heights, the ES would be equal in both examples because the underlying population of scores from which we obtained our samples would be identical. The sampling distributions, however, would be very different (recall from Figure 9.4 the influence of sample size on the sampling distribution and power). In this way, ES is not influenced by the size of the study, whereas the statistic and the p value are. Which leads us to the second important consequence of conceiving hypothesis testing as a product of ES and size of study: Rejecting the null hypothesis does not mean a large effect. In fact, very small effects can be statistically significant, whereas large effects can be nonsignificant. The statistic's absolute value and the p value are a function of both the effect and the size of the study. A large study investigating a very small effect could result in highly significant (very small) p value. A small study investigating a large effect could result in failing to reject the null hypothesis (a large p value). Therefore, it is important to conduct a sample size analysis prior to doing a study so you have a good chance of rejecting an incorrect null hypothesis, or of detecting an effect of a certain size.

Estimating Effect Size

Jacob Cohen provided the conceptual basis for effect size as well as one way to estimate ES, called "*d*" or "Cohen's *d*." It is actually a family of measures that estimate the *differ*ence between two distributions, or the degree of departure from the null hypothesis.

Returning to Figure 9.7 for a moment, we see that the ES is the difference in the measures of central tendency of the two distributions. However, we want to standardize the units of the differences. Thus, if we divide by σ, we arrive at the number of standard deviations that the distributions differ:

$$d = \frac{|M - \mu_0|}{\sigma}$$

In the women smokers' heights example, the computation of d is very easy:

$$d = \frac{|64.80 - 65.00|}{3.28} = 0.06$$

For interpretive purposes, Cohen suggested that .2 should be considered a small effect, .5 a moderate effect, and .8 a large effect. As you can see, the effect of smoking on women's heights is very small.

A simpler way to compute d starts with the formula for a z-score:

$$z = \frac{|M - \mu_0|}{\sigma_M} = \frac{|M - \mu_0|}{\sigma/\sqrt{n}}$$

or rearranging the terms a little:

$$z = \frac{|M - \mu_0|}{\sigma} \times \sqrt{n}$$

Substituting the formula for d, we see that

$$z = d \times \sqrt{n}$$

Or, that z is a function of the size of the effect and the size of the study. If we rearrange a bit more we find a simple way of calculating ES from the statistic and size of the study:

$$d = \frac{z}{\sqrt{n}}$$

Ways to Increase Effect Size?

Unfortunately, there are no ways to increase effect size. You can always increase power by increasing the sample size, but the ES cannot be increased. However, you may be able to modify your experiment or study such that the conditions favor a greater effect. Suppose that you are working with Dr. Baker's team on the Smoking Study. You are interested in the effect of Zyban on quitting smoking. Technically, you might be interested in the effects of a 6-month regimen of Zyban (Zyban supposedly helps with cravings). But, your experience and intuition tell you that a 6-month course of Zyban will probably have a very small effect, such that to have a good chance of rejecting a false null hypothesis, you will need a very large sample size. What if you extend the course of Zyban to 12 months? The longer the drug is taken, you presume, the more effective it will be. In this way, then, you have increased the effectiveness of your intervention, but now your study is about a 12-month course of the drug rather than a 6-month course.

As a second example, consider a clinical psychologist working with people with eating disorders. She thinks that her treatment method is better than the traditional method used to treat these disorders, but the effect is only moderate when administered over 10 weeks. She hypothesizes that if she can administer her therapy for 15 weeks, rather than 10, the effect will be larger. Once again, though, she is now looking at the effect size of 15 weeks of treatment, not 10.

In sum, it may be possible to "increase" the effect size by increasing the magnitude of your treatment, for example, longer therapy sessions, longer treatment regimens, and so forth. Keep in mind that this doesn't guarantee an increase in effect size and thereby an increase in power, as does an increase in sample size. Changing a study's parameters to increase the length of treatment and the like may come at great cost. In addition, some treatment regimens, drug therapies, for example, can have the opposite effect: Increasing the dosage of a drug may result in the loss of beneficial effects.

COMPUTING PROCEDURES FOR POWER AND SAMPLE SIZE DETERMINATION

We have seen that power analyses can be useful, but the computational procedures using z scores are cumbersome. Recently, however, computational procedures have been developed that take the drudgery out of power analyses. The procedures can be used to calculate power and to estimate the sample size needed to obtain a desired amount of power.

The computational procedures presented in this chapter apply only to testing hypotheses about a single population mean. These procedures generalize quite easily, however, to other types of hypothesis-testing situations. These generalizations will be presented in upcoming chapters.

Power for Testing Hypotheses About a Single Population Mean

Power analysis begins by specifying an effect size related to the numerical difference between the population means specified by H_0 and H_s. Then, the procedure answers the question, "Given my level of α, sample size, and the type of alternative hypothesis, what is the probability that I will be able to reject the null hypothesis *when the effect size is as specified?*"

Step 1 (d). As noted earlier, the two factors that affect power are the absolute numerical difference between means specified by H_0 and H_s and the variability of the distributions. These factors combine to give us d, the effect size. Recall that the computational formula for d is

$$d = \frac{|\mu_s - \mu_0|}{\sigma}$$

where μ_s is the mean specified by H_s, and μ_0 is the mean of the population specified by H_0.

In the IQ example, $H_0 : \mu = 100$, $H_1: \mu < 96$, $H_s: \mu = 96$, and $\sigma = 16$. Therefore,

$$d = \frac{|96 - 100|}{16} = .25$$

Recall that d is a type of z score, the number of standard deviations separating μ_s and μ_0. Note that d is not based on estimates obtained from samples; the formula uses population parameters. Of course, usually we do not really know μ_s (or σ, for that matter) or we would not bother with hypothesis testing. The point of the procedure is to determine power, assuming that the True mean is some specific value (μ_s). Then we can decide if the procedure has sufficient power to warrant our continuing, or if corrective steps need to be taken.

Because d is a type of z score, it can be estimated directly, rather than first specifying a value for μ_s and σ. Use a z score that reflects your belief as to the probable effect size. If you believe that the ES is relatively small, then use $d = .2$; if you think the ES is moderate, use $d = .5$; if you think the ES is large, use $d = .8$. The closer the estimate is to the real effect size, the closer the computed power will be to the real power of the statistical test.

Step 2 (δ). Another factor that affects power is the sample size, n. The sample size and ES(d) are combined to produce a quantity call δ (delta).

$$\delta = d\sqrt{n}$$

For our example in which $n = 64$,

$$\delta = .25\sqrt{64} = 2$$

Step 3 (power). Refer δ to Table B. The table is constructed to reflect the other factors that affect power, namely, α, and whether the alternative hypothesis is directional or nondirectional.

For the example problem, we used $\alpha = .05$ and a directional alternative. Find the row in Table B that begins with a δ of 2.0, and the column for $\alpha = .05$ for a directional test. The entry, .64, is the power of the statistical test. Note that the value of .64 is, except for rounding, identical to the .6368 we computed previously using z scores.

Sample Size Determination for Testing Hypotheses About a Single Population Mean

It is useful to know the power of a statistical test so that corrective action can be taken if power is too low. This section presents a procedure for taking that corrective action based on the relationship between power and n, the sample size. The procedure begins by specifying an effect size and a desired level of power. Then, the procedure answers the question, "Given my level of alpha and type of alternative hypothesis, how large of a sample do I need to achieve the desired power *if the effect size is as specified*?" This procedure has four steps.

Step 1 (d). The effect size may be estimated using standard values (for example, .2 for a small effect, .5 for a moderate effect, and .8 for a large effect), or by using the formula,

$$d = \frac{|\mu_s - \mu_0|}{\sigma}$$

For the IQ example,

$$d = \frac{|96 - 100|}{16} = .25$$

Step 2 (desired power). Determine the desired power of the statistical test. Because increases in power are paid for by (sometimes) costly increases in n, very high power is often too expensive to realize. A reasonable power is about .80 (see the following discussion of when to use power analysis).

Step 3 (δ). Enter Table B under the column appropriate for the level of α and the type of alternative hypothesis you propose to use. Read down the column until you find the desired power. Read across the row to find the value of δ corresponding to that level of power.

For the IQ example (directional alternative, $\alpha = .05$), to achieve a power of .8 requires that $\delta = 2.5$ (from Table B).

Step 4 (n). The formula for the sample size needed to obtain the desired level of power is

$$n = \left(\frac{\delta}{d}\right)^2$$

For the example,

$$n = \left(\frac{2.5}{.25}\right)^2 = 100$$

Thus, the educational psychologist will need a sample size of about 100 IQ scores to obtain a power of .80 (assuming that the effect size is .25).

WHEN TO USE POWER ANALYSES

Before Collecting Any Data

The most useful time for power analysis is before any data are collected, when the research is being planned. The goal of the analysis is to maximize the probability of rejecting H_0 when it is incorrect.

The most practical way to increase power is to reduce the variability of the sampling distribution. This reduction can be accomplished by using dependent sampling procedures (discussed in Chapter 15), using standard (and constant) measurement procedures, and increasing the sample size.

Given that it is always possible to increase the sample size to obtain more power, the question arises as to how much power is enough power. From a statistical standpoint, the more power the better; that is, the greater the power, the greater the probability of making a correct decision. Unfortunately, in real life, the sample size cannot be increased without bound. Data collection is not cheap; it can be expensive to conduct interviews, administer IQ tests, and so on. Additionally, often the resources of a single investigator or agency must be divided among several projects, and thus decisions must be made as to how many resources, and, therefore, how much power, can be devoted to each project. These decisions require consideration of the importance of the questions being asked of the data.

In judging the amount of resources to devote to a problem, we have to consider all of the possible outcomes of hypothesis testing listed in Figure 8.4 on page 161. In particular, we have to consider what can be gained by making the correct decision, what can be lost if an error is made, and the relative costs of Type I and Type II errors. These considerations are illustrated in two examples.

The first example involves the educational psychologist who investigates the effects of environmental pollution on IQ. In this example, a Type II error (not rejecting H_0 when it is incorrect) means not discovering the adverse affect of the pollution on IQ. This error would be extremely costly in lost human potential: The lives of the children affected by the pollution would be inexorably changed for the worse. A Type I error (rejecting H_0 when it is correct) means deciding that the average IQ for the school is less than the national average when it really equals the national average. This type of error would also be costly: Local industries might be required to undertake costly modifications that produce no benefit.

On balance, for this example most people would probably decide that a Type II error (resulting in a poorer quality of life because of lower IQs) is worse than a Type I error (resulting in reduced industrial profits), although this is clearly a value judgment, not a statistical judgment. Given this analysis, it is reasonable to devote many resources to increasing power to avoid a Type II error. The educational psychologist might also decide to increase α to buy a little more power, because the cost of a Type I error is judged to be less than the cost of a Type II error.

As a second example, consider a scientist who conducts basic research that has no immediate prospect for either increasing or decreasing the quality of life. Typically, scientists are rather cautious and do not jump to make new claims until there is little chance of error. Statistically, a new claim amounts to rejecting the null hypothesis (remember, the null hypothesis often states that there is no difference from a standard, so rejecting the null is tantamount to making the new claim that the standard no longer applies). Thus, scientific caution requires avoidance of Type I errors. Of course, Type II errors are also bad for the scientist, because a Type II error means that the scientist has missed a (potentially important) new finding.

Welkowitz, Ewen, and Cohen suggest a compromise that recognizes the caution of the scientist as well as the problem of missing new findings.[1] The compromise is to set α =

---

[1] Welkowitz, J., Ewen, R. B., & Cohen, J. (1982). *Introductory statistics for the behavioral sciences* (3rd ed.). New York: Academic Press.

.05, and to attempt to obtain power = .80 (β = .20). The low probability of a Type I error recognizes scientific caution; the reasonable level of power gives a fighting chance for making new discoveries. Of course, these are only general suggestions. The values of α and β should be set after a consideration of the merits of each situation.

Calculating Power After Failing to Reject H_0

Failing to reject H_0 is unsatisfying because it does not allow strong claims. As discussed in Chapter 8, failing to reject H_0 does not prove the null hypothesis true; the best that can be said is that there is not enough evidence one way or the other. Often, power analysis can help by demonstrating that the null hypothesis, although not proven true, may be close to true.

The general strategy has two steps. First, determine the power of the statistical test to detect a small effect size (for example, d = .1 or .2). Second, if the power is reasonably large (for example, power > .80), then you may conclude that even if H_0 is not proven true, it is unlikely to be wrong by very much. That is, because you have sufficient power to reject H_0 even when the effect size is small, but H_0 was not rejected, it is likely that the effect size is even smaller than your proposed ES. In other words, when power is high and you still do not reject H_0, then H_0 may well be close to the truth.

Power and the Consumer of Research

In our complex society, we are constantly presented with "scientific facts" that we must evaluate. (Should we lobby the government for stricter air pollution controls? Should we continue to use artificial food colorings?) Often, these facts are based on the results of statistical analyses. When someone makes a new claim (for example, pollution affects IQ) you should consider the level of α that was used. Might the claim be a Type I error? Similarly, when the result is that there is nothing to worry about (consumption of food with a coloring produces no more cancers than when no coloring is used), you should consider the power of the statistical test. Might the claim be a Type II error? Not only can we learn from data, we can also learn when the data are not convincing.

SUMMARY

Power is the probability of rejecting H_0 when it is incorrect. It is beneficial to use tests with high power because that increases the chances of making correct decisions. Five factors that affect power are: the value of α; the effect size, that is, the variability of the sampling distribution (which is affected by the variability in the population, the sample size, and the type of random sampling, as discussed in Chapters 13 and 15); the form of the alternative hypothesis; and the type of statistical test used (parametric or nonparametric).

Power analysis can improve research in at least three ways. First, the careful investigator can estimate the power of the statistical test before beginning the research. Costly mistakes can be avoided by discovering low power before too many resources are committed. Second, power analysis can be used to estimate the sample size needed to attain a desired level of power. Finally, when H_0 is not rejected, sometimes a power analysis can demonstrate that H_0 is unlikely to be very wrong.

EXERCISES

Terms   *Define these new terms and symbols.*

power	μ_s
effect size	d
β	δ
H_s	

Questions   *Answer the following questions.*

1. Describe in your own words why power increases when α increases.
2. Describe in your own words why power changes with changes in the standard error.
3. Describe why choice of the alternative hypothesis affects power.
4. Under what conditions would it be desirable to perform a power analysis before collecting any data?
5. Describe the logic that allows the use of a power analysis to determine that H_0 is not too wrong.
6. Use the z-score method to compute the power of the following statistical tests:
   a. $H_0: \mu = 17$; $H_1: \mu > 17$; $H_s: \mu = 23$; $\alpha = .05$; $\sigma = 18$; $n = 36$
   b. same as a, but $H_1: \mu \neq 17$
   c. same as a, but $\sigma = 36$
   d. same as a, but $n = 144$
†7. Solve the problems in Question 6 using the computational procedures for computing power.
†8. Given the following situation, determine the sample sizes needed to obtain a power of .5, .8, and .95:

$$H_0: \mu = .75; \ H_1: \mu \neq .75; \ H_s: \mu = .60; \ \alpha = .05; \ \sigma = .30$$

Logic of Parameter Estimation

*H*ypothesis testing is one approach to statistical inference; parameter estimation is another. Parameter estimation is used to estimate directly the value of a population parameter, rather than testing hypotheses about the parameter. This chapter begins with a brief discussion of point estimation—procedures for estimating an exact (pointlike) value for a population parameter. We will then consider interval estimation—a technique for calculating a range of values likely to include the population parameter. Finally, the chapter ends with a comparison of parameter estimation and hypothesis testing as alternative ways of learning from data.

The numerical techniques described in this chapter apply only to estimating a population mean (μ), and only when the standard deviation of the population (σ) is known, not estimated. Chapters 12–15 include methods for estimating μ when σ is estimated by s, and Chapter 16 includes a method for estimating a population variance (when, of course, σ is not known). Nonetheless, information in this chapter about how interval estimation works applies to all parameter estimation situations.

POINT ESTIMATION

Point Estimation Using M

If you have a random sample from a population, the single best guess for the mean of the population, μ, is the mean of the random sample, M. The mean of the sample is called a **point estimator;** that is, it provides a single point or value as an estimate of the population parameter. Thus, a particularly easy statistical inference is to compute the mean of a random sample and to use it as an estimate of the population mean.

Other statistics, such as the sample median and the sample mode, are also legitimate point estimators of μ. The advantage that M has over other estimators is that M is an unbiased estimator of μ.

> An **unbiased estimator** is a statistic that has a sampling distribution with a mean exactly equal to the population parameter being estimated.

As we know from Amazing Fact Number 1 (Chapter 8), the mean of the sampling distribution of the sample mean exactly equals μ. This is generally not the case for the sample median or mode.

An unbiased estimator has the useful property of being equally as likely an overestimate of the parameter as an underestimate. That is, it is not systematically too big or too small, but on the average just right. Caution is in order, however, because of the phrase "on the average." The actual estimator (for example, M) that you have at hand may be larger or smaller than the population parameter—not always just right.

Problems With Point Estimation

As you well know, it is unlikely that any specific M will actually equal μ exactly. In fact, because of variability in the sampling distribution of M, usually quite a range of Ms are possible, and most will not equal μ. A second problem with point estimation is that you do not even know how far off the estimate might be. For some random samples, the point estimator may be very close to the population parameter; however, for other random samples, the point estimator may be quite discrepant from the population parameter. It is only "on the average" that an unbiased point estimator (such as M) is guaranteed to equal the estimated parameter.

INTERVAL ESTIMATION

The problems just discussed are solved by using interval estimation to construct confidence intervals.

> A **confidence interval** is a range of values constructed to have a specific probability (the confidence) of including the population parameter.

For example, suppose that a random sample from a population produced an $M = 50$. The 95% confidence interval might range from 45 to 55. That is, the probability that the interval 45–55 includes μ is .95.

> The lower bound on the interval is called the **lower confidence limit,** and the upper bound is called the **upper confidence limit.**

In this example, the lower confidence limit is 45, and the upper confidence limit is 55.

Interval estimation provides solutions to both of the problems associated with point estimation. First, because an interval is specified rather than a single number, the interval is much more likely to include the population parameter than is a single point estimate. Second, the procedure produces a probability statement (the confidence of the confidence interval) of exactly how likely the interval really is to include the parameter.

CONSTRUCTING CONFIDENCE LIMITS FOR μ WHEN σ IS KNOWN

As with hypothesis testing, interval estimation requires a multistep procedure. This procedure is discussed within the context of an example, and it is summarized in Table 10.1 at the end of the chapter.

Remember the example from Dr. Baker's Smoking Study on heights of women smokers from Chapter 8? In that example, the 352 women's heights from the study had a mean height of 64.80 inches. The National Center for Health Statistics (NCHS) has determined that $\sigma = 3.28$ inches (in Chapter 12, we will learn how to deal with the situation when we don't know σ and have to use s as an estimate). How can we use a confidence interval to estimate the mean of the population of heights of women smokers?

Step 1: Assumptions (Requirements)

Confidence intervals are guaranteed to work (have the specified probability of including μ in the interval) only when several assumptions are met. For constructing a confidence interval for μ when σ is known, the assumptions are exactly the same as for testing hypotheses about μ when σ is known.

Population assumptions: The population is normally distributed or the sample size is large. Also, σ is known, not estimated by s.
Sampling assumption: An independent (within-sample) random sample is drawn from the population.
Data assumption: The data are measured on an interval or ratio scale. As with hypothesis testing, the data assumption is the least important.

Except for the sampling assumption these assumptions are met in the example. The implications of not meeting this assumption are discussed in Step 5.

Step 2: Set a Confidence Level

In hypothesis testing, you choose the significance level, α; in construction of a confidence limit, you choose the confidence level, $1 - \alpha$. The use of the symbol α in both contexts is more than coincidental; the relationship between hypothesis testing and interval estimation is discussed later.

The greater the confidence level $(1 - \alpha)$, the greater the probability that the interval will actually include μ. Unfortunately, there is a cost for having greater confidence: the greater the confidence, the wider the interval and, hence, the less precise the estimate. This result has an analogue in nonstatistical estimation. For example, if you are guessing someone's age, you may try "19" (analogous to a point estimate). You could increase confidence in the accuracy of your guess by specifying an interval, "18–20" (analogous to interval estimation). You could be even more confident that your guess includes the person's real age by expanding the interval to, say, "15–24."

Note that an increase in the width of the interval increases your confidence that you are correct, but reduces the precision of the estimate. Certainly, using 15–24 to estimate a person's age is less precise than using 18–20, and as such the wider interval conveys less information about the person. Similarly, a wide confidence interval for a population mean is less precise than a narrow interval, and as such the wide interval conveys less information about the population. For this reason, most confidence limits specify a confidence level of about .95, rather than the more confident (but consequently wider and less precise) .99 or .999.

In the example, suppose that we decide to construct a 95% confidence interval. That is, $1 - \alpha = .95$, and $\alpha = .05$.

Step 3: Obtain an Independent (Within-sample) Random Sample

As with hypothesis testing, estimation procedures require random samples. This step, although easy to describe in words, is often quite difficult to complete. Our sample of heights had $M = 64.80$ and $\sigma = 3.28$.

Step 4: Construct the Confidence Interval for μ

The formulas for computing the upper and lower $1 - \alpha$ confidence limits for μ are

<hr>

FORMULA 10.1   **Confidence Limits for μ**

$$\text{upper limit} = M + z_{\alpha/2} \times \sigma_M$$
$$\text{lower limit} = M - z_{\alpha/2} \times \sigma_M$$

and the $1 - \alpha$ interval is

$$\text{lower limit} \leq \mu \leq \text{upper limit}$$

In this formula, $z_{\alpha/2}$ is the z score that has $\alpha/2$ proportion of the z-score distribution above it. The σ_M is found using Amazing Fact Number 2,

$$\sigma_M = \sigma/\sqrt{n}$$

For constructing a 95% confidence interval (so that $\alpha = .05$), $z_{\alpha/2}$ is the z score having .025 (.05/2) of the distribution above it. That z score is 1.96. Next,

$$s_M = 3.28/\sqrt{352} = .175$$

Using Formula 10.1,

$$\text{upper limit} = 64.80 + 1.96 \times .175 = 65.14$$

$$\text{lower limit} = 64.80 - 1.96 \times .175 = 64.46$$

Thus, the 95% confidence interval is

$$64.46 \text{ inches} \leq \mu \leq 65.14 \text{ inches}$$

Step 5: Interpret the Confidence Interval

What does it mean to have a 95% confidence interval? The probability is .95 that the interval includes μ. For the example, there is a .95 probability that the interval 64.46 inches to 65.14 inches includes the real mean of the population. Keep in mind, however, that there is a small probability (.05) that the interval does not include μ.

You may recall from Chapter 6 that probability can be interpreted as relative frequency in the population. This relative frequency interpretation also applies to confidence intervals. Imagine taking many samples from the population and constructing a 95% confidence limit for each sample. As it turns out, 95% (relative frequency of .95) of the samples would have 95% confidence intervals that include the population mean. In most cases, we do not know for sure that the specific interval we constructed (64.46–65.14) actually includes μ; we can be 95% confident, not 100% confident. In this case, though, we do know μ. Recall that according to the NCHS, the mean height of women aged 18 and older in the United States is 65.00 inches. Note that μ is within our interval of 64.46 to 65.14. In other words, the confidence interval worked just as it should: The interval included the real μ.

An interpretation that sounds similar, but is incorrect, is to say that the probability is .95 that μ falls into the interval. Attaching the probability to μ implies (incorrectly) that μ changes from sample to sample. As you know, the mean of a population does not change; it is M, and, hence, the confidence interval that changes from sample to sample. Thus, the probability statement is attached to the interval, not μ: There is a $1 - \alpha$ probability that the *interval* constructed from a specific sample actually includes the mean of the population.

As with hypothesis testing, you should avoid overgeneralizing. The confidence interval is applicable only to estimating μ for the population from which you randomly sampled.

Recall, however, that we did not meet the sampling assumption, that is, the data are not from a *random* sample. Consequently, for this example, the interval provides only a rough sense of possible values for μ. The exact confidence (e.g., .95), only applies when all of the assumptions are met. For ease of exposition, we will ignore this inconvenient fact in the following discussion.

WHY THE FORMULA WORKS

In trying to understand how interval estimation works, it helps to begin with an example in which μ is known, and to demonstrate that the confidence intervals do include that value. Therefore, since we happen to know that the population mean of women's heights is 65.00, we will work through the example and then generalize the reasoning to the situation in which μ is not known.

Figure 10.1 presents an illustration of the sampling distribution of M. We know from Amazing Fact Number 3 that the sampling distribution is essentially normally distributed (regardless of the shape of the population). Furthermore, because we know $\sigma = 3.28$ and $n = 3.52$, we can, from Amazing Fact Number 2, calculate $\sigma_M = .175$. Finally, based on the fact that $\mu = 65.00$ (and Amazing Fact Number 1), we know that the mean of the sampling distribution is 65.00.

Now, consider a first random sample. It had $M = 65.12$, and the confidence interval extended from 64.78 to 65.46. This interval is illustrated in Figure 10.1 with the mean labeled M_1. This interval does include μ, as illustrated by the interval crossing the dashed line. Note that the range of values covered by the interval extends $1.96 \times \sigma_M$ units on either side of M_1. This "1.96" arises because we are dealing with the 95% interval, and 1.96 is $z_{\alpha/2}$.

Now, imagine taking a second random sample in which $M_2 = 64.96$. The 95% confidence interval will extend $1.96 \times \sigma_M$ units on either side of M_2, giving a confidence interval of 64.62 to 65.30. This interval also includes μ.

A third random sample from the same population might have $M_3 = 64.72$. Again, if the 95% interval is calculated, it will extend $1.96 \times \sigma_M$ units on either side, giving an interval of 64.36 to 65.06. As with the first two intervals, this interval also includes μ.

The fourth sample is more interesting. For this sample, $M_4 = 65.45$. The 95% interval extends $1.96 \times \sigma_M$ units on either side of M_4, giving an interval of 65.11 to 65.79. This interval does not include μ: M_4 is so far into the tail of the sampling distribution that $1.96 \times \sigma_M$ units on either side of M_4 simply does not extend far enough to include μ. In fact, *whenever M is more than $1.96 \times \sigma_M$ units away from μ, the 95% confidence limit will miss μ.*

On the other hand, any M that is within $1.96 \times \sigma_M$ units of μ will include μ in its 95% interval. Now, what is the probability that an M will be within $1.96 \times \sigma_M$ units of μ (and thus include μ in its 95% confidence limit)? This is a simple z-score problem. Referring to Table A, 95% of the distribution of Ms lies between -1.96 and $+1.96$ σ_M units of the mean.

Here is the point: 95% of all the Ms are within $1.96 \times \sigma_M$ units of μ. Therefore, 95% of the Ms will have 95% confidence intervals that include μ. Stated somewhat differently, the probability is .95 that the M you obtain in a random sample is one of the 95% in the middle of the sampling distribution and will, therefore, have a 95% confidence interval that includes μ.

FIGURE 10.1
Any of the 95% of the *M*s from the middle of the sampling distribution will have 95% confidence intervals that include μ. Each horizontal line indicates the confidence interval constructed around a particular *M*.

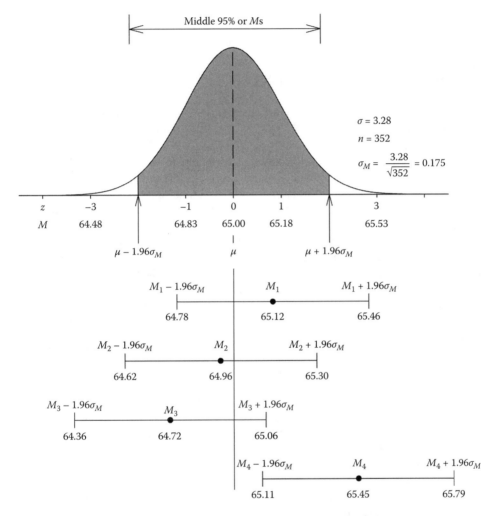

Now let's generalize this point. First, it doesn't depend on knowing that $\mu = 65$. Whatever value μ takes on, 95% of the *M*s will be within $1.96 \times \sigma_M$ units of μ. Furthermore, all of these middle 95% of the *M*s will have confidence intervals that include μ because the intervals themselves will extend $1.96 \times \sigma_M$ units on either side of the *M*s. Also, because the probability is .95 that any random sample will be among the middle 95%, the probability is .95 that any random sample will have a 95% confidence interval that includes μ.

We can also generalize the reasoning to apply to all confidence levels, rather than just the 95% level. This generalization requires restating the logic using $(1 - \alpha) \times 100\%$ in place of 95% and $z_{\alpha/2}$ in place of 1.96. The middle $(1 - \alpha) \times 100\%$ of the *M*s will be within $z_{\alpha/2} \times \sigma_M$ units of μ. All of these middle *M*s will have $(1 - \alpha) \times 100\%$ confidence intervals that include μ, because the intervals will extend $z_{\alpha/2} \times \sigma_M$ units on either side of M. Finally, because the probability is $1 - \alpha$ that any random sample will be among the middle $(1 - \alpha)$ $\times$ 100%, the probability is $1 - \alpha$ that any random sample will have a $(1 - \alpha) \times 100\%$ confidence interval that includes μ!

FACTORS THAT AFFECT THE WIDTH OF THE CONFIDENCE INTERVAL

Two factors affect the width of the confidence interval. One is the level of confidence, $1 - \alpha$. The other is the standard error, σ_M. We will discuss both of these within the context of a new example.

Suppose that a physiological psychologist is attempting to estimate the number of synapses (connections) between individual neurons in the cortex of the (rat) brain. Clearly, it would be impossible to count all the synapses on all the millions of neurons in even one cortex, let alone in all rat brains. Instead, the psychologist plans to sample relatively few ($n = 16$) neurons and to use parameter estimation techniques. For his sample, $M = 500$.

The first step in constructing a confidence interval is to check the assumptions. The first population assumption is that the population is normally distributed, or the sample size is large. Well, it is hard to argue that $n = 16$ is large. However, the physiological psychologist examined the relative frequency distribution of his sample to see if he could gain any information about the shape of the population. As it turned out, he could detect little evidence of skew or asymmetry in the sample, and so he presumed that the population was, if not normally distributed, at least not grossly non-normal. Under these conditions, the sampling distribution of M is essentially normally distributed (see Figure 7.3 on p. 132).

The second population assumption is that σ is known; estimating it from s is not good enough. To keep this example going, the value of σ will be given as 100. In the real world, not knowing σ would force the physiological psychologist to abandon this procedure and to use the interval estimation procedure based on the t distribution (see Chapter 12).

The sampling assumption is that an independent (within-sample) random sample is taken. This assumption is met.

The data assumption is that the data are measured on an interval or a ratio scale. Because each datum is an actual count (of synapses), a ratio scale is formed.

The second step is to set the level of confidence, $(1 - \alpha)$. The physiological psychologist decides to use the standard 95% interval.

The interval is constructed using Formula 10.1. For a 95% interval, $z_{\alpha/2} = 1.96$. For $\sigma = 100$ and $n = 16$,

$$\sigma_M = 100/\sqrt{16} = 25$$

Then,

$$\text{upper limit} = 500 + 1.96 \times 25 = 549$$

$$\text{lower limit} = 500 - 1.96 \times 25 = 451$$

The 95% confidence interval is

$$451 \le \mu \le 549$$

The probability is .95 that this interval includes μ. Now, how do the level of confidence and the size of σ_M affect the width of the interval?

Level of Confidence

The higher the confidence, the wider the confidence interval. As discussed in the context of guessing ages, this is a sensible relationship. It is also an unfortunate relationship: although it is desirable to have high confidence in the estimate of μ, a wide interval is less informative (a less precise estimate) than a narrow interval.

The effect of changing the level of confidence can be illustrated by constructing the 99% interval for the mean number of synapses in the rat brains. For the 99% interval, $1 - \alpha = .99$, so that $\alpha = .01$, $\alpha/2 = .005$, and $z_{\alpha/2}$ is the z score that has .005 of the distribution above it. Entering Table A, we find that the corresponding z score is 2.58.

$$\text{upper limit} = 500 + 2.58 \times 25 = 564.5 \qquad 1 - \alpha = .99$$

$$\text{lower limit} = 500 - 2.58 \times 25 = 435.5 \qquad \alpha = .01, \; \alpha/2 = .005$$

The 99% confidence limit is

$$435.5 \le \mu \le 564.5$$

Note that this interval is, indeed, wider than the 95% interval that extends from 451 to 549. We can have greater confidence that the 99% interval includes the population mean, but the cost is that the interval is wider so that it provides less information.

Size of σ_M

As σ_M decreases, so does the width of the confidence interval. Decreases in σ_M (and the width of the confidence interval) can be achieved by careful data collection to eliminate excess variability, dependent sampling (discussed in Chapters 13 and 15), and increasing the sample size.

Suppose the physiological psychologist had had the patience to count the synapses on 64 neurons, instead of 16. In that case,

$$\sigma_M = 100/\sqrt{64} = 12.5$$

For the 95% confidence interval,

$$\text{upper limit} = 500 + 1.96 \times 12.5 = 524.5$$

$$\text{lower limit} = 500 - 1.96 \times 12.5 = 475.5$$

This 95% confidence interval

$$475.5 \le \mu \le 524.5$$

is narrower (and more informative) than the 95% confidence interval based on $n = 16$

$$451 \le \mu \le 549$$

The fact that an increase in n results in a more informative confidence interval makes intuitive sense: Increasing n does provide more information about the population, so of course the confidence interval becomes more informative.

The relationship between n and the width of the confidence interval can be used to counter the growth in the width of the interval with high levels of confidence. If you want the luxury of high confidence (for example, .99) *and* a narrow interval, it can be obtained at the cost of a large n.

In the Media: Do Jews Have More Fun?

A point estimate of a population parameter, such as using the sample mean to estimate the population mean, can be difficult to interpret for several, often hidden, reasons. First, because of variability in the sampling distribution, the sample statistic is unlikely to be exactly equal to the population parameter. Second, the likely size of the difference between the two will depend on the variability of the measurements and the sample size: Both variability and sample size help to determine the width of the confidence interval. Unfortunately, even well-reported media articles rarely give enough data to construct a confidence interval.

On October 9, 1994, Tamar Lewin reported in the *New York Times* ("So, Now We Know What Americans Do in Bed. So?") some of the results of a study of sexual behavior. One set of results described in the article was the median number of sex partners since age 18 for members of different religious groups: No religion, 5; Mainline Protestant, 4; Conservative Protestant, 3; Catholic, 3; Jewish, 6; and Other Religion, 3. A quick glance at the data would indicate that Jews have twice as many sex partners as some Christians. Can this quick glance be trusted?

The statement, "Jews have twice as many sex partners as Christians," is an inference about the populations based on sample data. Do the data support this inference? One reason for caution revolves around sample size. Although the study as a whole had a large sample (3432), Jews are a small percentage (about 3%) of the U.S. population, so the number of Jews in the sample was probably close to 100 (3% of 3432). Furthermore, the smaller the sample size, the larger the width of the confidence interval. Consequently, because of the small sample size, we cannot have much faith in the accuracy of the point estimate for Jews, whereas the point estimates for the groups of Christians (which have much larger sample sizes) are probably close to the corresponding population parameters.

COMPARISON OF INTERVAL ESTIMATION AND HYPOTHESIS TESTING

Hypothesis testing (using the nondirectional alternative) and interval estimation are quite closely related. In fact, they provide exactly the same information about the population; they simply package it differently.[1] Suppose that the same sample is used to construct a confidence interval and to test hypotheses. The $(1 - \alpha)$ confidence interval indicates all the values of μ_0 (the value of μ specified by H_0) that would *not* be rejected using a nondirectional test with the probability of a Type I error set at α. For the physiological psychologist, the 95% confidence interval (using $n = 16$) was $451 \leq \mu \leq 549$. In terms of hypothesis testing, any null hypothesis specifying a value of μ_0 between 451 and 549 would not be rejected when using a nondirectional, $\alpha = .05$ test and the sample data (e.g., $M = 500$).

Errors in Interval Estimation

If hypothesis testing and interval estimation are informationally equivalent procedures, then we should be just as likely (or unlikely) to make errors using interval estimation as in hypothesis testing.

Consider first Type I errors. A Type I error is to reject the null hypothesis when it is correct (and so it should not be rejected). When the null is correct, a Type I error occurs with a probability of α.

An equivalent type of error can occur when using parameter estimation: The interval can fail to include μ. This is clearly an error, and interestingly enough, for the $1 - \alpha$ interval, this sort of error will occur exactly α proportion of the time. For example, for 95% confidence intervals, the probability is .05 that the interval will miss μ. This equivalence is why the same symbol, α, is used for the probability of a Type I error in hypothesis testing and for indicating the degree of confidence in interval estimation.

In hypothesis testing, a Type II error is to not reject the null hypothesis when it is incorrect (and so it should be rejected). You might think of this error as including too much (namely H_0) in the realm of possibility. An analogous error arises in interval estimation: including too much in the confidence interval. The interval may include μ, but the interval will also include many other values in addition to μ, and these values are all incorrect.

The analogy between Type II errors and the width of the confidence interval also extends to techniques for reducing the problem. Recall from Chapters 8 and 9 that two of the ways to reduce the probability of a Type II error (β) are (a) to increase α, and (b) to decrease σ_M. Both of these manipulations also reduce the width of the confidence interval, thereby reducing the number of incorrect possibilities included in the interval.

Choosing Between Hypothesis Testing and Interval Estimation

Because hypothesis testing and interval estimation are so closely related, the choice is usually just a matter of style. However, there are some guidelines. Hypothesis testing is often

---

[1] Actually, there are some highly technical differences, but these will be ignored.

used when a reasonable value for μ can be formulated before collecting any data (to serve as the null hypothesis), and when rejecting a specific null hypothesis would provide useful information. For example, in Chapter 8 one of the examples concerned a psychologist studying aggression of monkeys reared in a social environment. She was able to use as μ_0 the mean aggression of monkeys reared in isolation. Rejecting this particular null hypothesis indicates that rearing condition makes a difference. Hypothesis testing would have been inappropriate if she did not have a standard value to propose for the null hypothesis.

On the other hand, interval estimation is useful for providing an indication of the certainty that should be associated with inferences. The wider the interval, the less certainty there is as to the actual value of the population parameter.

In psychology, there is a clear preference for hypothesis-testing procedures over parameter estimation. This preference can be traced to two sources. First, many psychologists (and other scientists) believe that scientific progress can be made most quickly by testing and refining theories. By their very nature, theories make predictions, and these predictions can often serve as null hypotheses to be tested. Rejecting a theoretically based null hypothesis is a good signal that the theory needs to be refined (because it made a poor prediction). Thus, an emphasis on theory testing leads to a preference for hypothesis testing.

The second reason for preferring hypothesis-testing techniques is that they have been developed to analyze rather complex situations (for example, see the factorial analysis of variance discussed in Chapters 18 and 19). Although parameter estimation techniques could be used in these complex situations, they would be cumbersome.

SUMMARY

A point estimator is a single value computed from a sample that is used to estimate a population parameter. For an unbiased point estimator, the mean of the sampling distribution of the estimator is equal to the population parameter being estimated. The sample mean, M, is an unbiased point estimator of the population mean, μ. Unfortunately, because of variability in the sampling distribution, any single point estimate is likely to be wrong.

Interval estimation procedures compute a range of values for the population parameter called a confidence interval. When the assumptions are met, the confidence interval has a guaranteed probability of including the population parameter. Increasing confidence is bought at the expense of increasing the width of the interval. On the other hand, decreasing σ_M decreases the width of the interval without affecting the confidence that can be placed in the interval.

Interval estimation and hypothesis testing are alternative approaches to learning from data. They are, however, informationally equivalent, and so the choice of one technique or the other is often a matter of convenience or style.

The computational formulas described in this chapter are to be used only to estimate μ from M when σ is known. Nonetheless, three features hold for all confidence intervals. First, the confidence level indicates the probability that the interval includes the population parameter. Second, as the confidence level increases, the width of the interval increases, making the interval less informative. Third, the width of the interval can be decreased by decreasing variability.

TABLE 10.1
Confidence Interval for μ When σ Is Known

1. **Assumptions:**
   Population assumptions:
   a. The population is normally distributed, or the sample size is large.
   b. σ is known, not estimated.

   Sampling assumption:
   An independent (within-sample) random sample is obtained from the population.

   Data assumption:
   The data are measured using an interval or ratio scale.

2. **Set the confidence level, $1 - \alpha$.**

3. **Obtain a random sample from the population.**

4. **Construct the interval:**
   $$\textbf{upper limit} = M + Z_{\alpha/2} \times \sigma_M$$
   $$\textbf{lower limit} = M - Z_{\alpha/2} \times \sigma_M$$

   Where M is computed from the random sample, $z_{\alpha/2}$ is the z score with $\alpha/2$ of the distribution above it, and

   $$\sigma_M = \sigma / \sqrt{n}$$

   The $(1 - \alpha)$ confidence interval is
   $$\text{lower limit} \leq \mu \leq \text{upper limit}$$

5. **Interpretation:**
   The probability is $1 - \alpha$ that the interval includes the mean of the population from which the sample was selected. There is a probability of α that the interval does not include μ.

Table 10.1 summarizes the procedure for determining a confidence interval for μ when σ is known.

EXERCISES

Terms   *Define these new terms and symbols.*

point estimator   confidence interval
unbiased estimator   confidence limits
interval estimation $1 - \alpha$ interval

Questions   *Answer the following questions.*

1. A school administrator is planning to switch to a new math program for the fifth grade. The program he selects depends on the abilities of the current fourth-grade students (who will enter fifth grade for the new program). The administrator randomly selects $n = 49$ fourth-grade students for ability testing. Assume that the ability test results in interval data. $M = 27$, $\sigma = 21$. Should the administrator use hypothesis-testing or parameter = estimation techniques to learn about the population? Why?

2. A clinical psychologist is testing a drug that is supposed to decrease the frequency of acting-out behaviors in hospitalized patients with schizophrenia. She knows from historical records that the mean number of acting-out behaviors in a week is 6.3, and $\sigma = 4$. She randomly selects a group of 25 patients with schizophrenia, administers the drug to them, and then counts the number of acting-out behaviors during the test week. $M = 5.6$. Should the psychologist use hypothesis-testing or parameter-estimation techniques to learn about her population? Why?

†**3.** Using the data in Question 1, construct 80%, 90%, and 95% confidence intervals for μ. What happens to the size of the confidence interval as the confidence increases?

†**4.** Using the data in Question 2, construct confidence limits for μ using sample sizes of 25 and 100. What happens to the size of the confidence interval as the sample size increases?

5. For each of the confidence intervals constructed in Question 4, state a null hypothesis that could not be rejected and a null hypothesis that could be rejected by these data.

6. State in your own words why changes in level of confidence $(1 - \alpha)$ change the range of the confidence interval.

7. State in your own words why changes in σ_M change the range of the confidence interval.

8. Prove that the range of values included in the $1 - \alpha$ confidence interval are just those values of μ_0 that would not be rejected in a nondirectional test with the significance level set at α. (*Hint:* Start with the formula for the rejection region for the nondirectional test, and substitute for z the formula used to compute z.)

PART ***III***

Applications of Inferential Statistics

*T*his part of the book consists of 12 chapters to help you learn from data collected in specific, real situations. In each chapter, we examine a different type of situation.

The adjective *real* is used in contrast to the unlikely situations described in Part II. In all of those situations, to proceed with data analysis we had to know the population variance (σ^2)—a very unlikely situation. This unlikely condition was introduced because it simplifies the data analysis. In the remaining chapters, we will learn how to deal with situations in which σ^2 is unknown.

The majority of these chapters will have similar formats. First, typical situations are described for which techniques discussed in the chapter are appropriate. Second, the hypothesis-testing techniques are described. These techniques follow the six-step procedure introduced in Chapter 8. Third, an introduction to power analyses for the situation is presented. These analyses are modeled after those in Chapter 9. Fourth, parameter estimation (as in Chapter 10) is discussed.

The last part of each chapter introduces alternative (usually) nonparametric procedures (see Chapter 5 for the distinction between parametric and nonparametric hypothesis testing). When the situation does not meet the assumptions required for parametric statistical inference (for example, the population may be very skewed instead of normally distributed), these alternative procedures can be used instead.

The front endpapers of this book include a statistical selection guide that can be used to help you choose appropriate statistical procedures. To use the guide, you answer a series of questions to determine the most important statistical characteristics of the situation of interest. Once the situation has been characterized, the guide indicates the appropriate procedure and chapter. At this point, you may not be able to answer some of the questions (for example, regarding independent or dependent samples) because the distinctions have not yet been introduced. Nonetheless, it may be worthwhile to spend a few moments perusing the selection guide so that you know what is in store for you.

CHAPTER 11

Inferences About Population Proportions Using the z Statistic

*I*n this chapter we describe how to make inferences about the proportion (or relative frequency) of an event in a population. Inferences of this sort are often made in surveys and polls. For example, suppose that a newspaper commissions a poll to find out what proportion of the voters prefer Candidate A over Candidate B. If the poll is a random sample, then the proportion of voters favoring Candidate A in the poll can be used to infer the proportion of voters in the population that prefer Candidate A.

As another example, consider a question from the field of cognitive development. According to Piaget's theory of development, only children who have developed to the stage of "concrete operations" have the ability to conserve volume (the child realizes that the volume of water remains the same regardless of the shape of the container into which it is poured). A question might be, What proportion of 5-year-olds can conserve volume?

The voter preference example and the cognitive development example, although different on the surface, have a number of characteristics in common that make them amenable to the statistical procedures introduced in this chapter. We will proceed by describing the common characteristics and then the statistical analysis.

THE BINOMIAL EXPERIMENT

The procedures developed in this chapter can be used for situations that conform to a binomial experiment:

1. The binomial experiment consists of n observations (that is, the sample size is n).
2. Each observation can be classified into one of two mutually exclusive and exhaustive outcomes. For convenience, one outcome is called a success and the other a failure. Mutually exclusive means that each observation must fit into only one of the outcome categories—an observation cannot be classified as both a success and a failure. Exhaustive means that all of the observations fit into one of the two outcome categories—there is no middle ground.
3. The observations are obtained using independent (within-sample) random sampling; that is, measuring one observation does not influence the measurement of any other observation.
4. Interest centers on the proportion (or relative frequency) of successes in the population.

   The **parameter** π (the Greek letter *pi*) is the proportion of successes in the population. The statistic p is an unbiased estimator of the parameter π. p is simply the number of successes in the sample divided by n.

Both the voter opinion example and the cognitive development example are binomial experiments. In each example, there were n independent observations, and the observations fell into one of two mutually exclusive and exhaustive categories (for example, a child can conserve volume—a success, or not conserve—a failure). Finally, interest centered on π, the proportion of successes in the population (for example, the proportion of 5-year-olds who conserve).

Consider the following additional examples of binomial experiments. A coin is flipped 20 times and the number of heads counted. Is it a fair coin (in the population of flips, is the proportion of heads .5)? Here, $n = 20$. Each observation consists of a head (success) or a tail (failure). If the coin is flipped in the same manner for each observation (that is, the outcome of the previous flip does not influence the next), then the observations are independent. p is the number of heads divided by 20. Finally, the question of interest concerns the proportion of heads in the population (π).

For another example, consider asking a random sample of 10 people if they approve or disapprove of U.S. foreign policy. In this binomial experiment, $n = 10$; each observation is a success (approves) or a failure (disapproves); and if the observations all come from different people and are made discretely, then the observations are independent. In this example, p is the number of people expressing approval divided by 10, and π is the proportion of people in the population who approve of U.S. foreign policy.

Sometimes, observations that fall into more than two categories can be reclassified so that only two mutually exclusive and exhaustive categories are used. For example, suppose that the results of a poll consist of those who favor U.S. foreign policy, those who do not, and those with no opinion. By combining the latter two into a single category, the data are made to conform to a binomial experiment.

The Sampling Distribution of *p*

Binomial experiments are particularly valuable because mathematicians have determined the sampling distribution of p, the proportion of successes in the sample.[1] Remember, a sampling distribution is the probability distribution of a statistic computed from all possible random samples of the same size drawn from the same population. For binomial experiments, the statistic is p, the sample size is n, and the population is a population of binomial observations (such as the opinions regarding foreign policy). As it turns out, the sole determiners of the sampling distribution of p are the sample size and the proportion of successes in the population (π).

Consider the sampling distribution of p = proportion of people in a random sample of $n = 10$ who approve of U.S. foreign policy. Suppose that in the population the proportion of approvals is .50; that is, for this population, $\pi = .50$. Now suppose that in the first random sample there are six successes (approvals) so that $p = .6$. Selecting a second random sample of size 10 may produce a $p = .5$. In a third sample, $p = .5$ again; in a fourth $p = .4$, and so on.

After taking all possible random samples we would have many different ps, and these ps could be used to construct a relative frequency distribution of ps, which is the sampling distribution of p when $n = 10$ and $\pi = .50$. The sampling distribution is illustrated by the histogram in Figure 11.1.

The sampling distribution of p always has a range of 0.0 (when the sample contains no successes) to 1.0 (when the sample contains all successes). For the distribution in Figure 11.1, p changes in increments of .1 because $n = 10$. Finally, note that the distribution is symmetric. In fact, whenever $\pi = .5$, the sampling distribution of p is symmetric, and whenever $\pi \neq .5$, the distribution is skewed.

For a slightly different example, suppose that $\pi = .7$ (70% of the people approve of U.S. foreign policy) and $n = 20$. In the first random sample, the number of successes might be 12, so that $p = 12/20 = .60$. In the next sample, the number of successes might be 15, so that $p = .75$, and so on. The sampling distribution based on all possible random samples of $n = 20$, drawn from a population with $\pi = .7$, is illustrated by the histogram in Figure 11.2.

---

[1] The sampling distribution of p is closely related to the binomial distribution, the sampling distribution of the number of successes. For our purposes, it is more convenient to work with the sampling distribution of p.

FIGURE 11.1
The histogram is the sampling distribution of *p* when $\pi = .5$ and *n* = 10. The continuous curve
is the normal approximation with $\mu = .5$ and $\sigma = .158$.

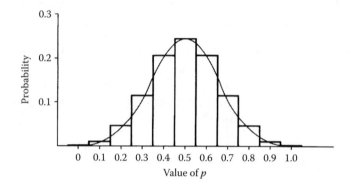

FIGURE 11.2
The histogram is the sampling distribution of *p* when $\pi = .7$ and *n* = 20. The continuous curve
is the normal approximation with $\mu = .7$ and $\sigma = .102$.

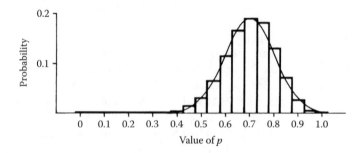

As must be, the distribution ranges from 0.0 to 1.0. This time the increments are in units
of .05 (1 success in 20), and the distribution is slightly skewed to the left: Because $\pi > .5$,
the most common values of *p* are those greater than .5. The infrequent *p*s less than .5 create
the long tail on the left.

Three Amazing Facts About the Sampling Distribution of *p*

In Chapter 7, we learned three amazing facts about the sampling distribution of *M*, and
those facts were put to good use in making statistical inferences. There are also three
amazing facts about the sampling distribution of *p*.

Fact Number 1. The mean of a sampling distribution of *p*s always equals π, the proportion of successes in the population. Another way of saying this is that *p* is an unbiased
estimator for π.

Fact Number 2. The standard deviation of a sampling distribution of *p*s, σ_p, is:

FORMULA 11.1   Standard Deviation of the Sampling Distribution of *p*

$$\sigma_p = \sqrt{\frac{\pi(1-\pi)}{n}}$$

Fact Number 3. The sampling distribution of *p*s approximates a normal distribution. The approximation improves as π gets closer to .5 and as *n* gets larger. How close to .5 does π have to be, and how large *n*, before the normal distribution is a reasonable approximation? As a rough guideline, if $(n)(\pi) \geq 5$, and $(n)(1 - \pi) \geq 5$, then the sampling distribution of π can be considered (for computational purposes) normally distributed.

These amazing facts are illustrated in Figures 11.1 and 11.2. The histogram in Figure 11.1 is the sampling distribution of *p* when $\pi = .5$ and $n = 10$. Note that the mean of the distribution is indeed $\pi = .5$. Also, although it is not as obvious,

$$\sigma_p = \sqrt{\frac{\pi(1-\pi)}{n}} = \sqrt{\frac{.5(1-.5)}{10}} = .158$$

For this distribution, $(n)(\pi) = (10)(.5) = 5$ and $(n)(1 - \pi) = (10)(1 - .5) = 5$, so that the distribution can be considered approximately normally distributed. The normal distribution with $\mu = .5$ and $\sigma = .158$ is superimposed on the histogram in Figure 11.1. You can see for yourself that the normal distribution is reasonably like the distribution of *p*s.

The sampling distribution illustrated by the histogram in Figure 11.2 is based on $\pi = .7$ and $n = 20$. The mean of the sampling distribution does indeed equal .7, and the standard deviation is indeed

$$\sigma_p = \sqrt{\frac{.7(1-.7)}{20}} = .102$$

For this distribution, $(n)(\pi) = (20)(.7) = 14$ and $(n)(1 - \pi) = (20)(1 - .7) = 6$. Because both quantities exceed 5, the normal distribution is again a reasonable approximation to the distribution of *p*s. Superimposed on the histogram in Figure 11.2 is the normal distribution with $\mu = .7$ and $\sigma = .102$. Note that even though the distribution of *p*s is slightly skewed, the normal distribution is a pretty good approximation.

TESTING HYPOTHESES ABOUT π

The basic hypothesis-testing strategy is to begin with a guess about the value of π in a population. This guess becomes the null hypothesis. The value of π specified by H_0 is used to construct the sampling distribution of *p* (which is approximated by the normal distribution). The sampling distribution is, in effect, a prediction of the likely values of p in a random sample from the population. If the value of p found in an actual random sample is consistent with the sampling distribution, then H_0 is supported (but not proven true). If the actual value of p is unlikely (given the predictions derived from H_0), then the hypothesis is rejected.

We will flesh out this strategy using the six-step procedure for hypothesis testing and illustrating it with an example. The six-step procedure is also summarized at the end of the chapter in Table 11.1. Now to the example.

Is the rate of cognitive development universal, or does it depend on specific character-istics of local culture such as education, diet, and so on? To begin to answer this question a psychologist might engage in cross-cultural research. Suppose that he knows that in the United States 40% of 5-year-olds are in the stage of concrete operations (can conserve volume); that is, for this population $\pi = .40$.

The psychologist obtains a random sample of 50 5-year-olds from a school district in Cancun, Mexico, and classifies each child as a conserver or a nonconserver. To answer the question about cognitive development the psychologist will determine if π in the Mexican population is any different from π in the United States; that is, is π in the Mexican popu-lation equal to .40? The six-step procedure for hypothesis testing is designed to answer questions just like this.

Step 1: Assumptions

There are three assumptions that need to be checked (and verified) before hypotheses about π can be tested legitimately. These assumptions ensure that the data conform to a binomial experiment.

Sampling Assumptions

1. The n observations are obtained by independent (within-sample) random sam-pling. If each child contributes only one observation, and the testing is done in a way so that one child's performance does not influence any other's, then this assumption is satisfied.
2. The sample size must be large. In particular, $(n)(\pi_0) \geq 5$ and $(n)(1 - \pi_0) \geq 5$, where π_0 is the value of π specified by H_0. This assumption insures that the normal distribution can be used to approximate the sampling distribution of p. In the example, $(50)(.40) = 20$ and $(50)(1 - .4) = 30$, so this assumption is satisfied.

Data Assumption

Each of the observations can be classified as either a success or a failure. This assumption is met because each child is classified as either a conserver (success) or a nonconserver (failure).

These assumptions are quite different from those needed to test hypotheses about a population mean. For example, we do not have to make assumptions about the type of data because even nominal data can be classified as success or failure. Also, we do not have to make assumptions about σ, because for binomial experiments, σ_p can be computed directly from π_0 and n.

Step 2: Hypotheses

As always, the null hypothesis states that there is no change from some standard, and it makes a specific proposal about the population. When testing hypotheses about the proportion of successes in the population, the null hypothesis is, of course, a specific proposal about π (not about μ). The general form is

$$H_0: \pi = \pi_0$$

For our example, a good standard to use for π_0 is the value of π in the United States. Thus,

$$H_0: \pi = .40$$

In words, the null hypothesis is: The proportion of successes (conservers) in the population of 5-year-old children in Cancun is .40.

The alternative hypothesis is about the same aspect of the population, π, as the null hypothesis, but the alternative is a general proposal that contradicts the null hypothesis. In testing hypotheses about π, three forms of the alternative are available. The nondirectional alternative is

$$H_1: \pi \neq \pi_0$$

The two directional alternatives are

$$H_1: \pi > \pi_0$$

$$H_1: \pi < \pi_0$$

Because the psychologist is interested in deviations from the null hypothesis in either direction (it would be interesting to find out if π for the Mexican population is greater or less than .40), the nondirectional alternative is most appropriate. Thus, for the example,

$$H_1: \pi \neq .40$$

Step 3: Sampling Distributions

This step has two parts. First, we will consider the sampling distributions of p when H_0 is presumed true and when H_1 is presumed true. Second, the z transformation will be used to transform the sampling distributions so that Table A can be used.

Presume for a moment that H_0 is correct. In that case, applying our three amazing facts about the sampling distribution of p:

1. Because $\pi = .4$ (assuming that H_0 is true), the mean of the sampling distribution will also equal .4.

2. The standard deviation of the sampling distribution is

$$\sigma_p = \sqrt{\frac{.4(1-.4)}{50}} = .069$$

3. The sampling distribution can be approximated by using the normal distribution.

The sampling distribution is illustrated in the center of Figure 11.3. This distribution is predicting what we will find in a random sample (if H_0 is correct). Namely, likely values of p (in the sample) are around .4. Values of p much greater than about .52 or much less than about .28 are very unlikely *when H_0 is correct*.

Now, presume for a moment that H_1 is correct. In this case, the sampling distribution of p will have a mean greater than .4 (as on the right of Figure 11.3) or less than .4 (as on the left). These distributions are also making predictions, namely, that the value of p in the sample will be discrepant with .4.

Now, consider finding a z score for each p in the sampling distribution corresponding to H_0. Remember, a z score is always a score minus the mean of the distribution divided by the standard deviation of the distribution. In this case, each value of p is a score, the mean of the distribution is π_0, and the standard deviation is σ_p. So, to transform ps into zs use Formula 11.2.

FORMULA 11.2 z-Score Transformation for p

$$z = \frac{p - \pi_0}{\sigma_p}$$

FIGURE 11.3
Normal approximations to the sampling distributions of p. The black curve is the sampling distribution when H_0: $\pi = .4$ is correct. The gray curves illustrate some of the sampling distributions when H_1: $\pi \neq .4$ is correct.

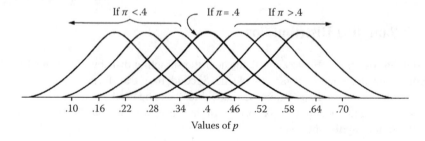

If we transformed every p into a z, we would have a distribution of z scores with (as always) a mean of zero and a standard deviation of 1.0. Furthermore, because the distribution of ps is normally distributed (see the second assumption), the distribution of z scores will be the standard normal distribution of Table A. The transformed distributions are illustrated in Figure 11.4.

These distributions of z scores are also making predictions. Suppose that we take a random sample, compute p, and then transform p into z. If H_0 is *correct*, then the most likely values of z are around zero (see the middle distribution in Figure 11.4). On the other hand, *if H_1 is correct*, then the most likely values of z are discrepant from zero.

Step 4: Set α and the Decision Rule

Setting the significance level (α) for testing hypotheses about π requires the same considerations as in testing hypotheses about μ. A small α corresponds to a small probability of a Type I error (rejecting H_0 when it is correct). Unfortunately, lowering α increases β, the probability of a Type II error (not rejecting H_0 when it is wrong). We will use the standard significance level of $\alpha = .05$.

Now that the significance level is set, we can generate the decision rule. Remember, the decision rule gives those values of the test statistic that, if they occur in the sample, will lead us to reject H_0 in favor of H_1. Thus, the rule states values of the test statistic that (a) have a low probability (α) of occurring when H_0 is correct and (b) have a high probability of occurring when H_1 is correct. For a nondirectional alternative hypothesis,

$$\text{Reject } H_0 \text{ if } z \geq z_{\alpha/2} \text{ or if } z \leq -z_{\alpha/2}$$

The symbol $z_{\alpha/2}$ stands for the value of z that has $\alpha/2$ of the distribution above it.

For the directional alternative, $H_1: \pi > \pi_0$, the decision rule is

$$\text{Reject } H_0 \text{ if } z \geq z_\alpha$$

FIGURE 11.4
Sampling distributions for the test statistic, z. The black curve is the sampling distribution when H_0 is correct; the gray curves illustrate some of the sampling distributions when H_1 is correct.

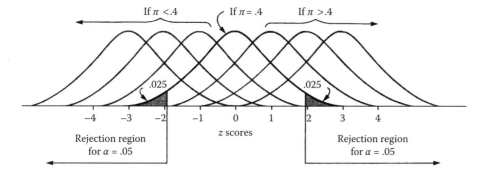

For the directional alternative, H_1: $\pi < \pi_0$ the decision rule is

$$\text{Reject } H_0 \text{ if } z \leq -z_\alpha$$

The symbol z_α stands for the value of z that has α proportion of the distribution above it.

The cognitive development example uses a nondirectional alternative with $\alpha = .05$. Thus $\alpha/2 = .025$, $z_{\alpha/2} = 1.96$ (from Table A), and the decision rule is

$$\text{Reject } H_0 \text{ if } z \geq 1.96 \text{ or if } z \leq -1.96$$

The rejection region is illustrated in Figure 11.4.

Step 5: Sample and Compute the Test Statistic

Now the psychologist actually measures each child to determine if the child is a conserver (success) or a nonconserver (failure). The psychologist must take care to ensure that the sample is indeed a random sample from the population (the population of conservation scores for 5-year-olds in Cancun, Mexico), and that the observations are independent of one another.

Suppose that of the $n = 50$ children, there are 30 successes, so that $p = 30/50 = .60$. Converting this p into a z score gives

$$z = \frac{p - \pi_0}{\sigma_p} = \frac{.6 - .4}{.069} = 2.90$$

As we noted in Chapter 8, it is now a recommended practice to include an estimate of the effect size (ES) when conducting a hypothesis test. For a z statistic:

$$\hat{d} = \frac{z}{\sqrt{n}} = \frac{2.90}{\sqrt{50}} = 0.41$$

Step 6: Decide and Draw Conclusions

The test statistic, 2.90, is greater than the critical value, 1.96, so the null hypothesis is rejected. The results are statistically significant (for $\alpha = .05$).

What does rejecting H_0 mean? Remember, H_0 stated that the population proportion of 5-year-old conservers in Cancun equals .40 (the same as in the United States). Because the null hypothesis is rejected, and because $p > .4$, we can conclude that the proportion of 5-year-old conservers in Cancun is greater than the proportion of 5-year-old conservers in the United States. Moreover, with $\hat{d} = .41$, we can say that the size of the effect of living in Cancun on conserving is a moderate one.

Now it is up to the psychologist to figure out *why* there is difference between the two populations. It might be because of differences in schooling, other experiences, or different genetic makeups. There is nothing in the statistical analysis that pinpoints the reason for the difference.

Be careful not to overgeneralize the results. For instance, it would be a mistake to claim that children develop faster in Mexico than in the United States. First, we do not know about all children in Mexico, only those in Cancun. Second, we do not know if these results hold for all aspects of development. After all, we examined only one type of development in 5-year-olds. We do know that the proportion of 5-year-old children in Cancun who conserve volume is greater than the proportion in the United States. Any claim beyond that may be correct, but it has no statistical justification.

Errors in Testing Hypotheses About π

As with all hypothesis testing, errors can be made. When the null hypothesis is rejected, there is some probability that you have made a Type I error (rejecting H_0 when it is really correct). Fortunately, when the assumptions are met, the probability of a Type I error is small, because it equals α.

When H_0 is not rejected, there is a probability (β) that you have made a Type II error. The value of β can be reduced (and power increased) by increasing α, increasing the sample size, decreasing variability by careful data collection procedures, and by appropriate use of directional alternative hypotheses. More formal power and sample size analyses are presented after the next example.

Reporting the Results

When reporting the results of a statistical analysis (in a research paper, for example), you should state enough of the elements of the statistical test for a reader to come to his or her own conclusions. These elements are the level of α, the value of the test statistic, the value of π_0, and whether or not you rejected the null hypothesis. Since a nondirectional test is typically used, the type of alternative hypothesis is not mentioned unless a directional alternative was used.

Thus, a report might read, "For a sample of $n = 50$, the proportion of conservers was .60. Using $\alpha = .05$, the null hypothesis that $\pi = .40$ was rejected, $z = 2.90$, $d = .41$."

TESTING A DIRECTIONAL ALTERNATIVE HYPOTHESIS ABOUT π

According to Drs. James Anthony and Fernando Echeagraray-Wagner (2000) of Johns Hopkins University, the rate of alcohol dependence in smokers in the United States is 6.9%. We might ask then: Is the prevalence of alcohol dependence in smokers universal, or does it vary from state to state? Recall that Dr. Baker's Smoking Study was conducted in Wisconsin. There may be cultural differences that affect the rate of alcohol dependence in Wisconsin when compared to other states in the United States. What proportion of the participants in Dr. Baker's Smoking Study are also alcohol-dependent? And, is this higher than would be expected?

We begin by defining a success as a participant in Dr. Baker's study who is also alcohol-dependent. Although being alcohol-dependent is not a good thing, we call it a "success" because it is a positive instance of the feature we are measuring. (Alcohol dependence is a serious problem and can be a life-threatening drug dependency.) A failure, in the present example, is a person in the study who is not alcohol-dependent. We count the number of successes in Dr. Baker's sample of 608 Wisconsin smokers, and determine if the π in the Wisconsin sample is equal to .069.

Assumptions   The assumptions for testing hypotheses about π are mostly satisfied here. Each measurement can be classified as a success or failure, and, given the value of π specified by the null hypothesis (below) and a sample size of 608, the normal approximation can be used (two participants did not answer the question of alcohol dependence, thus $n = 606$). However, because the smokers in Dr. Baker's study volunteered, rather than being randomly selected, the independent (within-sample) random sampling assumption is not fully met. Although we should probably stop at this point, we will continue and address this issue in Step 6 and Chapter 14.

Hypotheses   The most reasonable null hypothesis is H_0: $\pi = .069$. The value of .069 comes from the study by Drs. Anthony and Echeagraray-Wagner. The directional alternative, H_1: $\pi > .069$, is appropriate because we are interested in rates higher than average.

Sampling Distributions   The sampling distribution of p, assuming that H_0 is correct, is illustrated on the left of Figure 11.5. The distribution was constructed using the amazing

FIGURE 11.5
Normal approximations to the sampling distribution of p. The thick curve is the sampling distribution when H_0: $\pi = .069$ is correct. The lighter curves illustrate some of the sampling distributions when H_1: $\pi > .069$ is correct.

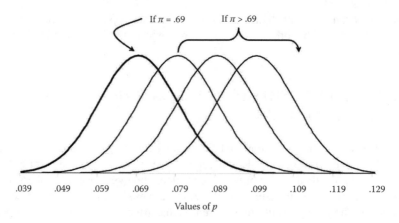

Values of p

fact about the sampling distribution of p. First, the mean of the distribution will equal π_0, which equals .069. Second, the standard deviation will equal

$$\sigma_p = \sqrt{\frac{.3(1-.3)}{20}} = .102$$

Some of the sampling distributions corresponding to the alternative hypothesis are also illustrated in Figure 11.5. These distributions are only on the right because the directional alternative specifies that $\pi > .069$. All of the distributions can be transformed using the z transformation:

$$z = \frac{p - \pi_0}{\sigma_p} = \frac{p - .3}{.102}$$

The transformed distributions are in Figure 11.6.

Set α and the Decision Rule   If we set $\alpha = .025$, the test will be less powerful and we will have a greater chance of making a Type II error. However, directional tests are generally more powerful than a nondirectional one, so we can take advantage of that extra power to decrease α without making power too low. We will check our reasoning in the next section on power analysis.

The decision rule with $\alpha = .025$ is

Reject H_0 if $z \geq 1.96$

The rejection region is illustrated in Figure 11.6.

The decision rule can also be stated as such:

Reject H_0 if p-value $< \alpha$

FIGURE 11.6
Sampling distribution for the test statistic, z. The thick curve is the sampling distribution when H_0; the lighter curves illustrate some of the sampling distributions when H_1 is correct.

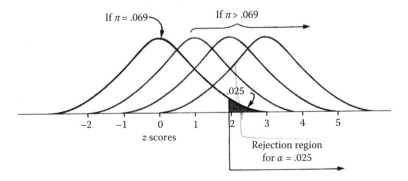

The advantage of stating the decision rule this second way is that many computer programs, including Excel, will compute both a test statistic's value and the probability (p value) associated with that statistic. Thus, you do not have to use a look-up table for a critical value. As you will see in later chapters, determining a test's p value is easier than finding the correct table for a critical value.

Sample and Compute the Test Statistic   Looking at the smoking data provided by Dr. Baker on the supplemental CD, you will find a column titled "DIAGALC," which indicates whether or not the participant has been diagnosed (the "DIAG" part) as alcohol-dependent (the "ALC" part of the variable label). The values in this column are either a 0 or 1, which is coded so that 0 = "no" and 1 = "yes." For the current purposes, a "1" is a success (a diagnosis of alcohol dependence is present) and a "0" is a failure (no alcohol dependence is present). If we now count the number of successes (or the number of "1s"), we see that there are 46 people in the Smoking Study who were alcohol-dependent. Note, though, that there are also 2 "*'s" in the spreadsheet denoting missing data. Therefore, there are 46/606 successes, so that $p = .076$. Converting this p into a z score gives:

$$z = \frac{p - \pi_0}{\sigma_p} = \frac{.076 - .069}{.01} = .70$$

To determine the probability of obtaining a z of .70 or less, we can use the "NORMSDIST" function in Excel (=NORMSDIST(0.70)) or Table A, which yields a p value of .7580.

Decide and Draw Conclusions   The test statistic, $z = .70$ is not in the rejection region, so the null hypothesis is not rejected (note also that $p(z = .70) = .758$, which is not less than α). What does not rejecting H_0 mean? Remember, H_0 stated that the population proportion of smokers in the smoking study that are alcohol dependent equals .069 (the same as the rest of the United States). Because the null hypothesis is not rejected, we don't have evidence that the population of smokers in Wisconsin is different from the general U.S. population of smokers, with respect to alcohol dependence and smoking. Note that we cannot conclude that π in Wisconsin is the same as for the U.S. population (that would mean that we would ACCEPT the null hypothesis); we just fail to reject the null. Even this conclusion must be moderated, however. Because the sample of smokers was not a random sample of Wisconsin smokers, the conclusion is at best tentative. Suppose, for example, that smokers who are alcohol-dependent tend not to volunteer. Thus, p in the Smoking Study will be biased and underestimate π. Chapter 14 discusses these issues in more depth.

POWER AND SAMPLE SIZE ANALYSES

Power is the probability of rejecting H_0 when it is incorrect and should be rejected. In other words, power is the probability of making a type of correct decision, and so we should try to maximize it. Another way to think about power is that it equals $1 - \beta$, where β is the probability of a Type II error. Thus, increasing power reduces the probability of a Type II error. This section presents procedures for estimating the power of a statistical test, and for estimating the sample size needed to achieve a desired level of power.

Power Analysis

The factors that affect power when testing hypotheses about π are the same as the factors that affect power when testing hypotheses about μ. First, power increases as α increases (that is, α and β are inversely related). Second, power increases the greater the discrepancy between π_0 (specified by H_0) and the true value of π. In other words, the more wrong H_0 is, the greater the probability of rejecting it. Third, power increases as variability in the sampling distribution is decreased. For testing hypotheses about π, the most effective way to reduce variability is to increase the sample size. Finally, power is increased by appropriate use of directional alternative hypotheses.

These factors are combined in the power analysis. The analysis begins by specifying an effect size—an estimate as to the discrepancy between the value of π specified by H_0 and a specific alternative value of π_s. Then, the analysis answers the question, "Given my sample size, value of π_s, and type of alternative hypothesis, what is the probability that I will be able to reject H_0 *if my guess for the effect size is correct?*"

Now, it may be of interest to specify a value for π_s, which is consistent with the alternative hypothesis; however, you might want to know the power of the hypothesis test you just conducted. Consider our smoking and alcohol dependence example from Dr. Baker's study. Remember that the rate of alcohol dependence in smokers, throughout the United States, is .069; thus the value specified by the null hypothesis, π_0, was .069. We used $n = 606$, $\alpha = .025$, and a directional hypothesis. Our computations determined that $p = .076$, $\sigma_p = .01$, $z = 0.70$, and $p(z) = .758$. Recall that we failed to reject the null. What was the power of our hypothesis test? In other words, given our sample size, type of alternative hypothesis, and value of p, what was the probability that we would be able to reject H_0 if there was an effect consistent with our obtained results?

Calculating the power of a test like the one we completed on smoking and alcohol dependence has already been introduced in Chapter 9. To review:

1. Specify H_s. (In this case it will be the obtained value of p.)
2. Find the values of π that constitute the rejection region (the critical value).
3. Calculate the probability of obtaining p based on the sampling distribution of H_s.

This result is the power of the test.

Figure 11.7 should help you follow the steps. The figure illustrates the sampling distribution assuming H_0 is correct (the dark curve) and the sampling distribution for H_s (the result from computing our statistic). These sampling distributions may be treated as distributions of p or z, depending on which abscissa (x-axis) is used.

Power is the shaded area in Figure 11.7. That area is the probability, when H_s is correct, that a random sample will produce a test statistic in the rejection region. Note that α is an area under the sampling distribution corresponding to H_0, because it is the probability of falling into the rejection region *when H_0 is correct.*

FIGURE 11.7
Power of the statistical test on the proportion of smokers in Dr. Baker's Smoking Study who are also alcohol-dependent.

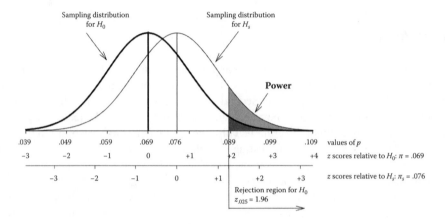

Step 2 is to find the value of p that constitutes the rejection region. Recall that this is a reverse z-score problem:

$$p = \pi_0 + (z)(\sigma_p)$$

$$p = .69 + (1.96)(0.01) = .0886$$

Thus, for any $p \geq .0886$, we would reject H_0, because the corresponding z score would be in the rejection region.

Step 3 is to calculate the probability of obtaining $p \geq .0886$, assuming that H_s is correct. What is the probability of obtaining a $p \geq .0886$ when $\pi = .076$? The z score is:

$$z = \frac{p - \pi_s}{\sigma_p} = \frac{.0886 - .076}{.01} = 1.26$$

Now, using either Table A or the NORMSDIST function in Excel, we see that the probability of z scores greater than 1.26 is $1 - .8962 = .1038$. Thus, the power of our statistic test was a measly .1038. Moreover, β, or the probability of a Type II error, was .8932. In other words, if the rate of alcohol dependence in smokers in Wisconsin is higher than 0.76 (i.e., higher than the .069 specified by H_0), we would have about a 1 in 10 chance of rejecting the null hypothesis, and a 9 in 10 chance of making a Type II error.

Completing this type of analysis might lead you to wonder: Is this informative? After all, we failed to reject the null hypothesis and all that the power analysis demonstrated was that we had a very small chance of rejecting. This type of "post hoc" or "observed" power analysis is of little consolation after conducting a hypothesis test. If you rejected the null, you had enough power; failing to reject the null probably means you had too little power. The point of the analysis of the smoking data is to demonstrate conceptually what power is and how it can be measured. The appropriate course of action is to conduct the power analysis first. Then we could have adjusted the data collection situation to increase power to an acceptable level.

Sample Size Analysis

Sample size analysis begins with a specification of the desired power and an estimate of the effect size. The analysis is designed to answer the question, "Given my level of α and the type of alternative hypothesis, how large a sample do I need to achieve the desired power given my estimate of effect size?"

So, let us say that we thought it highly probable that the incidence of alcohol dependence in smokers in Wisconsin was higher than the national average. After all, there are a number of large breweries in Wisconsin and we did not have a truly random sample. Thus, we might ask, "How large of a sample would we need to detect an effect consistent with our previous results?" First, we must estimate the effect size from our previous results:

$$\hat{d} = \frac{z}{\sqrt{n}} = \frac{.70}{\sqrt{606}} = .03$$

(This is a very small effect size estimate.)

Next, use α and the type of alternative to locate the appropriate column in Table B, then scan down the column until you find the desired power. Read the value of δ from the row containing the desired power. Finally, the sample size is given by:

$$n = \left(\frac{\delta}{\hat{d}}\right)^2$$

Let us suppose that we would be satisfied with a power of .80. For a directional test, $\alpha = .025$, .80 corresponds to a δ of 2.8 (on the left of the table). The sample size needed then is

$$n = \left(\frac{2.8}{.03}\right)^2 = 8711$$

Therefore, we would need a random sample of 8711 smokers in Wisconsin to obtain power close to .80, much more than the original 606.

There are three important lessons to be learned here. First, casual guesses as to the appropriate sample size may be very wrong. Second, sample size analyses can prevent a waste of time and effort. If we were indeed convinced that there is a higher incidence of alcohol dependence in Wisconsin smokers than in the United States in general, we wasted a lot of time and effort on data collection with a very low chance of finding significant results. Third, good research is not cheap. The cost of doing a study with 8711 participants would be an enormous undertaking. Whether it is worth the time and money to collect the data from 8711 people is not a statistical question, though. Rather, it is a question likely to be influenced by the current culture.

ESTIMATING π

Parameter estimation is often used in polls and in survey research. For example, a politician may commission a poll to estimate the proportion of voters (π) favoring the candidate. Or a research organization may conduct a survey to ascertain the proportion of a particular population that favors birth control, or simpler taxes, or nuclear disarmament, or striped toothpaste.

Because p is an unbiased estimator of π, p computed from a random sample is the best single (point) estimate of π. Unfortunately, it is unlikely that p will exactly equal π because of variability in the sampling distribution. Look again at Figure 11.5. Even when π is fixed at .069, the value of p varies from sample to sample (as illustrated by the sampling distribution at the left of the figure).

A confidence interval for π specifies a range of values that has a particular probability (confidence) of actually including π. We will review the five-step procedure for constructing confidence intervals within the context of a specific example. A summary of the procedure is included in Table 11.2 at the end of the chapter.

Confidence Interval for π

The county government has discovered that women in its employ are generally paid less than men, even when performing work requiring comparable levels of skill. The county supervisors have to decide whether to try to remedy the situation by adopting a program of "comparable worth," that is, increasing the salaries of women to the level of men doing work of comparable worth. The county supervisors commission you to estimate π, the proportion of registered voters who approve of comparable worth programs.

You decide to take a random sample of $n = 200$ from the population of opinions of registered voters. You select a random sample of names from voter registration lists, contact each voter, explain the issues, and ask each if they favor comparable worth or not.

Step 1: Assumptions

The assumptions for parameter estimation are very similar to those for hypothesis testing. The first sampling assumption is that independent (within-sample) random sampling is used. This requirement is achieved by using each person's opinion only once and collecting the data so that one person's opinion is not influenced by any other's. The second sampling assumption is that the sample size must be large. If $(n)(p)$ and $(n)(1 - p)$ are both greater than 20, this assumption is satisfied. The reason for the stricter sample size requirement for parameter estimation as opposed to hypothesis testing will be explained shortly.

The data assumption is that the observations need to be classified as a success (for example, favor comparable worth) or a failure (for example, do not favor comparable worth or no opinion).

Step 2: Set a Confidence Level, $(1 - \alpha)$

The greater the confidence level, the greater the probability that the interval will actually include π. The cost, however, is that the greater the confidence, the wider the interval, so the less specific information it provides. You decide to use the standard confidence level of 95% (so that $\alpha = .05$).

Step 3: Obtain a Random Sample

Suppose that of the 200 opinions, 76 were in favor of comparable worth. Thus, $p = 76/200 = .38$.

Step 4: Construct the Confidence Interval

The formula is very similar to that used for constructing a confidence limit for μ.

$$\text{upper limit} = p + z_{\alpha/2} \times \sigma_p$$
$$\text{lower limit} = p - z_{\alpha/2} \times \sigma_p$$

and the $1 - \alpha$ confidence interval is:

$$\text{lower limit} \leq \pi \leq \text{upper limit}$$

We know two of the three quantities in the formula. Namely, $p = .38$, and $z_{\alpha/2} = 1.96$ (for $\alpha = .05$). The problematic quantity is σ_p. Remember, $\sigma_\pi = \sqrt{\pi(1-\pi)/n}$, but we do not know π; in fact, that is exactly what we are trying to estimate. Fortunately, when the sample size is large (the last assumption), p can be used as an estimate of π when computing σ_p. There are two reasons why this works. First, the value of σ_p does not change much with small errors in estimating π. Second, when the sample size is large, p is a pretty good estimate of π.

So, using $p = .38$ in the formula for σ_p,

$$\sigma_p = \sqrt{\frac{.38(1-.38)}{200}} = .034$$

Then,

$$\text{upper limit} = .38 + 1.96 \times .034 = .447$$
$$\text{lower limit} = .38 - 1.96 \times .034 = .313$$

and the 95% confidence interval is

$$.313 \leq \pi \leq .447$$

Step 5: Interpretation

The probability is .95 that the interval .313 to .417 includes the real value of π. Stated differently, if this procedure of sampling and constructing a confidence interval were repeated 100 times, the interval would actually include π about 95 times. As usual, we do not know for certain that the interval we computed includes π this time, but we can be 95% confident.

The county supervisors should be concerned about these results. As our best guess, far fewer than half of the registered voters favor a program of comparable worth. If the supervisors plan to institute such a program, they may wish to precede it with an educational campaign designed to convince the public that the program is desirable.

Margin of Error

As people become more sophisticated in matters statistical, newspapers and other forms of mass media are beginning to report the results of polls along with information similar to confidence intervals. For example, on November 25, 1985, the *New York Times* reported the results of a *New York Times*/CBS News telephone poll on the views of 927 Americans (including 280 American Roman Catholics, who were of primary interest to the pollsters). The pollsters asked each respondent for views on various issues, such as the use of artificial birth control. One of the findings was that 70% of the sample favored the use of artificial birth control. The report includes the statement, "In theory, in 19 cases out of 20 the results based on such samples will differ by no more than three percentage points in either direction from what would have been obtained by interviewing all adult Americans … [but] the margin of sampling error for Catholics is plus or minus six percentage points."

The phrase "19 cases out of 20" refers to a 95% confidence interval (19/20 = .95). The three-percentage-point margin of error arises from the $\sigma_p \times z_{\alpha/2}$ part of the formula for confidence limits. In this case, using $p = .70$ to estimate π, $\sigma_p = \sqrt{.7(1-.7)/927} = .015$, and $\sigma_p \times z_{\alpha/2} = .029$, the three-percentage-point margin of error. Thus, the 95% confidence interval is .671 to .729. Note that the quote also indicates that the margin of error is greater for Catholics than for the sample as a whole. Remember (from Chapter 10) that for any given level of confidence, the smaller the sample size, the wider the interval has to be. Because the sample contained only 280 Catholics (as opposed to 927 respondents in all), the margin of error (width of the interval) will necessarily be larger.

Finally, note that even the *New York Times* can overgeneralize. The newspaper claims that the results represent the views of "all adult Americans." Technically, the population consists of the opinions of all adult Americans *who own telephones and who answer telephone polls*.

In the Media: An Ironically Erroneous Margin of Error

In the article "Truth Forsaken" (*Isthmus,* August 14, 1992), Charles Sykes attempts to use "margin of error" in a poll on sexual abuse for two purposes, to decry the "widespread statistical illiteracy among the media" and to note the "extraordinary willingness to suspend disbelief on sensitive issues involving society's victims." As it turns out, however, an erroneous calculation reveals an ironic "statistical illiteracy" in this article.

Sykes takes issue with the poll's figures on rape. "The widely reported estimate that 683,000 women were raped in 1990 was based on a survey of 4,008 women conducted for the National Victim Center. In that survey, 28 women, or 0.7% of the respondents, reported a forcible rape. That percentage was then multiplied by the approximately 96 million women in the United States to come up with the projection of 683,000 rapes.

"But the margin of error in a survey this size is plus or minus 1.5%, a caveat that is especially relevant in this case. Since the number of women reporting rape in the survey was less than 1%, it fell well within the survey's margin of error, making the report's conclusion highly suspect."

Margin of error in the media almost always means the size of half of a 95% confidence interval. Thus, if Sykes is correct, the confidence interval extends from $-.8\%$ to 2.2%. Because this interval includes 0.0% (and other very small numbers) as possible values for the population mean, the projected number of rapes in the United States could be much, much smaller than 683,000. But, is Sykes correct? To check on the computations, let's assume that the 4008 women comprised a random sample and that observations were independent of one another. Then $p = .007$ (28/4008), and $n \times p = 28$, which meets the sample size requirements. Using the formulas in Table 11.2, the confidence interval is $.007 \pm .0026$, or .0044 to .0096. That is, the margin of error is .0026, or .26%, far less than Sykes' 1.5%. Projecting from this confidence interval (and here the assumption of a random sample is critical), the estimated number of yearly rapes is tremendous: 422,400 to 921,600.

Why did Sykes report a margin of error of 1.5% instead of 0.26%? The maximum margin of error (maximum width of the confidence interval for a proportion) is always for $p = .5$. In this case, using $p = .5$, the margin of error is indeed 1.5%. Because the observed p (.007) is so different from .5, however, the confidence interval is also quite different. In any event, the error does seem to illustrate Sykes' claim of "widespread statistical illiteracy among the media."

RELATED STATISTICAL PROCEDURES

There are many situations involving proportions that are not covered by the procedures described in this chapter. Statistical analyses for some of these situations can be found in other chapters of this book and in more advanced texts.

Small Sample Sizes

All of the procedures discussed in this chapter have required relatively large sample sizes. There are, however, procedures for testing hypotheses about π that can be used with small samples. These procedures make use of the sampling distribution of the number of successes (rather than p) that is called the binomial distribution. The small sample procedures can usually be found in texts that include discussion of the binomial distribution.

More Than Two Mutually Exclusive and Exhaustive Categories

Procedures discussed in this chapter require binomial observations: Each observation must fall into exactly one of two categories (success or failure). Sometimes, however, data are not that accommodating. For example, a poll may ask for preference among Candidates A, B, or C. Analysis of nominal data that fall into more than two categories is discussed in Chapter 22.

Comparing Two Populations

Often the point of a statistical procedure is to compare the value of a parameter in two different populations. For example, a politician might want to compare the proportion of young voters favoring a policy compared to the proportion of older voters. Or a developmental psychologist may wish to compare the proportion of city-dwelling 5-year-olds who conserve volume to the proportion of non-city-dwelling 5-year-olds who conserve volume.

Three types of statistical procedures are available for comparing populations. First, comparison of population relative frequencies (including binomial proportions) can be made using procedures found in Chapter 22. Second, comparison of population means (μs) is discussed in Chapters 13, 15, and 17–19. Third, comparison of population variances (σs) may be found in Chapter 16.

SUMMARY

This chapter introduced procedures for making inferences about the proportion of successes in a population (π). The parameter π is of interest in many situations in which the data meet the assumptions of a binomial experiment. Examples include situations in which the answers to a poll result in one of two outcomes (success or failure), or when the response of an individual in an experiment can be classified as success or failure.

Two inferential procedures were discussed. Hypothesis testing is used to discriminate between a null hypothesis stating a specific value for π and an alternative hypothesis that contradicts the null. Power of this test can be calculated, and it is affected by the same factors that affect power in other situations. The second inferential procedure is parameter estimation. The point estimate for the parameter π is p, the proportion of successes in the sample. Interval estimation of π requires a relatively large sample so that the standard deviation of the sampling distribution of p, σ_p, can be accurately estimated. The size of the resulting interval is affected by the same factors that affect the interval in other situations, such as the sample size and the level of confidence. Table 11.1 summarizes the procedure for testing hypotheses about π, and Table 11.2 summarizes interval estimation of π.

TABLE 11.1

Testing Hypotheses About π, the Proportion of Successes in a Population

1. **Assumptions (requirements):**

   Sampling assumptions:
   a. The n observations are obtained by independent (within-sample) random sampling.
   b. The sample size must be large. In particular, $(n)(\pi_0) \geq 5$ and $(n)(1 - \pi_0) \geq 5$, where π_0 is the value of π specified by H_0.

   Data assumption:
   Each of the observations must be classified as either a success or a failure.

2. **Hypotheses:**

   Null hypothesis:
   $$H_0: \pi = \pi_0$$

   where π_0 is a specific value between 0.0 and 1.0.

   Alternative hypotheses available:
   $$H_1: \pi \neq \pi_0$$
   $$H_1: \pi > \pi_0$$
   $$H_1: \pi < \pi_0$$

3. **Test statistic and its sampling distribution:**

   $$z = \frac{p - \pi_0}{\sigma_p}$$

   $$\sigma_p = \sqrt{\frac{\pi_0(1 - \pi_0)}{n}}, \quad p = \frac{\text{number of successes}}{n}$$

   When H_0 is correct, the sampling distribution is the standard normal; thus, the most likely values of z are near zero. When H_1 is correct, the most likely values of z are discrepant from zero.

4. **Decision rule:**

   For $H_1: \pi \neq \pi_0$
   $$\text{Reject } H_0 \text{ if } z \geq z_{\alpha/2} \text{ or } z \leq - z_{\alpha/2}$$

   $$\text{Reject } H_0 \text{ if } p(z) \leq \alpha/2 \text{ or } 1 - p(z) \geq \alpha/2$$

   where $z_{\alpha/2}$ is the z score that has $\alpha/2$ of the distribution above it.

   Directional alternative:
   For $H_1: \pi \geq \pi_0$
   $$\text{Reject } H_0 \text{ when } z \geq z_\alpha$$
   or
   $$1 - p(z) \geq \alpha$$
   For $H_1: \pi \leq \pi_0$
   $$\text{Reject } H_0 \text{ when } z \leq -z_\alpha$$
   or
   $$p(z) \leq \alpha$$
   where z_α is the z score that has α proportion of the distribution above it.

5. **Randomly sample from the population and compute the test statistic.**

6. **Apply decision rule and draw conclusions.** If the null hypothesis is rejected, decide that the proportion of successes in the population is different from the proportion specified by H_0.

TABLE 11.2
Confidence Interval for π, the Proportion of Successes in a Population

1. **Assumptions (requirements):**
   Sampling assumptions:
   a. The n observations are obtained by independent (within-sample) random sampling.
   b. The sample size must be large. In particular, $(n)(p) \geq 20$ and $(n)(1 - p) \leq 20$.

   Data assumption:
   Each of the observations must be classified as either a success or a failure.

2. **Set confidence level, $(1 - \alpha)$.**

3. **Obtain a random sample from the population.**

4. **Construct the interval:**
   Upper limit $= p + z_{\alpha/2} \times \sigma_p$
   Lower limit $= p - z_{\alpha/2} \times \sigma_p$

$$p = \frac{\text{number of successes}}{n}$$

   $z_{\alpha/2}$ is the z score with $\alpha/2$ of the distribution above it

$$\sigma_p = \sqrt{\frac{p(1-p)}{n}}$$

   The $1 - \alpha$ confidence interval is:
$$\text{lower limit} \leq \pi \leq \text{upper limit}$$

5. **Interpretation:** The probability is $1 - \alpha$ that the interval includes the real value of π. There is a probability of α that the interval does not include the real value of π.

EXERCISES

Terms   *Define these new terms and symbols.*

binomial experiment	p
success	π
failure	σ_p
mutually exclusive	π_0
exhaustive	π_s

Questions   *Answer the following questions.*

1. If the assumptions are met, test H_0: $\pi = .65$ against the nondirectional alternative for these combinations of conditions.
   †**a.** $n = 50$, $\alpha = .05$, $p = .5$
   b. $n = 10$, $\alpha = .02$, $p = .6$
   c. $n = 25$, $\alpha = .01$, $p = .75$

†**2.** Redo Question 1 using $H_1: \pi > \pi_0$.

†**3.** Suppose that $\pi = .73$. What is the power of the statistical tests described in Questions 1 and 2?

†**4.** Determine the sample size need to obtain the desired power in each of the following situations. Assume that $H_0: \pi = .4$.

    a. $H_1: \pi \neq .4$, $\alpha = .05$, $\pi_s = .6$, power $= .8$.

    b. $H_1: \pi > .4$, $\alpha = .05$, $\pi_s = .6$, power $= .8$.

    c. $H_1: \pi \neq .4$, $\alpha = .01$, $\pi_s = .6$, power $= .8$.

    d. $H_1: \pi \neq .4$, $\alpha = .05$, $\pi_s = .7$, power $= .8$.

    e. $H_1: \pi \neq .4$, $\alpha = .05$, $\pi_s = .6$, power $= .5$.

†**5.** If the assumptions are met, construct 95% and 98% confidence intervals for π in each of the following situations:

    a. $n = 200$, $p = .25$

    b. $n = 400$, $p = .25$

    c. $n = 500$, $p = .98$

6. You are hired to conduct a survey of student opinion. In particular, the Board of Regents has to devise a plan to save money in the coming year. They ask you to determine if students prefer an increase of $50 a semester in tuition or a decrease of 25% in library hours. Describe how you would obtain the appropriate data, including the sample size.

    Suppose that $p = .75$, what would you conclude? How would you explain your conclusion to the board (which is composed of statistically unsophisticated people)?

7. You are asked to conduct a test of the efficacy of a new quality control procedure for a lightbulb manufacturer. Ordinarily, the lightbulbs have a failure rate of .001 (that is, one in a thousand does not work). The manufacturer institutes the new procedure for a month and wants you to determine if the new procedure actually reduces the failure rate. What would you do?

8. You are working for a psychologist who is testing a theory of motivation. According to the theory, when both hungry and thirsty, animals are more likely to work for a drink than for food. To test the theory, each of 30 rats is taught one response (Response A) to gain water, and a second response (Response B) to gain food. After 24 hours of neither food nor water, each rat is given the opportunity to make one response. Of the 30 rats, 20 made Response A and 10 made Response B. Use statistical hypothesis testing to test the theory. Report the results as you would in a research report.

9. What would you do in Question 8 if 20 rats made Response A, 7 rats made Response B, and 3 rats did not respond?

Inferences About μ When σ Is Unknown: The Single-sample t Test

*A*s discussed in Part II (Chapters 5–10), inferences about a single population mean can be made using a random sample from the population. However, all of the procedures discussed in those chapters required that you know σ, the population standard deviation. Unfortunately, in the real world σ generally is unknown.

In this chapter, we face the problem of making inferences about μ when σ is unknown. The solution is to use a new statistic, t, that does not require σ. As you shall see, the t statistic is used frequently in this book (Chapters 12, 13, 15, and 20), and it is used frequently in real-world statistical tasks.

Although we will be using a new statistic, the goal of statistical inference remains the same: Use a random sample to learn about the population from which the sample was drawn. In this chapter, the more specific goal is to learn about a population mean, through either hypothesis testing or parameter estimation. Some examples include an educational psychologist who tests hypotheses about the *mean* time-on-task during a standard arithmetic lesson; a hospital administrator who estimates the *mean* length of stay in hospitals following a standard surgical procedure; and a cognitive psychologist who estimates the *mean* number of pictures that can be remembered after a single exposure.

Because the procedure is used to make an inference about a single population mean based on a single sample, the procedure is called the "single-sample" t test.

WHY s CANNOT BE USED TO COMPUTE z

When making inferences about μ, the formula for z is

$$z = \frac{M - \mu_0}{\sigma_M}$$

In this formula, σ_M is the standard deviation of the sampling distribution of M. This standard deviation is (according to Amazing Fact Number 2)

$$\sigma_M = \frac{\sigma}{\sqrt{n}}$$

Note that this formula requires σ, which is usually unknown. You might think, "Because s is an unbiased estimator of σ, and s can be computed from a random sample, why not use s instead of σ?" In part your thinking is correct, and in part incorrect. The correct part is that using s in the formula for σ_M does result in something sensible, namely, the estimated standard error.

> The **estimated standard error** (or standard error for short) is an estimate of σ_M, the standard error of the sampling distribution of M. The estimated standard error is obtained by dividing s, the sample standard deviation, by the square root of the sample size.

FORMULA 12.1   The Estimated Standard Error of the Sampling Distribution of M

$$s_M = \frac{s}{\sqrt{n}}$$

Here is why s_M cannot be used to compute z, however. One purpose of the z transformation is to convert the sampling distribution of M into the standard normal distribution with a mean of 0.0 and a standard deviation of 1.0. To do this, each of the Ms in the sampling distribution must have μ subtracted from it and the difference divided by σ_M. Because σ_M is a parameter, it is the same for each sample M and z. Unfortunately, the estimated standard error, s_M, varies from sample to sample (that is, from M to M), because s varies from sample to sample. The result is a distribution with a standard deviation larger than 1.0, not a standard normal distribution. The resulting distribution is, however, a *t* distribution.

[handwritten: normal distribution mean = 0 standard deviation = 1]

THE *t* STATISTIC

In the early part of the 20th century, W. S. Gosset developed the sampling distribution of the *t* statistic. Because Gosset was writing under the pen name "Student," the statistic is often called Student's *t*.

> The *t* **statistic** is formed whenever a statistic that has a normal sampling distribution (such as *M*) is transformed by subtracting the mean of the sampling distribution and dividing by an *estimate* of the standard error.

Because there are multiple statistics that have normal sampling distributions, there are multiple ways of forming the *t* statistic. In this chapter, we will be concerned with only the following form:

[handwritten: so, s can not be used to compute z, but s can be used to compute t.]

FORMULA 12.2   The Single-sample *t* Statistic

[handwritten: sample]

$$t = \frac{M - \mu}{s_M}$$

[handwritten: — population]

Consider how the sampling distribution of the *t* statistic (that is, the *t* distribution) could be obtained. First, select a population (with a particular μ) and a sample size, *n*.[1] Next, draw a random sample (of size *n*) from the population and compute *M*, $s_M = s/\sqrt{n}$, and then *t* using Formula 12.2. Draw a second random sample and compute *M*, s_M, and *t* again. Do the same for a third random sample, a fourth, and so on, until all possible random samples have been selected. The relative frequency distribution of these *t*s is the sampling distribution of *t*.[2] *[handwritten: — what does this mean?]*

Comparison of *t* and *z* Distributions

Figure 12.1 illustrates the sampling distribution of the *t* statistic for sample sizes of 2 and 10, and the standard normal (*z*) distribution for comparison. The figure makes four important points. First, the means of the *t* distributions all equal zero, just like the mean of the *z* distribution. Second, the *t* distributions are all symmetric about the mean, just like the *z* distribution.

---

[1] Also, the population must be normally distributed. This constraint will be discussed along with the assumptions for hypothesis testing.

[2] We could have constructed the sampling distribution of *M* first, and then converted all of the *M*s into *t*s by using Formula 12.2. Because you are now familiar with sampling distributions, the extra step can be omitted and the sampling distribution of the *t* statistic constructed directly.

FIGURE 12.1

Comparison of standard normal and t distributions.

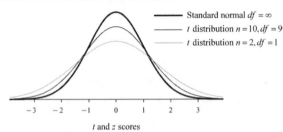

Third, the t distributions are more variable than the z distribution. (Note that the tails of the t distributions are higher than the tails of the standard normal. Because there are more scores in the tails of a t distribution than in the tails of the z distribution, there are more scores dispersed from the mean, producing greater variability.) The reason for the greater variability is easy to understand. When constructing the sampling distribution of z, the only quantity that varies from sample to sample is M; the μ_0 and the σ_M in the formula stay the same from sample to sample. However, when constructing a sampling distribution of t, both M and s_M vary from sample to sample. Because there are two sources of variability, the t statistic is more variable than the z statistic.

The fourth point to note about Figure 12.1 is that the shape of the t distribution changes with the sample size: As the sample size increases, the t distribution becomes more and more like a normal distribution. In fact, with an infinite sample size, the two are identical. Thus, unlike the standard normal, there is a different t distribution for every sample size.

These different t distributions are characterized by their degrees of freedom.

> The number of **degrees of freedom** (df) for a statistic equals the number of components in its calculation that are free to vary.

The concept of degrees of freedom is important, but rather technical. For our purposes, it is important to remember only that the degrees of freedom for the t statistic in Formula 12.2 equals $n - 1$, that is, one less than the sample size.[3]

Using the Table of t Statistics

Because the t distribution changes with the degrees of freedom (df), it is a little trickier to deal with than the standard normal distribution. One way to deal with the problem would be to have a table, similar to Table A, for each number of df. Of course, this would take up a lot of room. Another solution is to have a single table that includes only important critical values of t from each of the t distributions. That is the approach used in the table of t statistics, Table C.

---

[3] The degrees of freedom for other forms of the t statistic are computed differently. These computations will be discussed in later chapters.

FIGURE 12.2

Comparison of 95th percentiles for *t* distributions with 5 and 20 *df*.

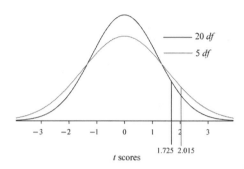

Turn now to Table C, and keep it marked with a finger. Each row gives critical values from a different *t* distribution specified by its *df* (given on the far left). Each critical value in the table is the *t* statistic that has a specific proportion of the scores in the distribution greater than it. The proportion is given by the heading of the column. As we will see shortly, these proportions correspond to various levels of *α*, the significance level.

Locate the critical values of the *t* distribution with 5 *df*, and find the number 1.476. At the top of the column is the heading ".10." This heading indicates that 10% of the scores (*t* statistics) in the distribution are greater than 1.476. That is, 1.476 is the 90th percentile. Moving over a column, 5% of the scores in the distribution are greater than the critical value of 2.015; it is the 95th percentile.

Now, look at the values for the *t* distribution with 20 degrees of freedom. In this distribution, 5% of the *t* statistics are greater than 1.725. Note that 1.725 is smaller than the 2.015, the corresponding critical value from the distribution with 5 *df*. The reason for this difference is illustrated in Figure 12.2.

The *t* score of 1.725 has above it 5% of the distribution with 20 *df*. The distribution with 5 *df* is more variable than the distribution with 20 *df*, however. Thus, to locate the upper 5% of the distribution with 5 *df*, we have to move farther out into the tail of the distribution, to 2.015.

Because the *t* distribution is symmetric, Table C can be used to obtain critical values for the lower tail by simply adding a negative sign. Thus, for 20 *df*, −1.725 is the critical value that has 5% of the scores in the distribution *below* it; in other words, −1.725 is the 5th percentile.

You may have noticed that not all values of *df* are listed in Table C. If the *df* you are working with is not in the table, you may use the next *lower* number of *df*. Using the lower number of *df* is somewhat conservative; that is, the probability of a Type I error will be a little lower than the stated value of *α*.

USING *t* TO TEST HYPOTHESES ABOUT *μ*

Hypothesis testing will be introduced in the context of a specific example. A summary of the procedure is provided in Table 12.3 at the end of the chapter.

A psychologist is studying the effects of moderate stress on life expectancy. He exposes a random sample of 31 rats to 15 minutes of loud noise (the stressor) every day. This is continued until the rats die, and the psychologist records their ages (in months) at the time of death. The data are in Table 12.1. Is there enough evidence to conclude that rats exposed to a moderate amount of stress have a life expectancy that differs from the unstressed population average of 37.5 months?

The question concerns the mean of a population. Namely, is the mean of the population of life expectancies of rats exposed to moderate stress different from 37.5 months? Because we have a random sample from the population, we can test hypotheses about μ using the six-step procedure.

Step 1: Assumptions

The single-sample t statistic should be used only when the following assumptions are satisfied.

Population Assumption The population is normally distributed. This is a difficult assumption to satisfy.[4] Clearly, the population of rat life expectancies is not normally distributed (a life expectancy cannot be less than zero). In fact, few real populations will be exactly normally distributed. Fortunately, the t statistic is robust in regard to this assumption.

> A statistic is **robust** if it gives fairly accurate results even when an assumption is violated.

Because t is robust, it can be used as long as the population is somewhat symmetric and mound shaped. If the sample is large enough, constructing the frequency distribution for the sample will give some indication as to the shape of the population. If the sample frequency distribution is not greatly skewed, then the t statistic can be used.

Figure 12.3 gives the frequency distribution for the data in Table 12.1. Because the data are not greatly skewed, we can count on the robustness of the t statistic to meet the population assumption.

Sampling Assumption The observations are collected using independent (within-sample) random sampling from the population. This assumption requires careful data collection so that the measurement of one observation does not influence the measurement of any other. For example, the rats should be housed separately so that infectious diseases are not spread.

---

[4] When using the z statistic, we could count on the Central Limit Theorem (Amazing Fact Number 3) to ensure that the sampling distribution of M was, for large samples, essentially normally distributed. To use the t statistic, the assumption requires the population of scores (not Ms) to be normally distributed. The reason is that the sampling distribution of the t statistic is computed assuming that each M and s_M are independent of one another, and this assumption is met when the population is normally distributed.

TABLE 12.1
Age of Death (in Months) for 31 Rats Exposed
to 15 Minutes of Noise Each Day

43	39	38	37	37
39	35	36	40	41
36	38	39	41	40
41	40	37	38	39
39	37	43	39	38
38	40	40	35	40
				41

$n = 31$

$$\sum X = 1205$$

$$\sum X^2 = 46969$$

$$M = \frac{\sum X}{n} = \frac{1205}{31} = 38.87$$

$$SS(X) = \sum (X - M)^2 = \sum X^2 - nM^2$$

$$SS(X) = 46969 - 31(38.87)^2 = 129.48$$

$$s^2 = \frac{SS(X)}{n-1} = \frac{129.48}{30} = 4.316$$

$$s = \sqrt{s^2} = \sqrt{4.316} = 2.08$$

FIGURE 12.3
Frequency distribution for the data in Table 12.1.

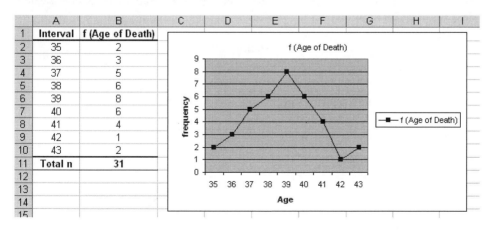

Data Assumption   The results will be easiest to interpret if the scores are measured on an interval or a ratio scale. As discussed in Chapter 3, computation of means and variances is most sensible when the data are interval or ratio. Although the t test can be used with ordinal (and even nominal) data, the results may not be sensible. The data in the example are ratio data.

Step 2: Hypotheses

As usual, the null hypothesis must state something specific about the population. For the single-sample t test, the null must propose a specific value for the population mean. The general form for the null hypothesis is

$$H_0: \mu = \mu_0$$

The symbol μ_0 stands for "the value of μ specified by the null hypothesis."

Typically, μ_0 is selected to imply no change from a standard. For our example, a good value for μ_0 is 38 months, the life expectancy of rats not exposed to noise stress. Thus, for this example

$$H_0: \mu = 38$$

Three forms of the alternative hypothesis are available:

$$H_1: \mu \neq \mu_0$$

$$H_1: \mu < \mu_0$$

$$H_1: \mu > \mu_0$$

Because the psychologist is interested in determining if moderate stress decreases or increases life expectancy, the nondirectional alternative is most appropriate for this example. Thus, the alternative hypothesis will be

$$H_1: \mu \neq 38$$

Step 3: Sampling Distributions

Substituting the value of μ_0 into the formula for t gives

$$t = \frac{M - \mu_0}{s_M} = \frac{M - 38}{s_M}$$

For the example, the t statistic has 30 df (because $n = 31$).

FIGURE 12.4
Sampling distributions of the t statistic with 30 df for testing H_0: $\mu = 38$ and H_1: $\mu \neq 38$. Also illustrated is the rejection region for $\alpha = .05$.

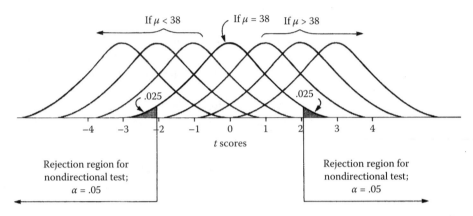

The middle distribution in Figure 12.4 illustrates the sampling distribution of t when H_0 is correct. Remember, when H_0 is correct, most random samples will have Ms around 38. When these Ms are put into the formula for t, the result will be a t around zero (because of subtracting $\mu_0 = 38$). Thus this distribution is predicting that when H_0 is correct the most likely value for t is around zero.

The flanking distributions in Figure 12.4 are all consistent with H_1. For example, if μ is really greater than 38, then most random samples will have Ms greater than 38. Putting these Ms into the formula for t will produce t values offset to the right. These distributions are predicting that when H_1 is correct the most likely values for t are different from zero.

Step 4: Set α and the Decision Rule

The factors that go into setting the significance level, α, are exactly the same as for other statistical tests. Namely, how do you wish to adjust the trade-off between Type I and Type II errors? Decreasing α will lower the probability of a Type I error, but it has the unfortunate side effect of increasing the probability of a Type II error (decreasing power). For this example, we will use the standard $\alpha = .05$.

The decision rule for the t test is identical to that used for the z statistic, except for the use of t instead of z. For the nondirectional alternative,

$$\text{Reject } H_0 \text{ if } t \geq t_{\alpha/2} \text{ or if } t \leq -t_{\alpha/2} \text{ or}$$
$$\text{Reject } H_0 \text{ if } p\text{-value} < \alpha$$

$t_{\alpha/2}$ is the value of t that has $\alpha/2$ of the distribution above it (so that the total probability of a Type I error is α when both tails are considered).

For the directional alternative H_0: $\mu > \mu_0$,

$$\text{Reject } H_0 \text{ if } t \geq t_\alpha$$

and for the directional alternative H_0: $\mu < \mu_0$,

$$\text{Reject } H_0 \text{ if } t \leq -t_\alpha$$

Here, t_α is the value of the t statistic that has α of the distribution above it.

As usual, these decision rules satisfy two criteria: Values of the test statistic that lead to rejection of H_0 are (a) unlikely when H_0 is correct and (b) very likely when H_1 is correct. Thus, obtaining one of these values of t from the random sample implies that H_0 is incorrect and H_1 is correct.

For the specific example, we need the nondirectional decision rule. Because $\alpha = .05$, $\alpha/2 = .025$, and for 30 df the critical value of t is 2.042 (from Table C). Thus, the decision rule is

$$\text{Reject } H_0 \text{ if } t \geq 2.042 \text{ or if } t \leq -2.042$$

This decision rule is illustrated in Figure 12.4. Note that it really is the case that values of t that lead to rejection of H_0 are unlikely when H_0 is correct, but very likely when H_1 is correct.

Step 5: Sample and Compute the Test Statistic

The formula for the t statistic is

$$t = \frac{M - \mu_0}{s_M}$$

The calculations of M (38.87) and s (2.08) are included in Table 12.1. The estimated standard error is

$$s_M = \frac{s}{\sqrt{n}} = \frac{2.08}{\sqrt{31}} = .37$$

Thus,

$$t = \frac{38.87 - 38}{.37} = 2.35$$

The p value of the test statistic, that is, the probability of obtaining a $t = 2.35$ assuming the null hypothesis were true, can be found using the Excel worksheet function "TDIST" or some other statistical computer program [TDIST (2.35, 30,2) = .026]. It is also important to report an estimate of the size of the effect. For a single-sample t test, the formula for $\hat{d}$ is

$$\hat{d} = \frac{|t|}{\sqrt{n}} = \frac{|2.35|}{\sqrt{31}} = .42$$

Step 6: Decide and Draw Conclusions

Because $t = 2.35$ is in the rejection region, the null hypothesis is rejected and the results are considered statistically significant (for $\alpha = .05$). The psychologist can claim that moderate stress has a moderate ($\hat{d} = .42$) effect on life expectancy, and appears to increase it (note that the age of the 31 stressed rats was longer than the average life expectancy of nonstressed rats).

Reporting the Results of a t Test

Research and statistical analyses are of little import if they are not communicated successfully to others. A good research report has many characteristics (see texts on experimental methodology, technical writing, or the *Publication Manual of the American Psychological Association*), one of which is clear reporting of data and statistical analyses. Chapters 2 and 3 covered some of this ground; here the concern is with communicating the results of hypothesis testing.

When reporting a statistical test, the goals of the communication are to present what you did clearly and concisely, with enough information so that the reader can draw appropriate conclusions. The conclusions a reader draws may differ from yours, because the reader may be using a different value of α. Nonetheless, you must communicate enough information for the reader to reach his or her own conclusions.

Generally, two types of information are required. First, you need to report the descriptive statistics that were used in hypothesis testing. For this example, report M and s (or s_M). When s is reported, it is often given in parentheses immediately following M. Second, information about the statistical test is given: the value of α, the value of the t statistic (and its df in parentheses), and whether or not the result is significant at the stated value of α. It is also now good practice to report the p value and an estimate of the effect size (like $\hat{d}$). The type of alternative is generally not mentioned unless a directional alternative is used.

Most of this information is presented compactly, in a single sentence. Thus, the psychologist might report, "Using an $\alpha = .05$, the observed mean of 38.87 (2.08) was significantly different from the hypothesized mean of 38, $t(30) = 2.35$, $p = .026$, $\hat{d} = .42$." Of course, after reporting the dry statistics, one goes on to report the substantive conclusions, either immediately following or in a discussion section.

Possible Errors

As with the z statistic, not all of the inferences you make using the t statistic will be correct; sometimes you will make Type I or Type II errors. Fortunately, we know how to minimize the probability of making errors. Rejecting H_0 when it is really correct is a Type I error. When the assumptions are met, the probability of making a Type I error equals α. To decrease the probability of a Type I error, simply decrease α.

Not rejecting H_0 when it really is wrong is a Type II error. In general, the probability of a Type II error, β, decreases as α increases, as the sample size increases, when careful measurement procedures are used to reduce variability, and with appropriate use of directional hypotheses. Actual computation of β is discussed in the section on power (remember, $\beta = 1 - $ power).

EXAMPLE USING A DIRECTIONAL ALTERNATIVE

If you recall from previous chapters, Drs. Janet Hyde and Marilyn Essex conducted a study on the effects of having a child on many family-related issues (the Maternity Study), including marital satisfaction. Due to the increased social, emotional, and financial demands on the family structure, does having a child decrease marital satisfaction for mothers after 1 year? To answer this question, we could take a random sample of mothers, compute the mean marital satisfaction score at 12 months, and compare it to the population mean. According to previous research $\mu = 1.75$; that is, the mean marital satisfaction (MARSAT) score for women is 1.75. We do not, however, know σ.

We start by obtaining a random sample of 36 MARSAT scores 12 months after giving birth. We assume that MARSAT scores are measured on an interval or ratio scale, and that they are not grossly skewed or non-normal. Thus, all the assumptions appear to be met.

The null hypothesis is H_0: $\mu = 1.75$. One could argue that the nondirectional alternative should be used. After all, we want to know if having a child decreases marital satisfaction, or if, contrary to our suspicions, having a child increases marital satisfaction. In this case, though, we are interested only in deviations from H_0 in one direction, and so the alternative hypothesis is H_1: $\mu < 1.75$.

Since we do not know σ, we will use the sampling distribution for the t statistic with 35 df $(n - 1)$. When H_0 is true, likely values of t will be around 0. On the other hand, when H_1 is likely true, values of t will be less than 0.

Analysis of the relative costs of Type I and Type II errors suggests that it may be appropriate to increase α in order to decrease β (increase power). A Type I error means that we would reject H_0 and conclude that having a child decreases marital satisfaction, when having a child really does not. Of course, it is never pleasant to make an error, but what are the consequences of this specific error? One consequence may be that married couples try to improve their relationship. On the other hand, a Type II error would be unfortunate. A Type II error would be made if there were truly a decrease in mother's marital satisfaction, but we failed to reject H_0 and concluded erroneously that there was no evidence of an effect of having a child on marital satisfaction. The consequence of having very unhappy women in marriages following childbirth may result in poor interactions with the child, increased frequencies of disputes with the husband, and so forth. Based on this analysis, we may decide to increase α from the standard .05 to .10.

We can state the decision rule in terms of a critical value for t (from Table C). However, we can also state the decision rule in terms of the probability of obtaining a particular value of t. Therefore, the decision rule for the directional alternative with $\alpha = .10$ and $df = 35$ is

$$\text{Reject } H_0 \text{ if } p(|t|_{35}) \leq .10$$

TABLE 12.2
MARSAT (Marital Satisfaction) Scores 1 Year After Childbirth for 36 Randomly Selected Women

2.653	1.959	1.541	2.502	2.443	0.725
−0.249	0.421	2.014	1.713	1.069	1.538
2.218	0.431	2.909	2.105	1.713	1.959
2.902	1.008	1.848	−0.499	1.045	0.904
0.242	−0.499	−1.964	2.579	1.976	−1.964
0.505	−0.237	1.653	2.562	1.981	1.146

In other words, we will reject H_0 if the probability of our obtained t, with 35 degrees of freedom, is less than or equal to .10 (our α).

Table 12.2 shows the 36 MARSAT scores at 12 months after birth. The t statistic is computed using Formula 12.2:

$$t = \frac{M - \mu_0}{s_M}$$

Although we could compute the mean and standard deviation of the data using a calculator or Excel, the easiest and most reliable way to compute t, p-value, and $\hat{d}$ is to use the LFD3 Analyses Add-in. Enter the data into Excel in a single column and click on Tools → LFD3 Analyses. Select "Single-Sample t test." After entering the appropriate range, alpha, the hypothesized mean, and clicking "OK" you should get an output that looks something like Figure 12.5. As you can see, the output provides a substantial amount of information. The most relevant, though, in terms of our hypothesis test is the t statistic, p value, and $\hat{d}$.

The decision is to reject the null hypothesis. Thus, we may report, "Using a directional hypothesis with $\alpha = .10$, the observed mean marital satisfaction score for mothers 12 months after childbirth of 1.243 was sufficiently low to reject the null hypothesis that the population mean was 1.75, $t(36) = -2.433$, $p = .01$. In addition, the estimated effect size was small to moderate, $\hat{d} = .41$."

POWER AND SAMPLE SIZE ANALYSIS

Power

Power is the probability of making the correct decision of rejecting H_0 when H_0 is wrong. Because power is the probability of a correct decision, we should attempt to make power as large as possible. All of the procedures for increasing power discussed in Chapters 8 and 9 apply to the t test. That is, power increases as α increases, the disparity between the True mean and μ_0 (the effect size) increases, variability decreases (for example, by increasing n), and when directional tests are used appropriately.

A power analysis is begun by proposing an effect size. Then, the analysis answers the question, "Given my α, sample size, and type of alternative, what is the probability that I

FIGURE 12.5
Excel output from LFD3 analyses Single-Sample t Test.

Single-Sample t Test

SUMMARY

Group	Number
MARSAT Scores	36

Single-Sample t Test	
Mean	1.245889
SS(X)	54.06681
Observations (n)	36
Variance	1.544766
Standard deviation	1.242886
SEM	0.207148
Hypothesized mean	1.75
df	35
t statistic	−2.43358
Tails	1
p Value	0.010098
d (est.)	0.405597

will reject H_0 *if my proposed effect size is correct?*" The answer provided by the procedure presented next is only approximate because the procedure uses the normal distribution instead of the t distribution.

In our first example, the psychologist was investigating the effects of moderate stress on life expectancy. The null hypothesis was that the mean life expectancy of the rats was 38 months ($\mu_0 = 38$ months). He used a nondirectional alternative with $\alpha = .05$ and $n = 31$.

Suppose that stress actually reduces the life expectancy to 37 months. This value provides a specific alternative to $\mu_0 = 38$—namely, $\mu_s = 37$ months—and this specific alternative is used to obtain d, the effect size.

$$d = \frac{|\mu_s - \mu_0|}{\sigma}$$

Note that the formula for d requires a value for μ_s (such as 37 months) and a guess as to the population standard deviation. Suppose that the psychologist had access to other data that suggested a standard deviation of 2 months. Thus,

$$d = \frac{|37 - 38|}{2} = .5$$

Alternatively, standard values for d may be used. Remember, d is the number of standard deviations (z scores) between μ_0 and μ_s. If you believe that the effect is relatively small, $d = .2$ is a reasonable guess. If you believe that the effect is of medium size, use $d = .5$. Finally, use $d = .8$ when you believe that the effect is relatively large.

The value of d is used to compute δ (*delta*),

$$\delta = d\sqrt{n}$$

For the example,

$$\delta = .5\sqrt{31} = 2.78$$

Entering Table B for $\alpha = .05$ and a nondirectional test, $\delta = 2.78$ corresponds to power of about .80. That is, *if the proposed effect size is correct,* then the probability of successfully rejecting H_0 is .80, a reasonable level of power.

Sample Size Analysis

Before beginning to collect data it is often important to determine, at least approximately, how large a sample is required to provide enough power to reject an incorrect H_0. The (approximate) procedure for determining sample size for the t test is the same as the procedure discussed in Chapter 9 for the z statistic.

The procedure begins by proposing an effect size, d, and a desired level of power. Then the analysis answers the question, "For my level of α and type of alternative hypothesis, how many observations do I need to have the desired power to reject H_0 *if the effect size is as proposed*?"

First, compute d, the effect size, using the formula

$$d = \frac{\left|\mu_s - \mu_0\right|}{\sigma}$$

Alternatively, because d is simply a z score indicating the number of standard deviations between μ_0 and μ_s, you may estimate d directly using values such as .8, .5, and .2, for large, medium, and small effects, respectively.

Next, go to Table B and locate the column corresponding to the appropriate α and type of alternative hypothesis. Scan down this column until you find the desired power, and then read off δ from the left of the table. Finally, the sample size is given by

$$n = \left(\frac{\delta}{d}\right)^2$$

Consider the second example from the Maternity Study. Suppose that Drs. Hyde and Essex desired a power of .90 to detect any effect of having a child, and that they believed that the effect was likely to be rather small, that is, $\delta = .2$.

Go to Table B for a directional test with $\alpha = .05$, and find .9 (the desired power) in the body of the table. The corresponding δ (at the left) is 2.9. The required sample size is

$$n = \left(\frac{2.9}{.2}\right)^2 = 210.25$$

You may recall that Drs. Hyde and Essex were able to reject H_0 with a much smaller sample size. Why? Although they guessed that the effect was rather small ($d = .2$), the estimated effect size was much greater.

ESTIMATING μ WHEN σ IS NOT KNOWN

An alternative to testing hypotheses about a population mean is to attempt to estimate it directly. As you already know, M is an unbiased estimator of μ, and therefore it makes the best point estimate. A single point estimate is unlikely to actually hit μ exactly, however. In this section, we will learn how to use the t statistic to construct a confidence interval for μ.

As an example, consider a clinical psychologist who is beginning to develop a new questionnaire to measure frequency of "fantasy life." She has constructed a series of statements describing various situations in which a person might fantasize; for example, "I often fantasize while reading textbooks." People answering the questionnaire check those statements that apply to themselves. The psychologist's first research goal is to estimate the mean number of items checked by noninstitutionalized people. She randomly selects 61 people from her university community and has each fill out the questionnaire. Her sample of 61 scores has $M = 34.3$ and $s = 18.8$.

Step 1: Assumptions

The assumptions are identical to those needed for hypothesis testing. The population assumption is that the population is normally distributed. However, because t is robust, you may consider the first assumption satisfied as long as the population is relatively mound-shaped and symmetrical. The sampling assumption is that the observations must be obtained using independent (within-sample) random sampling. The data assumption is that the scores are measured on an interval or a ratio scale.

Step 2: Set the Confidence Level, $(1 - \alpha)$

As usual, you have complete choice in setting the confidence level. The higher the confidence level (the lower the α), the greater the probability that the interval will actually include μ. However, high confidence results in a wide interval that is less useful than a narrow interval. Let us suppose that our psychologist wishes to construct a 95% confidence limit so that $\alpha = .05$.

Step 3: Obtain a Random Sample

In the psychologist's random sample, $n = 61$, $M = 34.3$, and $s = 18.8$.

Step 4: Construct the Interval

The formulas are

$$\text{upper limit} = M + t_{\alpha/2} \times s_M$$

$$\text{lower limit} = M - t_{\alpha/2} \times s_M$$

The symbol $t_{\alpha/2}$ is the value of t (with $n - 1$ df) that has $\alpha/2$ of the distribution above it.

From the data in the random sample, we know that $M = 34.3$. Because $s = 18.8$ and $n = 61$,

$$s_M = \frac{s}{\sqrt{n}} = \frac{18.8}{\sqrt{61}} = 2.41$$

Using the t distribution with $n - 1 = 61 - 1 = 60$ df, the value of t with .025 (that is, $\alpha/2$) of the distribution above it is 2.00. Plugging these numbers into the formula gives:

$$\text{upper limit} = 34.3 + 2.00 \times 2.41 = 39.12$$

$$\text{lower limit} = 34.3 - 2.00 \times 2.41 = 29.48$$

Thus, the 95% confidence interval is

$$29.48 \leq \mu \leq 39.12$$

Step 5: Interpretation

The probability is .95 that this interval actually includes the mean of the population. There is another way of saying this: If 100 random samples were taken from this population and one hundred 95% confidence intervals were constructed, about 95 of the 100 intervals would really include μ.

Do not overgeneralize. These results hold only for the population from which the random sample was selected. We can say (with 95% confidence) that the mean number of fantasy statements that would be checked is between 29.48 and 39.12 for members of the "university community." Whether or not this interval contains the mean of any other population is anybody's guess.

As always, interval estimation is comparable to hypothesis testing. The fact that the 95% confidence interval is 29.48–39.12 means that any null hypothesis specifying a mean between 29.48 and 39.12 could not be rejected using this random sample and a nondirectional, $\alpha = .05$ test.

SUMMARY

When σ is not known, the z statistic cannot be used to make inferences about μ. Using s as an estimate of σ produces the t statistic. The sampling distribution of t is more variable than the standard normal, although the variability decreases with the df (the sample size minus 1 for the single-sample t statistic in Formula 12.2). Other than using s instead of σ, having to consider df, and slightly different assumptions, t and z are remarkably similar in use and interpretation. Table 12.3 summarizes the single-sample t test, and Table 12.4 summarizes interval estimation of μ when σ is unknown.

EXERCISES

Terms   *Define these new terms and symbols.*

t statistic μ_0
df μ_s
s_M

Questions   *Assume for Questions 1–5 that all assumptions for the t statistic are met.*

1. Test H_0: $\mu = 4$ and H_1: $\mu \neq 4$ using $\alpha = .05$ for each of the following samples.
   †**a.** $M = 3$, $s = 5$, $n = 20$
   b. $M = 0$, $s = 5$, $n = 20$
   c. $M = 3$, $s = 1$, $n = 20$
   d. $M = 3$, $s = 5$, $n = 100$
†2. Using the data in Question 1, test H_0: $\mu = 4$ and H_1: $\mu < 4$, with $\alpha = .01$.
3. Suppose that you are planning research in which you will test H_0: $\mu = .58$ against the nondirectional alternative. The initial plan is to use $n = 35$ and $\alpha = .01$. Furthermore, you suspect that the effect is rather small. Should you continue? If not, what should you do? Why is it generally not reasonable to propose increasing the effect size?
4. Find approximate sample sizes needed for power of .7 and .9 in each of the following situations:
   †**a.** nondirectional alternative, $\alpha = .05$, small effect size
   b. nondirectional alternative, $\alpha = .05$, moderate effect size
   c. nondirectional alternative, $\alpha = .01$, small effect size
   d. directional alternative, $\alpha = .05$, small effect size
5. Find 95% and 99% confidence intervals for μ for each of the following samples:
   †**a.** $M = -.789$, $s = .51$, $n = 26$
   b. $M = 324$, $s = 35$, $n = 100$
   c. $M = 0$, $s = 5$, $n = 10$
   For each of the following situations, determine if the t test is appropriate. If it is, perform the t test, labeling each of the six steps, and report your results and conclusions.

TABLE 12.3
The Single-sample t Test for Testing Hypotheses About the Mean of a Population When σ Is Not Known

1. **Assumptions:**
   Population assumption: The population is normally distributed (but see discussion of robustness).
   Sampling assumption: The sample is obtained using independent (within-sample) random sampling.
   Data assumption: The data are measured using an interval or ratio scale.

2. **Hypotheses:**

   Null hypothesis:
   $$H_0: \mu = \mu_0$$
   where μ_0 is a specific number.

   Alternative hypotheses available:
   $$H_1: \mu \neq \mu_0$$
   $$H_1: \mu < \mu_0$$
   $$H_1: \mu > \mu_0$$

3. **Test statistic and its sampling distribution:**

   The test statistic is

   $$t = \frac{M - \mu_0}{s_M}, \; s_M = \frac{s}{\sqrt{n}}, \; s = \sqrt{\frac{\Sigma X^2 - (\Sigma X)^2/n}{n-1}} = \sqrt{\frac{SS(X)}{n-1}}$$

   The sampling distribution has $n - 1$ df. When H_0 is correct, the most likely values for t are close to zero. When H_1 is correct, the most likely values for t are discrepant from zero.

4. **Decision rule:**
   For $H_1: \mu \neq \mu_0$
   $$\text{Reject } H_0 \text{ if } t \geq t_{\alpha/2} \text{ or if } t \leq -t_{\alpha/2} \text{ or}$$
   $$\text{Reject } H_0 \text{ if } p\text{-value} \leq \alpha/2$$

   where $t_{\alpha/2}$ is the critical value of t with $n - 1$ df that has $\alpha/2$ of the distribution greater than it.

   For $H_1: \mu < \mu_0$
   $$\text{Reject } H_0 \text{ if } t \leq -t_\alpha \text{ or}$$
   $$\text{Reject } H_0 \text{ if } p\text{-value} \leq \alpha$$

   For $H_1: \mu > \mu_0$
   $$\text{Reject } H_0 \text{ if } t \geq t_\alpha \text{ or}$$
   $$\text{Reject } H_0 \text{ if } p\text{-value} \leq \alpha$$

   where t_α is the critical value of t with $n - 1$ df that has α of the distribution greater than it.

5. **Collect a random sample and compute M, s, and t** (or use the "Single-Sample t test" in "LFD3 Analyses").

6. **Apply decision rule and draw conclusions:**
   If H_0 is rejected, conclude that the population mean has a value greater or less than μ_0, depending on the sign of t. If H_0 is not rejected, conclude that there is insufficient evidence to decide whether or not H_0 is correct.

TABLE 12.4
Confidence Interval for μ When σ Is Not Known

1. **Assumptions:**
   Population assumption: The population is normally distributed (but see discussion of robustness).
   Sampling assumption: The sample is obtained using independent (within-sample) random sampling.
   Data assumption: The data are measured using an interval or ratio scale.

2. **Set the confidence level, $(1 - \alpha)$.**

3. **Obtain a random sample from the population.**

4. **Construct the interval:**

$$\text{Upper limit} = M + t_{\alpha/2} \times s_M$$
$$\text{Lower limit} = M - t_{\alpha/2} \times s_M$$

   where $t_{\alpha/2}$ is the critical value of the t statistic with $n - 1$ df that has $\alpha/2$ of the distribution above it:

$$s_M = \frac{s}{\sqrt{n}}, \; s = \sqrt{\frac{\Sigma X^2 - (\Sigma X)^2/n}{n-1}} = \sqrt{\frac{SS(X)}{n-1}}$$

   $1 - \alpha$ confidence interval is:

$$\text{lower limit} \le \mu \le \text{upper limit}$$

5. **Interpretation:**
   The probability is $1 - \alpha$ that the interval includes the mean of the population from which the sample was randomly drawn. There is a probability of α that the interval does not include μ.

---

6. A local legislator claims that more than 75% of his constituents support his attempt to ban the sale of pornographic materials within 300 feet of schools. You decide to test this claim by asking a random sample of 100 constituents if they do or do not support the ban. You find that 70 of those in the sample support the ban. What do you conclude about the legislator's claim?

†7. A sensational newspaper story claimed that students in the local high school drink, on average, the equivalent of a six-pack of beer a week. The school board asks you to test this claim. You select a random sample of 30 students and ask each student how many beers he or she consumed last week. (Of course, each student's confidentiality is assured.) You find that $M = .76$ and $s = .51$. What can you report to the school board?

8. Suppose that in Question 7, $s = 2.1$. Why might you decide not to perform a t test?

9. A clinical psychologist is devising a new program to help people stop smoking cigarettes. Two weeks after a standard therapy, the average number of cigarettes smoked is 5.3 per day. The psychologist selects a random sample of 10 people seeking therapy and gives them the new treatment. Two weeks after the new treatment, he counts the number of cigarettes smoked per day. The data are in Table 12.5. Is the new program a success?

10. A teacher wishes to compare the efficacy of two reading programs. She takes a random sample of 15 students and gives them Program A, and a random sample of 15 other students are given Program B. After the program, each student is

TABLE 12.5
Number of Cigarettes Smoked per Day
After 2 Weeks of the New Treatment

0	2
4	5
3	2
1	2
6	1

given a test of reading (assume that the test results in interval data). For the students given Program A, $M = 15.7$, $s = 4.5$; for the students given Program B, $M = 18.3$, $s = 5.1$. What should the teacher conclude about the programs?

11. A medical researcher suspects that a new medication affects blood pressure. The researcher randomly selects 10 participants and gives them the new medication for a month. The diastolic blood pressure of the 10 people was: 108, 76, 69, 78, 74, 85, 79, 78, 80, and 81. Does the new medication affect blood pressure ($\mu = 75$)?

12. A researcher knows that the mean number of symptoms exhibited by the population of people with unipolar depression, prior to diagnosis, is 9.5. She suspects that being told that one suffers from unipolar depression increases that number. She randomly selects 14 individuals already with the diagnosis of unipolar depression and counts the number of symptoms they exhibit. The number of depressive symptoms exhibited by the 14 participants was: 8, 9, 15, 19, 2, 8, 16, 14, 12, 13, 4, 15, 9, and 10. What can she conclude?

13. Andrzejewski, Cane, and Bersh ran an experiment where rats were exposed to 20-minute learning sessions each day. Alternating every minute, rats could earn sugar pellets by pressing a lever. In other words, during the 1st, 3rd, 5th, 7th, etc., minutes lever presses were reinforced with sugar pellets; during the 2nd, 4th, 6th, 8th, and so on, minutes lever presses did not produce sugar pellets. They divided the number of lever presses during the odd minutes by the total number of lever presses, to arrive at a proportion of reinforced responses. If the rats did not learn about the regularity of the sugar pellets, the proportion of reinforced responses would be .50.

   a. Eight rats produced proportions of: 0.67, 0.58, 0.46, 0.45, 0.69, 0.74, 0.66, and 0.61. What can you conclude from these data?

   b. Four other groups of eight rats were run in the same experiment, except that the experimenters interposed a delay (of varying lengths) between responses and reinforcers. Did any of the groups learn about the regularity of the reinforcers?

   Group B: 0.37, 0.43, 0.48, 0.47, 0.44, 0.40, 0.41, 0.43
   Group C: 0.64, 0.63, 0.46, 0.58, 0.65, 0.44, 0.64, 0.64
   Group D: 0.45, 0.44, 0.45, 0.46, 0.50, 0.41, 0.25, 0.37
   Group E: 0.63, 0.52, 0.46, 0.55, 0.51, 0.50, 0.57, 0.47

Comparing Two Populations: Independent Samples

*I*n the procedures discussed so far, testing hypotheses about the mean of a population has required a guess as to the value of the mean. This guess was used as μ_0, the value of the mean specified by the null hypothesis. For example, in Chapter 12 the psychologist examining the effects of moderate stress on life expectancy used as μ_0 the average life expectancy of rats that were not stressed (38 months). What would the psychologist have done if she did not know a reasonable value for μ_0? Indeed, when doing real research, this sort of information is often not available.

Although it sounds paradoxical, in many cases questions can be answered by making inferences about *two population means*, even when you have no information about either mean. A question that may be of interest for Drs. Hyde and Essex from the Maternity Study is whether the population of mother's marital satisfaction scores after having a girl baby (one population) is different from those scores after having a boy baby (the second population). The trick in these cases is to ask the question about a difference: Do the means of the two populations differ? How to answer this question is what the chapter is all about.

One of the most frequent uses of the statistical comparison of two populations is in the context of an experiment. Typically, an experiment involves two conditions, an experimental condition and a control condition, and one purpose of the experiment is to determine if the two conditions differ. In terms of the statistics, is the mean of the population from which the experimental observations were drawn different from the mean of the population from which the control observations were drawn?

The statistical analysis of the difference between two populations means uses a variant of the t test, the independent-sample t test. In this chapter, we also examine a number of related issues. Some of these, such as power analysis and parameter estimation, are familiar. Some new issues are also considered. These are the difference between naturally occurring and hypothetical populations; the distinction between independent and dependent sampling from two populations; and the use of a nonparametric test when the assumptions of the t test are violated.

COMPARING NATURALLY OCCURRING AND HYPOTHETICAL POPULATIONS

Consider these examples of the comparison of two population means. Do adults consume more alcohol per capita in small towns or in larger cities (statistically, is the mean of the population of alcohol consumption for adults in small towns different from the mean of the population of alcohol consumption for adults in larger cities)? Is one study technique more effective than another (statistically, is the mean of the population of achievement scores associated with one study technique different from the mean of the population of achievement scores associated with the other technique)? Is one type of cancer treatment more effective than another (is the mean of the population of survival rates following one treatment different from the mean of the population of survival rates following the other treatment)?

Some of these populations are naturally occurring, whereas others are hypothetical.

A naturally occurring population is one that is present without any intervention by the investigator.

For example, the amount of alcohol consumed in small towns and amounts consumed in large cities are two naturally occurring populations. Those amounts exist whether or not anyone chooses to investigate them. As we will see, the means of these populations can be compared by drawing a random sample from each of the populations.

The observations in a **hypothetical population** do not exist until they are actually measured.

Suppose that the learning coordinator at a school wishes to compare two new study methods: Method 1 and Method 2. The two populations to be compared are the achievement scores of students who use Method 1 and the achievement scores of students who use Method 2. These are both hypothetical populations because the students are not yet using either method. The learning coordinator could create these populations by having half of *all* the students study using Method 1 and half study using Method 2, and then measuring their achievement. Clearly this would be impractical.

Now consider an alternative procedure to determine if there is any difference between the two study methods. The learning coordinator takes a random *sample* of students and has them learn by Method 1, and he takes a second random *sample* of students and has them learn by Method 2. The achievement scores of both of these groups are then measured.

Conceptually, the learning coordinator has two random samples from two distinct, hypothetical populations. One is a random sample from the population of achievement scores of students who use Method 1. The second is a random sample from the population of achievement scores of students who use Method 2. Note that these are legitimate random samples from their respective (hypothetical) populations of achievement scores *even though the populations do not really exist;* only the samples exist. As we shall see, the means of these populations can be investigated by comparing the random samples. In this manner, the learning coordinator can compare the means of populations without going to the expense of actually creating the populations first.

An analogous case can be made for the cancer researcher. Suppose that the researcher wants to compare the mean number of years of survival following two forms of treatment. Because the treatments are untested, it would be unethical to actually create two full-fledged populations (by administering the treatments to many people). Instead, the researcher takes a random sample of patients and administers Treatment A, and she takes a second random sample of patients and administers Treatment B. The survival rates of these two groups form two random samples from two different populations of survival rates. Comparing these random samples will provide information about the respective populations. In this way, the researcher can determine the efficacy of the two treatments without having to create the populations first.

There are two points to this section. First, examining hypothetical populations (by using real random samples) is an extremely common technique because it is cheap, effective, and ethically much more sound than attempting to create populations. Second, all of the techniques discussed in this chapter can be applied to making inferences about naturally occurring populations and hypothetical populations. Statistically, they are treated identically.

INDEPENDENT AND DEPENDENT SAMPLING FROM POPULATIONS

The statistical procedures discussed in this chapter require two samples from two populations. When samples are selected from two (or more) populations, the samples can be independent of one another or dependent.[1] The statistical procedures discussed in this chapter apply only to independent samples; statistical techniques appropriate for dependent samples will be discussed in Chapter 15.

> Two (or more) random samples are **independent** when the scores included in one random sample are unrelated to the scores included in the other random sample.

Typically, independent samples arise when *different and unrelated* people contribute the scores in the two samples. For example, the learning coordinator had unrelated students study using Methods 1 and 2. Thus, the two samples of achievement scores are independent. Similarly, the cancer researcher used unrelated patients for the two treatments, resulting in independent samples.

> Two (or more) random samples are **dependent** when the scores included in one random sample are *systematically* related to the scores included in the other random sample.

Often, dependent samples are created when the same (or related) individuals contribute scores to the two samples. Suppose that the learning coordinator had each student study for one subject using Method 1 and study for a second subject using Method 2. In this case, the two samples of achievement scores would be dependent: The scores in one sample can be systematically matched with the scores in the second sample by pairing the scores that came from the same student.

The cancer researcher could also have used dependent samples. Suppose that the researcher began by pairing patients who were very similar in age, occupation, and type of cancer. One patient in each pair could be assigned to Treatment A and the other patient assigned to Treatment B. In this way, the two samples of survival rates are dependent; a score in one sample can be systematically paired with a score in the other sample.

As we will see in Chapter 15, using dependent samples has a number of important benefits. One is that dependent samples generally result in much more powerful statistical tests

---

[1] The concept of dependent samples is so important that it has many synonyms. Some of these are paired samples, correlated samples, matched samples, repeated measures, and within-subject sampling.

than independent samples. Nonetheless, for other equally good reasons (also discussed in Chapter 15), independent samples are often used in research.

Independent Samples, Dependent Samples, and Independent (Within-sample) Random Sampling

It is important to distinguish between two similar-sounding terms, independent samples and independent (within-sample) random sampling. When discussing independent samples, the important feature is the *relationship between the scores in two (or more) samples:* Independent samples are formed when the scores in the two samples are unrelated to one another.

In regard to independent (within-sample) random sampling, the important feature is the *relationship among the scores in any one sample:* Measurement of any other observation in the sample should not affect measurement of any other observation in the sample. Independent (within-sample) random sampling is ensured by careful data collection procedures. For example, how one person answers a questionnaire should not be allowed to influence how another person (contributing to the same sample) answers the questionnaire.

Even when dependent samples are used, the scores *within* each sample should be collected using independent (within-sample) random sampling. For example, the same students might contribute scores to two samples (so that the samples are dependent). Nonetheless, each student should work alone to ensure independent (within-sample) random sampling.

In summary, whether the two samples (from two populations) are independent samples or dependent samples, they should always be obtained by independent (within-sample) random sampling. For the remainder of this chapter, we will discuss making inferences only when the samples from the two populations are independent, and when both of the samples are obtained by independent (within-sample) random sampling.

SAMPLING DISTRIBUTION OF THE DIFFERENCE BETWEEN SAMPLE MEANS (INDEPENDENT SAMPLES)

When dealing with two populations, a frequently asked question is whether the means of the two populations differ. The null hypothesis is, typically,

$$H_0: \mu_1 - \mu_2 = 0$$

which implies that there is no difference.

As usual, the null hypothesis is evaluated by computing a test statistic and comparing the test statistic to its sampling distribution. If the null hypothesis really is correct, then the test statistic ought to be one of those that the sampling distribution predicts is highly probable.

The test statistic in this case is a t statistic based on $M_1 - M_2$. We will begin by examining the sampling distribution of $M_1 - M_2$. After getting a feel for it, we will progress to the sampling distribution of the related t statistic.

Using the Five-step Procedure to Construct the Sampling Distribution of $M_1 - M_2$

Figure 13.1 is a sampling distribution of $M_1 - M_2$. It could have been obtained using the five-step procedure for constructing sampling distributions. For example, suppose that you are the learning coordinator interested in comparing two study methods. You define one population as the population of social studies achievement scores for students in your school who study using Method 1. The second population is the population of social studies achievement scores for students in your school who study using Method 2. A random sample from each population is obtained by randomly choosing two samples of students, teaching them (at the beginning of the year) Method 1 (for those in Sample 1) or Method 2, and then measuring their achievement at the end of the year. Suppose that you decide to use $n_1 = 15$ and $n_2 = 15$. The difference between the sample means at the end of the year is one value of $M_1 - M_2$. Repeating this procedure a large number of times and obtaining a value of $M_1 - M_2$ each time would allow you to construct the sampling distribution of $M_1 - M_2$ (that is, the relative frequency distribution of all of the differences).

Like all sampling distributions, Figure 13.1 is making predictions about values of the statistic that are likely to be found in random sampling. For the distribution illustrated, the most likely values for $M_1 - M_2$ are around 15.0.

Characteristics of the Sampling Distribution of $M_1 - M_2$

Fortunately, because statisticians have determined the characteristics of the sampling distribution, we do not have to resort to repeated sampling. Like the sampling distribution of M, the sampling distribution of $M_1 - M_2$ can be described by three amazing facts:

1. The mean of the sampling distribution of $M_1 - M_2$ is always equal to $\mu_1 - \mu_2$, the difference between the means of the two populations from which the samples were drawn. Because the mean of the sampling distribution in Figure 13.1 is 15.0, the two populations of achievement scores must have means that differ by 15 points on the achievement test. For example, one population might have a mean of 60 and the other a mean of 75.

FIGURE 13.1
Sampling distribution of $M_1 - M_2$ when $\mu_1 - \mu_2 = 15$.

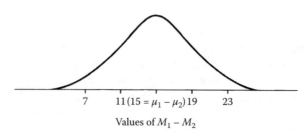

Values of $M_1 - M_2$

2. When the two populations have the same variance, σ^2, then the standard deviation (standard error) of the sampling distribution of $M_1 - M_2$ is given by Formula 13.1.

FORMULA 13.1   Standard Error of the Sampling Distribution of $M_1 - M_2$

$$\sigma_{M-M_2} = \sqrt{\sigma^2\left(\frac{1}{n_1} + \frac{1}{n_2}\right)}$$

Because the sample sizes are used as divisors, $\sigma_{M_1-M_2}$ (like σ_M) decreases as the sample sizes increase.

3. The Central Limit Theorem holds: If the two populations are normally distributed, then the sampling distribution of $M_1 - M_2$ will be normally distributed. Even if the two populations are not normally distributed, as the sample sizes increase, the sampling distribution approaches closer and closer to a normal distribution.

THE *t* DISTRIBUTION FOR INDEPENDENT SAMPLES

It is difficult to work with the sampling distribution of $M_1 - M_2$ directly because we do not have tabled values. One solution is to convert the distribution into the standard normal distribution and use Table A. Unfortunately, this maneuver requires that we know $\sigma_{M_1-M_2}$, which in turn requires that we know σ, which we usually do not know. Another solution is to convert the sampling distribution into the distribution of the *t* statistic, and this can be done.

In Chapter 12, we learned that the *t* statistic is formed whenever a statistic that is normally distributed (such as M) has the mean of its sampling distribution (such as μ_M) subtracted from it and the result divided by the estimate of the standard error (such as s_M). Thus, when dealing with a *single* sample from a *single* population, *t* is

$$t = \frac{M - \mu}{s_M}$$

Now, consider $M_1 - M_2$. Its sampling distribution is normally distributed, the mean of the sampling distribution is $\mu_1 - \mu_2$, and an estimate of the standard error of the sampling distribution is $s_{M_1-M_2}$. Thus, the *t* statistic is given in Formula 13.2.

FORMULA 13.2   The *t* Statistic for Independent Samples

$$t = \frac{(M_1 - M_2) - (\mu_1 - \mu_2)}{s_{M_1-M_2}}$$

Before continuing discussion of the t statistic, we need a brief digression to discuss $s_{M_1-M_2}$.

Estimating the Standard Error, $s_{M_1-M_2}$

The formula for $s_{M_1-M_2}$ is very similar to that for the standard error, $\sigma_{M_1-M_2}$. Compare Formula 13.1,

$$\sigma_{M_1-M_2} = \sqrt{\sigma^2\left(\frac{1}{n_1}+\frac{1}{n_2}\right)}$$

to the following formula for $s_{M_1-M_2}$.

FORMULA 13.3   Estimate of the Standard Error, $s_{M_1-M_2}$

$$s_{M_1-M_2} = \sqrt{s_p^2\left(\frac{1}{n_1}+\frac{1}{n_2}\right)}$$

The only new term is s_p^2, the symbol for the "pooled variance." Remember, Formula 13.1 assumes that the populations from which the random samples were drawn have equal variances. Likewise, Formula 13.3 is based on that assumption. When you have two random samples, however, and each provides its own estimate of the variance (s_1^2 and s_2^2), what are you to use for an estimate of the common population variance? The answer is intuitive: use of the average of s_1^2 and s_2^2. This average is the pooled variance, s_p^2.

The **pooled variance** is the weighted average of s_1^2 and s_2^2.

The formula for s_p^2 is

FORMULA 13.4   Pooled Variance

$$s_p^2 = \frac{s_1^2(n_1-1)+s_2^2(n_2-1)}{n_1+n_2-2} = \frac{SS(X_1)+SS(X_2)}{n_1+n_2-2}$$

Although this formula looks complicated, it is actually quite simple. When the sample sizes are equal, then the pooled variance really is just the average of s_1^2 and s_2^2.[2] When the sample sizes are unequal, the sample with the greater number of observations is given more weight. That is why each of the sample variances is multiplied by its sample size minus one (that is, the degrees of freedom in the sample variance).

---

[2] You can prove this yourself by equating n_1 and n_2 in Formula 13.4 and simplifying the expression.

To recap, the pooled variance, s_p^2, is computed by finding the (weighted) average of the sample variances obtained from Sample 1 and Sample 2. The pooled variance is an estimate of the common population variance (the two populations are assumed to have the same variance). The pooled variance is used to estimate the standard error of the sampling distribution (Formula 13.3), and this standard error is used to compute the t statistic for independent samples (Formula 13.2). Now back to the main story.

Characteristics of the t Distribution

We left the learning coordinator puzzling over the sampling distribution of $M_1 - M_2$. That distribution could have been obtained by taking a random sample from the population of achievement scores of students learning by Method 1 and a second random sample from the population of achievement scores of students learning by Method 2. The mean of one random sample was then subtracted from the mean of the second to produce one statistic, $M_1 - M_2$. After doing this often, the sampling (relative frequency) distribution of $M_1 - M_2$ was constructed.

Now suppose that each time that the learning coordinator computed $M_1 - M_2$, he went on to compute the t statistic described by Formula 13.2. When he had finished taking many samples and computing many t statistics, the sampling distribution of the t statistic could be constructed. (Of course, the learning coordinator does not really have to take multiple samples from the populations because Gosset, the discoverer of the t distribution, has already determined what the distribution will be like. But the learning coordinator could have done so, if he had the time and inclination.)

The sampling distribution of the t statistic has the following characteristics:

1. The distribution will be a t distribution with $n_1 + n_2 - 2$ degrees of freedom. The first sample has $n_1 - 1$ degrees of freedom and the second sample has $n_2 - 1$ degrees of freedom. Together the total degrees of freedom equals $n_1 + n_2 - 2$.
2. The distribution will be symmetric about the mean of 0.0. Look at the sampling distribution of $M_1 - M_2$ illustrated in Figure 13.1. The most likely value of $M_1 - M_2$ is $\mu_1 - \mu_2$. Therefore, the numerator of t, $(M_1 - M_2) - (\mu_1 - \mu_2)$, is likely to equal 0.0, regardless of values of the means of the original populations.

These characteristics are illustrated by the distribution on the right in Figure 13.2.

HYPOTHESIS TESTING

We now have enough background information to use the sampling distribution of the independent sample t statistic to solve some real problems. Remember, the goal of the independent sample t test is to make an inference about the means of two populations, namely, to determine whether the means are the same or different. As usual, the discussion will present general information on how to conduct an independent sample t test and illustrate it using a specific example. The procedure is summarized at the end of the chapter in Table 13.3.

FIGURE 13.2
Sampling distribution of t assuming H_0 is correct (black line), and distributions consistent with directional alternative (gray lines). Also illustrated is the $\alpha = .05$ rejection region.

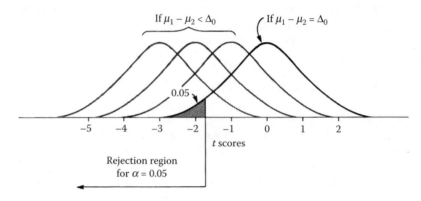

We will continue with a modification of the example of the learning coordinator. Suppose that he is trying to determine if there is a difference between two study methods—Method 1, the standard method taught at his school, and Method 2, a new method. In statistical terminology, he is trying to determine if the mean of the population of achievement scores of students who study using Method 1 is different from the mean of the population of achievement scores of students who study using Method 2. He could try to actually form these two populations, measure each observation, and then directly compare the means. Of course, this would be enormously time consuming, expensive, and probably unethical (if one of the study methods is really bad).

Instead, he uses random samples from the two populations to learn about the population means. Suppose that he takes a random sample of $n_1 = 15$ students, has them learn by Method 1, and then measures their achievement. He takes a second independent sample of $n_2 = 15$ students, has them learn by Method 2, and then measures their achievement. He then uses the six-step procedure of hypothesis testing to determine if the population means are likely to differ.

Step 1: Assumptions

The independent-sample t test has five assumptions that should be met to guarantee accurate results. If the assumptions cannot be met, an alternative procedure, the rank-sum test discussed later in this chapter, may be applicable.

Population Assumptions

1. The two populations are normally distributed. However, because the t statistic is robust, there is little loss of accuracy as long as the two populations are relatively mound-shaped and symmetrical. If you have reason to suspect that the populations are grossly skewed, then consider the rank-sum test.

2. The two populations have the same variance (homogeneity of variance). *When the sample sizes are equal (or close to equal)*, this assumption can be ignored with little loss of accuracy. If the sample sizes are not equal, and you have reason to believe that the population variances are not equal (for example, one sample variance is more than twice the other), then the rank-sum test should be considered.

Sampling Assumptions

1. The scores in the two samples must be independent of one another. This assumption is met because the students contributing to the two samples are unrelated. Procedures for dependent samples are discussed in Chapter 15.
2. Each of the samples must be obtained using independent (within-sample) random sampling from its population. This assumption is met as long as the students in each sample work alone.

Data Assumption   The results will be most interpretable if the scores are measured on an interval or ratio scale. If the scores are measured on an ordinal scale, then the rank-sum test is more appropriate.

Step 2: Hypotheses

The null hypothesis must propose a specific value for $\mu_1 - \mu_2$, the mean of the sampling distribution of $M_1 - M_2$. The symbol for the difference is Δ_0, the uppercase Greek *delta*. A Greek letter is used to indicate that the difference is a population parameter. An uppercase *delta* is used to distinguish it from the lowercase *delta* (δ) used in power analysis. Thus, the general form of the null hypothesis is:

$$H_0: \mu_1 - \mu_2 = \Delta_0$$

Typically, Δ_0 is zero, indicating that there is no difference between the means of the two populations (according to the null hypothesis). Nonetheless, other values can be used without changing any of the mathematics that follow. Other values should only be used for good reason, however, such as when testing a theory that specifies a value for Δ_0.

For our example, the most reasonable null hypothesis is

$$H_0: \mu_1 - \mu_2 = 0$$

That is, $\Delta_0 = 0$. According to the null hypothesis, the two study methods are equally effective. Rejecting this null hypothesis will be evidence that the two study methods are *not* equally effective.

The alternative hypothesis is also framed in terms of the difference between the population means, and it uses the same Δ_0 as specified by H_0. Because 0 is the most common value of Δ_0, the following discussion of alternative hypotheses assumes that $\Delta_0 = 0$.

As usual, three forms of the alternative hypothesis are available. The nondirectional alternative,

$$H_1: \mu_1 - \mu_2 \neq 0$$

states that there is a difference between the population means (because their difference is not zero), but does not specify the direction of the difference (which population mean is the larger). The directional alternative,

$$H_1: \mu_1 - \mu_2 > 0$$

implies that the mean of Population 1 is greater than the mean of Population 2, whereas the other directional alternative,

$$H_1: \mu_1 - \mu_2 < 0$$

implies that the mean of Population 1 is less than the mean of Population 2.

Choice among the three forms of the alternative, as always, depends on a frank assessment of what is of interest. Most often researchers select the nondirectional alternative because they are interested in rejecting the null hypothesis in either direction. On the other hand, if, for example, you are solely interested in finding out if μ_1 is less than μ_2, and you have absolutely no interest in the possibility that μ_2 is less than μ_1, then $H_1: \mu_1 - \mu_2 < 0$ is appropriate. If the null hypothesis is rejected, then you may claim that μ_1 is less than μ_2. Using this alternative precludes the possibility of finding out that μ_1 is larger than μ_2, however, because you cannot switch alternative hypotheses.

The learning coordinator is trying to decide if on average the new study method results in greater achievement (μ_2) than the old method (μ_1). In this situation a reasonable null hypothesis is the directional

$$H_1: \mu_1 - \mu_2 < 0.$$

If the new study method is more effective than the old, then the null hypothesis will be rejected in favor of this directional alternative. Because the learning coordinator has absolutely no interest in determining whether the new study method is actually worse than the old, he might as well gain the extra power associated with the directional alternative.[3]

Step 3: Sampling Distributions

The test statistic is the t statistic in Formula 13.2. Now that we have a null hypothesis that specifies a value for $\mu_1 - \mu_2$ (that is, Δ_0), the formula can be rewritten as follows:

$$t = \frac{(M_1 - M_2) - \Delta_0}{s_{M_1 - M_2}} = \frac{(M_1 - M_2) - 0}{s_{M_1 - M_2}}$$

---

[3] A slight change in the scenario makes the nondirectional alternative preferable. Suppose that some teachers had their students use Method 1 and other teachers had their students use Method 2. In this situation, the learning coordinator is interested in finding out whether Method 1 is better than Method 2 or Method 2 is better than Method 1. In this case, the nondirectional alternative is preferable.

The distribution on the right of Figure 13.2 illustrates the sampling distribution when the null hypothesis is correct. As discussed before, the most likely values of t are around zero. In other words, this distribution predicts that when H_0 is correct, values around zero are most likely for the t statistic actually computed from the random samples (one from each population).

Consider what would happen, however, if the alternative hypothesis were correct. The alternative is $H_1: \mu_1 - \mu_2 < 0$, implying that $\mu_1 < \mu_2$. Now, if μ_1 were really less than μ_2, then the most likely values for $M_1 - M_2$ would be values less than zero. Inserting these predominantly negative numbers into the numerator of the t statistic would cause the t statistic to be, predominantly, less than zero.

Sampling distributions consistent with the alternative hypothesis are illustrated on the left of Figure 13.2. Each of the distributions corresponds to a different (alternative) value of $\mu_1 - \mu_2$. These distributions also make predictions about the most likely value of t: When the alternative hypothesis is correct, the most likely value of t is substantially less than zero.

Step 4: Set α and the Decision Rule

The consideration that goes into setting the significance level is always the same, namely, weighing the different costs of Type I and Type II errors. We will assume that the learning coordinator has done this and has chosen $\alpha = .05$.

As usual, the decision rule states that if the probability of obtaining our statistic (p value), given that the null hypothesis is true, is less than α, we reject H_0 in favor of H_1. Thus, the rule is based on values of the statistic that (a) have a low probability ($<\alpha$) of occurring when H_0 is correct and (b) have a high probability of occurring when H_1 is correct.

For a nondirectional alternative hypothesis $H_1: \mu_1 - \mu_2 \neq 0$:

$$\text{Reject } H_0 \text{ if } p\text{-value} \leq \alpha/2$$

or, in terms of the values of t

$$\text{Reject } H_0 \text{ if } t \geq t_{\alpha/2} \text{ or } t \leq -t_{\alpha/2}$$

where $p(|t(df)|)$ is the probability of the absolute value of the t statistic with $n_1 + n_2 - 2$ degrees of freedom (df), and $t_{\alpha/2}$ is the value of t that has $\alpha/2$ of the distribution above it.

For the directional alternatives $H_1: \mu_1 - \mu_2 < 0$:

$$\text{Reject } H_0 \text{ if } p\text{-value} \leq \alpha$$

or in terms of the values of t,

$$\text{Reject } H_0 \text{ if } t \geq t_\alpha$$

For the directional alternative $H_1: \mu_1 - \mu_2 > 0$:

$$\text{Reject } H_0 \text{ if } p\text{-value} \leq \alpha$$

or in terms of the values of t,

$$\text{Reject } H_0 \text{ if } t \leq -t_\alpha$$

Here, t_α is the value of the t statistic that has α of the distribution above it.

For the learning coordinator example, the alternative hypothesis is H_1: $\mu_1 - \mu_2 < 0$, the degrees of freedom are $15 + 15 - 2 = 28$, and $\alpha = .05$. If you use Table C, the degrees of freedom define the row, whereas α identifies the column. The junction of 28 df and $\alpha = .05$ defines the critical value, $t_{.05} = 1.701$. Thus the decision rule can be stated as:

$$\text{Reject } H_0 \text{ if } p\text{-value} \leq \alpha \text{ or}$$

$$\text{Reject } H_0 \text{ if } t \leq -1.701$$

Step 5: Sample and Compute the Test Statistic

The first population is the population of achievement scores of students (in the learning coordinator's school) who study using Method 1 (the old method). The second population is the population of achievement scores of students who study using Method 2. These are hypothetical populations because no students have used Method 2, and no students have taken the achievement test yet. The learning coordinator can obtain random samples as follows. First, he obtains a random sample of 15 students to whom he teaches Method 1. He also obtains an independent random sample of students to whom he teaches Method 2. After the students in each sample have studied the materials, they are given achievement tests. These two samples of scores are random samples from the respective populations. The data are listed in Table 13.1.

Calculation of the independent-sample t statistic requires the mean and $SS(X)$ of each of the samples. These are computed in Table 13.1 using the standard computational formulas from Chapter 3.

The next step is to compute s_p^2, and then $s_{M_1-M_2}$.

$$s_p^2 = \frac{SS(X_1) + SS(X_2)}{n_1 + n_2 - 2} = \frac{2370.4 + 1677.73}{15 + 15 - 2} = 144.58$$

$$s_{M_1-M_2} = \sqrt{s_p^2 \left(\frac{1}{n_1} + \frac{1}{n_2} \right)} = \sqrt{144.58 \left(\frac{1}{15} + \frac{1}{15} \right)} = 4.39$$

The t statistic itself is computed using Formula 13.2:

$$t = \frac{(M_1 - M_2) - \Delta_0}{s_{M_1-M_2}} = \frac{(60.80 - 73.53) - 0}{4.39} = -2.90$$

TABLE 13.1
Achievement Scores for the Two Samples

Sample 1		Sample 2	
60	53	59	72
42	55	90	77
78	68	87	68
36	72	85	63
65	75	75	73
58	47	73	80
81	63	60	86
59		55	

$n_1 = 15$ $n_2 = 15$

$\Sigma X_1 = 912$ $\Sigma X_2 = 1103$

$\Sigma X_1^2 = 57820$ $\Sigma X_1^2 = 82785$

$M = \dfrac{\Sigma X_1}{n_1} = \dfrac{912}{15} = 60.80$ $M_2 = \dfrac{\Sigma X_2}{n_2} = \dfrac{1103}{15} = 73.53$

$SS(X_1) = \Sigma X_1^2 - n_1 M_1^2$ $SS(X_2) = \Sigma X_2^2 - n_2 M_2^2$

$SS(X_1) = 57820 - 15(60.80)^2 = 2370.4$ $SS(X_2) = 82785 - 15(73.53)^2 = 1677.73$

Using the Excel worksheet function "TDIST," the p-value of the t statistic can be computed; however, when using the worksheet function, Excel will recognize only positive values of t.

$$= \text{TDIST}(2.90, 28, 1) = 0.003591$$

Once again, an estimate of the effect size should accompany your computations. We can conceptualize our hypothesis test as:

$$\text{Test Statistic} = \text{Size of Effect} \times \text{Size of Study}$$

In the case of a t statistic, if we perform a little algebra, we see that

$$t = \frac{M_1 - M_2}{s_{M_1 - M_2}}$$

$$t = \frac{M_1 - M_2}{\sqrt{s_p^2 \left(\dfrac{1}{n_1} + \dfrac{1}{n_2} \right)}}$$

$$t = \frac{M_1 - M_2}{\sqrt{s_p^2}} \times \frac{1}{\sqrt{\left(\dfrac{1}{n_1} + \dfrac{1}{n_2}\right)}}$$

$$t = \frac{M_1 - M_2}{s_p} \times \sqrt{\frac{n_1 n_2}{n_1 + n_2}}$$

Thus, the size of the effect is given by the term $(M_1 - M_2)/s_p$ whereas the size of the study is indexed by the term $\sqrt{n_1 n_2 / (n_1 + n_2)}$. The effect size term we will call $\hat{d}$ as with previous tests. Thus,

$$t = \hat{d} \times \sqrt{\frac{n_1 n_2}{n_1 + n_2}}$$

$$\hat{d} = \frac{|t|}{\sqrt{\dfrac{n_1 n_2}{n_1 + n_2}}}$$

In the present example, we see that

$$\hat{d} = \frac{|-2.90|}{\sqrt{\dfrac{15(15)}{15 + 15}}} = 1.059$$

Step 6: Decide and Draw Conclusions

Applying the decision rule, H_0 is rejected in favor of the alternative hypothesis. In other words, there is enough evidence to conclude that the mean of the population of achievement scores associated with Method 2 is greater than the mean of the population of achievement scores associated with Method 1. Of course, statistically, this result holds only for the students in the learning coordinator's school, and it holds only for the particular achievement test used. Generalizations beyond these populations are not warranted by the statistics (although they may be correct).

Based on these data, the learning coordinator can make sound policy decisions. In particular, because the new method results in much greater achievement than the old method, he should work to get the new method adopted.

Reporting the Results

In reporting these results, include all of the important components used in the procedure, especially the values of the two sample means. The learning coordinator might report, "The mean achievement scores for the students who used Methods 1 and 2 were 60.80

and 73.53, respectively. With $\alpha = .05$, the two population means are significantly different, $t(28) = -2.90$, standard error $= 4.39$, $p = .003$, $\hat{d} = 1.059$."

Possible Errors

As always, there is some possibility of a Type I error when H_0 is rejected. A Type I error results from rejecting H_0 when it is really correct. Fortunately, the probability of a Type I error is exactly α, and you have complete control over its value.

A Type II error results from not rejecting H_0 when it really is incorrect. The probability of a Type II error, β, is affected by the same factors as usual. It decreases when α increases, when the sample size increases, when variability decreases, when the effect size increases, and with appropriate use of directional alternative hypotheses. The fact that β decreases as the effect size increases has some practical significance when dealing with hypothetical populations that a researcher constructs. That is, the researcher can attempt to construct the populations with maximally different means to maximize the effect size and thereby reduce β.[4]

Consider again the example with the learning coordinator. How long should the two groups of students use their respective study methods before they are given the achievement tests? If they study for too short a time, both groups will probably learn too little for there to be much of a difference on the achievement tests. On the other hand, if the groups study for too long a time, both groups will learn the material so completely that, again, there will be little difference in the population means. Picking an intermediate amount of study should maximize the difference between the population means (maximize the effect size) and decrease β (increase power). Another example of enhancing the effect size is provided in the next section.

A SECOND EXAMPLE OF HYPOTHESIS TESTING

Does having a baby girl or boy affect marital satisfaction for mothers? In the Maternity Study, Drs. Hyde and Essex asked about marital satisfaction 12 months after the baby's birth and documented the gender of the baby. So, we can conduct a hypothesis test to ask whether marital satisfaction scores following the birth of a baby girl are different from those following the birth of a boy. If we determine that all the assumptions of an independent-sample t test are satisfied, the question turns to the type of alternative hypothesis. Now, we might think that girls would be easier to raise (probably for sexist reasons, such as they are more "passive"), affecting marital satisfaction in a positive way. Conversely, we might think (probably, again, for sexist reasons, such as "dad's more likely to help out") that boys are easier, thereby affecting marital satisfaction in a positive way. The point is: There are likely scenarios that might increase or decrease marital satisfaction. It is probably best, therefore, to use the nondirectional alternative hypothesis:

---

[4] This reasoning assumes H_0: $\mu_1 - \mu_2 = 0$. If the value of Δ_0 is different from 0, then producing a large difference between the population means may make H_0 right rather than wrong.

$$H_0: \mu_G - \mu_B = 0$$

$$H_1: \mu_G - \mu_B \neq 0$$

where μ_G is the mean marital satisfaction score 1 year after having a girl and μ_B is the mean marital satisfaction score 1 year after having a boy.

Now, if we use all the data provided by the Maternity Study, we will have $n_G = 131$ and $n_B = 113$. Thus, the relevant sampling distribution is a t with 242 (131 + 113 − 2) df. According to this sampling distribution, the most likely values for the test statistic (independent-sample t) are around 0.0. If the alternative is correct, then likely values for t are much greater than 0 or much less than 0.

Using $\alpha = .05$ (so that $\alpha/2 = .025$), the decision rule is:

Reject H_0 if p-value $\leq .025$ or

using Table C (and interpolating)

Reject H_0 if $t \leq -1.970$ or $t \geq 1.970$

Before computing the necessary components of this t test by hand, consider trying to accurately compute the mean or $SS(X)$ of 131 scores. Accuracy is one of the many reasons that most contemporary researchers conduct their statistical analyses with the use of a computer. If you open the "Marital Satisfaction and Baby Gender.XLS" spreadsheet on your supplemental data CD, you'll see that we have copied the marital satisfaction scores from mothers 1 year after having a girl in Column A and the marital satisfaction scores 1 year following the birth of a boy in Column B. Copying and pasting data not only saves time, it may prevent a lot of data-entry errors.

From this point, you could compute the mean from each group, pooled variance, etc. However, like all of the computations in this book, there is an easier way. In the data analysis add-in (which is different from the LFD3 Analyses), there is an option "t-Test: Two-Sample Assuming Equal Variances." By selecting that option and filling in the relevant options, you should get an output that looks like that in Figure 13.3.

FIGURE 13.3   Output from "t-Test: Two-Sample Assuming Equal Variances" data analysis option in Excel on Marital Satisfaction and Baby Gender.

	A	B	C	D
1	t-Test: Two-Sample Assuming Equal Variances			
2				
3		Girl	Boy	
4	Mean	1.529239	1.496017	
5	Variance	0.806574	0.73677	
6	Observations	131	113	
7	Pooled Variance	0.774268		
8	Hypothesized Mean Difference	0		
9	df	242		
10	t Stat	0.294078		
11	P(T<=t) one-tail	0.384475		
12	t Critical one-tail	1.651174		
13	P(T<=t) two-tail	0.768951		
14	t Critical two-tail	1.969815		
15				
16				

Applying our decision rule, we do not reject the null (the *p*-value was not less than .025); the results are not statistically significant. We can conclude that there is not enough evidence to determine if the baby's gender affects marital satisfaction. Note that we were unable to reject the null hypothesis even though we had a large sample, and presumably good power.

POWER AND SAMPLE SIZE ANALYSES

Power is the probability of rejecting H_0 when it is wrong. It is equal to $1 - \beta$, where β is the probability of making a Type II error. Because rejecting H_0 when it is wrong is a correct decision, we attempt to increase power.

In general, the power of the independent-sample *t* test is enhanced by taking any of the actions discussed in Chapter 9. These actions are increasing α, increasing the effect size, decreasing variability (by, for example, increasing the sample sizes), and appropriate use of directional alternative hypotheses.

Calculating Power

Power analysis begins by proposing an effect size based on a value for $\mu_1 - \mu_2$ other than that specified by H_0. Then the analysis answers the question, "Given my α, sample size, and alternative hypothesis, what is the probability that I will reject H_0 *if my proposal for the effect size is correct?*" The answer given by the procedures described next is only approximate because the computational formulas use the standard normal distribution instead of the *t* distribution.

The effect size, *d,* can be estimated in either of two ways. One way requires guesses for σ, the common population variance (remember, the independent-sample *t* test assumes that $\sigma_1 = \sigma_2$), and a specific (alternative) difference between the population means, Δ_s. Then,

$$d = \frac{|\Delta_s - \Delta_0|}{\sigma}$$

In this formula, Δ_0 is the difference between the population means specified by the null hypothesis (typically, 0), whereas Δ_s is your guess for the difference between the population means when the null hypothesis is wrong. The other method for estimating *d* is to use standard values to represent small ($d = .2$), medium ($d = .5$) and large ($d = .8$) effects.

Next, compute δ using

$$\delta = d\sqrt{\frac{(n_1)(n_2)}{n_1 + n_2}}$$

Find in Table B the column corresponding to the type of alternative and value of α you are using. Then locate the row corresponding to δ. The approximate power is given at the intersection of the row and column.

As an example, let us calculate the power of the statistical test used in the second example in which we were interested in the effect of a baby's gender on the mother's marital satisfaction. Computing an estimate of the size of the effect, $\hat{d} = .037$, $n_1 = 131$, and $n_2 = 113$.

$$\delta = .037 \sqrt{\frac{131(113)}{131 + 113}} = .29$$

Looking in Table B, the closest value for δ is .3. The power corresponding to a nondirectional $\alpha = .05$ test is a measly .06. In other words, given a very small effect size estimate (.037), we had only a 6% chance of detecting it with the sample sizes we used.

There are at least three possible explanations of these findings: (a) There are small effects of a baby's gender on marital satisfaction which we need a lot more power to detect, or (b) there are no effects of a baby's gender on marital satisfaction, or (c) there are other variables that probably have larger effects on marital satisfaction (baby's health, father's involvement, and so on) than a baby's gender. Because research can be very costly, we, as researchers, may be confronted with the choice to drop a line of inquiry and pursue more potent variables. In the case of a baby's gender, it is likely that the effect is so small that it would take an enormous study (and probably the entire career of a researcher) to detect. At this point, it may be better to see the forest, instead of concentrating on a tree, and pursue another avenue of inquiry.

Sample Size Analysis

Sample size analysis begins with a specification of desired power and an estimate of the population effect size (d). The analysis answers the question, "Given my α and type of alternative hypothesis, what sample size do I need to obtain the desired power *if my estimate of the effect size is correct?*"

Estimate d using standard values or the formula

$$d = \frac{|\Delta_s - \Delta_0|}{\sigma}$$

Find the column in Table B corresponding to the type of alternative and α you are using. Scan down the column until you find the desired power and obtain the corresponding value of δ from the left of the table. Then,

$$n = 2 \left(\frac{\delta}{d} \right)^2$$

Note that n is the size of one of the independent samples. Considering both samples, the total number of observations needed is $2n$.

To follow up on the gender of a baby and marital satisfaction example, suppose that we would be happy with a power of .80. If we calculated an effect size estimate from the data provided, we see that $\hat{d} = .037$. Using Table B, locate the .80 in the column with $\alpha = .05$, nondirectional test. The δ (on the left) is 2.8. Then,

$$n = 2\left(\frac{2.8}{.037}\right)^2 = 11454$$

In sum, to detect an effect size of .037, we would need 22,908 (i.e., 2×11454) mother's marital satisfaction scores 1 year after birth in order to have a reasonable chance of rejecting H_0.

ESTIMATING THE DIFFERENCE BETWEEN TWO POPULATION MEANS

Testing hypotheses is not the only way to make an inference about the difference between two population means. An alternative is to estimate the difference directly.

The statistic $M_1 - M_2$ is an unbiased point estimator for $\mu_1 - \mu_2$; it is the best guess for $\mu_1 - \mu_2$ that can be obtained from random samples. Nonetheless, it will often be well off the mark, and so interval estimation is more practical. The procedure is summarized in Table 13.4 at the end of the chapter.

As an example, consider a comparative psychologist who is studying how captivity influences aggressive behavior in monkeys. She randomly selects eight monkeys from a population housed in a local zoo. She observes each animal for 15 minutes a day for a week and records the total number of fights with other animals. The mean is 13 fights with a variance of 16. Also, she obtains a grant from the National Science Foundation to make observations of the same breed of monkeys living in a South American forest. After locating a colony of monkeys, she randomly selects five for observation (it is much more difficult to observe the animals in the wild) and records the same information. The mean for the wild group is 8 fights, with a variance of 10. She uses these data to estimate $\mu_1 - \mu_2$, the difference between the mean of the population of number of fights for the captive animals and the mean of the population of the number of fights for the wild animals.

Step 1: Assumptions

The assumptions for constructing confidence intervals are exactly the same as for hypothesis testing. The first population assumption is that both populations are normally distributed. Because t is so robust, however, unless there is reason to believe that the populations are grossly non-normal, this assumption can be ignored.

The second population assumption is that the two populations have the same variance (the common population variance). If the sample sizes are equal, then this assumption can be ignored. When the sample sizes are not equal (as in the monkey example), then a good rule of thumb is to continue as long as one sample variance is not more than twice the other. In the example, the variances are 16 and 10. Because 16 is not more than twice 10, we can continue.

The two sampling assumptions are (a) the two samples are independent of one another and (b) each is obtained by independent (within-sample) random sampling. If dependent samples are used, then the procedure in Chapter 15 is appropriate.

The assumption that each sample is obtained by independent (within-sample) random sampling from its population could easily be violated in the example. Because monkeys that are attacked are likely to fight back, observing one animal fighting is not independent of observing other monkeys fighting. The psychologist can guard against nonindependence by the following precaution. She should observe only one animal during each 15-minute period. Thus, while observing Animal A, if it fights with Animal B (and B fights back), she would record only the fight for Animal A. Fights for Animal B would be recorded only during the 15-minute observation interval devoted to Animal B.

The data assumption is that the results are easiest to interpret if the data are interval or ratio.

Step 2: Set the Confidence Level, $1 - \alpha$

The confidence level is the probability that the interval constructed will include the real $\mu_1 - \mu_2$. The higher the confidence level, the wider the interval will be, and so the more likely that the interval will include $\mu_1 - \mu_2$. On the other hand, the wider the interval, the less information provided. That is, a wide interval is not very useful for pinpointing a value of $\mu_1 - \mu_2$.

The comparative psychologist reasons that the confidence interval will be relatively wide because the sample sizes are small. To roughly compensate, she chooses to form a 90% confidence interval ($\alpha = .10$), which will reduce the width of the interval compared to a 95% interval.

Step 3: Obtain the Random Samples

The comparative psychologist obtained two random samples, one from each of the populations. The data are $n_1 = 8$, $M_1 = 13$, $s_1^2 = 16$, and $n_2 = 5$, $M_2 = 8$, $s_2^2 = 10$.

Step 4: Construct the Confidence Interval

The formulas are:

$$\text{upper limit} = M_1 - M_2 + (s_{M_1-M_2} \times t_{\alpha/2})$$

$$\text{lower limit} = M_1 - M_2 - (s_{M_1-M_2} \times t_{\alpha/2})$$

The $1 - \alpha$ confidence limit is

$$\text{lower limit} \leq \mu_1 - \mu_2 \leq \text{upper limit}$$

In these formulas, $s_{M_1-M_2}$ is computed exactly as for the independent-sample t test, and so it requires s_p^2. The symbol $t_{\alpha/2}$ is the value of the t statistic (with $n_1 + n_2 - 2\ df$) that has $\alpha/2$ of the distribution above it.

For our example, s_p^2 is

$$s_p^2 = \frac{s_1^2(n_1-1) + s_2^2(n_2-1)}{n_1 + n_2 - 2} = \frac{(16)(7) + (10)(4)}{8 + 5 - 2} = 13.82$$

and the standard error is

$$s_{M_1-M_2} = \sqrt{s_p^2\left(\frac{1}{n_1} + \frac{1}{n_2}\right)} = \sqrt{13.82\left(\frac{1}{8} + \frac{1}{5}\right)} = 2.12$$

The t statistic has $8 + 5 - 2 = 11\ df$. For a 90% confidence interval, $\alpha = .10$ so that $\alpha/2 = .05$. The value of t that has .05 of the distribution above it is 1.796.

$$\text{lower limit} = (13 - 8) - (2.12 \times 1.796) = 1.19$$

$$\text{upper limit} = (13 - 8) + (2.12 \times 1.796) = 8.81$$

The 90% confidence interval is

$$1.19 \leq \mu_1 - \mu_2 \leq 8.81$$

Step 5: Interpretation

The comparative psychologist (and you) can be 90% confident that this interval includes the real value of $\mu_1 - \mu_2$. That is, if the psychologist repeated this procedure 100 times, about 90 times the interval would contain $\mu_1 - \mu_2$. It seems very likely that the two population means do in fact differ because the confidence interval does not include 0 (no difference) as a likely value for $\mu_1 - \mu_2$.

Because forming a confidence interval and hypothesis testing provide equivalent information, the comparative psychologist can also frame her results in the language of hypothesis testing. Any of the null hypotheses that propose a Δ_0 in the range 1.19 to 8.81 would *not* be rejected using a nondirectional, $\alpha = .10$ test. On the other hand, null hypotheses specifying a Δ_0 outside of this range would be rejected. For example, $H_0: \mu_1 - \mu_2 = 0$ would be rejected, and the psychologist can claim that the results are statistically significant for $\alpha = .10$.

At least for the populations sampled, it appears that monkeys in captivity are more aggressive than wild monkeys. This result opens a number of options for further action. For example, the psychologist may investigate why the captive animals are more aggressive, or she may suggest ways of reducing aggressiveness among the animals housed in the zoo.

THE RANK-SUM TEST FOR INDEPENDENT SAMPLES[5]

The independent-sample t test has three assumptions that might be difficult to meet: Both populations are normally distributed, the populations have the same variance, and the data are interval or ratio. We can trust to the robustness of the t statistic to overcome mild violations of the first two assumptions. However, when the assumptions are grossly violated, the t test becomes inaccurate so that the real level of α may be quite different from the stated level that you used in determining the rejection region. Thus, when the assumptions are grossly violated, a nonparametric test is called for.

In general, nonparametric tests do not require the estimation of any population parameters, and consequently do not require any assumptions about the population distributions. This advantage is paid for by two important disadvantages. First, nonparametric tests are less powerful than parametric tests. That is, for a given sample size, value of α, and form of the alternative hypothesis, the nonparametric test is more likely to produce a Type II error than the parametric test.

Second, the null hypothesis is more general for the nonparametric test than for the parametric test. The typical null hypothesis for the independent-sample t test is $H_0: \mu_1 - \mu_2 = 0$. When this null is rejected, you know exactly why: The population means are not equal. The typical null hypothesis for the nonparametric test is H_0: The two populations have the same relative frequency distribution. When this null is rejected, it may be because the populations differ in shape, central tendency, or variability. Thus, rejecting the null does not give much specific information about the populations other than that they differ. (As a practical matter, however, when the null hypothesis is rejected, it is likely to signify a difference in the central tendencies of the populations.)

Which should you use, parametric or nonparametric hypothesis testing? When the assumptions of the parametric test are met, then use it; it is more powerful and more informative than the nonparametric test. On the other hand, if the assumptions of the parametric test are grossly violated, then the nonparametric test is more accurate, and so it is preferred.

---

[5] The Mann–Whitney U statistic is similar, and it is discussed in many introductory statistics texts. The calculation of the rank-sum statistic T is easier, however.

The Rank-sum Statistic, *T*

The rank-sum test is a nonparametric procedure that corresponds to the independent-sample *t* test. That is, it is used to compare two populations when two independent samples, one from each population, are available. The test uses the *T* statistic computed as follows:

1. Combine the $n_1 + n_2$ scores from the two samples and order them from the smallest to the largest.
2. Assign the rank of 1 to the smallest score and the rank of $n_1 + n_2$ to the largest score. If there are ties, assign the average rank to all of the tied scores. For example, if the third and fourth scores are the same, assign each the rank of 3.5; if the eighth, ninth, and tenth scores are the same, assign each the rank of 9.
3. Sum the ranks corresponding to the scores in the first sample. This sum is the statistic *T*. As a check on your computations, the sum of the ranks in both groups should equal $(n_1 + n_2)(n_1 + n_2 + 1)/2$.

These computations are illustrated in Table 13.2.

The logic behind the rank-sum statistic is straightforward. When the null hypothesis is correct (and so the two populations have the same distributions), then both the high and the low ranks should be equally distributed across the two samples. On the other hand, when the null hypothesis is incorrect, then one of the samples should have the higher scores and the higher ranks, and the other sample should have the lower scores and the lower ranks. In this case, the sum of the ranks (*T*) will be very large for one sample and very small for the other. Therefore, to determine whether or not the null hypothesis is correct, we determine if the *T* statistic is very large or very small by comparing it to the sampling distribution of the statistic.

TABLE 13.2

Zoo-raised		Wild-raised	
Fear Rating	Rank	Fear Rating	Rank
3	1	17	7
8	2	20	9
10	3.5	40	12.5
10	3.5	48	14
15	5	53	15
16	6	55	16
20	9	61	17
20	9	72	18
21	11		
40	12.5		
	$T = 62.5$		108.5
Check: $62.5 + 108.5 = 171 = 18(18 + 1)/2$			

The T statistic, like all others, has a sampling distribution that could be obtained from repeated sampling from the two populations. However, we need not actually do the sampling. When the two sample sizes are both more than 7 and the null hypothesis is correct, the sampling distribution has some remarkable properties. First, the mean of the sampling distribution, μ_T, is

$$\mu_T = \frac{n_1(n_1 + n_2 + 1)}{2}$$

Second, the standard deviation of the sampling distribution, σ_T, is

$$\sigma_T = \sqrt{\frac{(n_1)(n_2)(n_1 + n_2 + 1)}{12}}$$

The 12 in the denominator is a constant, and it is not affected by the sample sizes. Third, the sampling distribution of T is approximately normally distributed.

Because the sampling distribution is approximately normally distributed and we know its means and standard deviation, we can convert the T statistic into a z score and use Table A. This conversion is

$$z = \frac{T - \mu_T}{\sigma_T}$$

When the null hypothesis is correct, then the T from the sample will be approximately equal to μ_T, and the z score will be close to zero. On the other hand, when the null hypothesis is incorrect, then T will be much larger or much smaller than μ_T. Consequently, z will be much larger or much smaller than zero.

Hypothesis Testing Using T

As usual, hypothesis testing will follow the six-step procedure. The procedure is summarized in Table 13.5 in the chapter summary. We begin with an example to make it concrete. A clinical psychologist studying fear is attempting to determine if fear of snakes is greater in wild-raised or zoo-raised animals. She takes a random sample of 10 zoo-raised monkeys who have never been exposed to snakes and another random sample of 8 wild-raised monkeys. Each monkey is exposed to a rubber snake and its reactions are rated on a scale of 0 (no fear) to 100 (enormous fear). The data are given in Table 13.2. Is there enough evidence to conclude that the population of fear reactions of zoo-raised monkeys is different from the population of fear reactions of wild-raised monkeys? Because the data are ordinal and because the data for the zoo-raised sample is so skewed (see Table 13.2), the psychologist concludes that the independent-sample t test is inappropriate. Instead, she decides to use the rank-sum test.

Step 1: Assumptions

Sampling Assumptions

1. The two samples are independent.
2. Each is obtained using independent (within-sample) random sampling.
3. Both samples have 8 or more observations so that the sampling distribution of the T statistic is approximately normally distributed. If only smaller samples are available, you should use the related Mann–Whitney U statistic.

Data Assumption   The data are ordinal, interval, or ratio. Because nominal data cannot be ranked sensibly, the rank-sum test should not be used with nominal data.

These assumptions are met by the data in Table 13.2. Note that there are no population assumptions. This is why the rank-sum test can be used with populations that are not normally distributed.

Step 2: Hypotheses

The hypotheses will look a little strange because they are not about population parameters, but about the population distributions. The hypotheses serve the same purpose as in parametric hypothesis testing, however.

The null hypothesis for the rank-sum test is always:

H_0: the two populations have identical relative frequency distributions

Three forms of the alternative hypothesis are available, the most common being the nondirectional:

H_1: the two populations do not have identical relative frequency distributions

The two directional alternatives are:

H_1: the scores in Population 1 tend to exceed the scores in Population 2

and

H_1: the scores in Population 2 tend to exceed the scores in Population 1

The nondirectional alternative is most appropriate for the clinical psychologist because she is interested in either outcome. Thus, she will test

H_0: the two populations have identical relative frequency distributions

H_1: the two populations do not have identical relative frequency distributions

Step 3: Sampling Distributions

When the null hypothesis is correct, the sampling distribution of the test statistic,

$$z = \frac{T - \mu_T}{\sigma_T}$$

will be a normal distribution with a mean of zero and a standard deviation of 1 (the standard normal distribution). Thus, the most likely values for z will be around 0.0. When the nondirectional alternative is correct, the most likely values for z will be different from 0.0—either much larger or much smaller.

Step 4: Set α and the Decision Rule

As usual, α is the probability of a Type I error and you can choose to set it at whatever level you wish. Remember, however, that there are consequences to your choices. Using a small α decreases the probability of a Type I error, but this increases the probability of a Type II error (decreases power). Let us suppose that the clinical psychologist chooses the standard $\alpha = .05$.

The decision rule for the nondirectional alternative is:

Reject H_0 if $1 - p$-value $\leq \alpha/2$

Or in terms of the values of z,

Reject H_0 if $z \leq -z_{\alpha/2}$ or if $z \geq z_{\alpha/2}$

Of course, $z_{\alpha/2}$ is the z score that has $\alpha/2$ of the distribution above it.

The decision rules for the directional alternatives are:

For H_1: The scores in Population 1 exceed the scores in Population 2

Reject H_0 if $1 - p$-value $\leq \alpha$

Or in terms of the values of z,

Reject H_0 if $z \geq z_\alpha$

For H_1: The scores in Population 2 exceed the scores in Population 1

Reject H_0 if p-value $\leq \alpha$

Or in terms of the values of z,

Reject H_0 if $z \leq -z_\alpha$

where z_α is the z score that has a proportion of α of the distribution above it.

For the example, using a nondirectional, $\alpha = .05$ test, the decision rule is

$$\text{Reject } H_0 \text{ if } 1 - p(|z|) \le \alpha/2$$

Or in terms of the values of z,

$$\text{Reject } H_0 \text{ if } z \le -1.96 \text{ or if } z \ge 1.96$$

Step 5: Sample and Compute the Test Statistic

The data are presented in Table 13.2, where they have been ranked and the sum of the ranks computed. The mean of the sampling distribution of T scores (when the null hypothesis is correct), μ_T, is

$$\mu_T = \frac{n_1(n_1 + n_2 + 1)}{2} = \frac{(10)(10 + 8 + 1)}{2} = 95$$

and the standard deviation, σ_T, is

$$\sigma_T = \sqrt{\frac{(n_1)(n_2)(n_1 + n_2 + 1)}{12}} = \sqrt{\frac{(10)(8)(10 + 8 + 1)}{12}} = 11.25$$

Based on these values, the z statistic is

$$z = \frac{T - \mu_T}{\sigma_T} = \frac{62.5 - 95}{11.25} = -2.89$$

To compute the p value of the z statistic, use the "NORMSDIST" function in Excel. First, calculate the p value of the absolute value of the z score ("=NORMSDIST(2.89)) which results in a proportion of .9981. If we subtract this proportion from 1, we arrive at the p value (.001), or the probability of obtaining a z of −2.89, when the null hypothesis is true.

Step 6: Decide and Draw Conclusions

Because the computed p value (.001) is less than $\alpha/2$ (.025), as well as the z statistic being less than −1.96, the null hypothesis should be rejected. Thus, we can conclude that the two populations do not have the same distribution. In fact, the scores in the zoo-raised population tend to be less than the scores in the wild-raised population. In other words, zoo-raised monkeys tend to be less fearful of the rubber snake than do wild-raised monkeys.

As with all inferential statistical tests, there is the possibility of errors. When the null hypothesis has been rejected, there is the possibility of a Type I error, but it is small because it equals α. When the null hypothesis is not rejected, there is the possibility of a Type II error. For the rank-sum test, the probability of a Type II error can be decreased (or power can be increased) by any of the now-familiar steps: Increase α, increase the effect size, decrease variability, or appropriate use of directional alternative hypothesis.

SUMMARY

A common approach to learning about the world is to compare two populations with the goal of learning whether or not they differ. These populations may be preexisting sets of scores, or they may be hypothetical populations that do not exist in full. In either case, the procedures for learning about the populations are identical: Obtain a random sample of (real) scores from each population and make inferences about the populations from the data in the samples.

The independent-sample t test and the rank-sum test are used when the samples from the two populations are independent. That is, the tests are appropriate only when the scores in one sample are completely unrelated to the scores in the other sample (dependent samples are discussed in Chapter 15). The t test is more powerful than the rank-sum test, but before the t test can be used, more restrictive assumptions must be met. In brief, the t test requires that both populations are normally distributed, that the populations have equal variances, and that the scores are measured on an interval or ratio scale. The rank-sum test does not require any of these conditions. Table 13.3 summarizes the independent-sample t test; Table 13.4 summarizes interval estimation of $\mu_1 - \mu_2$; and Table 13.5 summarizes the rank-sum test.

EXERCISES

Terms   *Define these new terms and symbols.*

independent samples	s_p^2
dependent samples	$\sigma_{M_1-M_2}$
independent (within-sample)	Δ_0
random sampling	Δ_s
hypothetical populations	T
$M_1 - M_2$	μ_T
$s_{M_1-M_2}$	σ_T

Questions   *Answer the following questions.*

†1. Use the data in Table 13.6 and the independent-sample t test to decide between $H_0: \mu_1 - \mu_2 = 0$ and $H_1: \mu_1 - \mu_2 \neq 0$. Use $\alpha = .01$. State the decision rule and your decision. Report the results as if you were writing a research report.

TABLE 13.3

Testing Hypotheses About the Difference Between Two Population Means:
Independent Sample *t* Test

1. **Assumptions:**

   Population assumptions:

   a. The populations are both normally distributed (but see discussion of robustness).

   b. The populations have the same variance (common population variance, see discussion of robustness).

   Sampling assumption:

   a. The two samples must be independent.

   b. Both samples must be obtained using independent (within-sample) random sampling.

   Data assumption

   Interpretation of the results is most clear-cut when the data are measured using an interval or ratio scale.

2. **Hypotheses:**

   Null hypothesis:

   $$H_0: \mu_1 - \mu_2 = \Delta_0$$

   where Δ_0 is a specific number, usually 0.

   Alternative hypotheses available:

   $$H_1: \mu_1 - \mu_2 \neq \Delta_0$$
   $$H_1: \mu_1 - \mu_2 > \Delta_0$$
   $$H_1: \mu_1 - \mu_2 < \Delta_0$$

3. **Test statistic and its sampling distribution:**

   The test statistic is

   $$t = \frac{(M_1 - M_2) - \Delta_0}{s_{M_1 - M_2}}$$

   $$s_{M_1 - M_2} = \sqrt{s_p^2 \left(\frac{1}{n_1} + \frac{1}{n_2} \right)}$$

   $$s_p^2 = \frac{SS(X_1) + SS(X_2)}{n_1 + n_2 - 2}$$

   The sampling distribution has $n_1 + n_2 - 2$ *df*. When H_0 is correct the most likely values for *t* are around zero.

4. **Decision rule:**

   For $H_1: \mu_1 - \mu_2 \neq \Delta_0$

   Reject H_0 if *p*-value $\leq \alpha/2$ or
   Reject H_0 if $t \geq t_{\alpha/2}$ or if $t \leq -t_{\alpha/2}$

   where $t_{\alpha/2}$ is the critical value of *t* with $n_1 + n_2 + 2$ *df* that has $\alpha/2$ of the distribution greater than it.

   For $H_1: \mu_1 - \mu_2 < \Delta_0$

   Reject H_0 if *p*-value $\leq \alpha$ or
   Reject H_0 if $t \leq -t_\alpha$

   For $H_1: \mu_1 - \mu_2 > \Delta_0$

   Reject H_0 if *p*-value $\leq \alpha$ or
   Reject H_0 if $t \geq t_\alpha$

   where t_α is the critical value of *t* with $n_1 + n_2 - 2$ *df* that has α of the distribution greater than it.

5. **Randomly sample and compute *t*** (or use "*t*-Test: Two-Sample Assuming Equal Variances" from the "Data Analysis" toolpak).

6. **Apply decision rule and draw conclusions.** If H_0 is rejected, conclude that the two population means differ by an amount other than Δ_0.

TABLE 13.4

Confidence Interval for $\mu_1 - \mu_2$: Independent Sampling

1. **Assumptions:**

   Population assumptions:
   a. The populations are both normally distributed (but see discussion of robustness).
   b. The populations have the same variance (common population variance, see discussion of robustness).

   Sampling assumption:
   a. The two samples must be independent.
   b. Both samples must be obtained using independent (within-sample) random sampling.

   Data assumption:
   Interpretation of the results is most clear-cut when the data are measured using an interval or ratio scale.

2. **Set the confidence level, $1 - \alpha$.**

3. **Obtain a random sample from each population.**

4. **Construct the interval:**

   Upper limit: $M_1 - M_2 + t_{\alpha/2} \times s_{M_1 - M_2}$
   Lower limit: $M_1 - M_2 - t_{\alpha/2} \times s_{M_1 - M_2}$

   where $t_{\alpha/2}$ is the critical value of the t statistic with $n_1 + n_2 - 2$ df that has $\alpha/2$ of the distribution above it, and

   $$s_{M_1 - M_2} = \sqrt{s_p^2 \left(\frac{1}{n_1} + \frac{1}{n_2} \right)}, \; s_p^2 \frac{SS(X_1) + SS(X_2)}{n_1 + n_2 - 2}$$

   $1 - \alpha$ confidence interval is:

   $$\text{lower limit} \leq \mu_1 - \mu_2 \leq \text{upper limit}$$

5. **Interpretation:**
   The probability is $1 - \alpha$ that the interval includes the actual difference between the means of the populations from which the samples were randomly drawn. There is a probability of α that the interval does not include the actual difference.

---

†2. Suppose that $d = .8$. What is the power of the statistical test used in Question 1? If the investigator wanted a power of .95, what would the sample size have to be?

†3. Use the data in Table 13.6 and the rank-sum test to decide between H_0: the two populations have identical distributions and H_1: the two populations have different distributions. State the decision rule for $\alpha = .01$ and your decision.

4. Why are the two decisions in Questions 1 and 3 different? When the assumptions for the t test and the rank-sum test are met, which decision is more likely correct? Why?

†5. Use the data in Table 13.6 to construct 95%, 99%, and 99.9% confidence intervals for $\mu_1 - \mu_2$. What is the interpretation of a confidence interval that includes zero?

For each of the following questions (6–10),

   a. *Determine the most appropriate statistical test (independent-sample t test, rank-sum test, single-sample t test, test of a population proportion).*

   b. *If enough data are given, perform the test. State the hypotheses, α, decision rule, and decision.*

TABLE 13.5

The Rank-sum Test for Testing Hypotheses About Two Populations: Independent Sampling

1. **Assumptions:**

   Sampling assumptions:

   a. The two samples must be independent of one another.

   b. Both must be obtained using independent (within-sample) random sampling.

   c. Both samples must include at least eight observations.

   Data assumption:

   The data must be measured using an ordinal, interval, or ratio scale.

2. **Hypotheses:**

   Null hypothesis:

   H_0: The two populations have the same relative frequency distributions.

   Alternative hypotheses available:

   H_1: The two populations do not have the same relative frequency distributions.

   H_1: The scores in Population 1 tend to exceed the scores in Population 2.

   H_1: The scores in Population 2 tend to exceed the scores in Population 1.

3. **Test statistic and its sampling distribution:**

   The test statistic is

   $$z = \frac{T - \mu_T}{\sigma_T}$$

   $$\mu_T = \frac{n_1(n_1 + n_2 + 1)}{2},$$

   $$\sigma_T = \sqrt{\frac{(n_1)(n_2)(n_1 + n_2 + 1)}{12}}$$

   T is computed by ranking (see text). The sampling distribution of z is the standard normal distribution. When H_0 is correct, the most likely values of z are around zero.

4. **Decision rule:**

   For H_1: the two populations do not have the same relative frequency distribution

   Reject H_0 if p-value $\leq \alpha/2$ or

   Reject H_0 if $z > z_{\alpha/2}$ or if $z < - z_{\alpha/2}$

   where $z_{\alpha/2}$ is the critical value of z that has $\alpha/2$ of the distribution greater than it.

   For H_1: the scores in Population 1 tend to exceed the scores in Population 2.

   Reject H_0 if p-value $\leq \alpha$ or

   Reject H_0 if $z > z_\alpha$

   For H_1: the scores in Population 2 tend to exceed the scores in Population 1.

   Reject H_0 if p-value $\leq \alpha$ or

   Reject H_0 if $z < -z_\alpha$

   where z_α is the critical value of z that has α of the distribution greater than it.

5. **Randomly sample and compute T and z** (or use "Rank Sum T" from "LFD3 Analyses").

6. **Apply decision rule and draw conclusions.** If H_0 is rejected, conclude that the two populations' relative frequency distributions are not identical. The most likely reason is that the populations differ in central tendency.

TABLE 13.6

Sample 1	6	7	3	8	2	5	4	5
Sample 2	11	5	10	9	8	7	6	8

TABLE 13.7

Method A	3	16	10	11	5.5	5.5	2	13
Method B	1	12	8	9	14	4	7	15

†6. A school psychologist wants to determine if reprimanding in public (in front of the class) or private is more effective for curbing behavior. He randomly selects 12 students whose teachers reprimand in private and 12 students whose teachers reprimand in public. At the end of the year, he determines the number of mis-behaviors for each student. For the public condition, $M = 7.7$ and $s = 4.1$; for the private condition, $M = 4.2$ and $s = 3.5$.

7. A clinical psychologist is comparing two methods of reducing anxiety. From among those attending an anxiety clinic, he randomly selects 8 people for Method A and 8 people for Method B. Following therapy, each of the 16 participants gives a speech in front of the others and they are ranked by amount of apparent anxiety from 1 (least anxious) to 16 (most anxious). The data are in Table 13.7.

8. A marriage counselor is comparing two methods of counseling. For each of 8 couples, she randomly assigns one spouse to Method A and one spouse to Method B. Following therapy, she ranks each in terms of "understanding of spouse." The data are in Table 13.7.

9. The psychology department is trying to determine whether or not to require a course in the history of psychology. Students in a random sample of 24 majors are asked whether or not the course should be required. A response of yes is scored as a 1, and a response of no is scored as a 0. A total of 15 students say yes ($M = .625$, $s = .102$). Is there enough evidence to conclude that more than half of the majors favor the requirement?

10. One psychological theory proposes that rewarding people for performing a task that is enjoyable may actually decrease the time people spend performing the task. A second theory proposes that rewarding people for performing a task always increases the time spent on the task. To test these theories a psychologist has 40 children spend 15 minutes coloring. Then, 20 children are given candy "for col-oring so well" and sent home. The other 20 children are sent home without any reward. The following week the same 40 children are brought back and asked to color. The psychologist measures the amount of time each child spends coloring. For the children previously given candy, $M = 10.3$ minutes and $s = 8.2$ minutes; for the other children, $M = 18.4$ minutes and $s = 10.3$.

11. A full-service brokerage firm claims that the stocks it picks will, on the aver-age, gain at least $2.50 more than the stocks picked by its nearest competitor. To test this claim the Securities and Exchange Commission hires you to randomly

sample 100 stock picks from the firm and 100 stock picks from the competitor. Test the firm's claim using the data given below. Be careful when setting up the null hypothesis.

Gains for the full-service firm: $M = \$1.25$, $s = \$12.95$

Gains for the competitor firm: $M = -\$1.52$, $s = \$10.50$

12. Make up a problem with data that can be analyzed using the independent-sample t test or the rank-sum test. Specify the populations and how the samples are obtained. Provide the data in a table. Show all six steps in hypothesis testing, and report the results as if preparing a manuscript for publication in a professional journal.

13. A clinical psychologist thinks that depression affects sleeping patterns. To test this idea, she randomly selects 9 people with depression and 8 people without depression (1 drops out of the study) and monitors their sleeping. The number of hours that each patient slept is presented below.

Depressed:	7.1	6.8	6.7	7.3	7.5	6.2	6.9	6.5	7.2
Not depressed:	8.2	7.5	7.7	7.8	8.0	7.4	7.3	6.5	

Using $\alpha = .05$, is there something to the psychologist's intuition? Do people with depression sleep less than normal people? Conduct a hypothesis test that people with depression sleep less than nondepressed people. What is the size of the effect?

14. A recent study tested the effects of MDMA ("ecstasy") on rats. Two groups of 15 rats were first trained to lever-press for sugar pellets. One group, the experimental group, then received an injection of MDMA prior to a test session, whereas the control group received a saline injection prior to the test session. The number of lever presses made by each group during the test session are presented below:

MDMA: 178, 562, 451, 622, 98, 557, 363, 259, 214, 541, 577, 171, 208, 180, 601
Saline: 335, 362, 401, 295, 420, 398, 345, 362, 344, 286, 387, 294, 312, 341, 350

Did MDMA have an effect on lever pressing?

14

Random Sampling, Random Assignment, and Causality

*A*ll of the inferential procedures we have considered (and will consider) require random samples. Surprisingly, however, random samples are rarely obtained in real-world investigations; it is just too difficult and expensive. Instead, in many experiments a procedure called random assignment is employed. The goals of this chapter are to help you understand how random sampling and random assignment differ, to discuss their primary uses, and, finally, to consider the conditions under which random assignment can be used instead of random sampling to satisfy the assumptions of inferential statistical procedures. This last goal is the most important. Without understanding how random assignment can substitute for random sampling, most applications of statistical inference that you read about (at least in psychology) will appear arbitrary, if not downright wrong.

RANDOM SAMPLING

Random sampling occurs when each and every observation in a population has an equal chance of occurring in the sample. As discussed in Chapter 5, procedures that ensure random sampling start by listing each observation in the population, and then use an unbiased method of choosing *n* observations from this listing. One unbiased method is to use a random number table. A second is to use a computer. Whenever some observations are systematically excluded from the sample (for example, telephone opinion polls may exclude the opinions of wives who do not list their own names) the sampling method is biased, not random.

The primary purpose of random sampling is to allow the laws of probability to work. Without random sampling, there is no guarantee that the sampling distribution of M will actually be normally distributed with a mean equal to μ; without random sampling there is no guarantee that the sampling distribution of the t statistic will be the t distribution described in Table C. In other words, without random sampling, none of the inferential procedures described in this book would work. That, of course, is why random sampling has been an assumption for every one of these procedures.

Here is the rub. It is extremely rare that psychologists and other behavioral scientists actually sample randomly from any population. The procedure of listing all of the observations in a population and ensuring no bias in selection is simply too difficult, too time consuming, and often unethical. Nonetheless, psychologists are always using statistical procedures that require random sampling. How can they get away with this? One answer is provided by the remainder of this chapter.

EXPERIMENTS IN THE BEHAVIORAL SCIENCES

Consider again the learning coordinator example from Chapter 13. He was attempting to discover if there is a difference between study Method 1 and study Method 2. He randomly sampled $n = 15$ students from his school and had them study using Method 1. The achievement test scores of these students are a random sample from the population of achievement test scores of students at the school who use Method 1. The learning coordinator also randomly sampled another group of $n = 15$ students from the school and had them study using Method 2. The achievement scores of these students are a random sample from a slightly different population, the population of achievement scores of students at the school who study using Method 2. Although the populations are hypothetical populations (that is, the whole population of scores does not really exist), the samples are legitimate random samples, so that generalizations about the means of those (hypothetical) populations can be made.

Contrast this idealized example to how such a study might actually be conducted by a psychologist. Rather than randomly sampling, the psychologist will probably grab the first 30 people who agree to participate in his study. These 30 people may be members of the psychologist's class, they may be recruited from a newspaper advertisement, and so on. One thing is for sure, they are *not* a random sample from any population.

The psychologist will take great care, however, to *randomly assign* the 30 individuals to the two conditions. For example, starting with the first person, the psychologist selects a number from a random number table and if the number is odd, he assigns that person to Method 1; if the number is even, he assigns that person to Method 2. For the next person, the psychologist moves to the next number in the table and assigns the person to Method 1 if the number is odd, and assigns that person to Method 2 if the number is even, and so on. The purpose of this sort of random assignment is best understood in the context of experiments.

Experiments Determine Causal Relationships

Experiments are conducted to determine causality: Only through experiments can we learn what *causes* what. The logic behind experiments is really quite simple. The basic experiment starts out with two groups that are exactly alike (or at least have no systematic differences). Then, the experimenter imposes one change so that the groups now differ in one respect. Following the change, if there is any (statistically significant) difference in the behavior of the two groups, then the difference must have been *caused* by the one change imposed by the experimenter. Why? Because the two groups are exactly alike except for that one change.

> The one change imposed on the groups is called the **independent variable** because it is imposed *independently* of the subject's wishes and behavior. For the two groups in an experiment, one group has one level of the independent variable imposed on it, and the other group has a different level of the independent variable imposed on it. The behavior that is measured (the observations that go into a statistical analysis) is called the **dependent variable,** because the behavior of the subjects *depends* on the level of the independent variable imposed.

In the study method example, study method is the independent variable. One level of the independent variable is Method 1; the other level is Method 2. Note that study method is imposed on the groups; students in the experiment do not have a choice as to which study method to use. The dependent variable is the score on the achievement test. The experiment is designed to determine if type of study method (the independent variable) causes changes in achievement score (the dependent variable).

We can now give a more formal definition of an experiment.

> **Experiments** are designed to determine if changes in the level of the independent variable *cause* changes in the dependent variable. The prime requirement for any experiment is that different levels of the independent variable are imposed on groups that have no other systematic differences.

Experiments and Random Assignment

Now, where does random assignment fit into all of this? Remember, the logic of an experiment depends on starting with two groups that are exactly alike (or at least have no systematic differences) before the independent variable is imposed. Random assignment is the procedure used to eliminate systematic differences between the groups.

> **Random assignment** is a procedure that is applied to people (or animals) to assign them to conditions of an experiment. For each individual, a random method (for example, a random number table) is used to determine the level of the independent variable imposed on that individual.

In the realistic version of the study method example, the psychologist took 30 people (not a random sample), and randomly assigned each individual to study Method 1 or 2. Because each individual is randomly assigned a study method, it is very unlikely that the groups are systematically different in any respect except for the level of the independent variable. Thus, the prime requirement of an experiment is met.

Contrast random assignment with other methods for assigning individuals to groups (levels of the independent variable). Suppose that the psychologist had assigned the first 15 people to Method 1 and the second 15 to Method 2. In this case, there might well be a systematic difference between the groups before the independent variable is assigned. The first 15 people might be more motivated (that is why they are first), or more interested in science, or more eager to please their professor. The first group might consist of early-risers, or older adults, or more intelligent individuals. Each of these factors is a potential confound.

> A **confound** is any *systematic* difference between two groups *other* than the independent variable. Confounds often arise due to differences between the groups that exist before the independent variable is imposed.

Factors such as motivation, eagerness to please, lifestyle, age, and intelligence are confounds that may occur when levels of the independent variable are not randomly assigned to individuals.

Here is the problem with confounds: If there is a systematic difference between the groups before the independent variable is assigned—that is, if there is a confound in the experiment—then any (statistically significant) difference in the behavior of the two groups may be caused by the confound, not by the independent variable. In other words, when a confound exists, you cannot know whether the independent variable caused the difference in behavior, or the confound caused the difference. The whole purpose of the experiment is undermined.

Review: Random Assignment and Random Sampling

An experiment is designed to determine if an independent variable causes change in a dependent variable. An experiment works by ensuring that the only systematic difference between two groups is the independent variable. If there is a confound (another systematic difference between the groups), then the logic of the experiment is undermined. Potential confounds due to characteristics of the subjects (for example, age, motivation) are eliminated by random assignment. Because each subject is randomly assigned to groups independent of the subject's characteristics, these characteristics are likely to be equally distributed among the groups, and are likely not to be a confound. In short, random assignment is a procedure used to eliminate confounds by randomly assigning individuals to groups (levels of the independent variable) in an experiment.

In contrast, random sampling is a procedure for selecting observations from a population so that each observation has the same probability of inclusion in the sample. The purpose of random sampling is to enable the laws of probability to work correctly so that generalizations can be made about the population.

Both procedures can be used at the same time. A learning coordinator could randomly *sample* 30 students from his school, and then randomly *assign* 15 students to Method 1 and 15 students to Method 2. The point, however, is that the two procedures accomplish different goals. If the null hypothesis is rejected, random sampling allows conclusions to be drawn about specific populations, namely, the populations from which the samples were randomly drawn. Random assignment allows conclusions as to what caused the difference; namely, the difference in the dependent variable is caused by the different levels of the independent variable.

RANDOM ASSIGNMENT CAN (SOMETIMES) BE USED INSTEAD OF RANDOM SAMPLING[1]

Make no mistake about it, random sampling and random assignment are different, and they accomplish different goals. Nonetheless, if you are willing to make a new assumption, and to appropriately limit your conclusions, random assignment can be used to substitute for random sampling. And it is a good thing, too, because much of psychological research uses random assignment, but not random sampling.

Assumption of Randomness of Biological Systems

Consider the following new assumption.[2] *The behavior of biological systems (such as people and animals) is, within limits, inherently random.* For example, when you study, you may generally spend about 1 hour reading statistics. On any given day, however, you may spend anywhere from 45 minutes to 75 minutes, and the actual amount of time spent is essentially random. That is, the actual amount of time depends on factors such as how much sleep you had the night before, the number of other assignments, whether or not there is a good program on television, who happens to be in the library, and so on. Your friend may be less variable, always studying between 58 minutes and 62 minutes, but even her behavior is random within these limits.

As another example, consider the words that you might use to answer a question such as "How ya doin'?" Although your choices are limited ("fine," "OK," "all right"), your actual choice on any given occasion is random.

For a final example, consider the performance of a subject in the experiment comparing study methods. That subject's achievement score may be constrained to within certain limits by his native intelligence and how much he studied. Nonetheless, within these limits, his actual score may be determined by a host of random factors, such as the type of breakfast he had, whether or not his journey to school was pleasant, where he was sitting in the classroom, and so on.

---

[1] This section owes much to discussions with my colleagues in the University of Wisconsin Department of Psychology.

[2] The rationale that follows develops from the analysis of variance notion that what is important is random sampling of error, not random sampling of people.

FIGURE 14.1

Top: **The six distributions represents six individuals' possible responses. The arrows indicate the actual responses included in the samples.** *Bottom:* **Composite population distributions, one for each condition in the experiment. Each composite distribution is composed of three individual distributions.**

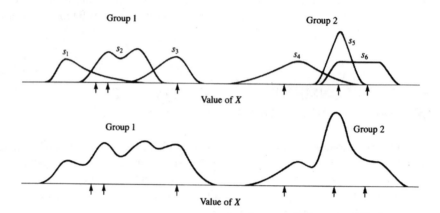

Another way of framing this new assumption is that an individual's particular behavior at a particular time is a random sample (of size 1) from a distribution of possible behaviors.

This new assumption is illustrated in the top panel of Figure 14.1 for three subjects in each of two groups (for example, study Method 1 and study Method 2). Each distribution corresponds to an individual's possible behaviors. The arrow in each distribution indicates the actual observation that the individual contributes to the experiment. By our new assumption, each observation (location of the arrow) is a *random sample* from the individual's population of possible responses.

The bottom of the figure summarizes the situation by combining the three individual distributions into one distribution for each group. Thus, for each group, the three $n = 1$ random samples may be considered a random sample of $n = 3$ from the combined distribution.

Using the *t* Test After Random Assignment

Can the independent-sample *t* test be used to compare the two populations illustrated in the bottom of Figure 14.1? The answer depends on whether or not the assumptions of the *t* test are met. The first population assumption is that the populations are normally distributed. Clearly, these populations are not. Remember, however, that the *t* statistic is robust. Therefore, as long as the populations are not horribly skewed, this assumption can be ignored without risking great loss of accuracy.

The second population assumption is that the two populations have the same variance. It is unlikely that the distributions illustrated have exactly the same variance. However, when the two samples have the same number of observations, this assumption can also be ignored.

The sampling assumption is that we have independent *random samples* from the two populations.[3] This assumption is met. Note that we meet this assumption not by traditional random sampling, but by assuming that biological systems are inherently random: The three responses obtained from the three individuals are assumed to be a random sample from the *population of possible behaviors of the three subjects*. In short, if the assumption of randomness of biological systems is correct, then the *t* test can be used to compare conditions after random assignment, even without traditional random sampling.

INTERPRETING THE RESULTS BASED ON RANDOM ASSIGNMENT

Extra caution is needed when interpreting a significant difference based on random assignment rather than traditional random sampling. When the null hypothesis is rejected, we can claim that the means of the two populations are not equal. But what are the populations?

In our example, one population consists of the *possible achievement scores of the three students* who studied using Method 1, and the other population consists of the *possible achievement scores of the three students* who studied using Method 2. But what good does the statistical test do if it holds only for the particular individuals used in the samples? There are three answers to this question.

First, some people may be willing to assume that there are no important differences between the individuals used in the samples and other individuals. In this case, the results can be generalized to a much broader population (for example, all students in the school). As discussed before, however, this type of (over) generalization is risky. There is nothing in the statistics that guarantees it.

Second, a significant difference based on random assignment indicates the potential importance of the research (after all, there is a significant difference for the specific individuals used in this study). Thus, the data can be used to justify a more expensive study, using traditional random sampling, that would determine if the results generalize to a broader population. On the other hand, if there is no significant difference in the study using random assignment, then you have learned, rather cheaply, not to bother conducting an expensive study using random sampling.

Third, and most important, because of random assignment, we know that the significant difference between the two populations is very likely to be due to the independent variable rather than a confound. Stated differently, the significant difference allows us to conclude that the *cause* of the difference between the population means is the independent variable. Thus, the statistical test, along with random assignment, can be used to demonstrate a causal link between an independent variable (such as study method) and a dependent variable (such as achievement score).

These types of causal links are of great importance in developing and testing scientific theories. Most scientific theories are formal statements of causal links. Thus, finding a causal link is just the stuff needed for developing a new theory. Similarly, finding causal

---

[3] Also, the observations within a sample should be independent of one another. Within-sample independence is approximated as the sample size increases.

links can be used to test theories so that those that are accurate can be kept, and those that are inaccurate can be discarded or modified.

For example, a theory of learning may propose a causal link between study method and performance on an achievement test. Finding such a link (a significant difference between the population means after random assignment) provides the data that support the theory. A second theory may propose that there is no causal link between study method and performance (for example, according to this theory, performance depends solely on amount of study, not type of study). Finding a causal link is just the evidence needed to demonstrate that this second theory is inaccurate and should be discarded or modified.

REVIEW

Random sampling and random assignment are not interchangeable. Random sampling must be used if you wish to make claims about specific populations. Only after random sampling from those populations does a significant difference warrant conclusions about those populations.

The purpose of random assignment is to aid in finding causal links. In an experiment, random assignment combined with a significant difference between conditions allows you to conclude that the independent variable causes a difference between the conditions. Finding causal links is often important for constructing and testing theories.

Random assignment can be used to substitute for random sampling when you are willing to make the new assumption that biological systems are inherently random. When this new assumption is met, the observations in the first group are a random sample from the population of possible scores that could be produced by the subjects in the first group, and the observations in the second group are a random sample from the population of possible scores that could be produced by subjects in the second group.

Random sampling and random assignment can be combined. In this case, because of random assignment, a significant difference indicates a causal link; and because of random sampling, the causal link can be generalized to a broader population.

A SECOND EXAMPLE

To help make these distinctions clearer, this section describes three ways of studying the relationship between type of television watched and aggressive behavior, and the different conclusions that can be drawn from each type of study.

First, suppose that a school system has surveyed its students in regard to the type of television watched. A psychologist randomly *samples* 20 elementary school children who watch 0–2 hours of violent television shows a week and randomly *samples* 20 elementary school children who watch 10–12 hours of violent television. Each child is given a test of aggressive behavior, and M for the children who watch more violent television is greater than M for the children who watch less. Using the independent-sample t test, the psychologist finds a significant difference (the null hypothesis specifying $\mu_1 - \mu_2 = 0$ is rejected).

What can the psychologist conclude? Except for the small chance of a Type I error (equal to her α), she can be certain that the mean of the population of aggressive behavior scores for children in the school system who watch 10–12 hours of violent television is greater than the mean of the population of aggressive behavior scores for children in the school system who watch 0–2 hours of violent television. In other words, because of random sampling, the psychologist can generalize to other children in this school system: Children in this school system who watch more violent television act more aggressively.

The psychologist may *not* conclude that watching violent television causes aggressive behavior. The two groups of children may have differed in many ways in addition to number of hours spent watching violent television, and any one of these confounding differences may have caused the difference in aggressive behavior. For example, the children who watch more violent television may, by nature, be more aggressive. They choose to watch violent television, but it is not violent television that makes them aggressive. Or, children who watch more violent television may be punished more, and that makes them more aggressive, and so on.

Consider now a psychologist who advertises in a local paper that she will pay $50 to each child's parent who allows the psychologist to completely control the child's television watching for 2 weeks. Forty parents volunteer their children. The psychologist randomly *assigns* 20 children to a group that watches 0–2 hours of violent television a week, and she randomly *assigns* 20 children to a group that watches 10–12 hours of violent television. After 2 weeks of this regimen, each child is tested for aggressive behavior, and once again the null hypothesis is rejected.

If the assumption of inherent randomness is correct, then because of random assignment the results demonstrate conclusively (except for the small chance of a Type I error) that there is a causal link between amount of violent television watched and aggressive behavior for these specific children. Any theory that says there is no link is incorrect. Unfortunately, because the psychologist did not use traditional random sampling, she does not know how far these data and conclusions can be generalized. Do they hold for all children? Do they hold for all children of parents who volunteer their children for a study? Do they hold for all children of parents who read the newspaper in which the psychologist advertised? Because the psychologist has not used traditional random sampling, she can draw conclusions only about the specific students used in her research.

As a third example, suppose that the psychologist begins with a *random sample* of 40 elementary school children from her school district. She *randomly assigns* each student to watch either 0–2 or 10–12 hours of violent television a week. After 2 weeks each child is given the aggressiveness test, and once again the null hypothesis is rejected. Because of random assignment, the psychologist can conclude that there is a causal link between amount of violent television watched and aggressive behavior. Furthermore, because of random sampling, she knows that this conclusion holds for all elementary school children in her school district.

SUMMARY

Random sampling should not be confused with random assignment. Random sampling is a procedure for obtaining, without bias, a sample from a population. The major purpose of random sampling is to allow the laws of probability to work so that inferences can be made about the populations. Random assignment is a procedure for creating groups with no systematic differences. The major purpose of random assignment is to eliminate confounds in an experiment so that changes in a dependent variable (whatever is measured) can be causally attributed to the independent variable (whatever is imposed on the two groups to make them different).

Nonetheless, if you are willing to accept an additional assumption about behavior, and if you are willing to limit your conclusions, random assignment can be used in place of random sampling. The additional assumption is that behavior is inherently random so that the observation of an individual in an experiment is a random sample (of size 1) from that individual's own distribution of possible behaviors. When the null hypothesis is rejected, the conclusion must be limited to the statement that the independent variable caused the change in the dependent variable for the particular individuals used in the research; nothing in the procedure warrants generalizing beyond these individuals. Often, this sort of conclusion is sufficient to demonstrate that one theory is wrong and that another is supported. Also, the results can be used to justify a study using traditional random sampling.

Of course, random sampling and random assignment can be used together. Then, the random assignment warrants conclusions about cause and effect, and the random sampling allows you to generalize these conclusions to the broader populations from which the random samples were obtained.

EXERCISES

Terms   *Define these new terms.*

experiment
independent variable
dependent variable
confound

causality
random sampling
random assignment

Questions   *For each of the following problems (a) determine the most appropriate null hypothesis and assume that it is rejected; (b) decide if causal statements are justified; and (c) indicate the populations for which the conclusions hold.*

†1. All students in a university fill out a questionnaire that classifies them as low or high prejudice in regard to Native Americans. A random sample of the low-prejudice individuals and a random sample of the high-prejudice individuals are chosen. Each of the sampled individuals is interviewed, and the dependent variable is the number of negative statements in the interview.

2. A psychologist is attempting to determine factors that control the confidence eyewitnesses have in their identifications. Forty students are asked to observe a videotape of a crime. Twenty students are randomly assigned to a condition in which they attempt to choose the criminal from a lineup consisting of 5 people. The other 20 choose from a lineup consisting of 10 people. After choosing, each

student is asked to rate confidence in his or her choice from 1 (low confidence) to 10 (high confidence). The dependent variable is the rating.

3. A developmental psychologist gives a memory test to a random sample of 20 college students and a random sample of 20 residents in a nursing home. The dependent variable is the number of words recalled on the memory test.

4. A researcher is studying the accuracy of polygraph ("lie detector") readers. A random sample of 20 polygraph readers is selected from a national directory. Ten are randomly assigned to a control condition in which they are asked to interpret a test polygraph record. The other 10 are given extensive additional training in noting peculiarities in polygraph records. These 10 then interpret the test record. The dependent variable is the number of errors in interpreting the test record.

5. A total of 40 students volunteered to serve in a study of the effects of caffeine on memory. Each student provided the researcher with an estimate of the number of cups of coffee consumed each day. Those above the median were assigned to the "high-caffeine" group. Those below the median were assigned to the "low-caffeine" group. Students in the "high-caffeine" group drank three cups of coffee, attempted to memorize a list of words, and then recalled the words. Students in the "low-caffeine" group drank one cup of coffee before memorizing and recalling the words. The dependent variable was number of words recalled.

6. Make up an experiment in which random assignment is used. Specify the null hypothesis and suppose that it is rejected. What conclusions can be drawn from the results? How might the experiment be changed so that random sampling is included? How would the conclusions change?

Comparing Two Populations: Dependent Samples

*C*omparing two populations (or experimental conditions) requires two samples, one from each population. The samples may be either independent (as discussed in Chapter 13) or dependent. This chapter focuses on the statistical analysis of dependent samples. As we will see, dependent sampling has an enormous benefit over independent sampling, increased power. Two methods of hypothesis testing with dependent samples are discussed in the chapter. One, the dependent-sample *t* test, is a parametric test that uses the *t* statistic. The other is the Wilcoxon T_m test, a nonparametric test that can often be used when the parametric assumptions are not met.

DEPENDENT SAMPLING

Dependent sampling is such an important procedure, discussed in so many contexts, that it has been given a variety of names. Some of these are paired sampling, correlated sampling, matched sampling, repeated measures, matched-group sampling, and within-subject sampling. For all intents and purposes, these can be treated alike statistically.

The basic requirement for dependent sampling is that the scores in the two samples are related to one another: There must be a consistent and logical method for matching each score in one sample with a corresponding score in the other sample. However, you must be able to do this matching without reference to the actual values of the scores. That is, simply arranging the scores in the samples from smallest to largest and matching smallest to smallest, next smallest to next smallest, and so on, will not do.

Examples of Dependent Sampling

There are two basic procedures for creating dependent samples. The simplest is to obtain two scores from each subject (the person or animal in an experiment).

> **A within-subjects design** is a form of dependent sampling in which each subject contributes a score to each sample (or condition in an experiment).

Consider a physician studying the effect of an amount of caffeine (the independent variable) on blood pressure (the dependent variable). He could collect data by administering a low level of caffeine to one group of people and a high level to a second group, and then measure the blood pressures. He would then have independent samples, one from the population of blood pressures after a low dose of caffeine and one from the population of blood pressures after a high dose. Alternatively, the physician could use a within-subjects design by administering both the low dose and the high dose to each person on separate days.[1] In this case, each subject contributes two scores—one to the sample of blood pressures after a low dose, and one to the sample of blood pressures after a high dose. The

---

[1] The purpose of waiting a day between doses is to allow the body to recover from the effects of the first dose before administering the second dose. This is a strategy for minimizing "carryover" effects discussed later in the chapter.

scores in the two samples can be matched: Simply pair each score in the low-dose sample with the score in the high-dose sample that came from the same person.

The second procedure for creating dependent samples is often called a matched-group design.

> **A matched-group design** requires pairs of subjects who are similar. One member of the pair is assigned to one of the samples (experimental conditions), and the other member of the pair is assigned to the second sample. Each subject contributes one score.

Consider a medical researcher who is studying the long-term effects of caffeine on blood pressure. She begins by selecting pairs of rats from the same litter (so that the rats are genetically similar). One animal in each pair is randomly assigned to the low-dose condition, and the other is assigned to the high-dose condition. Each rat is fed its dose daily, and the researcher measures blood pressure after a year. These blood pressure scores can be matched by pairing scores from the rats born in the same litter.

Advantages of Dependent Sampling Compared With Independent Sampling

There are two advantages of dependent sampling. The first applies particularly to within-subjects designs: Because each subject contributes scores to both conditions, only half the number of subjects are needed as with independent sampling. Clearly, this can represent a considerable savings in the time and expense associated with locating subjects, scheduling them, explaining procedures, and so on.

The second and more important advantage applies to all forms of dependent sampling: Dependent sampling generally results in a more powerful statistical test than independent sampling. That is, given the same number of observations, the dependent sample procedure is more likely to result in the correct rejection of the null hypothesis than is independent sampling.

As you know, power is affected by variability; the greater the variability of the sampling distribution of the test statistic, the lower the power. In Chapter 9, we noted that variability in the sampling distribution can be reduced by careful data collection procedures and by increasing the number of observations in the samples. Dependent sampling also achieves an increase in power by reducing variability in the sampling distribution.

Consider the data in Table 15.1 from an experiment investigating the long-term effects of caffeine on blood pressure in rats. Remember, one way to compare two populations is to make inferences regarding the difference between population means, and in this case the statistic of interest is $M_1 - M_2$.

If we (temporarily) treat the samples in Table 15.1 as independent, then the estimate of the standard error (standard deviation) of the sampling distribution of $M_1 - M_2$ is $s_{M_1 - M_2}$. In Table 15.1, this standard error (6.15) is sizable, so power is low. There are now two questions to be answered: Why is $s_{M_1 - M_2}$ so large? How does dependent sampling reduce the variance of the sampling distribution?[2]

---

[2] The explanation that follows is developed on intuitive grounds and is somewhat simplified. A more rigorous explanation can be found in most advanced statistics texts.

TABLE 15.1
Blood Pressure After Two Doses of Caffeine

High Dose	Low Dose	D
15	5	10
45	36	9
16	18	-2
41	25	16
7	10	-3
48	40	8
46	43	3
37	30	7
40	35	5
35	29	6

Independent-sample Calculations   *Matched-sample Calculations*

$\Sigma X = \quad 330 \quad = \quad 271$

$\Sigma X^2 = 12,850 \quad = 8,785$

$M = \quad 33 \quad = \quad 27.1$

$SS(X) = \quad 1960 \quad = 1440.9$

$s^2 = \quad 217.78 \quad = \quad 160.10$

$s_p^2 = 188.94$

$s_{M_1 - M_2} = 6.15$

$$t = \frac{M_1 - M_2}{s_{M_1 - M_2}} \frac{(33 - 27.1) - 0}{6.15}$$

$t = .96$

$\Sigma D = 59$

$\Sigma D^2 = 633$

$M_D = \Sigma D / n_p = 59/10 = 5.9$

$$s_D^2 = \frac{\Sigma D^2 - (\Sigma D)^2 / n_p}{n_p - 1} = \frac{633 - (59)^2/10}{9}$$

$s_D^2 = 31.65$

$s_{M_D} = \sqrt{s_{M_D}^2 / n_p} = \sqrt{31.65/10}$

$s_{M_D} = 1.78$

$$t = \frac{M_D - \Delta_0}{s_{M_D}} = \frac{5.9 - 0}{1.78}$$

$t = 3.32$

Why is $s_{M_1 - M_2}$ so large? This statistic is the estimate of the variance in the sampling distribution of $M_1 - M_2$, so let us consider why that sampling distribution is variable. When constructing the sampling distribution using repeated sampling (the five-step procedure), the larger the differences between successive values of $M_1 - M_2$, the greater the value of $s_{M_1 - M_2}$. For independent samples, the size of the differences between successive $M_1 - M_2$ is due in part to individual differences within each sample. (Computationally, these individual differences inflate s for each sample, s is used in computing s_p^2, and that is used in computing $s_{M_1 - M_2}$).

Take a look at the variability within each sample in Table 15.1. The scores in the high-dose sample vary from 7 to 48 ($s^2 = 217.78$), and the scores in the low-dose sample vary from

5 to 43 (s^2 = 160.10). These tremendous individual differences (variability) are reflected in the large value of $s_{M_1-M_2}$, and the consequent low power. Note that the independent-sample t is only $-.96$, too small to reject H_0 at any reasonable level of α.

With dependent samples, the matching of the scores is used to eliminate much of the variability associated with individual differences. To see how this works requires a reconceptualization of the problem. Suppose that there is no difference between the population means (that is, the null hypothesis is correct). In this case, we expect $M_1 - M_2$ to be about 0.0. Also, for dependent samples, we would expect the difference between each *pair* of scores to be about 0.0. In fact, we can reconceptualize the whole problem in terms of the differences between pairs of matched scores.

A difference score, D, is obtained by subtracting the value of one score in a pair from the other score in the pair, as in Table 15.1. If the null hypothesis is correct (the two population means are identical), then each of these Ds should be close to zero, and the mean of the sample of difference scores, M_D, should also be close to zero.

Note that each difference score indicates the amount of *change* from a baseline (from low dose to high dose in this example), and the amount of change within each matched pair is fairly stable from pair to pair; that is, there is little variability in the difference scores. Looking at Table 15.1, the range of the difference scores is 19 (from -3 to 16), whereas the range of the original (low-dose) scores is 38 (from 5 to 43). This difference in ranges is reflected in the difference in the variances: The variance of the difference scores, s_D^2, is only 31.65, whereas the variance of the low-dose scores is 160.1.

Here is the point: Individual differences in the baseline (low-dose) levels are a major source of variability. Difference scores remove this variability by focusing on the amount of *change* from the baseline. In doing so, the power of the statistical test is greatly enhanced.

Precautions When Using Dependent Sampling

There are two precautions to take when using dependent sampling—one that applies to the matched-group design in particular and one that applies to the within-subjects design. The first precaution is that matching will be effective only in increasing power when the difference scores are actually less variable than the original scores. When this condition is not met, matching may actually decrease power instead of increasing power.

The degree to which the difference scores are less variable than the original scores depends on how closely related the scores in the two samples actually are. If there is no relationship between the two sets of scores, then the difference scores will be just as variable as the original scores. You can enhance the relationship between the scores in the two samples by ensuring that the method used to match the scores is closely related to the scores being measured (the dependent variable).

Consider these examples. Suppose a mathematics instructor wishes to compare two learning methods using a matched-group design. He pairs students by matching the tallest with the second tallest, the third tallest with the fourth tallest, and so on. Then he randomly assigns one member of each pair to learning Method 1 and the other member of the pair to learning Method 2. After using the methods for 1 month, he gives each student a mathematics achievement test.

Matching by height is unlikely to result in any reduction in variability. Why? Because height is unrelated to mathematics achievement, the dependent variable. Thus, the difference scores are unlikely to be less variable than the original scores. (Matching by height would make sense if the dependent variable were basketball ability, for example.)

Suppose that the mathematics instructor had matched students on the basis of grade point average (GPA). The students with the two highest GPAs are paired, the students with the next two highest GPAs are paired, and so on. Again, one member of each pair is randomly assigned to each study method. This time, the matching is likely to produce some reduction in variability (and an increase in power) because the method of matching (using general intellectual ability) is related to the dependent variable—the score on the mathematics achievement test.

Finally, suppose that the instructor had matched students on the basis of grades in previous mathematics courses. This procedure is likely to produce a great reduction in variability, and, consequently, a great increase in power. The close relationship between the method of matching (grades in mathematics courses) and the dependent variable (mathematics achievement test score) will virtually guarantee that the difference scores will be less variable than the original scores.

The second precaution applies to within-subjects designs in particular. This precaution is to be wary of carryover effects.

> **A carryover effect** occurs in a within-subjects design when participation in one condition affects responding in the other condition.

For example, within-subjects designs are inappropriate for investigating clinical treatment methods. Once a patient has been treated with Method 1, that patient has been changed so that it is now impossible to apply Method 2 without any carryover from the first treatment. In general, carryover effects are a potential problem in experiments on treatments, therapies, drugs, and experiments that use any form of deception (because the same person is unlikely to be deceived more than once).

Random Sampling and Random Assignment

As discussed in Chapter 14, different conclusions are warranted by random sampling and random assignment. Exactly the same analyses apply when considering dependent sampling designs (either within-subjects or matched group). When (dependent) *random sampling* is used, rejecting the null hypothesis warrants conclusions about specific populations. When members of dependent pairs are *randomly assigned* to conditions, then rejecting the null hypothesis warrants conclusions about causal links. Of course, random sampling and random assignment can both be used.

Consider a psychologist who is studying how different presentation modalities (auditory or visual) affect memory for the material presented. She *randomly samples* 30 students from among those in an introductory psychology subject pool and creates 15 pairs of students by matching them on general memory performance (matched-group design). One member of each pair is *randomly assigned* to the auditory condition and the other to the visual condition. The psychologist collects memory scores in the two conditions and uses the samples to test the null hypothesis that the means of the populations of memory scores are identical.

If the null hypothesis is rejected, then because of random sampling she may conclude that the mean of the population of auditory memory scores (for all students in the introductory psychology subject pool) is different from the mean of the population of visual memory scores (for all students in the subject pool). The psychologist can also conclude that there is a causal link between modality of presentation and memory score. Because the students were randomly assigned to the two conditions, the level of the independent variable (auditory or visual presentation) is the only systematic difference between the groups. Thus, the independent variable is the only factor that could have caused the difference in memory scores (disregarding the possibility of a Type I error).

For another example, suppose that the psychologist selects 15 volunteers from a class and plans to use a within-subjects design to study modality differences. Each volunteer will memorize two sets of materials—one set presented audibly and the other presented visually. How can she randomly assign the same volunteer to the two conditions? For the within-subjects design, random assignment is often accomplished by randomly assigning the *order* of the two tasks.[3] In this case, for each student, the psychologist randomly determines whether the auditory or the visual material is presented first.

If the null hypothesis is rejected, then the psychologist can conclude that there is a causal link between modality and memory scores (because of random assignment). However, because she did not randomly sample from a well-specified population, the conclusion holds only for the populations of possible memory scores produced by these specific students.

The Before–After Design and Causality

A special case of within-subjects sampling is the before–after design. In this design, two measurements are obtained from each participant—one before some treatment and one after. For example, a psychologist might want to examine the efficacy of a new weight reduction counseling program. He randomly selects 20 participants attending a weight-loss clinic and measures their weight before the new program and after the new program. These measurements are matched (by participant) and used to test the hypothesis that the means of the before and after populations are identical. Suppose that the null hypothesis is rejected. What can the psychologist conclude? Because of random sampling, he can be certain that the mean of the population of weight scores before the new program is different from the mean after the new program.

---

[3] The topic of random assignment in within-subjects designs is complex, and a textbook on experimental design should be consulted before actually performing experiments of this sort. For example, should the same student study the same material under both auditory and visual presentation? This would obviously lead to carryover effects. Should the student study different material for auditory and visual presentation? This leads to a confound in that the two conditions differ not only in modality of presentation but also in what is presented. One solution is to begin with the two sets of materials. Then, for each student, randomly determine the order of presentation of the auditory and visual presentations and randomly determine which set of materials is used for auditory presentation and which for visual presentation.

He *may not* conclude that the new program caused the difference, because there was no random assignment. Unlike the example with learning in two modalities, the order of the measurements cannot be randomly assigned in the before–after design: The before measurements must precede the after measurements. To see the problem, consider that these people might have lost the weight spontaneously, not because of the counseling program. Or they might have lost the weight because of other measures they were taking (such as increased exercise), not because of the counseling. Without random assignment, it is impossible to determine the actual cause of the weight loss.[4]

SAMPLING DISTRIBUTIONS OF THE DEPENDENT-SAMPLE *t* STATISTIC

The difference score is the key intuition in thinking about the dependent-sample *t* statistic. Suppose that the means of two populations differ by Δ (that is, $\mu_1 - \mu_2 = \Delta$) as illustrated in the top of Figure 15.1. Now, imagine taking a dependent sample from the populations. To be concrete, imagine that the dependent sample is based on five pairs of scores. So, one member of each pair is obtained from Population 1 and the other member of each pair is obtained from Population 2. For each pair, calculate a difference score, *D,* by subtracting from the Population 1 score the Population 2 score. There will be five difference scores, one *D* for each of the original pairs. Each of these difference scores should be about equal to Δ. Also, the mean of the sample of difference scores, M_D, should be about equal to Δ.

Now, consider the sampling distribution of M_D. One M_D is obtained from the first dependent sample. Taking another dependent sample, we can compute a second M_D. With enough of these M_Ds we can construct the relative frequency (sampling) distribution of the M_Ds, as illustrated in the middle of Figure 15.1.

Now for some amazing facts. First, the mean of the sampling distribution of M_Ds is guaranteed to equal Δ, the difference between the means of the original populations. Therefore, testing hypotheses about the mean of this sampling distribution will give the same answer as testing hypotheses about the difference between the original population means.

Second, the standard error of the sampling distribution, σ, can be estimated from the standard deviation of a sample of difference scores (each sample of difference scores provides its own estimate). The first step is to compute the standard deviation of the difference scores in the sample, s_D. The computational formula for standard deviations (Chapter 3) can be used directly on the difference scores. For convenience, however, instead of *X*s in the equation, *D*s are used, to indicate difference scores.

---

[4] Causality can be determined in the before–after design by using an appropriate control group. See a textbook on experimental design for details.

FIGURE 15.1
Top: **Two populations whose means differ by** $\triangle$. *Middle:* **Sampling distribution of** M_D **when the original populations have means differing by** $\triangle$. *Bottom:* **Distribution of *t* statistic when null hypothesis** ($H_0: \mu_1 - \mu_2 = \triangle$) **is correct.**

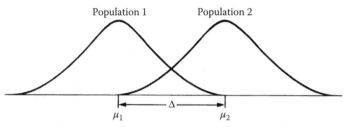

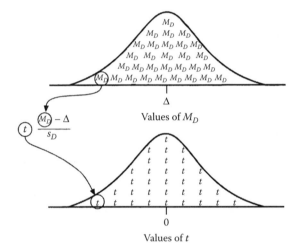

FORMULA 15.1   Standard Deviation of the Difference Scores

$$s_D = \sqrt{\frac{SS(D)}{n_p - 1}} = \sqrt{\frac{\Sigma D^2 - (\Sigma D)^2 / n_p}{n_p - 1}}$$

The term n_p stands for the number of pairs of observations, or, in other words, the number of difference scores in the sample.

The second step is to convert the s_D into an estimate of the standard error of the sampling distribution, σ_{M_D}. This is done using Formula 15.2.

FORMULA 15.2   Estimated Standard Error of the Sampling Distribution of M_D

$$s_{M_D} = \frac{s_D}{\sqrt{n_p}}$$

Now, the third amazing fact: When the original populations are normally distributed, then the sampling distribution of M_D is also normally distributed.

Given these three amazing facts, we have all the ingredients needed to construct a t statistic. Remember, t is formed whenever we take a statistic that is normally distributed (such as M_D), subtract from it the mean of its sampling distribution (such as Δ), and divide it by an estimate of the standard error of the sampling distribution (such as s_{M_D}).

FORMULA 15.3   Dependent-sample t Statistic

$$t = \frac{M_D - \Delta_0}{s_{M_D}}$$

$$df = n_p - 1$$

The sampling distribution of the t statistic is illustrated on the bottom of Figure 15.1. To understand what this sampling distribution is, imagine that all of the M_Ds that went into the sampling distribution of M_D (middle of the figure) were run through Formula 15.3 and transformed into the t statistic. All of these t statistics would form the distribution illustrated on the bottom of the Figure 15.1.

As usual, this sampling distribution is making predictions. When the null hypothesis is true—that is, when the real difference between the population means equals Δ—then the most likely value of t is around zero.

There is one more amazing fact about this sampling distribution. The distribution for the dependent-sample t statistic is virtually the same as the distribution for the single-sample t statistic discussed in Chapter 12. The only difference is that the dependent-sample t is based on a sampling distribution of M_Ds, whereas the single-sample t is based on a sampling distribution of Ms. Otherwise, in shape, logic, and use they are exactly alike. Because of this, you will notice an extraordinary similarity between the formulas presented in this chapter and those in Chapter 12. The only difference is in the use of D (or M_D) instead of X (or M).

HYPOTHESIS TESTING USING THE DEPENDENT-SAMPLE t STATISTIC

The six-step logic of hypothesis testing applies to the dependent-sample t test as in all other hypothesis-testing situations. As usual, the logic will be illustrated using a specific example. A summary may be found at the end of the chapter in Table 15.4.

For the example, we return to the researcher studying long-term effects of caffeine on blood pressure in rats. She had obtained 10 pairs of rats, one pair from each of 10 litters. One member of each pair was randomly assigned to a low-dose group and the other to a high-dose group. After a year on the caffeine regimens, she measured the blood pressure of each rat. The data are in Table 15.1 on page 314.

These data are samples from two populations, the population of blood pressures after a year of low doses of caffeine and the population of blood pressures after a year of high doses of caffeine. The question of interest is, "Do these population means differ?"

Step 1: Assumptions

The assumptions are virtually identical to those needed for the single-sample *t* test. When these assumptions cannot be met, the nonparametric Wilcoxon T_m test may be appropriate. It is discussed later in the chapter.

Population Assumption The population of difference scores is normally distributed. This assumption will be met if both of the original populations (populations of blood pressures) are normally distributed. Because of the robustness of the *t* statistic, this assumption can be ignored as long as the population of difference scores is not terribly skewed.

Examination of the data in Table 15.1 indicates that at least the sample of difference scores is not terribly skewed. Thus, there is no indication that the *t* test should not be used.

Sampling Assumptions

1. The two samples are dependent.
2. Each of the individual samples is obtained using independent (within-sample) random sampling (or random assignment is used with the assumption that biological systems are inherently random).

The two sampling assumptions can be rephrased and combined in the following way: The data must be pairs of observations in which each *pair* is obtained by independent (within-sample) random sampling.

Data Assumption Because the procedure requires calculation of means and variances, the results will be most readily interpretable if the data are interval or ratio. The scores in this example are ratio.

Step 2: Hypotheses

As usual, the null hypothesis must propose something specific about the populations because it is used in generating the sampling distribution. For the dependent-sample *t* test, the null hypothesis is

$$H_0: \mu_1 - \mu_2 = \Delta_0$$

That is, the difference between the populations means equals Δ_0, and thus the mean of the sampling distribution of M_D will also equal Δ_0.

Most often Δ_0 is zero. That is, the null hypothesis proposes that there is no difference between the population means. In fact, zero is the most reasonable value for Δ_0 for the caffeine problem. For ease of exposition, the remainder of this discussion will suppose that $\Delta_0 = 0$. Keep in mind, however, that any value can be used without changing the mathematics.

All three forms of the alternative hypothesis are available. The nondirectional alternative, $H_1: \mu_1 - \mu_2 \neq 0$, implies that the means of the two populations are not equal, but does not specify the direction of the difference. The directional alternative, $H_1: \mu_1 - \mu_2 < 0$, implies that μ_1 is less than μ_2 (so that the difference is less than zero). The other directional alternative, $H_1: \mu_1 - \mu_2 > 0$, implies that μ_1 is greater than μ_2. When used appropriately, the directional alternative is more powerful than the nondirectional alternative. Nonetheless, the nondirectional is often chosen because it examines deviations from H_0 in both directions.

For our example, the researcher chooses the nondirectional alternative. She is just as interested in finding out if long-term use of caffeine decreases or increases blood pressure (or has no effect). Thus, the hypotheses that will be tested are

$$H_0: \mu_1 - \mu_2 = 0$$

$$H_1: \mu_1 - \mu_2 \neq 0$$

Step 3: Sampling Distributions

The test statistic is the t statistic from Formula 15.3. For our example, now that Δ_0 is specified

$$t = \frac{M_D - \Delta_0}{s_{M_D}} = \frac{M_D - 0}{s_{M_D}}$$

Note that the sampling distribution has $n_p - 1$ degrees of freedom. For this example, because there are 10 pairs of scores, there are 9 df.

Consider the sampling distribution of this statistic when the null hypothesis is correct (that is, there really is not any difference between the population means). In this case, most of the difference scores will be around zero (more generally, around Δ_0), and with repeated sampling, most of the M_Ds will be around zero. When an M_D of zero is put into the formula for t, the result is $t = 0$. Hence, when H_0 is correct, most of the t statistics will be close to zero. The sampling distribution is illustrated in the middle of Figure 15.2.

Now consider what would happen if μ_1 were really much greater than μ_2 (so that H_0 is wrong). Most of the difference scores would now be greater than zero, and with repeated sampling, most of the M_Ds would be greater than zero. When an M_D greater than zero is put into the formula for t, the result will be a t statistic substantially greater than 0. Some of the resulting sampling distributions are illustrated on the right in Figure 15.2.

FIGURE 15.2
The black line illustrates the sampling distribution of *t* assuming that H_0 is correct. The gray lines illustrate distributions consistent with the nondirectional alternative. The rejection region for $\alpha = .05$ is also indicated.

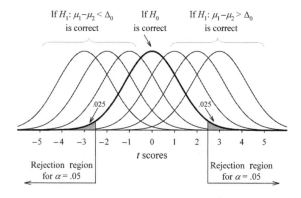

The point of this discussion is straightforward. When H_0 is correct, the most likely values for *t* are around zero. When H_1 is correct, the most likely values for *t* are either larger or smaller than zero.

Step 4: Set α and the Decision Rule

Choice of significance level is, as always, up to you. Smaller values of α will decrease the probability of a Type I error, but also decrease power (increase the probability of a Type II error). For our example, use the standard $\alpha = .05$, because there are no cogent reasons for using any other significance level.

The decision rule specifies the rejection region—those values of the test statistic that occur with a probability of only α when H_0 is true, but are very likely when H_1 is true. For the nondirectional alternative, these are the values of *t* far away from zero (see Figure 15.2).

Three forms of the decision rule correspond to the three forms of the alternative hypothesis. For the nondirectional alternative,

$$\text{Reject } H_0 \text{ if } p\text{-value} \leq \alpha/2 \text{ or}$$

$$\text{Reject } H_0 \text{ if } t \leq -t_{\alpha/2} \text{ or } t \geq t_{\alpha/2}$$

$t_{\alpha/2}$ is the value of *t* (with $n_p - 1$ *df*) that has a proportion of $\alpha/2$ of the distribution above it. Of course, critical values of *t* are obtained from Table C. For the directional alternative, $H_1: \mu_1 - \mu_2 > 0$,

$$\text{Reject } H_0 \text{ if } p\text{-value} \leq \alpha \text{ or}$$

$$\text{Reject } H_0 \text{ if } t \geq t_{\alpha}$$

and for the directional alternative H_1: $\mu_1 - \mu_2 < 0$,

$$\text{Reject } H_0 \text{ if } p\text{-value} \leq \alpha \text{ or}$$

$$\text{Reject } H_0 \text{ if } t \leq -t_\alpha$$

For the two directional alternatives, t_α is the value of t (with $n_p - 1$ df) that has α of the distribution above it.

Our example is using a nondirectional alternative, and because there are 10 pairs of scores, there are 9 df. Thus, the decision rule is

$$\text{Reject } H_0 \text{ if } p\text{-value} \leq .025 \text{ or}$$

$$\text{Reject } H_0 \text{ if } t \leq -2.262 \text{ or } t \geq 2.262$$

Step 5: Sample and Compute the Test Statistic

The data for this example are in Table 15.1. The first step in computing the dependent-sample t statistic is to form the difference scores. Then, the mean and variance of the difference scores are computed using the standard computational formulas (although the symbol D is used instead of X to remind us that we are dealing with difference scores).

$$M_D = \frac{\Sigma D}{n_p} = \frac{59}{10} = 5.9, \; s_D = \sqrt{\frac{\Sigma D^2 - (\Sigma D)^2/n_p}{n_p - 1}} = \sqrt{\frac{633 - (59)^2/10}{10 - 1}} = 5.63$$

Next, use Formula 15.2 to compute the estimate of the standard error of the sampling distribution of M_D.

$$s_{M_D} = \frac{s_D}{\sqrt{n_p}} = \frac{5.63}{\sqrt{10}} = 1.78$$

The dependent-sample t is computed using Formula 15.3:

$$t = \frac{M_D - \Delta_0}{s_{M_D}} = \frac{5.9 - 0}{1.78} = 3.32$$

The p value can be found by using the "TDIST" function in Excel (or some other statistical package). Entering the appropriate argument in Excel, we see that

$$= \text{TDIST}(3.32, 9, 2) = .00894$$

Finally, as we have done in previous examples, an estimate of the effect size should be included in any report. Beginning with the concept

$$\text{Test Statistic} = \text{Size of Effect} \times \text{Size of Study}$$

In the case of the dependent-sample *t*-test:

$$t = \frac{M_D - \Delta_0}{s_{M_D}} = \frac{M_D}{\frac{s_{M_D}}{\sqrt{n_p}}} = \frac{M_D}{s_{M_D}} \times \sqrt{n_p}$$

If we define the term $\frac{M_D}{s_{M_D}} = \hat{d}$, and then solving for $\hat{d}$

$$t = \hat{d} \times \sqrt{n_p}$$

$$\hat{d} = \frac{t}{\sqrt{n_p}}$$

In the current example, then

$$\hat{d} = \frac{3.32}{\sqrt{9}} = 1.11$$

Step 6: Decide and Draw Conclusions

The observed *t* of 3.32, which, if the null hypothesis were true, has a .00894 chance of occurring (remember the *p* value is the probability of the results given the null hypothesis is true), is in the rejection region. Hence, the null hypothesis should be rejected; the results are statistically significant. In addition, the researcher can claim that caffeine has a large effect on blood pressure in rats ($\hat{d} = 1.11$). Given the direction of the difference between the sample means, the researcher may conclude that the mean of the population of blood pressures after a year of high doses of caffeine is greater than the mean of the population of blood pressures after a year of low doses of caffeine. Furthermore, because of random assignment, the researcher may conclude that it is the caffeine that causes the difference in population means. Nonetheless, because she did not randomly sample, she has no statistical warrant to generalize the results beyond the population of possible blood pressures for the specific rats used in her research. What good, then, are the results? They demonstrate that caffeine does affect blood pressure for at least some animals. They also can be used to justify further study of the relationship between caffeine and blood pressure.

Reporting the Results

In reporting the results, the researcher should provide the reader with all of the important components of the statistical analysis. Often, in addition to reporting M_D, it is useful to report the original sample means. So a typical report might read, "The mean of the low-dose group was 27.10 (12.65), and the mean of the high-dose group was 33.00 (14.76).

Using an $\alpha = .05$, the difference between these means, 5.9, indicated a large and statistically significant effect of caffeine, $t(9) = 3.32$, $p = .0089$, $\hat{d} = 1.11$, estimated standard error = 1.78."

Possible Errors

The dependent-sample t test is not immune to errors. Type I errors result from rejecting H_0 when it is really correct. Of course, the probability of a Type I error is directly controlled by you when you set α.

Type II errors result from not rejecting H_0 when it really is incorrect. The probability of a Type II error is generally lower for the dependent-sample t test than for the corresponding independent-sample t test because the standard error is smaller. The probability of a Type II error can be reduced even further (or equivalently, power increased) by increasing α, increasing the sample size, reducing variability by careful data collection, and appropriate use of alternative hypotheses.

A SECOND EXAMPLE

So far, in using examples from the Maternity Study conducted by Drs. Hyde and Essex, we've concentrated on mothers' marital satisfaction. Recall that we have a measure of marital satisfaction for fathers before the baby was born and up to 1 year later. So, what happens to fathers' ratings of marital satisfaction after a baby is born? This is an example of a before–after study design, the data for which are provided in the file "Fathers' marital satisfaction before and after dep t-test.XLS" on the supplemental CD.

The assumptions for a dependent-sample t test seem to be met. First, the differences, although variable, are not skewed. Because of this, the population of differences is probably not too skewed. Second, the observations in the two samples are dependent, and within a sample the observations are independent of one another. Third, the data appear to be near interval scale (i.e., an "in-between" scale).

The null hypothesis is H_0: $\mu_B - \mu_A = 0$ (that is $\Delta_0 = 0$), where μ_B is fathers' marital satisfaction *B*efore a baby's birth and μ_A is marital satisfaction *A*fter the birth. Now, in thinking about the alternative hypothesis, it may be interesting if 1 year after a baby comes along, fathers' marital satisfaction has increased, but that finding would probably have few consequences. On the other hand, if fathers' marital satisfaction was lessened 1 year after a baby's birth, this may suggest that our health care community needs to look into supporting fathers more. Presumably, if marital satisfaction decreases enough, divorce would become more of an option, and this is probably not very good for the child. So, with the additional power provided by a directional alternative, we are interested only if father's marital satisfaction goes down after a baby's birth. Thus, the appropriate alternative is H_1: $\mu_B - \mu_A > 0$ (before scores are higher than after scores).

The sampling distribution, assuming the null hypothesis is correct, is the t distribution with $244 - 1 = 243$ *df*. When the null hypothesis is correct, likely values for t are around 0. When the alternative is correct, likely values of t are much less than 0.

FIGURE 15.3
Excel output from dependent-sample *t* test on father's marital satisfaction before and after a baby's birth.

t-Test: Paired Two Sample for Means

	F1 Marsat	F4 Marsat
Mean	1.649655607	1.438529411
Variance	0.509528212	0.710822448
Observations	244	244
Pearson correlation	0.601320229	
Hypothesized mean difference	0	
df	243	
t Stat	4.679959271	
P (T< = t) one-tail	2.38467E-06	
t Critical one-tail	1.651148978	
P (T< = t) two-tail	4.76933E-06	
t Critical two-tail	1.96977453	

For the standard $\alpha = .05$, the decision rule is

Reject H_0 if *p*-value $\leq .05$ or

from Table C (for 120 df rather than the more accurate 243 used by Excel),

Reject H_0 if $t \leq -1.658$

Looking at data provided in the Excel file, the task of computing the difference of the pairs of scores, as well as the standard deviation of the difference, appears a daunting task. Fortunately, a dependent-sample *t* test is one of the options provided in the data analysis toolpak ("*t*-Test: Paired Two-Sample for Means"). As in previous sections, select this option from the Data Analysis menu. Enter the appropriate data ranges and information. Your output should look something like Figure 15.3.

Computing an estimate of the effect size,

$$\hat{d} = \frac{t}{\sqrt{n_p}} = \frac{4.68}{\sqrt{243}} = .30$$

Because the $p(t = 4.68$ with 243 *df*$) = .000002$, we reject the null hypothesis; the results are statistically significant. However, although the results are highly statistically unlikely if the null hypothesis were true, the estimated effect size is small to moderate (remember Cohen described a small effect as .2 and a moderate effect as .5). This illustrates the principle that with a large sample (244 pairs of scores) we have substantial power, and enough to detect a small effect. What is the effect, though? Can we claim that having a baby *caused* a decrease in marital satisfaction for fathers? Unfortunately, we cannot make that claim.

We can say that in general fathers' marital satisfaction decreased following the birth of a child, but there are likely many causes of the effect. For example, the father is older after the birth than before, and the relationship is older. Either of these confounding factors may have caused the change. To find the cause of decreased marital satisfaction in fathers, additional study is needed.

POWER AND SAMPLE SIZE ANALYSES

Power

Power is the probability of rejecting H_0 when it is false; it is $1 - \beta$—that is, power is the inverse of the probability of a Type II error. Because rejecting H_0 when it is false is a correct decision, we always want to increase power (or, conversely, decrease β).

The dependent-sample t test is generally more powerful than the independent-sample t test because difference scores are generally less variable than the original scores. Power of the dependent-sample t test can be enhanced by careful matching (matching in a way related to the dependent variable) to eliminate variability due to different baselines. In addition, the usual procedures for increasing power apply to the dependent-sample t test. Power increases as the sample size increases; power increases as variability decreases; power increases as α increases; and power increases with appropriate use of directional alternative hypotheses. When testing the standard null hypothesis, $H_0: \mu_1 - \mu_2 = 0$ (that is, $\Delta_0 = 0$), power increases with the effect size, the actual difference between the population means. As discussed in Chapter 13, in some situations the effect size can be increased by judicious choice of the levels of the independent variable.

Computing Power

Power analysis is a procedure for estimating the power of a statistical test under certain specified conditions. You begin the analysis by proposing a value for the population effect size. Then, the analysis is designed to answer the question, "Given my α, sample size, and type of alternative hypothesis, what is the probability that I will reject H_0 *when my estimate of the effect size is correct?*"

The effect size, d, can be estimated using either of two methods. The first method requires a specification of a difference between μ_1 and μ_2, a quantity symbolized by Δ_s, and an estimate of σ_D, the standard deviation of the population of difference scores. Then,

$$d = \frac{|\Delta_s - \Delta_0|}{\sigma_D}$$

Remember, Δ_0 is the difference between the means specified by the null hypothesis.

The second method is to estimate the effect size directly, using standard deviation units. You may use any number of standard deviation units that you believe best approximate the real effect size. As a guideline, a small effect corresponds to about .2 units; a medium effect corresponds to about .5 units; and a large effect corresponds to about .8 units.

The second step is to compute δ using the following formula:

$$\delta = d\sqrt{n_p}$$

You will notice that the formula is virtually identical to the one used in Chapter 12 for the single-sample t test. The only difference is that n_p is used instead of n.

Find the value of δ in Table B and move to the column corresponding to the type of alternative and α. The number in this column is the approximate power of the statistical test.

As an example, suppose that a psychologist is using a matched-group design to test H_0: $\mu_1 - \mu_2 = 0$ against H_1: $\mu_1 - \mu_2 \neq 0$ with $\alpha = .05$. The number of pairs of observations is 30. Based on past research, the psychologist estimates that $\sigma_D = 5$ and that $\Delta_s = 4$. How much power does the statistical test have (what is the probability that H_0 will be rejected)?

$$d = \frac{4-0}{5} = .8$$

Alternatively, the psychologist could have begun by supposing that the effect is large, and using $d = .8$, without first estimating σ_D and Δ_s. Next,

$$\delta = .8\sqrt{30} = 4.38$$

Referring the value of δ to Table B, the power is .99, which is quite good. In other words, if the estimates for σ_D and Δ_s are accurate, then the statistical test is very likely to end up rejecting H_0.

Sample Size Analysis

Before beginning research, it is wise to estimate the sample size needed to attain a given degree of power. The estimation procedure begins with your statement of a desired power and an estimate of the effect size. Then, the analysis is designed to answer the question, "Given my α and type of alternative hypothesis, how large of a sample do I need to have the desired power of rejecting H_0 *when my estimate of the effect size is correct?*"

The effect size may be obtained by first estimating σ_D and Δ_s, and using the formula

$$d = \frac{|\Delta_s - \Delta_0|}{\sigma_D}$$

or the effect size can be estimated directly using ds of .2, .5, or .8 for small, medium, and large effects, respectively.

Then, find the column in Table B corresponding to the type of alternative and α you will be using. Scan down the column until you find the desired power and obtain the corresponding value of δ from the left of the table.

The final step is to compute n_p using the following formula:

$$n_p = \left(\frac{\delta}{d}\right)^2$$

As an example, suppose that a psychologist is testing H_0: $\mu_1 - \mu_2 = 0$ against the directional alternative, H_1: $\mu_1 - \mu_2 > 0$. She is using $\alpha = .05$ and desires a power of at least .75. She believes that the effect size is medium, so she uses $d = .5$.

Using Table B, δ corresponding to a power of .77 (close to .75) is 2.4.

$$n_p = \left(\frac{2.4}{.5}\right)^2 = 23.04$$

If her estimate of the effect size is correct, the psychologist can use as few as 23 pairs of observations and have a power of about .77. Unless it is extremely expensive to collect the data, she may wish to increase her sample size to obtain even more power. After all, even with power of .77 there is still a 1 in 4 (.23) probability that she will make a Type II error (when H_1 is correct).

A power of .9 corresponds to $\delta = 2.9$. Using the same effect size ($d = .5$),

$$n_p = \left(\frac{2.9}{.5}\right)^2 = 33.64$$

Thus, only 34 pairs of observations are needed to obtain a power of .9.

ESTIMATING THE DIFFERENCE BETWEEN TWO POPULATION MEANS

As an alternative to testing hypotheses, the difference between two population means can be estimated directly. For dependent samples, M_D is an unbiased estimator of $\mu_1 - \mu_2$. Thus, M_D can be used as a point estimate of the difference, or it can be used to construct a confidence interval for the difference.

As with other confidence intervals, the width of the interval will increase as confidence increases. Also, the width of the interval will decrease (and thus be more informative) as the variability of the sampling distribution (of M_D) decreases. This can be accomplished by increasing the sample size, by decreasing variability in the original data, and by matching subjects carefully so that there is a strong relationship between the method of matching and the dependent variable.

Consider this example. A physical therapist is interested in estimating the difference in coordination between the preferred hand (for most people the right hand) and the nonpreferred hand. She takes a random sample of 30 students from physical education classes. Each student is timed while tracing a complicated form. Two measurements are taken for each student, one measurement using the preferred hand and the other using the nonpreferred hand. For these data, $M_D = 5.7$ seconds and $s_D = 3.4$ seconds. She uses these statistics to construct a confidence interval. Table 15.5, at the end of the chapter, contains a summary of the procedure.

Step 1: Assumptions

The assumptions are exactly the same as for hypothesis testing. The population assumption is that the population of difference scores is normally distributed. Because the t statistic is robust, you may consider this assumption satisfied unless the population is grossly skewed. The sampling assumptions are that the two samples are dependent and each is obtained using independent (within-sample) random sampling (or random assignment is used with the assumption that biological systems are inherently random). The data assumption is that interpretation will be most meaningful if the data are interval or ratio. These assumptions are met in the example.

Step 2: Set the Confidence Level, $1 - \alpha$

Small values of α (corresponding to high confidence) increase the probability that the interval really does include $\mu_1 - \mu_2$. Unfortunately, the cost is a wide interval that does not help to pinpoint the value of the difference. Our therapist might reason that she has done a good job reducing variability in the sampling distribution because she used a within-subjects design and because she has a reasonably large sample size. Thus, she can afford the luxury of high confidence without the cost of a very wide interval. She sets $\alpha = .01$ to construct a 99% confidence interval.

Step 3: Obtain the Random Samples

This step has been completed for the example.

Step 4: Construct the Interval

The formulas for the limits are:

$$\text{lower limit} = M_D - s_{M_D} \times t_{\alpha/2}$$

$$\text{upper limit} = M_D + s_{M_D} \times t_{\alpha/2}$$

where $t_{\alpha/2}$ is the value of the t statistic with $n_p - 1$ degrees of freedom that has $\alpha/2$ of the distribution above it. Putting the limits together, the $1 - \alpha$ confidence limit is:

$$\text{lower limit} \leq \mu_1 - \mu_2 \leq \text{upper limit}$$

For the example, $M_D = 5.7$, and $s_D = 3.4$. Using Formula 15.2,

$$s_{M_D} = \frac{s_D}{\sqrt{n_p}} = \frac{3.4}{\sqrt{30}} = .62$$

$$\text{lower limit} = 5.7 - .62 \times 2.756 = 3.99$$

$$\text{upper limit} = 5.7 + .62 \times 2.756 = 7.41$$

The 99% confidence interval is

$$3.99 \leq \mu_1 - \mu_2 \leq 7.41$$

Step 5: Interpretation

The probability is .99 that the interval 3.99 to 7.41 includes the real difference between the population means. That is, the average difference in time between the preferred and the nonpreferred hand is very likely to be between 3.99 and 7.41 seconds. Of course, there is some probability that the interval does not include the real difference between the population means, but because that probability is equal to α, we know it is very small.

As usual, these results can also be interpreted in terms of hypothesis testing. Using a nondirectional, $\alpha = .01$ test, any null hypothesis specifying a value of Δ_0 outside the interval 3.99 – 7.41 would be rejected using these data. It is important to note that the null hypothesis H_0: $\mu_1 - \mu_2 = 0$ would be rejected, implying that there is a real difference between the population means.

THE WILCOXON T_m TEST

The Wilcoxon T_m test (the subscript m refers to "matched") is a nonparametric analogue of the dependent-sample t test. It is used to uncover differences between populations when the assumptions of the t test cannot be met. In particular, the Wilcoxon T_m test does not require assumptions about normality, nor does it require interval or ratio data. As with the rank-sum test (the nonparametric analogue for the independent-sample t test), the Wilcoxon test is not perfect: It is less powerful than the dependent-sample t test. Thus when the assumptions of both are met, the dependent-sample t test is preferred.

Computation of the Wilcoxon T_m statistic is best illustrated with an example. A textbook publisher is trying to determine which of two type styles, A or B, is preferred by readers.

TABLE 15.2
Ratings of Two Type Styles

Style A	Style B	D	R	R+	R−
8	15	−7	6		6
4	7	−3	4		4
17	17	0			
12	13	−1	1.5		1.5
10	8	2	3	3	
13	13	0			
3	2	1	1.5	1.5	
7	18	−11	8		8
8	12	−4	5		5
6	14	−8	7		7
				$T_m = 4.5$	31.5

$n_p = 8$ (deleting data for two subjects with $D = 0$)

Check: $\dfrac{n_p(n_p + 1)}{2} = 8(9)/2 = 36 = 4.5 + 31.5$

He obtains a sample of 10 student volunteers from a local college and has each student read two passages, one printed in Style A and one printed in Style B. Furthermore, for each student, he randomly assigns the style that is read first. After reading each style, the student rates the style using a scale of 1 (horrible) to 20 (magnificent). The data are in Table 15.2. Do these ratings provide enough evidence to conclude that the populations of ratings of the two type styles are different?

The first step in computing the Wilcoxon T_m statistic is to obtain the difference between each pair of scores (see Table 15.2). Now suppose that the null hypothesis is correct so that the populations are not different. What would we expect of the difference scores? First, about half of the differences should be positive and half negative. Furthermore, the size of the positive differences should be about the same as the size of the negative differences. The Wilcoxon T_m statistic is based on this latter expectation. When the null hypothesis is correct, the size of the positive and negative differences should be about the same; when the null hypothesis is incorrect, then either the positive differences will be much larger than the negative differences or the negative differences will be much larger than the positive.

The specific steps in computing the Wilcoxon T_m are as follows:

1. Obtain the difference between each pair of scores. Eliminate all pairs with differences of zero, and reduce n_p accordingly.
2. *Ignore the sign of the differences* and rank the differences from smallest (1) to largest (n_p). See column R in Table 15.2.
3. Separate the ranks based on positive differences (column R+) and the ranks based on negative differences (column R−).
4. Compute the sum of the positive ranks, T_m. As a check, the sum of the positive ranks plus the sum of the negative ranks should equal $n_p (n_p + 1)/2$.

Sampling Distribution of T_m

Imagine repeatedly taking pairs of random samples, one from one population and one from the other, and computing T_m. When the populations are identically distributed (the null hypothesis is correct), most of the T_m scores will be clumped around an average value, μ_{T_m}. When H_0 is correct,

$$\mu_{T_m} = \frac{n_p(n_p + 1)}{4}$$

Furthermore, the standard error of the sampling distribution of T_m scores (the real standard error, not just an estimate) is

$$\sigma_{T_m} = \sqrt{\frac{(2n_p + 1)\mu_{T_m}}{6}}$$

Note that the "4" in the formula for μ_{T_m} and the "6" in the formula for σ_{T_m} are constants. Finally, when n_p is larger than 7, the distribution of T_m scores is approximately normal.

Given these three facts, we can translate the sampling distribution of T_m into the standard normal distribution, and use it to test hypotheses. The transformation is given in Formula 15.4.

▬▬▬▬▬▬

FORMULA 15.4 z Transformation for T_m

$$z = \frac{T_m - \mu_{T_m}}{\sigma_{T_m}}$$

Note that this transformation subtracts from each value of T_m the most probable value, namely, μ_{T_m}. Thus, after the transformation, when the null hypothesis is correct, the most likely value for the test statistic (z) is zero. When the null hypothesis is incorrect, the most likely values for z are substantially different from zero.

HYPOTHESIS TESTING USING THE WILCOXON T_m STATISTIC

The example data are in Table 15.2. Recall that the question of interest is whether the two populations differ. That is, does the population of ratings for type Style A differ from the population of ratings for type Style B? The six-step procedure is illustrated next and summarized in Table 15.5 at the end of the chapter.

Step 1: Assumptions

Sampling Assumptions

1. The samples are dependent.
2. Each of the samples is obtained using independent (within-sample) random sampling (or random assignment is used along with the assumption that biological systems are inherently random).
3. The number of pairs should be at least eight to use the normal approximation presented here. If you have fewer pairs, consult a more advanced text presenting the exact distribution of T_m.

Data Assumption   The data are ordinal, interval, or ratio. The scores cannot be sensibly ranked (for computation of T_m) if they are nominal.

These assumptions are met in the current example. Note that there are no requirements regarding the shape of the population distributions. For this reason, Wilcoxon T_m is appropriate when population assumptions for the dependent-sample t test cannot be met.

Step 2: Hypotheses

The hypotheses are very similar to those tested by the rank-sum test (Chapter 13). The null hypothesis is always

H_0: the two populations have identical relative frequency distributions

Note that H_0 does not make any claims about specific population parameters such as the population means. Thus, rejecting H_0 does not allow you to make any definite claims other than the claim that the populations differ. Nonetheless, it is a fairly good bet that rejecting the null hypothesis indicates a difference in the population central tendencies.

The typical alternative hypothesis is the nondirectional:

H_1: the two populations do not have identical distributions

Nonetheless, the two directional alternatives are also available:

H_1: the scores in Population 1 tend to exceed the scores in Population 2

H_1: the scores in Population 2 tend to exceed the scores in Population 1

In the example, the publisher is interested in rejecting the null hypothesis in either direction. That is, he is interested in determining if the ratings of type Style A (Population 1) exceed those of type Style B, or vice versa. Thus, the nondirectional alternative is the most appropriate.

Step 3: Sampling Distributions

When the null hypothesis is correct, most of the T_m scores will equal μ_{T_m}, and, consequently, z is likely to be around zero. On the other hand, when the null hypothesis is incorrect, T_m is likely to be either much larger than μ_{T_m} (when the scores in Population 1 exceed the scores in Population 2) or much smaller than μ_{T_m} (when the scores in Population 2 exceed the scores in Population 1). Thus, when H_0 is incorrect, z will be much larger than zero, or much smaller than zero.

Step 4: Set α and the Decision Rule

As usual, the lower you set α, the smaller the chance that you will make a Type I error. Unfortunately, because of the inverse relationship between α and β, as you decrease α you increase β, the probability of a Type II error.

Because the sample size is relatively small (leading to low power), and because the Wilcoxon T_m statistic already has low power compared to the dependent-sample t test, the publisher decides to sacrifice protection against Type I errors for improved protection against Type II errors. Instead of the standard $\alpha = .05$, he chooses an $\alpha = .10$.

The decision rules are identical to those discussed in Chapters 8 and 11 (because the z statistic is used in all of these cases). For the nondirectional alternative hypothesis,

$$\text{Reject } H_0 \text{ if } p\text{-value} \leq \alpha/2 \text{ or}$$

$$\text{Reject } H_0 \text{ if } z \leq -z_{\alpha/2} \text{ or if } z \geq z_{\alpha/2}$$

where $z_{\alpha/2}$ is the z score that has $\alpha/2$ of the distribution above it.

For the directional alternative that the scores in Population 1 exceed the scores in Population 2 the decision rule is

$$\text{Reject } H_0 \text{ if } p\text{-value} \leq \alpha \text{ or}$$

$$\text{Reject } H_0 \text{ if } z \geq z_\alpha$$

For the directional alternative that the scores in Population 2 exceed the scores in Population 1 the decision rule is

$$\text{Reject } H_0 \text{ if } p\text{-value} \leq \alpha \text{ or}$$

$$\text{Reject } H_0 \text{ if } z \leq -z_\alpha$$

In both of these cases, z_α is the z score that has α of the distribution above it.

Given the nondirectional hypothesis and $\alpha = .10$, the decision rule for the example is

$$\text{Reject } H_0 \text{ if } p\text{-value} \leq .05 \text{ or}$$

$$\text{Reject } H_0 \text{ if } z \leq -1.65 \text{ or if } z \geq 1.65$$

Step 5: Sample and Compute the Test Statistic

The T_m statistic is computed as described at the beginning of this section and illustrated in Table 15.2. Next, μ_{T_m} and σ_{T_m} are computed (or use the "Wilcoxon T_m" option in the "LFD3 Analyses" Excel Add-in).

$$\mu_{T_m} = \frac{n_p(n_p+1)}{4} \qquad \sigma_{T_m} = \sqrt{\frac{(2n_p+1)\mu_{T_m}}{6}}$$

$$= \frac{8(8+1)}{4} \qquad = \sqrt{\frac{[(2)(8)+1](18)}{6}}$$

$$= 18 \qquad\qquad = 7.14$$

Finally, given $T_m = 4.5$ (Table 15.2), z is computed using Formula 15.4, as follows:

$$z = \frac{T_m - \mu_{T_m}}{\sigma_{T_m}} = \frac{4.5 - 18}{7.14} = -1.89$$

And using either NORMSDIST or the LFD3 Add-in, we find that the p-value = .029.

Step 6: Decide and Draw Conclusions

Because p-value $\le .05$ (or $z < -1.65$), the null hypothesis can be rejected, and the publisher can conclude that the ratings for type Style B tend to exceed the ratings for type Style A. In addition, because random assignment was used, he can conclude that it was type style that caused the difference in the populations.

Others might not be quite so comfortable with these conclusions, however. Remember, the probability of a Type I error (α) was set at .10. In fact, if a .01 significance level had been used, the publisher would have been unable to reject H_0 because the p value was .029. In that case, the only legitimate conclusion would be that there is not enough evidence to decide whether or not the two populations have identical distributions.

Even when the null hypothesis is rejected, because the publisher did not randomly sample, he does not know if these conclusions will generalize beyond the population of possible ratings produced by these subjects. Why, then, did he bother? One reason is that these data give some indication that preferences for the type styles do differ. Thus, the data can be used to justify a much larger (and expensive) investigation using random sampling from more relevant populations.

SUMMARY

Dependent-sample statistical techniques are used to compare two populations when the scores in the two samples (one from each population) are related to each other. The relationship between the samples may arise because the scores in the two samples come from the same people (within-subjects design). Alternatively, the relationship may arise because pairs of people are created by matching individuals on a characteristic closely related to the dependent variable (matched-group design), and one person in each pair is assigned to each of the samples. In either case, the dependent-sample design creates a powerful statistical test by focusing on difference scores that eliminate much of the variability due to individual differences.

As discussed in Chapter 14, random sampling warrants generalization to the population from which the samples were drawn, and random assignment is needed to discover causal links. The before–after design is a legitimate type of within-subjects design that can be statistically analyzed using the dependent-sample procedures. Nonetheless, because before and after conditions cannot be randomly assigned, causality cannot be determined.

The dependent-sample t test can be used for matched-group and within-subjects designs. The purpose of the test is to determine whether or not the two population means are identical. The t test assumes that the populations are normally distributed (or at least not grossly skewed), and because means and variances are computed, it is most easily interpreted when the data are interval or ratio. When these assumptions cannot be met, the nonparametric Wilcoxon test is available. The Wilcoxon test is not as powerful as the dependent-sample t test, but it can be used with ordinal data and it makes no assumptions about the population distributions. The purpose of the test is to determine whether or not two populations have identical distributions; however, rejecting the null hypothesis usually indicates a difference in population central tendencies.

The dependent-sample t test is summarized in Table 15.3, and the procedure for constructing a confidence interval for $\mu_1 - \mu_2$ is summarized in Table 15.4. The Wilcoxon T_m test is summarized in Table 15.5.

EXERCISES

Terms   *Identify these new terms and symbols.*

dependent samples	D
within-subjects design	M_D
matched-group design	s_D
before–after design	s_{M_D}

Questions   *Answer the following questions.*

†1. Use the data in Table 15.6 to perform a dependent-sample t test. Use $\Delta_0 = 0$ and a nondirectional alternative with $\alpha = .05$. Show all six steps.

2. Use the data in Table 15.6 to test the alternative $H_1: \mu_1 - \mu_2 > 0$. Again, $\Delta_0 = 0$ and $\alpha = .05$. Show all six steps.

†3. Use the data in Table 15.6 to perform a dependent-sample Wilcoxon test. Use a nondirectional alternative with $\alpha = .025$.

TABLE 15.3
Testing Hypotheses About the Difference Between Two Population Means:
Dependent-sample t Test

1. **Assumptions:**

   Population assumption: The population of difference scores is normally distributed (but see discussion of robustness).

   Sampling assumptions:
   a. The two samples are dependent.
   b. Each of the individual samples is obtained using independent (within-sample) random sampling (or random assignment is used with the assumption that biological systems are inherently random).

   Data assumption: The results will be most readily interpretable if the data are interval or ratio.

2. **Hypotheses:**

   Null hypothesis:

   $$H_0: \mu_1 - \mu_2 = \Delta_0$$

   where Δ_0 is a specific number, usually zero.

   Alternative hypotheses available:

   $$H_1: \mu_1 - \mu_2 \neq \Delta_0$$
   $$H_1: \mu_1 - \mu_2 > \Delta_0$$
   $$H_1: \mu_1 - \mu_2 < \Delta_0$$

3. **Test statistic and its sampling distribution:**

   The test statistic is

   $$t = \frac{M_D - \Delta_0}{s_{M_D}}$$

   $$M_D = \frac{\Sigma D}{n_p}, \; s_{M_D} = \frac{s_D}{\sqrt{n_p}}, \; s_D = \sqrt{\frac{\Sigma D^2 - (\Sigma D)^2 / n_p}{n_p - 1}}$$

   This t statistic has $n_p - 1$ df.

   When H_0 is correct, t is likely to be around 0.0. When H_1 is correct, t is likely to be discrepant from 0.0.

4. **Decision rule:**

   For $H_1: \mu_1 - \mu_2 \neq \Delta_0$

   $$\text{Reject } H_0 \text{ if } p\text{-value} \leq \alpha/2 \text{ or}$$
   $$\text{Reject } H_0 \text{ if } t \geq t_{\alpha/2} \text{ or if } t \leq -t_{\alpha/2}$$

   where $t_{\alpha/2}$ is the value of t with $n_p - 1$ df that has $\alpha/2$ of the distribution greater than it.

   For $H_1: \mu_1 - \mu_2 < \Delta_0$

   $$\text{Reject } H_0 \text{ if } p\text{-value} \leq \alpha \text{ or}$$
   $$\text{Reject } H_0 \text{ if } t \leq -t_\alpha$$

   For $H_1: \mu_1 - \mu_2 > \Delta_0$

   $$\text{Reject } H_0 \text{ if } p\text{-value} \leq \alpha \text{ or}$$
   $$\text{Reject } H_0 \text{ if } t \geq t_\alpha$$

   where t_α is the value of t with $n_p - 1$ df that has α of the distribution greater than it.

5. **Sample and compute t** (or use "t-Test: Paired Two-Sample for Means" in "Data Analysis" toolpak).

6. **Decide and draw conclusions:**

   If the null hypothesis is rejected, you may conclude that the means of the populations differ by an amount other than Δ_0. If the null hypothesis is rejected and random assignment was used, conclusions about causal links may be warranted.

TABLE 15.4
Confidence Interval for $\mu_1 - \mu_2$ Using Dependent Samples

1. **Assumptions:**

   Population assumption: The population of difference scores is normally distributed (but see discussion of robustness).

   Sampling assumptions:
   a. The two samples are dependent.
   b. Each of the individual samples is obtained using independent (within-sample) random sampling (or random assignment is used with the assumption that biological systems are inherently random).

   Data assumption: The results will be most readily interpretable if the data are interval or ratio.

2. **Set the confidence level, $1 - \alpha$.**

3. **Obtain dependent samples from the populations.**

4. **Construct the interval:**

   Upper limit: $M_D + t_{\alpha/2} \times s_{M_D}$
   Lower limit: $M_D - t_{\alpha/2} \times s_{M_D}$

   where $t_{\alpha/2}$ is the critical value of the t statistic with $n_p - 1$ df that has $\alpha/2$ of the distribution above it,

   $$M_D = \frac{\Sigma D}{n_p}, \; s_{M_D} = \frac{s_D}{\sqrt{n_p}}, \; s_D = \sqrt{\frac{\Sigma D^2 - (\Sigma D)^2 / n_p}{n_p - 1}}$$

   and the $1 - \alpha$ confidence interval is:

   $$\text{lower limit} \leq \mu_1 - \mu_2 \leq \text{upper limit}$$

5. **Interpretation:**

   The probability is $1 - \alpha$ that the interval includes the actual difference between the population means. There is a probability of α that the interval does not include $\mu_1 - \mu_2$.

†4. Use the data in Table 15.6 to construct a 95% confidence interval for $\mu_1 - \mu_2$. Interpret this interval in terms of the null hypotheses that can be rejected. How does this interpretation square with your answer to Question 1?

†5. Assuming that $\Delta_s = 10$ and that $\sigma_D = 15$, what is the power of the statistical test used in Question 1? What sample size is needed to increase the power to .95?

6. Assuming that the effect is of medium size, what is the power of the statistical test used in Question 2? What sample size is needed to increase the power to .99?

For Questions 7–13:
a. *Determine which statistical test is most appropriate. (Hint: Not all the tests are discussed in this chapter. Use the endpapers in the front of the book to help determine the most appropriate test.)*
b. *If dependent samples are used, determine whether a matched-group or within-subjects design was used.*
c. *If sufficient data are given, perform the statistical test showing all six steps.*
d. *For all of the situations, state the conclusion that could be drawn if the null hypothesis had been rejected. What are the populations to which the conclusion can be generalized? Can a causal link be established? If so, what is it?*

TABLE 15.5

The Wilcoxon T_m Test for Testing Hypotheses About Two Populations: Dependent Sampling

1. **Assumptions:**

   Sampling assumptions:
   a. The samples are dependent.
   b. Each of the samples is obtained using independent (within-sample) random sampling (or random assignment is used along with the assumption that biological systems are inherently random).
   c. The number of pairs should be at least eight to use the normal approximation.

   Data assumption:
   The data are ordinal, interval, or ratio.

2. **Hypotheses:**

   Null hypothesis:

   H_0: the two populations have the same relative frequency distributions.

   Alternative hypotheses available:

   H_1: the two populations do not have the same relative frequency distributions.
   H_1: the scores in Population 1 tend to exceed the scores in Population 2.
   H_1: the scores in Population 2 tend to exceed the scores in Population 1.

3. **Test statistic and its sampling distribution:**
   The test statistic is

   $$z = \frac{T_m - \mu_{T_m}}{\sigma_{T_m}}$$

   $$\mu_{T_m} = \frac{n_p(n_p+1)}{4}, \sigma_{T_m} = \sqrt{\frac{(2n_p+1)\mu_{T_m}}{6}}$$

   The statistic T_m is computed by ranking (see p. 000). The sampling distribution is the standard normal distribution. When H_0 is correct, the most likely values of z are around 0.0. When H_1 is correct, the most likely values of z are discrepant from 0.0.

4. **Decision rule:**
   For H_1: the two populations do not have the same distributions.

   Reject H_0 if p-value $\leq \alpha/2$ or
   Reject H_0 if $z \geq z_{\alpha/2}$ or if $z \leq -z_{\alpha/2}$

   where $z_{\alpha/2}$ is the critical value of z that has $\alpha/2$ of the distribution greater than it.
   For H_1: the scores in Population 1 tend to exceed the scores in Population 2.

   Reject H_0 if p-value $\leq \alpha$ or
   Reject H_0 if $z \geq z_\alpha$

   For H_1: the scores in Population 2 tend to exceed the scores in Population 1.

   Reject H_0 if p-value $\leq \alpha$ or
   Reject H_0 if $z \leq -\alpha_\alpha$

   where $z_{\alpha/2}$ is the critical value of z that has α of the distribution greater than it.

5. **Sample and compute T_m and z** (or use "Wilcoxon T_m" option provided in "LFD3 Analyses" for Excel).

6. **Decide and draw conclusions:**
   If H_0 is rejected, conclude that the population relative frequency distributions differ, and that the central tendencies probably differ too. If random assignment was used, conclusions about causal links may be warranted.

TABLE 15.6

Subject	1	2	3	4	5	6	7	8	9	10	11	12	13	14	15
Sample 1	160	172	123	147	191	167	144	143	166	167	135	120	173	155	190
Sample 2	150	185	103	117	191	155	149	121	160	167	151	120	150	136	159

TABLE 15.7
Number of Words Recalled in Two Conditions

Pair	1	2	3	4	5	6	7	8	9	10
Hypnosis	41	13	23	17	28	15	12	34	8	18
Normal	21	30	20	34	28	17	12	24	16	17

7. A researcher wishes to determine if gender is associated with extrasensory perception (ESP). He takes a random sample of 15 women psychology majors at Great Midwest University and 15 men psychology majors at GMU. Each subject is given a test of "sensitivity to ESP." The data for the women are $M = 53.8$, $s = 12.7$; the data for the men are $M = 57.0$, $s = 15.5$.

8. A psychologist decides to determine if hypnosis can help people recall more than would otherwise be possible. Grades on the last psychology test are obtained for each of 20 student volunteers. On the basis of these grades, the top two students are paired, the next two are paired, and so on. Next, all students are given 5 minutes to attempt to memorize a list of 50 unrelated words. One member of each pair of students is randomly assigned to recall the list of 50 words under hypnosis and the other member recalls in a normal state. The results are in Table 15.7. Propose a method for matching subjects that would be more effective than matching on the basis of grade on the last psychology exam. Why is your method more effective?

9. An engineering psychologist is studying how different types of computer screens influence reading speed. Each of eight student volunteers is timed while reading from two types of screens. Reading speeds (in words per minute) are given in Table 15.8.

†10. Do students at GMU study more than the national average? In a random sample of 24 GMU students, the average amount of time spent studying was 32.3 hours a week, and the standard deviation was 16 hours. The national average is 25.1 hours a week.

11. Findings from the psychological literature on memory indicate that memory for a list of unrelated words is better after distributed practice (two study intervals separated by a time period) than after massed practice (two adjacent study intervals). A statistics professor attempts to determine if these findings pertain to memory for statistics material. She instructed a randomly selected half of the class to study Chapter 1 using two consecutive (massed) study sessions; the other students studied Chapter 1 using two sessions separated by a 5-minute interval

TABLE 15.8
Reading Speeds (Words per Minute) for Two Types of Computer Screens

Student	1	2	3	4	5	6	7	8
Screen A	136	215	187	331	80	155	204	233
Screen B	134	221	196	328	400	162	208	241

TABLE 15.9
Performance After Two Types of Study

Student	1	2	3	4	5	6	7	8	9	10	11	12	13	14
Massed	86	75	91	60	53	68	68	73	75	75	62	67	84	80
Distributed	91	80	88	63	59	68	64	80	81	85	65	69	84	86

(distributed). For Chapter 2, each student studied using the other method. Each student then took a test on the two chapters. The data are in Table 15.9. How might the instructor try to increase power by increasing the effect size (increasing the difference between the means of the two populations)?

12. Make up an experiment that uses a dependent sampling procedure. Describe the experimental conditions, the samples, the populations, and the null hypothesis. Provide enough data to test the null hypothesis. Report the results as if preparing a manuscript for publication in a professional journal.

13. Andrzejewski, Spencer, and Kelley (2006) conducted an experiment on the effects of a drug injected into the hippocampus on eating and movement. Eight rats were injected with drug or saline prior to being placed in a small compartment for two sessions each. The experimenters measured the total amount of food eaten, the total number of times the rat moved across the compartment (locomotor counts), and the total number of time the rat stood up on its hind legs (rears). Did the drug affect behavior?

Rat	Amount Eaten		Locomotor Counts		Rears	
	Saline	Drug	Saline	Drug	Saline	Drug
1	6.7	2.9	22	20	13	17
2	1.3	4.8	26	25	26	22
3	3.9	3.8	21	25	27	32
4	5.6	6.5	17	12	27	8
5	3.8	6.6	25	17	30	19
6	5.7	4	15	16	18	15
7	4.5	5.7	33	17	27	18
8	6.7	4.1	26	14	26	15
9	7.8	5.6	50	33	38	12

16

Comparing Two Population Variances: The *F* Statistic

Two populations may have equal means, but still differ in shape or variability. In this chapter, we describe the *F* statistic, which is used to determine if two populations differ in variability. The *F* statistic is also used in the analysis of variance discussed in Chapters 17–19.

Consider the following situation. A clinical psychologist is investigating the effects of administering small amounts of mood-altering drugs to severely withdrawn patients in a psychiatric hospital. His goal is to increase social interactions initiated by these patients. He selects a random sample of patients and randomly assigns 15 to the experimental group and 11 to the control group.[1] Those in the experimental group are administered the test drug, whereas those in the control group are administered a placebo. Following drug administration, the number of social interactions initiated by each patient is recorded for 1 week. The data are in Table 16.1.

As you can see, the drug did not increase the average number of social interactions; in fact, the difference between the sample means is in the wrong direction. At first glance, these data are disappointing. A more careful look, however, reveals something interesting. The data for the experimental group appear to be much more variable than the data for

---

[1] It is usually best to have the same number of observations in each sample. Different sample sizes are used in this example to illustrate some of the peculiarities of the *F* distribution.

TABLE 16.1
Number of Social Interactions After Two Treatments

Experimental Group	Control Group
0	7
8	8
5	7
20	6
4	6
15	9
7	10
8	5
6	8
6	12
9	4
11	
3	
1	
7	
$n_1 = 15$	$n_2 = 11$
$\Sigma X = 110$	$\Sigma X = 82$
$\Sigma X^2 = 1176$	$\Sigma X^2 = 664$
$M_1 = 110/15 = 7.33$	$M_2 = 82/11 = 7.45$
$s_1^2 = \dfrac{1176 - (110)^2/15}{14}$	$s_2^2 = \dfrac{664 - (82)^2/11}{10}$
$= 26.38$	$= 5.27$

the control group. If the difference in variances is significant (that is, if the two *popula-tion* variances differ as well as the two *sample* variances), then the psychologist may have discovered something important. There may be two kinds of patients: those whom the drug helps and those whom it hurts. So, on the average, the drug does not improve matters; instead, it increases variability. We will return to this example after discussing the *F* statistic and how it can be used to test hypotheses about population variances.

THE *F* STATISTIC

The *F* statistic (named after Sir Ronald Fisher, a British statistician) is very easy to calculate. It is simply the ratio of two sample variances. Thus,

$$F = s_1^2/s_2^2$$

or

$$F = s_2^2/s_1^2$$

As we will soon see, the sampling distribution of the *F* statistic depends on both the degrees of freedom in s_1^2, $df_1 = n_1 - 1$, and the degrees of freedom in s_2^2, $df_2 = n_2 - 1$.

The sample variances can be computed in the usual way, using the computational formula,

$$s^2 = \frac{SS(X)}{n-1}, \text{ where } SS(X) = \sum (X - M)^2$$

To see how the *F* statistic can be used to make inferences, consider its sampling distribution when $\sigma_1^2 = \sigma_2^2$. Imagine two populations that have equal variances. Draw a random sample from each population and compute s_1^2 and s_2^2. The ratio s_1^2/s_2^2 is the first *F*. Now, draw two more random samples and compute *F* again; draw again and compute *F* again, and so on. After computing many *F*s, construct the relative frequency distribution of the *F* statistics. If you have computed *F* for all possible random samples from the populations, then the relative frequency distribution is the sampling distribution.

When the populations have the same variance, then s_1^2 will usually be about equal to s_2^2, and most of the *F*s (s_1^2/s_2^2) will be close to 1.0. Of course, in repeated sampling from the populations, s_1^2 and s_2^2 may not be exactly equal each time, so we would not be surprised to see *F* statistics that deviate from 1.0. Remember that variances can never be less than zero. Thus, the smallest value of *F* is zero (when $s_1^2 = 0.0$). On the other hand, when s_2^2 is very small, the value of *F* can be very large (because dividing by a small number produces a large result). Putting this together, we are led to expect a sampling distribution that is positively skewed: Most values of *F* will be about 1.0, the smallest will be zero, but the largest will be very large.

Two sampling distributions of the *F* statistic are presented in Figure 16.1. Note that the distributions are indeed positively skewed. Also, note that the exact shapes of the distributions depend on the degrees of freedom in both s_1^2 and s_2^2; that is, $n_1 - 1$ and $n_2 - 1$. Thus, like *t*, there are many *F* distributions, depending on the sample sizes.

Table D (in the Tables section at the end of the book) presents critical values for the *upper* tails of the various *F* distributions. Along the top of the table are listed degrees of freedom for the sample variance in the numerator. The left-hand column lists the degrees

FIGURE 16.1
The *F* distributions with 20, 4 *df* and 10, 10 *df*.

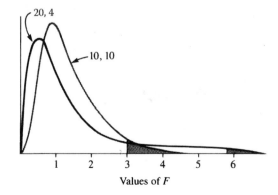

of freedom for the sample variance in the denominator. The intersection of each row and column specifies a particular F distribution. Two numbers are given at each intersection. The number in light type is the 95th percentile for the distribution. That is, it is the value of F that has .05 of the distribution above it. The number in the boldface type is the 99th percentile; it has .01 of the distribution above it.

The locations of some critical values are illustrated in Figure 16.1. For the F distribution with 20 and 4 df, 5.80 is the 95th percentile: All of the Fs with values above 5.80 contribute 5% to the distribution. For the distribution with 10 and 10 df, the 95th percentile is 2.97.

Note that there is a big difference between distributions that have the same degrees of freedom, but with the degrees of freedom for the numerator and the denominator switched. For the distribution with 20 df in the numerator and 4 df in the denominator, the 95th percentile is 5.80. For the distribution with 4 df in the numerator and 20 df in the denominator, the 95th percentile is 2.87.

As usual, the sampling distribution of F is making predictions. Namely, when the population variances are equal, then the actual value of F computed from two random samples is likely to be around 1.0. Very large values of F and very small values (near zero) are unlikely when the population variances are equal.

When using z or t, critical values for the lower tail can be found by adding a negative sign to the critical values in the tables. This works because those distributions are symmetric about zero. The procedure will not work for F, because the F distribution is not symmetric. Fortunately, as you will see shortly, we need only the upper tail of the F distribution, even when conducting a nondirectional test.

TESTING HYPOTHESES ABOUT POPULATION VARIANCES

The six-step procedure will be illustrated using the data from the social interaction experiment (Table 16.1). The procedure is summarized at the end of the chapter in Table 16.2.

Step 1: Assumptions

Population Assumption   Both of the populations must be normally distributed. Fortunately, the F statistic, like the t statistic, is robust in regard to this assumption. As long as the populations are relatively mound-shaped and not terribly skewed, you may consider this assumption met. The data in Table 16.1 do not give any indication of terrible skew, so this assumption appears to be met.

Sampling Assumptions

1. The two samples must be independent. The procedure does not work for dependent samples.
2. Both samples must be obtained using independent (within-sample) random sampling (or use random assignment and the assumption that biological systems are inherently random).

In the example, unrelated patients contributed to the two samples, so the samples are independent. However, because the psychologist is counting social interactions, there is danger that the scores *within* each sample are not independent of one another: When Patient 1 interacts with Patient 2, they influence each other so that there is the potential for nonindependence. One solution to this problem is to count social interactions only for a given patient during a specified interval during which that patient is being observed. So, when Patient 1 is being observed, an interaction with Patient 2 is counted as an interaction initiated by Patient 1. Any interactions then initiated by Patient 2 are ignored, until the specified time for observing Patient 2.

Data Assumption   The data should be measured using an interval or ratio scale. Of course, the mathematics can be performed on ordinal or nominal data, but it is not clear that the results will be interpretable. A count of the number of social interactions, the dependent variable in this study, results in a ratio scale.

Step 2: Hypotheses

The null hypothesis for comparing two population variances is always the same:

$$H_0: \sigma_1^2 = \sigma_2^2$$

Three forms of the alternative hypothesis are available: the nondirectional

$$H_1: \sigma_1^2 \neq \sigma_2^2$$

and the two directional alternative hypotheses

$$H_1: \sigma_1^2 > \sigma_2^2$$

$$H_2: \sigma_1^2 < \sigma_2^2$$

The usual factors enter into deciding which alternative to use. Most important, if the investigator is interested in rejecting H_0 in either direction (the most typical situation), then the nondirectional alternative should be chosen. However, appropriate use of the directional alternative results in a more powerful test.

Because the psychologist is interested in rejecting H_0 in either direction, the nondirectional hypothesis is appropriate. Remember, choice of the alternative should not be influenced by examination of the data (see Chapter 8). Thus, although the psychologist became interested in testing hypotheses about variances only after looking at the data, and at that point it was clear that, if anything, $\sigma_1^2 > \sigma_2^2$, choice of alternatives is dictated by the logical situation, not the actual data. In this situation, the psychologist is logically interested in rejecting H_0 in either direction; thus, the nondirectional alternative is appropriate.

Step 3: Test Statistic and Its Sampling Distribution

Because Table D gives only critical values of F in the upper tail, determining the appropriate test statistic and its sampling distribution is a little tricky. As we will see, it is the form of the alternative hypothesis that determines whether we use $F = s_1^2/s_2^2$ or $F = s_2^2/s_1^2$.

Suppose that you are testing the directional alternative

$$H_1: \sigma_1^2 > \sigma_2^2$$

For this alternative, the appropriate statistic is $F = s_1^2/s_2^2$. If this alternative is correct, then we are likely to find (in our random samples) large values for this F (because s_1^2 will be large relative to s_2^2). If the null hypothesis is correct (so that $\sigma_1^2 = \sigma_2^2$), then likely values for this F are around 1.0 and large values are unlikely. In other words, for this alternative, $F = s_1^2/s_2^2$ is just the statistic we need for constructing a rejection region: Large values of this F are (a) unlikely when H_0 is correct and (b) very likely when H_1 is correct.

Now suppose that you are testing the other directional alternative

$$H_1: \sigma_1^2 < \sigma_2^2$$

For this alternative, the appropriate statistic is the other form of the F statistic, $F = s_2^2/s_1^2$. This form of F is likely to be large when this alternative is correct and around 1.0 when H_0 is correct. Once again we have the conditions needed to form a rejection region: Large values of $F = s_2^2/s_1^2$ are (a) unlikely when H_0 is correct and (b) very likely when H_1 is correct.

What about the nondirectional alternative

$$H_1: \sigma_1^2 \neq \sigma_2^2$$

The nondirectional alternative does not indicate whether $F = s_1^2/s_2^2$ or $F = s_2^2/s_1^2$ is likely to be large, just that one of them should. The correct procedure is to form both F ratios, and to see if either of them exceeds its critical value. When H_0 is correct, both of these Fs should be close to 1.0. When H_1 is correct, one of these Fs should be large and exceed its critical value.

These analyses are reflected in construction of the decision rules discussed next.

Step 4: Set α and the Decision Rule

Setting α requires the same considerations as always. A small α protects against Type I errors (rejecting H_0 when it is correct), but increases the probability of a Type II error (decreases power). Thus, choosing α requires a consideration of the cost of the different types of errors.

Because administration of drugs is always dangerous, a Type I error would be very costly: The psychologist would conclude that the drug is effective (at least in changing variability), when it is not. Perhaps many patients would be needlessly given the drug before the error was discovered. Clearly, the psychologist should guard against Type I errors by using a small α.

Consider the decision rule for the directional alternative, $H_1: \sigma_1^2 > \sigma_2^2$. It is

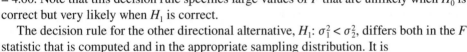

$$\text{Reject } H_0 \text{ if } F = s_1^2/s_2^2 \geq F_\alpha(df_1, df_2) \text{ or}$$

$$\text{Reject } H_0 \text{ if } p\text{-value} \leq \alpha$$

$F_\alpha(df_1, df_2)$ is the critical value of F, in the distribution specified by df_1 ($n_1 - 1$) in the numerator and df_2 ($n_2 - 1$) in the denominator, that has α proportion of the distribution above it. For the data in Table 16.1 (with 14 and 10 degrees of freedom), using $\alpha = .01$, $F_{.01}(14, 10) = 4.60$. Note that this decision rule specifies large values of F that are unlikely when H_0 is correct but very likely when H_1 is correct.

The decision rule for the other directional alternative, $H_1: \sigma_1^2 < \sigma_2^2$, differs both in the F statistic that is computed and in the appropriate sampling distribution. It is

$$\text{Reject } H_0 \text{ if } F = s_2^2/s_1^2 \geq F_\alpha(df_2, df_1) \text{ or}$$

$$\text{Reject } H_0 \text{ if } p\text{-value} \leq \alpha$$

For the data in Table 16.1, using $\alpha = .01$, $F_{.01}(10, 14) = 3.94$. Once again, the decision rule specifies values of F that are unlikely when H_0 is correct, but very likely when H_1 is correct.

The decision rule for the nondirectional alternative, $H_1: \sigma_1^2 \neq \sigma_2^2$, is

$$\text{Reject } H_0 \text{ if } F = s_1^2/s_2^2 \geq F_{\alpha/2}(df_1, df_2) \text{ or if } F = s_2^2/s_1^2 \geq F_{\alpha/2}(df_2, df_1) \text{ or}$$

$$\text{Reject } H_0 \text{ if } p\text{-value} \leq \alpha$$

Given the structure of Table D, .01 and .05 are the only choices for $\alpha/2$; thus, .02 and .10 are the only available levels of α for the nondirectional test (although more comprehensive tables may be used). If H_0 is correct, then both of the Fs should be around 1.0, but if H_1 is correct, then one of these Fs should exceed its critical value.

An α of .02 will be used in the example because a small probability of a Type I error is desired. Furthermore, because the nondirectional alternative is being used, the decision rule is

$$\text{Reject } H_0 \text{ if } F = s_1^2/s_2^2 \geq 4.60 \text{ or if } F = s_2^2/s_1^2 \geq 3.94 \text{ or}$$

$$\text{Reject } H_0 \text{ if } p\text{-value} \leq .02$$

Step 5: Sample and Compute the Test Statistic

The data are in Table 16.1, as well as the computations for $s_1^2 = 26.38$ and $s_2^2 = 5.27$. F is simply the ratio of the two sample variances, so

$$F = s_1^2/s_2^2 = 26.38/5.27 = 5.01$$

and

$$F = s_2^2/s_1^2 = 5.27/26.38 = 0.20$$

Step 6: Decide and Draw Conclusions

Because the first F exceeds its critical value (4.60; or use "FDIST" in Excel to find the p-value, which equals .01), the null hypothesis is rejected; the results are statistically significant. The psychologist may conclude that the variance of the population of scores of drugged patients exceeds the variance of the population of scores for the nondrugged patients. Also, because of random assignment, he may conclude that the drug caused the change in variability.

What is the psychologist to make of this difference? Clearly, he should not advocate use of the drug; on the average it did not increase the number of social interactions, it just increased variability in the number of social interactions. The results suggest an interesting possibility, however. Perhaps there are two (or more) types of patients who are socially withdrawn for different reasons. The drug helps one type initiate social interactions, but the drug makes another type even more withdrawn. Mixing the scores from these two types of patients produces the increase in variability. Thus, the psychologist may use these results to begin an investigation into these putatively different types of patients.

Reporting the Results

When reporting the results of an F test comparing variances, include the descriptive statistics (the sample variances) and the important components of the statistical test. Degrees of freedom are included in parentheses immediately following the symbol F. The psychologist might report, "The sample variances for the experimental and control groups were 26.38 and 5.27, respectively. The difference was significant with $\alpha = .02$, $F(14,10) = 5.01$, $p = .01$."

Possible Errors

As usual, there is some probability of making an error. When the null hypothesis is rejected, there is a small chance of making a Type I error (if the rejected null is really correct). Of course, you have complete control over the probability of a Type I error, because it equals the value of α you choose in Step 4.

When the null hypothesis is not rejected, there is some probability of making a Type II error (if the null really is wrong and should have been rejected). When testing hypotheses about population variances, the usual factors influence the probability of a Type II error: Decreasing α increases the probability of a Type II error; increasing the sample size and appropriate use of alternative hypotheses decrease the probability of a Type II error; increasing the effect size (the real difference between the population variances) also decreases the probability of a Type II error.

A SECOND EXAMPLE

Suppose that you are consulted by the engineer in charge of preventive maintenance in a large factory. The ball bearings in the factory have an average life span of 90 days, with a standard deviation of 30 days. Because unscheduled breakdown due to bearing failure is so costly, the engineer must change the ball bearings once a month just to make sure that one of the bearings with a short life span does not fail. Clearly, the problem here is variability. If the standard deviation of the bearing life spans were 7 days (rather than 30 days), then preventive maintenance could be scheduled every other month without increasing the chance of bearing failures. (If you do not follow this reasoning, draw two distributions of bearing life spans, one with a mean of 90 days and a standard deviation of 30 days, the other with a mean of 90 days and a standard deviation of 7 days. Then, using z scores, determine the life span corresponding to the 1% of the bearings that have the shortest life spans. The bearings with the shortest life spans determine the frequency of preventive maintenance.)

The engineer was told by a ball-bearing salesperson that a new (more expensive) bearing has a standard deviation substantially less than 30 days. The engineer wants you to test the salesperson's claim. In your position as consultant, you take a random sample of 25 of the new type of bearings and a random sample of 25 of the standard type. They are all subjected to a stress test, and the number of days before failure is recorded. For the new bearings, $M = 98$ days, $s_1 = 25$ days; for the standard bearings, $M = 93$ days, $s_2 = 31$ days.

If we assume that the population of bearing life spans is mound-shaped, without too much skew, then the assumptions are met. The null hypothesis is

$$H_0\colon \sigma_1^2 = \sigma_2^2$$

The most appropriate alternative is the directional,

$$H_1\colon \sigma_1^2 < \sigma_2^2$$

When H_0 is correct, the most likely value for $F = s_2^2/s_1^2$ is about 1.0. However, when the alternative is correct, $F = s_2^2/s_1^2$ should be substantially greater than 1.0 (because s_1^2 should be small).

Using an $\alpha = .05$, the decision rule is

$$\text{Reject } H_0 \text{ if } F = s_2^2/s_1^2 > 1.98 \text{ or}$$

$$\text{Reject } H_0 \text{ if } p\text{-value} \le .05$$

Note that the critical value is based on 24 and 24 *df*.

To compute *F*, the sample standard deviations (25 and 31) must be squared. Thus, the sample variances are 625 and 961, and $F = 961/625 = 1.54$.

There is not enough evidence to reject the null hypothesis. The preventive maintenance engineer should not be convinced that life spans of the more expensive bearings are less variable than the life spans of the standard bearings.

ESTIMATING THE RATIO OF TWO POPULATION VARIANCES

Instead of testing hypotheses, a confidence interval can be constructed for the ratio of two population variances, σ_1^2/σ_2^2. As usual, the greater the confidence, the greater the probability that the interval includes the real value of the ratio. However, the greater the confidence, the wider the interval, so the less specific information that it provides.

As an example, suppose that a researcher has obtained random samples of $n_1 = 15$ and $n_2 = 21$ observations with $s_1^2 = 63$ and $s_2^2 = 35$. The ratio of the sample variances is $63/35 = 1.8$. What is a likely range for the ratio of the *population* variances?

The first step is to check the assumptions for constructing the confidence interval, which are exactly the same as for hypothesis testing. Both populations must be normally distributed (although we can count on the robustness of the F statistic when this assumption is not met); the samples must be independent of one another, and the observations within each sample must be obtained by independent (within-sample) random sampling; finally, the procedure might not result in interpretable data if it is applied to ordinal or nominal data.

The second step is to choose a value for α. Because we will need $\alpha/2$ for the formulas, Table D limits our choice of α to .02 and .10. For the example, use $\alpha = .10$.

After randomly sampling from the populations, the formulas for the confidence limits are:

$$\text{upper limit} = s_1^2/s_2^2 \times F_{\alpha/2}(df_2, df_1)$$

$$\text{lower limit} = s_1^2/s_2^2 \times 1/F_{\alpha/2}(df_1, df_2)$$

Then, the confidence interval is

$$\text{lower limit} \leq \sigma_1^2/\sigma_2^2 \leq \text{upper limit}$$

In these formulas, $F_{\alpha/2}$ is the critical value of the F statistic that has $\alpha/2$ of the distribution above it. Note that one of the critical values is based on df_1 in the numerator and the other is based on df_2 in the numerator.

For the example,

$$\text{upper limit} = 63/35 \times 2.39 = 4.30$$

$$\text{lower limit} = 63/35 \times 1/2.23 = .81$$

and

$$.81 \leq \sigma_1^2/\sigma_2^2 \leq 4.30$$

The probability is .90 that the interval .81 to 4.30 includes the real value of the ratio of the population variances.

As usual, constructing a confidence interval is formally equivalent to hypothesis testing. Because this interval includes the ratio 1.0, the data would not be sufficient to reject H_0: $\sigma_1^2 = \sigma_2^2$ when tested against the nondirectional alternative with $\alpha = .10$.

SUMMARY

The F statistic is the ratio of two sample variances. It is used to make inferences about population variances. This chapter discussed two types of inferences: (a) testing hypotheses about the equality of two population variances given independent random samples (summarized in Table 16.2) and (b) forming a confidence interval for the ratio of the population variances (summarized in Table 16.3). The F statistic is also used in the analysis of variance procedure (see Chapters 17–19).

The shape of the sampling distribution is positively skewed because the smallest value of the statistic is zero, but the largest value is positive infinity. When the two populations have equivalent variances (so that the null hypothesis is correct), the most likely values for F are around 1.0.

EXERCISES

Questions   *Answer the following questions.*

†1. Use the data in Table 16.4 to test H_0: $\sigma_1^2 = \sigma_2^2$ against the nondirectional alternative. Specify your α, the decision rule, and your decision.

†2. Construct a 98% confidence interval for the ratio of the population variances using the data in Table 16.4.

For each of the following, (a) decide which statistical test is most appropriate; (b) if sufficient information is given, perform the statistical test specifying the hypotheses, alpha, the decision rule, and your decision. Include in your decision a description of the populations about which the inference was made, and whether or not the independent variable can be causally linked to changes in the dependent variable.

3. A social psychologist is trying to determine if positive moods increase helping behavior. Using a sample of 30 volunteers, half are randomly assigned to a positive mood condition and half are assigned to a neutral mood condition. Those in the positive mood condition read a series of pleasant statements, and those in the neutral mood condition read neutral statements. Next, each subject was asked to help the experimenter score data from a previous experiment. The amount of time spent helping score data was recorded for each subject. For the positive mood condition, $M = 14.4$ minutes, $s = 8.1$ minutes; for the neutral mood condition, $M = 6.3$ minutes, $s = 6.2$ minutes. Use a statistical test most appropriate for determining if mood affects the overall amount of helping behavior.

†4. A different social psychologist is studying how alcohol affects restaurant tipping. He randomly selected the checks and charge card receipts (being careful to preserve the confidentiality of the diners) of 51 dinner parties that included alcohol with the meal and 51 that did not. He computed the percentage of the bill that the tip was. For the alcohol group, $M = 18\%$ and $s = 9\%$; for the no-alcohol group, $M = 17\%$ and $s = 6\%$. Use statistical procedures that allow you to find any type of effect of alcohol on tipping.

TABLE 16.2
The F Statistic for Testing Hypotheses About Population Variances

1. **Assumptions:**

   Population assumption: The populations should be normally distributed (although see discussion of robustness).

   Sampling assumptions:
   a. The samples must be independent of one another.
   b. The observations in each sample must be obtained using independent (within-sample) random sampling (or use random assignment and the assumption that biological systems are inherently random).

   Data assumption:
   Interpretation of the results is most clear-cut when the data are measured using an interval or ratio scale.

2. **Hypotheses:**

   Null hypothesis:

   $$H_0:\ \sigma_1^2 = \sigma_2^2$$

   Alternative hypotheses available:

   $$H_1:\ \sigma_1^2 \neq \sigma_2^2$$
   $$H_1:\ \sigma_1^2 < \sigma_2^2$$
   $$H_1:\ \sigma_1^2 > \sigma_2^2$$

3. **Test statistic and its sampling distribution:**

   The test statistics are:

   $$F = s_1^2/s_2^2 \text{ which has } n_1 - 1,\ n_2 - 1\ df$$
   $$F = s_2^2/s_1^2 \text{ which has } n_2 - 1,\ n_1 - 1\ df$$

   When H_0 is correct the most likely values for F are around 1.0.

4. **Decision rule:**

   For $H_1:\ \sigma_1^2 \neq \sigma_2^2$

   $$\text{Reject } H_0 \text{ if } F = s_1^2/s_2^2 \geq F_{\alpha/2}(df_1, df_2)$$

   or

   $$\text{if } F = s_2^2/s_1^2 \geq F_{\alpha/2}(df_2, df_1) \text{ or if } p\text{-value} \leq \alpha$$

   $F_{\alpha/2}(df_1, df_2)$ is the value of F with df_1 for the numerator and df_2 for the denominator that has $\alpha/2$ of the distribution above it. In Table D, values of $\alpha/2$ are limited to .05 and .01, so that the nondirectional α must be .10 or .02.

   For $H_1:\ \sigma_1^2 < \sigma_2^2$

   $$\text{Reject } H_0 \text{ if } F = s_2^2/s_1^2 \geq F_{\alpha}(df_2, df_1) \text{ or if } p\text{-value} \leq \alpha$$

   $F_{\alpha}(df_2, df_1)$ is the value of F with df_2 for the numerator and df_1 for the denominator that has α of the distribution above it. In Table D, the values of α for a directional test are limited to .05 or .01.

   For $H_1:\ \sigma_1^2 > \sigma_2^2$

   $$\text{Reject } H_0 \text{ if } F = s_1^2/s_2^2 \geq F_{\alpha}(df_1, df_2) \text{ or if } p\text{-value} \leq \alpha$$

   $F_{\alpha}(df_1, df_2)$ is the value of F with df_1 for the numerator and df_2 for the denominator that has α of the distribution above it. In Table D, the values of α for a directional test are limited to .05 or .01.

5. **Sample and compute F** (or use "F-Test Two-Sample for Variances" option provided in "Data Analysis" toolpak).

6. **Decide and draw conclusions:**

   If H_0 is rejected, conclude that the population variances are not equal. If random assignment was used, conclusions about causal links may be warranted.

TABLE 16.3
Confidence Interval for the Ratio of Two Population Variances

1. **Assumptions:**
   Population assumption: The populations should be normally distributed (although see discussion of robustness).

   Sampling assumptions:
   a. The samples must be independent of one another.
   b. The observations in each sample must be obtained using independent (within-sample) random sampling (or use random assignment and the assumption that biological systems are inherently random).

   Data assumption:
   Interpretation of the results is most clear-cut when the data are measured using an interval or ratio scale.

2. **Set the confidence level, $1 - \alpha$.**
   When using Table D, limit choice of confidence to 90% and 98%.

3. **Obtain independent random samples from the populations.**

4. **Construct the interval:**
   $$Upper\ limit = s_1^2/s_2^2 \times F_{\alpha/2}(df_2, df_1)$$

   $F_{\alpha/2}(df_2, df_1)$ is the value of F with df_2 for the numerator and df_1 for the denominator that has $\alpha/2$ of the distribution above it. In Table D, values of $\alpha/2$ are limited to .05 or .01. $df_1 = n_1 - 1$ and $df_2 = n_2 - 1$.

   $$Lower\ limit = s_1^2/s_2^2 \times 1/F_{\alpha/2}(df_1, df_2)$$

   $F_{\alpha/2}(df_1, df_2)$ is the value of F with df_1 for the numerator and df_2 for the denominator that has $\alpha/2$ of the distribution above it. In Table D, values of $\alpha/2$ are limited to .05 and .01. $df_1 = n_1 - 1$ and $df_2 = n_2 - 1$.
   $1 - \alpha$ *confidence interval is:*
   $$Lower\ limit \leq \sigma_1^2/\sigma_2^2 \leq upper\ limit$$

5. **Interpretation:**
   The probability is $1 - \alpha$ that the interval includes the ratio of the variances of the populations from which the samples were randomly drawn. There is a probability of α that the interval does not include the actual ratio.

TABLE 16.4

Sample 1	110	110	105	108	112	115	117	102				
Sample 2	0	−35	−47	−4	18	40	41	20	−11	−8	14	6

5. A cognitive psychologist is studying how changing the environmental context affects memory. Of 40 volunteers, 20 are randomly assigned to the same context condition (study and recall of words in the same room), and 20 are randomly assigned to the different context condition (study in one room, recall in another). The dependent variable is number of words recalled. For the same context condition, $M = 28$, $s = 8$; for the different context condition, $M = 25$, $s = 14$. The psychologist is trying to test a theory that predicts that, relative to the same context, some people do better in a changed context because they try harder, whereas others in the changed context remember less well because they do not have any reminders from the original study room. How can the psychologist use the data to test the theory?

6. Suppose another psychologist is testing a theory that suggests that recall in a different context will suffer due to distraction. How would this psychologist use the data in Question 5 to test his theory?

CHAPTER 17

Comparing Multiple Population Means: One-factor ANOVA

*I*n the preceding few chapters, you have learned how to compare two populations by looking for a difference between the population means or the population variances. Whereas these procedures are useful, they are limited because they can be used only to compare two populations at a time. There are many situations, however, in which it is useful to compare more than two populations. For example, a social psychologist may wish to compare the marital satisfaction of mothers employed (outside of the home) full-time, part-time, or not at all 12 months after giving birth to their first baby. A school psychologist may wish to compare four different study methods; a developmental psychologist may wish to compare the rate of cognitive development in five different cultures.

One (unsatisfactory) procedure for comparing multiple populations is to perform multiple *t* tests. The social psychologists comparing marital satisfaction in women employed full-time, part-time, or not at all could use three *t* tests to compare full-time to part-time, full-time to none, and part-time to none. The school psychologist examining study Methods A, B, C, and D could use six *t* tests to compare A to B, A to C, A to D, B to C, B to D, and C to D. And the developmental psychologist testing Cultures A, B, C, D, and E could use 10 *t* tests to make all possible comparisons.

Note that each new population adds more than one more comparison. In fact, the addition of the *k*th population requires additional $k - 1$ comparisons to compare the *k*th population with other $k - 1$ populations. This explosion in the number of comparisons creates two problems. The first is that multiple *t* tests require a lot of work. The second is more serious. Each *t* test has a Type I error rate of α. However, over the *series* of multiple *t* tests, the overall Type I error rate does not stay at α but grows with each new comparison.[1] With 3 *t* tests, each performed with $\alpha = .05$, the overall probability of a Type I error is about .14; with 6 *t* tests it increases to about .26; and with 10 *t* tests it climbs to about .40. Clearly, these large probabilities of making an error are unacceptable.

The analysis of variance (ANOVA) is a procedure for comparing multiple populations that avoids the inflation of Type I error rates (and is less work than performing many *t* tests). The trick is that the ANOVA makes only one comparison (tests one null hypothesis) to determine if any of the populations differ from the rest. Because there is only one comparison, the Type I error rate remains exactly at α.

You might think that ANOVA is a procedure for comparing population variances. However, *the ANOVA compares population means*. It is true that the ANOVA examines variances, and it is true that the *F* statistic is used. Nonetheless, the null hypothesis is

---

[1] The probability of a Type I error over the series of multiple *t* tests is approximately equal to $1 - (1 - \alpha)^c$ where *C* is the number of paired comparisons. This formula is only approximate because it assumes that the comparisons are independent.

$$H_0: \mu_1 = \mu_2 = \mu_3 = \ldots = \mu_k$$

and rejecting H_0 indicates that at least one of the population *means* differs from the others.

FACTORS AND TREATMENTS

In this chapter, we discuss the one-factor ANOVA. The adjective "one-factor" means that the populations sampled are related on one dimension. For the social psychologist studying the mother's employment situation, the factor (dimension) is type of employment; for the school psychologist investigating four study methods, the factor is study method; and for the developmental psychologist, the factor is culture. Chapters 18 and 19 deal with the ANOVA for populations that differ on more than one factor. It is called the factorial ANOVA.

A factor is very much like an independent variable in an experiment (see Chapter 14). The only difference is that levels of the independent variable must be randomly assigned (for it to be an independent variable), whereas levels of a factor need not be randomly assigned. For example, in the study of cognitive development in different cultures, culture is not randomly assigned. Thus, culture is a factor, but not an independent variable.

A treatment distinguishes one population from another. The social psychologist investigating the three employment situations is sampling from three populations. Similarly, the school psychologist investigating four study methods is sampling from four populations or treatments. Thus, a one-factor ANOVA can have many treatments, each treatment defining a population that is sampled.[2]

As you will discover, one of the difficulties with the ANOVA is the terminology; it is almost like learning a new language. If you ignore the terminology, you are likely to get very confused. Instead, try this study strategy. Each time a new term is introduced, turn to the end of the chapter and review the list of new terms and symbols already introduced. Be sure that you can remember the distinctions among them.

The remainder of this chapter covers a number of issues related to the ANOVA. First, there is a discussion of how the one-factor ANOVA works, that is, how analyzing variances can inform us about population means. Next, the procedures for the independent-sample and dependent-sample one-factor ANOVAs are presented. Finally, two nonparametric tests (one for independent and one for dependent samples) are discussed. These tests are used when the assumptions of the ANOVA are not met.

HOW THE INDEPENDENT-SAMPLE ONE-FACTOR ANOVA WORKS

The independent-sample ANOVA has five assumptions that must be met. The assumptions are very similar to those required for the independent-sample *t* test (indeed, in many respects the ANOVA is simply an extension of the *t* test). The two population assumptions

---

[2] The specific populations are also called levels of the factors.

are that all of the populations are normally distributed, and that all of the populations have the same variance. The two sampling assumptions are that the samples are independent of one another, and that each sample is obtained by using independent (within-sample) random sampling. That is, we need one random sample from each of the k populations (treatments) examined. The sample sizes need not be the same, however. Finally, the outcome will be most interpretable if the data are measured on an interval or ratio scale.

Once these assumptions are met, the null and alternative hypotheses can be tested. The null hypothesis is always

$$H_0: \mu_1 = \mu_2 = \ldots = \mu_k$$

where μ_k is the mean of the kth population. The alternative hypothesis is always that at least one of the population means differs from at least one of the others. That is, they may all differ from one another, or only one may differ. Because there is no easy way of capturing this alternative in symbols, we will use

$$H_1: \text{The null is wrong}$$

Consider the social psychologist comparing three different employment situations of new mothers. Three random samples of new mothers are needed. The mothers in Sample A are employed full-time, the mothers in Sample B are employed part-time, and the mothers in Sample C do not work outside the home. The social psychologist measures marital satisfaction (MARSAT score) 12 months after giving birth. The three populations (treatments) are: (a) the population of MARSAT scores for all mothers who are fully employed, (b) the population of MARSAT scores for all mothers who are employed part-time, and (c) the population of MARSAT scores for all mothers who do not work outside the home. If the null hypothesis is correct, then the means of all three populations are equal (and the sample means should be close to one another too).

Suppose that each sample has only three observations (an unrealistic number for real research, but easy to illustrate). Figure 17.1 illustrates the situation when the assumptions are met and *the null hypothesis is correct*. The three distributions on the left correspond to the three populations (MARSAT scores). Each population is a normal distribution (Assumption 1), the variance of each equals σ^2 (Assumption 2), and random and independent samples have been drawn from each of the populations. The specific observations included in each sample are indicated by the arrows.

When H_0 is correct (as in Figure 17.1), the three populations have the same mean. In this case, the three populations are identical—they all have the same shape (normal), the same variance (σ^2), and the same mean (μ). Thus, statistically, drawing a sample from each of the three separate populations can just as easily be thought of as drawing three samples from the same population, as illustrated on the right of the figure.

Estimating σ^2: Mean Square Within (or Mean Square Error)

Now, let us begin to analyze the variance of the situation illustrated in Figure 17.1. The three populations all have the same variance, σ^2. Although we do not know the value of

FIGURE 17.1
Three populations that meet the assumptions of the ANOVA and illustrate the situation when H_0 is correct. The arrows indicate observations sampled from each of the populations.

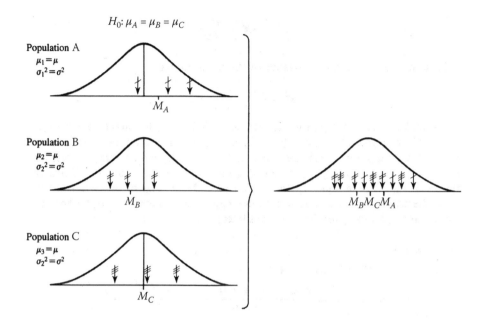

$H_0: \mu_A = \mu_B = \mu_C$

Population A
$\mu_1 = \mu$
$\sigma_1^2 = \sigma^2$

M_A

Population B
$\mu_2 = \mu$
$\sigma_2^2 = \sigma^2$

M_B

$M_B M_C M_A$

Population C
$\mu_3 = \mu$
$\sigma_2^2 = \sigma^2$

M_C

σ^2, it can be estimated in many different ways. First, the variance of Sample A, s_A^2, is a perfectly good estimate of σ^2 because the variance of a random sample is always an unbiased estimate of the population variance. So the first estimate of σ^2 is

$$s_A^2 = \frac{\sum (X - M_A)}{n_A - 1} = \frac{SS(X_A)}{n_A - 1}$$

The second estimate of σ^2 is the variance of Sample B,

$$s_B^2 = \frac{\sum (X - M_B)}{n_B - 1} = \frac{SS(X_B)}{n_B - 1}$$

The third estimate is the variance of Sample C,

$$s_C^2 = \frac{\sum (X - M_C)}{n_C - 1} = \frac{SS(X_C)}{n_C - 1}$$

It is unlikely that the three sample variances will be exactly equal to one another. To avoid having to pick just one (to estimate σ^2), a fourth estimate is obtained by pooling the three sample variances, just as we did with the independent-sample t test. When the sample sizes are equal, s_p^2 (the pooled variance) is the average of the individual s^2s. When the sample sizes differ, we must compute a weighted average of the s^2s. You can use the following formula to compute s_p^2 under either condition:

▇▇▇▇▇▇▇▇▇▇▇

FORMULA 17.1   Mean Square Within

$$MSW = s_p^2 = \frac{SS(X_A) + SS(X_B) + SS(X_C)}{n_A + n_B + n_C - 3}$$

The s_p^2 is an excellent estimate of σ^2, the variance of each of the populations. It is also known as mean square within or MSW (or mean square error or MSE). MSW, like any other variance, has associated with it a certain number of degrees of freedom. Because MSW is a pooled variance, we pool the degrees of freedom so that

$$df_w = (n_A - 1) + (n_B - 1) + (n_C - 1) = N - k$$

In this formula, N is the total number of observations (all the sample sizes added together) and k is the number of groups (or the number of samples).

As you can see from Formula 17.1, MSW is like other variances in that it is a quantity of sum of squares divided by some quantity related to the number of observations. Thus, the numerator of Formula 17.1 is sometimes called sum of squares within or SSW and the denominator is called degrees of freedom within or df_w. With a little algebra, you can see that

$$MSW = \frac{SSW}{df_W}$$

Here is the main point about MSW: The value of MSW does not depend on the differences between the sample means. The reason is that MSW is based on deviations within each sample (that is, s_A^2, s_B^2, and s_C^2). This means that *MSW is a legitimate estimate of σ^2 when H_0 is correct (and the sample means are similar) and when H_0 is incorrect (and the sample means are disparate)*.

Estimating σ^2: Mean Square Between (or Mean Square Treatment)

There is one more estimate of σ^2 that is needed to complete the analysis of variance. This estimate is based on the sample means.

Remember (from Chapter 7) the five-step procedure for constructing the sampling distribution of sample means. After choosing a population and a sample size, you draw multiple samples from the population and compute M for each sample. You may also remember that the variance of the sample means, σ_M^2, is related to the variance of the population by the equation

$$\sigma_M^2 = \frac{\sigma^2}{n}$$

Multiplying both sides of the equation by n (the sample size) gives

$$n\sigma_M^2 = \sigma^2$$

Now, you can see that σ^2 can be obtained from n times the variance of the sample means, so if we can only obtain an estimate of σ_M^2, then we can obtain another estimate of σ^2.

How can we estimate σ_M^2? Remember, σ_M^2 is the variance of the Ms obtained from multiple samples from the sample population. Now, look at the right-hand side of Figure 17.1. When the null hypothesis is correct, we have multiple (three) samples from the same population and each sample provides an M. The variance *between* these Ms, s_M^2, can be computed using the formula for variance (from Chapter 3)—simply treat the three Ms as three scores for which you will compute a variance. Then, because $\sigma^2 = n\sigma_M^2$, we can estimate σ^2 with ns_M^2.

■■■■■■■■■

FORMULA 17.2   Mean Square Between

$$MSB = ns_M^2$$

$$df_B = k - 1$$

This estimate of σ^2 is called mean square between (or MSB). The name reflects the fact that the estimate is based on differences *between* the Ms. Once again, since MSB is a type of variance, it can be computed as some quantity of sum of squares (called sum of squares between) divided by the appropriate degrees of freedom:

$$MSB = \frac{SSB}{df_B}$$

Here is the important point about MSB: MSB is a good estimate of σ^2 only when H_0 is correct so that, conceptually, all the samples are drawn from the same population, as in Figure 17.1.

So far, we have developed two main points. MSW, the pooled s^2, is based on the variability *within* each sample, not between the samples. Therefore, MSW is a legitimate estimate of σ^2 whether H_0 is correct or incorrect. MSB is also a legitimate estimate of σ^2, and based on variability *between* the means of the samples, but only when H_0 is correct and all

FIGURE 17.2
Three populations that meet the assumptions of the ANOVA and illustrate the situation when H_0 is incorrect. The arrows indicate observations sampled from each of the populations.

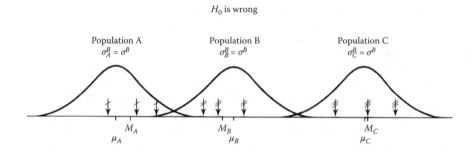

the samples can be considered samples from the same population. Therefore, when H_0 is correct, both *MSW* and *MSB* are estimates of σ^2. Furthermore, when H_0 is correct, *MSW* and *MSB* will be numerically similar and the ratio *MSB/MSW* will be about equal to 1.

Remember from Chapter 16 that the ratio of two variances is an *F* statistic. So, when H_0 is correct, $F = MSB/MSW$ is approximately 1. Even though the null hypothesis is about population means, it makes a clear prediction about the ratio of two estimates of σ^2.

MSW and *MSB* When H_0 Is Incorrect

Figure 17.2 illustrates the situation when the assumptions for ANOVA are met, but H_0 is incorrect. Note that the three population distributions have the same shape and the same variance, σ^2. They differ, however, in their means, so the populations cannot be combined as in Figure 17.1.

Once again, consider taking a random sample of three observations from each of the populations, and using the data in the samples to estimate σ^2. The observations included in the samples are indicated by the arrows.

As before, each of the sample variances, s_A^2, s_B^2, and s_C^2, provides a good estimate of σ^2, because each population has the same value of σ^2 (Assumption 2). Furthermore, pooling the sample variances will provide an even better estimate of σ^2, *MSW*. To reiterate, even when H_0 is incorrect, *MSW* is a good estimate of σ^2 because *MSW* is simply the (weighted) average of the individual s^2s.

Now, consider using *MSB* to estimate σ^2. Remember, *MSB* is the variance of the sample means times the sample size. Note in Figure 17.2 that when H_0 is incorrect, the sample means are likely to be far apart. Consequently, the variance of the sample means is likely to be quite large compared to σ^2. Then, multiplying the variance of the sample means by *n* (to get *MSB*) will make it even larger. Here is the point: When H_0 is incorrect, *MSB* is not a good estimate of σ^2; it is much too big. Furthermore, the greater the differences between the sample means, the larger *MSB*.

What happens when we form the statistic $F = MSB/MSW$? When H_0 is incorrect, *MSB* greatly overestimates σ^2, whereas *MSW* is a good estimate of σ^2. Thus, the *F* statistic will be much greater than 1.0.

The Logic of ANOVA

We can now appreciate how ANOVA works. When H_0 is correct (the population means are all equal), $F = MSB/MSW$ will be about 1.0, because both MSB and MSW are estimates of σ^2. On the other hand, when H_0 is incorrect (the population means differ), $F = MSB/MSW$ will tend to be larger than 1.0, because MSB overestimates σ^2. Furthermore, the larger the differences between the population (and sample) means, the greater the value of MSB and F. So, how can you tell if H_0 is correct of not? Form the ratio $F = MSB/MSW$ and see if it is substantially greater than 1.0. If it is, reject H_0. If it is not, do not reject H_0.

TESTING HYPOTHESES USING THE INDEPENDENT-SAMPLE ANOVA

This section uses the six-step procedure to formalize hypothesis testing by ANOVA. Also, computational formulas for MSB and MSW are given. The procedure will be illustrated using an example, and the procedure is summarized in Table 17.13 at the end of the chapter.

Suppose that a developmental psychologist is studying problem-solving ability across the life span. She decides to investigate how long it takes to solve a standard problem for people of four different ages. Using demographic data about her home city, she contacts random samples of 10 adolescents, 10 young adults, 10 middle-aged adults, and 10 older adults. She measures the amount of time required for each individual to solve the standard problem. Due to an error in the procedures, some of the data are not useable. The final samples are presented in Table 17.1. The goal is to use these sample data to determine if there are any differences among the population (treatment) means.

The psychologist will use the one-factor ANOVA to analyze her data. In this example, the one factor is age of the problem solver. This factor has four treatments: adolescents, young adults, middle-aged adults, and the older adults. (Note that the factor age is not an independent variable because it has not been randomly assigned.)

Step 1: Assumptions

Population Assumptions

1. All of the populations are normally distributed. Of course, this assumption is almost never met. However, because the F statistic is robust, as long as the populations are not too non-normal, this assumption can be ignored. If you have reason to believe that the populations are very non-normal, then the nonparametric Kruskal–Wallis procedure should be used (see p. 384).
2. All of the populations must have the same variance. This assumption is also called "homogeneity of variance." Now that you understand the logic of ANOVA, you can see the importance of this assumption: The whole procedure depends on being able to use the *pooled* s^2 to estimate σ^2, the common population variance. If all of the populations do not have approximately the same variance, the procedure will not work well.

TABLE 17.1
Time (in minutes) to Solve a Standard Problem

Adolescents (A)	Young Adults (Y)	Middle-aged Adults (M)	Old Adults (O)
7	5	7	13
10	6	5	11
11	6	8	12
9	8	4	11
8	7	6	14
12	4	9	9
13	6	3	10
6	9	6	11
	3	7	8
	7	4	
$n_A = 8$	$n_Y = 10$	$n_M = 10$	$n_O = 9$
$\Sigma X_A = 76$	$\Sigma X_Y = 61$	$\Sigma X_M = 59$	$\Sigma X_O = 99$
$\Sigma X_A^2 = 736$	$\Sigma X_Y^2 = 401$	$\Sigma X_M^2 = 371$	$\Sigma X_O^2 = 1117$
$M_A = 9.5$	$M_Y = 6.1$	$M_M = 5.9$	$M_O = 11.0$
$SS(X_A) = 42$	$SS(X_Y) = 28.9$	$SS(X_M) = 32.9$	$SS(X_O) = 28$
$s_A^2 = 6$	$s_Y^2 = 3.211$	$s_M^2 = 3.656$	$s_O^2 = 3.5$

$$M_G = \frac{\Sigma X}{N} = (7 + 10 + 11 + \cdots + 10 + 11 + 8)/37 = 7.973$$

$$SSW = \sum_{j=1}^{k} \left[\sum_{i=1}^{n} (X_{ij} - M_j)^2 \right] = \sum_{j=1}^{k} SS(X_k) = SS(X_1) + SS(X_2) + \cdots + SS(X_k)$$

$$df_W = (n_1 - 1) + (n_2 - 1) + \cdots + (n_k - 1) = N - k$$

$$SSW = SS(X_A) + SS(X_Y) + SS(X_M) + SS(X_O) = 42 + 28.9 + 32.9 + 28 = 131.8$$

$$df_W = 37 - 4 = 33$$

$$SSB = ns_M^2 = \sum_{j=1}^{k} n_j(M_j - M_G)^2 = \sum_{j=1}^{k} n_j M_j^2 - NM_G^2$$

$$df_B = k - 1$$

$$SSB = 8(9.5)^2 + 10(6.1)^2 + 10(5.9)^2 + 9(11.0)^2 - 37(7.973)^2 = 179.173$$

$$df_B = 4 - 1 = 3$$

Fortunately, when the sample sizes are about equal, mild violations of this assumption are acceptable. However, if you have evidence that suggests that the population variances are very different (for example, the sample variances are very different), then the nonparametric Kruskal–Wallis test should be used.

Sampling Assumptions

1. The samples must be independent of one another. Dependent samples are discussed later in the chapter.
2. Each sample must be obtained using independent (within-sample) random sampling. If random assignment is used instead of random sampling, then the additional assumption of the randomness of biological systems should be made.

Data Assumption   Because the procedure tests hypotheses about means, the results will be most interpretable for interval or ratio data.

The example meets these assumptions.

Step 2: Hypotheses

The null hypothesis for the ANOVA is always of the form

$$H_0: \mu_1 = \mu_2 = \ldots = \mu_k$$

Because the example compares four populations (treatments), the specific null is

$$H_0: \mu_A = \mu_Y = \mu_M = \mu_O$$

The alternative hypothesis is always

$$H_1: \text{The null is wrong}$$

This means that at least one of the population means differs from the others.

Step 3: Test Statistic and Its Sampling Distribution

The test statistic is $F = MSB/MSW$, with $k - 1$ df in the numerator and $N - k$ df in the denominator. When H_0 is correct, the most likely value for F is about 1.0, and large values of F are rare. When H_1 is correct, then $F = MSB/MSW$ will be large (because MSB overestimates σ^2). In other words, large values of F are (a) very unlikely when H_0 is correct and (b) very likely when H_1 is correct. Thus, large values of F form the rejection region. Note that small values of F (around 0.0) are inconsistent with both H_0 and H_1, so that small values of F are *not* useful for rejecting H_0 *in favor of* H_1.

There is an interesting "paradox" when using the F statistic in the ANOVA. The alternative hypothesis is nondirectional, in that it does not specify the direction of deviations from H_0. However, only the upper tail of the F distribution is important for rejecting H_0 in favor of H_1. The paradox is resolved when you realize that whenever the population means differ (so that H_0 is wrong), MSB will be larger than MSW. Thus, the nondirectional alternative hypothesis predicts that $F = MSB/MSW$ will be large, but never small.

Step 4: Set α and the Decision Rule

Choice of α is up to you (although limited to .01 or .05 when using Table D). As usual, lower αs decrease the probability of a Type I error, but increase the probability of a Type II error. You need not worry about inflating α because of multiple comparisons. The ANOVA makes only one comparison (*MSB* or *MSW*), so that the probability of a Type I error is exactly equal to α *no matter how many populations are sampled.*

For the example, there are no cogent reasons for departing from the standard significance level, $\alpha = .05$.

The decision rule for the ANOVA is

$$\text{Reject } H_0 \text{ if } F = MSB/MSW \geq F_\alpha(k - 1, N - k) \text{ or}$$
$$\text{Reject } H_0 \text{ if } p\text{-value} \leq \alpha$$

For the example (in Table 17.1), the F distribution has 3 $(k - 1)$ and 33 $(N - k)$ degrees of freedom. Because Table D does not have an entry for 33 *df* in the denominator, the critical value for the closest *lower df* is used. Using the critical value with *fewer df* results in a slightly conservative test; that is, α is a touch lower than stated. Thus, the decision rule is

$$\text{Reject } H_0 \text{ is } F = MSB/MSW \geq 2.90 \text{ or}$$
$$\text{Reject } H_0 \text{ if } p\text{-value} \leq .05$$

Step 5: Sample and Compute the Test Statistic

The goal of the computations is to produce an $F = MSB/MSW$. As is often the case, the definitional formulas are too cumbersome, so computational formulas are used. These computational formulas produce intermediate quantities. You should be familiar with many of them including $\sum X$, $\sum X^2$, n, M, $SS(X)$, and s^2. With ANOVA, we compute these terms for each group or sample. The term M_G is the grand mean; it is the mean of all of the observations. Then using these intermediate values, we compute SSW, df_w, SSB, and df_B. Recall that $MSW = SSW/df_W$ and $MSB = SSB/df_B$. In addition to the above quantities, we also compute the sum of squares total (or SST). SST is the sum of the squared deviations of each score from the grand mean:

$$SST = \sum_{j=1}^{k} \sum_{i=1}^{n} (X_{ij} - M_G)^2 = \sum X^2 - NM_G^2$$

In the present example, then

$$SST = [(7)^2 + (10)^2 + (11)^2 + \ldots + (11)^2 + (8)^2] - 37(7.973)^2 = 310.973$$

The ANOVA Summary Table

To help keep the different steps and results organized, it is traditional to use an ANOVA summary table. Table 17.2 is a schema for an independent-sample one-factor ANOVA

TABLE 17.2
General Summary Table for Independent-sample One-factor ANOVA

Source of Variation	SS	df	MS	F
Between	$\sum_{j=1}^{k} n_j M_j^2 - NM_G^2$	$k-1$	SSB/df_B	MSB/MSW
Within	$\sum_{j=1}^{k} SS(X_k)$	$N-k$	SSW/df_w	
Total	$\sum X^2 - NM_G^2$	$N-1$		

TABLE 17.3
ANOVA Table on Problem-solving Times

Source of Variation	SS	df	MS	F
Between	179.173	3	59.72	$59.72/3.99 = 14.95$
Within	131.8	33	3.99	
Total	310.973	36		

summary table. The summary table for the specific example is in Table 17.3. Each row corresponds to a "source of variation," and provides the components needed to compute the corresponding MS and F.

The table also helps in three checks of computational accuracy. First, all of the components should be positive. Second, SSB and SSW should add up to the SST. Third, the degrees of freedom for between and within should add up to the total degrees of freedom, $N-1$.

Step 6: Decide and Draw Conclusions

The actual value of F, 14.95, is greater than the critical value of 2.90, so the null hypothesis can be rejected. The developmental psychologist can conclude that the mean problem-solving times differ among the populations, not just among the samples.

Note that the psychologist may not conclude that age *causes* the differences, because subjects were not randomly assigned to the different ages (treatments). The observed differences might be due to motivation, or level of education, or general intelligence, or any of many other variables confounded with age.

When reporting the results of an ANOVA, it is important to provide the sample means on which it is based. Remember, a critical factor in determining whether or not the null hypothesis is rejected is the size of the differences between the sample means. When more than three means are involved, they are usually contained in a table. Then, the psychologist might report, "Using an $\alpha = .05$, the means (see Table 17.1) were significantly different, $F(3, 33) = 14.95$, $MSW = 3.99$." Note that MSW is reported as an index of variability because it is the pooled s^2. Usually, this statement of a significant difference is followed by a statement of which means differed, for example, that the older adults are slower than the middle-aged adults. This sort of statement depends on the results of specific comparisons, discussed shortly.

Possible Errors

When H_0 is rejected, there is a small probability of a Type I error that is exactly equal to α. As in other hypothesis-testing situations, you have complete control over the level of α.

When H_0 is not rejected, there is always a chance that a Type II error was made. All of the usual precautions (except using directional alternatives) can be taken to lower β (and thereby increase power): Increase α, increase the sample size, increase the effect size (differences between the population means) by judicious choice of the treatments, and reduce unwanted variability by careful data collection procedures.

COMPARISONS BETWEEN SELECTED POPULATION MEANS: THE PROTECTED t TEST

Rejecting H_0 tells us that at least one of the population means differs from the others. It does not tell us *which* means are different from the others. Fortunately, a variety of procedures have been developed to follow up on the ANOVA and provide comparisons between selected pairs of means. Choice of the best procedure is too technical to cover in any detail here. Instead, we will present a single procedure, the protected t test. This procedure has the advantages of being simple and powerful. In some situations, it has the disadvantage of allowing the Type I error rate to increase slightly over the stated value of α.

The protected t procedure has two main steps (and a twist). The first step is to conduct an ANOVA. Only if the outcome of the ANOVA is the rejection of the null hypothesis do you proceed to the second step. The second step is to perform independent-sample t tests on selected pairs of means.

You may recall that one of the advantages of the ANOVA is that it avoids the inflation of Type I error rates (past the stated value of α) brought about by multiple t tests. The protected t procedure avoids the inflation of Type I error rates by requiring rejection of H_0 by the ANOVA. Remember, Type I errors are a factor only when H_0 is correct. Rejecting H_0 in the ANOVA indicates that H_0 is (very likely) incorrect. Thus rejecting H_0 using the ANOVA "protects" the t tests against Type I errors. Nonetheless, the fewer comparisons made using the protected t procedure, the better.

After selecting a pair of means to compare, the protected t procedure is, except for a twist, identical to the independent-sample t test. The twist is to use MSW as s_p^2 in the t test. Using MSW has two benefits. First, it avoids having to recompute a new s_p^2. Second, because it is based on the data from all of the samples, it is a better estimate of σ^2 than could be obtained from just the two samples being compared, and this results in a more powerful t test. In part, this extra power is reflected in the degrees of freedom used in the protected *t* procedure: *Use the degrees of freedom associated with MSW,* even though far fewer observations will be involved in the specific comparisons you make.

As an example of the protected *t* procedure, suppose that the developmental psychologist is particularly interested in finding out if the mean for adolescents is different from the mean for young adults, and if the mean for middle-aged adults is different from the mean for the older adults. We begin with the first comparison.

The assumptions for the protected *t* are the same as for the ANOVA. Thus, meeting the assumptions in the first stage of the protected *t* test (performing the ANOVA) automatically guarantees they are met in the second stage.

For the first comparison, the hypotheses are

$$H_0: \mu_A - \mu_Y = 0$$

$$H_1: \mu_A - \mu_Y \neq 0$$

When the null hypothesis is correct, likely values of the *t* statistic will be around 0.0. When the alternative is correct, likely values for *t* are either much greater than 0.0 or much less than zero.

The decision rule is

$$\text{Reject } H_0 \text{ if } t \leq -t_{\alpha/2} \text{ or if } t \geq t_{\alpha/2} \text{ or}$$
$$\text{Reject } H_0 \text{ if } p\text{-value} \leq \alpha$$

Using $\alpha = .05$ (as in the ANOVA), with 33 *df* (in *MSW*), the decision rule is

$$\text{Reject } H_0 \text{ if } t \leq -2.042 \text{ or if } t \geq 2.042 \text{ or}$$
$$\text{Reject } H_0 \text{ if } p\text{-value} \leq .05$$

The formula for the *t* statistic is Formula 13.2 reproduced below.

$$t = \frac{(M_1 - M_2) - \Delta_0}{s_{M_1 - M_2}}$$

where $s_{M_1 - M_2}$ is computed using *MSW* as s_p^2,

$$s_{M_1 - M_2} = \sqrt{MSW\left(\frac{1}{n_1} + \frac{1}{n_2}\right)}$$

For the example, using the data in Table 17.1 and *MSW* from Table 17.3,

$$s_{MSW} = \sqrt{3.99\left(\frac{1}{8} + \frac{1}{10}\right)} = .947$$

and

$$t = \frac{(9.5 - 6.1) - 0}{.947} = 3.59$$

Because a t of 3.59 is in the rejection region, the null hypothesis can be rejected. The psychologist concludes that there is a real difference between the means of the two populations of problem-solving times. As usual, however, there is a small chance of a Type I error. The protected t procedure does not eliminate Type I errors; it only prevents the probability of a Type I error from increasing much beyond the stated level of α.

The second comparison is between the means of the populations of problem-solving times for the middle-aged adults and the older adults. The hypotheses are

$$H_0: \mu_M - \mu_O = 0$$

$$H_1: \mu_M - \mu_O \neq 0$$

The sampling distributions and the decision rule stay the same. The computations are

$$s_{M_1-M_2} = \sqrt{3.99\left(\frac{1}{10}+\frac{1}{9}\right)} = .918, \, t = \frac{(5.9-11.0)-0}{.918} = -5.56$$

Again, the null hypothesis can be rejected, indicating that there is a difference between these population means.

Of course, it is now up to the psychologist to do something substantial with the knowledge she has gained from the data. Why are older adults slower than middle-aged adults? Why are adolescents slower than young adults? What do these results imply about cognitive development across the life span? These substantive issues cannot be answered by statistical analyses. The statistics, however, have demonstrated that it is reasonable to ask the questions.

A SECOND EXAMPLE OF THE INDEPENDENT-SAMPLE ONE-FACTOR ANOVA

In the Maternity Study, Drs. Janet Hyde and Marilyn Essex were interested in whether employment status (outside the home) affected a new mother's marital satisfaction. From their data set of 244 participants, Drs. Hyde and Essex asked if MARSAT scores at 12 months were different for moms employed full-time, part-time, or not at all. The scores are presented in Table 17.4.

In this experiment, the independent variable (and factor) is employment status, with three types or levels. The dependent variable is the mother's MARSAT score at 12 months postpartum. The assumptions of ANOVA are that the populations are normally distributed, that they have homogeneous variances, that they contain interval- or ratio-level data, and that we obtained independent samples through independent random sampling. The assumptions are largely met here with the exception of the independent random sampling. Recall that families volunteered for the Maternity Study and were not selected randomly. Therefore, we must limit our conclusions to the groups studied.

The hypotheses are

TABLE 17.4
MARSAT Scores for Mothers 12 Months Postpartum

None			Part-time				Full-time			
2.49	2.33	1.59	2.90	1.06	1.00	1.44	1.31	1.15	2.35	−0.15
1.55	2.69	1.47	2.74	0.36	1.55	2.86	2.12	−0.82	1.42	2.37
1.64	2.40	2.02	0.16	1.06	0.37	−0.07	1.85	0.72	−0.25	2.49
2.11	1.55	1.86	2.35	0.49	1.70	1.79	2.95	1.80	0.46	1.06
2.84	1.33	0.80	1.14	2.64	1.52	−0.06	0.37	1.05	−0.33	1.46
−1.96	−0.50	2.34	2.11	1.48	1.56	1.98	1.96	2.35	2.56	1.07
2.68	1.09	2.15	2.90	1.52	1.01	1.16	0.02	1.65	1.71	1.04
0.90	2.50	1.10	1.18	1.55	1.62	1.67	1.67	2.05	−2.11	1.96
0.78	0.50	1.93	1.12	0.67	1.21	0.31	2.45	0.68	1.75	0.42
2.26	1.67	1.58	2.65	1.17	2.65	−0.25	1.54	2.42	1.65	
1.68	0.16		2.74	0.97	−0.37	1.16	1.12	1.14	2.43	
0.34	1.99		2.13	1.64	1.49	2.04	2.01	2.69	1.36	
1.85	0.56		1.76	1.08	1.94	2.43	2.22	2.39	0.73	
2.26	1.94		1.54	1.98	1.96	1.48	2.17	2.44	1.67	
2.06	0.90		0.68	2.68	1.54	1.56	−0.24	2.19	1.45	
2.23	2.17		1.47	1.87	1.65	0.25	−0.56	2.91	1.00	
0.43	0.72		1.06	1.40	2.21	1.08	2.22	2.32	2.23	
0.49	2.76		2.04	1.52	−0.13	2.01	1.86	1.25	1.97	
0.26	3.00		1.57	1.44	0.41	2.15	1.36	2.34	2.20	
1.47	1.50		1.76	0.35	1.52	1.94	−0.09	0.86	2.89	
2.06	1.51		1.24	2.63	0.14	0.47	0.31	2.12	2.84	
1.55	1.43		0.98	0.24	0.87	1.41	2.32	1.49	2.58	
2.56	1.34		1.45	2.95	1.93	1.67	1.19	2.08	0.11	
1.96	1.98		2.37	2.89	1.56	1.92	1.59	1.63	2.13	
1.42	1.87		2.50	1.71	2.00	2.50	1.92	1.16	1.29	

$$H_0: \mu_{\text{None}} = \mu_{\text{Part-time}} = \mu_{\text{Full-time}}$$

$$H_1: \text{the null is wrong}$$

When H_0 is correct, F will be around 1.0. When H_1 is correct, F will be substantially larger than 1.0.

Using $\alpha = .05$ and 2 and 241 df, the decision rule is

$$\text{Reject } H_0 \text{ if } F = MSB/MSW \geq 3.03$$

The critical values of F contained within Table D do not have a value for 241 df in the numerator. However, many statistical programs give the probability value associated with a particular statistic's value. Thus, we can also state the decision rule as

FIGURE 17.3
ANOVA output from Excel on MARSAT scores and employment status.

	A	B	C	D	E	F	G
1	Anova: Single Factor						
2							
3	SUMMARY						
4	Groups	Count	Sum	Average	Variance		
5	Full-time	84	125.5521	1.494667	0.941215		
6	Part-Time	100	149.6574	1.496574	0.634351		
7	None	60	94.17088	1.569515	0.784264		
8							
9							
10	ANOVA						
11	Source of Variation	SS	df	MS	F	P-value	F crit
12	Between Groups	0.24667	2	0.123335	0.158786	0.853268	3.033279
13	Within Groups	187.1932	241	0.776735			
14							
15	Total	187.4399	243				
16							
17							

Reject H_0 if p-value $\leq \alpha$

With such a large data set, performing the necessary calculations for an ANOVA are daunting. Moreover, you are likely to make errors that are imperceptible. In other words, it might take you hours to do all the calculations on these data and even after that, mistakes are likely, no matter how careful you are. Therefore, most researchers use a computer program to analyze data sets like this. Excel can easily perform an ANOVA on these data. If you open up the file "Mothers marital satisfaction and employment status.XLS," you will see the data in Table 17.4 arranged in columns. Using the Data Analysis Toolpak provided with Excel, select "Anova: One Factor" and fill in the necessary fields. Clicking on the "OK" button should give you something like Figure 17.3. As you can see, Excel gives you an ANOVA table much like the one shown earlier. Because the p-value (0.85) is not less than α (.05), we do not reject the null hypothesis. We must conclude that there is not enough evidence to reject H_0.

ONE-FACTOR ANOVA FOR DEPENDENT SAMPLES

Dependent-sample designs (within-subject and matched-group) are very popular because they increase power compared to independent-sample designs. The statistical analysis is somewhat complicated, however, and cannot be discussed in detail here. As a compromise, this section describes the dependent-sample ANOVA, the computational methods, and what you can learn from the ANOVA; no attempt is made to explain the details of how the analysis works.

In a dependent-sample design, the observations in one sample can be systematically related to the observations in all other samples. One method for creating dependent samples is to use a within-subjects design in which each subject contributes a score to each sample. Another method is to use matched groups of related subjects (for example, litter mates). Then, one member of each matched group is randomly assigned to each of the samples.

A **block** is the name for the collection of scores from a single subject, or the collection of scores from a single matched group of subjects in a matched group design. The dependent-sample ANOVA is sometimes called a randomized block ANOVA.

As with the independent-sample ANOVA, the goal of the dependent-sample ANOVA is to decide if there are any differences among the population means. Differences between the sample means (reflected in MSB) are a major factor contributing to the decision. The larger the differences between the sample means, the greater the likelihood of rejecting H_0 and concluding that there are differences between the population means. However, the dependent-samples ANOVA differs from the independent-samples ANOVA in one important way. Recall that in an independent-samples ANOVA, $F = MSB/MSW$. The denominator, MSW, is a legitimate estimate of σ^2 when either H_0 is correct or incorrect. In the dependent samples ANOVA, a different term, MSE, is used as the estimate of σ^2, and the denominator for the F-ratio.

The procedure is introduced with an example, and a summary of the steps is included in Table 17.12 at the end of the chapter.

Consider a health psychologist examining three different methods (treatments) for getting patients to take medication. The three treatments are (a) a lecture on the importance of the medication, (b) a digital watch that beeps whenever medication is to be taken, and (c) a control in which no special instructions or methods are used. The dependent variable is the actual frequency (over a month) that the medication is taken.

The psychologist forms eight blocks of matched triplets of patients so that the patients in each block are of the same sex, are approximately the same age and educational level, and take the same medication for the same medical problem. One member of each block is randomly assigned to each of the three treatments so that there are a total of eight patients in each sample (see Table 17.5). The data in the different samples are dependent (related) because an observation in one sample can be matched with observations from each of the other samples; just group together scores coming from patients in the same block.

Step 1: Assumptions

The assumptions for the dependent-sample ANOVA include all those for the independent-sample ANOVA (except, of course, that the samples should be dependent instead of independent) and one more. The additional assumption is that there is the same degree of relationship between the scores in all pairs of samples. The implications of this assumption are technical; for full understanding, refer to an advanced text. Although this assumption is as important as any other (and cannot be overcome by robustness), it is often ignored. If the assumptions cannot be met, the Friedman F_r test (see p. 388) may be appropriate.

Step 2: Hypotheses

The hypotheses are the same as for the independent-sample ANOVA:

$$H_0: \mu_1 = \mu_2 = \ldots = \mu_k$$

$$H_1: H_0 \text{ is wrong}$$

For the example, we are concerned with the means of three populations (the three treatments) and so the hypotheses are

$$H_0: \mu_1 = \mu_2 = \mu_3$$

$$H_1: H_0 \text{ is wrong}$$

Step 3: Sampling Distribution

The test statistic is $F = MSB/MSE$. When H_0 is correct, F will be close to 1.0. When H_1 is correct, F will be much larger than 1.0.

Step 4: Set α and the Decision Rule

Setting α involves the same trade-off as always: Decreasing α lowers the probability of a Type I error, but increases the probability of a Type II error (decreases power). For the example, we will use $\alpha = .05$.

The decision rule is

$$\text{Reject } H_0 \text{ if } F \geq F_\alpha (k - 1, (k - 1)(n - 1)) \text{ or}$$
$$\text{Reject } H_0 \text{ if } p\text{-value} \leq \alpha$$

Note that the degrees of freedom for the denominator are calculated differently than in the independent-sample ANOVA. For the example, the degrees of freedom in the F statistic are 2 and 14. Thus,

$$\text{Reject } H_0 \text{ if } F = MSB/MSE \geq 3.74 \text{ or}$$
$$\text{Reject } H_0 \text{ if } p\text{-value} \leq .05$$

Step 5: Sample and Compute the Test Statistic

The computations are given in Table 17.5 along with the data. The summary table schema for the dependent-sample one-factor ANOVA is in Table 17.6, and the ANOVA summary table for this example is in Table 17.7.

Computations of the total sum of squares (SST) and the sum of squares between (SSB) are just as in the independent-sample ANOVA (see Table 17.5).

The next step is to compute the sum of squares for blocks, $SSBl$. This term is obtained by squaring the total for all observations in a block (square each Bl_i), summing the squared totals, dividing by k (the number of treatment populations), and subtracting NM_G^2. This sum of squares represents the variability due to differences among the blocks. By removing this variability (in the next step), the power of the dependent-sample ANOVA is increased compared to the power of the independent-sample ANOVA.

TABLE 17.5
Frequency of Taking Medication Following Three Treatments

		Treatment			
				Block Totals	
Block	Lecture	Watch	Control	(Bl)	Bl^2
1	17	19	18	54	2916
2	16	17	19	52	2704
3	20	22	21	63	3969
4	25	23	24	72	5184
5	10	8	9	27	729
6	15	15	14	44	1936
7	18	17	16	51	2601
8	12	11	10	33	1089

$$n_L = 8 \qquad n_W = 8 \qquad n_C = 8 \qquad \sum Bl^2 = 21128$$

$$\sum X_L = 133 \qquad \sum X_W = 132 \qquad \sum X_C = 131$$

$$\sum X_L^2 = 2363 \qquad \sum X_W^2 = 2362 \qquad \sum X_C^2 = 2335$$

$$M_L = 16.625 \qquad M_W = 16.5 \qquad M_C = 16.375$$

$$SS(X_L) = 151.88 \qquad SS(X_W) = 184 \qquad SS(X_C) = 189.88$$

$$s_L^2 = 21.696 \qquad s_W^2 = 26.286 \qquad s_C^2 = 27.125$$

$$M_G = \sum X/N = 396/24 = 16.5$$

$$SST = \sum X^2 - NM_G^2 = 7060 - 6534 = 526$$

$$df_T = N - 1 = 24 - 1 = 23$$

$$SSB = \sum n_j M_j^2 - NM_G^2 = 8(16.625)^2 + 8(16.5)^2 + 8(16.375)^2 - 24(16.5)^2 = 0.25$$

$$df_B = k - 1 = 3 - 1 = 2$$

$$SSBl = k \sum_{j=1}^{k} (M_j - M_G)^2 = \frac{\sum Bl^2}{k} - NM_G^2$$

$$df_{Bl} = (Bl - 1)$$

$$SSBl = \frac{21128}{3} - 24(16.5)^2 = 508.67$$

$$df_{Bl} = (8 - 1) = 7$$

$$SSE = \sum_{j=1}^{m} \sum_{i=1}^{n} (X_{ij} - M_i - M_j - M_G)^2 = SST - SSB - SSBl$$

$$df_E = (k - 1)(n - 1)$$

$$SSE = 526 - 0.25 - 508.67 = 17.08$$

$$df_E = (3 - 1)(8 - 1) = 14$$

TABLE 17.6
General Summary Table for Independent-sample One-factor ANOVA

Source of Variation	SS	df	MS	F
Between	$\sum n_j M_j^2 - NM_G^2$	$k - 1$	SSB/df_B	MSB/MSE
Blocks	$\dfrac{\sum Bl^2}{k} - NM_G^2$	$Bl - 1$	$SSBl/df_{Bl}$	
Error	$SST - SSB - SSBl$	$(k - 1)(n - 1)$	SSE/df_E	
Total	$\sum X^2 - NM_G^2$	$N - 1$		

TABLE 17.7
ANOVA Table for Frequency of Taking Medication
Following Three Treatments

Source of Variation	SS	df	MS	F
Between	0.25	2	0.125	$0.125/1.22 = 0.10$
Blocks	508.67	7	72.67	
Error	17.08	14	1.22	
Total	526	23		

The sum of squares of error *SSE* is obtained by subtracting *SSB* and *SSBl* from the Total *SST*.

As indicated in the summary table schema (Table 17.6), the mean squares are obtained by dividing each of the sum of squares by its degrees of freedom. Finally, the *F* statistic is obtained by dividing *MSB* by *MSE*.

The summary table in Table 17.7 organizes the results of the ANOVA and provides a check on computations. All sums of squares should be positive; the sum of squares for between, blocks, and error should sum to the total sum of squares; the degrees of freedom for between, blocks, and error should sum to the total degrees of freedom.

Step 6: Decide and Draw Conclusions

Because *F* (0.10; see Table 17.7) does not exceed the critical value (3.74), the null hypothesis cannot be rejected. The only conclusion is that there is insufficient evidence to reject H_0, not that H_0 is correct. Thus the health psychologist cannot tell if there is a difference (in the population μs) among the methods of instructing patients in how to take their medicines. Certainly, the data offer little evidence in favor of such a difference.

When reporting the results, give the sample means, as well as the critical components of the ANOVA. Assuming that the means are given in a table, the report might read, "Using an $\alpha = .05$, the null hypothesis could not be rejected, $F(2, 14) = 0.10$, $MSE = 1.22$."

Specific populations can be compared using the protected t procedure, after the ANOVA H_0 has been rejected. In the example, the ANOVA H_0 was not rejected, and so the protected t procedure cannot be used (the t test is not protected). An illustration of the protected t procedure will follow the next example.

Possible Errors

As always, when H_0 is not rejected, there is some probability of making a Type II error. With the dependent-sample ANOVA, that probability is generally smaller than with the independent-sample ANOVA. Of course, if H_0 had been rejected, there would be a probability of a Type I error. But that probability is always small and equal to α.

Power of the one-factor ANOVA can be enhanced (and thus the probability of a Type II error decreased) in a variety of ways. Increasing α will increase power, as will increasing the sample size (number of blocks). As with the dependent-sample t test, power will also increase the closer the relationship between the scores in the samples (the greater the similarity among the scores in a block). Finally, power will increase with the distance between the population means (the effect size). Often, the effect size can be enhanced by careful choice of the populations sampled (treatments).

A SECOND DEPENDENT-SAMPLE ONE-FACTOR ANOVA

In planning the Maternity Study, Drs. Hyde and Essex wondered what would happen to marital satisfaction over time. Thus, they obtained MARSAT scores for mothers during the 5th month of pregnancy, and at 1 month, 4 months, and 12 months postpartum to see if marital satisfaction scores changed. Since each mother contributes four MARSAT scores, the scores are systematically related, the samples are dependent.

In this experiment, then, the independent variable is time and it corresponds to the factor in the one-factor ANOVA. The factor has four levels (before birth, 1 month, 4 months, and 12 months postpartum). The dependent variable is the MARSAT score. As noted earlier, it appears that all the assumptions of ANOVA are met except the independent random-sampling assumption. We will note this in our conclusions.

The hypotheses are:

$$H_0: \mu_{\text{Before}} = \mu_{1\text{mo}} = \mu_{4\text{mo}} = \mu_{12\text{mo}}$$

$$H_1: H_0 \text{ is wrong}$$

When H_0 is correct, $F = MSB/MSE$ will be around 1.0. When H_1 is correct, F will be much larger than 1.0.

The decision rule for $\alpha = .05$ and 3 $(k-1)$ and 729 $((k-1)(n-1))$ df is

$$\text{Reject } H_0 \text{ if } F = MSB/MSE \geq 2.62$$

FIGURE 17.4
Excel output for dependent-sample ANOVA on MARSAT scores over time.

	ANOVA						
	Source of Variation	SS	df	MS	F	P-value	F crit
57	Rows	445.4835	243	1.833265	7.435362	5E-99	1.183252
58	Columns	11.69768	3	3.899227	15.81449	5.69E-10	2.617121
59	Error	179.7425	729	0.24656			
60							
61	Total	636.9236	975				
62							
63							

Once again, Table D does not provide a critical value for 729 df (although you can interpolate). The decision rule can be stated as

$$\text{Reject } H_0 \text{ if } p\text{-value} \leq \alpha$$

Because each of 244 mothers provided four MARSAT scores in this experiment, the complete data set is too large to reproduce here. Moreover, doing the computations by hand would take a very long time. Therefore, we have provided the complete data set on your data CD ("Marital satisfaction over time.XLS"). Using Tools → Data Analysis in Excel, choose "Anova: Two-factor without replication." Input the required fields. Excel will provide a lot of output. At the bottom should be the ANOVA table.

Deciphering the output from Excel may require a bit of consideration. In earlier examples, we computed four terms: SSB, $SSBl$, SSE, and SST. Excel computed SS(Rows), SS(Columns), SS(Error) and SS(Total). It is easy to figure out that $SSE = SS$(Error) and $SST = SS$(Total), but "Rows" and "Columns"? Which one is sum of squares blocks ($SSBl$) and which one is sum of squares between (SSB)? The answer depends on your data. If you entered blocks of scores in a row, as was provided on the data CD, then $SSBl = SS$(Rows) and $SSB = SS$(Columns); however, Excel can handle data entered in the other direction as well. Nevertheless, since Figure 17.4 was obtained from the data provided, Columns is the between-groups factor. Because that F (15.81) is much larger than the critical value of 2.62, we reject H_0. These data suggest that, among new mothers in Wisconsin who volunteered for the Maternity Study, at least one of the population means differs from at least one of the others. Looking at the means in the Excel output, it appears that there is a steady decline in marital satisfaction over time. To check on specific comparisons between the time periods, we can use the protected t procedure.

Comparison Between Selected Population Means

The protected t test can be performed only after the ANOVA H_0 has been rejected. Rejecting H_0 is just what "protects" you against the inflation of Type I errors when performing multiple t tests. Unlike the protected t following the independent-sample ANOVA, the protected t following the dependent-sample ANOVA does *not* use MSE. Instead, the t test described in Chapter 15 is used directly. It will be illustrated by comparing the mean of the before-birth treatment to the 12-month treatment.

The assumptions of the dependent t are met by virtue of meeting the assumptions for the ANOVA. The first pair of hypotheses to be examined are

$$H_0: \mu_{\text{Before}} = \mu_{12\text{mo}}$$

$$H_1: \mu_{\text{Before}} > \mu_{12\text{mo}}$$

Using an $\alpha = .05$ and 243 ($n_p - 1$) df, the decision rule is

Reject H_0 if $t \geq 1.65$ or

Reject H_0 if p-value $\leq \alpha$

The computations use Formula 15.3 (see Table 15.7) based on differences between the matched scores in each sample. Use the data from the "MARSAT 5 mo before" column and the "MARSAT 12 mo after" column in the Excel file provided to obtain the differences between the pairs of scores, then

$$M_D = \frac{\sum D}{n_p} = \frac{71.11}{244} = 0.29$$

$$s_D = \sqrt{\frac{SS(D)}{n_p - 1}} = \sqrt{\frac{125.77}{243}} = 0.72, \ s_{M_D} = \frac{s_D}{\sqrt{n_p}} = \frac{0.72}{\sqrt{244}} = 0.046$$

$$t = \frac{M_D - \Delta_0}{s_{M_D}} = \frac{0.29}{0.046} = 6.30$$

Because t is greater than 1.65, the null hypothesis that MARSAT scores 5 months before birth are equal to MARSAT scores 12 months after birth can be rejected. In other words, there is sufficient evidence to conclude that MARSAT scores 12 months after birth are lower than MARSAT scores 5 months before birth, in new mothers from Wisconsin who volunteer for psychological studies. Additional pairs of hypotheses may be tested with the same procedure; however, with each comparison comes less "protection." In other words, the protected t test should be used only in a limited number of comparisons, not all of the possible ones in a study.

The above conclusions may be worded in an odd way, but because we did not have a truly random sample, we cannot conclude that marital satisfaction decreases after the birth of the first child for all women. However, these data strongly suggest that the birth of a child affects, in a negative way, marital satisfaction over time for new mothers. Which populations of new moms might or might not be affected (for example, women who live in California, women who do not normally volunteer for psychological studies, and so on) is the subject for additional research.

KRUSKAL–WALLIS *H* TEST: NONPARAMETRIC ANALOGUE FOR THE INDEPENDENT-SAMPLE ONE-FACTOR ANOVA

When the assumptions of the independent-sample ANOVA cannot be met, an alternative procedure is the nonparametric Kruskal–Wallis *H* test. Because the *H* test is not as powerful as the ANOVA, it should not be used when the ANOVA assumptions are tenable.

The *H* test is an extension of the rank-sum test discussed in Chapter 13, and like the rank-sum test, the null hypothesis is about the population distributions, not a specific population parameter. Although the null hypothesis may be rejected due to any of a variety of differences between the populations, the test is most sensitive to differences in the population central tendencies.

As an example, consider the data in Table 17.8. The data come from an industrial psychologist's investigation of the effects of type of handicap on interviewer evaluations. Each interviewer was randomly assigned a résumé of a prospective employee that included information on one of four types of handicaps (none, physical, mental, emotional). The interviewer then rated the employee for job suitability. Do the populations (of ratings) differ for the four types of handicaps? Because the data are ordinal, and because one of the samples (emotional handicap) seems to have much greater variability than the others (contradicting the equal-variance assumption of the ANOVA), the psychologist decides to perform a Kruskal–Wallis test rather than an ANOVA.

TABLE 17.8
Interview Evaluations (rank in parentheses)

			Type of Handicap				
None	*(R)*	*Physical*	*(R)*	*Mental*	*(R)*	*Emotional*	*(R)*
75	(21.5)	60	(10)	51	(6.5)	33	(1)
86	(27)	70	(17)	48	(4)	87	(28)
66	(14)	65	(13)	63	(12)	42	(2)
73	(19)	56	(9)	54	(8)	68	(15)
79	(23)	75	(21.5)	45	(3)	74	(20)
81	(26)	80	(24.5)	61	(11)	51	(6.5)
70	(17)	70	(17)	50	(5)	80	(24.5)
$T_1 = 147.5$		$T_2 = 112$		$T_3 = 49.5$		$T_4 = 97$	
$n_1 = 7$		$n_2 = 7$		$n_3 = 7$		$n_4 = 7$	

Check: $\displaystyle\sum_{j=1}^{k} T_k = \frac{N(N+1)}{2} = \frac{(28)(29)}{2} = 406$

$$= 147.5 + 112 + 49.5 + 97 = 406$$

$$SSB = \sum \frac{(T_j)^2}{n_j} - \frac{N(N+1)^2}{4} = \frac{(147.5)^2}{7} + \frac{(112)^2}{7} + \frac{(49.5)^2}{7} + \frac{(97)^2}{7} - \frac{(28)(29)^2}{4} = 707.21$$

$$H = \frac{12SSB}{N(N+1)} = \frac{12(707.21)}{(28)(29)} = 10.45$$

In this example, the independent variable (factor) is type of handicap, with four treatments. The treatments define the four populations from which the samples are drawn. The dependent variable is the rating. Because treatment is randomly assigned to each interviewer, causal links may be inferred if the null hypothesis is rejected. Furthermore, because each interviewer makes only one rating, and because there is no systematic way of matching the ratings across the samples, the samples are independent.

Step 1: Assumptions

Sampling Assumptions

1. The samples are independent of one another.
2. Each sample is obtained using independent (within-sample) random sampling. If random assignment has been used instead, then the inherent randomness of biological systems must be assumed.
3. If there are three treatments, then each sample must have at least five observations. If there are more than three treatments, each sample must have at least two observations. The sampling distribution used below approximates the distribution of the *H* statistic when the sample sizes are large. Exact tables of *H*, which can be used with smaller sample sizes, are available in more advanced books.

Data Assumption   The data must be ordinal, interval, or ratio. The *H* statistic is based on ranking, and nominal data cannot be sensibly ranked.

The example meets these assumptions. Note that there are no population assumptions. That, of course, is why the Kruskal–Wallis procedure can be used when the population assumptions for the independent-sample ANOVA cannot be met.

Step 2: Hypotheses

H_0: The population relative frequency distributions are identical

H_1: The null is wrong

The nondirectional alternative states that at least one of the population distributions is different from the others. It does not specify how many differences there may be, or which populations differ. If the null is rejected, more specific information can be obtained by using the protected rank-sum test to compare specific populations.

Step 3: Test Statistic and Its Sampling Distribution

The first step in computing *H* is to rank all of the data (regardless of group) from lowest (1) to highest (*N*). Next, using the ranks, *SSB* is computed.

$$SSB = \sum \frac{(T_j)^2}{n_j} - \frac{N(N+1)^2}{4}$$

T_j is the total of the ranks for the jth sample, and n_j is the number of observations in the jth sample. The uppercase N is the total number of observations. The "4" in the formula is a constant that does not depend on the sample sizes or the number of treatments.

The final step is to compute H using the formula

$$H = \frac{12SSB}{N(N+1)}$$

The 12 in the numerator is a constant. This statistic has $k - 1$ degrees of freedom, where k is the number of populations (treatments) sampled.

Thus H, like MSB in the ANOVA, is an index of the variability between the treatments. When H_0 is correct, the variability should be modest. When H_1 is correct, the variability should be large and H should be large.

As usual, the question is how large is large? And as usual, the answer depends on the sampling distribution of H assuming that H_0 is correct. When the sample sizes are not too small, the sampling distribution of H can be approximated by the sampling distribution of another statistic called *chi-square* (χ^2). This statistic and its sampling distribution are discussed in greater detail in Chapter 22.

Table G (in the Tables section at the back of the book) tabulates critical values of the χ^2 statistic. Turn to the table now. Each row in the table gives the critical values for a different distribution corresponding to the degrees of freedom on the left. Each critical value is the value of the statistic that has a particular proportion of the distribution above it. Thus, in the distribution with 5 *df*, 9.24 has 10% of the distribution above it, and 15.09 has 1% of the distribution above it.

When H_0 is correct, it is unlikely that H will exceed the critical value. On the other hand, when H_1 is correct, H is likely to be very large and exceed the critical value. Thus, values of H greater than the critical value are evidence against H_0 and evidence in favor of H_1.

Step 4: Set α and the Decision Rule

As always, α is the probability of a Type I error, and you may set it at whatever value strikes the best trade-off between Type I and Type II errors. Because the Kruskal–Wallis test examines a single null hypothesis, the value of α does not change with the number of populations (as would be the case when using multiple rank-sum tests).

The decision rule is

Reject H_0 if $H \geq \chi^2_\alpha(k - 1)$ or
Reject H_0 if p-value $\leq \alpha$

The symbol $\chi^2_\alpha(k - 1)$ is the critical value of the χ^2 statistic (from Table G) for a particular value of α and $k - 1$ degrees of freedom, where k is the number of populations sampled.

For the example, $k = 4$ so $df = 3$. Using $\alpha = .05$, the decision rule is

$$\text{Reject } H_0 \text{ if } H \geq 7.81$$

Step 5: Sample and Compute the Test Statistic

The rankings are given in Table 17.9. Note that tied values are given the average of the ranks. Also, as a check on your ranking, the total of all the ranks should equal $N(N + 1)/2$. Computation of SSB and H are illustrated in Table 17.9.

Step 6: Decide and Draw Conclusions

Because the value of H (10.45) exceeds the critical value, the null hypothesis can be rejected, and the psychologist can conclude that at least one of the populations of ratings differs from the others. Note, however, that the alternative does not specify which populations differ.

Specific information as to which populations differ can be obtained by using the protected rank-sum procedure. That is, after the Kruskal–Wallis null hypothesis has been rejected, multiple comparisons can be made using the rank-sum procedure (described in Chapter 13) without fear of greatly inflating the Type I error rate.

Possible Errors

Like any other statistical test, the Kruskal–Wallis test is subject to Type I errors (when H_0 is rejected) and Type II errors (when it is not). Fortunately, the probability of a Type I error can be kept low by using a small α. The probability of a Type II error can be decreased (power increased) by increasing α, by increasing the sample size, by increasing the effect size (by judicious choice of treatments), and by careful data collection procedures that eliminate unwanted variability.

FRIEDMAN F_r TEST: NONPARAMETRIC ANALOGUE FOR THE DEPENDENT-SAMPLE ONE-FACTOR ANOVA

The Friedman test may be appropriate when the assumptions for the dependent-sample ANOVA cannot be met. Because the Friedman test is not as powerful as the ANOVA, it should be used only when the ANOVA cannot be used.

As an example, consider a researcher studying memory in pigeons. Each animal is placed in a cage with two different-colored disks. While the pigeon is restrained, one of the disks is illuminated for a short period of time. The pigeon is released after a 0-, 10-, 20-, or 40-second retention interval and allowed to peck at one of the disks. If the pigeon pecks at the previously lit disk, it is rewarded.

TABLE 17.9
Correct (out of 10) at Each of Four Retention Intervals

Pigeon	Intervals (and ranks)							
	0	*(R)*	*10*	*(R)*	*20*	*(R)*	*40*	*(R)*
1	10	(4)	5	(2)	6	(3)	1	(1)
2	10	(4)	8	(3)	2	(2)	0	(1)
3	8	(3.5)	8	(3.5)	1	(1.5)	1	(1.5)
4	7	(4)	2	(3)	0	(1)	1	(2)
5	9	(4)	4	(3)	1	(1.5)	1	(1.5)
6	9	(3)	10	(4)	2	(2)	0	(1)
7	9	(4)	3	(3)	2	(2)	1	(1)
8	8	(4)	6	(3)	4	(2)	0	(1)
	$T_1 = 30.5$		$T_2 = 24.5$		$T_3 = 15$		$T_4 = 10$	

Check: $\displaystyle\sum_{j=1}^{k} T_k = \frac{bl(k)(k+1)}{2} = \frac{(8)(4)(5)}{2} = 80$

$= 30.5 + 24.5 + 15 + 10 = 80$

$SSB = \dfrac{\sum(T_j)^2}{bl} - \dfrac{bl(k)(k+1)^2}{4} = \dfrac{(30.5)^2 + (24.5)^2 + (15)^2 + (10)^2}{8} - \dfrac{(8)(4)(5)^2}{4} = 31.94$

$F_r = \dfrac{12SSB}{k(k+1)} = \dfrac{12(31.94)}{(4)(5)} = 19.16$

Each of eight pigeons is given 10 trials at each of the four retention intervals. The order of the various retention intervals is randomly determined for each pigeon. The data in Table 17.10 are the number of times (out of 10) each pigeon pecked the correct disk.

In this experiment, retention interval is an independent variable (and factor) with four treatments corresponding to the populations sampled. One population is the number of correct pecks (out of 10) after a 0-second retention interval, another is the number of correct pecks after a 10-second interval, and so on. Because each pigeon contributed an observation to each sample, the factor was manipulated within subjects (that is, this is a dependent-sample design). The four scores associated with each pigeon comprise a block, and because there are eight pigeons, the experiment has eight blocks. Of course, the question of interest is whether the populations differ.

At first glance, it appears that the dependent-sample ANOVA would be appropriate. Note, however, that compared to the other conditions, there is very little variability in the 40-second retention interval condition. Thus, the equal variance assumption of the ANOVA is probably violated, and the psychologist decides to use the Friedman F_r statistic instead.

Step 1: Assumptions

Sampling Assumptions

1. The samples are dependent (related to each other).

2. Each sample is obtained by independent (within-sample) random sampling. If random assignment has been used instead, then the inherent randomness of biological systems must be assumed.

3. If there are three treatments, then each sample must have at least five observations (five blocks). If there are more than three treatments, each must have at least three observations (three blocks). The sampling distribution used below approximates the distribution of the F_r statistic when the sample sizes are large. Exact tables of F_r, which can be used with smaller sample sizes, are available in more advanced books.

Data Assumption   The data must be ordinal, interval, or ratio. The F_r test is based on ranking, and nominal data cannot be ranked sensibly.

The example meets these assumptions.

Step 2: Hypotheses

H_0: The population relative frequency distributions are identical

H_1: The null is wrong

The nondirectional alternative states that at least one of the population distributions is different from the others. It does not specify how many differences there may be, nor which populations differ. If the null is rejected, more specific information can be obtained by using the protected Wilcoxon T_m test to compare specific populations.

Step 3: Test Statistic and Its Sampling Distribution

There are three steps to the calculation of F_r. First, rank the observations within each block (see Table 17.9), and sum the ranks in each sample. A method to check on the rankings is provided in the table.

The second step is to compute SSB.

The third step is to compute F_r, as illustrated in Table 17.9. This statistic has $k - 1$ degrees of freedom, where k is the number of populations from which you have samples.

Because F_r is based on SSB, it will be small when H_0 is correct and large when H_1 is correct. In fact, just like the Kruskal–Wallis H, when H_0 is correct, the distribution of F_r is approximated by the χ^2 distribution with $k - 1$ degrees of freedom. Thus, critical values for the F_r statistic can be obtained from Table G. Finding an F_r greater than the critical value is unlikely when H_0 is correct, but very likely when H_1 is correct.

Step 4: Set α and the Decision Rule

As usual, α should be set after considering the trade-off between Type I and Type II errors. The decision rule is

$$\text{Reject } H_0 \text{ if } F_r \geq \chi_\alpha^2(k-1) \text{ or}$$
$$\text{Reject } H_0 \text{ if } p\text{-value} \leq \alpha$$

For example, using $\alpha = .05$ and 3 df, the decision rule is

$$\text{Reject } H_0 \text{ if } F_r \geq 7.81 \text{ or}$$
$$\text{Reject } H_0 \text{ if } p\text{-value} \leq .05$$

Step 5: Sample and Compute the Test Statistic

The rankings are included in Table 17.9. Note the check to make sure that the rankings are correct. The value of F_r from Table 17.9 is 19.16.

Step 6: Decide and Draw Conclusions

Because F_r exceeds the critical value, the null hypotheses can be rejected, and the psychologist can conclude that at least one of the populations differs from the others. Apparently, pigeon short-term memory declines over a retention interval, much as does human short-term memory.

Specific comparisons between treatments can be made using the protected Wilcoxon T_m procedure. First, reject H_0 using the Friedman test. This provides protection against the inflation of Type I error rates that would otherwise accompany multiple comparisons. Then, compare specific pairs of means using the Wilcoxon procedure described in Chapter 15.

Possible Errors

As always, an erroneous decision might be made. Using the Friedman procedure, the probability of a Type I error is exactly α, regardless of the number of treatments compared. This probability can be set at whatever level you desire, but remember, decreasing α will increase β.

The probability of a Type II error can be decreased (that is, power increased) by increasing α, by increasing the sample sizes, by increasing the effect size (by sampling populations with very different distributions), and by good control over data collection procedures to reduce excess variability.

SUMMARY

The ANOVA is a procedure used to compare population means. Rejecting the null hypothesis (that all population means are equal) implies that at least one of the population means differs from the others. The major advantages of the ANOVA over multiple t tests are that it is less work, and it avoids the inflation of the Type I error rate past the stated level of α.

The ANOVA works by obtaining two different estimates of the variance common to all of the populations. MSW is the pooled s^2 based on deviations within each sample. When the assumptions are met, MSW is a good estimate of σ^2. MSB is based on deviations between the sample means. When H_0 is correct, MSB is also an estimate of σ^2, but when H_1 is correct, MSB is much larger than σ^2. Therefore, when H_0 is correct, $F = MSB/MSW$ is likely to be around 1.0, but when H_1 is correct, $F = MSB/MSW$ is likely to be much larger than 1.0.

Rejecting H_0 does not specify which population means differ. Specific comparisons may be made using the protected t procedure. This procedure has two steps. First, reject H_0 using the ANOVA. Because Type I errors can be made only when H_0 is correct, rejecting H_0 using the ANOVA protects the t tests against Type I errors. The second step is to conduct t tests between pairs of populations of interest. For independent samples, MSW and its degrees of freedom can be used for s_p^2. For dependent samples, the t test should be conducted exactly as in Chapter 15.

The Kruskal–Wallis test is a nonparametric analogue for the independent-sample one-factor ANOVA. After rejecting its null hypothesis, specific comparisons may be made using the protected rank-sum test. The Friedman test is a nonparametric analogue for the dependent-sample, one-factor ANOVA. It may be followed by the protected Wilcoxon T_m test.

A summary of the independent-sample one-factor ANOVA is provided in Table 17.10, and the dependent-sample one-factor ANOVA is summarized in Table 17.11. The Kruskal–Wallis test is summarized in Table 17.12, and the Friedman test is summarized in Table 17.13.

EXERCISES

Terms Define these new terms and symbols.

ANOVA	factor
treatment	independent variable
dependent variable	s_p^2
MSB	MSW
MSE	SST
SSW	SSB
SSE	Block
protected t	H
χ^2	protected rank-sum test
F_r	protected Wilcoxon T_m

Questions *Answer the following questions.*

†1. Analyze the data in Table 17.14 using the independent-sample ANOVA. Organize the components of the analysis in an ANOVA summary table. If appropriate, use the correct procedure to compare the third and the fifth populations.

TABLE 17.10

The Independent-sample One-factor ANOVA

1. Assumptions:

Population assumptions:

a. The k populations (treatments) must be normally distributed (but see discussions of robustness).

b. Homogeneity of variance: The populations must all have the same variance (but see discussion of equal sample sizes).

Sampling assumptions:

a. The k samples must be independent of one another.

b. Each sample must be obtained using independent (within-sample) random sampling. If random assignment is used instead of random sampling, then the additional assumption of the randomness of biological systems should be made.

Data assumption:

The results will be most interpretable if the data are interval or ratio.

2. Hypotheses:

$$H_0: \mu_1 = \mu_2 = \ldots = \mu_k$$

$$H_1: \text{The null is wrong}$$

3. Test statistic and its sampling distribution:

The test statistic is

$$F = MSB/MSW \text{ which has } k - 1 \text{ and } N - k \, df$$

When H_0 is correct, the most likely values for F are around 1.0. When H_1 is correct, the most likely values for F are much greater than 1.0.

4. Decision rule:

$$\text{Reject } H_0 \text{ if } F = MSB/MSW \geq F_\alpha(k - 1, N - k) \text{ or}$$
$$\text{Reject } H_0 \text{ if } p\text{-value} \leq \alpha$$

$F_\alpha(k - 1, N - k)$ is the value of F with $k - 1$ df in the numerator and $N - k$ df in the denominator that has α of the distribution above it.

5. Sample and compute F **using formulas in Table 17.2** (or use "ANOVA: Single Factor" in "Data Analysis" toolpak).

6. Decide and draw conclusions:

If H_0 is rejected, conclude that the means of the populations are not all equal. The protected t test can be used to compare specific population means only after the ANOVA H_0 is rejected.

---

†**2.** Analyze the data in Table 17.14 using the dependent-sample ANOVA. Treat each row as a block. Organize the components of the analysis in an ANOVA summary table. If appropriate, use the correct procedure to compare the third and the fifth populations.

†**3.** Analyze the data in Table 17.14 using the Kruskal–Wallis test. If appropriate, use the correct procedure to compare the third and the fifth populations.

†**4.** Analyze the data in Table 17.14 using the Friedman test. If appropriate, use the correct procedure to compare the third and the fifth populations.

5. Note that the *SST* is exactly the same in Questions 1 and 2, and the value of *MSB* is exactly the same. Nonetheless, the values of F are quite different. Why? What does this comparison indicate about the relative advantages of independent- and dependent-sample designs?

TABLE 17.11
The Dependent-sample One-factor ANOVA

1. **Assumptions:**

Population assumptions:
   a. The k populations (treatments) must be normally distributed (but see discussions of robustness).
   b. Homogeneity of variance: the populations should all have the same variance σ^2 (but see discussion of equal sample sizes).
   c. The scores in all pairs of populations should have the same degree of relationship.

Sampling assumptions:
   a. The k samples must be dependent (related).
   b. Each of the samples must be obtained using independent (within-sample) random sampling. If random assignment is used instead of random sampling, then make the assumption that biological systems are inherently random.

Data assumption:
The results will be most interpretable if the data are interval or ratio.

2. **Hypotheses:**
$$H_0: \mu_1 = \mu_2 = \cdots = \mu_k$$

$$H_1: \text{The null is wrong}$$

3. **Test statistic and its sampling distribution:**
The test statistic is

$$F = MSB/MSE \text{ which has } k - 1 \text{ and } (k - 1)(n - 1) \ df$$

When H_0 is correct, the most likely values for F are around 1.0. When H_1 is correct, the most likely values for F are much greater than 1.0.

4. **Decision rule:**
$$\text{Reject } H_0 \text{ if } F = MSB/MSE \geq F_a(k - 1, (k - 1)(n - 1)) \text{ or}$$
$$\text{Reject } H_0 \text{ if } p\text{-value} \leq \alpha$$

$F_a(k - 1, (k - 1)(n - 1))$ is the value of F with $k - 1$ df in the numerator and $(k - 1)(n - 1)$ df in the denominator that has α of the distribution above it.

5. **Sample and compute F using formulas in Table 17.7** (or use "ANOVA: Two-Factor Without Replication" in "Data Analysis" toolpak).

6. **Decide and draw conclusions:**
If H_0 is rejected, conclude that the means of the populations are not all equal. The protected t test can be used to compare specific populations only after the ANOVA H_0 is rejected.

---

6. Suggest six ways in which power can be increased in the following situation. Comment on how your suggestion increases power.

For an independent research project, a student is investigating whether different types of soft drinks are effective in combating sleepiness during study. Each of 12 volunteers is randomly assigned to one of three groups. In one group, subjects drink diet caffeine-free Cola A while studying; students in a second group drink diet caffeine-free Cola B; and in the third group students drink diet caffeine-free Cola C. Each student is allowed to study whatever subject he or she chooses. The experimenter measures how long each student studies before falling asleep, and then rates the amount of time from 1 (immediately) to 100 (never

---

TABLE 17.12
The Kruskal–Wallis *H* Test: A Nonparametric Alternative for the Independent-sample One-factor ANOVA

1. **Assumptions:**
    Sampling assumptions:
    a. The samples from the *k* populations must be independent of each other.
    b. Each of the samples must be obtained using independent (within-sample) random sampling. If random assignment is used instead of random sampling, then the additional assumption of the randomness of biological systems should be made.
    c. If *k* = 3 then all samples should have at least five observations. If *k* > 3 then all samples should have at least two observations.

    Data assumption:
    The data must be ordinal, interval, or ratio.

2. **Hypotheses:**

    H_0: The populations have identical distributions

    H_1: The null is wrong

3. **Test statistic and its sampling distribution:**
    The test statistic is

    $$H = \frac{12SSB}{N(N+1)} \text{ with } k-1 \, df, \, SSB = \sum \frac{(T_j)^2}{n_j} - \frac{N(N+1)^2}{4}$$

    T_j = total ranks of in the *j*th sample; n_j = number of observations in the *j*th sample; *N* = total number of observations.

    First rank all *N* scores, then calculate *SSB* as in ANOVA, but use the ranks in place of the original scores. When H_0 is correct, the most likely values for *H* are around *k* − 1. When H_1 is correct, the most likely values for *H* are much greater than *k* − 1.

4. **Decision rule:**

    Reject H_0 if $H \geq \chi^2_\alpha(k-1)$ or
    Reject H_0 if *p*-value $\leq \alpha$

    $\chi^2_\alpha(k-1)$ is the value of the χ^2 statistic with *k* − 1 *df* that has α of the distribution above it.

5. **Sample and compute *H*** (or use "Kruskal-Wallis H" in "LFD3 Analyses").

6. **Decide and draw conclusions:**
    Although H_0 may be rejected because of any difference among the populations, rejection of H_0 most likely reflects a difference in the population central tendencies. If H_0 is rejected, the protected rank-sum test can be used to compare specific populations.

---

succumbs). Because the dependent variable is a rating, the experimenter uses the Kruskal–Wallis procedure and sets $\alpha = .01$.

For each of the following situations determine the most appropriate inferential statistical procedure. If enough data are given, perform the test, include comparisons of specific treatments when warranted, report your results (both verbally and using an ANOVA table where appropriate), and draw appropriate conclusions. Note: You may have to use procedures not discussed in this chapter. Use the Statistical Selection Guide (see the endpapers) to help you choose the appropriate procedure.

TABLE 17.13

The Friedman F_r Test: A Nonparametric Alternative for the Dependent-sample One-factor ANOVA

1. **Assumptions:**

   Sampling assumptions:

   a. The samples from the k populations must be dependent.

   b. Each of the samples must be obtained using independent (within-sample) random sampling. If random assignment is used instead of random sampling, then make the additional assumption that biological systems are inherently random.

   c. If $k = 3$ then all samples should have at least five observations. If $k > 3$ then all samples should have at least three observations.

   Data assumption:

   The data must be ordinal, interval, or ratio.

2. **Hypotheses:**

   $$H_0: \text{The populations have identical distributions}$$

   $$H_1: \text{The null is wrong}$$

3. **Test statistic and its sampling distribution:**

   The test statistic is

   $$F_r = \frac{12SSB}{k(k+1)} \text{ with } k-1 \ df, SSB = \frac{\sum (T_j)^2}{bl} - \frac{bl(k)(k+1)^2}{4}$$

   T_j = total of the ranks in the jth sample; bl = number of blocks (observations per sample); k = number of groups.

   Within each block rank the scores from 1 to k. Then, calculate SSB and then F_r.

   When H_0 is correct, the most likely values for F_r are around $k - 1$. When H_1 is correct, the most likely values for F_r are much greater than $k - 1$.

4. **Decision rule:**

   $$\text{Reject } H_0 \text{ if } F_r \geq \chi^2_\alpha(k-1) \text{ or}$$
   $$\text{Reject } H_0 \text{ if } p\text{-value} \leq \alpha$$

   $\chi^2_\alpha(k - 1)$ is the value of the χ^2 statistic with $k - 1$ df that has α of the distribution above it.

5. **Sample and compute F_r** (or use "Friedman F_r" in "LFD3 Analyses").

6. **Decide and draw conclusions:**

   Although H_0 may be rejected because of any difference among the populations, rejection of H_0 most likely reflects a difference in the population central tendencies. If H_0 is rejected, the protected Wilcoxon T_m test can be used to compare specific populations.

7. An anthropologist believes that some cultures foster diversity in basic cognitive abilities, whereas other cultures foster uniformity. To test her idea she randomly selects 35 equally well-educated adults in each of two cultures. The memory span (number of digits that can be remembered in order perfectly, half of the time) of each participant is measured. For the two cultures, $M_1 = 6.1$, $s_1 = 1.3$, and $M_2 = 6.3$, $s_2 = 1.9$.

†8. A psychologist used rats to study fetal alcohol syndrome. Thirty pregnant rats were randomly assigned to each of three treatments: no alcohol, daily doses, and weekly doses. After giving birth, an offspring of each rat was tested in a maze,

TABLE 17.14

		Samples		
1	*2*	*3*	*4*	*5*
1	1	2	2	3
15	14	17	16	18
10	8	11	10	13
11	7	13	12	13
3	4	5	5	6

TABLE 17.15
Number of Errors in Maze Learning Following Three Levels of Maternal Alcohol Consumption

No Alcohol	7	3	10	7	8	6	5	9	6	8
Daily Doses	7	15	23	8	5	5	12	17	14	*
Weekly Doses	7	10	9	8	9	11	6	8	9	12

* After 25 trials this rat has not learned the maze.

and the number of errors made learning the maze was recorded. The data are in Table 17.16. Does alcohol cause differences in learning ability of offspring?

†9. A psychologist was studying how repetition influences the believability of statements. Each of eight volunteers listened to a long list of statements such as "The Amazon is the longest river in the world." Twenty statements were presented once, 20 twice, 20 four times, and 20 six times. For each volunteer, the statements were randomly assigned to the levels of the repetition variable and order of presentation. After listening to the list, each volunteer checked off the statements believed true. The data in Table 17.16 are, for each volunteer, the number of statements (out of 20) checked in each repetition condition.

†10. A psychologist was studying how birds recognize and respond to variations in their songs. Each of seven birds listened to three types of variations in its song. The variations were none, different pitch, and different rhythm. Fifteen trials were given on each type of variation, and the psychologist counted the number of times the bird approached the sound source (a loudspeaker). The order of the three types of variations was randomly determined for each bird. The data are in Table 17.17.

†11. A clinical psychologist compared four "brief" therapies for short-term depression. Forty mildly depressed student volunteers were randomly assigned to four different 90-minute therapies (10 in each therapy). After the therapy, an interval measure of depression was made for each student. Because the measure was lengthy, two students had to leave before completion. The data are in Table 17.18.

†12. A sports psychologist was investigating how personality factors influence recovery from injury. The psychologist contacted 20 college athletes who had broken a

TABLE 17.16
Number of Believed Statements in Four Presentation Conditions

	Number of Presentations			
Volunteer	*1*	*2*	*4*	*6*
1	3	6	5	7
2	11	11	14	15
3	7	5	8	8
4	10	13	12	12
5	6	10	13	18
6	4	8	10	12
7	9	10	11	11
8	12	12	14	11

TABLE 17.17
Frequency of Approach Responses to Three Types of Songs

	Song Variation		
Bird	*None*	*Pitch*	*Rhythm*
1	8	6	10
2	6	6	12
3	7	5	9
4	9	8	6
5	8	4	5
6	9	7	3
7	7	4	7

bone in competition. Athletes were assigned to a high-anxious group ($n_1 = 11$) or a low-anxious group ($n_2 = 9$) on the basis of answers to a questionnaire. The dependent variable was the number of weeks before the athlete returned to competition. The data are $M_1 = 8.3$, $s_1 = 2.3$, and $M_2 = 7.9$, $s_2 = 2.4$.

13. Andrzejewski, Spencer, Kelley, and Berridge trained eight rats in a signal detection procedure. That is, the rats had to respond on two levers (left or right) signifying whether they had just seen a tiny green light or not. Prior to test sessions, each of the rats was given a drug injection. The dependent variable was the percentage of trials in which they responded correctly.

   The researchers hypothesized that since amphetamine and Ritalin are used therapeutically to improve attention in humans, it might improve signal detection in rats. What would you conclude? Table 17.19 contains the data from this experiment.

14. Using the data provided on the companion CD, does the father's marital satisfaction change over time after the birth of a child?

TABLE 17.18
Depression Scores After Four Different Therapies

	Therapy		
1	*2*	*3*	*4*
15	35	24	20
23	29	35	26
36	17	18	34
28	21	34	18
19	33	27	23
25	16	16	16
33	23	22	22
17	14	24	35
24	23	15	27
	22	24	

TABLE 17.19
Percentage of Correct Responses After Five Different Drug Injections

		Drug			
Rat	Saline	0.1 mg/kg Amphetamine	0.25 mg/kg Amphetamine	0.5 mg/kg Ritalin	1.0 mg/kg Ritalin
1	84%	84%	84%	88%	88%
2	90%	90%	90%	88%	91%
3	84%	83%	94%	89%	89%
4	92%	92%	87%	94%	90%
5	92%	93%	97%	96%	92%
6	88%	78%	88%	90%	93%
7	88%	88%	94%	94%	94%
8	80%	82%	87%	83%	82%

Introduction to Factorial Designs

*T*he one-factor ANOVA is an advance over the *t* test because it compares more than two populations. Nonetheless, it is limited in that it asks only one question (that is, it has one null hypothesis): Are the means of the populations corresponding to the factor different? The factorial ANOVA examines populations from two (or more) factors and asks a series of questions: Are the means of the populations corresponding to the first factor different from one another? Are the means of the populations corresponding to the second factor different from one another? And, finally, how do the factors act in concert? This last question is about the **interaction** of factors. As you will see, it is the information about interactions that makes the factorial ANOVA a great advance over the one-factor ANOVA.

This chapter has two goals. The first is to provide you with an understanding of a factorial experiment and how you might design one. The second goal is to acquaint you with what can be learned from the factorial experiment when its data are analyzed using the factorial ANOVA. The actual mechanics of how to perform the factorial ANOVA are discussed in Chapter 19.

THE TWO-FACTOR FACTORIAL EXPERIMENT:
COMBINING TWO EXPERIMENTS INTO ONE

Suppose that a cognitive psychologist is investigating the relationship between mood and memory. To induce a sad, neutral, or pleasant mood, she has 6 volunteers read a series of sad statements, 6 read neutral statements, and 6 read pleasant statements, for a total of 18 volunteers. Once the mood has been established, the volunteers memorize and recall a list of words.

In this experiment, the independent variable (factor) is mood, with three treatments. The populations corresponding to these treatments are sampled independently because different people contribute data to each treatment. The dependent variable is number of words recalled. These data can be analyzed using the independent-sample one-factor ANOVA (from Chapter 17) to determine if the means of any of the populations (of number of words recalled under different mood states) differ from one another.

The psychologist might also be interested in how word type influences memory: Are people better at remembering emotional words (such as *love* and *hate*) or nonemotional words (such as *shoe* and *tree*)? In a second experiment, 9 volunteers memorize emotional words, and 9 memorize nonemotional words (for a total of 18 volunteers). The independent variable is word type (emotional or nonemotional), and it is sampled independently. The dependent variable is number of words recalled. The data from this experiment can be analyzed using the independent-sample *t* test.

In total, the psychologist has conducted two experiments (using $18 + 18 = 36$ volunteers), and she has learned the answers to two questions by testing two null hypotheses. Both of these experiments are adequate. Nonetheless, they can be improved (in regard to efficiency and amount that can be learned) by combining them into one factorial experiment.

A **factorial** experiment has the following characteristics:

1. A factorial experiment must have at least two factors, and each factor must have at least two levels.
2. Each treatment (population that is sampled) is formed by combining one level from each of the factors (but never by combining levels from the same factor).
3. The total number of treatments is equal to the product of the levels of all of the factors.
4. Each sample (one from each treatment) must contain at least two observations.

The two memory experiments can be combined into a factorial experiment as follows. The first factor, Mood (M), has three levels: sad (m_1), neutral (m_2), and happy (m_3). The second factor, Word Type (W), has two levels: emotional words (w_1) and nonemotional words (w_2). The six (three levels times two levels) treatments are created by forming all possible combinations of the levels of the two factors. These combinations are listed in Table 18.1.

Each of these treatments corresponds to a condition in the factorial experiment. For example, in condition m_1w_1 volunteers in a sad mood (m_1) memorize emotional words (w_1); in condition m_3w_2 volunteers in a happy mood (m_3) memorize nonemotional words (w_2). Also, each of these treatments corresponds to a population that is sampled. The data in treatment m_1w_1 are a sample from the population of the number of words recalled by volunteers in a sad mood who memorize emotional words; and the data in treatment m_3w_2

TABLE 18.1
Treatments in a 3 × 2 Factorial Experiment

Word Type	Mood		
	Sad (m_1)	Neutral (m_2)	Happy (m_3)
Emotional (w_1)	m_1w_1	m_2w_1	m_3w_1
Nonemotional (w_2)	m_1w_2	m_2w_2	m_3w_2

TABLE 18.2
Data from 3 × 2 Factorial Experiment

Word Type	Mood			
	Sad (m_1)	Neutral (m_2)	Happy (m_3)	
Emotional (w_1)	5	7	16	
	7 $\overline{m_1w_1} = 5$	8 $\overline{m_2w_1} = 7$	8 $\overline{m_3w_1} = 12$	$\overline{w_1} = 8$
	3	6	12	
Nonemotional (w_2)	10	6	8	
	6 $\overline{m_1w_2} = 8$	7 $\overline{m_2w_2} = 8$	7 $\overline{m_3w_2} = 8$	$\overline{w_2} = 8$
	8	11	9	
	$\overline{m_1} = 6.5$	$\overline{m_2} = 7.5$	$\overline{m_3} = 10$	

are a sample from the population of the number of words recalled by volunteers in a happy mood who study nonemotional words.

Note the distinction between a factor level and a treatment. A **level** is one of the conditions that constitute a factor. For example, m_1 (sad mood) is a level of the Mood factor. In the one-factor ANOVA, levels and treatments are synonymous. In the factorial experiment, the term **treatment** refers to the combination of levels from different factors. For example, a sad mood (level m_1) combined with memorization of emotional words (level w_1) forms one of the six treatments (m_1w_1).

Suppose that each of the six samples (one for each treatment) consists of three observations, each from a different volunteer. In total, 18 volunteers are needed. Data from such an experiment are given in Table 18.2. The table also presents the means for each treatment and factor level.[1]

Note that this experiment meets all of the criteria for a factorial experiment: It has two factors, each with at least two levels; the treatments consist of all combinations of levels of the different factors; each treatment sample has at least two observations.

The factorial experiment is much more efficient than the two single-factor experiments. In the single-factor experiments, a total of 36 volunteers were needed to obtain six observations contributing to each of the mood state means ($\overline{m}_1$, $\overline{m}_2$, and $\overline{m}_3$) and nine observations

---

[1] In this chapter and the next, we use an older method to symbolize the mean of a sample, namely putting a bar over the symbol for a treatment or level. For example, $\overline{m}_1 = M_{m_1}$. We adopted this method to avoid multiple levels of subscripts.

contributing to each of the word type means ($\bar{w}_1$ and $\bar{w}_2$). In the factorial experiment, only 18 volunteers were used, but there are still six observations contributing to each of the mood states and nine observations contributing to each of the word types (count them in Table 18.2).

LEARNING FROM A FACTORIAL EXPERIMENT

Compared to multiple single-factor experiments, the factorial experiment actually increases the amount of information that can be learned. Information about **main effects** corresponds exactly to what can be learned from the single-factor experiments. Information about **interactions** is a bonus that can be obtained only from factorial experiments.

Main Effects

In a factorial experiment, each factor is tested separately for a main effect.

> The **main effect of a factor** is tested by the null hypothesis specifying no difference between the means of the populations corresponding to the factor levels. If the null hypothesis is rejected, then the factor has a main effect and the conclusion is that the population means are different.

The general form for the null and alternative hypotheses for a main effect is

$$H_0: \mu_{a_1} = \mu_{a_2} = \cdots = \mu_{a_k}$$

$$H_1: \text{The null is wrong}$$

where k is the number of levels of the factor (Factor A) being tested for a main effect.

Evidence against H_0 comes from differences between the level means; if the differences are large enough (so that MSB is large enough), then H_0 will be rejected.

Note that the hypotheses for a main effect are exactly the same as the hypotheses tested in a single-factor experiment. Indeed, tests of main effects in factorial experiments give the identical information as single-factor experiments.

In the example, the main effect for Mood is tested by examining

$$H_0: \mu_{m_1} = \mu_{m_2} = \mu_{m_3}$$

$$H_1: \text{The null is wrong}$$

Evidence against this null hypothesis (evidence for the main effect of Mood) comes from differences between the means of the levels of Mood ($\bar{m}_1$, $\bar{m}_2$, and $\bar{m}_3$). Because the Mood level means (6.5, 7.5, and 10) are not identical, there is some *evidence* for a main effect of Mood. To determine whether there really is a main effect, you must perform the statistical test (see Chapter 19); if the null hypothesis is rejected, then you may conclude that there is a main effect for Mood.

In the example, the main effect for Word Type is tested by examining

$$H_0: \mu_{w_1} = \mu_{w_2}$$

$$H_1: \text{The null is wrong}$$

Evidence against this null (and in favor of the main effect of Word Type) comes from differences between the Word Type level means ($\bar{w}_1$ and $\bar{w}_2$). Because the sample means for the levels of Word Type are equal (see Table 18.2), there is no evidence for a main effect of Word Type.

To summarize, each factor in a factorial experiment is tested for a main effect. The information provided by these tests corresponds exactly to the information provided by the single-factor experiments. If there is a significant main effect for a factor (the null hypothesis is rejected), then there is enough evidence to conclude that there are differences among the means of the *populations* corresponding to the levels of that factor.

Interactions: How Factors Act Together

Careful examination of the data in Table 18.2 reveals something rather curious: In the sad mood, emotional words are recalled less well than the nonemotional words (5 vs. 8); in the neutral mood, the emotional words and the nonemotional words are recalled to about the same degree (7 vs. 8); in the happy mood, the emotional words are recalled better than the nonemotional words (12 vs. 8). That is, the difference in recall between emotional and nonemotional words *depends* on the level of Mood. This dependency between the effect of one factor (Word Type) on the level of the other factor (Mood) is evidence for an interaction.

More formally,

> The **effect** of a factor corresponds to the size(s) of the differences among the means of the levels of the factor.

At level m_1 (sad mood), the effect of Word Type is −3 (5 − 8); at level m_2 (neutral mood), the effect of Word Type is −1 (7 − 8), and at level m_3 (happy mood), the effect of Word Type is +4 (12 − 8).

> Evidence for an **interaction** consists of changes in the *effect* of one factor at different *levels* of the other factor.

In the example, there is *evidence* for a Mood by Word Type interaction, because the effect of Word Type changes with the level of Mood (from −3 to −1 to +4). Whether that evidence is strong enough to claim that there is an interaction depends on whether the interaction null hypothesis is rejected.

In general, the interaction null hypothesis and its alternative are

H_0: There is no A by B interaction

H_1: The null is wrong

For our example, the null hypothesis for the interaction of Mood and Word Type is

H_0: There is no Mood by Word Type interaction

The null hypothesis can also be framed in terms of effects:

H_0: The effect of Word Type is the same at all levels of Mood

In symbols,

$$H_0: \mu_{m_1w_1} - \mu_{m_1w_2} = \mu_{m_2w_1} - \mu_{m_2w_2} = \mu_{m_3w_1} - \mu_{m_3w_2}$$

H_1: The null is wrong

The first term $(\mu_{m_1w_1} - \mu_{m_1w_2})$ is the effect of Word Type (difference in recall between emotional and nonemotional words) at level m_1 (sad mood), the second term is the effect of Word Type at level m_2, and the third term is the effect of Word Type at level m_3. The null hypothesis specifies that the effects are all equal (but not necessarily zero).

For each pair of factors, there is only one interaction: If the effect of Word Type depends on the level of Mood, then (and only then) will the effect of Mood depend on the level of Word Type. Look again at Table 18.2. We have already noted that the effect of Word Type changes with the level of Mood. Now look at the effect of Mood at the different levels of Word Type. At level w_1 (emotional words), the effect of Mood is an increase of two units from m_1 to m_2, and an increase of 5 units from m_2 to m_3. Now look at the effect of Mood at level w_2 (nonemotional words). The difference between m_1 and m_2 is zero, and the difference between m_2 and m_3 is zero. Clearly, the effect of Mood depends on the level of Word Type, so there is evidence for an interaction. Is the evidence strong enough to reject the interaction null hypothesis? That remains to be seen.

Table 18.3 illustrates the outcome of an experiment in which there is no evidence for an interaction. As in Table 18.2, there is evidence for a main effect of Mood ($\bar{m}_1$, $\bar{m}_2$, and $\bar{m}_3$ differ), and there is no evidence for a main effect of Word Type ($\bar{w}_1 = \bar{w}_2$).

Now look for evidence of an interaction. The effect of Word Type at level m_1 is zero ($6.5 - 6.5$), the effect of Word Type at level m_2 is zero ($7.5 - 7.5$), and the effect of Word Type at level m_3 is zero ($10 - 10$). There is no evidence for an interaction because the effect of Word Type does not change with the level of Mood. Similarly, there is no evidence for an interaction because the effect of Mood does not change with the level of Word Type: At level w_1, the effect of Mood is a 1-unit increase from m_1 to m_2, and a 2.5-unit increase from m_2 to m_3. At level w_2, the effect of Mood is also a 1-unit increase from m_1 to m_2 and a 2.5-unit increase from m_2 to m_3.

To reiterate, there is only one interaction between Mood and Word Type. If the effect of Word Type depends on the level of Mood (as in Table 18.2), then the effect of Mood will also depend on the level of Word Type. On the other hand, if the effect of Word Type is the

TABLE 18.3
Alternative Data From 3 × 2 Factorial Experiment

Word Type	Mood			
	Sad (m_1)	_Neutral_ (m_2)	_Happy_ (m_3)	
Emotional (w_1)	$\overline{m_1 w_1} = 6.5$	$\overline{m_2 w_1} = 7.5$	$\overline{m_3 w_1} = 10$	$\overline{w}_1 = 8$
Nonemotional (w_2)	$\overline{m_1 w_2} = 6.5$	$\overline{m_2 w_2} = 7.5$	$\overline{m_3 w_2} = 10$	$\overline{w}_2 = 8$
	$\overline{m}_1 = 6.5$	$\overline{m}_2 = 7.5$	$\overline{m}_3 = 10$	

same at all levels of Mood (as in Table 18.3), then the effect of Mood will be the same at all levels of Word Type.

Comparison of Tables 18.2 and 18.3 illustrates another point regarding interactions: Interactions and main effects can come in all combinations. An interaction may be found when there are no main effects, when there is one main effect, or when there are two main effects (see Question 1 on p. 422). Interactions are truly new and independent information that you cannot learn about from examining main effects alone.

When an interaction is significant, it is often necessary to change your interpretation of a main effect. Turn back to Table 18.2 and suppose that there is a significant main effect of Mood and a significant interaction between Mood and Word Type. Examining the means for the three moods, a reasonable interpretation of the main effect is that more is recalled in a happy mood than a sad mood. Because the interaction is significant, however, this interpretation must be modified: More _emotional_ words are recalled in a happy mood than in a sad mood, but there is no difference for the _nonemotional_ words. In fact, this change of interpretation gets at the crux of the matter: An interaction indicates that the effect of one factor depends on the level of the other factor.

In summary, there are four points to remember about interactions. First, the interaction null hypothesis is about population means. Second, for a pair of factors (such as Mood and Word Type), there is only one interaction. Third, interactions do not depend on main effects. Fourth, significant interactions often require reinterpretation of main effects.

Importance of Interactions

Interactions are of the utmost importance in all aspects of science and technology. Consider for a moment the different interpretations for the data depending on whether there is no interaction (as in Table 18.3) or there is an interaction (as in Table 18.2). Given the data in Table 18.3, the proper interpretation is that mood affects memory for all types of materials. One implication of this finding is that whenever it is desirable to help people to remember (such as during a test, or in a court, or in psychotherapy), make them happy.

The data in Table 18.2 paint a different picture. If the interaction null hypothesis is rejected (so that there is a significant interaction), then how mood state affects memory depends on what is being remembered. When trying to remember emotional events, a happy mood is beneficial; for nonemotional events, mood makes little difference.

TABLE 18.4
Improvement During Therapy for Two Types
of Patients and Two Types of Psychotherapies

	Type of Therapy	
Type of Patient	*Cognitive*	*Behavior*
Cooperative	20	10
Uncooperative	5	10

TABLE 18.5
Test Performance Following Two Study
Methods for Two Subject Matters

	Subject Matter	
Study Method	*Mathematics*	*Psychology*
Rote	40	70
Discovery	60	90

Consider the following examples of the importance of interactions. In another factorial experiment, the factors are Type of Psychotherapy and Type of Patient (Table 18.4). The psychotherapy factor has two levels, cognitive therapy and behavior therapy, and the Type of Patient factor also has two levels, cooperative and uncooperative. The dependent variable is amount of improvement over the course of therapy. Look at Table 18.4. There is evidence for an interaction between Type of Patient and Type of Therapy because the effect of therapy (difference in improvement between cognitive therapy and behavior therapy) depends on the Type of Patient: The cognitive therapy produced greater improvements for the cooperative patients, but the behavior therapy produced greater improvements for the uncooperative patients. If statistically significant, an interaction of this sort would be very important for determining the most effective sort of therapy for a given individual.

For the next example, consider a factorial experiment investigating Study Method (rote and discovery) and Subject Matter (mathematics and psychology), in which the dependent variable is performance on a test. The treatment means are in Table 18.5. In this experiment, there is no evidence for an interaction: The effect of Study Method (discovery better than rote) is the same for both levels of Subject Matter.

As a final example, consider an engineer who is investigating the amount of air pollutants (dependent variable) produced by different types of Gasolines and different types of Engine Designs (see Table 18.6). Here there is evidence for an interaction because Gasoline 1 results in the lowest pollution for Engine Design 1, but Gasoline 3 results in the lowest pollution for Engine Designs 2 and 3. That is, the effect of Gasoline (on pollution) depends on the level of Engine Design.

The point is that interactions are very important not just for psychology, but for all sciences and technologies. Furthermore, interactions can be discovered only in factorial experiments, and that is what makes factorial experiments so important.

TABLE 18.6
Amount of Pollutants (in mg) Generated by Three
Engine Designs for Three Types of Gasolines

Engine Designs	Gasolines		
	1	*2*	*3*
1	3	8	9
2	15	15	8
3	20	25	10

TABLE 18.7
Mean Weight Loss Under Different Treatments

Percentage of Protein	Amount of Exercise (minutes)				
	0	*10*	*20*	*40*	*M*
0%	0.0	1.3	5.9	7.8	3.75
5%	1.0	2.0	7.0	9.0	4.75
10%	2.0	3.0	7.9	10.1	5.75
M	1.0	2.1	6.9	9.0	

A SECOND EXAMPLE OF A FACTORIAL EXPERIMENT

In trying to understand how to effectively produce weight losses, a physiological psychologist manipulates two factors in the diet of rats. The first is Percentage of Protein in the diet: 0%, 5%, or 10%. The second is amount of forced Exercise in minutes a day: 0, 10, 20, or 40 minutes. The dependent variable is number of grams lost in a month. Ten rats are randomly assigned to each of the 12 (3 × 4) treatments. The mean weight loss in each of the treatments is given in Table 18.7.

Is there any evidence for a main effect of Exercise? Because the means of the levels (1.0, 2.1, 6.9, and 9.0) are not all equal, there is evidence for this main effect. If the level means are far enough apart, then the null hypothesis will be rejected (there will be a main effect). In that case, there would be enough evidence to conclude that the population means are different.

Is there any evidence for a main effect of Percentage of Protein? There are differences among the means of the factor levels (3.75, 4.75, and 5.75), although the differences are not very large. Thus, there is some evidence for a main effect. Whether or not the main effect is significant depends on whether or not the null hypothesis is rejected.

Is there any evidence for an interaction? Does the effect of Percentage of Protein depend on the amount of Exercise? Focus on the weight loss means for 0 minutes of exercise. The effect of Percentage of Protein is 1 gram from 0% to 5%, and 1 gram from 5% to 10%. Now look at the means for the 10-minute exercise group. The effect of Percentage of Protein is again about 1 gram (actually .7) from 0% to 5%, and 1 gram from 5% to 10%. In fact, for all different levels of the exercise variable, the difference in weight lost from 0% to 5% Percentage of Protein is about 1 gram, and the difference in weight loss from 5% to 10% Percentage of Protein is about another 1 gram. Thus, the effect of Percentage of Protein does *not* depend on the level of Exercise, and there is very little evidence for an interaction.

GRAPHING THE RESULTS OF A FACTORIAL EXPERIMENT

The results of a factorial experiment can be complex and difficult to grasp from a data table alone. In many cases, a graph of the results can be helpful in determining if there is evidence for main effects and interactions, and in understanding significant effects.

Figure 18.1 illustrates the weight loss data from Table 18.7. Four rules are used in constructing a graph of the results of a factorial experiment:

1. The ordinate (*y*-axis) is marked off in units of the dependent variable. Note that this is quite different from the graphs in Chapter 2, in which the ordinate always represented frequency or relative frequency.
2. The abscissa (*x*-axis) is labeled with the levels of one of the factors. Traditionally, the abscissa is labeled with the levels of the factor with the most levels.
3. Each *treatment* is represented by a single point. The height of the point (on the ordinate) indicates the mean of the treatment; the location of the point (on the abscissa) indicates the level of one of the factors (the factor marked off on the abscissa). For example, consider the treatment with 0% of protein and 20 minutes of exercise. The mean of the treatment is 5.9 (from Table 18.7). This treatment mean is represented by the dot over the 20-minute mark (on the abscissa) at a height of 5.9.

FIGURE 18.1
Plot of the treatment means from Table 18.7, the weight-loss experiment.

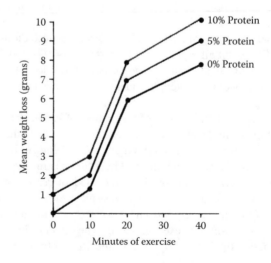

4. Now, consider the factor that does *not* label the abscissa (Percentage of Protein in Figure 18.1). Points representing treatments from the same level of this factor are connected by lines. Thus, all of the points representing 0% protein are connected together. Similarly, all of the points representing 5% protein are connected together. For clarity, different types of lines can be used to connect the points from different levels, and each line is labeled with the level of the factor.

Graphs of this sort are particularly useful for judging if there is evidence for an interaction. Evidence for an interaction is indicated by nonparallel lines; the greater the deviation from parallel lines, the greater the evidence for an interaction. For example, in Figure 18.1 the lines are almost exactly parallel, indicating little evidence for an interaction.

A graph can also be used to judge evidence for a main effect. Remember, evidence for a main effect of a factor is that the means of the *levels* of the factor differ from one another. However, what is plotted in the graph are treatment means, not level means. So the level means will have to be estimated before you can judge whether or not there is evidence for main effects.

Start with the Percentage of Protein factor. The mean of the 0% level is given by the average of all of the treatment means having 0% protein. Conveniently, all of these treatment means are connected by the same line (see Figure 18.1). Thus, the mean for the 0% protein corresponds to the average height of this line. Similarly, the means for the 5% and 10% protein levels correspond to the average heights of the 5% and the 10% lines, respectively.

Is there evidence for a main effect of Percentage of Protein (do the level means differ)? Note that the 10% line is always above the 5% line, which in turn is always above the 0% line. Thus, the average heights of the three lines do differ, and there is evidence for a main effect of Percentage of Protein.

Is there evidence for a main effect of amount of Exercise? To judge, compare the means of the levels of this factor. The mean for the 0-minute level can be estimated by the average height of the three dots located above the 0-minute mark. Use your pencil to put a cross on the graph, above the 0-minute mark at the average height of the three dots. Next, put a cross above the 10-minute mark at the average height of the three dots located above that mark, and do the same for the 20-minute and 40-minute marks. Because the heights of the four crosses differ from one another (indicating that the level means differ from one another), there is evidence for a main effect of amount of exercise. If the differences are large enough (as evaluated by a factorial ANOVA), then the null hypothesis will be rejected.

The data in Figure 18.2 are the means from Table 18.2 (mood and memory experiment). Is there evidence for an interaction? Indeed there is. The lines are not parallel, indicating that the effect of one variable (for example, Word Type) changes with the level of the other variable (Mood).

Is there evidence for a main effect of Word Type? The average height of the line for the emotional words (average of 5, 7, and 12) is exactly the same as the average height of the line for nonemotional words (average of 8, 8, and 8); thus, there is no evidence for a main effect of Word Type.

Is there evidence for a main effect of Mood? Place a cross at the average height of the dots above each mark on the abscissa. Because the average heights of the crosses change (from 6.5 to 7.5 to 10), there is evidence for a main effect of Mood.

FIGURE 18.2
Plot of the treatment means from Table 18.2, the mood experiment.

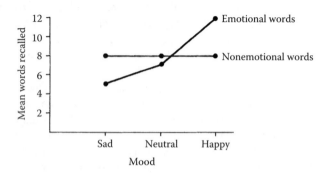

DESIGN OF FACTORIAL EXPERIMENTS

In designing a factorial experiment, you must decide between independent and dependent sampling for each factor. To review: The levels of a factor are sampled independently when different subjects contribute to each level. Dependent samples are formed when the observations contributing to each level are related to one another. A common way of forming dependent samples is to use a within-subject design in which each subject contributes data to each and every level of the factor.

Each factor is treated separately. Thus, independent sampling can be used for both factors, dependent samples can be used for both factors, or one factor can be sampled independently and one factor sampled dependently.

The data from Table 18.2 are reproduced in Table 18.8 along with an indication of the subject that contributed each observation. Mood is sampled independently because different subjects contributed to the different levels of the Mood factor. For example, Subjects 1–6 contributed to the sad mood, whereas Subjects 7–12 contributed to the neutral mood. Word Type is also sampled independently because different subjects contributed to the different levels of the Word Type factor.

TABLE 18.8
3×2 Factorial Experiment: Independent Sampling

Word Type	Mood						
	Sad (m_1)		*Neutral (m_2)*		*Happy (m_3)*		
Emotional (w_1)	S_1:5 S_2:7 S_3:3	$\overline{m_1 w_1} = 5$	S_7:7 S_8:8 S_9:6	$\overline{m_2 w_1} = 7$	S_{13}:16 S_{14}:8 S_{15}:12	$\overline{m_3 w_1} = 12$	$\overline{w}_1 = 8$
Nonemotional (w_2)	S_4:10 S_5:6 S_6:8	$\overline{m_1 w_2} = 8$	S_{10}:6 S_{11}:7 S_{12}:11	$\overline{m_2 w_2} = 8$	S_{16}:8 S_{17}:7 S_{18}:9	$\overline{m_3 w_2} = 8$	$\overline{w}_2 = 8$
	$\overline{m}_1 = 6.5$		$\overline{m}_2 = 7.5$		$\overline{m}_3 = 10$		

TABLE 18.9
3 × 2 Factorial Experiment: Mixed Design

Word Type	Sad (m_1)		Neutral (m_2)		Happy (m_3)		
					Mood		
Emotional (w_1)	S_1:5 S_2:7 S_3:3	$\overline{m_1w_1} = 5$	S_4:7 S_5:8 S_6:6	$\overline{m_2w_1} = 7$	S_7:16 S_8:8 S_9:12	$\overline{m_3w_1} = 12$	$\overline{w_1} = 8$
Nonemotional (w_2)	S_1:10 S_2:6 S_3:8	$\overline{m_1w_2} = 8$	S_4:6 S_5:7 S_6:11	$\overline{m_2w_2} = 8$	S_7:8 S_8:7 S_9:9	$\overline{m_3w_2} = 8$	$\overline{w_2} = 8$
	$\overline{m_1} = 6.5$		$\overline{m_2} = 7.5$		$\overline{m_3} = 10$		

TABLE 18.10
3 × 2 Factorial Experiment: Dependent Sampling (within-subjects) Design

Word Type	Sad (m_1)		Neutral (m_2)		Happy (m_3)		
					Mood		
Emotional (w_1)	S_1:5 S_2:7 S_3:3	$\overline{m_1w_1} = 5$	S_1:7 S_2:8 S_3:6	$\overline{m_2w_1} = 7$	S_1:16 S_2:8 S_3:12	$\overline{m_3w_1} = 12$	$\overline{w_1} = 8$
Nonemotional (w_2)	S_1:10 S_2:6 S_3:8	$\overline{m_1w_2} = 8$	S_1:6 S_2:7 S_3:11	$\overline{m_2w_2} = 8$	S_1:8 S_2:7 S_3:9	$\overline{m_3w_2} = 8$	$\overline{w_2} = 8$
	$\overline{m_1} = 6.5$		$\overline{m_2} = 7.5$		$\overline{m_3} = 10$		

Table 18.9 illustrates how the experiment could be designed with one factor sampled independently and one sampled dependently. The Mood factor is sampled independently: Note that different subjects contribute to the sad, neutral, and happy moods. Dependent (within-subjects) sampling is used for the Word Type factor: Every subject contributes to both levels of the Word Type factor.

How might this design have been realized? First, each subject would be randomly assigned to a level of the Mood factor (so that the factor is sampled independently), and the subject would be read statements to induce the appropriate mood. Next, each subject would memorize both emotional words and nonemotional words, and the subject would attempt to recall the words. Thus, each subject would contribute a score for number of emotional words recalled and number of nonemotional words recalled.

Table 18.10 illustrates how the experiment could be designed with dependent sampling for both factors. Each subject (for example, Subject 1) contributes to all levels of the mood factor and all levels of the word type factor. Put differently, each subject contributes an observation to each treatment.

To realize this design, the psychologist might have randomly determined, for each subject, the order of the three moods. For example, for the first subject, on the first day, the neutral mood might be induced, and the subject would memorize and recall both emotional and nonemotional words. On the second day, that subject might receive the sad mood, and the subject would memorize and recall (a different set of) emotional and nonemotional words. Finally, the happy mood would be induced on the third day.

Considerations in Designing a Factorial Experiment

The basic decision is which factor(s) should be sampled independently and which should be sampled dependently. As always, dependent sampling has two advantages over independent sampling. First, with the same number of observations, the dependent-sample design is more powerful than the independent-sample design. Second, compared to independent sampling, within-subject sampling requires fewer subjects to obtain the same number of observations. In Table 18.8, 18 subjects were needed to obtain 18 observations (3 in each of the 6 treatments); in Table 18.10, only 3 subjects were needed to obtain 18 observations.

Dependent sampling is not always the best choice, however. First, within-subject designs may generate carryover effects (see Chapter 15). Second, matched-group designs require careful selection of blocks of subjects to ensure a close relationship between the scores in the samples.

The choice of type of sampling must be made after careful consideration of all of these points. As a general rule of thumb, however, if carryover effects can be minimized, dependent sampling is preferred because of the potential for increased power.

THREE-FACTOR FACTORIAL EXPERIMENT

A factorial experiment is not limited to two factors. Indeed, a factorial experiment can have any number of factors, although, for practical reasons, there are rarely more than three or four. Much of what you have learned about two-factor experiments applies directly to three-factor experiments. We begin with an example to focus the discussion.

The psychologist investigating mood state and memory is also interested in how sex enters into the equation. Do men and women recall emotional and nonemotional words in the same way? To find out, she includes in the experiment a third factor, Gender (G), with two levels (male, g_1, and female, g_2). The data in Table 18.11 are from this experiment (note that the data in Table 18.2 have been reproduced to serve as the data for the males).

The three-factor factorial experiment is constructed by applying the same rules as for the two-factor experiment. First, each factor has at least two levels. Second, each treatment is formed by combining one level from each of the factors, and these treatments correspond to populations sampled in the experiment. For example, the treatment $m_2w_1g_2$ corresponds to the population of number of emotional (w_1) words recalled by females (g_2) while in a neutral mood (m_2). The three scores 8, 9, and 10 (see Table 18.11) are a sample

TABLE 18.11
Data From 3 × 2 × 2 Factorial Experiment

Males (g_1)

Word Type	Sad (m_1)		Neutral (m_2)		Happy (m_3)	
		Mood				
Emotional (w_1)	5		7		16	
	7	$\overline{m_1 w_1 g_1} = 5$	8	$\overline{m_2 w_1 g_1} = 7$	8	$\overline{m_3 w_1 g_1} = 12$
	3		6		12	
Nonemotional (w_2)	10		6		8	
	6	$\overline{m_1 w_2 g_1} = 8$	7	$\overline{m_2 w_2 g_1} = 8$	7	$\overline{m_3 w_2 g_1} = 8$
	8		11		9	

Females (g_2)

Word Type	Sad (m_1)		Neutral (m_2)		Happy (m_3)	
		Mood				
Emotional (w_1)	7		8		13	
	9	$\overline{m_1 w_1 g_2} = 8$	9	$\overline{m_2 w_1 g_2} = 9$	11	$\overline{m_3 w_1 g_2} = 11.67$
	8		10		11	
Nonemotional (w_2)	9		13		13	
	11	$\overline{m_1 w_2 g_2} = 10$	11	$\overline{m_2 w_2 g_2} = 11$	13	$\overline{m_3 w_2 g_2} = 13.67$
	10		9		15	

from this population. Third, the total number of treatments is equal to the product of the number of levels of each factor (in this case, $3 \times 2 \times 2 = 12$). Fourth, each sample (from each treatment) has at least two observations.

For each factor, you are free to choose to sample independently or to use a form of dependent sampling. Of course, except under rather extreme and bizarre conditions, a factor like Gender cannot be sampled using within-subjects sampling.

The yield of a three-factor experiment can be divided into main effects and interactions. As with the two-factor experiment, each factor is tested for a main effect, and the evidence going into the test is the differences among the means of the levels of that factor. The interactions are a little more complex. In a multifactor experiment, there is a possible interaction between each pair of factors, a possible interaction between each triplet of factors, and, if more factors are used, a possible interaction between each n-tuple of factors. Interactions move from possible to actual when the associated null hypothesis is rejected.

Evaluating Main Effects

The general form of a main effect null hypothesis is exactly like that used in the two-factor experiment.

$$H_0: \mu_{a_1} = \mu_{a_2} = \cdots \mu_{a_k}$$

H_1: The null is wrong

In the example, Mood has three levels, so the specific null is

$$H_0: \mu_{m_1} = \mu_{m_2} = \mu_{m_3}$$

As always in the ANOVA, the null hypothesis is about population means. Evidence in regard to this null hypothesis is obtained from the sample means—in this case, the means of the levels of Mood.

The mean of a level is found by taking the average of all scores that are in treatments including that level. For the example, the mean of Level m_1 will be the average of all the scores in treatments $m_1w_1g_1$, $m_1w_1g_2$, $m_1w_2g_1$, and $m_1w_2g_2$. Thus,

$$\bar{m}_1 = (5 + 7 + 3 + 10 + 6 + 8 + 7 + 9 + 8 + 9 + 11 + 10)/12 = 7.75$$

$$\bar{m}_2 = (7 + 8 + 6 + 6 + 7 + 11 + 8 + 9 + 10 + 13 + 11 + 9)/12 = 8.75$$

$$\bar{m}_3 = (16 + 8 + 12 + 8 + 7 + 9 + 13 + 11 + 11 + 13 + 13 + 15)/12 = 11.33$$

Is there evidence for a main effect of Mood? Yes, because the level means differ. If the level means are different enough, then the null hypothesis will be rejected. In that case, the appropriate conclusion is that there are differences among the means of the *populations* corresponding to the levels of Mood. That is, more words are recalled in a happy mood than in a sad mood.

The main effect of Word Type is tested by

$$H_0: \mu_{w_1} = \mu_{w_2}$$

H_1: The null is wrong

Evidence for this main effect is found by comparing the means of the levels of Word Type,

$$\bar{w}_1 = (5 + 7 + 3 + 7 + 8 + 6 + 16 + 8 + 12 + 7 + 9 + 8 + 8$$
$$+ 9 + 10 + 13 + 11 + 11)/18 = 8.78$$

$$\bar{w}_2 = (10 + 6 + 8 + 6 + 7 + 11 + 8 + 7 + 9 + 9$$
$$+ 11 + 10 + 13 + 11 + 9 + 13 + 13 + 15)/18 = 9.78$$

Because these means are not the same, there is some evidence for a main effect of Word Type.

The hypotheses tested to determine if there is a main effect of Gender are

$$H_0: \mu_{g_1} = \mu_{g_2}$$

H_1: The null is wrong

Evidence for the main effect is found by comparing the means of the levels of Gender.

$$\bar{g}_1 = (5 + 7 + 3 + 7 + 8 + 6 + 16 + 8 + 12 + 10$$
$$+ 6 + 8 + 6 + 7 + 11 + 8 + 7 + 9)/18 = 8.0$$

$$\bar{g}_2 = (7 + 9 + 8 + 8 + 9 + 10 + 13 + 11 + 11 + 9$$
$$+ 11 + 10 + 13 + 11 + 9 + 13 + 13 + 15)/18 = 10.56$$

Thus, there is some evidence for a main effect of Gender. If the evidence is strong enough to reject H_0, then you may conclude that the means of the two populations are different. In this case, the mean of the population of memory scores for women is higher than the mean for men (under the conditions of this experiment).

Evaluating Interactions

In a factorial experiment, there is a separate interaction for each pair of factors, each triplet of factors, and so on. Thus, for a three-factor experiment, we evaluate interactions for Factors A and B, Factors A and C, Factors B and C, and Factors A, B, and C.

In the example, an interaction between Mood and Word Type would mean that the effect of Word Type changes with the level of Mood (and vice versa). The interaction is significant if the following null hypothesis can be rejected:

H_0: There is no Mood by Word Type interaction

H_1: The null is wrong

An equivalent set of hypotheses can be framed in terms of effects:

$$H_0: \mu_{m_1w_1} - \mu_{m_1w_2} = \mu_{m_2w_1} - \mu_{m_2w_2} = \mu_{m_3w_1} - \mu_{m_3w_2}$$

H_1: The null is wrong

Evidence used in evaluating the Mood by Word Type hypothesis comes from the six means formed by the factorial combination of the Mood and Word Type factors. These means are presented in Table 18.12. The individual scores in each cell of this table are the individual scores from Table 18.11. They have been reorganized, however, into the six groups relevant to the interaction.

Note that the effect of Word Type does change with the level of Mood. The difference between the means for the emotional and the nonemotional words is −2.5 in the sad mood, −1.5 in the neutral mood, and +1 in the happy mood. Evidence for the interaction can also be seen in a graph of the six means in Figure 18.3. Note that the lines are not parallel.

If the changes in the effect of Word Type at different levels of Mood are large enough, then the null hypothesis will be rejected. In that case, the appropriate conclusion would be: The difference in recall between emotional and nonemotional words depends on the mood of the rememberer.

TABLE 18.12
Evaluation of the Mood by Word Type Interaction From Table 18.11

Word Type	Sad (m_1)			Neutral (m_2)			Happy (m_3)		
									Mood
Emotional (w_1)	5	7		7	8		16	13	
	7	9	$\overline{m_1w_1} = 6.5$	8	9	$\overline{m_2w_1} = 8.0$	8	11	$\overline{m_3w_1} = 11.8$
	3	8		6	10		12	11	
Nonemotional (w_2)	10	9		6	13		8	13	
	6	11	$\overline{m_1w_2} = 9.0$	7	11	$\overline{m_2w_2} = 9.5$	7	13	$\overline{m_3w_2} = 10.8$
	8	10		11	9		9	15	

There is also a possible interaction between Mood and Gender. The hypotheses tested are:

H_0: There is no Mood by Gender interaction

H_1: The null is wrong

In terms of the population means,

$$H_0: \mu_{m_1g_1} - \mu_{m_1g_2} = \mu_{m_2g_1} - \mu_{m_2g_2} = \mu_{m_3g_1} - \mu_{m_3g_2}$$

H_1: The null is wrong

To determine if there is evidence for the Mood by Gender interaction, form the table of means corresponding to the factorial combination of these two factors. Table 18.13 illustrates the procedure.

Note that the effect of Gender is virtually the same at each level of Mood: At Level m_1 the effect of Gender is –2.5 (6.5 – 9), at Level m_2 the effect of Gender is –2.5 (7.5 – 10),

FIGURE 18.3
Plot of the means that determine the evidence for the Mood by Word Type interaction. Data are from Table 18.12.

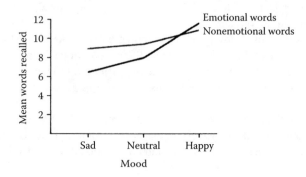

TABLE 18.13
Evaluation of the Mood by Gender Interaction From Table 18.11

Gender	Mood								
	Sad (m_1)			Neutral (m_2)			Happy (m_3)		
Males (g_1)	5	10		7	6		16	8	
	7	6	$\overline{m_1g_1} = 6.5$	8	7	$\overline{m_2g_1} = 7.5$	8	7	$\overline{m_3g_1} = 10.0$
	3	8		6	11		12	9	
Females (g_2)	7	9		8	13		13	13	
	9	11	$\overline{m_1g_2} = 9.0$	9	11	$\overline{m_2g_2} = 10.0$	11	13	$\overline{m_3g_2} = 12.7$
	8	10		10	9		11	15	

and at Level m_3 the effect of Gender is −2.7 (10 − 12.7). In terms of a graph (Figure 18.4), the lines are almost parallel.

Because the effect of Gender is so similar at each level of Mood, there is very little evidence for a Mood by Gender interaction. Assuming that H_0 will not be rejected, the appropriate conclusion is that there is *little evidence* for an interaction. Do not conclude that there is no interaction, because that conclusion implies that the null hypothesis has been proved true.

For the Word Type by Gender interaction, the hypotheses are

H_0: There is no Word Type by Gender interaction

H_1: The null is wrong

Stated in terms of population means for this example,

$$H_0: \mu_{w_1g_1} - \mu_{w_1g_2} = \mu_{w_2g_1} - \mu_{w_2g_2}$$

H_1: The null is wrong

FIGURE 18.4
Plot of the means that determine the evidence for the Mood by Gender interaction. Data are from Table 18.13.

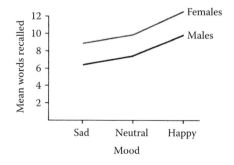

TABLE 18.14
Evaluation of the Word by Gender Interaction From Table 18.11

Word Type	Gender								
	Males (g_1)				Females (g_2)				
Emotional (w_1)	5	7	16		7	8	13		
	7	8	8	$\overline{w_1 g_1} = 8.0$	9	9	11	$\overline{w_1 g_2} = 9.56$	
	3	6	12		8	10	11		
Nonemotional (w_2)	10	6	8		9	13	13		
	6	7	7	$\overline{w_2 g_1} = 8.0$	11	11	13	$\overline{w_2 g_2} = 11.56$	
	8	11	9		10	9	15		

FIGURE 18.5
Plot of the means that determine the evidence for the Gender by Word Type interaction. Data are from Table 18.14.

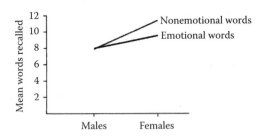

The evidence used in evaluating these hypotheses is the table of means (Table 18.14) formed by the factorial combination of Word Type and Gender.

At Level g_1 the effect of Word Type is 0 (8 – 8), and at level g_2 the effect of Word Type is –2 (11.56 – 9.56). Because the effect of Word Type is different at the two levels of Gender, there is evidence for an interaction. In a graph of the two factors (Figure 18.5), you can see that the lines are not parallel. If the null hypothesis is rejected, then you may conclude that, in general, females show a larger difference in recall between the emotional and nonemotional words than do males.

Three-factor Interactions

In general, the hypotheses for testing a three-factor interaction are

H_0: There is no A by B by C interaction

H_1: The null is wrong

As with the other ANOVA hypotheses, these can be formulated in terms of population means, but the formulations are rather complex.

FIGURE 18.6

Plot of the treatment means from Table 18.11, the three-factor mood experiment.

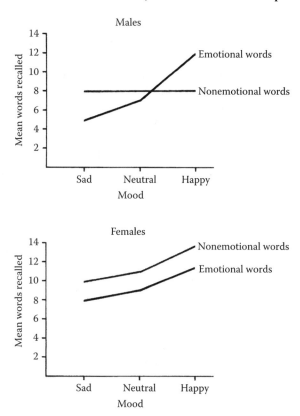

When this null hypothesis is rejected (using the ANOVA), you may conclude that there is a three-factor interaction. This means that the form of the interaction between any two of the factors changes with the level of the third factor. For example, if there is an AB interaction at Level c_1, but no AB interaction at Level c_2, then there is an ABC interaction.

For the three-factor, Mood by Word Type by Gender interaction, the hypotheses are

H_0: There is no Mood by Word Type by Gender interaction

H_1: The null is wrong

Figure 18.6 is a graph of the means from the three-factor experiment (from Table 18.11). For clarity, this graph uses two sets of axes (one set for males and one set for females); however, all of the means could have been plotted on one set of axes. Note that there is evidence for a Mood by Word Type interaction for the males (Level g_1), because the lines are not parallel. For the females (Level g_2) there is no evidence for a Mood by Word Type interaction. Because the form of the Mood by Word Type interaction depends on the level of Gender, there is *evidence* for a three-factor, Mood by Word Type by Gender, interaction.

We noted earlier that a significant two-factor interaction may require reinterpretation of a main effect. Similarly, a significant three-factor interaction may require reinterpretation of two-factor interactions as well as main effects. For example, suppose that the Mood by Word Type by Gender interaction is significant and that the Mood by Word Type interaction is also significant. Examining the graph for the Mood by Word Type interaction (Figure 18.3), it appears that the nonemotional words are recalled better than the emotional words, except in a happy mood. But looking at the graph of the three-factor interaction (Figure 18.6), we can see that the Mood by Word Type interaction holds only for the males. For the females, the nonemotional words are always recalled better than the emotional words.

There is only one Mood by Word Type by Gender interaction. If there is evidence that the Mood by Word Type interaction depends on the level of Gender, then there is also evidence that the Mood by Gender interaction depends on the level of Word Type, and there is evidence that the Word Type by Gender interaction depends on the level of Mood. Evidence for each of these claims can be demonstrated by an alternative plot of the data (see Question 3 at the end of the chapter). Furthermore, if there is *no* evidence for the three-factor interaction, then the form of the Mood by Word Type interaction will be the same at all levels of Gender, and the form of the Mood by Gender interaction will be the same at all levels of Word Type, and the form of the Word Type by Gender interaction will be the same at all levels of Mood.

The pairs of graphs on the top of Figure 18.7 show various ways in which there can be evidence for a three-factor (ABC) interaction. In each pair, the form of the AB interaction changes with the level of Factor C. Included are cases where there is an AB interaction at one level of Factor C and not at the other level (Panel a), and cases where there is an AB interaction at both levels of Factor C, but the forms of the interactions are different (Panel b).

The pairs of graphs on the bottom of Figure 18.7 illustrate cases where there is no ABC interaction. In each case, the form of the AB interaction is the same at each level of Factor C. Note that this does not mean that the graphs within a pair will look exactly alike. Differences between a pair of graphs may indicate evidence for a main effect of Factor C (as in Panel f); or a two-factor interaction (A and C interact in Panel d; AC and BC interact in Panel g). The only consideration in determining evidence for an ABC interaction is whether the form of the AB interaction depends on the level of Factor C. For example, in Panel g there is no evidence for an AB interaction at Level c_1. Similarly, there is no evidence for an AB interaction at Level c_2. Therefore, the form of the AB interaction does not change with the level of Factor C, and so there is no evidence for an ABC interaction.

Higher Order Interactions

A factorial experiment with f factors can have significant interactions between each pair of factors, each triplet, and so on, up to all f factors. Interpretation of these higher order interactions follows the same reasoning as interpretation of three-factor interactions. That is, a significant f-factor interaction indicates that the form of the $f - 1$ factor interaction changes with the levels of the fth factor.

Most experiments do not include more than two or three factors, however. The problem is that higher order interactions are difficult to conceptualize and interpret. Thus, in the absence of a theory that predicts (and thereby helps to interpret) higher order interactions, most investigators do not bother to seek them.

FIGURE 18.7
Panels a–c each depict situations in which there is evidence for a three-factor interaction. In Panels d–g, there is no evidence for a three-factor interaction.

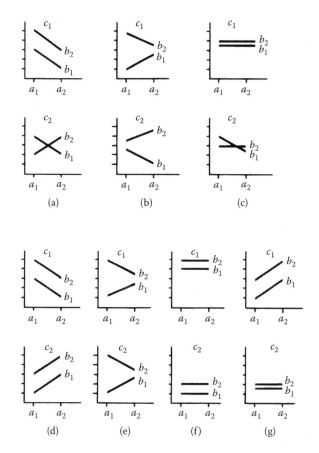

What can you learn from all of this? As usual, the statistical analyses tell you what differences are found in populations, not what those differences mean. But knowing about differences in population means is often important. Furthermore, examination of interactions tells you whether an effect (differences between population means) depends only on factor levels or on other factors too. So you might learn that the effectiveness of particular psychotherapies depends on the type of patient (Table 18.4), or that the cleanliness of an engine depends on the type of gasoline (Table 18.6). It is your job to ask an important question, then the statistics help you to find the answer.

SUMMARY

A factorial experiment examines the effects of at least two factors, each having at least two levels. The number of treatments (populations) sampled is given by the product of the levels of all of the factors. Independent sampling or dependent sampling can be used for the factors, and in any combination.

Each factor is tested for a main effect. If the null hypothesis is rejected, you can conclude that there are differences among the means of the populations corresponding to the factor levels.

A major benefit of a factorial experiment is that it provides information about interactions between factors. A significant two-factor interaction indicates that the effect of one factor changes with the level of the other factor. A significant three-factor interaction indicates that the form of the interaction between any two of the factors changes with the level of the third factor. Interactions can be found both in the absence of main effects and when the main effects are significant. When significant interactions are found, the main effects of the interacting factors (and lower order interactions) may need reinterpretation.

EXERCISES

Terms   *Define these new terms.*

level   interaction
treatment   factor
main effect   effect of a factor

Questions   *Answer the following questions.*

†1. Determine if there is any evidence for a main effect of Factor A, a main effect for Factor B, and an interaction for each of the six individual plots in Panels a–c of Figure 18.7.

†2. Determine if there is any evidence for main effects and for interactions in each of the pairs of graphs in Panels d–g of Figure 18.7.

 3. Replot the data in Figure 18.6 (Table 18.11) to determine if the form of the Mood by Gender interaction changes with the level of Word Type. Then replot the data to determine if the form of the Word Type by Gender interaction changes with the level of Mood.

 4. Use the data in Table 18.15 to determine if there is any evidence for main effects or interactions. Plot the treatment means.

TABLE 18.15
Data From a Two-factor Experiment

	b_1	b_2	b_3
a_1	1,2,0	3,5,1	6,4,5
a_2	3,5,1	2,2,5	4,3,2

TABLE 18.16
Data From a Three-factor Experiment

	a_1				a_2			
	b_1		b_2		b_1		b_2	
Subject	c_1	c_2	c_1	c_2	c_1	c_2	c_1	c_2
1	4	6	7	2	4	8	2	7
2	5	5	8	3	2	6	3	6
3	6	4	6	4	3	7	4	8

5. Assume that the data in Table 18.15 are from an experiment in which Factor A is sampled using independent samples and Factor B is sampled using within-subjects sampling. Indicate which scores came from which subjects.

†6. The data in Table 18.16 are from a three-factor experiment in which all the factors are sampled using within-subject sampling. Determine if there is any evidence for main effects or interactions. Plot the treatment means.

7. Redesign the experiment that led to the data in Table 18.16 so that two of the factors are sampled independently. Indicate which scores came from which subjects.

8. A social psychologist studying impression formation has each of 10 subjects listen to descriptions of four potential roommates. One description is of a smoker who likes to read; another is of a smoker who likes to play music; a third is of a non-smoker who likes to read; and a fourth is of a nonsmoker who likes to play music. The dependent variable is rated likeableness.
   a. How many factors are in this experiment, and what are they?
   b. How are the factors sampled?
   c. List all null and alternative hypotheses that would be tested in an ANOVA.

9. Suppose that in Question 8 half of the subjects were male and half were female. Answer Parts a–c again.

10. Describe three situations in which information about interactions is at least as important as information about main effects.

11. Design a factorial experiment having at least three factors with one factor having at least three levels. Describe the factors, levels, and treatments. Assign subjects independently to at least one factor, and use within-subjects sampling for at least one factor. Be sure to have at least two observations per treatment. Make up the raw data and present it in a table showing the individual observations in each treatment.

   List all null and alternative hypotheses. Determine if there is any evidence for each main effect and interaction. Display, in either a table or a graph, the means that make up the evidence for each main effect and interaction.

   Make a guess as to which main effects and interactions would be significant in an ANOVA. State the implications of these findings for the populations from which you sampled. That is, state how the populations differ and the conclusions you draw from these differences.

12. A clinical psychologist is investigating four types of treatments for obsessive eaters. The treatments are (a) wait-list control, (b) behavior therapy, (c) Freudian psychotherapy, and (d) Jungian psychotherapy. Five different patients are assigned to each therapy. After a month of therapy, the number of binge-eating episodes is recorded.

a. What is (are) the factor(s) in this experiment?

b. What is the dependent variable?

c. What are the statistical hypotheses that are tested?

d. Describe the populations sampled.

19

Computational Methods for the Factorial ANOVA

*C*hapter 18 described how factorial experiments are designed, the advantages of factorial experiments over single factor experiments, and how to learn from the factorial ANOVA. This chapter presents the computational procedures for the two-factor, independent-sample factorial ANOVA. The computational procedures for dependent-sample ANOVAs and for mixed ANOVAs are more complicated; an advanced text should be consulted for these designs.

As usual, the procedures will be discussed within the context of the six-step logic of hypothesis testing. A summary of the six steps is presented in Table 19.5, at the end of the chapter.

TWO-FACTOR FACTORIAL ANOVA

A social psychologist is studying jury decision making. In particular, he is interested in determining if Age of the defendant and the severity of the Charge against the defendant influence the amount of time a juror spends deciding on a verdict (dependent variable). The

FIGURE 19.1
Treatment means for the juror decision-making study.

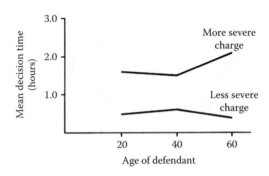

Age factor has three levels ($a_1 = 20$, $a_2 = 40$, and $a_3 = 60$ years old), and the Severity factor has two levels ($s_1 = $ lesser severity, such as manslaughter, and $s_2 = $ greater severity, such as murder). These factors are factorially combined to produce six treatments. Because a two-factor factorial experiment is easily represented in a table, with one factor representing rows and the other factor representing columns, we will call Factor A the "Rows" factor and Factor B the "Columns" factor. Thus, the number of rows (R) is the number of levels of Factor A whereas the number of columns (C) is the number of levels of Factor B. The combination of factors, called treatments, are also called "cells."

The psychologist randomly assigns 10 volunteer jurors to each treatment or cell, and each juror views a videotape of a trial. The videotapes for the six treatments differ only in respect to the severity of charge stated at the beginning and the end of the trial and the age of the defendant. After viewing a tape, each juror is asked to reach a verdict. The psychologist measures the amount of time before the juror signals that he or she has reached a verdict.

The means are depicted in Figure 19.1. Judging from the figure, (a) there is evidence for a main effect of Severity of the charge, (b) there is little evidence for a main effect of Age of the defendant, and (c) there is some evidence for an interaction. Which of these effects are statistically significant? The answer is provided by the ANOVA.

Step 1: Assumptions

Population Assumptions

1. All of the treatment populations are normally distributed. Although we do not know if the populations are normally distributed, we can trust to the robustness of the F statistic as long as the populations are relatively symmetrical.
2. All of the treatment populations have the same variance, σ^2. If the sample sizes are all the same (as they must be for the procedures described in Step 5) and if the treatment sample variances are approximately equal, then we can trust to the robustness of F to meet this assumption. Examination of the data (see Table 19.1) indicates that the sample variances are all comparable.

TABLE 19.1
Juror Decision Times (in hours)

Severity of Charge	Age of Defendant									
	20 (a_1)			40 (a_2)			60 (a_3)			
Less Severe Charge (s_1)	.1	.2	$n = 10$	.3	.7	$n = 10$	.1	.1	$n = 10$	$n_{s_1} = 30$
	.9	1.1	$\Sigma X = 5$	1.2	.8	$\Sigma X = 6$	.9	.8	$\Sigma X = 4$	$\Sigma X = 15$
	.5	.6	$\Sigma X^2 = 3.58$	.7	.6	$\Sigma X^2 = 4.68$	.4	.5	$\Sigma X^2 = 2.42$	$M_{s_1} = 0.5$
	.7	.1	$M = 0.5$	.2	1.0	$M = 0.6$	.1	.6	$M = 0.4$	
	.6	.2	$SS(X) = 1.08$	.3	.2	$SS(X) = 1.08$	.4	.1	$SS(X) = 0.82$	
			$s^2 = 0.12$			$s^2 = 0.12$			$s^2 = 0.09$	
More Severe Charge (s_2)	1.7	1.3	$n = 10$	1.2	1.1	$n = 10$	1.8	1.8	$n = 10$	$n_{s_2} = 30$
	1.8	2.2	$\Sigma X = 16$	2.1	1.9	$\Sigma X = 15$	2.6	2.5	21	$\Sigma X = 52$
	1.6	1.7	$\Sigma X^2 = 26.68$	1.6	1.5	$\Sigma X^2 = 23.58$	2.1	2.2	$\Sigma X^2 = 44.92$	$M_{s_2} = 1.73$
	2.0	1.2	$M = 1.6$	1.1	1.7	$M = 1.5$	1.8	2.3	$M = 2.1$	
	1.2	1.3	$SS(X) = 1.08$	1.2	1.6	$SS(X) = 1.08$	2.1	1.8	$SS(X) = 0.82$	
			$s^2 = 0.12$			$s^2 = 0.12$			$s^2 = 0.09$	
			$n_{a_1} = 20$			$n_{a_2} = 20$			$n_{a_3} = 20$	
			$\Sigma X = 21$			$\Sigma X = 21$			$\Sigma X = 25$	
			$M_{a_1} = 1.05$			$M_{a_2} = 1.05$			$M_{a_3} = 1.05$	

Sampling Assumptions

1. The samples (one for each treatment) are independent of one another. Computational procedures for the dependent-sample ANOVA and the mixed-sample ANOVA are more complicated; an advanced text should be consulted for those procedures.
2. Each sample is obtained by independent (within-sample) random sampling (or random assignment and the assumption of randomness of biological systems is made).
3. Each sample has at least two observations, and all of the samples have the same number of observations. Consult an advanced statistics text for procedures for analyzing factorial experiments with differing numbers of observations in each treatment.

The sampling assumptions are met for this example: Because different (unrelated) volunteers were assigned to each cell, the samples are independent of one another; random assignment was used; and there are an equal number of observations in each sample. Note that the assumption of independent observations within each sample would have been violated if all of the jurors within a treatment met as a single jury and came to one decision. In that case, the observation for one of the jurors would have been completely dependent on (the same as) the observation for any other juror in that sample.

Data Assumption   The observations are measured using an interval or a ratio scale. If this assumption is not met, then the results may not be interpretable.

Step 2: Hypotheses

There is a pair of hypotheses for each factor (the test of the main effect of the factor), and a pair of hypotheses for the interaction. These hypotheses are always about population means, although the means may not be stated explicitly.

For a two-factor ANOVA, the hypotheses for the main effects are:
For Factor A,

$$H_0: \mu_{A_1} = \mu_{A_2} = ... = \mu_{A_R}$$

$$H_1: \text{The null is wrong}$$

where R is the number of levels of Factor A.
For Factor B,

$$H_0: \mu_{B_1} = \mu_{B_2} = ... = \mu_{B_C}$$

$$H_1: \text{The null is wrong}$$

where C is the number of levels of Factor B.

Note that the alternative hypothesis is always nondirectional. It asserts that at least one of the population means is different from at least one of the others (they are not all equal), but it does not specify which mean is different nor the direction of the difference.

For the jury example, the hypotheses for the main effect of Severity ($R = 2$ levels) are:

$$H_0: \mu_{s_1} = \mu_{s_2}$$

$$H_1: \text{the null is wrong}$$

The hypotheses for the main effect of Age ($C = 3$ levels) are:

$$H_0: \mu_{a_1} = \mu_{a_2} = \mu_{a_3}$$

$$H_1: \text{the null is wrong}$$

The interaction hypotheses are:

$$H_0: \text{There is no Severity by Age interaction}$$

$$H_1: \text{The null is wrong (there is an interaction)}$$

Step 3: Sampling Distributions of the Test Statistics

We will begin by reviewing the logic of the ANOVA from Chapter 17. The test statistic is $F = MSB/MSW$. MSW is the pooled variance, that is, the average of the s^2s from each of the samples. As such, MSW is always a good estimate of σ^2, the variance of the populations (remember, all the populations are assumed to have the same variance).

MSB is an index of the variability among the treatment means. When H_0 is correct, MSB is a good estimate of σ^2, and so $F = MSB/MSW$ should be about 1.0. When H_0 is not correct, MSB will be much larger than σ^2. In this case, $F = MSB/MSW$ will be much greater than 1.0. In short, large values of F indicate that H_0 is probably wrong.

Similar reasoning applies to the factorial ANOVA. MSW is the average (pooled) s^2 from all of the treatments. It is always a good estimate of σ^2. Instead of a single MSB, however, there is a separate MS for each factor and for the interaction. For example, MS_{Age} is used to test the null hypothesis concerning Age. It is an index of the variability among the sample means corresponding to the levels of Age. When the null hypothesis for Age is correct, MS_{Age} is a legitimate estimate of σ^2, and $F = MS_{Age}/MSW$ will be about 1.0. When the null hypothesis for Age is incorrect, MS_{Age} is much larger than σ^2, and $F = MS_{Age}/MSW$ will be much larger than 1.0. In short, large values of MS_{Age}/MSW indicate that H_0 for Age is probably incorrect. Similarly, large values of $F = MS_{Severity}/MSW$ indicate that H_0 for Severity is probably incorrect, and large values of $F = MS_{Age\ by\ Severity}/MSW$ indicate that H_0 for the interaction is probably incorrect.

To summarize, there are three test statistics, one for each H_0. The statistics are $F = MS_{Age}/MSW$, $F = MS_{Severity}/MSW$, and $F = MS_{Age\ by\ Severity}/MSW$. For each statistic, values around 1.0 indicate that H_0 is probably correct, whereas large values indicate that H_0 is probably incorrect.

Step 4: Set α and the Decision Rules

Each pair of hypotheses has a separate decision rule. Traditionally, the same value of α is used for all of the decision rules in the ANOVA. Table D (the table of the F statistic) can be used for either $\alpha = .05$ or $\alpha = .01$. For the example, we will use $\alpha = .05$.

The decision rules all take the form

$$\text{Reject } H_0 \text{ if } F \geq F_\alpha(df_1, df_2) \text{ or}$$
$$\text{Reject } H_0 \text{ if } p\text{-value} \leq \alpha$$

That is, reject H_0 if the value of F is greater than the critical value (from Table D) for the specified α, degrees of freedom in the numerator (df_1), and the degrees of freedom in the denominator (df_2).

The degrees of freedom for MSs in the independent-sample ANOVA can be found using three rules:

1. The degrees of freedom in the MS for a factor equals the number of levels of the factor -1 ($R - 1$ for Factor A and $C - 1$ for Factor B). For Age, $df = 3 - 1 = 2$; for Severity, $df = 2 - 1 = 1$.

2. The degrees of freedom in the *MS* for an interaction equals the product of the *df* in the factors included in the interaction ($[R-1] \times [C-1]$). For the Severity by Age interaction, $df = 2 \times 1 = 2$.

3. The degrees of freedom in *MSW* equals the total number of observations minus the number of treatments ($N - RC$). For example, the *df* in *MSW* equal $60 - 6 = 54$.

Critical values are found using Table D. Remember, the critical value depends on the degrees of freedom in both the numerator (df_1) and the denominator (df_2). For the main effect of Age, the critical value is based on 2 and 54 *df*. For $\alpha = .05$ it is

$$\text{Reject } H_0 \text{ if } F = MS_{\text{Age}}/MSW \geq 3.18 \text{ or}$$
$$\text{Reject } H_0 \text{ if } p\text{-value} \leq .05$$

The decision rule for Severity (with 1 and 54 *df*) is

$$\text{Reject } H_0 \text{ if } F = MS_{\text{Severity}}/MSW \geq 4.03 \text{ or}$$
$$\text{Reject } H_0 \text{ if } p\text{-value} \leq .05$$

The decision rule for the interaction (with 2 and 54 *df*) is

$$\text{Reject } H_0 \text{ if } F = MS_{\text{Age by Severity}}/MSW \geq 3.18 \text{ or}$$
$$\text{Reject } H_0 \text{ if } p\text{-value} \leq .05$$

For convenience, the critical values are listed in the last column of the ANOVA summary table (Table 19.3).

Step 5: Sample and Compute the Test Statistics

The data are in Table 19.1, and the calculations are in Table 19.2. Table 19.3 is the ANOVA summary table for this example. Finally, Table 19.4 is a general summary table for the two-factor ANOVA that presents all of the equations. Note: Although the hypotheses are about means, the computational formulas are based on totals.

As in the one-factor ANOVA, the computational strategy is to compute intermediate quantities and then sum of squares (*SS*). Then, each *SS* is divided by its *df* to produce the *MS*. For example, the sum of squares for Age (SS_{Age}) is divided by the degrees of freedom for Age to produce the mean square for Age (MS_{Age}).

As we have done with many statistics, the first step in the ANOVA is to compute some basic descriptive statistics for each treatment or cell including: n, ΣX, ΣX^2, M, $SS(X)$, and s^2. For each Row and Column, n, ΣX, and M are then calculated. Computation of the grand mean (M_G) completes the preliminary calculations.

To start the computations of the Sum of Squares, notice that the *SST* and *SSW* for a two-factor ANOVA are computed in an identical fashion to the one-factor independent sample ANOVA. Next, the Sum of Squares Rows (*SSR*) and Sum of Squares Columns (*SSC*) use some of the intermediate values already computed. For *SSR,* simply take the sum of all the scores in each row (ΣX_R), square them ($(\Sigma X_R)^2$), and sum them up ($\Sigma (\Sigma X_R)^2$). Divide by the number of observations in a row (n_R) and subtract from that the total number of observations in the whole study (N) times the grand mean squared (M_G^2). In the juror times example, the sum of the scores in row 1 (R_1) is 15 and the sum of the scores in row 2 (R_2) is 52. Squaring these row totals, adding them together, and dividing that total by the number

TABLE 19.2
ANOVA Computations on Juror Decision Times

$$M_G = \frac{\sum X}{N} = (.1 + .9 + .5 + \cdots + 2.2 + 2.3 + 1.8)/60 = 1.117$$

$$SST = \sum (X - M_G)^2 = \sum X^2 - NM_G^2 = .1^2 + .9^2 + .5^2 + \cdots + 2.2^2 + 2.3^2 + 1.8^2 - 60(1.117)^2 = 31.04$$

$$SSW = \sum SS(cell) = 1.08 + 1.08 + 1.08 + 1.08 + 0.82 + 0.82 = 5.96$$

$$SSR = \sum n_R (M_R - M_G)^2 = \frac{\sum \left(\sum X_R \right)^2}{n_R} - NM_G^2$$

$$SSR = \frac{(15)^2 + (52)^2}{30} - (60)(1.117)^2 = 97.63 - 74.86 = 22.77$$

$$SSC = \sum n_C (M_C - M_G)^2 = \frac{\sum \left(\sum X_C \right)^2}{n_C} - NM_G^2$$

$$SSC = \frac{(21)^2 + (21)^2 + (25)^2}{20} - (60)(1.117)^2 = 75.35 - 74.86 = 0.49$$

$$SSR \times C = SST - SSW - SSR - SSC$$

$$SSR \times C = 31.04 - 5.96 - 22.77 - 0.49 = 1.82$$

TABLE 19.3
ANOVA Summary Table for Juror Decision Times

Source of Variation	SS	df	MS	F	$F_{.05}$
Rows (Severity)	22.77	1	22.77	207.00	4.03
Columns (Age)	0.49	2	0.25	2.27	3.18
Rows × Columns	1.82	2	0.91	8.27	3.18
Within	5.96	54	0.11		
Total	31.04	59			

of observations per row (30) yields a value of 97.63. From this, the total number of observations ($N = 60$) is multiplied by the grand mean squared ($M_G^2 = (1.117)^2$) is subtracted, resulting in $SSR = 22.77$.

The Sum of Squares Columns is computed in similar fashion except that the column totals are used instead of row totals ($SSC = 0.49$). The Sum of Squares Rows by Columns is computed by taking the subtracting SSW, SSR, and SSC from SST.

Mean squares (MSs) are computed by dividing each SS by the appropriate df. Once this is done, Fs can be calculated by dividing MSR, MSC, and $MSR \times C$ by MSW.

Step 6: Decide and Draw Conclusions

From the ANOVA summary table (Table 19.3), we can see which F ratios exceed their critical values, and thus which effects are statistically significant. The main effect of Severity

TABLE 19.4
Computational Formulas for the Two-factor Independent-sample ANOVA

Source of Variation	SS	df	MS	F
Rows	$\dfrac{\sum\left(\sum X_R^2\right)}{n_R} - NM_G^2$	$R-1$	$\dfrac{SSR}{df_R}$	$\dfrac{MSR}{MSW}$
Columns	$\dfrac{\sum\left(\sum X_C^2\right)}{n_C} - NM_G^2$	$C-1$	$\dfrac{SSC}{df_C}$	$\dfrac{MSC}{MSW}$
Rows × Columns	$SST - SSW - SSR - SSC$	$(R-1)(C-1)$	$\dfrac{SSR \times C}{df_{R\times C}}$	$\dfrac{MSR \times C}{MSW}$
Within	$\sum SS(cell)$	$N - RC$	$\dfrac{SSW}{df_W}$	
Total	$\sum X^2 - NM_G^2$	$N-1$		

is statistically significant: For this population of jurors, the mean time spent deciding is greater for the more severe charge than for the less severe charge. The main effect of Age is not statistically significant; there is not enough evidence to decide if age of the defendant (by itself) affects the time the jurors spend deciding. However, because the interaction is significant, these main effects need reinterpretation.

The interaction can be described in either of two ways (see Figure 19.1). First, the interaction indicates that the effect of Severity of Charge depends on the defendant's Age: The effect of Severity is to increase mean decision time by 1.1 hours (1.6 − .5) for the 20-year-old defendant, .9 hours for the 40-year-old defendant, and 1.7 hours for the 60-year-old defendant. Alternatively, the interaction can be described as a change in the effect of Age of the defendant for the two types of charges: For the less severe charge, there is little effect of the age of the defendant; for the more severe charge, more time is spent deciding when the defendant is older.

Because jurors were randomly assigned to conditions, we can make statements regarding the causes of these effects. Assuming there are no confounds in the experiment, then Severity of Charge *causes* an increase in decision time. Similarly, the interaction is *caused* by the joint action of Severity and Age.

Reporting the Results of a Factorial ANOVA

Be sure that a table or figure containing the treatment means is available. Without the means, the statistical results are often uninterpretable. Traditionally, the test of main effects is reported first, followed by interactions. The social psychologist might report, "The treatment means are illustrated in Figure 19.1. The main effect of Severity was significant, $F(1,54) = 22.81$, $MSW = .11$, indicating that more time was spent deciding for the more severe charge. The age factor was not significant, $F(2,54) = 2.41$, $MSW = .11$. As illustrated in the figure, the interaction between Severity and Age of the defendant was significant, $F(2,54) = 7.91$, $MSW = .11$." This report is, of course, followed by a discussion of what these data mean.

Possible Errors

For each null hypothesis tested, the Type I error rate is α, regardless of the number of levels in the factor. This, of course, is one of the major advantages of the ANOVA over multiple *t* tests. Nonetheless, across the factorial ANOVA, the chances of making a Type I error are greater than α. The test of each null hypothesis provides a separate opportunity to make a Type I error. Therefore, in the two-factor ANOVA, there are three opportunities to make a Type I error; and the probabilities cumulate to a total probability greater than α. In recognition of this, some statisticians recommend reducing the individual αs (for example, to .01) to keep the overall Type I error rate low. A more advanced text should be consulted for details on this procedure.

Type II errors can also occur in the factorial ANOVA; each time a null hypothesis is *not* rejected, you may be making a Type II error. The probability of a Type II error (β) can be decreased, or equivalently, power increased, by any of the procedures discussed in Chapter 9 (except for using directional alternative hypotheses). To review, β can be decreased by (a) increasing α, (b) increasing the sample size, (c) decreasing excess variability by careful data collection methods, (d) using dependent sampling (consult a more advanced text for the dependent-sample factorial ANOVA), and (e) increasing the effect size. For the juror decision-making example, the effect of age might have been increased by increasing the range of the defendants' ages.

COMPARING PAIRS OF MEANS: THE PROTECTED *t* TEST

A significant main effect indicates that at least one of the population means is different from the others, but no information is given as to which is (are) different. One (unsatisfactory) way of finding differences is to use multiple *t* tests to compare all pairs of means. This procedure inflates the Type I error rate over the stated value of α.

The protected *t* test can be used to compare pairs of means, but only after finding significant effects using the ANOVA. The significant effect guards against the inflation of Type I errors by (virtually) assuring that H_0 is *incorrect,* so that Type I errors (rejecting a *correct* H_0) are rare.

Two forms of the protected *t* test are available. One is used to compare the populations corresponding to the levels of a single factor. This form is generally used when there are no interactions. The second form is used to compare treatments (combinations of factor levels). This form can be used legitimately only when there is a significant interaction.

The Protected *t* Test for Main Effects

This procedure is used to compare the means corresponding to the levels of a specific factor. It should be used only after obtaining a significant main effect for the factor in the ANOVA.

The assumptions are exactly the same as the ANOVA assumptions. The hypotheses are:

$$H_0: \mu_{f_i} - \mu_{f_j} = 0$$

$$H_1: \mu_{f_i} - \mu_{f_j} \neq 0$$

The symbol μ_{f_i} refers to the mean of the population corresponding to level i of Factor F. As long as there is a significant main effect for Factor F, you may compare any of its levels.

The test statistic is the independent-sample t statistic using MSW for the s_p^2. The formula is

$$t = \frac{(\bar{f}_i - \bar{f}_j) - 0}{s_{M_1 - M_2}}, \quad s_{M_1 - M_2} = \sqrt{\frac{2\ MSW}{\text{number of observations in a level of Factor } F}}$$

where $\bar{f}_i$ is the mean for the ith level of Factor F.

Three aspects of this formula are notable. First, MSW is always multiplied by 2. Second, the divisor of MSW is the number of observations in one of the sample means being tested. Third, the t statistic has the same degrees of freedom as MSW, $N - RC$.

The decision rule is

Reject H_0 if $t \leq -t_{\alpha/2}$ or if $t \geq t_{\alpha/2}$ or
Reject H_0 if p-value $\leq \alpha$

where $t_{\alpha/2}$ is the t statistic with $N - RC$ degrees of freedom that has $\alpha/2$ of the distribution above it.

If the null hypothesis is rejected, you may conclude that the mean of the population corresponding to level f_i is different from the mean of the population corresponding to level f_j.

There is no need to use this form of the protected t test for the juror decision-making example. The main effect of Severity is significant, but there are only two levels; thus, the significant main effect must be due to a difference between the means of the populations corresponding to these two levels, and no t test is needed. The main effect for Age was not significant, so the procedure is inappropriate for comparing levels of this factor.

The Protected t Test Following a Significant Interaction

The next form of the protected t test is used to compare the means of populations corresponding to specific treatments (combinations of factor levels). It should be used only after finding a significant interaction, because the interaction (virtually) guarantees that there is at least one difference between treatment means.

Examining the juror decision-making data in Figure 19.1, the social psychologist supposes that the age of the defendant (40 vs. 60) affects decision time for the more severe charge, but for the less severe charge the age of the defendant makes little difference (and that is why there is a significant interaction). Statistically, his supposition translates into two t tests. One t test compares the means of a_2s_2 and a_3s_2 (the effect of age for the more severe charge), and the other compares the means of a_2s_1 and a_3s_1 (the effect of age for the less severe charge). Because the interaction was significant, the psychologist can make these specific comparisons without fear that the Type I error rate will be inflated.

The assumptions are exactly the same as for the ANOVA. The general form of the hypothesis is

$$H_0\colon \mu_{A_iB_j} - \mu_{A_kB_l} = 0$$

$$H_1\colon \mu_{A_iB_j} - \mu_{A_kB_l} \neq 0$$

As long as there is a significant interaction, you may choose to compare whichever treatment means are of interest to you. Your choice determines the values of the subscripts i, j, k, and l.

For the example, the hypotheses for the two t tests are:
For the more severe charge,

$$H_0\colon \mu_{s_2a_3} - \mu_{s_2a_2} = 0$$

$$H_1\colon \mu_{s_2a_3} - \mu_{s_2a_2} \neq 0$$

For the less severe charge,

$$H_0\colon \mu_{s_1a_3} - \mu_{s_1a_2} = 0$$

$$H_1\colon \mu_{s_1a_3} - \mu_{s_1a_2} \neq 0$$

The general form of the test statistic is

$$t = \frac{(\overline{A_iB_j} - \overline{A_kB_l}) - 0}{s_{M_1-M_2}}, s_{M_1-M_2} = \sqrt{\frac{2\,MSW}{n}}$$

Again, three aspects of this formula are notable. First, the multiplier of MSW, the "2," is a constant. Second, the divisor of MSW is the number of observations in one of the sample means being tested, n. Third, the degrees of freedom are the same as the degrees of freedom in MSW, $N - RC$.

The decision rule is

$$\text{Reject } H_0 \text{ if } t \le -t_{\alpha/2} \text{ or if } t \ge t_{\alpha/2} \text{ or}$$
$$\text{Reject } H_0 \text{ if } p\text{-value} \le \alpha$$

where $t_{\alpha/2}$ is the t statistic with $N - RC$ df that has $\alpha/2$ of the distribution above it. For the example, using $\alpha = .05$ (as in the ANOVA) and 54 df,

$$\text{Reject } H_0 \text{ if } t \le -2.021 \text{ or if } t \ge 2.021$$

For the two example t tests,

$$s_{M_1-M_2} = \sqrt{\frac{(2)(.11)}{10}} = .15$$

For the more severe charge,

$$t = \frac{(1.60 - 2.10) - 0}{.15} = -3.38$$

For the less severe charge,

$$t = \frac{(.50 - .40) - 0}{.15} = -.68$$

For the more severe charge (Level s_2), the null hypothesis can be rejected: Jurors spend more time deciding for the 60-year-old defendant than for the 40-year-old defendant. For the less severe charge (Level s_1), the null hypothesis cannot be rejected: There is not enough evidence to conclude that age of the defendant influences jury decision times.

A SECOND EXAMPLE OF THE FACTORIAL ANOVA

In conducting the Maternity Study, Drs. Hyde and Essex were interested in several questions, some of which were: (a) Does a mother's marital satisfaction depend on whether she is satisfied with the household division of labor, (b) does a mother's marital satisfaction depend on her employment status, and (c) do employment status and division of household labor somehow combine to affect marital satisfaction? These are questions for a two-factor factorial ANOVA. The first factor is household division of labor, with two levels, either satisfied or dissatisfied; an F can determine the main effect of division of labor (Question 1). The second factor is employment status, with three levels, full-time, part-time, and none; an F can determine the main effect of employment status (Question 2). Lastly, the factors combine to form six treatments, or cells; an F can determine if there is an interaction between the two factors (Question 3). The dependent variable is MARSAT score at 12 months postpartum.

Because the Maternity Study was such a large study, the data are not reproduced here, but are provided on the companion CD in a file "MARSAT Division of Labor and Employment Status.XLS." Also, whereas there were 244 participants in the original study, we have pared the data set down such that all cells have equal numbers of observations. If you want to complete a factorial ANOVA with unequal sample (cell) sizes, please consult a more advanced textbook. Thus, each cell in the data set has 27 observations.

The population and data assumptions of ANOVA, including homogeneity of variance, normally distributed measurements, and interval-ratio level of measurement, appear to be met here. However, since the Maternity Study did not use a random sample, we must constrain our conclusions to the groups studied, namely new mothers in Wisconsin who volunteer for psychological research.

The hypotheses for main effects are:

$$H_0: \mu_{\text{Satisfied}} = \mu_{\text{Dissatisfied}}$$

H_1: The null for Rows is wrong

$$H_0: \mu_{\text{Full-time}} = \mu_{\text{Part-time}} = \mu_{\text{None}}$$

H_1: The null for Columns is wrong

The hypotheses for the interaction are:

$$H_0: \text{There is no interaction}$$

$$H_1: \text{The null is wrong}$$

The three test statistics are $F = MSR/MSW$, $F = MSC / MSW$, and $F = MSRxC / MSW$. For each, when H_0 is correct, the most likely value is around 1.0, but when H_1 is correct, the most likely value is much greater than 1.0.

With $\alpha = .05$, the decision rules can all be stated in the form:

$$\text{Reject } H_0 \text{ if } p\text{-value} \leq \alpha$$

Although this example could be completed "by hand," it is likely that we would make computation errors. Therefore, it is always best to conduct this sort of analysis using a computer program like Excel. By clicking on "Tools" and selecting "Data Analysis," you can use the "Anova: Two-Factor With Replication" to analyze these data. Entering the appropriate information should yield results like those in Figure 19.2.

Note that the p-value for "Sample" is 3.38E − 05, which translates to 3.38×10^{-5}, or .000038, which is less than α (.05). Thus, we reject the null for the "Sample," which is also the Rows factor. However, the null hypotheses for Columns or Interaction cannot be rejected. So, women who are satisfied with the household division of labor generally have a higher marital satisfaction than women who are not satisfied with the household division of labor (this is the main effect of the rows factor), in the populations sampled. There is not enough evidence to claim that employment status affects marital satisfaction (no evidence of a main effect of the columns factor). Lastly, there is not enough evidence that employment status and satisfaction with household division of labor interact to influence marital satisfaction (no evidence of an interaction).

SUMMARY

The computational procedures described in this chapter are used for the independent-sample two-factor ANOVA. There is a separate null hypothesis for each factor (the test for the main effect of that factor) and the interaction between the factors. Each null hypothesis is

FIGURE 19.2
Two-factor ANOVA summary from Excel on marital satisfaction with employment status and division of household labor as factors.

	A	B	C	D	E	F	G
1	Anova: Two-Factor With Replication						
2							
3	SUMMARY	Full-Time	Part-Time	None	Total		
4	*Satisfied*						
5	Count	27	27	27	81		
6	Sum	45.01435411	45.9689	52.02609	143.0093		
7	Average	1.6671983	1.702552	1.926892	1.765547		
8	Variance	0.665590105	0.512133	0.427446	0.53507		
9							
10	*Dissatisfied*						
11	Count	27	27	27	81		
12	Sum	30.9259515	34.90824	30.41034	96.24453		
13	Average	1.145405611	1.292898	1.126309	1.188204		
14	Variance	1.269798881	0.597893	0.96821	0.927279		
15							
16	*Total*						
17	Count	54	54	54			
18	Sum	75.94030561	80.87714	82.43643			
19	Average	1.406301956	1.497725	1.526601			
20	Variance	1.01878729	0.587287	0.847918			
21							
22							
23	ANOVA						
24	*Source of Variation*	SS	df	MS	F	P-value	F crit
25	Sample	13.49967545	1	13.49968	18.2384	3.375E-05	3.901761
26	Columns	0.425946651	2	0.212973	0.287732	0.75035942	3.053998
27	Interaction	1.094060617	2	0.54703	0.739052	0.47923101	3.053998
28	Within	115.4678539	156	0.740179			
29							
30	Total	130.4875366	161				
31							

tested using an F ratio composed of the appropriate mean square divided by MSW. If the F ratio exceeds its critical value, the null hypothesis is rejected. When the null hypothesis for the interaction is rejected, you may conclude that the effect of one factor depends on (changes with) the levels of the other factor. A significant interaction often requires reinterpretation of any main effects. Significant main effects and interactions may be followed by protected t tests to determine exactly which means differ.

Although this chapter has focused on computations, keep in mind that the ultimate goal of data collection is not to simply determine which effects are significant and which are not. The statistical analysis is only a tool used to learn about (and perhaps change) the world by learning from the data. Table 19.5 contains a summary for the factorial ANOVA.

EXERCISES

Terms   *Define these new symbols.*

SSR	MSR
SSC	MSC
$SSR{\times}C$	$MSR{\times}C$

Questions   *For each of the following problems, list the hypotheses, provide a complete ANOVA summary table, and describe the results as if writing a research paper.*

†1. Complete the ANOVA for the data in Table 18.2 (p. 401). If appropriate, use the protected t test to compare the means of m_1w_1 and m_1w_2, and the means of m_3w_1 and m_3w_2.

TABLE 19.5
The Independent-sample Factorial ANOVA

1. **Assumptions:**

   Population assumptions:
   a. All of the treatment populations are normally distributed (but see discussion of robustness).
   b. All of the treatment populations have the same variance, σ^2 (but see discussion of equal sample sizes).

   Sampling assumptions:
   a. All samples are independent.
   b. Each sample is obtained by independent (within-sample) random sampling (or random assignment and the assumption of randomness of biological systems is made).
   c. Each sample has at least two observations, and all of the samples have the same number of observations.

   Data assumption:
   The observations are measured using an interval or ratio scale.

2. **Hypotheses:**

   Main effects:

   $$H_0 : \mu_{A_1} = \mu_{A_2} = \cdots = \mu_{A_k}$$

   H_1: The null is wrong

   $$H_0: \mu_{B_1} = \mu_{B_2} = \cdots = \mu_{B_l}$$

   H_1: The null is wrong

   Interaction:

   H_0: There is no interaction

   H_1: The null is wrong

3. **Test statistics and their sampling distributions:**

   The three test statistics are $F = \dfrac{MSR}{MSW}, F = \dfrac{MSC}{MSW}$ and $F = \dfrac{MSR \times C}{MSW}$. In each case, F will be approximately 1.0 if H_0 is correct, but F will be much greater if H_1 is correct.

4. **Decision rule:**

   $$\text{Reject } H_0 \text{ if } F \geq F_\alpha (df_1, df_2) \text{ or}$$
   $$\text{Reject } H_0 \text{ if } p\text{-value} \leq \alpha$$

   $F_\alpha(df_1, df_2)$ is the value of F with df_1 in the numerator and df_2 in the denominator that has α of the distribution above it.

5. **Sample and compute *F*s using formulas in Table 19.4** (or use "ANOVA: Two factor with Replication" from "Data Analysis" toolpak).

6. **Decide and draw conclusions:**
   Refer each value of F to its decision rule and decide whether or not to reject H_0. Draw conclusions about the means of the populations from which the samples were randomly selected. If H_0 is rejected, the protected t test can be used to compare specific populations.

---

†**2.** A clinical psychologist studied the effectiveness of various therapies for reducing cigarette smoking. He randomly assigned four smokers to each of the 12 groups formed by the factorial combination of three types of therapy (control, verbal, and drug) and four durations of therapy (1, 2, 3, and 4 weeks). After therapy, he measured the number of cigarettes smoked in the following week. The data are in Table 19.6. If warranted, use the protected t test to compare the verbal and drug therapies after 1 week, and compare the verbal and drug therapies after 4 weeks.

TABLE 19.6
Number of Cigarettes Smoked by Each of Four People in 12 Therapies

Type of Therapy	Duration of Therapy (weeks)							
	1		**2**		**3**		**4**	
Control	140,	98	156,	110	110,	132	150,	132
	120,	130	87,	137	90,	88	140,	102
Verbal	110,	92	80,	95	53,	22	0,	15
	115,	83	104,	41	65,	24	40,	37
Drug	100,	150	90,	120	95,	50	91,	83
	95,	95	50,	100	65,	70	50,	56

Report the results as if writing a journal article. Include in your report conclusions about the effectiveness of therapies; use the protected t tests to help you draw these conclusions.

Describing Linear Relationships: Regression

*P*revious chapters have described techniques for determining if populations differ. For example, Chapters 13 and 15 presented the *t* test for determining if two population means differ. **Linear regression** and **correlation** are procedures for describing how the scores in two populations are *related*, not how they differ.[1]

---

[1] The term *regression* comes from Sir Francis Galton's work on heredity in the 19th century. He noted that tall fathers tended to have sons who were not quite as tall. That is, the average height of the sons was closer to the mean of the population of heights than was the average height of the fathers. Similarly, short fathers tended to have sons who were not quite as short. This tendency is called "regression toward the mean."

Sometimes it makes no sense to ask if two populations are different. Consider the population of family incomes in the United States and the population of IQ scores of children. Clearly these populations are different; they are measured on completely different scales. It is hard to imagine why anyone would want to compare the mean of one of the populations to the mean of the other. Nonetheless, one might be curious about a *relationship* between these populations: Is family income related to IQ scores of the children?

Here are some other examples of pairs of populations for which it is sensible to ask if they are related, but not as sensible to ask if they are different (because they are measured using different scales).

Population X	Population Y
number of cigarettes smoked per day	age at death
hours studied for test	score on test
speed of playing a musical piece	number of errors in playing piece

Sometimes the scores in two populations are measured using the same scale, but the question, "Are the populations related?" is still of interest. For example,

Population X	Population Y
today's weather	tomorrow's weather
high school grade point average	college grade point average
IQ of parent	IQ of child

Correlation is used to quantify the strength of the relationship between the scores in two samples (or populations). It is discussed in Chapter 21. Linear regression, the topic of this chapter, is used (a) to describe the relationship between two samples (or populations), and (b) to predict one score (for example, the score on the test) from the other score (for example, number of hours studied).

The predictive aspect of regression is often important in making practical decisions. For example, can a college admissions officer accurately predict college grade point average from high school grade point average? If so, then he can make good decisions regarding whom to admit. Is there a predictive relationship between the amount of a particular food additive (for example, saccharin) and susceptibility to disease? If so, then you (or the government) can decide how much of the additive is healthy.

The chapter begins with a review of dependent sampling, the only type of sampling amenable to regression analysis. This review is followed by a discussion of the mathematics of straight lines (because we will be discussing *linear* relationships). In the next section we discuss descriptive techniques, that is, how to describe the linear relationship between two samples (or two populations). The final sections describe procedures for making inferences about relationships between populations.

DEPENDENT SAMPLES

This section reviews material covered in greater detail in Chapter 5 (independent [within-sample] random sampling), Chapter 13 (independent samples), and Chapter 15 (dependent samples).

Independent (Within-sample) Random Sampling

A sample is a subset of scores from a population of scores. Typically, we deal with samples because they are much easier to obtain than all of the scores in a population.

An important type of sample is a random sample. Only random samples can be used to make inferences about populations. Random samples are defined not by their content, but by the procedure used to obtain the sample from the population: A random sample is obtained when each observation in the population has an equal chance of being included in the sample. Otherwise the sample is biased.

One procedure for obtaining random samples makes use of a random number table, such as Table H. First, each observation in the population is assigned a unique number. Second, a starting location is chosen (randomly) in the random number table. Third, starting from that location, find the first *n* numbers assigned to observations in the population, where *n* is the sample size. These *n* observations are chosen for the random sample.

The procedure just described results in independent (within-sample) random samples: Each observation within the sample is independent of the other observations within the sample. In other words, the occurrence of one score in the sample is completely unaffected by the other scores in the sample. When there is communication or cooperation among the participants during data collection, the sample data are often not independent. For example, if a group of people are working together to solve a problem, the time one person takes to solve the problem is *not* independent of the time another person takes to solve the problem.

All of the inferential statistical techniques described in this book require independent (within-sample) random samples. Note carefully: The term independent (within-sample) random sampling applies to a single sample, and indicates that the observations within that sample are unrelated.

Independent Samples

When sampling from two (or more) populations, the scores in the two samples can be unrelated or related. When the scores in the two samples are unrelated, they are called independent samples. Do not confuse "independent samples," which applies to scores in two samples, with the term "independent (within-sample) random sampling," which applies to the scores within a single sample.

Usually, independent samples arise when different (and unrelated) people contribute to the two samples. For example, suppose you were conducting a project to determine if caffeine influences problem-solving speed. You time half of the participants while they solve a problem without caffeine, and you time half of the participants while they solve a problem with caffeine. Because different (and unrelated) participants contributed to the two conditions, the samples are independent.

Dependent Samples

The samples from two (or more) populations are dependent when the scores in one of the samples are related to the scores in the other sample(s). The scores are related if there is a logical method for pairing each score in one sample with a score in the other sample.

Consider the problem-solving example once again. Suppose that each person attempts to solve a problem with caffeine on one day, and that same person attempts to solve a problem without caffeine on another day. Because each score in one sample can be logically paired with a score in the other sample (the scores from the same person can be paired), the samples are dependent. When the same people contribute to both samples, this type of dependent sampling is called within-subject sampling.

Dependent samples can also be obtained from closely matched people. For example, suppose you begin the caffeine and problem-solving project by carefully forming pairs of people matched on characteristics you think might be related to problem-solving ability. For example, the people in each pair may be matched in regard to intelligence, occupation, education, age, and sex. One person in each pair is randomly assigned to solve the problem with caffeine, and the other person in each pair is assigned to solve the problem without caffeine. The scores in one sample can be logically paired to the scores in the other sample, so the samples are dependent. This procedure for obtaining dependent samples is called matched-group sampling.

Linear Regression and Dependent Sampling

Linear regression techniques always require dependent samples (either within-subject or matched-group). There is an obvious reason: Linear regression attempts to describe the relationship between the two samples and there will be a relationship to describe only if the samples are dependent.

When using regression as a descriptive technique, the samples need not be obtained by independent (within-sample) random sampling: Whether the samples are random or not, regression procedures will describe any linear relationship between the scores in the samples. However, if you are going to make inferences about the relationship between the populations, then the two dependent samples must be obtained using independent (within-sample) random sampling. That is, *within each sample* the scores should be independent of one another, even while the scores are related across the two samples.

Return one last time to the problem-solving example. Even when using dependent sampling, you would not want the people in the same condition working together. If they did, then the scores within the sample would not be an independent (within-sample) random sample, and inferential statistical techniques would be precluded.

FIGURE 20.1
Four types of linear relationships between hours studied (X) and score on test (Y) for four students.

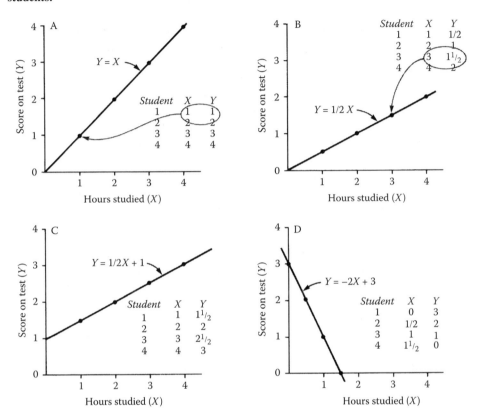

MATHEMATICS OF STRAIGHT LINES

Imagine a situation in which you have dependent samples from two populations. For example, for each of four students you might have number of hours studied (Sample 1) and performance on an exam (Sample 2). For generality, we will use X as the label for the number of hours studied, and Y as the label for the performance scores. The label X is usually used for the variable that is logically or temporally first, and the label Y is used for the variable that may be predicted from the X scores.

Figure 20.1A contains the sample of Xs and Ys for four students, and a graph representing the four pairs of scores. Note that the graph is different from any of the others we have run across. In particular, the Y-axis (the ordinate) is used to indicate the *value* of particular Y scores, not frequency as in Chapter 2, and not means as in Chapter 18. In the graph, a *pair* of scores from one student is represented by a *single* point at the intersection of the X value (number of hours studied) and the Y value (performance on the exam).

In Figure 20.1A, all of the points fall on a straight line, which has the formula $Y = X$. This formula generates all of the points on the line, and *only* points on the line.

The formula $Y = X$ can be used in two ways. First, it is a succinct description of the relationship between the sample of Xs and the sample of Ys; whatever the value of X, Y is exactly the same. Second, if the formula holds for the population of Xs and Ys, then it can be used to predict a new Y from a new X. For example, suppose that a fifth student tells you that he studied 2 hours for the exam. Using the formula $Y = X$, you would be able to predict for this student a score on the exam of 2.

Figure 20.1B illustrates a slightly more complex relationship between the sample of Xs and Ys. In this case, the formula for the line describing the relationship is $Y = 1/2(X)$. Again, the formula can be used to describe the relationship between the two samples, and if the relation holds in the populations, the formula can be used to predict a new Y from a new X.

Figures 20.1C and 20.1D illustrate still more complex straight-line relations between the two samples. The relation portrayed in Figure 20.1D is unfortunate as well as complex: The more time spent studying, the worse the performance.

Figures 20.1A to 20.1D are called scatter plots.

> A **scatter plot** is a graph of the relationship between a sample of Xs and a sample of Ys. The graph shows the "scatter" of the points. Two variables (X and Y) are **linearly related** if the scatter of the points can be approximated by a straight line.

The scatter plots in Figure 20.1 all illustrate linear relationships.

Now consider Figure 20.2. This scatter plot illustrates a **curvilinear** relationship. Although the Xs and the Ys are related, the relation is not approximated by a straight line. An advanced statistics book should be consulted for techniques for dealing with curvilinear relationships.

FIGURE 20.2

Curvilinear relationship between hours studied (X) and score on test (Y) for four students.

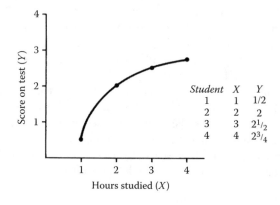

Characteristics of Straight Lines

The formula for a straight line can always be put in the form

$$Y = mX + b$$

The complete formula for the line in Figure 20.1A is $Y = (1)X + 0$. That is, for this line, $m = 1$ and $b = 0$. For the line in Figure 20.1D, $m = -2$ and $b = 3$ so that $Y = (-2)X + 3$.

> m is called the **slope** of the line.

The slope of a line determines its slant. Lines with positive slopes slant upward from left to right, as in Figures 20.1A to 20.1C. Lines with negative slopes slant downward from left to right, as in Figure 20.1D. The absolute value of the slope indicates the steepness of the line: the larger the absolute value, the steeper the slant of the line. When the slope is zero ($m = 0$), the line is horizontal, as in Figure 20.3.

The slope of a line is important in describing the relationship between a sample of Xs and Ys. A positive slope signals a "positive" or "direct" relationship between the two samples. When the slope is positive, an increase in X is accompanied by an increase in Y. A negative slope signals a "negative" or "indirect" relationship between the two samples. In this case, an increase in X is accompanied by a *decrease* in Y. Finally, a zero slope indicates *no* relationship between the samples: Whatever the value of X, Y is always the same. (For this reason, $m = 0$ is often a null hypothesis about the populations of Xs and Ys. *Rejecting* this null hypothesis indicates that there *is* a linear relationship.)

When all of the points fall on a single straight line (as in Figure 20.1), the slope can be calculated easily. Select any two points, and compute

$$m = \frac{Y_2 - Y_1}{X_2 - X_1}$$

FIGURE 20.3
There is no relationship between hours studied (X) and score on test (Y), because the value of Y is the same regardless of the value of X.

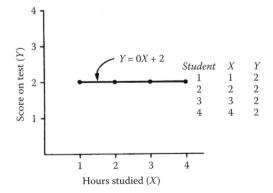

In words, the formula computes the change in Y ($Y_2 - Y_1$) for a corresponding change in X, or how much the line goes up for each change horizontally.

For practice, compute the slope of the line in Figure 20.1A. Using the data from the first two students,

$$m = \frac{2-1}{2-1} = \frac{1}{1} = 1$$

Any two points (students) can be used. For the slope of the line in Figure 20.1D, use Students 2 and 4.

$$m = \frac{2-0}{\frac{1}{2}-1\frac{1}{2}} = \frac{2}{-1} = -2$$

The other component of a straight line is b.

> b is called the **Y-intercept**. It is the value of Y when $X = 0$. When the axes are drawn so that they meet at the point 0,0, then the line crosses the Y-axis at the Y-intercept.

In Figures 20.1A and 20.1B, the Y-intercept (b) is 0: The line crosses the Y-axis at the origin. In Figure 20.1C, $b = 1$, and the line crosses the Y-axis at 1. Finally, in Figure 20.1D, $b = 3$, and, indeed, the line crosses the Y-axis at 3.

The Y-intercept is useful for precisely describing the form of the linear relationship between the two samples. Nonetheless, it is often not as important as the slope. Remember, the slope determines whether or not there is any linear relationship (whether or not $m = 0$), as well as the direction of the relation.

DESCRIBING LINEAR RELATIONSHIPS: THE LEAST-SQUARES REGRESSION LINE

The formula for the slope given above can be used only when all of the points fall on a straight line. Unfortunately, that is extremely rare when dealing with real data.

The scatter plots in Figure 20.4 are more typical of real data. Note that even though all the points do not fall onto straight lines, some of the graphs suggest linear relationships. For example, the scatter plot in Figure 20.4A suggests a linear relationship with a positive slope, and the scatter plot in Figure 20.4B suggests a negative linear relationship. The scatter plot in Figure 20.4C suggests that there is no relationship between the Xs and the Ys ($m = 0$). The scatter plot in Figure 20.4D illustrates a curvilinear relationship between the Xs and the Ys. Application of *linear* regression techniques to these data would be a mistake, because the relationship is not *linear*.

FIGURE 20.4
Scatter plots indicating (A) a direct linear relationship, (B) an indirect linear relationship, (C) no linear relationship, and (D) a curvilinear relationship.

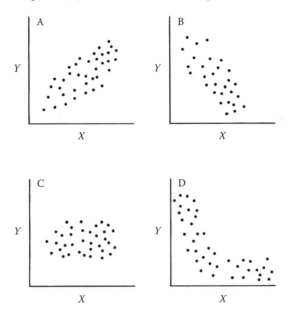

The Least-squares Criterion

Given that the data points suggest a linear relationship but do not all fall on a straight line, how can a line be used to describe the data? The answer is to find a line that "best fits" the linear trend in the scatter plot. The procedure for finding the best-fitting line is illustrated within the context of an example.

Suppose that the data in Table 20.1 (and the scatter plot in Figure 20.5) were obtained by a sociologist investigating the relationship between the number of years mothers attend college and the number of years their daughters attend college. The sociologist first obtained a listing of all mothers with daughters old enough to have attended college. Then he randomly selected six mothers and asked each the number of years she had attended college.[2] He then determined the number of years each mother's oldest daughter had attended college. This procedure results in two dependent (matched-group) samples, one from the population of number of years of college attended by mothers and one from the population of number of years attended by daughters. The observations were obtained by independent (within-sample) random sampling (the mothers are unrelated to each other and the daughters are unrelated to each other). Each sample has six observations. We will use the symbol n_p for the number of pairs of observations; thus, for this example, $n_p = 6$.

---

[2] A sample size of six is usually not large enough to learn anything significant (in either sense of the word). It is convenient for illustrating computations, however.

TABLE 20.1
Years of College Attended

Pair	Mothers (X)	Daughters (Y)	XY
1	0	0	0
2	0	1	0
3	1	2	2
4	2	3	6
5	2	4	8
6	3	5	15
	$n_X = 6$	$n_Y = 6$	$\Sigma\,XY = 31$
	$\Sigma X = 8$	$\Sigma Y = 15$	
	$\Sigma X^2 = 18$	$\Sigma Y^2 = 55$	
	$M_X = 1.333$	$M_Y = 2.5$	
	$SS(X) = 7.333$	$SS(Y) = 17.5$	

$$SP_{XY} = \Sigma XY - n_p M_X M_Y = 31 - 6(1.333)(2.5) = 11$$

$$\hat{m} = \frac{SP_{XY}}{SS(X)} = \frac{11}{7.333} = 1.5$$

$$\hat{b} = M_Y - \hat{m}M_X = 2.5 - 1.5(1.333) = 0.5$$

$$\hat{Y} = 1.5X + 0.5$$

$$s_{Y\bullet X} = \sqrt{\frac{1}{n_p - 2}\left(SS(Y) - \frac{SP_{XY}^2}{SS(X)}\right)} = \sqrt{\frac{1}{4}\left(17.5 - \frac{11^2}{7.333}\right)} = 0.5$$

The first step in constructing a regression line is to examine the scatter plot. Most important, does the scatter plot suggest that *linear* regression is appropriate? In this case, the answer is yes.

Now the task is to find the best-fitting straight line. But what, precisely, is meant by the best-fitting line? Look at the scatter plot in Figure 20.5. Each circle represents an actual pair of observations. The closer a line comes to each circle, the better fitting the line. The best-fitting line is the one that, on the average, comes closest to all of the circles.

The term "best-fitting" can also be given a mathematical interpretation. In Figure 20.5, each arrow indicates the distance between a data point and the line. This distance is $Y - \hat{Y}$, where Y is the actual value of Y (the circle), and $\hat{Y}$ is the "predicted" value of Y on the regression line (pronounced "Y-hat"). The smaller the difference $Y - \hat{Y}$, the closer the line comes to the actual data point. Squaring the difference gets rid of the sign, because when $\hat{Y}$ misses Y, it matters not if $\hat{Y}$ is too large or too small. Thus, for each data point, we can think of a squared deviation between the actual value of Y and the predicted value, $\hat{Y}$. In symbols, the squared deviation is $(Y - \hat{Y})^2$. The smaller the squared deviation, the closer the line comes to that point.

FIGURE 20.5
Scatter plot for data in Table 20.1.

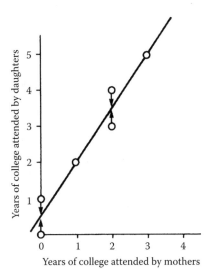

According to the **least-squares criterion,** the best-fitting straight line is the one that minimizes the sum of the squared deviations between the actual Y values and the predicted values. In symbols, the best-fitting straight line is the one with the minimum

$$\Sigma(Y - \hat{Y})^2$$

The sum of the squared deviations is also called **sum of squares of error** or **SSE.**

The least-squares regression line, the line that minimizes SSE, is found by calculating the least-squares slope, $\hat{m}$, and the least-squares Y-intercept, $\hat{b}$. The symbol "^" (a hat) is used to indicate that these are statistics, not parameters.

FORMULA 20.1   Least-squares Slope, $\hat{m}$

$$\hat{m} = \frac{n_p \Sigma XY - \Sigma X \Sigma Y}{n_p \Sigma X^2 - (\Sigma X)^2} = \frac{SP_{XY}}{SS(X)}$$

$$SP_{XY} = \Sigma XY - n_p M_X M_Y$$

The quantity ΣXY is found by multiplying each X by the corresponding Y and summing the products.

▌▌▌▌▌▌▌

FORMULA 20.2   Least-squares Y-intercept, $\hat{b}$

$$\hat{b} = M_y - \hat{m}M_x$$

M_x is, of course, the mean of the Xs, and M_y is the mean of the Ys.

Then, the least-squares regression line is

$$\hat{Y} = \hat{m}X + \hat{b}$$

Because regression analyses can require calculations using very large numbers, it is best to do as little rounding as possible. Use of these formulas is illustrated in Table 20.1. Thus for the example, the least-squares regression line is

$$\hat{Y} = 1.5(X) + .5$$

Drawing the Regression Line

The regression line can be superimposed on the scatter plot. Because a straight line is completely determined by any two of its points, the regression line is drawn by connecting any two points that satisfy the formula $\hat{Y} = \hat{m}X + \hat{b}$.

One point on the line is the Y-intercept, given by $\hat{b}$. That is, the point at $X = 0$, $Y = \hat{b}$ will always be on the line. In our example, $\hat{b} = .5$, so one point on the line is $X = 0$, $Y = .5$. To find a second point on the regression line, insert any value for X in the regression equation and solve for $\hat{Y}$. For the example, if we insert a "2" for X,

$$\hat{Y} = (1.5)(2) + .5 = 3.5$$

Thus, a second point on the line is $X = 2$, $Y = 3.5$. The line connecting these two points is guaranteed to minimize SSE; that is, the line minimizes the distances between the line (values of $\hat{Y}$) and the real values of Y.[3]

Standard Error of Estimate

Even though the regression line is the "best-fitting," not all of the data points fall on the straight line. In other words, SSE is not zero. The standard error of estimate, $s_{y \cdot x}$ (read s y dot x) is an index of the spread of the points around the line. The definitional formula is

---

[3] The least-squares regression line will also pass through the point (M_x, M_y); thus, this point can also be used in constructing the line.

$$s_{Y \cdot X} = \sqrt{\frac{SSE}{n_p - 2}}$$

The subscript $Y \cdot X$ is used to distinguish this standard deviation from related ones. Note that $s_{Y \cdot X}$ is *not* the standard deviation of the real Ys, nor is it the standard deviation of the real Xs, nor is it the standard deviation of the $\hat{Y}$ s. Instead, it is an index of the deviations between the real Ys and the $\hat{Y}$ s (the line). You may think of it as approximating the average deviation of each point from the line.

The standard error of estimate can be used as a descriptive statistic to convey the spread of the points around the line: the smaller the spread of the points around the line, the smaller the value of $s_{Y \cdot X}$ and the better fitting the line. As we will see shortly, $s_{Y \cdot X}$ is also used in making statistical inferences.

The definitional formula for $s_{Y \cdot X}$ is deceptively simple, but applying it to real data can be very tiresome; note that it requires computing a $\hat{Y}$ for each data point, getting a difference, and squaring the difference. The computational formula is frightful looking, but much less work.

▬▬▬▬▬▬

FORMULA 20.3   Computational formula for $s_{Y \cdot X}$

$$s_{Y \cdot X} = \sqrt{\frac{1}{n_p - 2}\left(SS(Y) - \frac{SP_{XY}^2}{SS(X)}\right)}$$

Use of this formula is illustrated in Table 20.1.

Interpreting the Regression Line

The regression line describes the linear relationship between the Xs (number of years of college attended by mothers) and the Ys (number of years of college attended by their daughters). Like any other descriptive statistic, the regression line holds only for these specific samples: Until you have completed inferential statistical tests demonstrating that the populations are linearly related, you should not make any claims regarding the populations. In addition, you should not attempt to predict a Y value for a new X (a mother not in the sample) until you demonstrate that the linear relation holds in the populations.

Even so, the regression line provides an informative description of the relationship between X and Y in these samples. First, there is a direct linear relationship: The more years a mother (in the sample) attended college, the more years her daughter tends to attend college. Furthermore, from the specific value of $\hat{m}$, we learn that these daughters tend to go to college for longer than their mothers: For each year a mother spends in college, her daughter tends to spend 1.5 years in college. From $\hat{b}$ we can tell that the daughters tend to go to college, even when their mothers do not: Even when the mothers do not attend college ($X = 0$), the daughters tend to attend some college ($\hat{b} = .50$).

Do these results imply a causal link between X and Y? For two reasons, the answer is no. First, claims about causal links require the demonstration that the relation holds in the populations, not just the samples. Second, claims about causal links require experimental control, and, in particular, random assignment to conditions (see Chapter 14). In this study, mothers were not randomly assigned to number of years of college attended, nor were the daughters randomly assigned to the mothers. Thus, there is no warrant for making causal claims. Linear relationships and causality are discussed again at the end of the next section and in Chapter 21 in the section, Correlation Does Not Prove Causation.

PRECAUTIONS IN REGRESSION (AND CORRELATION) ANALYSIS

Regression (and correlation) analysis should not be applied blindly; there are situations in which application of the formulas will lead to inaccurate descriptions of the data. In this section, we discuss some of these situations.

Linear Regression (and Correlation) Measure Only Linear Relationships

Formulas 20.1 and 20.2 will always give the slope and the intercept of the best-fitting line, but sometimes a line is an inappropriate description of the relationship (see Figures 20.2 and 20.4D). You can avoid this problem by constructing a scatter plot. If the relation between X and Y is curvilinear, consult a more advanced textbook for suggestions on describing the relationship.

Restricted Range

Figure 20.6 illustrates a linear relationship. Suppose, however, that the sample of Xs had been restricted to the values between the two vertical lines. Within this range, there is little linear relationship. Analysis of the data from this restricted range would be accurate in that it would indicate no linear relationship (within that range). However, the analysis is inaccurate to the extent that it misses the linear relationship over the whole range. Restricting the range of the Ys has the same unfortunate effect.

As an example, suppose that there is a linear relationship between age (X) and problem-solving ability (Y). A developmental psychologist investigating problem solving may miss this relationship if the sample of ages is restricted to, say, children 10–13 years of age, whereas a less restricted range of ages, say, 5–15, may well reveal the relationship.

Extreme Scores

Figure 20.7 illustrates a situation in which application of Formulas 20.1 and 20.2 would indicate a linear relationship when, for the most part, there is none. The single extreme

FIGURE 20.6
A linear relationship may go undetected if the sample contains a restricted range of X values or Y values.

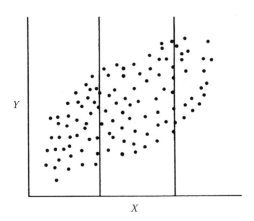

FIGURE 20.7
An extreme score (in the upper right) may simulate a linear relationship when there is none for the majority of the scores.

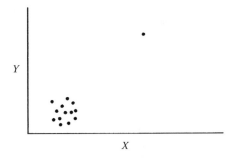

score in the upper right-hand corner is enough to pull up the regression line so that it has a nonzero slope.

The situation illustrated in Figure 20.7 might arise for a variety of reasons. One reason is that an observation from a different population is inadvertently included in the scores. Also, this situation is more likely to occur when the sample size is small. With large samples, the majority of the observations will overwhelm the extreme score. As with curvilinear relationships, the problem can be detected by examining the scatter plot.

Combined Groups

Combining scores from different groups can greatly distort a regression analysis. The problem is illustrated (with hypothetical data) in Figure 20.8. This figure indicates a generally positive relationship between the age of widowers and their desire to remarry (the

FIGURE 20.8
Combining data from different groups may distort linear relationships. In this figure, two positive relationships produce a negative relationship when combined.

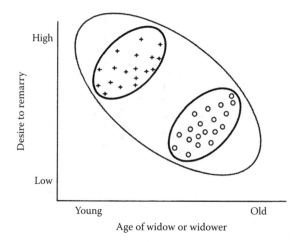

Age of widow or widower

crosses). The figure also indicates a generally positive relationship between the age of widows and their desire to remarry (the circles). However, when the two groups are combined, the relationship between age and desire to remarry is negative!

Once again, a scatter plot (in which different symbols are used for the different groups) should be used to detect the problem. Be cautious: Inappropriate combination of data across groups can lead to every imaginable type of distortion.

In the Media: Making Money With Regression

If only we could accurately predict the future, imagine how rich we could become by making just the right moves in the stock and bond markets. Regression is designed for prediction, and because of that it is a favorite tool of economists, as illustrated in an article by Louis Uchitelle, "Putting a Number to the Monthly Gyration in Bonds," reported in the *New York Times,* August 3, 1996. The article describes work by Alan B. Krueger, a labor economist at Princeton University, who developed an equation for predicting changes in the 30-year Treasury bond using monthly data from 1979. The data consisted of pairs of observations for each month, in which the X-variable is a fraction of the difference between the predicted number of new jobs (for the next month) and the actual number of new jobs announced by the Labor Department. The Y-variable is the change in bond rate. Although the article does not state this explicitly, it is almost certainly the case that Krueger used least-squares regression to develop the equation. According to the article, "For every difference of 200,000 jobs between the forecast and the actual number, the interest rate on the 30-year Treasury bond moves 8 basis points—or eight-hundredths of a percentage point—going down when the forecasters overestimate job creation and up when more jobs are created than the forecasters had expected." This description is a bit confusing, but it can be translated into a simple regression equation. First, consider the X-variable: X = (actual number of jobs created – predicted number of jobs)/200,000. Remember that the slope of a line indicates the change in y for each change in X. According to the article, for each difference of 200,000 jobs (the X-variable), there is a change in the Treasury rate of "eight-hundredths of a percentage point" or .0008, and that is the $\hat{m}$. Because there is no mention in the article of anything corresponding to a Y-intercept, $\hat{b}$ is likely to be 0.0. So, the regression equation is:

$$\text{Change in bond interest rate} = .0008X + 0.0$$

Thus, we can use this formula to predict monthly changes in the bond interest rate. Should you use this formula to bet your life savings on the bond market? There are several reasons to be skeptical. First, accurate prediction depends on having a random sample from the populations. Instead, the formula is based on data from a particular time period, rather than a random sample from all time periods (past, present, and future!). Second, prediction depends on rejecting the null hypothesis so that you have some confidence that the equation holds for the populations, not just this sample. The article does not indicate whether any null hypothesis has been rejected (yet alone a value for α). Third, the formula gives only a point estimate, whereas a much more informative predictor would a confidence interval. The article does not provide enough information (for example, $s_{y \cdot x}$) needed to construct a confidence interval. To its credit, the rest of the article does raise some cautionary notes related to these three reasons for skepticism. "Right off, Mr. Krueger, ever the cautious academic, makes clear that his method ... does not always work, particularly in these days of great skittishness and emotion over the economy. 'There is a lot of unexplained movement in the markets,' Mr. Krueger said, acknowledging that no formula, no matter how well founded in scholarship, can factor in uncertainty."

INFERENCES ABOUT THE SLOPE OF THE REGRESSION LINE

This section discusses the procedures for using random samples to make inferences about the slope of the regression line relating the scores in two populations. The procedure is discussed within the framework of a new example, and the procedure is summarized at the end of the chapter in Table 20.4.

A clinical psychologist is investigating the claim that there is a relationship between the amount of sugar eaten and hyperactivity in young children. He obtains a random sample of 20 children (and their parents) from among the volunteers at a local school district. Each parent is asked to record everything the child eats during a 1-week observation period. From this record, the psychologist determines the amount of sugar consumed. Each parent also records the activity level of the child: Each night of the week, the parent measures the amount of time the child is active (locomoting) during a 30-minute observation period. For each child, the amount of sugar consumed is X, and the time active is Y. The data are in Table 20.2 and the scatter plot in Figure 20.9.

Because the scatter plot indicates that the relationship is approximately linear, Formulas 20.1 and 20.2 can be used to find the least-squares regression line. The computations

TABLE 20.2
Sugar Consumption and Activity Scores for 20 Children

Child	Amount of Sugar (X)	Activity Score (Y)	XY
1	1	4	4
2	4	24	96
3	3	11	33
4	1	18	18
5	2	6	12
6	5	24	120
7	1	8	8
8	1	9	9
9	5	16	80
10	3	20	60
11	1	11	11
12	2	15	30
13	3	16	48
14	1	13	13
15	3	15	45
16	5	23	115
17	5	22	110
18	4	12	48
19	5	28	140
20	1	14	14
	$n_X = 20$	$n_Y = 20$	$\Sigma XY = 1014$
	$\Sigma X = 56$	$\Sigma Y = 309$	
	$\Sigma X^2 = 208$	$\Sigma Y^2 = 5583$	
	$M_X = 2.80$	$M_Y = 15.45$	
	$SS(X) = 51.2$	$SS(Y) = 808.95$	

$$SP_{XY} = \Sigma XY - n_p M_X M_Y = 1014 - 20(2.80)(15.45) = 148.8$$

$$\hat{m} = \frac{SP_{XY}}{SS(X)} = \frac{148.8}{51.2} = 2.906$$

$$\hat{b} = M_Y - \hat{m}M_X = 15.45 - 2.906(2.80) = 7.313$$

$$\hat{Y} = 2.906X + 7.313$$

$$s_{Y \cdot X} = \sqrt{\frac{1}{n_p - 2}\left(SS(Y) - \frac{SP_{XY}^2}{SS(X)}\right)} = \sqrt{\frac{1}{18}\left(808.95 - \frac{148.8^2}{51.2}\right)} = 4.573$$

are in Table 20.2, and the resulting regression line is illustrated in Figure 20.9. There is a positive (direct) relationship between the samples of Xs and the Ys: the more sugar consumed, the more active the child.

FIGURE 20.9
Scatter plot for data in Table 20.2, and the least-squares regression line.

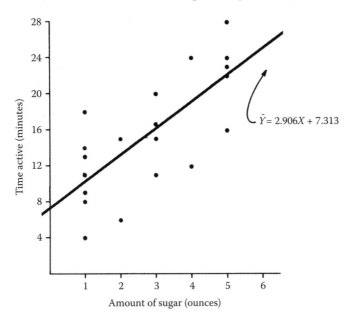

Now, is there enough evidence to conclude that the linear relationship holds in the populations as well as in these samples? The six-step logic of hypothesis testing will be used to answer this question. The null hypothesis will be about the slope of the regression line relating the two populations. Remember, if the slope is not zero, then there is a linear relationship.

Step 1: Assumptions

Population Assumptions

1. The population of Xs and the population of Ys are normally distributed.[4] Because the t statistic (which we will use) is robust, you may ignore this assumption as long as the populations are relatively mound-shaped and symmetrical.
2. The variance of the Ys is the same at each value of X. This condition is called **homoscedasticity.** The robustness of the t statistic can be counted on to overcome mild violations of this assumption.

Looking at the scatter plot in Figure 20.9, it appears that homoscedasticity in the populations is a good bet. Note that the spread of the Y values is about the same at each value of X.

---

[4] Technically, the assumption is more constraining: The distribution of the Ys should be normal at each value of X.

Sampling Assumptions

1. The samples must be dependent. This assumption is met because each child's sugar consumption score (X) can be matched with that child's activity score (Y).
2. Both samples must be obtained using independent (within-sample) random sampling. This assumption is met because the sugar consumption scores are unrelated to each other (they come from unrelated children), and the activity scores are unrelated to each other.

Data Assumption   The observations are measured using an interval or a ratio scale. Meeting this assumption guarantees that the results will be interpretable. In the example, both the Xs and the Ys are measured using ratio scales.

Step 2: Hypotheses

The general form of the null hypothesis is

$$H_0: m = m_0$$

The symbol m without "^" stands for the slope of the regression line relating the two populations. The symbol m_0 is the value of m specified by H_0. Although any value can be used for m_0, usually it is 0. Thus, for our example,

$$H_0: m = 0$$

If this null is rejected, then we conclude that there is a linear relationship between the scores in the two populations.

The alternative hypothesis can be any of three forms,

$$H_1: m \neq m_0$$
$$H_1: m < m_0$$
$$H_1: m > m_0$$

As usual, choose a directional alternative only if you have absolutely no interest in the outcome if the other directional alternative is correct.

For the sugar and activity example, the nondirectional alternative is the most reasonable, because it would be interesting to find a positive or a negative relationship between sugar consumption and activity. You may object that the data in Figure 20.9 indicate a positive relationship between X and Y, so why not use the directional alternative to gain power? Remember, however, that logically choice of the alternative (in Step 2) comes before examination of the data (in Step 5), and that the choice should reflect your sincere interests, not the form of the data. Because the psychologist is interested in detecting a positive or a negative relationship between the two populations, the nondirectional alternative is appropriate, even if he suspects that the relationship is positive.

Step 3: Sampling Distributions

Amazingly, the sampling distribution of the statistic $\hat{m}$ is normally distributed.[5] What is more, when the null hypothesis is correct, the mean of the sampling distribution is guaranteed to equal m_0. And, finally, an estimate of the standard deviation of the sampling distribution, $s_{\hat{m}}$, can be computed.

Recall from Chapter 12 that whenever you have a statistic that has a normal sampling distribution, and you know the mean of the sampling distribution, and you can estimate the variance, then you can form the t statistic. Indeed, in this case,

$$t = \frac{\hat{m} - m_0}{s_{\hat{m}}}$$

$$df = n_p - 2$$

In other words, although you are testing hypotheses about the slope of the regression line, the test statistic is the t statistic.

When the null hypothesis is correct, the most likely values for t are around 0.0. However, when H_0 is incorrect and the alternative is correct, the most likely values of t are discrepant from zero. Stated differently, a t discrepant from 0.0 is evidence against H_0, whereas a t near 0.0 is consistent with H_0.

Step 4: Set α and the Decision Rule

As usual, setting α is a personal decision: What probability of Type I errors are you willing to tolerate? And, as always, your decision has both obvious and hidden consequences. Obviously, you want to make α small to avoid Type I errors. Nonetheless, decreasing α increases β, the probability of a Type II error. Let us suppose that the psychologist sets $\alpha = .05$ for the sugar and activity data.

The decision rule is, except for the degrees of freedom, exactly as in Chapter 12 for the single-sample t test. For the nondirectional alternative,

Reject H_0 if $t \le -t_{\alpha/2}$ or if $t \ge t_{\alpha/2}$ or
Reject H_0 if p-value $\le \alpha$

where t has $n_p - 2$ degrees of freedom.

For the directional alternative H_1: $m < m_0$,

Reject H_0 if $t \le -t_\alpha$ or
Reject H_0 if p-value $\le \alpha$

and for H_1: $m > m_0$

---

[5] Imagine taking many pairs of dependent samples from the population of Xs and the population of Ys. For each pair of samples, compute $\hat{M}$. With enough pairs of samples, the relative frequency distribution of $\hat{M}$ is virtually guaranteed to be a normal distribution.

$$\text{Reject } H_0 \text{ if } t \geq t_\alpha \text{ or}$$
$$\text{Reject } H_0 \text{ if } p\text{-value} \leq \alpha$$

For the example, the alternative is nondirectional, $\alpha = .05$, and $\alpha/2 = .025$. For 18 $(n_p - 2)$ df, $t_{\alpha/2} = 2.101$. Therefore,

$$\text{Reject } H_0 \text{ if } t \leq -2.101 \text{ or if } t \geq 2.101 \text{ or}$$
$$\text{Reject } H_0 \text{ if } p\text{-value} \leq .025$$

Step 5: Sample and Compute the Test Statistic

The formula for t is

$$t = \frac{\hat{m} - m_0}{s_{\hat{m}}}$$

We have already calculated $\hat{m}$ (see Table 20.2) and $m_0 = 0$ (as specified by H_0). The only remaining term is $s_{\hat{m}}$, the estimate of the standard deviation of the sampling distribution of $\hat{m}$. The formula is

$$s_{\hat{m}} = s_{Y \cdot X} \sqrt{\frac{1}{SS(X)}}$$

Using the value of $s_{Y \cdot X}$ computed in Table 20.2,

$$s_{\hat{m}} = 4.573 \sqrt{\frac{1}{51.2}} = 0.639$$

The t statistic for the example is

$$t = \frac{2.906 - 0}{.639} = 4.547$$

Step 6: Decide and Draw Conclusions

The test statistic is in the rejection region, so the null hypothesis can be rejected. We can conclude that in the populations there is a positive (or direct) relationship between amount of sugar consumed and time spent active: the more sugar consumed, the more time the child is active.

Of course, you would not want to overgeneralize. Statistically, the results apply only for the populations sampled, that is, only for the children in the specific school system, and, really, only for the children of parents who volunteered for the study.

If there is a linear relationship between the Xs and the Ys, why are most of the data points off the regression line (see Figure 20.9)? There are two sources of "error variability" that move the points off the line. First, there is variability produced by errors in measurement.

In this example, it would be difficult to measure exactly the amount of sugar consumed (suppose one of the children ate a candy bar unobserved) and the time spent active (does sliding from one end of a couch to the other count as locomotion?). Second, there is variability introduced by individual differences. For example, some children may be more sensitive to sugar than others. Thus, the linear relation is one that holds in general, whereas a specific individual may deviate from the regression line.

Possible Errors

As always, the inferences made using hypothesis testing may be in error. Given that H_0 is rejected, there is some probability of a Type I error (concluding that there is a linear relationship between the populations when there really is none). Of course, this probability is small because it equals α.

When H_0 is not rejected, there is some probability of a Type II error (not rejecting H_0 when there really is a linear relationship in the populations). The probability of a Type II error can be decreased (power increased) by many of the usual procedures: Increase α, increase the sample size, decrease variability by careful measurement of the Xs and the Ys, and appropriately use directional alternatives.

Some of the problems discussed in the section Precautions in Regression (and Correlation) Analysis (p. 454) can also reduce the probability of detecting a linear relationship between populations. In particular, the restricted range and combined-groups problems may hide real linear relationships. A more formal power analyses for detecting linear relationships is presented in Chapter 21.

Regression and Causation

The significant linear relationship between amount of sugar and activity does not imply a causal link. To demonstrate a causal link you need experimental control, including random assignment. Without experimental control, the relationship between the Xs and the Ys may arise for any of three reasons.

1. It *may* be that changes in X cause changes in Y. For the example, it may be that eating sugar causes an increase in activity.
2. It *may* be that changes in Y cause changes in X. It may be that an increase in activity causes eating of sugar—because the children are so active, they become hungry and eat more.
3. It *may* be that a third variable produced the relationship between X and Y. For example, some parents may encourage both consumption of sugar and active play.

The point is that demonstrating a linear relationship in the populations (rejecting H_0: $m = 0$) is not sufficient to demonstrate a causal link. Experimental procedures, random assignment in particular, are also needed.

Based on the statistical analysis, the psychologist could tell parents of hyperactive children that a decrease in sugar *might* help their children to be less active. Because a causal link has not been established, however, there is no guarantee that limiting sugar will have the desired effect.

USING THE REGRESSION LINE FOR PREDICTION

Regression analysis can be followed by construction of confidence intervals for the slope, the Y-intercept, predictions of means (for example, the mean amount of time active for all children who eat 4 ounces of sugar), and predictions of individual scores (for example, the amount of time active for a particular child who eats 4 ounces of sugar). In this section, we address only the last of these options.

One of the major uses of regression analyses is for prediction. Once a linear relation is established for the populations, the regression line can be used to predict a $\hat{Y}$ for a new X drawn from the same population as that used to establish the line. As examples, regression is used in weather prediction, college admissions (predicting grades in college from high school grades), and economic forecasting.

The general procedure for prediction has three steps. First, determine that there is a linear relationship in the populations (reject H_0 using the t test). Second, use the regression line to compute a point estimate, $\hat{Y}$, for the new X. Finally, construct a confidence interval around $\hat{Y}$. This interval will have a specific probability (the confidence) of including the real value of Y, and thus constitutes your prediction. The procedure is summarized in Table 20.5 at the end of the chapter.

Point Estimation

For concreteness, consider the following example. An industrial psychologist is designing a screening test to help a large computer company select creative programmers. His plan is to first gather data on the relationship between performance on the screening test and creativity. If the relationship is linear, he will use that relationship to help select creative programmers in the future.

For the test, the psychologist times 15 new programmers while they attempt to correct faulty computer programs. During the next year, a supervisor counts the number of creative programming solutions developed by each of the 15 new employees. The 15 pairs of scores are listed in Table 20.3, and the scatter plot is shown in Figure 20.10.

The psychologist used Formulas 20.1 and 20.2 to compute the regression line (see Table 20.3). He tested

$$H_0: m = 0$$

$$H_1: m \neq 0$$

using $\alpha = .05$. The decision rule was

$$\text{Reject } H_0 \text{ if } t \leq -2.16 \text{ or if } t \geq 2.16$$

TABLE 20.3
Test Score (in minutes) and Number of Creative Solutions the Next Year for 15 New Programmers

Programmer	Test Score (X)	Number of Solutions (Y)	XY
1	15	8	120
2	21	7	147
3	56	5	280
4	50	4	200
5	75	2	150
6	46	5	230
7	69	3	207
8	20	3	60
9	73	4	292
10	32	5	160
11	63	6	378
12	21	8	168
13	60	3	180
14	30	7	210
15	22	6	132
	$n_X = 15$	$n_Y = 15$	$\Sigma XY = 2914$
	$\Sigma X = 653$	$\Sigma Y = 76$	
	$\Sigma X^2 = 34951$	$\Sigma Y^2 = 436$	
	$M_X = 43.533$	$M_Y = 5.067$	
	$SS(X) = 6523.73$	$SS(Y) = 50.883$	

$$SP_{XY} = \Sigma XY - n_p M_X M_Y = 2914 - 15(43.533)(5.067) = -394.73$$

$$\hat{m} = \frac{SP_{XY}}{SS(X)} = \frac{-394.73}{6523.73} = -0.60$$

$$\hat{b} = M_Y - \hat{m}M_X = 5.067 - (-0.06)(43.533) = 7.679$$

$$\hat{Y} = -0.06X + 7.679$$

He then computed

$$s_{Y \cdot X} = \sqrt{\frac{1}{n_p - 2}\left(SS(Y) - \frac{SP_{XY}^2}{SS(X)}\right)} = \sqrt{\frac{1}{13}\left(50.883 - \frac{(-394.73)^2}{6523.73}\right)} = 1.441$$

$$s_{\hat{m}} = s_{Y \cdot X}\sqrt{\frac{1}{SS(X)}} = 1.441\sqrt{\frac{1}{6523.73}} = 0.018$$

and

FIGURE 20.10
Scatter plot for data in Table 20.3, the least-squares regression line, and the 95% confidence interval for Y when $X = 32$.

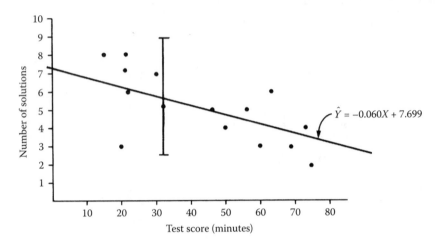

$$t = \frac{-.060 - 0}{.018} = -3.38$$

Because t is in the rejection region, he concluded that there is a linear relationship between the population of test scores and the population of number of creative solutions.[6]

Now, suppose that the computer company wishes to hire a new employee, and the psychologist is told to be sure to hire a programmer who is likely to produce at least two creative solutions a year. How can the psychologist predict the number of creative solutions for a new programmer?

The psychologist gives the screening test to a prospective new employee. Suppose her score is 32 minutes. Using the regression equation (from Table 20.3), the psychologist can predict (estimate) the number of creative solutions for that employee,

$$\hat{Y} = (-.060)(32) + 7.699$$

$$= 5.779$$

Given the data on hand, this point estimate is the single best guess for the number of creative solutions this prospective employee will contribute. As with other types of point

---

[6] Note that this conclusion is not strictly warranted, because the random sampling assumption was not met. That is, no attempt was made to randomly sample from the population of the scores of new programmers. In this case, the regression equation provides a description of the linear relationship between the two *samples,* but it is a leap of faith to conclude, even after the "significant" t test, that the linear relationship holds for the populations.

estimates, however, it is unlikely to be exactly correct. In fact, looking at Figure 20.10, you can see that other employees who scored around 32 minutes on the screening test had a range of creative solutions.

Confidence Interval for Predictions

The confidence interval for the prediction specifies a range (interval) of Y values and a confidence. The confidence is the probability that the interval will include the actual Y value (that we are trying to predict).

The width of the interval is affected by three factors. First, the greater the confidence, the wider the interval. Second, the greater the deviations of the points around the regression line (as reflected by $s_{Y \cdot X}$), the wider the interval. If the actual Y values are all close to the regression line (the predicted values), then the interval need not be very wide to be likely to include the actual Y value for the new X. On the other hand, if the real Y values are scattered about the line (as in Figure 20.10), then the confidence interval must be wide if it is to have a high probability of including the actual Y value for the new programmer. Third, the width of the interval depends on the particular value of X for which a prediction is being made. This particular value of X is called X_p. The greater the distance between X_p and M_x, the wider the confidence interval.

As usual, choice of level of confidence, $1 - \alpha$, is up to you. Once that decision is made, the formulas are

■■■■■■■■■

FORMULA 20.3   Confidence Limits for Y

$$\text{Upper Limit} = \hat{Y} + (t_{\alpha/2})(s_{Y \cdot X})\sqrt{1 + \frac{1}{n_p} + \frac{(X_p - M_X)}{SS(X)}}$$

$$\text{Lower Limit} = \hat{Y} - (t_{\alpha/2})(s_{Y \cdot X})\sqrt{1 + \frac{1}{n_p} + \frac{(X_p - M_X)}{SS(X)}}$$

$t_{\alpha/2}$ is the t statistic with $n_p - 2$ df that has $\alpha/2$ of the distribution above it.

The confidence interval is

$$\text{Lower Limit} \leq Y \leq \text{Upper Limit}$$

Note that the confidence interval is for the real value of Y, even though its computation used the predicted value, $\hat{Y}$.

The psychologist must determine if the prospective programmer is likely to produce at least two creative solutions a year. He decides that "likely" means a probability of at least .95, and thus he constructs a 95% confidence interval. For the 95% interval, $\alpha = .05$, and $t_{\alpha/2} = 2.16$. This t value is based on 13 df ($n_p - 2$) because the regression line we are using for prediction was constructed from 15 pairs of observations (see Table 20.3). Using

$s_{Y \cdot X} = 1.441$ (calculated previously) and $X_p = 32$ (the prospective employee's score on the screening test),

$$\text{Upper Limit} = 5.779 + (2.16)(1.441)\sqrt{1 + \frac{1}{15} + \frac{(32 - 43.533)^2}{6523.73}} = 9.024$$

$$\text{Lower Limit} = 5.779 - (2.16)(1.441)\sqrt{1 + \frac{1}{15} + \frac{(32 - 43.533)^2}{6523.73}} = 2.533$$

So, the 95% confidence interval is

$$2.533 \leq Y \leq 9.024$$

Interpreting the Confidence Interval

Remember, the probability statement attaches to the confidence interval, not to the quantity being estimated. Thus, when the assumptions are met, the probability is .95 that the interval includes the *real* number of creative solutions (Y not $\hat{Y}$) that the prospective employee will make.

Should the psychologist hire the prospective employee? Is she likely to produce at least two creative solutions in a year? The psychologist's best guess for the number of creative solutions the programmer will produce in the next year is 5.779, and the lower confidence limit extends down to 2.533. Because the lower limit is greater than 2.0, the psychologist can be confident (95% confidence) that this programmer will produce at least two creative solutions.

Precautions When Predicting

Prediction is fraught with possible pitfalls. Just consider how often weather predictions and stock market predictions, both of which use sophisticated forms of regression, are in error. Taking the following precautions will help you to avoid some pitfalls.

First, examine the scatter plot for signs of nonlinearity, extreme scores, or distortion due to combining data across groups. If there are any of these signs, prediction based on linear regression should not be used.

Second, make predictions only after rejecting H_0: $m = 0$, and thereby demonstrating that a linear relationship holds in the populations. Meeting the assumptions for testing H_0 guarantees that the assumptions are met for prediction.

Third, construct confidence intervals for your predictions. Generating a point estimate gives a false sense of accuracy. The confidence interval will illustrate the range of probable values for Y.

Fourth, make predictions for values of X only from the original population. This is another way of saying do not overgeneralize. Rejecting H_0 demonstrates a linear relationship between the populations randomly sampled, but no others. It would be foolhardy to attempt to use the regression equation to make predictions for other populations. Consider again the programming example. Because experienced programmers were not included in the population sampled (population of scores of new programmers), there is no guarantee that the regression equation will accurately predict creative solutions for experienced programmers.

Fifth, do not make predictions for values of X outside the range of X values in the original sample. Because the relationship may be nonlinear outside of the original range, predictions are not warranted. For example, suppose that the prospective computer programmer finished the test in 5 minutes, a test score outside the range of the original test scores (see Figure 20.10). If the relationship between test score and creativity is linear down to 5 minutes, then we would predict many creative solutions for this programmer. However, suppose the linear relationship breaks down for short test times because the short times indicate people who do not take the test seriously. In this case, a score of 5 minutes on the test may be associated with few creative solutions. The point is that we cannot determine if the linear relationship holds outside the range of the original X values, so prediction is inappropriate.

Sixth, do not use the same regression line to predict X from a new Y. Remember, the regression line is constructed to minimize deviations of $\hat{Y}$ from the real values of Y. However, this regression line does not necessarily minimize the deviations of predicted values of X from real values of X. If you wish to make predictions for X, switch the labels on the variables (so that what was X is now Y), and recompute the regression line and $s_{Y \cdot X}$.

MULTIPLE REGRESSION

Up to now, we have discussed finding a relationship between a single predictor variable, X, and the predicted variable, Y. Multiple regression is a procedure for finding relations between many predictor variables (X_1, X_2, and so on) and Y.

For example, predictions of college grade point average (Y) can be based on high school grade point (X_1), class rank (X_2), and an index of quality of high school program (X_3). For another example, predictions of satisfaction with salary (Y) can be based on actual salary (X_1), years of training (X_2), and standard of living (X_3).

When using multiple regression, the regression equation takes the general form

$$\hat{Y} = \hat{m}_1 X_1 + \hat{m}_2 X_2 + \ldots + \hat{m}_i X_i + b$$

The coefficients (for example, $\hat{m}_1$ and $\hat{m}_2$) are generally not the same values that would be obtained if you calculated a separate regression for each predictor variable. Instead, these coefficients indicate the relationship between the individual predictor variable and Y, taking into account the relationship between all of the other predictor variables and Y. The sign of a coefficient does indicate, however, whether the predictor variable has a direct or indirect relationship to Y.

Multiple regression has a major advantage over single-variable regression: Predictions of Y will generally be more accurate using multiple regression because more data go into making the prediction. An advanced text should be consulted for the many details involved in multiple regression.

SUMMARY

As a descriptive statistical technique, linear regression is used to find the best-fitting linear relationship between two dependent samples. The relationship is linear if the scatter plot can be approximated by a straight line of nonzero slope. According to the least-squares criterion, the best-fitting straight line is the one that minimizes the differences between the real data points in the scatter plot and the line. When the slope is positive, the relationship between X and Y is positive or direct; when the slope is negative, the relationship is negative or indirect.

Rejecting H_0: m = 0 using the t test indicates that the linear relationship holds in the populations. Without experimental control (random assignment in particular), however, you cannot conclude that the relationship is casual; X may cause Y, Y may cause X, or a third variable may cause both. Table 20.4 summarizes the procedure for testing hypotheses about m.

After demonstrating a linear relationship in the populations, the regression line may be used to predict values of Y for new values of X. The confidence interval for the prediction is a range of values with a guaranteed probability (the confidence) of including the actual Y. Table 20.5 summarizes the procedure for constructing a confidence interval for Y.

EXERCISES

Terms   *Define these new terms and symbols.*

linear regression	Y-intercept
correlation	m
slope	b
scatter plot	$\hat{m}$
direct or positive relationship	$\hat{b}$
indirect or negative relationship	$\hat{Y}$
homoscedasticity	m_0
restricted range	X_p

Questions   *Answer the following questions.*

†1. Find the least-squares regression line for the data in Table 20.6.

†2. Assuming that random samples were drawn, use the data in Table 20.6 to determine if a linear relationship exists in the populations.

†3. Use the data in Table 20.6 to construct 90% and 95% confidence intervals for predictions of Y when $X = 15$ and when $X = 45$. Compare the widths of the intervals.

TABLE 20.4
Testing for a Linear Relationship

1. **Assumptions:**

   Population assumptions:

   a. The population of Xs and the population of Ys are normally distributed (but see discussion of robustness).

   b. Homoscedasticity: the variance of the Ys is the same at each value of X (but see discussion of robustness).

   Sampling assumptions:

   a. The samples must be dependent.

   b. Both samples must be obtained using independent (within-sample) random sampling.

   Data assumption:

   The observations are measured using an interval or a ratio scale.

2. **Hypotheses:**

   Null hypothesis:

   $$H_0: m = m_0$$

   where m_0 is typically zero but can be any value.

   Alternatives available:

   $$H_1: m \neq m_0$$

   $$H_1: m < m_0$$

   $$H_1: m > m_0$$

3. **Test statistic and its sampling distribution:**

   The test statistic is

   $$t = \frac{\hat{m} - m_0}{s_{\hat{m}}}$$

   $$df = n_p - 2, \quad \hat{m} = \frac{SP_{XY}}{SS(X)}, \quad s_{\hat{m}} = s_{Y \cdot X} \sqrt{\frac{1}{SS(X)}}$$

   $$s_{Y \cdot X} = \sqrt{\frac{1}{n_p - 2}\left(SS(Y) - \frac{SP_{XY}^2}{SS(X)}\right)}$$

   When H_0 is correct, the most likely values for t are around 0.0. When H_1 is correct, the most likely values for t are discrepant with 0.0.

4. **Decision rule:**

   For $H_1: m \neq m_0$:

   $$\text{Reject } H_0 \text{ if } t \leq -t_{\alpha/2} \text{ or if } t \geq t_{\alpha/2}$$

   For $H_1: m < m_0$:

   $$\text{Reject } H_0 \text{ if } t \leq -t_\alpha$$

   For $H_1: m > m_0$:

   $$\text{Reject } H_0 \text{ if } t \geq t_\alpha \text{ or}$$
   $$\text{Reject } H_0 \text{ if } p\text{-value} \leq \alpha$$

5. **Sample and compute t.**

6. **Decide and draw conclusions:**

   If $H_0: m = 0$ is rejected, conclude that there is a linear relationship between the scores in the two populations. Positive values of $\hat{m}$ imply a positive or direct relationship; negative values of $\hat{m}$ imply a negative or indirect relationship. Causal links are not demonstrated unless random assignment has been used.

TABLE 20.5
Confidence Interval for the Prediction of Y

1. **Assumptions:**

   Population assumptions: The null hypothesis, H_0: $m = 0$, has been rejected.

   Sampling assumption: The new X (for which Y is being predicted) is sampled from the same population as that used to construct the regression line.

2. **Set the confidence level, $1 - \alpha$.**

3. **Sample the new value of X, X_p.**

4. **Construct the interval:**

$$\text{Upper Limit} = \hat{Y} + (t_{\alpha/2})(s_{Y \cdot X})\sqrt{1 + \frac{1}{n_p} + \frac{(X_p - M_X)}{SS(X)}}$$

$$\text{Lower Limit} = \hat{Y} - (t_{\alpha/2})(s_{Y \cdot X})\sqrt{1 + \frac{1}{n_p} + \frac{(X_p - M_X)}{SS(X)}}$$

$$s_{Y \cdot X} = \sqrt{\frac{1}{n_p - 2}\left(SS(Y) - \frac{SP_{XY}^2}{SS(X)}\right)}$$

where $\hat{Y}$ is computed using the regression equation, and $t_{\alpha/2}$ is the t statistic (with $n_p - 2$ df) that has $\alpha/2$ of the distribution above it.

The $1 - \alpha$ confidence interval is:

$$\text{Lower Limit} \leq Y \leq \text{Upper Limit}$$

5. **Interpretation:**

   The probability is $1 - \alpha$ that the interval includes the real value of Y for the particular value of $X(X_p)$. There is a probability of α that the interval does not include the real value of Y.

TABLE 20.6

Pair	X	Y	Pair	X	Y	Pair	X	Y
1	73	34	11	19	15	21	87	37
2	82	42	12	66	20	22	52	18
3	14	0	13	68	40	23	52	11
4	56	28	14	51	20	24	15	1
5	43	15	15	40	6	25	85	45
6	47	20	16	60	30	26	41	11
7	85	50	17	70	14	27	23	5
8	86	30	18	39	18	28	77	28
9	24	0	19	28	6	29	42	10
10	33	8	20	69	17	30	60	21

TABLE 20.7
Patient's Belief in Doctor's Competence and Number of Days of Therapy

Patient	Patient's Belief	Number of Days	Patient	Patient's Belief	Number of Days
1	5	8	14	9	6
2	8	6	15	3	11
3	8	8	16	1	10
4	7	5	17	9	7
5	6	9	18	8	6
6	4	11	19	3	9
7	2	9	20	9	7
8	9	6	21	9	8
9	10	5	22	5	12
10	8	9	23	6	10
11	7	8	24	4	11
12	7	8	25	8	6
13	8	7			

4. Explain why rejecting H_0: $m = 0$ indicates a linear relationship between the populations.

5. Why is it necessary to reject H_0: $m = 0$ before using the regression line to make predictions?

6. Make up four sets of data (each with $n_p = 6$) illustrating direct, indirect, curvilinear, and no relationship between the Xs and the Ys.

7. Using a random sample of married couples, a psychologist found a direct and statistically significant relationship between the husband's yearly income and the wife's satisfaction with the marriage. The psychologist argued that the most reasonable interpretation is that increases in the husband's income cause an increase in the wife's satisfaction with the marriage. What other causal links are just as consistent with these data? Formulate a reasonable context for each causal link.

For Questions 8–13, determine the most appropriate inferential statistical procedure, execute the procedure (be sure to indicate all components such as hypotheses, α, decision rule, and so on), and report your results and conclusions.

†**8.** Does the effectiveness of a drug depend on the patient's belief in the competence of his or her doctor? A psychologist studied a random sample of 25 patients undergoing a drug therapy. The psychologist measured the number of days needed for the drug to work and the patient's belief in the doctor's competence. The data are in Table 20.7.

†**9.** The data in Table 20.8 relate high school grade point average to college grade point average for a random sample of 10 students. You are asked to predict college grade point average for a student from the original population with a high school grade point average of 2.86.

†**10.** A psychologist measured the time to solve a problem under two conditions: with caffeine (from coffee) and without caffeine. Each of 15 randomly selected people

TABLE 20.8
GPAs for 10 Students

Student	High School GPA	College GPA
1	2.3	2.0
2	3.6	3.2
3	3.8	3.7
4	2.7	3.0
5	2.7	2.5
6	2.8	2.4
7	2.5	2.5
8	2.4	2.5
9	2.1	1.7
10	3.2	2.9

TABLE 20.9
Problem-solving Times (in minutes) for Two Conditions

Person	Time With Caffeine	Time Without Caffeine
1	14	7
2	8	6
3	11	6
4	12	5
5	15	14
6	13	10
7	10	9
8	9	7
9	11	8
10	12	11
11	16	13
12	7	11
13	8	10
14	8	9
15	9	13

was timed in both conditions on two separate days. The order of the conditions was randomly assigned for each person. The data are in Table 20.9. Determine if caffeine causes a difference in problem-solving time.

†11. Using the data in Table 20.9, determine if there is a linear relationship between problem solving with caffeine and problem solving without caffeine.

†12. You are investigating a possible connection between arthritis and alcohol consumption. You take a random sample of 10 patients with various degrees of arthritis and measure both the severity of arthritis and daily consumption of alcohol. The data are in Table 20.10. Is there a relationship between alcohol consumption and arthritis? Is there a causal link?

TABLE 20.10
Measured Arthritis and Alcohol Consumption for 10 Patients

Patient	Degree of Arthritis	Alcohol Consumption
1	3	0
2	7	5
3	5	8
4	7	6
5	4	6
6	2	4
7	3	3
8	1	0
9	6	7
10	2	2

TABLE 20.11
Measured Arthritis in Rats Fed Two Diets

Standard Ration	Alcohol + Standard Ration
0	4
1	2
3	6
2	3
2	4
3	2
1	4
4	5
0	3
2	1

†**13.** You are investigating a possible connection between arthritis and alcohol consumption. You take a random sample of 10 rats and feed them alcohol each day along with standard rations. Another random sample of 10 rats is fed only the standard rations. The data in Table 20.11 are the measured amount of arthritis in each rat. Is there a relationship between alcohol consumption and arthritis (does amount of alcohol consumed affect degree of arthritis)? Is there a causal link?

CHAPTER 21

Measuring the Strength of Linear Relationships: Correlation

*R*egression and correlation are both used to describe the relationship between two dependent samples (or populations). Regression is used to find the best-fitting straight line that relates the scores. Correlation is used to describe the *strength* of the linear relationship. In effect, correlation is a measure of how well the best-fitting straight line actually fits.

This chapter begins with a discussion of linear correlation and how to interpret correlation coefficients. The next section discusses making inferences about the correlation in populations. The chapter concludes with a presentation of alternative measures of correlation.

CORRELATION: DESCRIBING THE STRENGTH OF A LINEAR RELATIONSHIP

Many interesting scientific, medical, and societal questions can be framed in terms of correlations or relationships between two variables. For some examples, is there a relationship between a planet's chemical composition and its size? Is there a relationship between diet and susceptibility to particular diseases? Is there a relationship between the federal government's monetary policies and inflation? The correlation coefficient can be used as a measure of the strength of any of these relationships.

Measuring correlations is often used when random assignment is impossible or when many variables need to be considered. For example, it is difficult to imagine how planets could be randomly assigned chemical compositions (to determine if that causes their sizes). Also, consider all of the early experience variables that might influence an adult's behavior. You can determine which of these many early experience variables are actually related to adult behavior by computing the correlation between each early experience variable and adult behavior.

Although it has many advantages, correlational research has one great disadvantage compared to experimental research. Without random assignment, correlational research (including regression analyses) cannot be used to determine causal links. This fact is developed in detail in the section Correlation Does Not Prove Causation on page 489.

As with regression, correlational analyses can be applied only when the samples are dependent. Furthermore, when making inferences about populations, the samples should be obtained using independent (within-sample) random sampling. That is, the scores within a particular sample should be unrelated.

The Pearson Product–moment Correlation

The Pearson correlation is a measure of the strength of a linear relationship between two variables.[1] It can be applied to samples or populations. The letter r is used as the symbol for the statistic, and the Greek letter ρ (rho) is used as the symbol for the corresponding parameter. Both r and ρ have the following properties:

1. The correlation is always between −1 and 1, inclusive.
2. The sign of the correlation always corresponds to the sign of the slope of the regression line; regression lines with positive slopes always have positive correlation coefficients, regression lines with negative slopes always have negative correlation coefficients, and regression lines with zero slopes (no linear relationship) have a correlation of 0.0.

---

[1] Karl Pearson developed the correlation coefficient, building on the work of Francis Galton.

3. The strength of the linear relationship is indicated by the absolute value of the correlation (or, as we will see shortly, by the correlation squared). A perfect linear relationship is indicated by r or ρ equal to 1 or −1; no linear relationship is indicated by r or ρ equal to 0; intermediate levels of association between the variables are indicated by intermediate values of r or ρ. Because the sign indicates direction of the relationship, not strength, a correlation of −.9 is just as strong as a correlation of .9, and a correlation of −.1 is just as weak as a correlation of .1.

Strong linear relationships correspond to scatter plots in which the points are all close to the regression line (so that $s_{Y \cdot X}$ is small). Consider the scatter plots in Figure 21.1. Panel A illustrates a strong positive linear relationship between high school grade point average and college grade point average. The GPAs are strongly related in the sense that one can be accurately predicted from the other—all the points are close to the regression line. Note that the correlation is positive (corresponding to the slope of the regression line) and close to 1.0.

Panel B of Figure 21.1 illustrates a strong negative linear relationship between daily temperatures in Madison, Wisconsin, and Buenos Aires, Argentina. Buenos Aires is about as far south of the equator as Madison is north of the equator. Thus, when it is summer (and warm) in Madison, it is winter (and cold) in Buenos Aires. Although the correlation is negative, the relationship is a strong one, as indicated by the absolute value of the correlation.

Panel C illustrates a weak positive correlation between IQ and weight (undernourished children are more likely to have low IQs than are well-nourished children). Note that the scatter about the regression line ($s_{Y \cdot X}$) is considerable, indicating that weight and IQ are not strongly related. Consequently, the value of r is low.

FIGURE 21.1
Illustrations of correlations and their scatter plots.

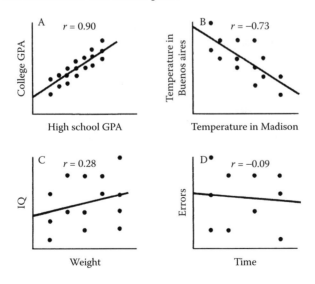

Finally, Panel D illustrates a weak negative correlation between time taken to perform a task (for example, perform a piece of music) and number of errors made in the performance: taking more time reduces the errors.

Interpretation of r^2

Although the absolute value of r or ρ provides an index of the strength of the linear relationship, they have no direct interpretation. On the other hand, r^2 and ρ^2 can be given a precise interpretation in terms of variances: The correlation squared is the proportion of Y variance associated with X variance. This interpretation is illustrated in Figure 21.2.

Figure 21.2A illustrates a perfect linear relationship: All of the points fall on the regression line and so r and $r^2 = 1.0$. Note further that each change in Y (for example, from $Y = 2$ to $Y = 3.5$) is accompanied by a change in X, for example, from $X = 2$ to $X = 3$). Stated differently, because all of the points fall on the regression line, every change in Y is *necessarily* accompanied by a change in X. Remember, changes in Y indicate variability in Y, and changes in X indicate variability in X. Therefore, because changes in Y are *necessarily* accompanied by changes in X, 100% of the Y variance is associated with X variance. In other words, $r^2 = 1.0$ is the proportion of Y variance associated with X variance.

Now look at Panel B in Figure 21.2. In this panel, there is no linear relationship (the slope, $\hat{m}$, is zero), and so $r = 0$ and $r^2 = 0$. Note that changes in Y occur at each value of X (for example, at $X = 2$, Y varies from 1 to 4). In fact, the same changes in Y occur whether or not X changes. Thus, none of the changes in Y are necessarily accompanied by changes in X, or, stated differently, none of the Y variance is associated with X variance. Thus, $r^2 = 0.0$ is the proportion of Y variance associated with X variance.

Now look at Panel C in Figure 21.2. There is some linear relationship between the Xs and the Ys, but it is not perfect. Thus, the proportion of Y variance associated with X variance should be somewhere between 0.0 (no relationship) and 1.0 (perfect relationship). In fact, for this panel, $r = .775$ so that $r^2 = .60$. What does it mean to say that 60% of the Y variance is associated with the X variance? Note that the total range of Y is from 1 to 6. At any given value of X, however, the range of Y is much less (for example, at $X = 2$, Y changes from 1 to 3). Thus, some of the change in Y occurs *without changes* in X, and some of

FIGURE 21.2
The closer the data points are to the regression line, the larger the correlation. Note that the regression lines are exactly the same in Panels A and C, but that the correlations differ.

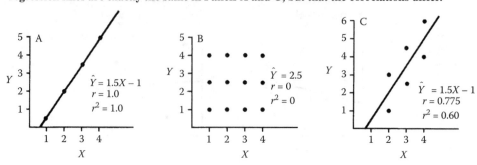

the changes in Y occur only *with* changes in X. $r^2 = .60$ is the proportion of changes in Y accompanied by changes in X, or, stated differently, $r^2 = .60$ is the proportion of Y variance associated with X variance.

This discussion can be summarized mathematically by examining a definitional formula for ρ^2. It is

$$\rho^2 = \frac{\sigma_y^2 - \sigma_{Y \cdot X}^2}{\sigma_y^2} = \frac{Y \text{ Variance Associated with } X \text{ Variance}}{\text{Total } Y \text{ Variance}}$$

The symbol σ_y^2 (in both the numerator and the denominator) is the total variance of the population of the Ys. The other term, $\sigma_{Y \cdot X}^2$, is a little harder to describe. Remember, the scatter about the regression line is measured by the standard error of estimate, $\sigma_{Y \cdot X}$. The greater the scatter, the greater $\sigma_{Y \cdot X}$. Squaring this term gives $\sigma_{Y \cdot X}^2$, and this is the variance of the Ys *not* associated with changes in X. Why? Because the scatter about the line indicates the degree to which there are changes in Y without changes in X.

Because σ_y^2 is the total variance of the Ys, subtracting $\sigma_{Y \cdot X}^2$, the variance of the Ys not associated with X, leaves the variance of the Ys that is associated with X, and that is just what the numerator is. Dividing by the total variance of Y, σ_y^2, gives the proportion of Y variance associated with X variance.

The major point of this section is that r^2 and ρ^2 have a direct interpretation, the proportion of Y variance associated with X variance, whereas the unsquared correlation does not have a direct interpretation. Thus, if you read that a particular correlation is, say, .5, do not think that it is half of a perfect correlation. Instead, square the correlation to obtain .25, which indicates that the linear relationship is only 25% of a perfect linear relationship. This is particularly important in judging the practical significance of statistically significant correlations. A correlation of .2 may be statistically significant, but practically, the linear relationship between X and Y is very weak—only 4% (.04) of the changes in Y are associated with changes in X.

Computational Formula for r

The definitional formula for ρ^2 is convenient for thinking about the meaning of a correlation, but it cannot be used for computing r, and it provides no indication of the direction (sign) of the linear relationship. The computational formula for r solves both of these problems. Once you have computed r using the computational formula, it can be squared to produce r^2, the proportion of Y variance associated with X variance.

FORMULA 21.1   Computation Formula for r

$$r = \frac{n_p \sum XY - \sum X \sum Y}{\sqrt{\left[n_p \sum X^2 - \left(\sum X \right)^2 \right] \left[n_p \sum Y^2 - \left(\sum Y \right)^2 \right]}} = \frac{SP_{XY}}{\sqrt{SS(X)SS(Y)}}$$

Use of the formula is illustrated in Table 21.1.

FACTORS THAT AFFECT THE SIZE OF *r*

Blind application of Formula 21.1 can lead to a misleading description of the relationship between the *X*s and the *Y*s. The factors of which you should be wary are exactly the same as those that lead to problems in regression (see the section Precautions in Regression [and Correlation] Analysis, in Chapter 20). To review, these factors are:

- *Nonlinear relationship.* Linear correlation measures only the degree of linear relationship. If the *X*s and the *Y*s are nonlinearly related, *r* may be zero even though the two variables are related (nonlinearly).
- *Restricted range.* Restrictions on the range of either *X* or *Y* will reduce *r*.
- *Extreme scores.* A single extreme score may produce evidence for a correlation when none exists for the majority of the scores.
- *Combining groups.* There may be no correlation within either group, but combining the groups can give the illusion of a linear correlation. Also, combining groups can change the direction of the correlation.

These problems can be avoided by careful examination of the scatter plot. See Chapter 20 for details.

TESTING HYPOTHESES ABOUT ρ

The statistic *r* can be used to make many types of inferences about ρ. For example, confidence intervals for ρ can be constructed; two *r*s can be compared to determine if the corresponding ρs differ; a single *r* can be tested to determine if the corresponding ρ is different from a hypothesized value. This section includes discussion of only the last of these inferences; discussion of the others may be found in more advanced texts.

The six-step procedure for testing hypotheses about ρ is illustrated using two examples, and the procedure is summarized in Table 21.3 at the end of the chapter. There are two mathematically equivalent ways of performing the computations. The first, based on the *t* statistic, is illustrated in the first example. The second procedure is illustrated in the second example.

Testing Hypotheses Using *t* as the Test Statistic

As an example, imagine that you are a developmental psychologist studying the effects of early experience on reading ability. You want to determine if there is a linear relationship between the amount of time a child was read to when the child was young and the child's current reading ability. You take a random sample of 10 children in the sixth grade of

TABLE 21.1
Relationship Between Early Experience and Reading Test Score

Child	Early Experience (X)	Reading Test Score (Y)	XY
1	0	34	0
2	10	14	140
3	20	40	600
4	5	71	355
5	20	89	1780
6	15	40	600
7	0	55	0
8	10	50	500
9	15	67	1005
10	5	14	70

$$n_X = 10 \qquad n_Y = 10 \qquad \sum XY = 5250$$

$$\sum X = 100 \qquad \sum Y = 474$$

$$\sum X^2 = 1500 \qquad \sum Y^2 = 27724$$

$$M_X = 10 \qquad M_Y = 47.4$$

$$SS(X) = 500 \qquad SS(Y) = 5256.4$$

$$SP_{XY} = \sum XY - n_p M_X M_Y = 5250 - 10(10)(47.4) = 510$$

$$\hat{m} = \frac{SP_{XY}}{SS(X)} = \frac{510}{500} = 1.02$$

$$\hat{b} = M_Y - \hat{m}M_X = 47.4 - 1.02(10) = 37.2$$

$$r = \frac{SP_{XY}}{\sqrt{SS(X)SS(Y)}} = \frac{510}{\sqrt{(500)(5256.4)}} = .315$$

your school system. The parents of each child are asked to estimate the average number of minutes a day they read to the child when the child was 5 years old (X), and each child is given a score for his or her current reading ability (Y). The data are in Table 21.1, and the scatter plot is in Figure 21.3.

Judging from Figure 21.3, there is a positive linear trend in the samples of Xs and Ys. Now, how strong is the linear relationship? The computation of r is given in Table 21.1. Because $r = .315$, $r^2 = .099$; that is, only 9.9% of the variance of the Ys is associated with X. Is there enough evidence to conclude that there is a linear relationship in the populations? In other words, is there enough evidence to conclude that ρ is different from zero?

This question is almost identical to the one asked when testing hypotheses about m, the slope of the regression line. In fact, the two hypothesis-testing procedures are mathematically equivalent and will always give the same answer. If there is enough evidence to conclude that m is not zero, then there will be enough evidence to conclude that ρ is not zero. Choice of test is mainly a matter of convenience.

FIGURE 21.3
Relationship between early experience and reading test score.

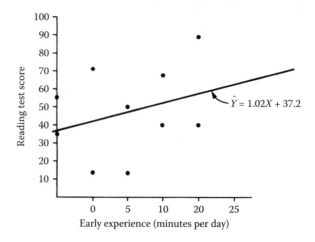

Step 1: Assumptions

Population Assumptions

1. The population of Xs and the population of Ys are normally distributed.[2] Because the t statistic (which we will be using) is robust, you may ignore this assumption as long as the populations are relatively mound-shaped and symmetrical.
2. The variance of the Ys is the same at each value of X. This condition is called **homoscedasticity.** The robustness of the t statistic can be counted on to overcome mild violations of this assumption.

Sampling Assumptions

1. The samples must be dependent. This assumption is met because each early experience score (X) can be matched systematically to a reading test score (Y)—simply match the scores pertaining to the same child.
2. Both samples must be obtained using independent (within-sample) random sampling. This assumption is met because the early experience scores are unrelated to each other (they come from unrelated children), and the reading test scores are unrelated to each other.

Data Assumption   The Xs and the Ys are measured using interval or ratio scales. The X variable, time parents spend reading, is a ratio measure. The scale of the reading test score (Y) depends on how reading is assessed. We will assume that the scores are, if not strictly, interval, at least close (an "in-between" scale).

---

[2] Technically, the distribution of X is normal, and the distribution of Y is normal at each value of X.

Step 2: Hypotheses

The general form of the null hypothesis is

$$H_0: \rho = \rho_0$$

where ρ_0 is any value between −1 and 1. However, if ρ_0 is any value other than 0, special procedures are required. Thus, the procedures described here are confined to testing

$$H_0: \rho = 0$$

Three forms of the alternative are available:

$$H_1: \rho \neq 0$$
$$H_1: \rho < 0$$
$$H_1: \rho > 0$$

In the example, we are interested in discovering if the populations are positively or negatively related; therefore, the nondirectional alternative is most appropriate.

Step 3: Test Statistic and Its Sampling Distribution

When H_0 is correct (so that $\rho = 0$), the sampling distribution of r is approximately normally distributed.[3] Furthermore, the mean of the sampling distribution is 0.0, and the standard deviation can be estimated by s_r (a formula for s_r will be given below). As you know, these are just the ingredients needed to form the t statistic. Indeed, the test statistic is

$$t = \frac{r - 0}{s_r}$$
$$df = n_p - 2$$

The formula for s_r is surprisingly simple:

$$s_r = \sqrt{\frac{1 - r^2}{n_p - 2}}$$

Thus, the t statistic can be rewritten as

---

[3] Imagine taking dependent samples from the two populations and computing r. Do this over and over again, each time computing a new r. When the null hypothesis is correct (and the assumptions are met), the relative frequency distribution of these rs approximates a normal distribution.

███████████

FORMULA 21.2   Computational Formula for *t*

$$t = \frac{r - 0}{\sqrt{\dfrac{1 - r^2}{n_p - 2}}}$$

When H_0 is correct, t is likely to be around zero. When H_0 is incorrect, the value of t is likely to be discrepant from zero. Stated differently, if the t you compute from your data is very different from zero, that is good evidence against H_0.

Step 4: Set α and the Decision Rule

As always, you have complete control over the value of α. Small values of α will reduce the probability of a Type I error, but also decrease power (that is, increase the probability of a Type II error). In this example, because the sample size is small, power is low. To roughly compensate, use $\alpha = .10$. Because of the larger than usual probability of a Type I error, if H_0 is rejected, it might be best to treat this as a preliminary result, one that should not be completely trusted until it is confirmed by further research.

The decision rule for the nondirectional alternative is

$$\text{Reject } H_0 \text{ if } t \le -t_{\alpha/2} \text{ or if } t \ge t_{\alpha/2} \text{ or}$$
$$\text{Reject } H_0 \text{ if } p\text{-value} \le \alpha$$

For the directional alternative $H_0: \rho < 0$, the decision rule is

$$\text{Reject } H_0 \text{ if } t \le -t_{\alpha} \text{ or}$$
$$\text{Reject } H_0 \text{ if } p\text{-value} \le \alpha$$

and for the directional alternative $H_0: \rho > 0$, the decision rule is

$$\text{Reject } H_0 \text{ if } t \ge t_{\alpha} \text{ or}$$
$$\text{Reject } H_0 \text{ if } p\text{-value} \le \alpha$$

For all of these decision rules, the t statistic has $n_p - 2$ *df*.

For the example, using the nondirectional alternative with $\alpha = .10$, $\alpha/2 = .05$, and with 8 *df*, $t_{\alpha/2} = 1.860$. Thus,

$$\text{Reject } H_0 \text{ if } t \le -1.860 \text{ or if } t \ge 1.860$$

Step 5: Sample and Compute the Test Statistic

For the data in Table 21.1, $r = .315$. The computations for t are

$$t = \frac{.315 - 0}{\sqrt{\dfrac{1 - (.315)^2}{10 - 2}}} = .939$$

Step 6: Decide and Draw Conclusions

The null hypothesis cannot be rejected; there is not enough evidence to conclude that there is a linear relationship between the populations. As usual, we have not proved the null hypothesis; thus, we cannot claim that there is no linear relationship, only that the data do not allow us to decide.

Possible Errors

Whenever H_0 is not rejected, there is a possibility of a Type II error (not rejecting H_0 when there is a linear correlation in the populations). For this example, that possibility seems large. Remember that the sample size was small (implying low power). Furthermore, the measurement process probably generated excess variability (which reduces power). Each parent was asked to estimate the number of minutes per week that the child was read to many years ago. These estimates are probably affected by the parents' memories, their desire to be perceived as "good" parents, and so on. A more accurate (but more expensive) procedure would have been to actually measure the time spent reading to the child when the child was young.

In general, β, the probability of a Type II error, can be decreased (or power increased) by most of the standard procedures: Increase α, increase the sample size, decrease excess variability introduced by measurement procedures, and appropriately use the directional alternative. Also, the problem of restricted range should be avoided. Formal power analyses are described later in the chapter.

When H_0 is rejected, there is, of course, a probability that a Type I error is made. Fortunately, when the assumptions are met, the probability of a Type I error is determined by α, so that it can be kept small.

Reporting the Results

The important components to include in a report are the values of r, t, df, s_r, and α. Thus, you might write, "For these data, $r = .315$. The correlation was not statistically significant at $\alpha = .10$, $t(8) = .939$, $s_r = .336$."

In the Media: Even the Experts Get Confused

When considering correlations, an important distinction is between the value of the correlation coefficient (e.g., r) and its square (e.g., r^2). The correlation coefficient is useful because the sign (+ or −) gives the direction of the relation (direct or indirect).

The correlation squared is a good index of the strength of the relation because it is the proportion of Y variance associated with X variance. Apparently, Geoffrey Cowley, the author of "Testing the Science of Intelligence" (*Newsweek,* October 24, 1994), has gotten the distinction confused. In discussing the link between IQ scores and genetics, Cowley writes, "By computing a value known as the correlation coefficient, a scientist can measure the degrees of association between any two phenomena that are plausibly linked. The correlation between unrelated variables is 0, while phenomena that vary in perfect lock step have a correlation of 1. A correlation of .4 would tell you that 40 percent of the variation in one thing is matched by variation in another, while 60 percent is not." Because Cowley has confused correlation and correlation squared, it is impossible to interpret the rest of the article. For example, consider his statement, "These twins exhibited IQ correlations of .7, suggesting that genetic factors account for fully 70 percent of the variation in IQ." Is it the case that $r = .7$ so that that $r^2 = .49$ (that Is, 49% of the variance is shared), or that $r^2 = .7$ so that $r = .84$? Also, if such a basic distinction was confused by the author (or the editors), what other aspects of the article might be incorrect?

Testing Hypotheses Using r as the Test Statistic

This example illustrates an alternative procedure for testing the statistical significance of r. The alternative procedure is simpler, but it hides the statistical reasoning based on sampling distributions. Because this alternative is mathematically equivalent to the t test, the two procedures will always give the same answer. Thus, choice of procedure can be based solely on convenience.

A clinical psychologist is studying personality characteristics that might be related to the development of schizophrenia. She develops two questionnaires. One provides an interval measure of hedonism (pleasure seeking); the other provides an interval measure of tendency toward schizophrenia. She randomly samples 100 volunteers from introductory psychology and administers both questionnaires to each student.

Initial examination of the scatter plot indicates that the relationship between the two variables is approximately linear and homoscedastistic. Using Formula 21.1, she calculates $r = -.281$. Is there enough evidence to conclude that there is a linear relationship between the population of hedonism scores and the population of tendency to schizophrenia scores?

The hypotheses are

$$H_0: \rho = 0$$

$$H_1: \rho \neq 0$$

Note that the nondirectional alternative is appropriate. The psychologist is interested in detecting deviations from H_0 in either direction. The fact that she knows that r is negative is irrelevant: Logically, formation of the hypotheses (Step 2) precedes calculation of the test statistic (Step 5).

Using the alternative procedure, the test statistic is the value of r itself. Look at Formula 21.2, and you will see that t is based solely on r and its degrees of freedom ($n_p - 2$). Therefore, after some algebraic manipulation, a table can be constructed (Table E, in the Tables section at the end of the book) that directly indicates critical values of r that are statistically significant. Do not be fooled: You are performing a t test, but the mechanics are hidden in Table E.

Using Table E, the decision rule is formulated as follows. For the nondirectional alternative,

$$\text{Reject } H_0 \text{ if } r \leq -r_\alpha \text{ or if } r \geq r_\alpha$$

Note that the critical value, r_α, is read directly from the table after finding the column corresponding to the nondirectional test and the row corresponding to the appropriate degrees of freedom. There is no need to find $r_{\alpha/2}$ because the table incorporates the distinction between directional and nondirectional tests.

For the directional alternative, H_1: $\rho < 0$, the decision rule is

$$\text{Reject } H_0 \text{ if } r \leq -r_\alpha$$

and for the alternative H_1: $\rho > 0$, the decision rule is

$$\text{Reject } H_0 \text{ if } r \geq r_\alpha$$

For both of these cases, be sure to read r_α from the column corresponding to directional tests.

Suppose that the clinical psychologist chooses to use $\alpha = .05$. For a nondirectional test with 98 ($100 - 2$) *df*, the decision rule is

$$\text{Reject } H_0 \text{ if } r \leq -.2050 \text{ or if } r \geq .2050$$

Because $-.281$ (the actual value of r) is in the rejection region, the null hypothesis can be rejected. The psychologist can conclude that for the populations sampled, there is a negative linear relation between hedonism and tendency toward schizophrenia: the greater the hedonism, the less the tendency toward schizophrenia. Of course, rejecting H_0 might be a Type I error; but the probability of a Type I error is small.

Note that hedonism is not the whole story behind tendency toward schizophrenia: Hedonism accounts for only about 8% ($-.281$ squared is .079) of the variability in tendency to schizophrenia. Probably, many other factors (such as upbringing, age, heredity) are needed to account for the rest of the variability in the tendency toward schizophrenia scores. This should not be surprising when dealing with anything as complicated as tendency toward schizophrenia.

CORRELATION DOES NOT PROVE CAUSATION

The aphoristic title of this section should be etched indelibly into your brain (right next to "You can't prove the null hypothesis"). Demonstrating a relationship, either through correlational analysis or through regression analysis, does not establish a causal link between the two populations.

Causal links can be established only by using experimental methodology (discussed more fully in Chapter 14). The key aspect of an experiment is collecting data in two conditions that are exactly alike (or at least have no systematic differences) except for the level of the independent variable. One condition has one level of the independent variable and the other condition has a different level. Because the conditions have no systematic differences except for the level of the independent variable, any statistically significant difference on the dependent variable must be *caused* by the independent variable (or a Type I error).

Remember, to ensure that the conditions have no systematic differences, random assignment must be used. That is, each individual from whom a measurement is taken must be randomly assigned to one or the other level of the independent variable. When random assignment is not used, as in most correlational studies, causality cannot be determined.

Consider how this reasoning applies to the hedonism and tendency toward schizophrenia example. The clinical psychologist measured the naturally occurring levels of the hedonism variable; she did not randomly assign students to levels of the hedonism variable. Because random assignment was not used, she cannot determine if there is a causal link between hedonism and tendency toward schizophrenia.

A statistically significant correlation or regression analysis indicates that any of the following three possibilities holds (ignoring the possibility of a Type I error):

1. *X may* be a cause of *Y*. For the example, engaging in pleasure seeking may cause a reduction in tendency toward schizophrenia.
2. *Y may* be a cause of *X*. For example, the tendency toward schizophrenia may cause students to engage in fewer pleasure-seeking behaviors.
3. Both *X* and *Y* may be caused by a third variable, *Z*. For example, perhaps a specific form of anxiety causes a tendency toward schizophrenia and a reduction in pleasure seeking.

Consider an example from outside of psychology. Suppose that an economist notes a significant positive relationship between the price of shares on the stock market and inflation: When inflation is low, the price of shares is low; when inflation is high, the price of shares in high. Does this demonstrate a causal relationship between inflation and the stock market? No. It may be that high inflation causes an increase in stock prices, or it may be that high stock prices cause inflation, or it may be that a third factor (for example, interest rates charged by the Federal Reserve bank) causes both stock prices and inflation to fluctuate together.

Let us return to the hedonism and tendency toward schizophrenia example to discuss the implications of causal links. In that example, the negative relationship between the two variables indicates that low hedonism is associated with a high tendency toward schizophrenia. Should the psychologist recommend students become more hedonistic to ward off schizophrenia? No. This recommendation assumes that there is a causal relationship between hedonism and tendency toward schizophrenia; it assumes that increasing hedonism will *cause* a decrease in schizophrenia. Because the causal link has not been established, there is little justification for this recommendation.

On the other hand, there is justification for continuing to study the relationship between hedonism and tendency toward schizophrenia: Because there is a statistically significant correlation, there *might* be a causal link. To investigate this hypothetical link, the psychologist could conduct an experiment contrasting two types of psychotherapy. One condition of the experiment would be a standard therapy, and the other condition would be the standard therapy plus a therapy designed to increase hedonism. Students seeking therapy would be *randomly assigned* to these conditions, and the dependent variable would be tendency toward schizophrenia measured after therapy. Then, if there were a statistically significant difference (in tendency toward schizophrenia) between the two conditions, the psychologist would be in a better position to conclude that there is a causal link between hedonism and tendency toward schizophrenia.[4] After demonstrating such a link, it is legitimate (or at least logical) to recommend an increase in pleasure seeking to decrease any tendency toward schizophrenia.

Some students mistakenly believe that whenever they perform a two-sample *t* test or an ANOVA they have demonstrated a causal link, and they believe that whenever they compute a correlation coefficient or a regression equation they have not demonstrated a causal link. These beliefs are mistaken because the *form* of the statistical test has absolutely no bearing on whether or not causal links are established. It is application of experimental methodology, not a particular statistical test, that determines whether or not causal links are established. The confusion probably arises because most experiments are followed by *t* tests or ANOVAs, whereas many nonexperimental studies are not. Nonetheless, it is the logic of the situation, not the form of the statistical test, that is important for establishing causal links.

THE SPEARMAN RANK-ORDER CORRELATION

Testing the significance of ρ requires that two population assumptions be met: The populations of Xs and Ys should be normally distributed, and the populations should be homoscedastic. When these assumptions cannot be met, the Spearman rank-order correlation (r_s) may be appropriate.

The Spearman r_s is the Pearson r applied to ranks. For example, suppose that the Xs in Table 21.1 are ranked from 1 (least amount of early experience) to 10 (most amount of early experience), and the Ys are ranked from 1 (lowest score on the reading test) to 10 (highest score). Applying the formula for the Pearson r (Formula 21.1) to the ranks will generate the Spearman r_s. As we will see shortly, however, because ranks are used, there is an easier computational formula for r_s.

Interpretation of r_s is exactly analogous to interpretation of r. Namely,

1. r_s is always between -1 and 1, inclusive.
2. The sign of r_s always corresponds to the sign of the slope of the regression line.

---

[4] Actually, she has demonstrated causal link between type of therapy and tendency toward schizophrenia, not hedonism and tendency toward schizophrenia.

3. The strength of the linear relationship (between the ranks) is best indicated by r_s^2. A perfect linear relationship is indicated by $r_s^2 = 1.0$, and the absence of a linear relationship is indicated by $r_s^2 = 0.0$.

The major advantage of r_s is that hypothesis testing does not require any population assumptions. Thus, it is often used when testing hypotheses about ρ is inappropriate. A major disadvantage of r_s is that significance testing based on ranks (ordinal data) is often less powerful than significance testing based on interval or ratio data. Thus, the Pearson correlation is preferred when its assumptions are met.

Hypothesis Testing Using r_s

The procedure is illustrated within the context of a specific example. The procedure is summarized in Table 21.4 at the end of the chapter.

A biological psychologist is interested in the relationship between social dominance and successful mating in baboons. He begins by selecting a random sample of 10 male baboons for study. For each baboon he counts the number of confrontations won by that baboon (X). He also counts the number of times each baboon successfully mates (Y). The data are in Table 21.2 and Figure 21.4. Is there enough evidence to conclude that there is a linear relationship between the two populations?

The scatter plot highlights the fact that one of the X scores is rather extreme, indicating that the population of Xs may be skewed, not normal. Also, the figure provides evidence of nonhomoscedasticity; note that the range of Y values appears much greater at the moderate levels of X than at either the higher or lower levels of X. For these two reasons, the psychologist decides that significance testing based on r_s is more appropriate than significance testing based on r.

FIGURE 21.4

Relationship between number of confrontations won and success in mating.

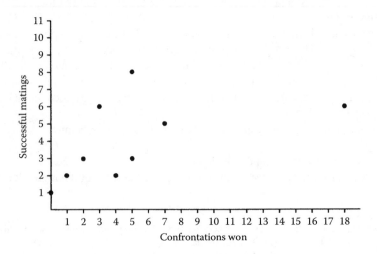

TABLE 21.2
Relationship Between Confrontations and Mating

Baboon	Confrontations Won (X)	Successful Matings (Y)	Rank of $X(R_X)$	Rank of $Y(R_Y)$	$D = R_Y - R_X$	D^2
1	0	0	1.5	1	−.5	.25
2	3	6	5	8.5	3.5	12.25
3	4	2	6	3.5	−2.5	6.25
4	5	8	7.5	10	2.5	6.25
5	0	1	1.5	2	.5	.25
6	2	3	4	5.5	1.5	2.25
7	5	3	7.5	5.5	−2.0	4.00
8	18	6	10	8.5	−1.5	2.25
9	1	2	3	3.5	.5	.25
10	7	5	9	7	−2.0	−4.00
			$\Sigma R_X = 55$	$\Sigma R_Y = 55$	$\Sigma D = 0.0$	$\Sigma D^2 = 38$

Check: $\Sigma R_X = \Sigma R_Y = \dfrac{(n_p)(n_p+1)}{2} = \dfrac{(10)(11)}{2} = 55$

$\Sigma D = 0$

$r_s = 1 - \dfrac{6\Sigma D^2}{n_p^3 - n_p}$

$= 1 - \dfrac{(6)(38)}{10^3 - 10}$

$= 1 - .230$

$= .770$

Step 1: Assumptions

Sampling Assumptions

1. The two samples are dependent.
2. Each sample is obtained by independent (within-sample) random sampling.

Data Assumption   The data are ordinal, interval, or ratio. Nominal data should not be used because the scores must be ranked (in Step 5). (See the next section on other correlation coefficients for how to handle nominal data.)

Step 2: Hypotheses

The null hypothesis is

$$H_0: \rho_s = 0$$

All three alternative hypotheses are available:

$$H_1: \rho_s \neq 0$$

$$H_1: \rho_s > 0$$

$$H_1: \rho_s < 0$$

For this example, the nondirectional alternative is the most appropriate.

Step 3: Test Statistic and Its Sampling Distribution

When H_0 is correct, r_s will be around 0.0. When H_1 is correct, r_s will be discrepant from zero. In other words, the greater the absolute value of r_s, the more evidence against H_0.

Step 4: Set α and the Decision Rule

Critical values for r_s are listed in Table F (in the Tables section at the end of the book). To use the table, first locate the row with the appropriate n_p (not df). Next, find the critical value in the column headed by the α and type of alternative being used. The decision rule for the nondirectional alternative is

$$\text{Reject } H_0 \text{ if } r_s \leq -r_{s\alpha} \text{ or if } r_s \geq r_{s\alpha}$$

For $H_1: \rho_s < 0.0$, the decision rule is

$$\text{Reject } H_0 \text{ if } r_s \leq -r_{s\alpha}$$

and for $H_1: \rho_s > 0.0$,

$$\text{Reject } H_0 \text{ if } \rho_s \geq r_{s\alpha}$$

For the example, set $\alpha = .05$. Then, using Table F, for $n_p = 10$ and a nondirectional test,

$$\text{Reject } H_0 \text{ if } r_s \leq -.649 \text{ or if } r_s \geq .649$$

Note that the table provides critical values only for up to $n_p = 30$. If you have more than 30 pairs of observations, the t statistic (Formula 21.2, substituting r_s for r) may be used. The t will have $n_p - 2$ df.

Step 5: Sample and Compute the Test Statistic

The procedure for computing r_s is illustrated in Table 21.2. The first step is to rank the Xs from 1 to n_p, and to rank the Ys from 1 to n_p. Note that observations of the same score are given the average of the ranks (for example, Baboon 1 and Baboon 5).

At this point, Formula 21.2 (the computational formula for r) could be applied to the ranks to obtain r_s. An easier procedure is based on the differences between the ranks. The formula is

■■■■■■■■■

FORMULA 21.3   Spearman r_s

$$r_s = 1 - \frac{6\Sigma D^2}{n_p^3 - n_p}$$

The "6" in the formula is a constant; it does not depend on n_p or any other aspect of the procedure.

Table 21.2 shows how the rankings can be checked in two ways. First, the sum of the ranks for the Xs should equal the sum of the ranks for the Ys, and they should both equal

$$\frac{(n_p)(n_p + 1)}{2}$$

Second, the sum of the differences between the rankings should equal 0.0.

Step 6: Decide and Draw Conclusions

The value of r_s is .77 (see Table 21.2). Because .77 is in the rejection region, the null hypothesis is rejected: There is enough evidence to conclude (with $\alpha = .05$) that there is a positive linear relationship between the *ranks* of scores in the two populations. In other words, for the populations sampled, the animals that tend to win more confrontations also tend to mate more often. Note that claims about causation should not be made.

Possible Errors

As always, when H_0 is rejected, the probability of a Type I error is equal to α, which we can make comfortably small.

When H_0 is not rejected, a Type II error is possible. The probability of a Type II error can be reduced by taking any of the precautions discussed in relation to the Pearson r. These include (a) increasing α, (b) increasing the sample size, (c) reducing excess variability by using careful measurement procedures, and (d) appropriate use of directional alternatives. In addition, the problem of restricted range should be avoided. A more formal power-analysis procedure is presented after the next section.

OTHER CORRELATION COEFFICIENTS

The Pearson r is best used when both the X and Y variables are continuous and measured on an interval or ratio scale. The Spearman r_s can be used for ordinal data, including rankings and ratings. Other correlation coefficients have been developed to accommodate various types of situations. Each of these has its own peculiarities, so a more advanced text should be consulted regarding application and interpretation of the statistics.

Point-biserial Correlation

The **point-biserial correlation coefficient** is used when one of the variables is continuous and the other is dichotomous. Dichotomous means that the variable takes on only two values, such as male or female, voter or nonvoter, and so on. Generally, the dichotomous variable is measured using a nominal scale.

For example, you might be interested in discovering if there is a relationship between voting and years of education. For each person in the sample you record if he or she voted in the last election (1) or not (0), and the number of years of formal education. The degree of relationship between the two variables is measured by the point-biserial correlation.

As with r, the point-biserial correlation ranges from -1 to 1, and the correlation squared has a direct interpretation: It is the proportion of Y variance associated with X variance.

The *phi* Coefficient

The *phi* coefficient is used when both of the variables are dichotomous (and generally measured using a nominal scale). For example, suppose that you are interested in assessing the strength of the relationship between gender and smoking. Each person in the sample is classified as male (0) or female (1), and each is classified as a nonsmoker (0) or a smoker (1). The *phi* coefficient measures the strength of the relationship from 0 (no relationship) to 1 (perfect relationship). The sign of *phi* is not reported, because direction is irrelevant when using nominal scales. As with r, the coefficient squared indicates the proportion of Y variance associated with X variance.

The maximum value of the *phi* correlation is constrained by the proportion of scores of 1 on the two dichotomous variables. When the proportions are not equal, the correlation cannot reach its maximum value of 1. Thus, caution is required in interpreting this correlation coefficient.

The *phi* coefficient is closely related to the *chi-square* statistic that is discussed in Chapter 22.

POWER AND SAMPLE SIZE ANALYSES

The techniques described below are appropriate for all of the correlation coefficients discussed in this chapter: Pearson correlation, Spearman rank-order correlation, point-biserial correlation, and *phi* correlation.

Power Analysis

Power is the probability of making the correct decision of rejecting H_0 when it is wrong. As such, power is the inverse of the Type II error probability (power $= 1 - \beta$). Anything you do to reduce β automatically increases power. The goal of power analysis is to determine if there is a reasonable probability that an incorrect H_0 will be rejected. If not, steps should be taken to increase power. These steps include increasing α, increasing the sample size, decreasing excess variability introduced by measurement procedures, and using the directional alternative appropriately.

You begin the power analyses by proposing a *specific* value, ρ_{sp}, for the linear relationship between the populations. Then, the power analysis answers the question, "Given my α, sample size, and type of alternative hypothesis, what is the probability that I will reject H_0 if $\rho = \rho_{sp}$?" If you have no information regarding an appropriate value for ρ_{sp}, you may use $\rho_{sp} = .10$ if you believe that the linear relationship is rather weak, $\rho_{sp} = .30$ for a medium-size effect, and $\rho_{sp} = .50$ for a strong relationship.

The value of ρ_{sp} is used directly as the effect size. Thus, we do not have to compute a different value for d, as in other power analyses. Combining ρ_{sp} with the sample size produces

$$\delta = \rho_{sp}\sqrt{n_p - 1}$$

Refer the quantity δ to Table B to find power.

In the first example of the chapter, we were looking at the relationship between early experience and reading ability in the sixth grade. There were $n_p = 10$ pairs of scores (see Table 21.1), $\alpha = .10$, and a nondirectional alternative was used. Now, suppose that we suspected that the relationship between early experience and reading ability was of moderate strength ($\rho_{sp} = .30$). What is the probability of rejecting $H_0: \rho = 0$, when ρ really does equal .30?

First, find δ:

$$\delta = .30\sqrt{10 - 1} = .9$$

Entering Table B with $\delta = .9$, and using the column for $\alpha = .10$, nondirectional test, the power is a very low .23. Thus, even when H_0 is really wrong, we have only about a one in four chance of making the correct decision. Clearly, remedial action, such as increasing the sample size, is called for.

Sample Size Analysis

Sample size analysis begins by specifying a desired level of power (for example, .8), and an estimate of the size of the correlation in the population (ρ_{sp}). Then the analysis is designed to answer the question, "Given my α and alternative hypothesis, how many pairs of observations do I need to have the desired level of power if $\rho = \rho_{sp}$?"

Locate the desired power in the body of Table B, and find the value of δ corresponding to that power. Then,

$$n_p = 1 + \left(\frac{\delta}{\rho_{sp}}\right)^2$$

The "1" in the formula is a constant.

For the early experience and reading example, suppose that we would like a power of .80, and that we believe that the strength of the relationship is moderate, so that $\rho_{sp} = .30$. Scan down the column in Table B corresponding to $\alpha = .10$ and a nondirectional test until you find .80. The corresponding value of delta is 2.5. Next,

$$n_p = 1 + \left(\frac{2.5}{.30}\right)^2 = 70.44$$

Thus, we need about 70 or 71 pairs of observations to have a reasonable chance of rejecting H_0, far more than the 10 pairs used initially.

SUMMARY

The Pearson correlation is a measure of the strength of the linear relationship between two variables, X and Y. The correlation is always between −1 and 1 (inclusive). The sign of the correlation is the same as the sign of the regression line, so positive correlations indicate positive relations and negative correlations indicate negative relations.

The size of the correlation is related to the spread of the observations around the regression line. When the data points are close to the regression line, the correlation is close to its maximum values of −1 or 1. When the linear relationship is weak and the data points are widely scattered about the regression line, the correlation is close to 0. More technically, r^2 is the proportion of Y variance associated with X variance, and it provides the most directly interpretable measure of the strength of the correlation.

Testing the null hypothesis H_0: $\rho = 0$ is mathematically equivalent to testing the null hypothesis about the slope of the regression line, H_0: $m = 0$. Thus, whenever there is enough evidence to conclude that the regression line has a nonzero slope, there will also be enough evidence to conclude that the correlation is different from zero.

Correlation does not prove causation. In the absence of experimental methodology (random assignment in particular), a significant correlation may be due to X causing Y, Y causing X, or a third variable causing both X and Y to change together.

When the population assumptions needed for testing the statistical significance of ρ cannot be met, the Spearman r_s correlation may be appropriate. Testing the significance of r_s does not require that any population assumptions be made.

EXERCISES

Terms   *Define these new terms and symbols.*

r	ρ_{sp}
r^2	Pearson correlation
ρ	Spearman rank-order correlation
ρ^2	point-biserial correlation
r_s	phi correlation

TABLE 21.3
Testing H_0: $\rho = 0$

1. **Assumptions:**

   Population assumptions:

   a. The population of Xs and the population of Ys are normally distributed (but see discussion of robustness).

   b. Homoscedasticity: The variance of the Ys is the same at each value of X (see discussion of robustness).

   Sampling assumptions:

   a. The samples must be dependent.

   b. Both samples must be obtained using independent (within-sample) random sampling.

   Data assumption:

   The observations are measured using an interval or a ratio scale.

2. **Hypotheses:**

   Null hypothesis:
   $$H_0: \rho = 0$$

   Alternatives available:
   $$H_1: \rho \neq 0$$
   $$H_1: \rho < 0$$
   $$H_1: \rho > 0$$

3. **Test statistic and its sampling distribution:**

   The test statistic is
   $$t = \frac{r - 0}{s_r}, \; df = n_p - 2$$

   $$s_r = \sqrt{\frac{1 - r^2}{n_p - 2}}, \; r = \frac{SP_{XY}}{\sqrt{SS(X)SS(Y)}}$$

   $$SP_{XY} = \sum XY - n_p M_X M_Y, \; SS(X) = \sum X^2 - nM_X^2, \; SS(Y) = \sum Y^2 - nM_Y^2$$

   When H_0 is correct, the most likely values for t are around 0.0. When H_1 is correct, the most likely values for t are discrepant with 0.0.

4. **Decision rule:**

   For $H_1: \rho \neq 0$:
   $$\text{Reject } H_0 \text{ if } t \leq -t_{\alpha/2} \text{ or if } t \geq t_{\alpha/2}$$

   For $H_1: \rho < 0$:
   $$\text{Reject } H_0 \text{ if } t \leq -t_{\alpha}$$

   For $H_1: \rho > 0$:
   $$\text{Reject } H_0 \text{ if } t \geq t_{\alpha}$$

   Or, a critical value for r can be obtained from Table E.

5. **Sample and compute r** (or use "Correlation" from "Data Analysis" toolpak).

   Collect dependent random samples and compute r. Then, either compute t as given above, or refer to Table E.

6. **Decide and draw conclusions:**

   If H_0 is rejected, conclude that there is a linear relationship between the scores in the two populations. Positive values of r imply a positive or direct relationship; negative values of r imply a negative or indirect relationship. r^2 is the best index of the strength of the relationship. Causal links are not demonstrated unless random assignment has been used.

TABLE 21.4
Hypothesis Testing Using the Spearman Rank-order Correlation

1. **Assumptions:**
   Sampling assumptions:
   a. The samples are dependent.
   b. Both samples are obtained using independent (within-sample) random sampling.

   Data assumption:
   The data must be ordinal, interval, or ratio.

2. **Hypotheses:**
   Null hypothesis:
   $$H_0: \rho_s = 0$$

   Alternatives available:
   $$H_1: \rho_s \neq 0$$
   $$H_1: \rho_s < 0$$
   $$H_1: \rho_s > 0$$

3. **Test statistic and its sampling distribution:**
   The test statistic is
   $$r_s = 1 - \frac{6\Sigma D^2}{n_p^3 - n_p}$$

   where D is the difference between the ranks assigned to a pair of observations.

   When H_0 is correct the most likely values for r_s are around 0.0. When H_1 is correct, the most likely values for r_s are discrepant with 0.0.

4. **Decision rule:**

   For $H_1: \rho_s \neq 0$
   $$\text{Reject } H_0 \text{ if } r_s \leq -r_{s\alpha} \text{ or if } r_s \geq r_{s\alpha}$$

   For $H_1: \rho_s < 0$:
   $$\text{Reject } H_0 \text{ if } r_s \leq -r_{s\alpha}$$

   For $H_1: \rho_s > 0$:
   $$\text{Reject } H_0 \text{ if } r_s \geq r_{s\alpha}$$

   In all cases, $r_{s\alpha}$ is a critical value found in Table F, using n_p, the type of alternative, and α.

5. **Sample and compute r_s** (or use "Spearman's Rho" from "LFD3 Analyses").

6. **Decide and draw conclusions:**
   If H_0 is rejected, conclude that there is a linear relationship between the ranks in the two populations. Positive values of r_s imply a positive or direct relationship; negative values imply a negative or indirect relationship. r_s^2 is the best index of the strength of the relationship. Causal links are not demonstrated unless random assignment has been used.

TABLE 21.5

X	75	16	42	43	21	36	25	63	59	33	54	63
Y	143	30	95	70	20	50	68	131	118	61	99	144

Questions *Answer the following questions.*

†1. Compute the Pearson r for the data in Table 21.5.

†2. Compute the Spearman r_s for the data in Table 21.5. Why does it differ from r?

†3. Use the data in Table 21.5 to test H_0: $\rho = 0$. Formulate the decision rule using the t statistic. Use $\alpha = .01$.

†4. Reformulate the decision rule using Table E, and test the significance of r. Did you reach the same conclusion as in Question 3?

†5. Use the data in Table 21.5 to test H_0: $\rho_s = 0$. use $\alpha = .01$.

6. Put the following correlations in order from the weakest to the strongest linear relationship: .5, −.8, .03, −.04, 1.0.

7. Explain why a statistically significant correlation of .15 may not have much practical significance.

8. Explain why correlation does not prove causation.

9. Suppose that a statistically significant correlation is found for each of the following pairs of variables. Write a short scenario that reveals how X could cause Y, how Y could cause X, and how a third variable could produce the relationship between X and Y. For example, in Pair a, Y may cause X if people who have many traffic accidents drink to calm themselves after each accident.

    a. X = alcohol consumption, Y = number traffic accidents

    b. X = time spent studying, Y = performance on a test

    c. X = amount of protein in diet, Y = grade point average

10. Determine power for each of the following situations.

    †**a.** $\rho = .2$, $\alpha = .01$, $n_p = 50$, nondirectional alternative

    b. $\rho = .5$, $\alpha = .01$, $n_p = 50$, nondirectional alternative

    c. $\rho = .2$, $\alpha = .05$, $n_p = 50$, nondirectional alternative

    d. $\rho = .2$, $\alpha = .01$, $n_p = 100$, nondirectional alternative

    e. $\rho = .2$, $\alpha = .01$, $n_p = 50$, directional alternative

†11. For each situation in Question 10, determine the sample size necessary to improve power to about .75.

    For Questions 12–16, determine the appropriate inferential statistical procedure. If enough data are given, carry out the procedure. Be sure to specify all components involved in the six steps.

†12. A psychologist is trying to determine if there is any relationship between people's beliefs about their knowledge and ability to apply their knowledge. He has a random sample of students study a textbook chapter in preparation for a test. After reading the chapter, each student rates his or her understanding of the material from 1 (very poor) to 10 (very good), and then takes the test. The ratings and the scores on the test are in Table 21.6. Is there enough evidence to conclude that there is a linear relationship between ratings of knowledge and performance on the test? Report your results and conclusions as if writing a journal article.

13. Using $\alpha = .05$ and a nondirectional test, what is the power of the situation in Question 12 to detect $\rho = .35$?

†14. A city planner is trying to decide on the maximum number of parking places to include in an urban renewal project. She visits a random sample of similar-size

TABLE 21.6
Ratings of Understanding and Test Scores

Student	Rated Understanding	Test Score
1	5	90
2	7	100
3	7	50
4	8	64
5	6	80
6	5	50
7	9	77
8	10	88
9	6	60
10	5	75
11	7	83
12	8	92
13	9	76
14	4	91
15	3	82

TABLE 21.7
City Populations and Number of Parking Spaces

City	Population (in thousands)	Parking Spaces
1	150	1200
2	58	850
3	36	460
4	43	400
5	77	990
6	65	700
7	110	1000
8	97	1100
9	28	425
10	38	450

cities that have successful parking programs and records for each city the population and the number of parking places. The data are in Table 21.7. If her city has a population of 50,000, how many parking places should she include to be fairly confident there are enough?

†15. An industrial psychologist is studying the relationship between work productivity and sleep. He asks each person in the random sample the number of hours slept the night before, and he counts the number of parts constructed during the day. The data are in Table 21.8. Is there a significant relationship? Report your results and conclusions as if writing a journal article.

TABLE 21.8
Number of Hours Slept and Number
of Parts Constructed the Next Day

Worker	Hours Slept	Parts Constructed
1	6	15
2	9	18
3	7	11
4	8	22
5	8	17
6	7	16
7	6	12
8	4	10
9	7	10
10	8	19
11	9	15
12	7	16
13	6	14
14	5	13
15	7	17

TABLE 21.9
Errors in Maze Learning for Rats on Two Types of Diets

Pair	High-protein Diet	Low-protein Diet
1	8	10
2	14	14
3	9	11
4	7	7
5	10	9
6	11	15
7	12	16
8	9	9
9	17	18
10	13	15

†**16.** The data in Table 21.9 come from an investigation of the relationship between diet and learning ability. Ten pairs of rat littermates were used. One member of each pair was randomly assigned to a high-protein diet; the other member was assigned to a low-protein diet. After 6 months on the diets the rats were taught to run a maze. The number of errors made before learning was used as a measure of maze-learning ability. Is there a significant relationship between diet and maze-learning ability (is there a significant influence of diet on maze-learning ability)? Report your results and conclusions as if writing a journal article.

Inferences From Nominal Data: The χ^2 Statistic

Most inferential procedures require ordinal, interval, or ratio data, and thus are inappropriate for nominal data. The only exceptions discussed so far (Chapter 11) are the techniques for making inferences about a population proportion. This chapter provides two additional techniques for analyzing nominal data, both of which use the χ^2 ("chi-square") statistic.

The first use of χ^2 is in testing hypotheses about relative frequencies in a population. This procedure is sometimes called a "goodness-of-fit" test, because the procedure determines if the relative frequency distribution specified by the null hypothesis matches or fits the real population relative frequency distribution.

Consider this example. A political scientist is trying to determine the distribution of political affiliations of freshmen at Great Midwestern University. He takes a random sample of 50 freshmen, and asks each if he or she is a Democrat, a Republican, a Socialist, or other. These nominally scaled data can be used to test the "goodness of fit" of hypotheses about the distribution of political affiliations in the population. For example, the political scientist might test the hypothesis that the relative frequencies in the population are .4, .3, .1, and .2, for Democrats, Republicans, Socialists, and others, respectively.

The second use of χ^2 is in determining if there are differences between two or more population relative frequency distributions. In this case, the null hypothesis is that all of the population relative frequency distributions are the same.

Consider a slightly different example. The political scientist is trying to determine if political affiliations differ between freshmen and seniors. To answer this question he might collect a random sample of the political affiliations of 50 freshmen and a random sample of the political affiliations of 50 seniors. These two samples can be used to test the hypothesis that the relative frequencies of Democrats, Republicans, Socialists, and others are the same in the two populations.

This chapter is divided into four main sections. The first section reviews the concept of nominal data. The second presents the goodness-of-fit test. The last two sections discuss comparison of two or more population relative frequency distributions.

NOMINAL, CATEGORICAL, ENUMERATIVE DATA

Measurement is the process of assigning numbers to observations to differentiate the observations with respect to some property. When the numbers assigned have no meaning except to categorize the observations, the data are nominal.

For example, assigning numbers to indicate political affiliation (1 = Democrat, 2 = Republican, and so on), classifies the observations into categories, but the magnitudes of the numbers have no meaning. Other examples of nominal scales include classifying by gender, make of car, and nationality.

Because the numbers assigned have no meaning other than to categorize, the numbers themselves are often omitted. Thus, coding observations as Democrat or Republican, male or female, Ford or Toyota, all produce nominal data, even though numbers may not be assigned. For this reason, nominal data are sometimes referred to as **categorical** data.

Most summary descriptive measures, such as the mean, the median, and the variance, are inappropriate for nominal data. This is because these statistics indicate "how much" of the measured quantity is inherent in the observations. For example, in a sample of people, we might want to know "how much" weight or height or IQ or aggressiveness there is on average. Determining "how much" requires that the measurements have at least the magnitude property (corresponding to an ordinal scale). With nominal data, however, the very notion of measuring "how much" makes no sense; a nominally scaled observation either has the distinguishing attribute or it does not. Returning to the examples, an observation is either a Republican or it is not, is either male or it is not, is either a Ford or it is not; the question of "how much" Republican or male or Ford is nonsensical. For nominal data, instead of "how much," the appropriate question is "how many": How many of the observations are Republican and how many Democrat, how many are male and how many female, and how many are Ford and how many Toyota.

For these reasons, the most common summary of nominal data is a frequency or relative frequency distribution, that is, a count of how many. Also for these reasons, inferential statistics applied to nominal data are used to make inferences about population relative frequency distributions. Because a frequency distribution is simply a count or an enumeration of the number of observations occurring at each score value (category), nominal data are sometimes called **count** or **enumerative data.**

The χ^2 procedures can be used to test hypotheses about the relative frequency distributions of ordinal, interval, and ratio data, as well as nominal data. However, using χ^2 for non-nominal data may be a mistake. Ordinal, interval, and ratio data are richer than nominal data, and inferential techniques that require these scales are designed to take advantage of this richer information. Using the χ^2 procedures with these scales disregards this extra information, making the inferential procedure less powerful and the outcome less informative. Thus, unless you are specifically interested in the relative frequency distribution, the χ^2 procedures should be reserved for nominal data.

χ^2 GOODNESS-OF-FIT TEST

This procedure is used when a single population is sampled. The null hypothesis specifies a relative frequency distribution, and the χ^2 statistic is used to assess the goodness of fit between this relative frequency distribution and the real population relative frequency distribution. The six-step hypothesis-testing procedure is discussed within the context of a particular example, and the procedure is summarized at the end of the chapter in Table 22.6.

As an example, consider a theory that predicts the relative frequencies of various personality traits in the general population. In particular, the theory predicts a .50 (50%) relative frequency of Type A personalities, a .25 relative frequency of Type B personalities, and a .25 relative frequency of Type C personalities. To investigate this theory, a psychologist takes a random sample of 60 introductory psychology students and classifies each as Type A, Type B, or Type C. In his sample, he finds 40 (.67) Type A personalities, 5 (.08) Type B personalities, and 15 (.25) Type C personalities.

How well do the data and the theory "fit"? The theory does predict a preponderance of Type A personalities (.50), but there are even more in this sample (.67) than predicted. Are these data so inconsistent with the theory that they indicate the theory does not apply to this population, or do the differences between the predicted and observed relative frequencies only reflect sampling error? The χ^2 procedure is used to answer this question.

Step 1: Assumptions

Sampling Assumptions

1. Each observation is obtained using independent (within-sample) random sampling. In particular, the procedure is inappropriate when a given individual contributes more than one observation (dependent sampling).

2. Each observation must be placed in one and only one category.

3. The sample size cannot be small. The test statistic is only an approximation of χ^2, and that approximation is poor when the sample size is too small. We will discuss shortly how small "too small" is.

Note that there are no population assumptions, nor are there any data assumptions.

The example situation appears to meet all of the requirements: The sample was obtained using independent (within-sample) random sampling, each observation is counted as contributing to only one category, and the sample size is large.

Step 2: Hypotheses

The goodness-of-fit procedure does not provide a standard format for the null hypothesis. Instead, you must propose a complete relative frequency distribution to serve as the null hypothesis. For the example, the theory of personalities provides the relative frequencies.

$$H_0: \text{relative frequency of Type A} = .50,$$

$$\text{relative frequency of Type B} = .25,$$

$$\text{relative frequency of Type C} = .25$$

Note that the sum of the relative frequencies must, of course, equal 1.0.

The only alternative hypothesis is the nondirectional,

$$H_1: H_0 \text{ is wrong}$$

Rejecting H_0 means that there is enough evidence to conclude that the population relative frequency distribution is different from the one specified by H_0. In this case, that would mean that the personality theory is incorrect (at least for this population).

Step 3: Test Statistic and Its Sampling Distribution

The χ^2 statistic measures how well the null hypothesis relative frequencies (**expected frequencies**) match up to the observed frequencies in the sample. Because the statistic is based on differences between the expected and the observed frequencies, the better the match, the smaller the value of χ^2.

The first step in computing χ^2 is to obtain an expected frequency for each of the categories in the relative frequency distribution.

> The **expected frequency** for a category is the number of observations in the sample that should be in the category *if the null hypothesis is correct*.

When H_0 is correct, what is the expected number of observations in each category? It is the relative frequency specified by H_0 times the sample size, n. For the example, according to H_0, we should observe in the sample of 60 personalities about

$$.50 \times 60 = 30 \text{ Type A personalities}$$

$$.25 \times 60 = 15 \text{ Type B personalities}$$

$$.25 \times 60 = 15 \text{ Type C personalities}$$

In terms of a formula,

$$f_e = rf_H \times n$$

That is, the expected frequency in a category (f_e) is the relative frequency of that category specified by H_0 (rf_H) times the sample size (n). Note that the sum of the expected frequencies must equal the sample size.

The formula for χ^2 is

███████████

FORMULA 22.1 χ^2 **Statistic**

$$\chi^2 = \sum \frac{(f_o - f_e)^2}{f_e}$$

degrees of freedom = number of categories − 1

The symbol f_o stands for the observed frequency in each category. According to this formula, for each category you obtain the difference between the observed and the expected frequencies, square the difference, divide each squared difference by f_e for that category, and sum the results across the categories.

When the null hypothesis is correct, the observed frequencies should be about the same as the expected frequencies. Thus, the squared deviations will be small and χ^2 will be small. In fact, when H_0 is correct, the mean of the χ^2 sampling distribution equals the degrees of freedom.[1] On the other hand, when H_0 is wrong, the expected frequencies and the observed frequencies should be quite discrepant. Thus, the squared deviations will be large and the χ^2 statistic will be large. Stated differently, large values of χ^2 are evidence against H_0, whereas values of χ^2 near the degrees of freedom are consistent with H_0.

Although the alternative is always nondirectional, only large values of χ^2 are evidence against H_0; small values of χ^2 are consistent with H_0. The situation is analogous to the ANOVA, in which the nondirectional alternative implied large values of F, but not small values.

One of the assumptions is that the sample size is large. The minimum sample size is related to the degrees of freedom and the expected frequencies. For 1 df, the expected

---

[1] Imagine taking a random sample of size n from a population and computing χ^2. Then, take another sample and compute χ^2 again. Do this many, many times. The relative frequency distribution of the χ^2 statistics is the χ^2 sampling distribution. When H_0 is correct, the mean of the χ^2s will equal the degrees of freedom.

frequencies in each category should be at least 5; for 2 *df,* the expected frequencies should all be at least 3; for 3 or more *df,* the expected frequencies should all be at least 1.

Step 4: Set α and the Decision Rule

As always, α is the probability of a Type I error, so small values should be used. Nonetheless, because the probability of a Type II error (β) increases as α decreases, it is foolhardy to set α too close to zero. Let us suppose that the personality psychologist chooses the standard $\alpha = .05$.

The decision rule is

$$\text{Reject } H_0 \text{ if } \chi^2 \geq \chi^2_\alpha \ (df) \text{ or}$$
$$\text{Reject } H_0 \text{ if } p\text{-value} \leq \alpha$$

where $\chi^2_\alpha \ (df)$ is the critical value obtained from Table G (in the Tables section at the end of the book) for a particular level of α and a particular *df.*

In the example, there are three categories (Type A, Type B, and Type C), so $df = 3 - 1 = 2$. Using Table G, the critical value for $\alpha = .05$ is 5.99, so

$$\text{Reject } H_0 \text{ if } \chi^2 \geq 5.99 \text{ or}$$
$$\text{Reject } H_0 \text{ if } p\text{-value} \leq .05$$

Step 5: Sample and Compute the Test Statistic

Using the expected frequencies computed before,

$$\chi^2 = \sum \frac{(f_o - f_e)^2}{f_e} = \frac{(40 - 30)^2}{30} + \frac{(15 - 15)^2}{15} + \frac{(5 - 15)^2}{15} = 10.0$$

To find the *p*-value, use CHIDIST in Excel, in which case the *p*-value = .007.

Step 6: Decide and Draw Conclusions

Because the observed value of χ^2 is in the rejection region (and thus the *p*-value is less than α), the null hypothesis can be rejected. There is sufficient evidence (with $\alpha = .05$) to conclude that the population relative frequency distribution is different from the one specified by H_0 (and the theory). In other words, the theory does not "fit" the population sampled. At least for this population, the theory will have to be revised.

The theory might not fit other populations either, but we cannot be certain from these results. Conclusions should be made only about the population (introductory psychology students) randomly sampled. In the case of personality variables, it would seem particularly inadvisable to overgeneralize: The distribution of personality types among psychology students may well be different than the distribution of personality types in other populations.

Reporting the Results

When reporting a χ^2 goodness-of-fit test, it is important to give the observed frequencies, the relative frequencies specified by H_0, and the values of α, df, and χ^2. Thus, the psychologist might write, "The theory specifies relative frequencies of .5, .25, and .25 for Type A, Type B, and Type C personalities, respectively. The corresponding observed frequencies of 40, 5, and 15 were sufficient to reject this theory $\chi^2(2) = 10.00$, $p = .006$."

Possible Errors

Whenever H_0 is rejected, there is the possibility of a Type I error (rejecting H_0 when it is correct). Fortunately, when the assumptions are met, the probability of a Type I error can be kept small because it is exactly equal to α.

When H_0 is not rejected, there is the possibility of a Type II error (not rejecting H_0 when it is wrong). Many of the techniques for reducing β (increasing power) can be applied to the χ^2 goodness-of-fit test. In particular, β can be reduced by increasing α, increasing the sample size, and decreasing excess variability by using careful measurement techniques.

A SECOND EXAMPLE OF THE χ^2 GOODNESS-OF-FIT TEST

In the absence of a theory that specifies the relative frequencies for H_0, it may be appropriate for H_0 to specify that the relative frequencies in the different categories are all equal. This technique can be useful in dealing with the results of polls. As an example, suppose that four candidates, A, B, C, and D, are running for a seat on the school board. You are commissioned by the local newspaper to determine whether or not the electorate has a clear preference. A reasonable null hypothesis is that the relative frequencies of voters preferring each candidate are all .25.

You decide to take a random sample of 40 registered voters to test the hypothesis. In addition to being random, the observations are independent if you are careful not to ask any person's opinion twice and if you are careful to collect the opinions discretely so that one person's opinion does not influence any other's. Also, you must be sure that each voter contacted states a preference for one and only one candidate. Finally, note that the sample size is adequate: The expected frequency is 10 (.25 × 40) in each of the categories.

The hypotheses are

H_0: relative frequency for Candidate A = .25,
relative frequency for Candidate B = .25,
relative frequency for Candidate C = .25,
relative frequency for Candidate D = .25
H_1: The null is wrong

The test statistic will have 3 (4 − 1) df. If the null hypothesis is correct, χ^2 should be about 3; if H_0 is not correct, χ^2 should be much larger than 3.

Using $\alpha = .05$, the decision rule is

$$\text{Reject } H_0 \text{ if } \chi^2 \geq 7.81 \text{ or}$$
$$\text{Reject } H_0 \text{ if } p\text{-value} \leq .05$$

To find the expected frequencies, apply the formula

$$f_e = rf_H \times n$$

Because the null hypothesis specifies $rf_H = .25$ for each category, all expected frequencies are

$$f_e = .25 \times 40 = 10$$

Suppose that the observed frequencies of voters preferring Candidates A, B, C, and D are 7, 10, 8, and 15, respectively. Then, applying Formula 22.1 for χ^2,

$$\chi^2 = \sum \frac{(f_o - f_e)^2}{f_e} = \frac{(7-10)^2}{10} + \frac{(10-10)^2}{10} + \frac{(8-10)^2}{10} + \frac{(15-10)^2}{10} = 3.8$$

p-value = .28

Because 3.8 is not part of the rejection region (and thus the p-value is not less than α), the null hypothesis cannot be rejected. However, because we have not proved H_0 correct, we cannot claim that the voter opinions are evenly divided among the four candidates. Instead, we can state only that there is insufficient evidence to determine if there is a voter preference.

Relationship Between Goodness-of-fit Test and z Test on Proportions

Chapter 11 discussed the use of the z statistic to test hypotheses about the population proportion. For example, in an election context, you might test the null hypothesis that the proportion of voters favoring Candidate A (over all others) is .50. For a different example, in a sociological context, you might test the null hypothesis that the proportion of teenagers favoring a decrease in the legal drinking age is .65. The data used to test either of these hypotheses about population proportions could also be used to compute a χ^2 statistic. For the latter example, the goodness-of-fit null hypothesis would specify relative frequencies of .65 (in favor of lowering the drinking age) and .35 (not in favor).

There is a remarkable relationship between the z test described in Chapter 11 and the χ^2 goodness-of-fit test. When the nondirectional alternative is used for both, and when there are only two categories (so that the χ^2 $df = 1$), the two tests are exactly equivalent and will always result in the same conclusion. In fact, when $df = 1$, $\chi^2 = z^2$.

When there are more than two categories in the frequency distribution, the χ^2 test is usually appropriate. When there are exactly two categories, either test is appropriate, and the choice is arbitrary. Remember, however, the z statistic can be used to construct confidence limits for the population proportion.

TABLE 22.1
Classification by Type of Injury and Type of Disability

Frequencies				
	Type of Disability			
Hemisphere Injured	*None*	*Verbal*	*Motor*	*Multiple*
Left (n = 30)	4	18	7	1
Right (n = 50)	6	14	26	4
Total	10	32	33	5

Relative Frequencies				
	Type of Disability			
Hemisphere Injured	*None*	*Verbal*	*Motor*	*Multiple*
Left (n = 30)	.133	.600	.233	.033
Right (n = 50)	.120	.280	.520	.080

COMPARISON OF MULTIPLE POPULATION DISTRIBUTIONS

The χ^2 statistic can also be used to compare multiple population relative frequency distributions. The question incorporated in H_0 is, "Do the populations all have the same distribution?" This procedure is sometimes called an analysis of contingency (independence or dependence) of classification schemes. The contingency analysis terminology is introduced in the next section.

Consider a neuropsychologist who is studying the effects of brain trauma caused by accident. The question she has is whether injury to different parts of the brain is associated with different types of disability. She takes a random sample of patients with left cerebral hemisphere injury and classifies them as having no disability, verbal disability, motor disability, or multiple disabilities. She also takes a random sample of patients with right cerebral hemisphere injury and classifies them using the same nominal scale. The data are in Table 22.1.

The frequency distributions in the upper half of Table 22.1 are a little difficult to compare because the samples are of different sizes. The relative frequencies (lower half of Table 22.1) highlight what appear to be large differences in the types of disability associated with injury to the different hemispheres. Note that for the left-hemisphere patients, the relative frequency of verbal impairment is greater than the relative frequency of motor impairment. Just the opposite is the case for the right-hemisphere patients. The inferential statistical question is whether these differences in the samples reflect differences in the population relative frequency distributions.

Step 1: Assumptions

Sampling Assumptions

1. The samples from each population must be independent of one another.
2. Each sample must be obtained by independent (within-sample) random sampling.
3. Each observation must be assigned to one and only one category.
4. The sample sizes must be large. For 1 *df*, the expected frequencies in each category should be at least 5; for 2 *df*, the expected frequencies should all be at least 3; for 3 or more *df*, the expected frequencies should all be at least 1.

The data in Table 22.1 meet all of these assumptions.

Step 2: Hypotheses

The null hypothesis is always

H_0: The populations have identical relative frequency distributions

The alternative hypothesis is always the nondirectional

H_1: The null is wrong

Step 3: Test Statistic and Its Sampling Distribution

The χ^2 statistic is computed using the same formula as before,

$$\chi^2 = \sum \frac{(f_o - f_e)^2}{f_e}$$

In this case, the summation is over each category for each population.

The major problem, however, is where the expected frequencies (f_e) come from. Remember, in the goodness-of-fit test, the null hypothesis provided relative frequencies that were used to compute expected frequencies. When comparing multiple population relative frequency distributions, the null states only that the relative frequencies are the same. It does not state what they are.

Fortunately, we have a way of estimating the expected frequencies *assuming that H_0 is correct*. Note in the top of Table 22.1 that there are really three frequency distributions: the frequency distribution for the left-hemisphere injuries, the frequency distribution for the right-hemisphere injuries, and the frequency distribution for both combined (based on a total of 80 observations). When H_0 is correct, the combined distribution can be used to estimate the frequencies in the individual distributions. For example, in the combined distribution there are 10 patients out of 80 with "no disability," for a relative frequency of

.125 (10/80). If H_0 is correct, each of the individual distributions should also have a relative frequency of "no disability" of about .125. Thus, the expected frequency of left-hemisphere patients in the "no disability" category is .125 × 30 = 3.75. Similarly, the expected frequency of right-hemisphere patients in the "no disability" category is .125 × 50 = 6.25.

To continue, in the combined distribution there are 32 patients in the "verbal" disability category, for a relative frequency of .40 (32/80). When H_0 is correct, the expected frequency of left-hemisphere patients in the "verbal disability" category is .40 × 30 = 12, and the expected frequency of right-hemisphere patients in the "verbal disability" category is .40 × 50 = 20.

This reasoning can be summarized in a formula for the expected frequency of any cell in the table:

$$f_e = \text{(column total)(row total)}/N$$

where N is the total number of observations in all of the samples. The formula works because "(row total)/N" is the relative frequency of a category in the combined distribution.

Once all of the expected frequencies are computed, the formula for χ^2 is used,

$$\chi^2 = \sum \frac{(f_o - f_e)^2}{f_e}$$

$$\text{degrees of freedom} = (R - 1)(C - 1)$$

For each cell in the table, subtract the expected frequency from the observed frequency, square the difference, and divide by the expected frequency. The sum across all categories is the test statistic. This statistic has $(R - 1)(C - 1)$ df, where R is the number of rows (populations sampled) and C is the number of columns (categories).

When the null hypothesis is correct, the deviations between the observed and the expected frequencies should be small. In fact, when H_0 is correct, the most likely value of χ^2 is equal to its degrees of freedom. However, when H_0 is incorrect, the deviations are likely to be large and χ^2 will be large. Thus, a value of χ^2 much larger than the degrees of freedom is evidence against H_0.

Step 4: Set α and the Decision Rule

As always, α is the probability of a Type I error, and it should be set to reflect your analysis of the relative costs of Type I and Type II errors (because lowering α increases β). Once α is set, the decision rule is the same as for the goodness-of-fit test,

Reject H_0 if $\chi^2 \geq \chi^2_\alpha$ (df) or
Reject H_0 if p-value $\leq \alpha$

For the example, suppose that $\alpha = .05$. The degrees of freedom equal $(2 - 1)(4 - 1) = 3$. Using Table G the critical value of χ^2 is 7.81; thus,

Reject H_0 if $\chi^2 \geq 7.81$ or
Reject H_0 if p-value $\leq .05$

TABLE 22.2
χ^2 Test Using the Injury Data

Observed (and Expected) Frequencies

Hemisphere Injured	Type of Disability			
	None	*Verbal*	*Motor*	*Multiple*
Left ($n = 30$)	4 (3.750)	18 (12.000)	7 (12.375)	1 (1.875)
Right ($n = 50$)	6 (6.250)	14 (20.000)	26 (20.625)	4 (3.125)
Total	10	32	33	5

Computation of $\chi^2 = \Sigma(f_o - f_e)^2/f_e$

f_o	f_e	$f_o - f_e$	$(f_o - f_e)^2$	$(f_o - f_e)^2/f_e$
4	3.750	.250	.062	.017
18	12.000	6.000	36.000	3.000
7	12.375	−5.375	28.891	2.395
1	1.875	−8.75	.766	.408
6	6.250	−.250	.063	.010
14	20.000	−6.000	36.000	1.800
26	20.625	5.375	28.891	1.401
4	3.125	.875	.766	.245
				$\chi^2 = 9.215$

Step 5: Sample and Compute the Test Statistic

The top of Table 22.2 presents the observed frequencies and the expected frequencies (in parentheses) for each cell. Note that the sum of the expected frequencies in any row equals the sum of the observed frequencies for that row. Also, the sum of the expected frequencies for any column equals the sum of the observed frequencies for that column. These sums can be used as a check on the computations of the expected frequencies. The computation of χ^2 is illustrated in the lower part of the table. Also, using Excel we find that the p-value = .03.

Step 6: Decide and Draw Conclusions

Because the value of χ^2 (9.215) is in the rejection region (and thus the p-value is less than .05), the null hypothesis can be rejected. The neuropsychologist should conclude that the relative frequency distributions (of types of disability) differ for the two populations (left- or right-hemisphere injury). Judging from the sample relative frequencies (Table 22.1), a major difference between the two populations is that patients with left-hemisphere injuries are more likely to have a verbal disability than a motor disability, whereas patients with right-hemisphere injuries are more likely to have a motor disability than a verbal disability. These data are consistent with the theory that the left hemisphere is predominant in control of verbal behavior and the right hemisphere is predominant in control of motor behavior.

TABLE 22.3
Observed (and Expected) Frequencies of Smokers

Gender	Smoker	Nonsmoker
Male ($n = 50$)	14 (12)	36 (38)
Female ($n = 50$)	10 (12)	40 (38)
Total	24	76

Computation of $\chi^2 = (f_o - f_e)^2/f_e$

f_o	f_e	$f_o - f_e$	$(f_o - f_e)^2$	$(f_o - f_e)^2/f_e$
14	12	2	4	.333
36	38	−2	4	.105
10	12	−2	4	.333
40	38	2	4	.105
				$\chi^2 = .876$

Technically, because random assignment was not used, the neuropsychologist cannot claim that left-hemisphere injuries *cause* verbal disabilities, nor can she claim that right-hemisphere injuries *cause* motor disabilities. Although these causal links are certainly likely, there are other possibilities consistent with the data and the statistics.

Possible Errors

When H_0 is rejected, there is always the possibility of a Type I error. Fortunately, when the assumptions are met, that possibility is very small (α). When H_0 is not rejected, there is always the possibility of a Type II error. As with the χ^2 goodness-of-fit test, the probability of a Type II error can be reduced by increasing α, increasing the sample size, and reducing variability by using careful measurement procedures.

SECOND EXAMPLE OF USING χ^2 TO COMPARE MULTIPLE DISTRIBUTIONS

A medical researcher is investigating gender and smoking: Is the relative frequency of smokers the same or different for males and females? He takes a random sample of 50 adult males and a random sample of 50 adult females. Each individual is categorized as a smoker or a nonsmoker. The data are in Table 22.3.

The assumptions are met. The hypotheses are

H_0: The populations have identical relative frequency distributions

H_1: The null is wrong

The test statistic is χ^2 with $(2 - 1)(2 - 1) = 1$ df. If H_0 is correct, the value of χ^2 should be about 1.0; if H_0 is incorrect, the value of χ^2 should be much larger. Using $\alpha = .05$, the decision rule is

Reject H_0 if $\chi^2 \geq 3.84$ or Reject H_0 if p-value $\leq .05$

The computations are illustrated in Table 22.3. Remember, the expected frequencies are obtained by using

$$f_e = \text{(column total)(row total)}/N$$

Because $\chi^2 = .876$ is not in the rejection region, the null hypothesis cannot be rejected. Clearly, these data offer little support for the claim of a difference in the relative frequency of smokers among men and women. The null hypothesis is not proved, however, because whenever the null is not rejected, there is the possibility of a Type II error. In this example, the samples are sizeable, however, so there is probably sufficient power to detect large differences between the populations. Therefore, if there are any differences between the populations, they are likely to be small.

In the Media: Using Chi-square to Answer Questions About Dementia

---

The point of research is to find out about what is true in the world, even when that truth is surprising or unexpected, as reported by Patricia Sims in "Hormone Therapy, Dementia Risk Linked" (*Wisconsin State Journal*, May 28, 2003). Sims described a study examining the effects on women over 65 who were taking a combination of estrogen and progestin (a type of hormone replacement therapy) in an attempt to reduce the incidence of dementia. Surprisingly, the data seemed to show just the opposite: Taking the hormones increased the incidence of dementia. At first glance, the data supporting this conclusion seem thin. "Out of about 4500 women, 61 developed probable dementia, but two-thirds of those cases were among women taking estrogen and progestin." Are these data strong enough to reject the null hypothesis that the two populations (population of dementia scores in women taking the hormones and population of dementia scores in women not taking the hormone) have the identical relative frequency distributions?

To check the assumptions, we have to make several guesses about details of the study. Assumption 1: It is likely that the samples are independent of one another. Assumption 2: Although it is not likely that the women were randomly sampled to participate, it may well be the case that they were randomly assigned to the two conditions (hormone replacement and no replacement) so that we can call upon the assumption of randomness of biological systems (see Chapter 14). Assumption 3: Almost certainly each observation is assigned to one and only one category (dementia or not). Assumption 4: The sample sizes must be large. Here there is a bit of difficulty, because although the article reports a sample size of "about 4500," it does not indicate the number of women in each condition. As a reasonable guess, let's assume that 2250 women were in each condition. Similarly, we have to do some guesswork as to the exact number of women who developed dementia. According to the article, "two-thirds [of the 61 cases] were among women taking estrogen and progestin." Let's guess that 40 cases of dementia occurred in the hormone group and 21 cases occurred in the other group.

With these assumptions and guesses, we have enough information to test the null hypothesis using the chi-square statistic. The table of frequencies (with expected frequencies in parentheses) is:

Condition

Dementia	Hormone replacement	No replacement
Observed	40 (30.5)	21 (30.5)
Not Observed	2210 (2219.5)	2229 (2219.5)
Total	2250	2250

Note that all of the expected frequencies exceed 5, so Sampling Assumption 4 is met. Setting alpha at .05 (no information about alpha was given in the article), with 1 df, the critical value is 3.84; that is, H_0 should be rejected if the value of χ^2 exceeds 3.84. In fact, the value of χ^2 is 5.999, and so the null hypothesis can be rejected.

What does this all mean? First, note that in the sample data, the incidence of dementia is higher for women taking the hormones (40 out of 2210, or 1.8%) than for women not taking the hormones (21 out of 2250, or 0.9%) contrary to the original hypothesis that hormone therapy would reduce dementia. Second, although the data seemed thin, in fact with reasonable assumptions and a reasonable value of alpha, the null hypothesis can be rejected. But, for whom does this conclusion hold? Because random sampling was unlikely, technically the conclusion applies only to these 4500 women (see Chapter 14). Nonetheless, a prudent person would probably discontinue the hormone therapy if it were being used solely to reduce the probability of dementia. Finally, the surprising data may hold important clues for figuring out the causes of dementia by investigating just how the hormones used in the study affect the brain.

AN ALTERNATIVE CONCEPTUALIZATION:
ANALYSIS OF CONTINGENCY

The comparison of population relative frequency distributions is often called an analysis of contingency, and tables such as Tables 22.1 and 22.3 are called contingency tables. Understanding this terminology requires a reconceptualization of the problem.

For concreteness, let us begin with the gender and smoking example. The example was originally framed by saying that a medical researcher took a random sample of males and classified them as smokers or nonsmokers, and that he took a random sample of females and classified them as smokers or nonsmokers. The purpose of the statistical analysis was to determine if the relative frequencies of smokers and nonsmokers were the same for the populations of males and females.

Now, look at Table 22.3 and note that the problem could have been framed differently: The researcher could have said that he took a random sample of smokers and classified them as male or female, and that he took a random sample of nonsmokers and classified

TABLE 22.4
Data Illustrating a Contingency (or Dependency)
Between Two Classification Systems

Gender	Smoker	Nonsmoker
Male ($n = 50$)	10	40
Female ($n = 50$)	40	10
	50	50

them as male or female. Thus, the χ^2 test could have been described as determining if the relative frequencies of males and females were the same for smokers and nonsmokers.

Now consider a third way of describing the same data. The researcher may have taken a single random sample from a population and classified each person in two ways: Each person is classified as male or female, and each person is classified as a smoker or a nonsmoker. Given this reconceptualization of the problem, the question becomes, "Are the two classification systems *independent* of one another or *dependent* on one another?" In this context, independent means "not affected by."

In Table 22.3, the relative frequency of "smoker" is about the same for males (.28) and females (.20). Thus, classification by smoker or nonsmoker is independent of (not affected by) classification by gender. In statistical terminology, independent and *noncontingent* are synonyms, as are dependent and *contingent*. The data in Table 22.3 illustrate noncontingent (independent) classification systems.

Although there are multiple ways of framing the question posed by the data in Table 22.3, only one χ^2 test is needed, and the result of that test is valid for any of the ways of framing the question. In fact, speaking statistically, there is only one question. Because the null hypothesis was not rejected, we can say that there is little evidence for a difference in the relative frequency of smokers among men and women, or there is little evidence for a difference in the relative frequency of men among smokers and nonsmokers, or there is little evidence for a contingency between classification by gender and by smoking.

Table 22.4 illustrates how the gender and smoking data might have looked if the classification systems had been dependent (contingent). The relative frequency of smoker or nonsmoker depends on (is affected by) classification by gender: For males, nonsmokers are far more prevalent; for females, smokers are far more prevalent.

Except for statement of the null hypothesis, the statistical analysis of contingency proceeds exactly as the χ^2 analysis for comparing multiple population relative frequency distributions. The new null hypothesis is

H_0: The classification systems are independent

Thus, rejecting the null hypothesis indicates that classification systems are dependent. The next example illustrates use of the contingency terminology in the χ^2 analysis.

A social psychologist is investigating how members of different religious groups view abortion. She will use her data to answer the questions, "Are religious affiliation and attitude toward abortion independent or dependent?" She took a random sample of 150 people and classified each person as to religious affiliation and attitude toward abortion. The results are in Table 22.5.

TABLE 22.5
Relationship Between Religion and Attitude Toward Abortion

Religion	Attitude Toward Abortion		
	Approve	*Neutral*	*Disapprove*
Catholic ($n = 50$)	10	10	30
Protestant ($n = 75$)	30	20	25
Jewish ($n = 15$)	5	5	5
Other ($n = 10$)	2	8	0
Total	47	43	60

f_o	f_e	$f_o - f_e$	$(f_o - f_e)^2$	$(f_o - f_e)^2/f_e$
10	15.67	−5.66	32.11	2.05
10	14.33	−4.33	18.78	1.31
30	20.00	10.00	100.00	5.00
30	23.50	6.50	42.25	1.80
20	21.50	−1.50	2.25	.10
25	30.00	−5.00	25.00	.83
5	4.70	.30	.09	.02
5	4.30	.70	.49	.11
5	6.00	−1.00	1.00	.17
2	3.13	−1.13	1.28	.41
8	2.87	5.13	26.35	9.18
0	4.00	−4.00	16.00	4.00
				$\chi^2 = 24.98$

The six-step procedure is exactly the same (except for statement of the null hypothesis) as the χ^2 test for comparing multiple populations.

Assumptions The assumptions are met: Each observation is obtained through independent (within-sample) random sampling; each observation is classified in one and only one cell; and as we shall see shortly, the sample size is large enough to produce expected frequencies larger than 1.0 in each cell (note that there are 6 *df*, so that the expected frequencies need only be larger than 1.0).

Hypotheses

H_0: The classification systems are independent (noncontingent)

H_1: The null is wrong

Test Statistic and Its Sampling Distribution The χ^2 statistic will have $(4 - 1)(3 - 1) = 6$ *df*. When H_0 is correct, the value of χ^2 will be around 6.0. When H_0 is incorrect, the value of χ^2 should be much larger.

Set α and the Decision Rule

For $\alpha = .05$, the decision rule is

Reject H_0 if $\chi^2 \geq 12.59$ or
Reject H_0 if p-value $\leq .05$

Sample and Compute the Test Statistic   As before, the expected frequencies are obtained using the formula,

$$f_e = (\text{row total})(\text{column total})/N,$$

where N is the total number of observations in the table. Then,

$$\chi^2 = \sum \frac{(f_o - f_e)^2}{f_e}$$

The computations are illustrated in Table 22.5. Further, we can find the p-value using Excel, in which case the p-value = .0003.

Decide and Draw Conclusions   Because the value of the test statistic (24.98) is in the rejection region, the null hypothesis can be rejected. Thus, classification by attitude toward abortion is contingent on (depends on) classification by religious affiliation, or equivalently, classification by religious affiliation is contingent on attitude toward abortion.

Causal links cannot be determined from these data because there was no random assignment. As with a significant correlation (Chapter 21), it may be that religious affiliation causes attitude toward abortion, attitude toward abortion causes religious affiliation, or some third factor causes both to vary together.

SUMMARY

The χ^2 statistic can be used to make inferences about population relative frequency distributions. Because the relevant data are simply a count of how many observations fall into each category of the distribution, the procedures are appropriate for nominal (count or enumerative) data. The "goodness-of-fit" procedure is used to make inferences about the relative frequency distribution of a single population. The null hypothesis must specify a complete relative frequency distribution. Then, the χ^2 statistic provides an index of the "fit" between the hypothesized distribution and the real population relative frequency distribution. Small values of χ^2 (near the df) imply a good fit; large values of χ^2 indicate that the null hypothesis is probably wrong. The goodness-of-fit procedure is summarized in Table 22.6.

The χ^2 statistic is also used to compare multiple population relative frequency distributions. The null hypothesis states that the relative frequency distributions are identical. Large values of χ^2 indicate that this hypothesis is probably wrong. This procedure is also called a contingency table analysis. It is summarized in Table 22.7.

TABLE 22.6
χ^2 Goodness-of-fit Test

---

1. **Assumptions:**
   Sampling assumptions:
   a. Each observation must be obtained using independent (within-sample) random sampling.
   b. Each observation must be classified in only one category.
   c. All expected frequencies must exceed 5 for 1 *df*, 3 for 2 *df*, and 1 for 3 *df*.

2. **Hypotheses:**

   H_0 must specify a complete relative frequency distribution
   H_1: The null is wrong

3. **Test statistic and its sampling distribution:**
   The test statistic is

$$\chi^2 = \sum \frac{(f_o - f_e)^2}{f_e}$$

   $f_e = rf_h \times n$, rf_h = relative frequency specified by H_0

   The *df* is one less than the number of categories in the relative frequency distribution (specified by H_0).

   When H_0 is correct, the most likely values for χ^2 are near its *df*. When H_1 is correct, the most likely values for χ^2 are much larger than the *df*.

4. **Decision rule:**

   Reject H_0 if $\chi^2 \geq \chi^2_\alpha$ (*df*) or
   Reject H_0 if *p*-value $\leq \alpha$

   where χ^2_α (*df*) is the critical value from Table G for the particular α and *df*.

5. **Sample and compute χ^2** (or use the "CHITEST" worksheet function in Excel).

6. **Decide and draw conclusions:**
   If H_0 is rejected, conclude that the relative frequency distribution specified by H_0 is not a good description of the population relative frequency distribution.

EXERCISES

Terms   *Define these new terms and symbols.*

enumerative data	contingency table
count data	χ^2
independent classification systems	f_e
dependent classification system	f_o
contingent	rf_h
noncontingent	

TABLE 22.7
Comparing Multiple Population Relative Frequency Distributions:
The Analysis of Contingency Tables

1. **Assumptions:**
   Sampling assumptions:
   a. The samples from each population must be independent of one another.
   b. Each sample must be obtained by independent (within-sample) random sampling.
   c. Each observation must be assigned to one and only one category.
   d. All expected frequencies must exceed 5 for 1 *df*, 3 for 2 *df*, and 1 for 3 *df*.

2. **Hypotheses:**

   H_0: The populations have identical relative frequency distributions
   H_1: The null is wrong

   or the equivalent:

   H_0: The classification systems are independent
   H_1: The null is wrong

3. **Test statistic and its sampling distribution:**
   The test statistic is

   $$\chi^2 = \sum \frac{(f_o - f_e)^2}{f_e}$$

   $$f_e = \frac{\text{(row total)(column total)}}{N}, N = \text{total number of observations}$$

   $df = (R - 1)(C - 1)$, where R is the number of rows and C the number of columns in the contingency table. When H_0 is correct, the most likely values for χ^2 are near its *df*; when H_1 is correct, the most likely values for χ^2 are much larger than the *df*.

4. **Decision rule:**

   Reject H_0 if $\chi^2 \geq \chi^2_\alpha (df)$

   where $\chi^2_\alpha (df)$ is the critical value from Table G for the particular α and *df*.

5. **Sample and compute χ^2.**

6. **Decide and draw conclusions:**
   If H_0 is rejected, conclude that the populations do not have identical relative frequency distributions. An equivalent conclusion is that the classification systems are contingent or dependent.

Questions   *Answer the following questions.*

†**1.** A school administrator believes that 75% of the students would prefer to eliminate final exams. In a random sample of 60 student opinions, he finds that 35 of the students wish to do away with final exams. Is there sufficient evidence to reject his belief that 75% of the students in the school would prefer to eliminate final exams? Use the goodness-of-fit procedure to answer the question.

2. Answer Question 1 using the *z* test described in Chapter 11. Is the answer the same? What is the relation between the value of *z* and the value of χ^2?

3. The goodness-of-fit procedure can be used as one test of the randomness of a random number table (or a computer's random number generator). Take a random sample of 100 digits from Table H by starting at a random location and choosing

TABLE 22.8
Favorite Leisure-time Activities

Watch TV	Play With a Friend	Play Alone	Other
15	8	7	2

TABLE 22.9
Punishments Used by Mothers and Fathers

Mothers	2	0	2	0	4	2	1	0	0	2	2	1	2	0	1	4	3	3	4	3
Fathers	4	2	4	2	3	3	4	1	2	2	3	3	4	1	4	0	4	3	2	3

the next 100 single digits. Count the number of occurrences of $0, 1, \ldots, 9$. Test the hypothesis that each of the digits occurs with the same relative frequency.

†4. A political scientist believes that there is little unanimity among voters on many issues of international economics. He takes a random sample of 40 voters in his congressional district and asks each if he or she is in favor of, opposes, or has no opinion in regard to use of protective tariffs. He finds that 15 are in favor, 12 are opposed, and 13 have no opinion. Test the hypothesis that the categories have the same relative frequency.

†5. Another political scientist believes that there is greater agreement among voters when international economic issues tap into moral values. He takes a random sample of 60 voters and asks each if he or she is in favor, opposes, or has no opinion in regard to use of economic sanctions against countries that engage in torture. He finds that 45 are in favor of sanctions, 10 oppose sanctions, and 5 have no opinion. Use the data from Questions 4 and 5 to determine if the relative frequencies of voter opinions depend on the issue.

In Questions 6–12, pick the most appropriate inferential procedure. If enough data are given, complete the analysis and report your conclusions.

6. For a study of children's leisure-time activities, each of a random sample of 20 children is asked to pick his or her favorite activity from the choices: watch TV, play with a friend, play alone, other. Because some children could not decide on a favorite activity, they were allowed to indicate more than one activity. The data are in Table 22.8. Is there sufficient evidence to claim that the categories differ in relative frequency?

†7. A psychologist asked a random sample of 20 mothers and 20 (unrelated) fathers the type of punishment they most frequently use on recalcitrant offspring. The data are in Table 22.9: 0 = no punishment, 1 = deprive of a privilege, 2 = deprive of affection, 3 = corporal punishment, 4 = other. Is there enough evidence to conclude that type of punishment differs between mothers and fathers?

†8. A psychologist asked a random sample of 20 mothers and 20 (unrelated) fathers the number of times per month he or she used some form of punishment on a recalcitrant offspring. Use the data in Table 22.9, but treat each number as the monthly frequency of punishment. Is there enough evidence to conclude that frequency of punishment (the mean number of punishments) differs for mothers and fathers?

9. What are some of the factors that may account for why the results were significant in Question 8 but not in Question 7?

†10. A psychologist asked a random sample of 20 wives and their husbands the number of times per month she or he used some form of punishment on a recalcitrant offspring. Use the data in Table 22.9, but treat the numbers as frequency of punishment and assume that the scores in the same column are from a married couple. Is there enough evidence to conclude that there is a relationship between the frequencies with which wives and husbands punish their offspring?

†11. The dean of students is trying to encourage equal representation of freshmen, sophomores, juniors, and seniors on student–faculty committees. He takes a random sample of 60 student committee members and determines each student's year in college. There were 10 freshmen, 15 sophomores, 25 juniors, and 10 seniors. Is it likely that the dean has reached his goal?

†12. A clinical psychologist is studying development of fear of snakes in monkeys. She tests random samples of 5 wild-born monkeys, 10 zoo-born monkeys who have never seen snakes before, and 10 zoo-born monkeys who have seen other monkeys react fearfully to snakes. The number of monkeys showing a fear of snakes in each group is 5, 2, and 8, respectively. Does the relative frequency of fear of snakes depend on experience?

Glossary of Symbols

English and Greek letters are listed separately in their approximate alphabetical order. Numbers in parentheses indicate the chapter in which the symbol is first used.

Greek Letters

α alpha, the probability of a Type I error, also called the significance level (8)

$1 - \alpha$ the probability that a confidence interval includes the value of the parameter being estimated (10)

β beta, the probability of a Type II error (8)

χ^2 chi-square, the statistic that follows the χ^2 distribution (17 and 22)

$\chi^2_\alpha (df)$ the value of the χ^2 statistic (with a specified number of degrees of freedom) that has α of the distribution above it (17 and 22)

δ delta, a quantity used in the computation of power (9)

Δ_s capital delta-sub s, the difference between two population means proposed in the specific alternative hypothesis used in computing power (13)

Δ_0 capital delta-sub zero, the difference between two population means proposed in the null hypothesis (13)

μ mu, the mean of a population (3)

μ_m mu-sub m, the mean of the sampling distribution of the sample mean (7)

μ_s mu-sub s, the population mean proposed in the specific alternative hypothesis used in computing power (9)

μ_T mu-sub T, the mean of the sampling distribution of the rank-sum T statistic when the null hypothesis is correct (13)

μ_0 mu-sub zero, the population mean proposed in the null hypothesis (8)

μ_{T_m} mu-sub $T m$, the mean of the sampling distribution of the Wilcoxon T_m statistic when the null hypothesis is correct (14)

μ_z mu-sub z, mean of a population of z scores (4)

π pi, the proportion of successes in a binomial population (11)

π_s pi-sub s, the value of π proposed in the specific alternative used in computing power (11)

π_0 pi-sub zero, the value of π proposed in the null hypothesis (11)

ρ rho, the population Pearson product–moment correlation coefficient (21)

ρ_s rho-sub s, the population Spearman rank-order correlation coefficient (21)

ρ_{sp} rho-sub sp, the value of ρ proposed in the specific alternative used in computing power (21)

ρ_0 rho-sub zero, the value of ρ proposed in the null hypothesis (21)

σ sigma, the standard deviation of a population (3)

σ^2 sigma-squared, the variance of a population (3)

σ_m sigma-sub m, the standard deviation of the sampling distribution of the sample mean (7)

σ_p sigma-sub p, the standard deviation of the sampling distribution of p (11)

$\sigma_{m_1-m_2}$ sigma-sub m_1 minus m_2, the standard deviation of the sampling distribution of the difference between two sample means (13)

σ_T sigma-sub T, the standard deviation of the sampling distribution of the rank-sum T statistic (13)

σ_{T_m} sigma-sub T sub m, the standard deviation of the sampling distribution of the Wilcoxon T_m statistic (14)

$\sigma_{Y\cdot X}$ sigma-Y dot X, the population standard error of estimate (20)

σ_z sigma-sub z, the standard deviation of a population of z scores (4)

Σ capital sigma, direction to sum the quantities that follow it (3)

English Letters

ANOVA   analysis of variance (17)

b the Y-intercept of the regression line relating the scores in two populations (it is a parameter) (20)

$\hat{b}$ the Y-intercept of the regression line relating the scores in two samples (it is a statistic) (20)

CM correction for the mean (17)

D difference between a pair of scores from dependent samples (14)

d Cohen's d, measure of effect size

$\hat{d}$ d-hat, an estimate of the effect size (Cohen's d)

df degrees of freedom, the number of components of a statistic that are free to vary (12)

df_1 df-one, the degrees of freedom for the first sample (16)

df_2 df-two, the degrees of freedom for the second sample (16)

f_e f-sub e, the expected frequency of a category (22)

f_o f-sub o, the observed frequency of a category (22)

F the statistic that follows the F distribution (16)

$F_\alpha(df_1, df_2)$ the value of the F statistic (with df_1 degrees of freedom in the numerator and df_2 degrees of freedom in the denominator) that has α of the distribution above it (16)

$F_\alpha(df_2, df_1)$ the value of the F statistic (with df_2 degrees of freedom in the numerator and df_1 degrees of freedom in the denominator) that has α of the distribution above it (16)

$F_{\alpha/2}(df_1, df_2)$ — the value of the F statistic (with df_1 degrees of freedom in the numerator and df_2 degrees of freedom in the denominator) that has $\alpha/2$ of the distribution above it (16)

$F_{\alpha/2}(df_2, df_1)$ — the value of the F statistic (with df_2 degrees of freedom in the numerator and df_1 degrees of freedom in the denominator) that has $\alpha/2$ of the distribution above it (16)

F_r — F-sub r, the statistic for the Friedman test (17)

H — the statistic for the Kruskal-Wallis test (17)

H_s — H-sub s, the specific alternative used in computing power (9)

H_0 — H-sub 0, the null hypothesis (8)

H_1 — H-sub one, the alternative hypothesis (8)

k — the number of populations sampled from a single factor (11)

l — the number of populations sampled from the second factor in a factorial ANOVA

m — the slope of the regression line relating the scores in two populations (it is a parameter) (20)

m_0 — m-sub zero, the value of the slope as proposed in the null hypothesis (20)

$\hat{m}$ — m-hat, the slope of the regression line relating the scores in two samples (it is a statistic) (20)

M — the mean of a sample (3)

M_D — mean of a sample of Ds (14)

MS — mean square (17)

MSB — Mean Square Between (17)

MSC — Mean Square Columns in factorial ANOVA (19)

MSE — Mean Square Error (17)

MSR — Mean Square Rows in factorial ANOVA (19)

$MSR{\times}C$ — Mean Square Rows by Columns; Mean Square for interaction in factorial ANOVA (19)

MSW — Mean Square Within (17), another name for s_p^2

n — number of measurements in a sample (2)

n_p — n-sub p, number of pairs of scores in dependent samples (14)

N — number of observations in a population (3); also, the total number of observations in a multigroup experiment (17)

p — the proportion of success in a sample of binomial observations (11)

p-value — probability of a statistic assuming H_0 is true; values lower than α permit rejection of H_0

$P\%$ — percentile rank, the percentage of observations in a distribution below a given score (2)

$p(x = event)$ — probability that in a to-be-taken random sample of $n = 1$, x (the variable sampled) has a specific value (the event) (6)

$p(A|B)$ — conditional probability; the probability of A given B

r — the sample Pearson product-moment correlation coefficient (21)

r_α	r-sub alpha, the critical value for testing the significance of r (21)	SS	sum of squares (17)
		SSB	Sum of Squares Between (17)
		$SSBl$	Sum of Squares Blocks (17)
rf_H	rf-sub H, the relative frequency of a category as specified in the null hypothesis (22)	SSC	Sum of Squares Columns (19)
		SSE	Sum of Squares Error (17)
		SSR	Sum of Squares Rows (19)
r_s	the sample Spearman rank-order correlation coefficient (21)	$SSR{\times}C$	Sum of Squares Rows by Columns; Interaction Sum of Squares (19)
$r_{s\alpha}$	the critical value for testing the significance of r_s (21)	SST	Sum of Squares Total (17, 19)
		SSW	Sum of Squares Within (17, 19)
s	sample standard deviation (3)	t	the statistic that follows the t distribution (12)
s^2	s-squared, sample variance (3)		
s_D	s-sub D, standard deviation of a sample of difference scores (14)	t_α	t-sub alpha, the t statistic that has α of the distribution above it (12)
s_M	s-sub M, the standard error, an estimate of the standard deviation of the sampling distribution of the sample mean (12)	$t_{\alpha/2}$	t-sub alpha slash two, the t statistic that has $\alpha/2$ of the distribution above it (12)
		T	the rank-sum statistic (13)
$s_{M_1-M_2}$	s-sub M one minus sub M two, estimate of the standard deviation of the sampling distribution of the difference between two sample means (13)	T_m	T-sub m, the matched T statistic for the Wilcoxon test (14)
		X	a score in a sample or population (3)
s_{M_D}	s-sub M sub D, estimate of the standard deviation of the sampling distribution of $\bar{D}$ (14)	X_p	X-sub p, the particular value of X for which Y is predicted (20)
		Y	a score in a sample or population (20)
$s_{\hat{m}}$	s-sub m-hat, estimate of the standard deviation of the sampling distribution of $\hat{m}$ (20)	$\hat{Y}$	Y-hat, a predicted value for Y (20)
s_p^2	pooled s-squared, weighted average of two or more sample variances (13)	z	standard score or z score, number of standard deviations between a score and the mean of the distribution (4)
s_r	s-sub r, estimate of the standard deviation of the sampling distribution of r (21)	z_α	z-sub alpha, the z score that has α of the distribution above it (8)
$s_{Y{\bullet}X}$	s-sub Y dot X, the sample standard error of estimate (20)	$z_{\alpha/2}$	z-sub alpha slash two, the z score that has $\alpha/2$ of the distribution above it (8)

Tables

TABLE A
Standard Unit Normal Distribution

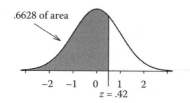

.6628 of area

$z = .42$

	0.00	0.01	0.02	0.03	0.04	0.05	0.06	0.07	0.08	0.09
−3.0	.0014	.0013	.0013	.0012	.0012	.0011	.0011	.0011	.0010	.0010
−2.9	.0019	.0018	.0018	.0017	.0016	.0016	.0015	.0015	.0014	.0014
−2.8	.0026	.0025	.0024	.0023	.0023	.0022	.0021	.0021	.0020	.0019
−2.7	.0035	.0034	.0033	.0032	.0031	.0030	.0029	.0028	.0027	.0026
−2.6	.0047	.0045	.0044	.0043	.0041	.0040	.0039	.0038	.0037	.0036
−2.5	.0062	.0060	.0059	.0057	.0055	.0054	.0052	.0051	.0049	.0048
−2.4	.0082	.0080	.0078	.0075	.0073	.0071	.0069	.0068	.0066	.0064
−2.3	.0107	.0104	.0102	.0099	.0096	.0094	.0091	.0089	.0087	.0084
−2.2	.0139	.0136	.0132	.0129	.0125	.0122	.0119	.0116	.0113	.0110
−2.1	.0179	.0174	.0170	.0166	.0162	.0158	.0154	.0150	.0146	.0143
−2.0	.0228	.0222	.0217	.0212	.0207	.0202	.0197	.0192	.0188	.0183
−1.9	.0287	.0281	.0274	.0268	.0262	.0256	.0250	.0244	.0239	.0233
−1.8	.0359	.0351	.0344	.0336	.0329	.0322	.0314	.0307	.0301	.0294
−1.7	.0446	.0436	.0427	.0418	.0409	.0401	.0392	.0384	.0375	.0367
−1.6	.0548	.0537	.0526	.0516	.0505	.0495	.0485	.0475	.0465	.0455
−1.5	.0668	.0655	.0643	.0630	.0618	.0606	.0594	.0582	.0571	.0559
−1.4	.0808	.0793	.0778	.0764	.0749	.0735	.0721	.0708	.0694	.0681
−1.3	.0968	.0951	.0934	.0918	.0901	.0885	.0869	.0853	.0838	.0823
−1.2	.1151	.1131	.1112	.1093	.1075	.1056	.1038	.1020	.1003	.0985
−1.1	.1357	.1335	.1314	.1292	.1271	.1251	.1230	.1210	.1190	.1170
−1.0	.1587	.1562	.1539	.1515	.1492	.1469	.1446	.1423	.1401	.1379
−0.9	.1841	.1814	.1788	.1762	.1736	.1711	.1685	.1660	.1635	.1611
−0.8	.2119	.2090	.2061	.2033	.2005	.1977	.1949	.1922	.1894	.1867
−0.7	.2420	.2389	.2358	.2327	.2296	.2266	.2236	.2206	.2177	.2148
−0.6	.2743	.2709	.2676	.2643	.2611	.2578	.2546	.2514	.2483	.2451
−0.5	.3085	.3050	.3015	.2981	.2946	.2912	.2877	.2843	.2810	.2776
−0.4	.3446	.3409	.3372	.3336	.3300	.3264	.3228	.3192	.3156	.3121
−0.3	.3821	.3783	.3745	.3707	.3669	.3632	.3594	.3557	.3520	.3483
−0.2	.4207	.4168	.4129	.4090	.4052	.4013	.3974	.3936	.3897	.3859

TABLE A (*Continued*)
Standard Unit Normal Distribution

	0.00	0.01	0.02	0.03	0.04	0.05	0.06	0.07	0.08	0.09
−0.1	.4602	.4562	.4522	.4483	.4443	.4404	.4364	.4325	.4286	.4247
−0.0	.5000	.4960	.4920	.4880	.4840	.4801	.4761	.4721	.4681	.4641
0.0	.5000	.5040	.5080	.5120	.5160	.5199	.5239	.5279	.5319	.5359
0.1	.5398	.5438	.5478	.5517	.5557	.5596	.5636	.5675	.5714	.5753
0.2	.5793	.5832	.5871	.5910	.5948	.5987	.6026	.6064	.6103	.6141
0.3	.6179	.6217	.6255	.6293	.6331	.6368	.6406	.6443	.6480	.6517
0.4	.6554	.6591	.6628	.6664	.6700	.6736	.6772	.6808	.6844	.6879
0.5	.6915	.6950	.6985	.7019	.7054	.7088	.7123	.7157	.7190	.7224
0.6	.7257	.7291	.7324	.7357	.7389	.7422	.7454	.7486	.7517	.7549
0.7	.7580	.7611	.7642	.7673	.7704	.7734	.7764	.7794	.7823	.7852
0.8	.7881	.7910	.7939	.7967	.7995	.8023	.8051	.8078	.8106	.8133
0.9	.8159	.8186	.8212	.8238	.8264	.8289	.8315	.8340	.8365	.8389
1.0	.8413	.8438	.8461	.8485	.8508	.8531	.8554	.8577	.8599	.8621
1.1	.8643	.8665	.8686	.8708	.8729	.8749	.8770	.8790	.8810	.8830
1.2	.8849	.8869	.8888	.8907	.8925	.8944	.8962	.8980	.8997	.9015
1.3	.9032	.9049	.9066	.9082	.9099	.9115	.9131	.9147	.9162	.9177
1.4	.9192	.9207	.9222	.9236	.9251	.9265	.9279	.9292	.9306	.9319
1.5	.9332	.9345	.9357	.9370	.9382	.9394	.9406	.9418	.9429	.9441
1.6	.9452	.9463	.9474	.9484	.9495	.9505	.9515	.9525	.9535	.9545
1.7	.9554	.9564	.9573	.9582	.9591	.9599	.9608	.9616	.9625	.9633
1.8	.9641	.9649	.9656	.9664	.9671	.9678	.9686	.9693	.9699	.9706
1.9	.9713	.9719	.9726	.9732	.9738	.9744	.9750	.9756	.9761	.9767
2.0	.9772	.9778	.9783	.9788	.9793	.9798	.9803	.9808	.9812	.9817
2.1	.9821	.9826	.9830	.9834	.9838	.9842	.9846	.9850	.9854	.9857
2.2	.9861	.9864	.9868	.9871	.9875	.9878	.9881	.9884	.9887	.9890
2.3	.9893	.9896	.9898	.9901	.9904	.9906	.9909	.9911	.9913	.9916
2.4	.9918	.9920	.9922	.9925	.9927	.9929	.9931	.9932	.9934	.9936
2.5	.9937	.9939	.9941	.9942	.9944	.9946	.9947	.9949	.9950	.9952
2.6	.9953	.9954	.9956	.9957	.9958	.9959	.9960	.9962	.9963	.9964
2.7	.9965	.9966	.9967	.9968	.9969	.9970	.9971	.9971	.9972	.9973
2.8	.9974	.9975	.9975	.9976	.9977	.9978	.9978	.9979	.9980	.9980
2.9	.9981	.9981	.9982	.9983	.9983	.9984	.9984	.9985	.9985	.9986
3.0	.9986	.9986	.9987	.9987	.9988	.9988	.9988	.9989	.9989	.9989

TABLE B
Power as a Function of δ and Significance Level (α)

	Directional test α						Directional test α			
	.05	.025	.01	.005			.05	.025	.01	.005
	Nondirectional test α						Nondirectional test α			
δ	.10	.05	.02	.01		δ	.10	.05	.02	.01
0.0	.10*	.05*	.02	.01		2.5	.80	.71	.57	.47
0.1	.10*	.05*	.02	.01		2.6	.83	.74	.61	.51
0.2	.11*	.05	.02	.01		2.7	.85	.77	.65	.55
0.3	.12*	.06	.03	.01		2.8	.88	.80	.68	.59
0.4	.13*	.07	.03	.01		2.9	.90	.83	.72	.63
0.5	.14	.08	.03	.02		3.0	.91	.85	.75	.66
0.6	.16	.09	.04	.02		3.1	.93	.87	.78	.70
0.7	.18	.11	.05	.03		3.2	.94	.89	.81	.73
0.8	.21	.13	.06	.04		3.3	.96	.91	.83	.77
0.9	.23	.15	.08	.05		3.4	.96	.93	.86	.80
1.0	.26	.17	.09	.06		3.5	.97	.94	.88	.82
1.1	.30	.20	.11	.07		3.6	.97	.95	.90	.85
1.2	.33	.22	.13	.08		3.7	.98	.96	.92	.87
1.3	.37	.26	.15	.10		3.8	.98	.97	.93	.89
1.4	.40	.29	.18	.12		3.9	.99	.97	.94	.91
1.5	.44	.32	.20	.14		4.0	.99	.98	.95	.92
1.6	.48	.36	.23	.16		4.1	.99	.98	.96	.94
1.7	.52	.40	.27	.19		4.2	.99	.99	.97	.95
1.8	.56	.44	.30	.22		4.3	**	.99	.98	.96
1.9	.60	.48	.33	.25		4.4		.99	.98	.97
2.0	.64	.52	.37	.28		4.5		.99	.99	.97
2.1	.68	.56	.41	.32		4.6		**	.99	.98
2.2	.71	.59	.45	.35		4.7			.99	.98
2.3	.74	.63	.49	.39		4.8			.99	.99
2.4	.77	.67	.53	.43		4.9			.99	.99
						5.0			**	.99
						5.1				.99
						5.2				**

* Values inaccurate for directional test by more than .01.
** The power at and below this point is greater than .995.

From *Introductory Statistics for the Behavioral Sciences,* Third Edition, by Joan Welkowitz, Robert B. Ewen, and Jacob Cohen, Copyright © 1982 by Harcourt Brace Jovanovich, Inc. Reprinted by permission of the publisher.

TABLE C
Critical Values of *t*

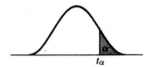

t_α

df	$t_{.100}$	$t_{.050}$	$t_{.025}$	$t_{.010}$	$t_{.005}$	$t_{.0005}$	df
1	3.078	6.314	12.706	31.821	63.657	636.619	1
2	1.886	2.920	4.303	6.965	9.925	31.598	2
3	1.638	2.353	3.182	4.541	5.841	12.924	3
4	1.533	2.132	2.776	3.747	4.604	8.610	4
5	1.476	2.015	2.571	3.365	4.032	6.869	5
6	1.440	1.943	2.447	3.143	3.707	5.959	6
7	1.415	1.895	2.365	2.998	3.499	5.408	7
8	1.397	1.860	2.306	2.896	3.355	5.041	8
9	1.383	1.833	2.262	2.821	3.250	4.781	9
10	1.372	1.812	2.228	2.764	3.169	4.587	10
11	1.363	1.796	2.201	2.718	3.106	4.437	11
12	1.356	1.782	2.179	2.681	3.055	4.318	12
13	1.350	1.771	2.160	2.650	3.012	4.221	13
14	1.345	1.761	2.145	2.624	2.977	4.140	14
15	1.341	1.753	2.131	2.602	2.947	4.073	15
16	1.337	1.746	2.120	2.583	2.921	4.015	16
17	1.333	1.740	2.110	2.567	2.898	3.965	17
18	1.330	1.734	2.101	2.552	2.878	3.922	18
19	1.328	1.729	2.093	2.539	2.861	3.883	19
20	1.325	1.725	2.086	2.528	2.845	3.850	20
21	1.323	1.721	2.080	2.518	2.831	3.819	21
22	1.321	1.717	2.074	2.508	2.819	3.792	22
23	1.319	1.714	2.069	2.500	2.807	3.767	23
24	1.318	1.711	2.064	2.492	2.797	3.745	24
25	1.316	1.708	2.060	2.485	2.787	3.725	25
26	1.315	1.706	2.056	2.479	2.779	3.707	26
27	1.314	1.703	2.052	2.473	2.771	3.690	27
28	1.313	1.701	2.048	2.467	2.763	3.674	28
29	1.311	1.699	2.045	2.462	2.756	3.659	29
30	1.310	1.697	2.042	2.457	2.750	3.646	30
40	1.303	1.684	2.021	2.423	2.704	3.551	40
60	1.296	1.671	2.000	2.390	2.660	3.460	60
120	1.289	1.658	1.980	2.358	2.617	3.373	120
∞	1.282	1.645	1.960	2.326	2.576	3.291	∞

Note: Each value in the table is a *t* score (t_α) that has α proportion of the distribution above it.
Reprinted with permission from William H. Beyer (Editor), *Handbook of Tables for Probability and Statistics,*
Second Edition (1968). Copyright The Chemical Rubber Co., CRC Press, Inc., Boca Raton, Florida.

TABLE D
The F Distribution

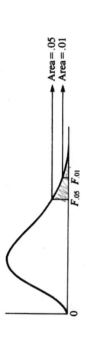

Area = .05
Area = .01

$F_{.05}$ $F_{.01}$

0

between

within

Degrees of Freedom: Denominator		Degrees of Freedom: Numerator																						
		1	2	3	4	5	6	7	8	9	10	11	12	14	16	20	24	30	40	50	75	100	200	500	∞
1	.05	161	200	216	225	230	234	237	239	241	242	243	244	245	246	248	249	250	251	252	253	253	254	254	254
	.01	4,052	4,999	5,403	5,625	5,764	5,859	5,928	5,981	6,022	6,056	6,082	6,106	6,142	6,169	6,208	6,234	6,258	6,286	6,302	6,323	6,334	6,352	6,361	6,366
2	.05	18.51	19.00	19.16	19.25	19.30	19.33	19.36	19.37	19.38	19.39	19.40	19.41	19.42	19.43	19.44	19.45	19.46	19.47	19.47	19.48	19.49	19.49	19.50	19.50
	.01	98.49	99.00	99.17	99.25	99.30	99.33	99.34	99.36	99.38	99.40	99.41	99.42	99.43	99.44	99.45	99.46	99.47	99.48	99.48	99.49	99.49	99.49	99.50	99.50
3	.05	10.13	9.55	9.28	9.12	9.01	8.94	8.88	8.84	8.81	8.78	8.76	8.74	8.71	8.69	8.66	8.64	8.62	8.60	8.58	8.57	8.56	8.54	8.54	8.53
	.01	34.12	30.82	29.46	28.71	28.24	27.91	27.67	27.49	27.34	27.23	27.13	27.05	26.92	26.83	26.69	26.60	26.50	26.41	26.35	26.27	26.23	26.18	26.14	26.12
4	.05	7.71	6.94	6.59	6.39	6.26	6.16	6.09	6.04	6.00	5.96	5.93	5.91	5.87	5.84	5.80	5.77	5.74	5.71	5.70	5.68	5.66	5.65	5.64	5.63
	.01	21.20	18.00	16.69	15.98	15.52	15.21	14.98	14.80	14.66	14.54	14.45	14.37	14.24	14.15	14.02	13.93	13.83	13.74	13.69	13.61	13.57	13.52	13.48	13.46
5	.05	6.61	5.79	5.41	5.19	5.05	4.95	4.88	4.82	4.78	4.74	4.70	4.68	4.64	4.60	4.56	4.53	4.50	4.46	4.44	4.42	4.40	4.38	4.37	4.36
	.01	16.26	13.27	12.06	11.39	10.97	10.67	10.45	10.27	10.15	10.05	9.96	9.89	9.77	9.68	9.55	9.47	9.38	9.29	9.24	9.17	9.13	9.07	9.04	9.02
6	.05	5.99	5.14	4.76	4.53	4.39	4.28	4.21	4.15	4.10	4.06	4.03	4.00	3.96	3.92	3.87	3.84	3.81	3.77	3.75	3.72	3.71	3.69	3.68	3.67
	.01	13.74	10.92	9.78	9.15	8.75	8.47	8.26	8.10	7.98	7.87	7.79	7.72	7.60	7.52	7.39	7.31	7.23	7.14	7.09	7.02	6.99	6.94	6.90	6.88
7	.05	5.59	4.47	4.35	4.12	3.97	3.87	3.79	3.73	3.68	3.63	3.60	3.57	3.52	3.49	3.44	3.41	3.38	3.34	3.32	3.29	3.28	3.25	3.24	3.23
	.01	12.25	9.55	8.45	7.85	7.46	7.19	7.00	6.84	6.71	6.62	6.54	6.47	6.35	6.27	6.15	6.07	5.98	5.90	5.85	5.78	5.75	5.70	5.67	5.65
8	.05	5.32	4.46	4.07	3.84	3.69	3.58	3.50	3.44	3.39	3.34	3.31	3.28	3.23	3.20	3.15	3.12	3.08	3.05	3.03	3.00	2.98	2.96	2.94	2.93
	.01	11.26	8.65	7.59	7.01	6.63	6.37	6.19	6.03	5.91	5.82	5.74	5.67	5.56	5.48	5.36	5.28	5.20	5.11	5.06	5.00	4.96	4.91	4.88	4.86

TABLE D (*Continued*)
The *F* Distribution

Degrees of Freedom: Denominator	\ Numerator: 1	2	3	4	5	6	7	8	9	10	11	12	14	16	20	24	30	40	50	75	100	200	500	∞
9	5.12 / **10.56**	4.26 / **8.02**	3.86 / **6.99**	3.63 / **6.42**	3.48 / **6.06**	3.37 / **5.80**	3.29 / **5.62**	3.23 / **5.47**	3.18 / **5.35**	3.13 / **5.26**	3.10 / **5.18**	3.07 / **5.11**	3.02 / **5.00**	2.98 / **4.92**	2.93 / **4.80**	2.90 / **4.73**	2.86 / **4.64**	2.82 / **4.56**	2.80 / **4.51**	2.77 / **4.45**	2.76 / **4.41**	2.73 / **4.36**	2.72 / **4.33**	2.71 / **4.31**
10	4.96 / **10.04**	4.10 / **7.56**	3.71 / **6.55**	3.48 / **5.99**	3.33 / **5.64**	3.22 / **5.39**	3.14 / **5.21**	3.07 / **5.06**	3.02 / **4.95**	2.97 / **4.85**	2.94 / **4.78**	2.91 / **4.71**	2.86 / **4.60**	2.82 / **4.52**	2.77 / **4.41**	2.74 / **4.33**	2.70 / **4.25**	2.67 / **4.17**	2.64 / **4.12**	2.61 / **4.05**	2.59 / **4.01**	2.56 / **3.96**	2.55 / **3.93**	2.54 / **3.91**
11	4.84 / **9.65**	3.98 / **7.20**	3.59 / **6.22**	3.36 / **5.67**	3.20 / **5.32**	3.09 / **5.07**	3.01 / **4.88**	2.95 / **4.74**	2.90 / **4.63**	2.86 / **4.54**	2.82 / **4.46**	2.79 / **4.40**	2.74 / **4.29**	2.70 / **4.21**	2.65 / **4.10**	2.61 / **4.02**	2.57 / **3.94**	2.53 / **3.86**	2.50 / **3.80**	2.47 / **3.74**	2.45 / **3.70**	2.42 / **3.66**	2.41 / **3.62**	2.40 / **3.60**
12	4.75 / **9.33**	3.88 / **6.93**	3.49 / **5.95**	3.26 / **5.41**	3.11 / **5.06**	3.00 / **4.82**	2.92 / **4.65**	2.85 / **4.50**	2.80 / **4.39**	2.76 / **4.30**	2.72 / **4.22**	2.69 / **4.16**	2.64 / **4.05**	2.60 / **3.98**	2.54 / **3.86**	2.50 / **3.78**	2.46 / **3.70**	2.42 / **3.61**	2.40 / **3.56**	2.36 / **3.49**	2.35 / **3.46**	2.32 / **3.41**	2.31 / **3.38**	2.30 / **3.36**
13	4.67 / **9.07**	3.80 / **6.70**	3.41 / **5.74**	3.18 / **5.20**	3.02 / **4.86**	2.92 / **4.62**	2.84 / **4.44**	2.77 / **4.30**	2.72 / **4.19**	2.67 / **4.10**	2.63 / **4.02**	2.60 / **3.96**	2.55 / **3.85**	2.51 / **3.78**	2.46 / **3.67**	2.42 / **3.59**	2.38 / **3.51**	2.34 / **3.42**	2.32 / **3.37**	2.28 / **3.30**	2.26 / **3.27**	2.24 / **3.21**	2.22 / **3.18**	2.21 / **3.16**
14	4.60 / **8.86**	3.74 / **6.51**	3.34 / **5.56**	3.11 / **5.03**	2.96 / **4.69**	2.85 / **4.46**	2.77 / **4.28**	2.70 / **4.14**	2.65 / **4.03**	2.60 / **3.94**	2.56 / **3.86**	2.53 / **3.80**	2.48 / **3.70**	2.44 / **3.62**	2.39 / **3.51**	2.35 / **3.43**	2.31 / **3.34**	2.27 / **3.26**	2.24 / **3.21**	2.21 / **3.14**	2.19 / **3.11**	2.16 / **3.06**	2.14 / **3.02**	2.13 / **3.00**
15	4.54 / **8.68**	3.68 / **6.36**	3.29 / **5.42**	3.06 / **4.89**	2.90 / **4.56**	2.79 / **4.32**	2.70 / **4.14**	2.64 / **4.00**	2.59 / **3.89**	2.55 / **3.80**	2.51 / **3.73**	2.48 / **3.67**	2.43 / **3.56**	2.39 / **3.48**	2.33 / **3.36**	2.29 / **3.29**	2.25 / **3.20**	2.21 / **3.12**	2.18 / **3.07**	2.15 / **3.00**	2.12 / **2.97**	2.10 / **2.92**	2.08 / **2.89**	2.07 / **2.87**
16	4.49 / **8.53**	3.63 / **6.23**	3.24 / **5.29**	3.01 / **4.77**	2.85 / **4.44**	2.74 / **4.20**	2.66 / **4.03**	2.59 / **3.89**	2.54 / **3.78**	2.49 / **3.69**	2.45 / **3.61**	2.42 / **3.55**	2.37 / **3.45**	2.33 / **3.37**	2.28 / **3.25**	2.24 / **3.18**	2.20 / **3.10**	2.16 / **3.01**	2.13 / **2.96**	2.09 / **2.89**	2.07 / **2.86**	2.04 / **2.80**	2.02 / **2.77**	2.01 / **2.75**
17	4.45 / **8.40**	3.59 / **6.11**	3.20 / **5.18**	2.96 / **4.67**	2.81 / **4.34**	2.70 / **4.10**	2.62 / **3.93**	2.55 / **3.79**	2.50 / **3.68**	2.45 / **3.59**	2.41 / **3.52**	2.38 / **3.45**	2.33 / **3.35**	2.29 / **3.27**	2.23 / **3.16**	2.19 / **3.08**	2.15 / **3.00**	2.11 / **2.92**	2.08 / **2.86**	2.04 / **2.79**	2.02 / **2.76**	1.99 / **2.70**	1.97 / **2.67**	1.96 / **2.65**
18	4.41 / **8.28**	3.55 / **6.01**	3.16 / **5.09**	2.93 / **4.58**	2.77 / **4.25**	2.66 / **4.01**	2.58 / **3.85**	2.51 / **3.71**	2.46 / **3.60**	2.41 / **3.51**	2.37 / **3.44**	2.34 / **3.37**	2.29 / **3.27**	2.25 / **3.19**	2.19 / **3.07**	2.15 / **3.00**	2.11 / **2.91**	2.07 / **2.83**	2.04 / **2.78**	2.00 / **2.71**	1.98 / **2.68**	1.95 / **2.62**	1.93 / **2.59**	1.92 / **2.57**
19	4.38 / **8.18**	3.52 / **5.93**	3.13 / **5.01**	2.90 / **4.50**	2.74 / **4.17**	2.63 / **3.94**	2.55 / **3.77**	2.48 / **3.63**	2.43 / **3.52**	2.38 / **3.43**	2.34 / **3.36**	2.31 / **3.30**	2.26 / **3.19**	2.21 / **3.12**	2.15 / **3.00**	2.11 / **2.92**	2.07 / **2.84**	2.02 / **2.76**	2.00 / **2.70**	1.96 / **2.63**	1.94 / **2.60**	1.91 / **2.54**	1.90 / **2.51**	1.88 / **2.49**
20	4.35 / **8.10**	3.49 / **5.85**	3.10 / **4.94**	2.87 / **4.43**	2.71 / **4.10**	2.60 / **3.87**	2.52 / **3.71**	2.45 / **3.56**	2.40 / **3.45**	2.35 / **3.37**	2.31 / **3.30**	2.28 / **3.23**	2.23 / **3.13**	2.18 / **3.05**	2.12 / **2.94**	2.08 / **2.86**	2.04 / **2.77**	1.99 / **2.69**	1.96 / **2.63**	1.92 / **2.56**	1.90 / **2.53**	1.87 / **2.47**	1.85 / **2.44**	1.84 / **2.42**
21	4.32 / **8.02**	3.47 / **5.78**	3.07 / **4.87**	2.84 / **4.37**	2.68 / **4.04**	2.57 / **3.81**	2.49 / **3.65**	2.42 / **3.51**	2.37 / **3.40**	2.32 / **3.31**	2.28 / **3.24**	2.25 / **3.17**	2.20 / **3.07**	2.15 / **2.99**	2.09 / **2.88**	2.05 / **2.80**	2.00 / **2.72**	1.96 / **2.63**	1.93 / **2.58**	1.89 / **2.51**	1.87 / **2.47**	1.84 / **2.42**	1.82 / **2.38**	1.81 / **2.36**

df																								
22	4.30 / 7.94	3.44 / 5.72	3.05 / 4.82	2.82 / 4.31	2.66 / 3.99	2.55 / 3.76	2.47 / 3.59	2.40 / 3.45	2.35 / 3.35	2.30 / 3.26	2.26 / 3.18	2.23 / 3.12	2.18 / 3.02	2.13 / 2.94	2.07 / 2.83	2.03 / 2.75	1.98 / 2.67	1.93 / 2.58	1.91 / 2.53	1.87 / 2.46	1.84 / 2.42	1.81 / 2.37	1.80 / 2.33	1.78 / 2.31
23	4.28 / 7.88	3.42 / 5.66	3.03 / 4.76	2.80 / 4.26	2.64 / 3.94	2.53 / 3.71	2.45 / 3.54	2.38 / 3.41	2.32 / 3.30	2.28 / 3.21	2.24 / 3.14	2.20 / 3.07	2.14 / 2.97	2.10 / 2.89	2.04 / 2.78	2.00 / 2.70	1.96 / 2.62	1.91 / 2.53	1.88 / 2.48	1.84 / 2.41	1.82 / 2.37	1.79 / 2.32	1.77 / 2.28	1.76 / 2.26
24	4.26 / 7.82	3.40 / 5.61	3.01 / 4.72	2.78 / 4.22	2.62 / 3.90	2.51 / 3.67	2.43 / 3.50	2.36 / 3.36	2.30 / 3.25	2.26 / 3.17	2.22 / 3.09	2.18 / 3.03	2.13 / 2.93	2.09 / 2.85	2.02 / 2.74	1.98 / 2.66	1.94 / 2.58	1.89 / 2.49	1.86 / 2.44	1.82 / 2.36	1.80 / 2.33	1.76 / 2.27	1.74 / 2.23	1.73 / 2.21
25	4.24 / 7.77	3.38 / 5.57	2.99 / 4.68	2.76 / 4.18	2.60 / 3.86	2.49 / 3.63	2.41 / 3.46	2.34 / 3.32	2.28 / 3.21	2.24 / 3.13	2.20 / 3.05	2.16 / 2.99	2.11 / 2.89	2.06 / 2.81	2.00 / 2.70	1.96 / 2.62	1.92 / 2.54	1.87 / 2.45	1.84 / 2.40	1.80 / 2.32	1.77 / 2.29	1.74 / 2.23	1.72 / 2.19	1.71 / 2.17
26	4.22 / 7.72	3.37 / 5.53	2.98 / 4.64	2.74 / 4.14	2.59 / 3.82	2.47 / 3.59	2.39 / 3.42	2.32 / 3.29	2.27 / 3.17	2.22 / 3.09	2.18 / 3.02	2.15 / 2.96	2.10 / 2.86	2.05 / 2.77	1.99 / 2.66	1.95 / 2.58	1.90 / 2.50	1.85 / 2.41	1.82 / 2.36	1.78 / 2.28	1.76 / 2.25	1.72 / 2.19	1.70 / 2.15	1.69 / 2.13
27	4.21 / 7.68	3.35 / 5.49	2.96 / 4.60	2.73 / 4.11	2.57 / 3.79	2.46 / 3.56	2.37 / 3.39	2.30 / 3.26	2.25 / 3.14	2.20 / 3.06	2.16 / 2.98	2.13 / 2.93	2.08 / 2.83	2.03 / 2.74	1.97 / 2.63	1.93 / 2.55	1.88 / 2.47	1.84 / 2.38	1.80 / 2.33	1.76 / 2.25	1.74 / 2.21	1.71 / 2.16	1.68 / 2.12	1.67 / 2.10
28	4.20 / 7.64	3.34 / 5.45	2.95 / 4.57	2.71 / 4.07	2.56 / 3.76	2.44 / 3.53	2.36 / 3.36	2.29 / 3.23	2.24 / 3.11	2.19 / 3.03	2.15 / 2.95	2.12 / 2.90	2.06 / 2.80	2.02 / 2.71	1.96 / 2.60	1.91 / 2.52	1.87 / 2.44	1.81 / 2.35	1.78 / 2.30	1.75 / 2.22	1.72 / 2.18	1.69 / 2.13	1.67 / 2.09	1.65 / 2.06
29	4.18 / 7.60	3.33 / 5.42	2.93 / 4.54	2.70 / 4.04	2.54 / 3.73	2.43 / 3.50	2.35 / 3.33	2.28 / 3.20	2.22 / 3.08	2.18 / 3.00	2.14 / 2.92	2.10 / 2.87	2.05 / 2.77	2.00 / 2.68	1.94 / 2.57	1.90 / 2.49	1.85 / 2.41	1.80 / 2.32	1.77 / 2.27	1.73 / 2.19	1.71 / 2.15	1.68 / 2.10	1.65 / 2.06	1.64 / 2.03
30	4.17 / 7.56	3.32 / 5.39	2.92 / 4.51	2.69 / 4.02	2.53 / 3.70	2.42 / 3.47	2.34 / 3.30	2.27 / 3.17	2.21 / 3.06	2.16 / 2.98	2.12 / 2.90	2.09 / 2.84	2.04 / 2.74	1.99 / 2.66	1.93 / 2.55	1.89 / 2.47	1.84 / 2.38	1.79 / 2.29	1.76 / 2.24	1.72 / 2.16	1.69 / 2.13	1.66 / 2.07	1.64 / 2.03	1.62 / 2.01
32	4.15 / 7.50	3.30 / 5.34	2.90 / 4.46	2.67 / 3.97	2.51 / 3.66	2.40 / 3.42	2.32 / 3.25	2.25 / 3.12	2.19 / 3.01	2.14 / 2.94	2.10 / 2.86	2.07 / 2.80	2.02 / 2.70	1.97 / 2.62	1.91 / 2.51	1.86 / 2.42	1.82 / 2.34	1.76 / 2.25	1.74 / 2.20	1.69 / 2.12	1.67 / 2.08	1.64 / 2.02	1.61 / 1.98	1.59 / 1.96
34	4.13 / 7.44	3.28 / 5.29	2.88 / 4.42	2.65 / 3.93	2.49 / 3.61	2.38 / 3.38	2.30 / 3.21	2.23 / 3.08	2.17 / 2.97	2.12 / 2.89	2.08 / 2.82	2.05 / 2.76	2.00 / 2.66	1.95 / 2.58	1.89 / 2.47	1.84 / 2.38	1.80 / 2.30	1.74 / 2.21	1.71 / 2.15	1.67 / 2.08	1.64 / 2.04	1.61 / 1.98	1.59 / 1.94	1.57 / 1.91
36	4.11 / 7.39	3.26 / 5.25	2.86 / 4.38	2.63 / 3.89	2.48 / 3.58	2.36 / 3.35	2.28 / 3.18	2.21 / 3.04	2.15 / 2.94	2.10 / 2.86	2.06 / 2.78	2.03 / 2.72	1.98 / 2.62	1.93 / 2.54	1.87 / 2.43	1.82 / 2.35	1.78 / 2.26	1.72 / 2.17	1.69 / 2.12	1.65 / 2.04	1.62 / 2.00	1.59 / 1.94	1.56 / 1.90	1.55 / 1.87
38	4.10 / 7.35	3.25 / 5.21	2.85 / 4.34	2.62 / 3.86	2.46 / 3.54	2.35 / 3.32	2.26 / 3.15	2.19 / 3.02	2.14 / 2.91	2.09 / 2.82	2.05 / 2.75	2.02 / 2.69	1.96 / 2.59	1.92 / 2.51	1.85 / 2.40	1.80 / 2.32	1.76 / 2.22	1.71 / 2.14	1.67 / 2.08	1.63 / 2.00	1.60 / 1.97	1.57 / 1.90	1.54 / 1.86	1.53 / 1.84
40	4.08 / 7.31	3.23 / 5.18	2.84 / 4.31	2.61 / 3.83	2.45 / 3.51	2.34 / 3.29	2.25 / 3.12	2.18 / 2.99	2.12 / 2.88	2.07 / 2.80	2.04 / 2.73	2.00 / 2.66	1.95 / 2.56	1.90 / 2.49	1.84 / 2.37	1.79 / 2.29	1.74 / 2.20	1.69 / 2.11	1.66 / 2.05	1.61 / 1.97	1.59 / 1.94	1.55 / 1.88	1.53 / 1.84	1.51 / 1.81
42	4.07 / 7.27	3.22 / 5.15	2.83 / 4.29	2.59 / 3.80	2.44 / 3.49	2.32 / 3.26	2.24 / 3.10	2.17 / 2.96	2.11 / 2.86	2.06 / 2.77	2.02 / 2.70	1.99 / 2.64	1.94 / 2.54	1.89 / 2.46	1.82 / 2.35	1.78 / 2.26	1.73 / 2.17	1.68 / 2.08	1.64 / 2.02	1.60 / 1.94	1.57 / 1.91	1.54 / 1.85	1.51 / 1.80	1.49 / 1.78

(The value 3.22 / 5.15 in the row for df = 42 is circled.)

TABLE D (*Continued*)
The *F* Distribution

Degrees of Freedom: Numerator

Each cell lists the .05 value (top) and the .01 value (bold, bottom).

Denominator	1	2	3	4	5	6	7	8	9	10	11	12	14	16	20	24	30	40	50	75	100	200	500	∞
44	4.06 / **7.24**	3.21 / **5.12**	2.82 / **4.26**	2.58 / **3.78**	2.43 / **3.46**	2.31 / **3.24**	2.23 / **3.07**	2.16 / **2.94**	2.10 / **2.84**	2.05 / **2.75**	2.01 / **2.68**	1.98 / **2.62**	1.92 / **2.52**	1.88 / **2.44**	1.81 / **2.32**	1.76 / **2.24**	1.72 / **2.15**	1.66 / **2.06**	1.63 / **2.00**	1.58 / **1.92**	1.56 / **1.88**	1.52 / **1.82**	1.50 / **1.78**	1.48 / **1.75**
46	4.05 / **7.21**	3.20 / **5.10**	2.81 / **4.24**	2.57 / **3.76**	2.42 / **3.44**	2.30 / **3.22**	2.22 / **3.05**	2.14 / **2.92**	2.09 / **2.82**	2.04 / **2.73**	2.00 / **2.66**	1.97 / **2.60**	1.91 / **2.50**	1.87 / **2.42**	1.80 / **2.30**	1.75 / **2.22**	1.71 / **2.13**	1.65 / **2.04**	1.62 / **1.98**	1.57 / **1.90**	1.54 / **1.86**	1.51 / **1.80**	1.48 / **1.76**	1.46 / **1.72**
48	4.04 / **7.19**	3.19 / **5.08**	2.80 / **4.22**	2.56 / **3.74**	2.41 / **3.42**	2.30 / **3.20**	2.21 / **3.04**	2.14 / **2.90**	2.08 / **2.80**	2.03 / **2.71**	1.99 / **2.64**	1.96 / **2.58**	1.90 / **2.48**	1.86 / **2.40**	1.79 / **2.28**	1.74 / **2.20**	1.70 / **2.11**	1.64 / **2.02**	1.61 / **1.96**	1.56 / **1.88**	1.53 / **1.84**	1.50 / **1.78**	1.47 / **1.73**	1.45 / **1.70**
50	4.03 / **7.17**	3.18 / **5.06**	2.79 / **4.20**	2.56 / **3.72**	2.40 / **3.41**	2.29 / **3.18**	2.20 / **3.02**	2.13 / **2.88**	2.07 / **2.78**	2.02 / **2.70**	1.98 / **2.62**	1.95 / **2.56**	1.90 / **2.46**	1.85 / **2.39**	1.78 / **2.26**	1.74 / **2.18**	1.69 / **2.10**	1.63 / **2.00**	1.60 / **1.94**	1.55 / **1.86**	1.52 / **1.82**	1.48 / **1.76**	1.46 / **1.71**	1.44 / **1.68**
55	4.02 / **7.12**	3.17 / **5.01**	2.78 / **4.16**	2.54 / **3.68**	2.38 / **3.37**	2.27 / **3.15**	2.18 / **2.98**	2.11 / **2.85**	2.05 / **2.75**	2.00 / **2.66**	1.97 / **2.59**	1.93 / **2.53**	1.88 / **2.43**	1.83 / **2.35**	1.76 / **2.23**	1.72 / **2.15**	1.67 / **2.06**	1.61 / **1.96**	1.58 / **1.90**	1.52 / **1.82**	1.50 / **1.78**	1.46 / **1.71**	1.43 / **1.66**	1.41 / **1.64**
60	4.00 / **7.08**	3.15 / **4.98**	2.76 / **4.13**	2.52 / **3.65**	2.37 / **3.34**	2.25 / **3.12**	2.17 / **2.95**	2.10 / **2.82**	2.04 / **2.72**	1.99 / **2.63**	1.95 / **2.56**	1.92 / **2.50**	1.86 / **2.40**	1.81 / **2.32**	1.75 / **2.20**	1.70 / **2.12**	1.65 / **2.03**	1.59 / **1.93**	1.56 / **1.87**	1.50 / **1.79**	1.48 / **1.74**	1.44 / **1.68**	1.41 / **1.63**	1.39 / **1.60**
65	3.99 / **7.04**	3.14 / **4.95**	2.75 / **4.10**	2.51 / **3.62**	2.36 / **3.31**	2.24 / **3.09**	2.15 / **2.93**	2.08 / **2.79**	2.02 / **2.70**	1.98 / **2.61**	1.94 / **2.54**	1.90 / **2.47**	1.85 / **2.37**	1.80 / **2.30**	1.73 / **2.18**	1.68 / **2.09**	1.63 / **2.00**	1.57 / **1.90**	1.54 / **1.84**	1.49 / **1.76**	1.46 / **1.71**	1.42 / **1.64**	1.39 / **1.60**	1.37 / **1.56**
70	3.98 / **7.01**	3.13 / **4.92**	2.74 / **4.08**	2.50 / **3.60**	2.35 / **3.29**	2.23 / **3.07**	2.14 / **2.91**	2.07 / **2.77**	2.01 / **2.67**	1.97 / **2.59**	1.93 / **2.51**	1.89 / **2.45**	1.84 / **2.35**	1.79 / **2.28**	1.72 / **2.15**	1.67 / **2.07**	1.62 / **1.98**	1.56 / **1.88**	1.53 / **1.82**	1.47 / **1.74**	1.45 / **1.69**	1.40 / **1.62**	1.37 / **1.56**	1.35 / **1.53**
80	3.96 / **6.96**	3.11 / **4.88**	2.72 / **4.04**	2.48 / **3.56**	2.33 / **3.25**	2.21 / **3.04**	2.12 / **2.87**	2.05 / **2.74**	1.99 / **2.64**	1.95 / **2.55**	1.91 / **2.48**	1.88 / **2.41**	1.82 / **2.32**	1.77 / **2.24**	1.70 / **2.11**	1.65 / **2.03**	1.60 / **1.94**	1.54 / **1.84**	1.51 / **1.78**	1.45 / **1.70**	1.42 / **1.65**	1.38 / **1.57**	1.35 / **1.52**	1.32 / **1.49**
100	3.94 / **6.90**	3.09 / **4.82**	2.70 / **3.98**	2.46 / **3.51**	2.30 / **3.20**	2.19 / **2.99**	2.10 / **2.82**	2.03 / **2.69**	1.97 / **2.59**	1.92 / **2.51**	1.88 / **2.43**	1.85 / **2.36**	1.79 / **2.26**	1.75 / **2.19**	1.68 / **2.06**	1.63 / **1.98**	1.57 / **1.89**	1.51 / **1.79**	1.48 / **1.73**	1.42 / **1.64**	1.39 / **1.59**	1.34 / **1.51**	1.30 / **1.46**	1.28 / **1.43**
125	3.92 / **6.84**	3.07 / **4.78**	2.68 / **3.94**	2.44 / **3.47**	2.29 / **3.17**	2.17 / **2.95**	2.08 / **2.79**	2.01 / **2.65**	1.95 / **2.56**	1.90 / **2.47**	1.86 / **2.40**	1.83 / **2.33**	1.77 / **2.23**	1.72 / **2.15**	1.65 / **2.03**	1.60 / **1.94**	1.55 / **1.85**	1.49 / **1.75**	1.45 / **1.68**	1.39 / **1.59**	1.36 / **1.54**	1.31 / **1.46**	1.27 / **1.40**	1.25 / **1.37**
150	3.91 / **6.81**	3.06 / **4.75**	2.67 / **3.91**	2.43 / **3.44**	2.27 / **3.14**	2.16 / **2.92**	2.07 / **2.76**	2.00 / **2.62**	1.94 / **2.53**	1.89 / **2.44**	1.85 / **2.37**	1.82 / **2.30**	1.76 / **2.20**	1.71 / **2.12**	1.64 / **2.00**	1.59 / **1.91**	1.54 / **1.83**	1.47 / **1.72**	1.44 / **1.66**	1.37 / **1.56**	1.34 / **1.51**	1.29 / **1.43**	1.25 / **1.37**	1.22 / **1.33**
200	3.89 / **6.76**	3.04 / **4.71**	2.65 / **3.88**	2.41 / **3.41**	2.26 / **3.11**	2.14 / **2.90**	2.05 / **2.73**	1.98 / **2.60**	1.92 / **2.50**	1.87 / **2.41**	1.83 / **2.34**	1.80 / **2.28**	1.74 / **2.17**	1.69 / **2.09**	1.62 / **1.97**	1.57 / **1.88**	1.52 / **1.79**	1.45 / **1.69**	1.42 / **1.62**	1.35 / **1.53**	1.32 / **1.48**	1.26 / **1.39**	1.22 / **1.33**	1.19 / **1.28**

df																							
400	3.86	3.02	2.62	2.39	2.23	2.12	2.03	1.96	1.90	1.85	1.81	1.78	1.72	1.67	1.60	1.54	1.49	1.42	1.38	1.32	1.28	1.22	1.16	1.13
	6.70	**4.66**	**3.83**	**3.36**	**3.06**	**2.85**	**2.69**	**2.55**	**2.46**	**2.37**	**2.29**	**2.23**	**2.12**	**2.04**	**1.92**	**1.84**	**1.74**	**1.64**	**1.57**	**1.47**	**1.42**	**1.32**	**1.24**	**1.19**
1000	3.85	3.00	2.61	2.38	2.22	2.10	2.02	1.95	1.89	1.84	1.80	1.76	1.70	1.65	1.58	1.53	1.47	1.41	1.36	1.30	1.26	1.19	1.13	1.08
	6.66	**4.62**	**3.80**	**3.34**	**3.04**	**2.82**	**2.66**	**2.53**	**2.43**	**2.34**	**2.26**	**2.20**	**2.09**	**2.01**	**1.89**	**1.81**	**1.71**	**1.61**	**1.54**	**1.44**	**1.38**	**1.28**	**1.19**	**1.11**
∞	3.84	2.99	2.60	2.37	2.21	2.09	2.01	1.94	1.88	1.83	1.79	1.75	1.69	1.64	1.57	1.52	1.46	1.40	1.35	1.28	1.24	1.17	1.11	1.00
	6.64	**4.60**	**3.78**	**3.32**	**3.02**	**2.80**	**2.64**	**2.51**	**2.41**	**2.32**	**2.24**	**2.18**	**2.07**	**1.99**	**1.87**	**1.79**	**1.69**	**1.59**	**1.52**	**1.41**	**1.36**	**1.25**	**1.15**	**1.00**

Note: Each value in the table corresponds to an F ratio $[F_\alpha(df_1, df_2)]$ that has α proportion of the distribution above it. Values in roman type are for $\alpha = .05$, and values in **boldface** are for $\alpha = .01$. Reprinted by permission from *Statistical Methods*, Seventh Edition, by George W. Snedecor and William G. Cochran © 1980 by Iowa State University Press, 2121 South State Avenue, Ames, Iowa 50010.

TABLE E
Critical Values of the Pearson Product–moment Correlation Coefficient (r_a)

	Values of α for a directional test				
	.05	.025	.01	.005	.0005
	Values of α for a nondirectional test				
$df = n_p - 2$	.10	.05	.02	.01	.001
1	.9877	.9969	.9995	.9999	1.0000
2	.9000	.9500	.9800	.9900	.9990
3	.8054	.8783	.9343	.9587	.9912
4	.7293	.8114	.8822	.9172	.9741
5	.6694	.7545	.8329	.8745	.9507
6	.6215	.7067	.7887	.8343	.9249
7	.5822	.6664	.7498	.7977	.8982
8	.5494	.6319	.7155	.7646	.8721
9	.5214	.6021	.6851	.7348	.8471
10	.4973	.5760	.6581	.7079	.8233
11	.4762	.5529	.6339	.6835	.8010
12	.4575	.5324	.6120	.6614	.7800
13	.4409	.5139	.5923	.6411	.7603
14	.4259	.4973	.5742	.6226	.7420
15	.4124	.4821	.5577	.6055	.7246
16	.4000	.4683	.5425	.5897	.7084
17	.3887	.4555	.5285	.5751	.6932
18	.3783	.4438	.5155	.5614	.6787
19	.3687	.4329	.5034	.5487	.6652
20	.3598	.4227	.4921	.5368	.6524
25	.3233	.3809	.4451	.4869	.5974
30	.2960	.3494	.4093	.4487	.5541
35	.2746	.3246	.3810	.4182	.5189
40	.2573	.3044	.3578	.3932	.4896
45	.2428	.2875	.3384	.3721	.4648
50	.2306	.2732	.3218	.3541	.4433
60	.2108	.2500	.2948	.3248	.4078
70	.1954	.2319	.2737	.3017	.3799
80	.1829	.2172	.2565	.2830	.3568
90	.1726	.2050	.2422	.2673	.3375
100	.1638	.1946	.2301	.2540	.3211

Table E is taken from Table VII of Fisher and Yates, *Statistical Tables for Biological, Agricultural, and Medical Research*, published by Longman Group Ltd., London (previously published by Oliver and Boyd, Ltd., Edinburgh), and by permission of the authors and publishers.

Note: If the observed value of *r* is *greater than or equal to* the tabled value for the appropriate α (columns) and degrees of freedom (rows), then reject H_0. The critical values in the table are both + and – for nondirectional (two-tailed) tests.

TABLE F
Critical Values for the Spearman Rank-order Correlation Coefficient (r_{s_α})

n_p	Values of α for a directional test			
	.05	.025	.005	.001
	Values of α for a nondirectional test			
	.10	.05	.01	.002
5	.900	1.000		
6	.829	.886	1.000	
7	.715	.786	.929	1.000
8	**.643**	.715	.881	.953
9	.600	.700	.834	.917
10	.564	.649	.794	.879
11	.537	.619	.755	**.845**
12	.504	.588	.727	.826
13	.484	.561	.704	.797
14	.464	.539	.680	.772
15	.447	.522	.658	.750
16	.430	.503	.636	.730
17	.415	.488	.618	.711
18	.402	.474	.600	.693
19	.392	.460	.585	.676
20	.381	.447	.570	.661
21	.371	.437	.556	.647
22	.361	.426	.544	.633
23	.353	.417	.532	.620
24	.345	.407	.521	.608
25	.337	.399	.511	.597
26	.331	.391	.501	.587
27	.325	.383	.493	.577
28	.319	.376	.484	.567
29	.312	.369	.475	.558
30	.307	.363	.467	.549

Glasser, G. J., and R. F. Winter, "Critical Values of the Coefficient of Rank Correlation for Testing the Hypothesis of Independence," *Biometrika,* 48, 444 (1961). Reprinted by permission of the Biometrika Trustees.

Note: If the observed value of r_s is *greater than or equal* to the tabled value for the appropriate α, reject H_0. Note that the left-hand column is the number of pairs of scores, not the number of degrees of freedom. The critical values listed are both + and − for nondirectional tests.

TABLE G
The χ^2 Distribution

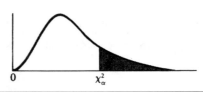

df	$\chi^2_{.995}$	$\chi^2_{.99}$	$\chi^2_{.975}$	$\chi^2_{.95}$	$\chi^2_{.90}$	$\chi^2_{.10}$	$\chi^2_{.05}$	$\chi^2_{.025}$	$\chi^2_{.01}$	$\chi^2_{.005}$
1	.000039	.00016	.00098	.0039	.016	2.71	3.84	5.02	6.63	7.88
2	.010	.020	.051	.10	.21	4.61	5.99	7.38	9.21	10.60
3	.072	.11	.22	.35	.58	6.25	7.81	9.35	11.34	12.84
4	.21	.30	.48	.71	1.06	7.78	9.49	11.14	13.28	14.86
5	.41	.55	.83	1.15	1.61	9.24	11.07	12.83	15.09	16.75
6	.68	.87	1.24	1.64	2.20	10.64	12.59	14.45	16.81	18.55
7	.99	1.24	1.69	2.17	2.83	12.02	14.07	16.01	18.48	20.28
8	1.34	1.65	2.18	2.73	3.49	13.36	15.51	17.53	20.09	21.96
9	1.73	2.09	2.70	3.33	4.17	14.68	16.92	19.02	21.67	23.59
10	2.16	2.56	3.25	3.94	4.87	15.99	18.31	20.48	23.21	25.19
11	2.60	3.05	3.82	4.57	5.58	17.28	19.68	21.92	24.72	26.76
12	3.07	3.57	4.40	5.23	6.30	18.55	21.03	23.34	26.22	28.30
13	3.57	4.11	5.01	5.89	7.04	19.81	22.36	24.74	27.69	29.82
14	4.07	4.66	5.63	6.57	7.79	21.06	23.68	26.12	29.14	31.32
15	4.60	5.23	6.26	7.26	8.55	22.31	25.00	27.49	30.58	32.80
16	5.14	5.81	6.91	7.96	9.31	23.54	26.30	28.85	32.00	34.27
17	5.70	6.41	7.56	8.67	10.09	24.77	27.59	30.19	33.41	35.72
18	6.26	7.01	8.23	9.39	10.86	25.99	28.87	31.53	34.81	37.16
19	6.84	7.63	8.91	10.12	11.65	27.20	30.14	32.85	36.19	38.58
20	7.43	8.26	9.59	10.85	12.44	28.41	31.41	34.17	37.57	40.00
21	8.03	8.90	10.28	11.59	13.24	29.62	32.67	35.48	38.93	41.40
22	8.64	9.54	10.98	12.34	14.04	30.81	33.92	36.78	40.29	42.80
23	9.26	10.20	11.69	13.09	14.85	32.01	35.17	38.08	41.64	44.18
24	9.89	10.86	12.40	13.85	15.66	33.20	36.42	39.36	42.98	45.56
25	10.52	11.52	13.12	14.61	16.47	34.38	37.65	40.65	44.31	46.93
26	11.16	12.20	13.84	15.38	17.29	35.56	38.89	41.92	45.64	48.29
27	11.81	12.88	14.57	16.15	18.11	36.74	40.11	43.19	46.96	49.64
28	12.46	13.56	15.31	16.93	18.94	37.92	41.34	44.46	48.28	50.99
29	13.12	14.26	16.05	17.71	19.77	39.09	42.56	45.72	49.59	52.34
30	13.79	14.95	16.79	18.49	20.60	40.26	43.77	46.98	50.89	53.67
40	20.71	22.16	24.43	26.51	29.05	51.81	55.76	59.34	63.69	66.77
50	27.99	29.71	32.36	34.76	37.69	63.17	67.50	71.42	76.15	79.49
60	35.53	37.48	40.48	43.19	46.46	74.40	79.08	83.30	88.38	91.95
70	43.28	45.44	48.76	51.74	55.33	85.53	90.53	95.02	100.42	104.22
80	51.17	53.54	57.15	60.39	64.28	96.58	101.88	106.63	112.33	116.32
90	59.20	61.75	65.65	69.13	73.29	107.56	113.14	118.14	124.12	128.30
100	67.33	70.06	74.22	77.93	82.36	118.50	124.34	129.56	135.81	140.17
120	83.85	86.92	91.58	95.70	100.62	140.23	146.57	152.21	158.95	163.64

Note: Each value in the table is a χ^2 score [χ^2_α (*df*)] that has α proportion of the distribution above it.

Modified from Table 8: E. Pearson, and H. Hartley, *Biometrika Tables for Statisticians*, Vol. 1, 3rd ed., University Press, Cambridge, 1966, with permission of the Biometrika Trustees.

TABLE H
Random Numbers

25380	98133	90446	14191	20389	61342	50468	77128	68175	11318	18708	88915	93308	32372	56668	73870
55366	67663	50484	09840	95749	63840	63904	82571	86100	35834	11892	30785	47791	76939	18701	94365
47985	85850	03883	67513	46832	43057	98562	78681	24580	31428	91236	70140	45569	13181	67906	75991
75804	02402	68781	74205	63099	83101	65117	52369	51327	86857	29231	68246	70408	86781	98081	41317
49094	76309	26574	94537	85110	68005	92335	99885	80907	75294	37475	55053	53461	23729	73194	64348
08051	70453	69708	56462	80010	94619	85475	21844	86426	49722	28082	41323	85114	97453	97255	21816
81327	89940	89483	01894	68576	44159	43385	62802	76298	77745	77425	46727	49221	05989	27062	87548
16679	67465	76075	51097	74827	21211	61444	80875	58549	63905	70227	05065	09673	26962	69259	89962
93803	01163	15616	91348	41502	35982	93043	21536	10550	68219	53547	88354	75790	60997	86174	63161
33488	23765	93861	68383	49736	42664	83898	42362	93634	67806	52583	52812	92445	99247	81762	36099
91321	39454	23233	53439	78294	64851	87225	91798	98006	19001	62714	94503	76186	80978	01368	73998
56639	61404	90072	16143	87080	66402	63945	81115	59288	66026	57334	86691	59725	72091	18308	67851
01538	11221	47234	80180	11563	56104	56276	05066	38958	38427	18835	36021	46817	54458	48828	77817
12120	58377	54938	48573	11787	67135	53658	36289	07140	94133	14457	68496	69757	89630	48717	11062
54708	94920	28227	71406	83044	12237	44727	08273	52528	39568	92563	55155	59542	04516	72555	30637
32843	79996	64972	53692	42927	81707	74261	08936	70770	80809	67491	13624	97871	59827	32283	34336
59245	59801	43948	20791	06522	01258	29293	95217	72056	23708	68232	32553	31565	77702	78670	28355
07027	04473	88187	15327	19456	82587	48172	45549	78452	88135	97855	67764	54911	46179	61065	83739
68334	94207	98726	21960	99119	85799	38997	06076	81093	85584	88925	13900	94221	99635	34606	48479
08057	19989	42051	24775	47022	73380	63050	12602	16451	43624	62875	25847	81474	73483	06198	87870
91884	64103	31153	07325	42711	88035	46918	61557	21865	94206	73562	61212	19455	35199	44207	87080
43122	62352	83637	75081	04511	11494	73478	21629	97350	62381	20412	78755	58441	85044	58181	58069
23133	15093	39813	76669	24269	38222	95836	26022	65273	62729	18520	64814	39659	19017	47208	22990
98535	99879	40782	45593	11379	55747	40283	98755	27103	31441	58731	22111	42100	65878	51946	99205
44327	21590	99530	39588	68478	79494	10042	38350	33696	62874	21447	90210	51072	84929	14013	02977
55812	05456	74436	93021	73154	81545	11858	08620	74787	17888	64791	38969	45927	82123	91697	20949
43372	36292	62331	52053	45581	86198	87022	20988	50812	38533	68137	60956	09252	17612	00354	72952
38088	52284	54321	73407	06367	35814	89417	06169	88075	48194	10711	29269	87214	65370	14060	58424
97708	49949	07776	68837	00982	87684	39280	80556	11306	83459	43012	47277	04617	89156	94188	39743
53108	28260	77405	63153	73898	78956	79677	75817	68589	34848	32167	59704	43968	10036	53045	19713
21224	45760	44980	91323	81481	44925	21830	90444	67887	29482	11615	71602	38446	13534	00103	28736
57591	53605	34037	09594	95754	84441	06204	02974	36769	12376	81570	49821	02469	66170	91453	87547
59045	24685	93300	91525	05824	13640	54001	53870	30334	26615	86596	42570	74500	47843	65391	92724
54340	48622	69973	68171	86024	71035	87306	25143	32949	95548	91991	71442	56890	44739	77735	61134
74543	19644	73012	92805	85638	01629	36794	96382	14865	09318	75636	25185	35797	03468	98227	39556
91960	41110	66409	34570	67838	01085	78688	88649	36282	39100	78326	20722	44144	32621	65774	25768
10374	14641	99267	23235	57827	77816	49201	16507	16782	85065	70477	98385	15642	02682	30331	48724
07461	30372	90702	75854	73787	22288	34436	74702	78143	97281	61390	35123	56314	69867	72798	78504
28398	89665	47137	70613	65242	96030	00202	11930	57733	13550	30463	98933	12376	94794	64872	59080
52553	50902	73828	45543	72004	47980	85555	72938	52322	59937	28993	15449	33851	26045	18013	89776
08119	75252	67940	22401	24701	41648	68931	08635	23089	61549	19972	63225	77691	83156	08215	62145
31702	00627	68457	07846	13124	67880	22002	26428	53407	43921	25368	78277	52498	45374	04653	46381
74067	95231	66476	31242	75676	23800	99983	14446	39117	37423	96922	52084	75435	34995	24156	95798
21142	58761	71623	10067	03526	51143	86358	77011	85243	51421	15234	05570	58691	62205	68416	12918
97863	87595	31062	90511	59291	28249	10598	57632	55249	66321	44135	71942	69865	07810	79335	70082
48548	80621	50198	79683	08617	22428	45713	22681	83816	91119	78636	74116	47794	90449	20921	15900
52892	63706	59323	61539	89794	47504	10982	64355	33605	40051	45468	97088	43728	28077	96498	52399
66984	38136	12753	35855	73630	10027	88449	07054	77675	85846	61710	59545	80471	27615	96158	06088
19700	97238	05254	60794	23918	69467	72444	47569	50996	24548	03100	08751	02746	53807	82703	72159
70815	35580	44724	53214	65066	57939	64976	31327	51660	51106	10389	39836	37587	14616	60562	68085

Appendix A.
Variables From the Stop Smoking Study

Variable	Description

Experimental Variables

ID	An arbitrary number used to protect an individual's identity
COND	Experimental condition (0 = placebo pill and gum; 1 = active pill [bupropion SR] and placebo gum; 2 = active pill and gum [nicotine replacement])
CO_EOT	Carbon monoxide level at end of treatment measured in parts per million
ABSTAIN	At end of treatment, person stated that he or she was not smoking and CO (carbon monoxide) measure was low (0 = relapse; 1 = abstain)

Smoking Variables

AGEFRST	Age of first cigarette
AGEDAY	Age when started smoking daily
YRSMK	Total number of years smoking daily
TYPCIG	Type of cigarette smoked (1 = regular filter; 2 = regular no filter; 3 = light; 4 = ultra light; 5 = other)
CIGDAY	Average number of cigarettes a day
CHEW	Smokeless tobacco use (0 = never; 1 = past only; 2 = once a month now; 3 = once a week now; 4 = a couple of times a week now; 5 = daily now)
SPOUSE	Spouse or partner smokes (0 = no; 1 = yes)
FRIENDS	Friends who smoke? (0 = none; 1 = less than half; 2 = about half; 3 = more than half; 4 = all)
HOUSE	Must smoke outside at home (0 = no; 1 = yes)
WORK	Smoking allowed at work (0 = no; 1 = some areas; 2 = all areas; 9 = not applicable)
QUIT	Number of times tried to quit smoking
LONG	Longest time without smoking (1 = less than a day; 2 = 1–7 days; 3 = 8–14 days; 4 = 15 days to a month; 5 = 1–3 months; 6 = 3–6 months; 7 = 6–12 months; 8 = more than a year)

Drugs and Alcohol

ONEDRK	At least 1 drink of any alcoholic beverage in last 30 days (0 = no; 1 = yes)
NUMDRK	Number of days in last 30 with at least 1 drink
DIAGALC	Ever diagnosed or treated for alcoholism or had a problem with alcohol (0 = no; 1 = yes)
DIAGDRG	Ever diagnosed or treated for drug use or had a problem with drug use (0 = no; 1 = yes)

Personal and Demographic Variables

AGE	Age in years
GENDER	gender (0 = male; 1 = female)
HISPANIC	Hispanic (0 = no; 1 = yes)
RACE	Race (1 = White; 2 = Black/African American; 3 = American Indian; 4 = Alaska Native; 5 = Asian, Pacific Islander; 6 = other)
MARITAL	Current marital status (1 = married; 2 = divorced; 3 = widowed; 4 = separated; 5 = never married; 6 = not married but living with partner)
EDUC	Highest grade completed (1 = no school or kindergarten; 2 = grades 1–8; 3 = grades 9–11; 4 = grade 12 or GED, 5 = 1–3 years of college; 6 = 4 or more years of college)
EMPLOY	Current work situation (1 = employed for wages; 2 = self-employed; 3 = out of work for more than 1 year; 4 = out of work for less than 1 year; 5 = homemaker; 6 = student; 7 = retired; 8 = unable to work)
INCOME	Annual household income (1 = less than $10,000; 2 = $10,000–$19,999; 3 = $20,000–$24,999; 4 = $25,000–$34,999; 5 = $35,000–$49,999; 6 = $50,000–$74,999; 7 = $75,000 or more)
HEIGHT	Height in inches

Physical and Psychological Health

HEALTH	Self-rated health (1 = excellent; 2 = very good; 3 = good; 4 = fair; 5 = poor; 6 = don't know)
DEPRESS	Ever diagnosed for depression (0 = no; 1 = yes)
WISDM	Wisconsin Inventory of Smoking Dependence Motives, ratings on 65 questions such as "Smoking makes a good mood better." Ratings from 1 (Not true of me at all) to 7 (Extremely true of me).
CESD	Center for Epidemiologic Studies Depression scale, total of ratings on 20 questions such as "I felt lonely." Ratings from 0 (rarely or none of the time during the past week) to 3 (most of the time during the past week).
CO_BASE	Average carbon monoxide at baseline

Appendix B.
Variables From the Wisconsin Maternity Leave and Health Project and the Wisconsin Study of Families and Work

Variable	Description
ID[1]	An arbitrary number used to protect an individual's identity
INCOME	Household income at T1[2] (1 = <$5,000; 2 = $5,000–$7,999; 3 = $8,000–$9,999; 4 = $10,000–$14,999; 5 = $15,000–$19,999; 6 = $20,000–$24,999; 7 = $25,000–$24,999; 8 = $35,000–$49,999; 9 = $50,000–$64,999; 10 = $65,000–$79,999; 11 = $80,000+)
MEDUCAT	Mother's education (11 = Less than high school; 12 = High school degree; 13 = Specific training post-high school; 14 = Some college; 15 = (omitted); 16 = College degree; 17 = 1+ years after college; 18 = (omitted); 19 = Professional degree)
F1MARSAT[3]	Father's marital satisfaction at T1
M1MARSAT	Mother's marital satisfaction at T1
GENDER	Child's gender (0 = male; 1 = female)
F2MARSAT	Father's marital satisfaction at T2
M2MARSAT	Mother's marital satisfaction at T2

---

[1] The names of some of these variables have been changed from those used in the original study.

[2] T1 is time 1, the 5th month of pregnancy; T2 is time 2, 1 month postpartum; T3 is time 3, 4 months postpartum; T4 is time 4, 12 months postpartum; T7 is time 7, 4.5 years.

[3] MARSAT, that is, marital satisfaction, is derived as follows. First, the mother and the father separately rated (1 = not at all; 4 = extremely) a series of questions regarding rewarding aspects of the marriage (e.g., "When you think about your relationship right now, how rewarding is it because your partner appreciates you") and concerns of the marriage ("How concerned are you because your partner does not understand who you really are"). An average was computed for the rewarding aspects and an average was computed for the concerns. Then, the marital satisfaction score is computed as the rewards average minus the concerns average.

F3MARSAT	Father's marital satisfaction at T3
M3MARSAT	Mother's marital satisfaction at T3
F4MARSAT	Father's marital satisfaction at T4
M4MARSAT	Mother's marital satisfaction at T4
MHOURSWK	Mother's hours of work per week at T4
MEMPLOY	Mother's employment status at T4
MSDIVLAB	Mother's satisfaction with division of household labor at T4 (0 = satisfied; 1 = dissatisfied)
MPOS	Sum of ratings (1 = none; 5 = characteristic) on 11 components of mother's positive affect during 15 minutes of free play at T4
MNEG	Sum of ratings (1 = none; 5 = characteristic) on 5 components of maternal negative affect during 15 minutes of free play at T4
MINTRU	Sum of ratings (1 = none; 5 = characteristic) on 8 components of maternal intrusiveness or insensitivity during 15 minutes of free play at T4
IPOSE	Sum of ratings (1 = none; 5 = characteristic) on 8 components of infant positive affect during 15 minutes of free play at T4
IQUAL	Sum of ratings (1 = none; 5 = characteristic) on 10 components of infant quality of play, interest, and attention during 15 minutes of free play at T4
IDYS	Sum of ratings (1 = none; 5 = characteristic) on 6 components of infant dysregulation and irritability during 15 minutes of free play at T4
DMUT	Sum of ratings (1 = none; 5 = characteristic) on 4 components of dyadic mutuality (such as mutual involvement and joint attention) during 15 minutes of free play at T4
DTEN	Sum of ratings (1 = none; 5 = characteristic) on 5 components of dyadic tension during 15 minutes of free play at T4
M7EXT	Sum of mother's ratings (0 = does not apply; 1 = sometimes applies; 2 = frequently applies) at T7 on 11 components of child's externalizing behavior (e.g., "Fights with other children").
M7HYP	Sum of mother's ratings (0 = does not apply; 1 = sometimes applies; 2 = frequently applies) at T7 on 4 components of child's hyperactivity and inattention (e.g., "Inattentive")
M7INT	Sum of mother's ratings (0 = does not apply; 1 = sometimes applies; 2 = frequently applies) at T7 on 9 components of child's internalizing behavior (e.g., "Tends to be fearful or afraid of new things or new situations")

Answers to Selected Exercises

Chapter 1

3b. Both. This set of scores is a population when the investigator is interested only in family incomes of Wisconsin residents. If the investigator is interested in a larger set of scores (such as the family incomes of all families in the United States), then this set is a sample, but not a random sample.

5. Ratio measures are preferred, because they incorporate more information than the other scale types. For example, a ratio measure of a variable includes equal interval information, whereas ordinal measures do not. Using a ratio scale allows more statements to be made about relationships in the data (e.g., one score indicates twice as much of the quantity being measured as another score), and opens the data to a greater variety of descriptive and inferential statistical procedures.

7b. Ordinal scale, because most rating scales yield ordinal data.

measurement scale as an ordinal scale of discrimination, then the minority couple is discriminated against more frequently than the majority couple (the minority couple has the higher scores).

5. Set 2: 82.75; 95.96; 108.44; 116.33

6. Set 2: .77; 37.7; 87.9

7. 19; Because number of bus rides is a discrete variable, the number of bus rides must be an integer. Therefore, the measurements cannot be spread evenly throughout the interval as Assumption 2 requires. A better value for the median would be zero.

9. Percentile ranks are a measure of relative standing in a particular distribution; they cannot be used to directly compare scores across distributions. Your friend is closer to the top of the remedial math class than you are to the top of your statistics class. But it cannot be determined from these data which of you is actually better in mathematics.

Chapter 2

2b. Relative frequency is more appropriate because the two sample sizes differ.

d. Children who participated in the school lunch program have, on average, lower IQs than children who did not participate. Is this a reliable finding? That is, will it hold for other children in this population? Procedures in Chapter 13 are designed to answer this question.

4b. Minority and majority couples seem to be treated differently. If we treat the

Chapter 3

1. Set B: a. 28.5, 25.5, 21, and 25
   b. 62
   c. 62/4 = 15.5
   d. $\alpha = 13.86$

   Set C: a. .33, .395, interval .40 to .49
   b. .53
   c. .53/4 = .13
   d. $s = .18$

2. 13.3, 1.08

7a. Yes. The variance of a distribution is independent of the mean, because the variance is the average deviation from the mean (see Formula 3-2). The important consideration is whether the scores tend to cluster around the mean (small average deviation, so a small variance) or whether the scores are distant from the mean (large average deviation, so a large variance). The actual value of the mean is not important.

Chapter 4

1a. 97.72%; d. 68.3

2a. 15.87%; d. 19.25

4. The distribution must be skewed because there are more scores above the mean than below the mean (thus the mean is not the median). Because the distribution is skewed, it cannot be normally distributed, and Table A cannot be used for computing percentiles. You must proceed by getting the whole distribution and using the formulas in Chapter 2.

6. It is possible if one (or both) of the distributions is very skewed. Suppose that the distribution of scores from Jane's history exam is symmetric so that the mean and the median are the same score value. Then her z score of 0.0 indicates that she is right at the mean, which is also the median, which gives her a percentile rank of 50%. Suppose that the distribution of scores from Bill's math exam is positively skewed, so that the median is below the mean. Then his z score of $-.1$ indicates that he is below the mean, but he might still be above the median. In that case, his percentile rank would be greater than 50%. It is more likely, however, that the z score of 0.0 corresponds to a greater percentile rank than does a z score of $-.1$.

9. 1116.5 hours

10. 918 students

Chapter 5

5a. The sample is biased because it systematically excludes the running times of rats that are more difficult to catch (that are perhaps faster or smarter).

Chapter 6

1. $\mu = 4.67$; $\sigma^2 = 10.67$

2b. $7/30 = .23$

e. $12/30 = .40$

3a. $4/52 = .08$

c. $2/52 = .04$

e. $26/52 = .50$

4a. .6915

d. .1056

e. These events are not mutually exclusive.

5a. .0228

b. Cannot be determined

c. .1498

e. These events are not mutually exclusive.

Chapter 7

1a. .1915

b. 4332

2a. Part c can be answered because the sample size is large, thus the sampling distribution of $\bar{X}$ will be close to normally distributed. If the population is not too non-normal, then Part b can also be answered.

4. For $\mu = 20$, .0474.

Chapter 8

1. Nondirectional:

For $\alpha = .04$, reject H_0 if $z \leq -2.05$ or if $z \geq 2.05$

Directional:

For $\alpha = .04$, reject H_0 if $z \leq 1.75$

3. Nondirectional:

For $\alpha = .04$, reject H_0 for zs $= -3.0, 2.25,$ and 4.0

Directional:

For $\alpha = .04$, reject H_0 for zs $= 1.92, 2.25,$ and 4.0

11. All the assumptions appear to be met.

H_0: $\mu = 3.5$ minutes

H_1: $\mu \neq 3.5$ minutes (both directions are of interest)

For $\alpha = .05$,

reject H_0 if $z \leq -1.96$ or if $z \geq 1.96$.

$\sigma_{\bar{x}} = 645$, $z = .465$,

do not reject H_0.

a. Not rejecting H_0 may be a Type II error. It cannot be a Type I error.

b. The population consists of GMU sophomores' social interaction scores (times) for interacting with a stranger after reading favorable information about the stranger.

c. The only conclusion is that there is not enough evidence to rule out the possibility that $\mu = 3.5$ minutes.

Chapter 9

7b. .52

8. Power = .8, $n = 31$

Chapter 10

3. 80%: $23.16 \le \mu \le 30.84$

4. $n = 25$: $4.032 \le \mu \le 7.168$

Chapter 11

1a. Reject H_0 if $z \ge 1.96$ or $z \le -1.96$
    $z = -2.22$, reject H_0.

2c. Reject H_0 if $z \ge 2.33$
    $z = 1.05$, do not reject H_0.

3. 1a: .26.

4a. 47

5a. 95%: $.190 \le \pi \le .31$
    98%: $.179 \le \pi \le .321$

Chapter 12

1a. Reject H_0 if $t \ge 2.093$ or if $t \le -2.093$
    $t = -.89$, do not reject H_0.

2a. Reject H_0 if $t \le -2.539$
    $t = -.89$, do not reject H_0.

4a. .7: $n = 156$; .9: $n = 272$

5a. 95%: $-.995 \le \mu \le -.583$
    99%: $-1.068 \le \mu \le -.510$

7. $t = -56.34$, reject H_0

Chapter 13

1. $t = -3.00$

2. 16

3. $z = -2.42$

5. 99%: $-5.977 \le \mu_1 - \le \mu_2 -.023$

6a. Independent-sample t test

6b. H_0: $\mu_1 - \mu_2 = 0$
    H_1: $\mu_1 - \mu_2 \ne 0$
    For $\alpha = .05$, reject H_0 if $t(22) \le -2.074$ or $t(22) \ge 2.074$
    $t = 2.24$, reject H_0.

Chapter 14

1a. H_0: $\mu_{\text{low}} - \mu_{\text{high}} = 0$

b. Causal statements are not justified because there is no random assignment.

c. The populations are the number of negative statements made by low-prejudice students and the number of negative statements made by high-prejudice students.

Chapter 15

1. $t = 2.42$

3. $z = -2.12$

4. $1.05 \le \mu_1 - \mu_2 \le 17.48$

5. Power is approximately .74. A sample size of about 29 pairs of observations is needed to increase power to .95.

7a. If we assume that the population and sample size assumptions are met, then use the independent-sample t test. Otherwise, use the rank-sum test.

c. H_0: $\mu_{\text{women}} - \mu_{\text{men}} = 0$; H_1: $\mu_{\text{women}} - \mu_{\text{men}} \ne 0$.
    For $\alpha = .05$,
    reject H_0 if $t(28) \le -2.048$ or if $t(28) \ge 2.048$
    $t = -.618$, do not reject H_0

d. The populations are the sensitivity to ESP scores for men and women psychology majors at GMU. If H_0 had been rejected, conclude that the population means differ. No causal links can be established.

8. $t = -.28$

10. $t = 2.20$

Chapter 16

1. $F = s_2^2/s_1^2 = 28.96$

2. $007 \le \sigma_1^2/\sigma_2^2 \le .226$

4a. The independent-sample t test could be used to look for differences between the population means, and the F test can be used to look for differences between the population variances. Because the difference between the means is so small, concentrate on finding a difference between the variances.

b. $H_0:\sigma_1^2 = \sigma_2^2$; $H_1:\sigma_1^2 \neq \sigma_2^2$

For $\alpha = .10$, reject H_0 if $F = s_1^2/s_2^2 \geq 1.60$ or if $F = s_2^2/s_1^2 \geq 1.60$.

$F = s_1^2/s_2^2 = 2.25$, reject H_0.

The populations are the tip sizes for meals that include alcohol and the tip sizes for the meals that do not include alcohol. The variance of the first population is larger than that of the second. No causal statements can be made.

Chapter 17

1. | Source | SS | df | MS | F |
|---|---|---|---|---|
| Treatment | 42.8 | 4 | 10.7 | .331 |
| Error | 647.2 | 20 | 32.4 | |
| Total | 690.0 | 24 | | |

2. | Source | SS | df | MS | F |
|---|---|---|---|---|
| Treatment | 42.8 | 4 | 10.7 | 12.97 |
| Blocks | 634.0 | 4 | 158.5 | |
| Error | 13.2 | 16 | .8 | |
| Total | 690.0 | 24 | | |

Protected t test:

For $\alpha = .05$, reject H_0 if $t(4) \geq 2.776$ or ≤ -2.776.

$t = -3.16$, reject H_0.

3. H_0: The populations have identical relative frequency distributions.

H_1: The null is wrong.

For $\alpha = .05$, reject H_0 if $H \geq 9.49$.

$CM = 4225$, $SST = 83.6$, $H = 1.54$

Do not reject H_0; do not compare third and fifth groups because H_0 from the Kruskal–Wallis test was not rejected.

4. H_0: The populations have identical relative frequency distributions.

H_1: The null is wrong.

For $\alpha = .05$, reject H_0 if $F_r \geq 9.49$.

$CM = 225$, $SST = 43.8$, $F_r = 17.52$

Reject H_0. Because there are fewer than eight pairs of observations, do not compare the third and fifth groups using the normal approximation for the Wilcoxon T_m test described in Chapter 14. Another text may be consulted for tables of the T_m statistic that can be used in situations such as this.

8. $H = 5.67$, do not reject H_0 with $\alpha = .05$.
9. Reject H_0 with $\alpha = .05$.
10. For $\alpha = .05$, do not reject H_0.
11. With $\alpha = .05$, do not reject H_0.
12. With $\alpha = .05$, do not reject H_0.

Chapter 18

1. Panel a, top: evidence for main effect of A and main effect of B; bottom: evidence for AB interaction.

2. Panel d: evidence for main effect of B and AC interaction.

Panel e: evidence for main effect of B and AB interaction.

6. There is evidence for a main effect of C, the AC interaction, the BC interaction, and the ABC interaction.

Chapter 19

1. | Source | SS | df | MS | F | $F_{.05}$ |
|---|---|---|---|---|---|
| Mood | 39 | 2 | 19.5 | 3.55 | 3.88 |
| Word Type | 0 | 1 | 0 | 0 | 4.75 |
| Mood by Word | 39 | 2 | 19.5 | 3.55 | 3.88 |
| Error | 66 | 12 | 5.5 | | |
| Total | 144 | 17 | | | |

2. | Source | SS | df | MS | F | $F_{.05}$ |
|---|---|---|---|---|---|
| Weeks | 12,430 | 3 | 4143.3 | 7.77 | 2.86 |
| Therapy | 28,296 | 2 | 14,148.0 | 27.20 | 3.26 |
| Interaction | 8299 | 6 | 1383.2 | 2.66 | 2.36 |
| Error | 18,723 | 36 | 500.1 | | |
| Total | 67,748 | 47 | | | |

Chapter 20

1. $\hat{Y} = .527X - 7.888$
2. $t = 9.095$
3. For $X = 15$, 90% interval:

$-12.74 \leq Y \leq 12.77$

For $X = 45$, 90% interval:

$3.60 \leq Y \leq 28.05$

8. $t = -5.179$
9. 95% confidence interval is $2.07 \leq Y \leq 3.30$
10. $t = 1.84$
11. $t = .98$
12. $t = 3.05$
13. $t = -2.53$

Chapter 21

1. $r = .948$
2. $r_s = .946$
3. $t = 9.42$
4. Reject H_0.
5. Reject H_0.

10a. .12

11a. 273

12. $r_s = .023$

14. To be 95% confident that there are enough parking spaces, the planner should plan on 940 spaces.

15. $t = 2.92$

16. $t = -2.58$
    Reject H_0.

Chapter 22

1. $\chi^2 = 8.89$, reject H_0.

4. H_0: relative frequency in favor = .33
   relative frequency opposed = .33
   relative frequency no opinion = .33

H_1: The null is wrong.
For $\alpha = .05$, reject H_0 if $\chi^2 \geq 5.99$.
$\chi^2 = .35$, do not reject H_0.
There is not sufficient evidence to claim that the relative frequencies differ.

5. H_0: The classification by voter opinion and classification by type of issue are independent.
H_1: The null is wrong.
For $\alpha = .05$, reject H_0 if $\chi^2 \geq 5.99$.
$\chi^2 = 15.35$, reject H_0; the classification systems are dependent.
There is enough evidence to conclude that the relative frequencies of voter opinions depend on the issues.

7. $\chi^2 = 4.96$

8. $t = -2.21$

10. $t = .52$

11. $\chi^2 = 10.0$

12. $\chi^2 = 11.67$

Index